CRITICAL SURVEY
OF
LONG FICTION

CRITICAL SURVEY
OF
LONG FICTION

Foreign Language Series

Authors
Don-Lag

2

Edited by
FRANK N. MAGILL

Academic Director
WALTON BEACHAM

SALEM PRESS
Englewood Cliffs, N. J.

LIBRARY OF CONGRESS CATALOG CARD NUMBER: 84-51791

Complete Set: ISBN 0-89356-369-2
Volume 2: ISBN 0-89356-371-4

PRINTED IN THE UNITED STATES OF AMERICA

LIST OF AUTHORS IN VOLUME 2

CRITICAL SURVEY
OF
LONG FICTION

JOSÉ DONOSO

Born: Santiago, Chile; October 5, 1924

Principal long fiction

Coronación, 1957 (*Coronation*, 1965); *Este domingo*, 1966 (*This Sunday*, 1967); *El lugar sin límites*, 1966 (*Hell Has No Limits*, 1972); *El obsceno pájaro de la noche*, 1970 (*The Obscene Bird of Night*, 1973); *Tres novelitas burguesas*, 1973 (novellas; *Sacred Families*, 1977); *Casa de campo*, 1978 (*A House in the Country*, 1984); *La misteriosa desaparición de la marquesita de Loria*, 1980; *El jardín de al lado*, 1981.

Other literary forms

José Donoso is a superb storyteller, and his first literary efforts were in the area of the short story (curiously, his first stories were written in English and published in the Princeton University literary review, *MSS*). His collections of stories include *Veraneo y otros cuentos* (1955; summer vacation and other stories); *Dos cuentos* (1956; two stories); *El Charleston* (1960; abridged edition, *Cuentos*, 1971; *Charleston and Other Stories*, 1977); and *Los mejores cuentos de José Donoso* (1965; the best stories of José Donoso). He also excels in the area of the novella, with *Sacred Families*. Little if any significant thematic or technical distinction can be drawn between Donoso's novels and shorter fiction, other than those imposed by the limits of the genres themselves. Regardless of length, all are superb blends of sociological observation and psychological analysis, in which realism never quite manages to eliminate fantasy, where madness, the supernatural, and the unknown hover just beyond the bounds of consciousness and reason. Donoso has also written essays of literary criticism and attracted attention with *Historia personal del "boom"* (1972; *The Boom in Spanish American Literature: A Personal History*, 1977). His *Poemas de un novelista* (1981) is a collection of thirty poems with a twelve-page authorial introduction explaining the personal circumstances that occasioned the verse.

Achievements

Each of Donoso's novels has had its special success, and the writer's prestige has grown with each stage of his career. Despite a slow beginning (he came to the novel at thirty-three), Donoso has published no novel which could be classed a failure by critics or the public, and several of his works have received awards, the most acclaimed being *The Obscene Bird of Night* (a favorite of reviewers and literary critics) and *A House in the Country*, which received the Spanish Critics' Prize, a coveted award despite its lack of endowment, since it reflects the esteem of the country's professional critics as a whole.

Donoso has been the recipient of two grants from the Guggenheim Foundation for the furthering of works in progress, has served as writer-in-residence at various American universities, with stints at the University of Iowa Writers' Workshop (1965-1967) and teaching positions at Princeton University and Dartmouth College. In demand as a distinguished lecturer, he also has held a number of editorial posts. His powers of sociopsychological penetration, his marvelous irony and skillful use of allegory, together with his masterful handling of existential themes and the abnormal or psychotic narrative perspective, place Donoso in the forefront of international fiction.

Biography

José Donoso, Chile's most widely known living writer of prose fiction and one of the most outstanding and prestigious figures of his generation of narrators in Latin America, was born into an upper-middle-class family of Spanish and Italian descent in Santiago. His father (for whom Donoso was named) was a physician; his mother, Alicia Yáñez, came from a prominent Chilean family. It was she who, with the couple's servant, Teresa Vergara, reared Donoso and his two brothers. Until her death in 1976, Donoso's mother continued to live in the spacious home where the future novelist was born, and the atmosphere of decrepitude and decay in the labyrinthine mansion (property of Dr. Donoso's three elderly great-aunts) haunts his fiction. When the boy was seven, his father hired an English governess, the foundation of his excellent knowledge of the language, which he continued to study at The Grange, an English school in Santiago, from 1932 to 1942. During this period, José's maternal grandmother returned from Europe to make her home with the family, an event which (together with her deteriorating mental and physical condition) left a mark on the future writer's development. A teenage rebel who disliked school and his father's imposition of the British sports ethic (personified in a boxing instructor), José began feigning stomachaches, which led to a real appendectomy and subsequently an equally real ulcer. Never serious about religion, he proclaimed himself an atheist at the age of twelve. Equally cavalier about classes, he cared only for reading, and in 1943, he dropped out of school. After two years during which he had not managed to hold a job for more than a few months, he set out for Magallanes at the southern tip of Chile, where he worked as a sheepherder on the pampas for about a year, subsequently hitchhiking through Patagonia to Buenos Aires, where he lived as a dockhand until he contracted measles, which obliged him to return home. He finished high school in 1947, enrolling in the University of Chile with a major in English and completing his B.A. at Princeton in 1951. His study with Allen Tate and his discovery of Henry James, as well as his introduction to the great paintings of the world, would all influence his future writings.

Returning to Chile, Donoso worked as a teacher, journalist, and literary critic but found himself estranged from his homeland and dissatisfied with his work. His ulcer returned, and he began psychoanalysis. He collaborated in launching the news magazine *Ercilla*, which he edited, and in 1954, his first short story written in Spanish ("China") was included in an anthology of Chilean short fiction. The following year, his first book, the collection *Veraneo y otros cuentos*, was published and had a favorable critical reception, winning the Santiago Municipal Short Story Prize. This success and that of his first novel notwithstanding, Donoso found Chilean society oppressive and moved on to Buenos Aires, where he met his future wife and stayed for two years. He published his second collection of short stories upon his return to Santiago, and became a leading literary critic, which led to teaching in the Writers' Workshop at the University of Iowa; he abandoned this position in order to move to Spain and finish a novel begun years before, which would become *The Obscene Bird of Night*.

Donoso and his wife, María del Pilar Serrano, whom he had married in 1961, adopted an infant daughter in Madrid and settled in Mallorca in 1967. His first Guggenheim award (1968) was followed by a lectureship at Colorado State University (1969), where his hemorrhaging ulcer required surgery; because of his inability to tolerate painkilling drugs, he subsequently went through a period marked by hallucinations, schizophrenia, and paranoia that resulted in suicide attempts. He returned to Mallorca, moved his family to Barcelona, and began to rewrite his novel, incorporating his nightmarish illness. Subsequently, still recuperating, he bought a seventeenth century home in Calaceite, remodeled it, and in 1971, moved to this village of some two thousand inhabitants in the center of Spain; both his critical history *The Boom in Spanish American Literature* and his novellas in *Sacred Families* were published in Spain. Donoso's second Guggenheim Fellowship, in 1973, enabled him to work on *A House in the Country*; his first trip to Chile in some nine years had to be canceled because of the military coup there (an event which colors both *A House in the Country* and *El jardín de al lado*). His next move, to the Mediterranean fishing and resort village of Sitges (1976), has obvious resonances in *El jardín de al lado*, which, like all of the author's fiction, has a strong autobiographical substratum.

Analysis

José Donoso's first two novels are similar in a number of ways, which makes it convenient to consider them together, despite significant and perhaps fundamental differences in the level of style and technique. Both involve upper-class, traditional Chilean families, a decaying mansion, and the problem of the "generation gap"; both treat psychological abnormalities in a rigidly stratified society where a rich, decadent minority is contrasted with an impoverished lower class, and in both, members of the aristocracy become emotionally involved with members of the lower class. In *This Sunday*, however, there is a more adroit utilization of innovative techniques and more subtle thematic development, a contrapuntal effect and stream-of-consciousness narration rather than the omniscient narrator of *Coronation*, who summarizes events and describes places and people in photographic fashion, sharpening the narrative perspective and involving the reader's collaborative effort, using secondary characters as third-person reflectors. Time in *Coronation* is treated in a linear, chronological manner, but in *This Sunday* it is subjected to a more fluid handling, reflecting the philosophical and literary theories of Henri Bergson and Marcel Proust while intensifying the latent Freudian and existential concepts of the first effort, with the result that the aesthetic and intellectual density of *This Sunday* is considerably greater.

Misiá Elisa Grey de Abalos in *Coronation* is a wealthy, demented nonagenarian who lives with her fiftyish bachelor grandson, Andrés, an asexual aesthete whose life is a prime example of abulia and existential inauthenticity, a man addicted to French history and collecting canes (possibly symbolic of his not standing on his own in life). Andrés' world, like that of his grandmother, is hermetic, monotonous, isolated from the "real" workaday world; virtually his only human contact is his lifelong friend, Dr. Carlos Gros. The two aging servants, Rosario and Lourdes, have devoted their lives to the service of the Abalos family but become unable to cope with and care for the bedridden Misiá Elisa; Estela, a sensual country wench, is brought in to care for her, introducing a new element into the previously closed system. Estela is something of a catalyst, awakening Andrés' dormant sexuality and introducing the neighboring shantytown's societal dregs into the mansion (and the novel) via her affair with Mario (whose older half brother, René, is a link with the criminal element).

Coronation is traditional in its technique and employs an almost Naturalistic cause-and-effect sequence, portraying most of the characters as products of their environment, although Donoso's interest in psychological analysis transcends the usual Naturalistic characterization. Social determinism underlies the formation both of Andrés, who studied law in his youth because it was the thing for young men of his class to do, and of Misiá Elisa, who is pathologically repressed, molded by the religious education and bourgeois puritanism of her family. A similar social determinism is responsible for Mario's fear of entrapment (partly cultural, partly based upon his brother's unhappy marriage); Estela's pregnancy thus inspires in Mario panic and instinctive flight.

Following Freudian psychology, Donoso stresses the importance of early childhood experiences, the power of the unconscious, and the central role of sexuality in other areas of human life, with much of the characters' conduct being irrational, neurotic, or motivated by repressed erotic urges. In her senile dementia, Misiá Elisa becomes overpoweringly obsessed with sexuality, which she suppressed during most of her life, and gives way to obscene outbursts.

Obsessions are a recurring motif in *Coronation* and in Donoso's fiction as a whole, and often are associated with recurring symbols, false rituals, repetitive or symbolic dreams, existential themes, and rigid daily routines which acquire an unconscious, magical, or supernatural character for the participants. Any break in the routine, therefore, is a transcendent disruption of order—hence the ultimately catastrophic ramifications of bringing Estela, the new servant, into the rigid and ritualistic existence of the mansion.

Misiá Elisa's conversations with Estela include warnings of the dangers of seduction and reveal that she considers all men "pigs" while considering herself a saint (having never let her husband see her naked). Life for the old lady is a gutter, a sewer, a cesspool from which religion is the only escape; thus she is also obsessed with sin, although for her, sexuality and sin are essentially identical. His grandmother's stern warnings and prohibitions and the inculcation of childhood fears and exaggerated taboos fill the boy Andrés with dread and apprehension, leading ultimately to his falsifying his first confession and, disappointed that instant fire and brimstone is not the result, to a loss of faith and rejection of religion, without any accompanying loss of inhibitions.

Plagued by a recurring nightmare in which a long bridge over an abyss suddenly ends, precipitating him into the void, Andrés experiences extreme existential anguish as he comes to realize the inability of philosophy or science to replace the security promised by faith and to assuage the fear of death, of the infinite, and of nothingness. Existentially, he is also radically alone, his solitude and loneliness so extreme that his abulia and inability to act are the visible result of the isolation and meaninglessness of his life. More than two decades spent in idle alienation, avoiding any engagement with life, end abruptly for Andrés when the terror inspired by his grandmother's approaching death is combined with the disturbing attraction of Estela's presence, bringing the realization that he has never really lived (in contrast with his friend, Carlos Gros, who represents an acceptance of life and love, believes both in science and religion, and exemplifies an existential exercise of free will). Where Misiá Elisa sees life as a sewer, Andrés sees it as chaos, terror, absurdity, a mad trick played upon mankind by an unjust or insane god. Both grandmother and grandson thus exemplify alienation so extreme that it borders upon the psychotic, their fragile equilibrium maintained by a series of obsessive routines and rituals—as in the case of Andrés limiting his cane collection to ten.

Donoso employs an indirect, third-person narration or monologue (comparable to the procedure of Henry James) to plumb the psychological depths of his characters and thereby to provide a multiplicity of perspectives, augment dramatic intensity, and allow the reader to identify more directly with a given character's viewpoint. The novel raises serious psychological, social, and philosophical issues, often through Andrés' very avoidance of them (an ironic technique which requires that the reader face the conclusions which Andrés has refused to contemplate), but Donoso also employs humor and numerous aesthetic ingredients. Incongruity is essential to many moments of humor, with the best examples involving Misiá Elisa, who, in her madness, swings like a pendulum from prudishness to obscenities to exaggerated religiosity. Similarly, the ironic contrast between Andrés' adolescent ignorance (in flashbacks to his childhood and youth) and the mature knowledge of narrator and reader provides much black comedy; for example, the young Andrés imagined that there was some connection between hell and the school restroom because the latter was a filthy place, and it was there that he first overheard a conversation about sex.

One of the recurring symbols or images of Donoso's fiction is the decaying mansion, often a Victorian monstrosity replete with gables and turrets, balconies whose only function is decorative, passages leading nowhere, closed or walled-up rooms, and other elements representative of a decadent or outmoded life-style. The mansion in *Coronation*, similarly constructed, also exemplifies Donoso's fascination with Art Nouveau—with its opulence of detail, decorative floral borders, and curving lines—while the depictions of the grandmother, her "coronation" and death (amid rococo bows, streamers, and billowing folds of cloth), function to complement and emphasize the theme of conspicuous consumption. The decadent mansion is a transparent allegory of a decadent upper class, while on an individual, psychological level, it also frequently symbolizes existential or emotional emptiness, isolation or alienation, and lack of contact with reality.

Another important symbol in *Coronation* is Andrés' collection of canes, rigidly limited to ten to exteriorize or make visible the rigid, self-imposed limits on his sterile, monotonous, routine existence. When the existential crisis provoked by confrontation with two of life's most powerful forces— love and death, both of which he has previously avoided—obliges Andrés to take radical measures, the one step he is able to visualize is raising the limit on his cane collection. His visit to the home of an antique dealer whose wife— with her pink shawl and naked palms, evoking a powerful subconscious association with Estela—profoundly disturbs him; thus brought to an awareness of his desire for Estela, he resolves to win her, a decision which, if carried out, would constitute his first step toward existential engagement and authenticity. As he returns home, however, an accidental glimpse of the girl with her lover beneath a streetlight mortifies him and brings realization of his own absurdity and that of his situation; unable to return to his once-comfortable abulia and solitude, he gradually retreats into madness (a denouement which, in Naturalistic terms, might be implicit in his heredity), succumbing to the pernicious influence of his grandmother, whose pervasive madness has gradually undermined his own rationality. Similarly, Mario's fear of becoming a criminal, arising from his brother's criminal nature, the family's increasingly desperate financial straits, and the injustices of society, presages his fall into crime: He is induced to participate in the theft of the Abalos family silver, thereby setting the stage for the grotesque denouement which combines the frustrated robbery attempt, Andrés' madness, and Misiá Elisa's death.

The themes of alienation and existential anguish reappear in *This Sunday*, but Donoso's interest in abnormal psychology and exploration of his protagonists' unconsciouses are much more visible than in the earlier novel. Don Alvaro Vives and his wife, Chepa, a wealthy, middle-aged couple, live in another of Donoso's mansions, where they are visited by their five grandchildren (one of whom narrates portions of the novel). Other characters include Violeta, a retired former servant of the Vives household and onetime mistress of Alvaro; Maya, a lower-class psychopath who has been convicted of murder; Marujita, a peddler; and Mirella, Violeta's illegitimate daughter, and her husband, Fausto.

In brief, the plot revolves around the activities of Chepa, as a volunteer welfare worker, her infatuation with Maya and use of the family's influence to obtain his parole. Settled by Chepa in Violeta's house, Maya is both attracted to his benefactress and fearful of her, and his pathology determines a path of escape through violence once again—this time through the murder of Violeta, which allows him to return to the comfortable alienation of prison, where no existential decisions are required. Rather than a straightforward narrative, *This Sunday* employs an ironic alternation between the naïve or limited vision of characters—first-person narrators who are participants in the action—and the occasional interventions of an omniscient narrator, thereby stressing the characters' ingenuousness, self-deception, or unawareness. Much of the narrative is retrospective, via the use of Proustian flashbacks (for example, Alvaro's recollections of the beginning of his affair with Violeta are stimulated by the smell of meat pastries, experienced years previously when he had gone to her house). Free association and indirect third-person, stream-of-consciousness narrative are combined in reconstructing Alvaro's life as a weak young man whose social position enabled him to exploit Violeta without assuming responsibilities, avoiding the threats represented by both university girls and prostitutes while preventing the servant girl from living an authentic existence of her own. A victim of the social conventions by which "decent" girls of his own class were sacred, meant only for marriage, Alvaro is unable truly to love Chepa and other upper-class girls, although on the basis of established mores, he assumes that he will love her; actually, he manages to consummate the marriage only by closing his eyes and imagining that he is making love to Violeta.

In their fifties, Alvaro and Chepa have ceased sleeping together, and both live behind masks, maintaining a façade which serves as a substitute for authentic relationships as well as an escape from unpleasant reality. Alvaro's inability to love having become more pronounced with time, he appears as narcissistic, withdrawn, and slightly ridiculous—aspects emphasized by his grandchildren's nicknaming him the Doll, his interminable games of chess/ solitaire, his deafness, his lack of concern for things other than his health, and his rituals. Chepa, a victim of a loveless marriage which has increased her basic insecurity, provides a self-portrait in a number of interior mono- logues, most of them precipitated by contact with Maya. As a lonely, aging woman whose children have left home, she seeks to give some meaning to her existence by works of charity—by helping the poor and through her work at the prison—in an attempt to compensate for the knowledge that for Alvaro she is an object devoid of significance. A good deal of sadomasochism inheres in Chepa's relationships with "her" poor; she imagines herself as "a littered bitch" with a compulsive need to feed the hungry mouths fastened to her. Her philanthropy is a substitute for the normal human relationships which are lacking in her life as well as a mask for less admirable motivations of her own, the desire to dominate or control, and to indulge her more (or less) than maternal interest in Maya. She helps him to set up a leather-goods shop, but her vigilance arouses his resentment and desire to escape; despite his derangement, Maya intuits in Chepa the devouring female, the Jungian evil mother.

Seeking Maya at Violeta's house, Chepa learns both that he has become Violeta's lover and that Violeta had an affair with Alvaro before his marriage to Chepa, provoking the latter's decision to throw off convention and look for Maya in the shantytown. Unfamiliar with the sprawling slums, she becomes lost in the twilight maze of alleys, but she fortuitously encounters Maya's mistress, Marujita, whose revelations of Maya's mixed emotions concerning Chepa inflame her and bring on a surrealistic, nightmarish experience as she is set upon by slum children who rob her of her furs and purse and leave her exhausted, on a trash heap. The inferno of the slums into which Chepa descends is a symbolic, expressionistic representation of her own subconscious with its hidden, conflicting sexual desires. Maya's murder of Violeta has been seen by critics as an instance of transferring his repressed aggression for Chepa to one socially weaker; the murder frees him from his obligations to her as benefactress, and to society.

The differences between Alvaro and Chepa are not so marked as the grand- children imagine; their inability to communicate with Alvaro leads them to see him as cold, absurd, and slightly grotesque, while the grandmother is perceived in an unrealistically positive fashion as generous and loving (perhaps a result of her own altruistic self-image), a participant in the children's games of fantasy. Actually, both Alvaro and Chepa suffer from inauthenticity, soli- tude, and unfulfilled emotions, but Chepa is close to achieving authenticity when she recognizes and accepts her desire for Maya and determines to seek him, while Alvaro has lived so long in egotistic aloofness, exploiting without giving, that no self-redemption appears possible. The novel's title refers to the family's habitual Sunday gatherings for dinner at the grandparents' residence, highlighting an incident of one specific Sunday, when Chepa searches for Maya, returning from the slums so traumatized that her subsequent life is almost that of a catatonic. Maya's murder of Violeta, who is vicariously Chepa, symbolically signals Chepa's death, and although she lives for many years, she spends them in isolation, essentially as dead to her grandchildren as if she were deceased. The rituals in the lives of adults are paralleled by the children's games, and additional parallels and contrasts throughout the novel lend symmetry: Alvaro's relationship with Violeta is socially similar to that of Chepa with Maya (a superior-inferior involvement); Alvaro and Violeta are passive, inert, making no effort to change their lives, while Chepa and Maya are active, attempting to improve their situations or to change them. *This Sunday* explores more complicated relationships, with more tragic repercussions, than those plumbed in *Coronation*, and does so in a more objective fashion, given the lessening of authorial intervention. Both novels, however, re-create the surrealistic and nightmarish effects of subconscious, irrational, or instinctive forces, achieving especially memorable portraits in the matriarchs (Misiá Elisa and Chepa), who undoubtedly hark back to the mental deterioration of Donoso's own maternal grandmother.

Hell Has No Limits, which was published in the same year as *This Sunday*, provides a departure from the novelist's previous urban settings, being set in a somber, sordid brothel in a backwater rural winegrowing area. Although the existential issues of authenticity and alienation, solitude, and incommunication found in the earlier novels are again present to some degree, there is an increased emphasis on absurdity and the grotesque, and Donoso begins to employ mythic elements and ambiguity, symbolically alluding to biblical myths of the Creation and the Fall in depicting the results of a failed economic experiment by a local politician, Don Alejo, who is a sort of local god, even said to resemble the Lord.

The village, Estación El Olivo, created by Don Alejo, a wealthy landowner and area boss, was touted as an earthly paradise at its inception, but some twenty years later, during the novel's present, it has become a caricature of itself, where physical and moral stagnation make it something of a hell on earth. Don Alejo had originally owned the brothel, but as the result of a bet between himself and the madam, Big Japonesa, he signed the property over to her (the wager involved Japonesa's managing to seduce "Manuela," a homosexual and transvestite who imagines that he is a flamenco dancer). Japonesa won, thanks to her astuteness in manipulating Manuela's erotic fantasy and a promise to make him her partner in the brothel, but during the incident she became pregnant and subsequently gave birth to an unattractive girl, Japonesita, who operated the brothel business following her mother's death. Japonesita, at twenty still a virgin despite her managing a house of prostitution, is a rival of her homosexual father in a subliminal competition for the affections of Pancho Vega, a truck driver, bully, and latent homosexual whose return precipitates the novel's climax.

Although Don Alejo, as "creator" of Estación El Olivo, is a benign god-figure, he is ambiguous by reason of being politically and morally corrupt (he also plots the destruction of the town, since he has decided to convert the whole area to vineyards). His wager, the precipitating factor that brings Manuela's family into being, is a parodic perversion of the concept of Christian marriage, and his association with the powers of evil is symbolized by four vicious black dogs which accompany him (similar dogs appear in *The Obscene Bird of Night*). The ambiguity of Manuela is primarily sexual, for he desires ardently to be a woman; some similar ambiguity appears in Pancho, who is muscular and seemingly virile but in reality is cowardly and a latent homosexual. The ambiguity of Japonesita, virgin madam of the bordello, is underlined by her lack of sexual maturity, her exaggerated thrift, and illusions which hinge upon buying a phonograph, a pathetically unrealistic hope, given the reality of her economic situation.

The catalyst in *Hell Has No Limits* is Pancho, who decides after a meeting with Don Alejo that he will enjoy one last spree at the brothel. He makes sexual advances toward Japonesita, but having aroused her (all the while thinking of his truck—both a Freudian sexual symbol and an instrument of suicidal escape), he sadistically rejects her for Manuela, whose dance provokes him, not so much to sexual desire as to murderous fantasies of disemboweling and leaving "her" lifeless.

The novel's brutal climax resolves Manuela's existential identity crisis (brought on by age and the depressing material situation): Leaving the brothel with Pancho and his brother-in-law, Octavio, after the flamenco performance, Manuela makes the mistake of kissing Pancho, who fears exposure of his latent homosexuality; this unleashes a nightmarish flight-and-pursuit sequence in which Manuela is beaten and attempts to seek refuge in the home of Don Alejo. Caught and beaten again, Manuela is sodomized by Pancho and Octavio and left nearly dead by the river. Whether this episode is fatal is also ambiguous; the novel ends on a note of pessimism as Japonesita extinguishes the brothel light and retires to the howling of Don Alejo's dogs and the sobs of a prostitute's child, traditional motifs of doom which combine with the blackness of night to underscore the impression of impending death and oblivion. Because of his psychological complexity, existential revolt, and commitment to ideals of art and beauty, Manuela is one of Donoso's most memorable characters.

The Obscene Bird of Night, considered by critics an antinovel because of Donoso's abandonment of traditional plot, character, and thematic development in favor of a more spontaneous depiction of reality and a virtuosic display of stylistic artistry, is the author's most complex work. Filled with grotesque fantasies, characters with multiple and fluctuating identities or protean, disintegrating personalities, the novel does away with conventions of logic and of mimetic literature, discarding any portrayal of objective reality to present the dilemma of modern man before the existential void.

Humberto Peñaloza, narrator and protagonist, begins as an incipient or would-be writer whose poverty obliges him to accept the job of secretary to Don Jerónimo Azcoitía, a wealthy aristocrat and influential politician. Jerónimo's wife, Inés, inspires Humberto's erotic fantasies, although her witchlike old servant, Peta Ponce, intrudes upon many of them, preventing the consummation—even in his mind—of Humberto's desire. When Jerónimo and Inés fail to have a son to carry on the family's distinguished name, Peta Ponce supposedly arranges for Humberto to have intercourse with Inés, who conceives and gives birth to Boy, a repugnant little monster, deformed to such an extreme that Jerónimo has him reared on an isolated, distant estate which is placed under the direction of Humberto. Whether Humberto fathers Boy is highly questionable; it may be only another fantasy, as are many other incidents in the novel (the ultimate reality of Boy is also questionable).

The distant estate, La Rinconada, peopled by monsters—gathered by Jerónimo so that Boy will not believe himself "abnormal"—is a grotesque, absurd mirror image of the Azcoitía estate and a possible expressionist allegory of Chilean society. Years later, after surgery for an ulcer, Humberto becomes obsessed with the notion that his physician, Dr. Azula, has removed eighty percent of his organs; Humberto abandons La Rinconada to take refuge in La Casa—a former convent which has become a domicile for retired female servants—where he retreats into silence and is called Mudito (mute).

Inés, now aging and frustrated in her aspirations to maternity, fails in a mission to the Vatican in which she seeks symbolic perpetuity via the quest for beatification of a homonymic forebear and also takes refuge in La Casa, where she spends her time despoiling the grotesque old inmates of their few miserable belongings in a dog-racing game which she always wins. Or does she? The visionary and phantasmagoric world of the protagonist-narrator is so fluctuating, so surrealistic and ambiguous, that the reader assumes the narrative consciousness to be schizophrenic or psychotic and mistrusts his representation of events. Humberto's schizophrenic symptoms include withdrawal from reality, hallucinations, living in a world of fantasy, systems of false selves, masks or personas, fear or terror of engulfment by others or the world, a feeling of imprisonment, and the imagining of himself as an infant. Donoso's uncanny capturing of the schizophrenic's perceptions undoubtedly owes something to his own experience of mental illness, with transient schizophrenia and paranoia induced by his inability to tolerate the painkillers given him after his operation. It is possible—and even plausible—that most of the novel's characters are phantoms generated by Humberto's deteriorating mind, and that the two worlds of the Azcoitía estate and the isolation of La Rinconada respectively represent the rational world of visible reality and the dangers of the invisible world of the unconscious.

Although the labyrinthine, dilapidated Casa has been seen as an archetypal Jungian symbol of terror, it may also be related to Donoso's use of the decaying mansion throughout his fiction as a symbol of Chilean society with its archaic social structures and decadence. Yet another such house, a seemingly limitless labyrinth with miles of underground passages, secret rooms, false or hollow walls, and hidden doors, appears in *A House in the Country*, seen by some as an allegory of Chilean politics and referring concretely to the military coup of 1973, following in the wake of other novels about Latin American dictators, such as Alejo Carpentier's *El recurso del método* (1974; *Reasons of State*, 1976), Augusto Roa Bastos' *Yo el Supremo* (1974), and Gabriel García Márquez' *El otoño del patriarca* (1975). If this is true, Donoso's novel does not present the biography of a dictator so much as the ideological configurations of a historical event, alluding to the opponents, victims and villains, the personal concentration of power and attendant aspiration to perpetuity, physical and intellectual repression, official rhetoric, and external intervention, with the house or mansion and its surrounding outbuildings constituting a metaphor for the totalitarian state, especially for the political prison, concentration camp, or detention center.

Beyond allusions to specific concepts or historically recognizable persons, *A House in the Country* is significant for its portrayal of a general problem in Latin America, a vast complex transcending geographical and political boundaries and involving the unholy alliance between oligarchies and foreign interests, militarism and dictatorships, the exploitation of the lower class and the lack of freedom of speech and of the press. It is an abstract political allegory of the abuse of power based upon bureaucratic structures, the novel of a family dynasty whose fortune is based upon mining in a remote rural area of lush vegetation and unreal, stylized geography, with significant subthemes such as adolescent rebellion, the conflict between idealism and materialism, the generation gap, psychosexual repression, conformism and hypocrisy, inauthentic values and life-styles, and radical solitude and the inability to communicate. Set in an imaginary country whose flora and fauna appear to be drawn from all of South America, *A House in the Country* employs a vague chronology, as befits its mythic and ahistorical nature. As something of a dystopia with strong existentialist undercurrents, it portrays a Kafkaesque world where utopia has gone awry via the symbolic narration of a "revolution": Children who take advantage of their elders' absence on an extended and unexplained trip take over the estate and set up their own regime, instituting some reforms among the natives but eventually quarreling among themselves and finally being discovered and chastised after a parental display of force involving the use of troops. *A House in the Country* is thus no more a realistic portrayal of recognizable reality than is *The Obscene Bird of Night*, although powerful realities of another order are captured and conveyed with forceful impact.

Donoso's later novels also display vanguardist tendencies, employing variants of the metanovel and self-conscious fiction, whose purpose is to erase the boundaries between the real and fictitious worlds, with the author being simultaneously creator and novelistic character, his novel both that which the reader peruses and another work whose genesis is subject or problem of the text at hand. The problem of the relationship among author, text, and reader is a leitmotif in *The Obscene Bird of Night*, *A House in the Country*, and *El jardín de al lado*, where it assumes preponderant proportions. In an encounter between the novelist and one of the Ventura dynasty in *A House in the Country*, the character criticizes many details of the narrative, a situation elaborated in *El jardín de al lado*; in both works, Donoso presents his literary theories or comments upon them, burlesques the expectations of the reader of conventional novels, parodies literary convention, and repeatedly destroys the mimetic illusion in favor of an investigation into the problems of the novel as genre, thereby further separating his last three novels from those of the 1950's and 1960's. Without ceasing to write of Chile, he has become more cosmopolitan in his choice of settings and characters; without abandoning social concerns, he has incorporated broader themes and more universal literary preoccupations.

Major publications other than long fiction

SHORT FICTION: *Veraneo y otros cuentos*, 1955; *Dos cuentos*, 1956; *El Charleston*, 1960 (abridged as *Cuentos*, 1971; *Charleston and Other Stories*, 1977); *Los mejores cuentos de José Donoso*, 1965.

POETRY: *Poemas de un novelista*, 1981.

NONFICTION: *Historia personal del "boom,"* 1972 (*The Boom in Spanish American Literature: A Personal History*, 1977).

Bibliography

Achugar, Hugo. *Ideología y estructuras narrativas en José Donoso*, 1979.

Bendezú, Edmundo. *José Donoso: La destrucción de un mundo*, 1975.

Coleman, Alexander. "Some Thoughts on Donoso's Traditionalism," in *Studies in Short Fiction*. VIII (Winter, 1971), pp. 155-158.

Gutierrez Mouat, Ricardo. *José Donoso: Impostura e impostación*, 1983.

McMurray, George. *José Donoso*, 1979.

Magnarelli, Sharon. "Amidst the Illusory Depths: The First Person Pronoun and *El obsceno pájaro de la noche*," in *Modern Language Notes*. XCIII (1973), pp. 267-284.

_____ . "The Baroque, the Picaresque and *El obsceno pájaro de la noche*," in *Hispanic Journal*. II, no. 2 (Spring, 1981), pp. 81-93.

_____ . "The Dilemma of Disappearance and Literary Duplicity in José Donoso's *Tres novelitas burguesas*," in *Prismal/Cabral*. III, no. 4 (Spring,

1979), pp. 29-46.

_____ . "From *El obsceno pájaro* to *Tres novelitas burguesas*: Development of a Semiotic Theory in the Works of Donoso," in *The Analysis of Literary Texts: Trends in Methodology*, 1980. Edited by Randolph Pope.

Nielson, Melvin Lee. "Ironic Portraiture in the Novels of José Donoso," in *Dissertation Abstracts International*. XXXVI (1979), 6793A.

Quain, Estelle. "Children and Their Games: Fiction and Reality in the Works of José Donoso," in *Requiem for the "Boom"—Premature? A Symposium*, 1980. Edited by Rose Minc and Marilyn Frankenthaler.

Quinteros, Isis. *José Donoso: Una insurrección contra la realidad*, 1978.

Stabb, Martin S. "The Erotic Mask: Notes on Donoso and the New Novel," in *Symposium*. XXX, no. 3 (Summer, 1976), pp. 170-179.

Janet Pérez

FYODOR DOSTOEVSKI

Born: Moscow, Russia; November 11, 1821
Died: Saint Petersburg, Russia; February 9, 1881

Principal long fiction

Bednye lyudi, 1846 (*Poor Folk*, 1887); *Dvoynik*, 1846 (*The Double*, 1956); *Unizhennye i oskorblyonnye*, 1861 (*The Insulted and Injured*, 1887); *Zapiski iz myortvogo doma*, 1861-1862 (*Buried Alive: Or, Ten Years of Penal Servitude in Siberia*, 1881; better known as *The House of the Dead*, 1915); *Zapiski iz podpolya*, 1864 (*Letters from the Underworld*, 1913; better known as *Notes from the Underground*, 1954); *Igrok*, 1866 (*The Gambler*, 1949); *Prestupleniye i nakazaniye*, 1866 (*Crime and Punishment*, 1886); *Idiot*, 1868 (*The Idiot*, 1887); *Besy*, 1871-1872 (*The Possessed*, 1913; also as *Devils*, 1953); *Podrostok*, 1875 (*A Raw Youth*, 1916); *Bratya Karamazovy*, 1879-1880 (*The Brothers Karamazov*, 1912); *The Novels*, 1912-1920 (12 volumes).

Other literary forms

The collected works of Fyodor Dostoevski are available in many Russian editions, starting from 1883. The most carefully prepared, nearing completion and comprising thirty volumes, is the Leningrad Nauka edition (1972-   ). A wide variety of selected works is also available in English. While the novels dominate Dostoevski's later creative period, he began his career with sketches, short stories, novellas, and short novels, and he continued to write shorter pieces throughout his working life. These works do not exhibit the same unity of theme as the major novels, though many of them in one way or another involve Dostoevski's favorite topic, human duality.

Dostoevski's nonfictional writing is diverse. In his monthly *Dnevnik pisatelya* (1873-1874, 1876, 1877-1881; *Pages from the Journal of an Author*, 1916; better known as *Diary of a Writer*, 1949), he included commentary on sociopolitical issues of the time, literary analyses, travelogues, and fictional sketches. He also contributed many essays to his own journals and other publications. The nonfictional writings often clash with the views expressed in the novels and consequently enjoy wide circulation among specialists for comparative purposes. Equally popular is his correspondence, comprising several volumes in his collected works. The notebooks for the major novels, as well as other background comments, are also included in the collection. They became available in English in editions published by the University of Chicago Press during the 1960's and 1970's.

Achievements

Both Leo Tolstoy and Fyodor Dostoevski, the giants of the Russian novel during the era preceding the 1917 Revolution, are firmly part of the Western literary tradition today, but while Tolstoy's outlook is solidly rooted in the nineteenth century, Dostoevski's ideas belong to modern times. His novels go far beyond the parameters of aesthetic literature; they are studied not only by literary historians and critics but also by psychologists, philosophers, and theologians the world over. Each discipline discerns a different drift in Dostoevski's work and few agree on what his basic tenets are, but all claim him as their hero. His contemporaries, too, were at a loss to categorize him, primarily because his style and subject matter had little in common with accepted literary norms. Russia's most prominent writing, as espoused by Ivan Turgenev and Tolstoy, was smooth and lyric. While Turgenev analyzed topical social problems in a restrained, faintly didactic manner, and Tolstoy presented panoramic visions of certain Russian social classes and their moral problems, Dostoevski brought an entirely new style and content to Russian writing. He disregarded his colleagues' logically progressing, chronological narrative mode and constructed his stories as mosaics or puzzles, often misleading the audience, experimenting with peculiar narrative voices, allowing his pathological figures to advance the plot in disconcertingly disorienting ways and in general forcing the reader to reevaluate and backtrack constantly. Dostoevski was also revolutionary in his choice of subjects, introducing characters whose perception of outside reality essentially mirrored their own skewed personalities.

Dostoevski thus rendered obsolete both his contemporaries' classical realism and the prevailing superficial treatment of the human psyche. In his choice of settings, he disdained the poetic landscapes preferred by others and concentrated on the teeming tenements of the city or the starkly barren aspects of the countryside. Because of this preference for the seamy side of life, he is often linked to Nikolai Gogol, but Dostoevski's descriptions of deviant behavior have a decidedly more modern flavor. During his enforced proximity to criminals, Dostoevski applied his powers of observation to their perverted worldview and, in the process, developed a new approach to literary portraiture; Sigmund Freud praised him for anticipating modern psychological approaches, and twentieth century psychologists on the whole have accepted Dostoevski's observations as valid.

Dostoevski tended to be conservative and didactic in his nonfictional writings, though his often cantankerous and controversial assertions contributed to the lively journalistic interplays of the time; to this day, there is disagreement over whether he affected a conservative public stance in order to be trusted with censorially sensitive material in his fiction or whether conflicting elements were actually integral to his personality. In either case, Dostoevski is responsible for leading Russian literature away from its often tranquilly harmonious narratives, with their clearly discernible authorial points of view, to a polyphonic plane.

During Joseph Stalin's reign as leader of the newly formed Soviet Union, severe censorial strictures limited the average Soviet reader's access to Dostoevski, yet interest in him remained undiminished, and he returned to his prominent place after Stalin's death. Outside his homeland, Dostoevski's influence has been immeasurable. Albert Camus—to cite only one among countless examples of twentieth century writers awed by the power of Dostoevski's metaphysical dialectics—transformed *The Possessed* into a gripping play, *Les Possédés* (1959; *The Possessed*, 1960), because he saw in Dostoevski's tortured protagonists the forerunners of today's Existentialist heroes. Dostoevski's work thus has remained topical and continues to appeal to widely divergent views.

Biography

There was little in the childhood of Fyodor Mikhailovich Dostoevski to presage his achievements as a writer of world-famous novels. Born into a middle-class family of few cultural pretensions, he received a mediocre education. His father, a physician at a Moscow hospital for the poor, ruled the family with a strict hand and enforced observance of Russian Orthodox ritual at home. When Dostoevski entered the Saint Petersburg Military Engineering School in 1838, he found himself unprepared for academic life; nevertheless he enjoyed his first exposure to literature and soon immersed himself in it. The elder Dostoevski's murder at the hands of his serfs (he had in the meantime become a modest landowner) and the first signs of his own epilepsy upset Dostoevski's academic routine, delaying his graduation until 1843.

Dostoevski worked only briefly as a military engineer before deciding to pursue a literary career. When the efforts of acquaintances resulted in the publication of his first fictional work, *Poor Folk*, his excitement knew no bounds, and he envisioned a promising writing career. His initial success led easily to publication of several additional pieces, among them his first novelistic attempt, the uncompleted *Netochka Nezvanova* (1849; English translation, 1921), and the psychologically impressive *The Double*. While these works are not considered primary by Dostoevski scholars, they hint at what was to become the author's fascination with humankind's ambiguous inner world.

The perfecting of this artistic vision was interrupted by Dostoevski's encounter with the realities of czarist autocracy under Nicholas I. Dostoevski was active in the Petrashevsky Circle, one of many dissident groups engaged in underground dissemination of sociopolitical pamphlets. Dostoevski's arrest and death sentence in 1849, commuted at the last moment to prison and exile, initiated a terrible period for the young author. On Christmas Eve of that year, he left Saint Petersburg in chains to spend four years in the company of violent criminals in Omsk, Siberia. The inhuman conditions of his imprisonment severely taxed his mental stability, especially because he was forbidden to write or even read anything, except religious matter. He later recorded these experiences graphically in *The House of the Dead* (initially translated as *Buried Alive: Or, Ten Years of Penal Servitude in Siberia*), immediately catching public attention for his psychological insight into pathological and criminal behavior. He spent an additional five years (1854-1859) as a political exile in a Siberian army contingent.

In 1857, after recovering somewhat from the ravages of incarceration, which had exacerbated his epilepsy, Dostoevski married a widow, Maria Isayeva, and hesitantly resumed his writing career. Upon his return to Saint Petersburg in 1859, he was drawn into a hectic pace of literary activity. Turgenev and Tolstoy occupied first place among writers, leaving the unfortunate ex-convict to rebuild his career almost from scratch. To facilitate the serial printing of his work, he ventured into publishing. Together with his brother Mikhail, he started the journal *Vremya* in 1861, using it as a vehicle to publish his not very successful novel *The Insulted and Injured*, which he had written primarily to alleviate financial pressures. When he visited Western Europe for the first time in 1862, his observations also appeared in *Vremya* as "Zimnie zametki o letnikh vpechatleniyakh" (1863; "Winter Notes on Summer Impressions," 1955). Before he could reap substantial material benefit from his enterprise, government censors closed the magazine in 1863 because a politically sensitive article on Russo-Polish affairs had appeared in its pages.

At this inopportune moment, Dostoevski indulged himself somewhat recklessly by revisiting Europe on borrowed funds in order to pursue a passionate love interest, Apollinaria Suslova, and to try his luck at German gaming tables. Unsuccessful in both pursuits, he returned to Russia in 1864 to risk another publishing venture, the periodical *Epokha*, which folded in less than a year, though he managed to print in it the initial installments of his first successful longer fiction, *Notes from the Underground*, before its demise. His personal life, too, did not proceed smoothly. The deaths of his wife, with whom he had shared seven unhappy years, and of his brother and business partner Mikhail in 1864 brought enormous additional debts and obligations, which led him to make hasty promises of future works. To extricate himself from one such contract, he interrupted work on *Crime and Punishment* and hastily put together a fictional version of his gambling experiences and his torrid love affair with Suslova. To speed the work, he dictated the text to a twenty-year-old stenographer, Anna Snitkina. With her expert help, *The Gambler* was delivered on time. Dostoevski and Snitkina married in 1867, and she is generally credited with providing the stability and emotional security that permitted the author to produce his last four novels at a more measured pace.

Despite the success of *Crime and Punishment*, Dostoevski still ranked below Turgenev and Tolstoy in popular esteem by the end of the 1860's, partly because their wealth allowed them leisure to compose carefully edited works that appealed to the public and their gentry status opened influential doors, and partly because Dostoevski's writings were uneven, alternating between strange psychological portraits and journalistic polemics, all produced in a frantic haste that seemed to transmit itself to the text. Dostoevski spent the first four years after his marriage to Snitkina in Europe, largely to escape creditors but also to feed his gambling mania, which kept the family destitute. He completed *The Idiot* abroad and accepted a publisher's large advance in 1871 to facilitate return to his homeland. His remaining ten years were spent in more rational pursuits.

Between 1873 and 1874, he edited the conservative weekly *Grazhdanin* and initiated a popular column, *Diary of a Writer*, which in 1876 he turned into a successful monthly. The appearance of the politically provocative *The Possessed* and of *A Raw Youth* kept him in the public eye, and he was finally accorded some of the social acknowledgments previously reserved for his rivals Turgenev and Tolstoy. The duality of his writings, at once religiously conservative and brilliantly innovative, made him acceptable to government, Church, and intellectuals alike. This philosophical dichotomy remained characteristic of Dostoevski to the end. In 1880, he delivered an enthusiastically received speech during the dedication of the Alexander Pushkin monument in Moscow, in which he reiterated patriotic sentiments of a rather traditional tenor. At the same time, his last novel, *The Brothers Karamazov*, expressed doubts about a single, traditional view of life. When he died two months after completing the novel, an impressive public funeral attested his stature as a major Russian writer.

Analysis

Fyodor Dostoevski's creative development is roughly divided into two stages. The shorter pieces, preceding his imprisonment, reflect native and foreign literary influences, although certain topics and stylistic innovations, which became Dostoevski's trademark, were already apparent. The young author was fascinated by Gogol's humiliated Saint Petersburg clerks and their squalid surroundings, teeming with marginal, grotesque individuals. These elements are so abundant in all of Dostoevski's fiction that he labeled himself a disciple of Gogol. Traces of E. T. A. Hoffmann's fantastic tales are evident in the young Dostoevski's preference for Gothic and Romantic melodrama. What distinguishes Dostoevski from those influences is his carnivalistically exaggerated tone in describing or echoing the torments of the lower classes. Not only does he imbue them with frantic emotional passions and personality quirks in order to make them strangers to their own mediocre setting, he also endows them with precisely the right balance between eccentricity and ordinariness to jar the reader into irritated alertness. While other writers strove to elicit public sympathy for the poor, Dostoevski subtly infused an element of ridiculousness into his portrayals, thereby reducing the social efficacy of the genre while enhancing the complexity of literary expression.

In Dostoevski's later, post-Siberian novels, this delicate equilibrium between empathy and contempt for the downtrodden is honed to perfection. The author supplements his gallery of mistreated eccentrics with powerful, enigmatic, ethically neutral supermen—highly intelligent loners, whose philosophies allow simultaneously for self-sacrifice and murder. Other favorite types are passionate females, aborting good impulses with vicious inclinations, and angelic prostitutes, curiously blending religious fanaticism with coarseness.

This multiplicity is the dominant characteristic of Dostoevski's style. It is for the most part impossible to discern in his works an authorial point of view. By using a polyphonic approach, Dostoevski has characters arguing diametrically opposed concepts so convincingly and in such an intellectually appealing fashion that readers are prevented from forming simplistic judgments. Most readers are held spellbound by the detective quality of Dostoevski's writing. On the surface, the novels appear to be thrillers, exhibiting the typical tricks of that genre, with generous doses of suspense, criminal activity, confession, and entrapment by police or detectives. While viewing the works from this angle alone will not yield a satisfactory reading, it eases the way into the psychologically complex subtext. Not the least of Dostoevski's appeal lies in his original development of characters, prominent among them frantically driven types who bare their psyche in melodramatic confessions and diaries while at the same time confusing the reader's expectations by performing entirely contradictory deeds. Superimposed on these psychological conflicts are other metaphysical quandaries, such as passionate discussions about good and evil, Church and State, Russia and Western Europe, free will and determinism. These struggles often crowd the plot to the point of symbolic overload, thereby destroying any semblance of harmony.

That Dostoevski is avidly read by the general public and specialists alike attests his genius in fusing banalities with profound intellectual insights. Nevertheless, a certain unevenness in language and structure remains. The constant pressure under which Dostoevski worked resulted in incongruities and dead spots that were incompatible with expert literary craftsmanship, while the installment approach forced him to end a segment with suspense artificially built up to ensure the reader's continuing interest. Some of these rough spots were edited out in later single-volume editions, but the sense of rugged style persists, and reading Dostoevski is therefore not a relaxing experience. No reader, however, can easily forget the mental puzzles and nightmarish visions generated by Dostoevski's work.

Notes from the Underground, Dostoevski's first successful longer work, already contained many elements found in the subsequent novels. The nameless underground man is a keenly conscious misogynist who masks excessive pride with pathological submissiveness. In his youth, his need for self-esteem led him into disastrous social encounters, from which he usually emerged the loser. For example, his delusion of being ignored by a social superior, who is not even aware of him, has caused him to spend years planning a ridiculous, and in the end miscarried, revenge. Dostoevski liked to use noncausal patterning in his compositional arrangements to enhance a sense of discontinuity. Thus, *Notes from the Underground* begins with the forty-year-old protagonist already withdrawn from society, spewing hatred, bitter philosophy, and ridicule at the imaginary reader of his journals. Only in the second part of the novel, which contains the underground man's actual confrontations, does it become clear that he has no choice but to hide himself away, because his twisted personality is incapable of even a casual positive human interaction. His very pronouncement is a contradiction, uttered in a continuous stream without developing a single argument, so that the overall effect is one of unordered dialectical listing.

On one level, *Notes from the Underground* was written to counter Nikolay Chernyshevsky's *Chto delat'?* (1863; *What's to Be Done?*, 1886), which stresses the benefits of scientific thinking and considers self-interest beneficial to all society. Through the underground man's irrational behavior and reasoning, Dostoevski ridicules Chernyshevsky's assumptions. He makes his hero a living refutation of scientific approaches. If human logic can be corrupted by the mind's own illogic, no strictly logical conclusions are possible. By indulging in actions injurious to himself, the underground man proves that human beings do not act solely out of self-interest, that they are, in part at least, intrinsically madcap. Thus, any attempt to structure society along scientific lines, as suggested by Chernyshevsky, is doomed to failure. The duality of the hero is such, however, that rational assertions, too, receive ample exposure, as the underground man refutes his own illogic and spins mental webs around the imaginary listener. *Notes from the Underground* is difficult to read, especially for those unfamiliar with Chernyshevsky's novel. The unprogressively flowing illogicalities, coupled with an elusive authorial voice, render the narrative undynamic and tax even the intellectually committed reader. Dostoevski himself realized an insufficiency, but blamed it partly on censorial editing of an obscure religious reference, according to which the hero saw a glimmer of hope for himself in Christianity. The deleted comments, however, do not carry such a weighty connotation, and Dostoevski made no effort to restore the cut text later, when he might have done so. In its emphasis on the dual qualities of human endeavor, *Notes from the Underground* is firmly linked to the subsequent novels, in which this theme is handled with more sophistication.

The wide appeal of *Crime and Punishment* results partly from its detective-story elements of murder, criminal investigation, evasion, confession, and courtroom drama. Yet Dostoevski immediately broadens the perspective of the genre. Readers not only know from the outset who the murderer is but are at once made part of his thinking process, so that his reasonings, motivations, and inclinations are laid bare from the start. The enigmatic element enters when readers come to realize, along with the murderer, and as slowly and painfully as the murderer, that he cannot assign a purpose to the crime, that human motivation remains, in the end, an unsolved mystery.

The very name of the hero, Raskolnikov, is derived from the Russian word for "split," and his entire existence is characterized by a swiftly alternating, unsettling duality. Raskolnikov is introduced as an intense ex-student who is about to put a carefully constructed theory into action. The opening chapters chronicle the confused state of his mental processes. He plans to rid the world of an evil by killing a pawnbroker who is gradually ruining her customers, Raskolnikov among them, and plans to use her hoarded wealth for philanthropical purposes in justification of the crime. Almost immediately, other motives call the first into question. Raskolnikov's mother threatens to sacrifice her daughter to ensure his financial well-being. An encounter with a derelict drunkard, Marmeladov, strengthens Raskolnikov in his resolve to kill, for Marmeladov keeps himself in drink and out of work by drawing on the pitiful earnings of his young daughter, Sonia, whom he has sent into prostitution. Raskolnikov notes in horror that he may force his sister into a similar situation through the legal prostitution of a sacrificial marriage. The crime itself renders all of Raskolnikov's musings invalid. He brutally murders a second, innocent victim, takes very little money, does not spend what he does steal, and will have nothing to do with his family.

From this point on, the novel focuses on Raskolnikov's struggle within himself. His prominently present but long repressed humanity asserts itself against his will to demolish arguments against confession provided by the proud part of his personality. Dostoevski uses the device of multiple alter egos in projecting Raskolnikov's dichotomy onto other characters. At one extreme pole stands the personification of Raskolnikov's evil impulses, the suspected killer and seducer Svidrigaïlov. Time and again, Raskolnikov confronts the latter in attempts to develop a psychological affinity with him. Raskolnikov's subconscious moral retraints, however, prevent such a union. Svidrigaïlov, and by extension Raskolnikov, cannot bring himself to perform planned abominations or live peacefully with already committed ones. Svidrigaïlov exits through suicide at about the same time that Raskolnikov is more urgently drawn to his other alter ego, the self-sacrificing, gentle prostitute Sonia.

While Svidrigaïlov is a sensually vibrant figure, Sonia is basically colorless and unbelievable, but as a symbol of Raskolnikov's Christian essence, she turns out to be the stronger influence on him. She is not able to effect a moral transformation, yet she subtly moves into the foreground the necessity of confession and expiation. Raskolnikov never truly repents. He has, however, been forced to take a journey into his psyche, has found there an unwillingness to accommodate murder, and, almost angrily, has been forced to acknowledge that each life has its own sacramental value and that transgression of this tenet brings about psychological self-destruction. The final pages hint at Raskolnikov's potential for spiritual renewal, a conclusion which many critics find artistically unconvincing.

Intertwined with this primary drama are related Dostoevskian themes. Raskolnikov, in one of his guises, imagines himself a Napoleonic superman, acting on a worldwide stage on which individual killings disappear in the murk of historical necessity. On another plane, Dostoevski weaves Raskolnikov's mother, his landlady, and the slain pawnbroker into a triangle which merges the figures in Raskolnikov's confused deliberations, so that murderous impulses toward one are sublimated and redirected toward another. Similarly, the figures of Sonia, Raskolnikov's sister Dounia, and the pawnbroker's sister Lizaveta, also killed by Raskolnikov, are symbolically linked. Raskolnikov directs Dounia away from his lecherous alter ego Svidrigaïlov toward his proper, goodhearted embodiment and friend, Razumihin, while he himself, in expiation for killing Lizaveta, becomes a brotherly friend to Sonia. An important and cleverly presented role is reserved for the detective Porfiry, whose cunning leads Raskolnikov to confess a moral as well as a legal transgression. *Crime and Punishment* remains Dostoevski's most popular novel.

The author's narrative mode does not differ drastically in the remaining novels. Though each work is built on a different drama, all are developed along Dostoevski's favorite lines of human duality, alter ego, and authorial ambiguity. These qualities find expression in a most controversial way in *The Idiot*, the incongruous, almost sacrilegious portrayal of a Christ-like figure. While the devout and selfless Sonia of *Crime and Punishment* occupied a position secondary to that of the central hero and thus lacked extensive development, Dostoevski makes the similarly self-sacrificing Prince Myshkin into the pivotal character of *The Idiot*. Through him, the author unfolds the notion that compassion and goodness, no matter how commendable on a theological plane, are insufficient to counter the less desirable aspects of reality.

The manner of Myshkin's presentation immediately challenges the reader's expectation of a "perfectly beautiful human being," as Dostoevski called his hero in preparatory notes. Myshkin—the name derives from the root for "mouse"—enters the novel as an insecure, epileptic, naïve young man, characterized by boundless goodwill, an immense capacity for humiliation, and a willingness to take the blame for the loathsome actions of others. He is a rather vapid personality, totally out of tune with existing human realities. Socially inept because of a long absence from Russia, ill at ease and inexperienced in confrontation with women, Myshkin is unable to establish satisfactory relationships. His kindness and empathy with suffering cause him to intervene repeatedly in other affairs, only to run afoul of the intense passions motivating his friends, and his interventions eventually lead to tragedy all around. Far from serving as counselor and redeemer, Myshkin is the cause of several calamities. Unversed in the intricacies of human interaction, created insufficiently incarnate by Dostoevski, the hapless protagonist leaves a path of misery and destruction before sinking totally into idiocy.

As he blunders his way through many unhappy encounters, several other themes emerge. The virginal hero actually has a sexually vicious and otherwise offensive double in Rogozhin, with whom he retains a close bond to the end, when both seemingly merge into one over the body of their mutual love, Nastasya Filipovna, freshly murdered by Rogozhin. Dostoevski assured outraged moralist critics that he had intended to create a perfect saint in Myshkin and implied that he had perhaps failed to create believable separate identities for Myshkin and Rogozhin, but Dostoevski's public assertions often contradicted the thrust of his novels, and it is more likely that here, too, he employed his favorite device of embodying the multifaceted human psyche in diametrically opposed figures.

In most of Dostoevski's novels, male characters are placed at center stage, leaving women to embody a given alter ego, highlight certain aspects of the protagonist, or echo other major concerns. *The Idiot* differs in presenting Nastasya Filipovna as Myshkin's primary antagonist. She is given scope and complexity in bringing to the surface Myshkin's temperamental inadequacy, in revenging herself for having been made concubine to the man appointed to be her guardian, in being torn by pride, guilt, and frustration, in vacillating between Myshkin and Rogozhin, and finally in orchestrating her own destruction. The other major female, Aglaya, receives less psychological expansion, but even here Dostoevski gives an interesting portrayal of a goodly woman unable to accept the humiliations associated with being Myshkin's companion. Dostoevski favored females of devious intensity, as typified by Nastasya Filipovna. In *Crime and Punishment* and *The Brothers Karamazov*, this type is marked by the identical name of "Katerina Ivanovna." Analysts interested in linking biography to plot perceive in these women an echo of Dostoevski's equally cruel and passionate friend, Apollinaria Suslova, as well as traits of his first wife, Maria Isayeva.

The preparatory notes to the novel reveal that Dostoevski changed perspective several times in shaping his guiding theme. In early drafts, Myshkin is a genuine double, possessed of many violent traits later transferred to Rogozhin. As Myshkin is stripped of negative features in later versions, he acquires the characteristics of a "holy fool," a popular type in pre-nineteenth century Russian literature, which depicts mental defectives as sweet, innocent, and specially favored by God. In the end, however there emerges the idea that an overflow of goodwill cannot vouchsafe positive results and can easily have the opposite effect. A certain meandering in the second part of the novel still reflects the author's hesitation in deciding on a direction. Earlier scholarship, unwilling to accept the fact that Dostoevski had depicted a failed saint in such a controversial manner, saw in *The Idiot* an unsuccessful attempt to portray a wholly Christian figure, but careful study of the text and background material reveals an intentional and original portrayal of a Christian dilemma. In succeeding works, too, Dostoevski's integrity as novelist took precedence over personal theological convictions.

In *The Possessed*, Dostoevski centered his attention on a very different type, the emerging Russian nihilist-atheist generation of the latter half of the nineteenth century. While the political aspect of the work occupies the general background, metaphysical and moral issues soon find their way into the narrative, as do satiric portraits of prominent Russians, among them a caricature of Turgenev, depicted in the ridiculous figure of Karmazinov. On the political level, Dostoevski demonstrates that revolutionary nihilism inevitably turns into a greater despotism than the order it intends to replace. One unscrupulous gang member, Shigalev, advocates a dictatorship of select revolutionaries and absolute submission on the part of the governed. For this reason, *The Possessed* faced long censorial repression in the Soviet Union, whose critics still find it awkward to present credible analyses of the novel.

The novelistic conspiracy is headed by a bloodthirsty degenerate, Pyotr Verkhovensky. Like Raskolnikov's murder in *Crime and Punishment*, Verkhovensky's killing is based on an actual event, the extermination of a student by the political terrorist Sergey Nechaev in 1869. Dostoevski's correspondence reveals that he was disturbed by the perverse publicity attending Nechaev's notoriety and intended to incorporate the incident into *The Possessed* for the purpose of deglamorizing such nihilistic misdeeds. In this he succeeded without question. Verkhovensky is shown to manipulate followers whose brutality and narrowmindedness easily fashion them into blindly obedient puppets.

The focus of the novel, however, is on an enigmatic atheist, Stavrogin, who is only passively interested in external events. Stavrogin has no plans, preferences, illusions, beliefs, or passions, and his actions are accordingly illogical. For example, he engages in duels, although he does not believe in them; marries a mental defective on a wager; bites his host, the governor of the province, on the ear; and calmly accepts a slap in the face from a subordinate. His very indifference to everyone and everything has made him into a charismatic figure, whom Verkhovensky and his revolutionaries revere as a deity.

Stavrogin is depicted in such a shadowy manner that no coherent portrait emerges. The notebooks for *The Possessed* record the author's difficulties in creating the character: In early versions, Stavrogin is more fleshed out and clarified, but in the end Dostoevski chose to present him as a riddle, to demonstrate that an incorporeal image, by its very nature, exacts the deepest loyalties. Stavrogin's disinterest in the world eventually leads to inner dissatisfaction and suicide. An interesting part of his portrayal, his confession to a priest that he is responsible for the death of a child whom he raped, was excised by the censors and never restored by Dostoevski. Omission of this episode strips Stavrogin of the feeling of regret implied in the confession and intensifies the impression of absolute ethical neutrality assigned to his personality. Stavrogin is the opposite of Prince Myshkin in every respect, uninvolved rather than concerned, bored rather than active, cruel and unpredictable rather than steadfastly compassionate, yet their endeavors lead to the same tragic end. Neither manages to cope with reality and both abandon the world, Myshkin through madness, Stavrogin through suicide.

Another major character carrying a symbolic burden is Kirillov, whose inner conflicts about the existence or nonexistence of God also drive him to self-extinction. Kirillov is Western-educated, influenced by the scientific discoveries of the age, and therefore an avowed atheist, who transfers godlike attributes to himself. As Dostoevski traces Kirillov's inner reasonings, he reveals Kirillov to be a philosophical extremist. Because he no longer believes in an afterlife but is inexplicably afraid of death, he conquers that fear by annihilating himself. His opposite, Shatov, a believer in the Orthodox Church and in the special status of the Russian people, ends as a victim of the conspirators; once more, the author's plot line follows two diametrically opposed figures to the same fatal end.

Both *The Idiot* and *The Possessed* lack a hopeful view of the future. The society and mores in which the major figures operate reflect moral confusion and material corruption, a Babylonian atmosphere which Dostoevski subtly ascribes to erosion of faith. As always, it is difficult to say exactly where the author stands. Clearly, he refutes the terrorism exercised by Verkhovensky and his gang. Their political intrigue assumes the metaphysical quality of biblical devils, "possessed" by love of ruin and chaos. The grisly demise of the other major characters suggests that Dostoevski also considered their approaches inadequate. The philosophical arguments, however, are presented with such conviction and honesty that no point of view is totally annihilated.

For most of the 1870's, Dostoevski was able to work at a leisurely pace, free from the material wants and deadline pressures of the preceding decades. It is all the more surprising, then, that *A Raw Youth*, composed in those tranquil years, is his least successful major novel. The reasons are painfully clear. The author overloaded the plot with poorly integrated, unrelated themes. What is worse, he let the rhetorical expression of his pet ideas overwhelm the artistic structure. The basic story deals with the illegitimate "raw youth" Arkady Dolgoruky, who is engaged in winning some recognition or affection from his biological father, Versilov. The narrative soon shifts to Versilov, a typical Dostoevskian dual type, motivated simultaneously by cruel passions and Christian meekness. Versilov carries additional symbolic burdens relating to Russia's alleged spiritual superiority over Western Europe. While Dostoevski failed to tie the many strands into a believable or even interesting panorama, he did attempt a symbolic scheme. Arkady's mother, Sofia, embodies "Mother Russia." She is on one side linked by marriage to a traditional peasant, Makar Ivanitch. At the same time, Sofia has been seduced and continues to be involved with Versilov, the representative of the Western-educated nobility. The hapless Arkady, the disoriented offspring of this unconsecrated union, is driven to drastic schemes in an effort to find his place in life.

Together with *Crime and Punishment*, *The Brothers Karamazov* continues to be Dostoevski's most widely read and discussed work. The author introduces no new concepts or literary devices, but this time he is successful in casting his themes into a brilliantly conceived construct. The conflict between a cruelly uncaring father and his vengeance-bound sons receives the artistic treatment missing in *A Raw Youth*. The metaphysical arguments, especially the dialectic between atheism and Christianity, are dealt with at length. Finally, the behavioral complexities of bipolar personalities are depicted in a most sophisticated manner.

The plot of the novel revolves around parricide. Four brothers, one illegitimate, have been criminally neglected by their wanton father, Fyodor Pavlovich, and subconsciously strive to avenge this transgression. The abominations of old Karamazov, some brutally indulged in the children's presence and partly involving their respective mothers, settle in the brothers' subconscious and motivate all of their later action and behavior. For most of the novel, none of the adult brothers is ever completely aware of the now-sublimated parricidal impulses, but all silently play their parts in seeing the old man murdered. The three legitimate brothers cope by nurturing father substitutes, with whom they enter into complicated relationships. The oldest, Dmitri, fights his surrogates, almost murdering one, while the youngest, Alyosha, a novice, faces deep mental anguish in cultivating a father figure in his spiritual superior, Father Zossima. Ivan, the middle brother, has transferred his hatred of his father to a metaphysical plane, where he spars with a cruel God about the injustice of permitting mistreatment of children. In his prose poem, "The Legend of the Grand Inquisitor," Ivan creates a benevolent father figure who shields his human flock from such suffering. Only Smerdyakov, the illegitimate offspring, keeps his attention focused on the primary target and actually kills old Karamazov, though his inner understanding of the factors motivating him is equally fuzzy. In desperation at not being fraternally acknowledged by his brothers, even after murdering for them, Smerdyakov implicates them in the crime and removes himself through suicide. The other three undergo painful self-examination, from which they emerge as better human beings, but not victorious. Dmitri, officially convicted of the crime, faces long imprisonment; Ivan's mind has given way as hallucinations plague him; and Alyosha seeks ways to combine his faith in a merciful God with the catastrophes of his actual experience.

Dostoevski has the major characters respond in different ways to their situation, developing each in terms of a specific psychological or metaphysical problem. Through Ivan, the author demonstrates the inadequacy of intellect where subconscious motivation is concerned. Ivan is educated, rational, atheistic, given to abstraction, loath to enter into close personal relationships, and proud of his intellectual superiority. Yet his wish to see his father dead is so powerful that it leads him into a silent conspiracy with Smerdyakov, whom he despises on a rational plane. The author attaches a higher moral value to Dmitri's type of personality. Dmitri represents an emotionally explosive spirit, quick to engage in melodramatic outbursts and passionate displays of surface sentiment. He instinctively grasps the moral superiority of the earthy, morally lax Grushenka to the socially superior, moralizing Katerina Ivanovna. His reckless nature leads him into many transgressions and misjudgments, but at a crucial point, when he has sought after opportunity to murder his parent, a deeply embedded reverence for life stays his hand. Alyosha acts as Dostoevski's representative of the Christian faith, and like all other Dostoevskian Christian heroes, he is subjected to severe spiritual torments. His faith is tested as the externals and rituals of religion, to which he clings, prove elusive, if not false, and he is made to reach for a more profound Christian commitment within himself in order to survive the violence engendered by the Karamazov heritage. He is given the privilege, rare among Dostoevskian heroes, of affecting his environment in a wholesome fashion, especially at the end of the novel.

Each of the three brothers is rendered more complex in the course of his spiritual odyssey. The atheistic Ivan defends the cause of the Orthodox Church in his formal writings and in the end loses all pride and reason as he humbles himself in a futile attempt to save the innocent Dmitri from imprisonment. Dmitri acquires a measure of philosophical introspection as he learns to accept punishment for a murder he ardently desired but did not commit. Alyosha, too, despite largely positive patterning, is shown to let hidden desire neutralize religious conviction. Charged by Father Zossima with acting as Dmitri's keeper, the otherwise conscientious and compassionate Alyosha simply "forgets" the obligation and thereby fails to prevent his father's murder and his brother's entrapment. Dostoevski envisioned a larger role for Alyosha in a sequel to *The Brothers Karamazov*, which never materialized. For this reason, Alyosha exits the work somewhat incomplete, incongruously engaged to a cunning, cruel cripple, Liza, who serves as his own unholy alter ego in the parricidal scheme.

The work abounds in secondary plots and figures, all interconnected and echoing the primary drama in intricate ways. Prominent among these plots is the legend of the Grand Inquisitor and its refutation by Father Zossima. Through the Grand Inquisitor, Dostoevski argues that Christian ideals are set too high for ordinary mortals, who prefer security and comfort to difficult individual choices. The Grand Inquisitor, in a dramatic encounter with Christ, thoroughly defends a benign kingdom on earth as most suitable for the masses. This argument is countered by Zossima's restatement of basic Christian theology, which does not answer the Grand Inquisitor's charges but simply offers traditional belief and practice of Christian tenets as an alternative perspective. The very type of behavior which proved ruinous to Prince Myshkin is in Zossima's actions converted into a richly beneficial model. By presenting the discourse in this fashion, Dostoevski cleverly juxtaposed humanistic and Christian arguments without resolving them. He thus once more implied that all so-called issues contain their own contradictions, that life and truth are indeed multiple.

By devoting his novels to the exploration of the mind, Dostoevski extended the intellectual horizons of his day. Though publicly a conservative of Russian Orthodox conviction, his long fiction continuously challenges the notion that atheism inevitably engenders wanton amorality. It is this recognition of human complexity, coupled with a fascinating narrative style, that gives Dostoevski his modern flavor.

Major publications other than long fiction
SHORT FICTION: *The Gambler and Other Stories*, 1914; *White Nights and Other Stories*, 1918; *An Honest Thief and Other Stories*, 1919; *The Short Novels of Dostoevsky*, 1945; *Best Short Stories*, 1965; *Great Short Works*, 1968.
NONFICTION: "Zimnie zametki o letnikh vpechatleniyakh," 1863 ("Winter Notes on Summer Impressions," 1955); *Dnevnik pisatelya*, 1873-1874, 1876, 1877-1881 (*Pages from the Journal of an Author*, 1916; also as *Diary of a Writer*, 1949); *Letters and Reminiscences*, 1923; *The Letters of Dostoevsky to His Wife*, 1930; *Letters*, 1961; *Occasional Writings*, 1963; *The Unpublished Dostoevsky: Diaries and Notebooks, 1860-1881*, 1973.
MISCELLANEOUS: *Polnoe sobranie sochineii v tritsati tomach*, 1972-   (30 volumes).

Bibliography
Curle, R. *Characters of Dostoevsky: Studies from Four Novels*, 1950.
Gibson, A. Boyce. *The Religion of Dostoevsky*, 1973.
Ivanov, V. *Freedom and the Tragic Life: A Study in Dostoevsky*, 1957.
Jones, John. *Dostoevsky*, 1983.
Mochulsky, K. V. *Dostoevsky: His Life and Work*, 1967.
Peace, Richard. *Dostoevsky: An Examination of the Major Novels*, 1971.
Wasiolek, Edward. *Dostoevsky: The Major Fiction*, 1964.
Wellek, R., ed. *Dostoevsky: A Collection of Critical Essays*, 1962.

Margot K. Frank

ALEXANDRE DUMAS, *père*

Born: Villers-Cotterêts, France; July 24, 1802
Died: Puys, France; December 5, 1870

Principal long fiction

Acté, 1838 (English translation, 1904); *Le Capitaine Paul*, 1838 (*Captain Paul*, 1848); *La Salle d'Armes*, 1838 (includes *Pauline* [English translation, 1844]; *Pascal Bruno* [English translation, 1837]; *Murat* [English translation, 1896]); *La Comtesse de Salisbury*, 1839; *Le Capitaine Pamphile*, 1840 (*Captain Pamphile*, 1850); *Othon l'Archer*, 1840 (*Otho the Archer*, 1860); *Aventures de Lyderic*, 1842 (*Lyderic, Count of Flanders*, 1903); *Le Chevalier d'Harmental*, 1843 (with Auguste Maquet; *The Chevalier d'Harmental*, 1856); *Ascanio*, 1843 (with Paul Meurice; English translation, 1849); *Georges*, 1843 (*George*, 1846); *Amaury*, 1844 (English translation, 1854); *Une Fille du Régent*, 1844 (with Auguste Maquet; *The Regent's Daughter*, 1845); *Les Frères corses*, 1844 (*The Corsican Brothers*, 1880); *Gabriel Lambert*, 1844 (*The Galley Slave*, 1849; also as *Gabriel Lambert*, 1904); *Sylvandire*, 1844 (*The Disputed Inheritance*, 1847; also as *Sylvandire*, 1897); *Les Trois Mousquetaires*, 1844 (*The Three Musketeers*, 1846); *Le Comte de Monte-Cristo*, 1844-1845 (*The Count of Monte-Cristo*, 1846); *La Reine Margot*, 1845 (with Auguste Maquet; *Marguerite de Navarre*, 1845; better known as *Marguerite de Valois*, 1846); *Vingt Ans après*, 1845 (with Auguste Maquet; *Twenty Years After*, 1846); *La Guerre des femmes*, 1845-1846 (*Nanon*, 1847; also as *The War of Women*, 1895); *Le Bâtard de Mauléon*, 1846 (*The Bastard of Mauléon*, 1848); *Le Chevalier de Maison-Rouge*, 1846 (with Auguste Maquet; *Marie Antoinette: Or, The Chevalier of the Red House*, 1846; also as *The Chevalier de Maison-Rouge*, 1893); *La Dame de Monsoreau*, 1846 (*Chicot the Jester*, 1857); *Les Deux Diane*, 1846 (with Paul Meurice; *The Two Dianas*, 1857); *Mémoires d'un médecin*, 1846-1848 (also as *Joseph Balsamo*, with Auguste Maquet; *Memoirs of a Physician*, 1846); *Les Quarante-cinq*, 1848 (with Auguste Maquet; *The Forty-five Guardsmen*, 1847); *Le Vicomte de Bragelonne*, 1848-1850 (with Auguste Maquet; *The Vicomte de Bragelonne*, 1857; also as three volumes: *The Vicomte de Bragelonne*, 1893, *Louise de la Vallière*, 1893, *The Man in the Iron Mask*, 1893); *La Véloce*, 1848-1851; *Le Collier de la reine*, 1849-1850 (with Auguste Maquet; *The Queen's Necklace*, 1855); *La Tulipe noire*, 1850 (with Auguste Maquet and Paul Lacroix; *The Black Tulip*, 1851); *Conscience l'Innocent*, 1852 (*Conscience*, 1905); *Olympe de Clèves*, 1852 (English translation, 1894); *Ange Pitou*, 1853 (*Taking the Bastille*, 1847; also as *Ange Pitou*, 1894); *Isaac Laquedem*, 1852-1853; *La Comtesse de Charny*, 1853-1855 (*The Countess de Charny*, 1858); *Catherine Blum*, 1854 (*The Foresters*, 1854; also as *Catherine Blum*, 1861); *Ingénue*, 1854 (English translation, 1855); *Le Page du Duc de Savoie*, 1854 (*Emmanuel Philibert*, 1854; also as *The Page of the Duke of*

Savoy, 1861); *El Saltéador*, 1854 (*The Brigand*, 1897); *Les Mohicans de Paris*, 1854-1855, and *Salvator*, 1855-1859 (*The Mohicans of Paris*, 1875; abridged version); *Charles le Téméraire*, 1857 (*Charles the Bold*, 1860); *Les Compagnons de Jéhu*, 1857 (*Roland de Montrevel*, 1860; also as *The Companions of Jéhu*, 1895); *Les Meneurs de loups*, 1857 (*The Wolf Leader*, 1904); *Ainsi-soit-il!*, 1858 (also as *Madame de Chamblay*, 1862; *Mme. de Chamblay*); *Le Capitaine Richard*, 1858 (*The Twin Captains*, 1861); *L'Horoscope*, 1858 (*The Horoscope*, 1897); *Le Chasseur de Sauvagine*, 1859 (*The Wild Duck Shooter*, 1906); *Histoire d'un cabanon et d'un chalet*, 1859 (*The Convict's Son*, 1905); *Les Louves de Machecoul*, 1859 (*The Last Vendée*, 1894; also as *The She Wolves of Machecoul*, 1895); *Le Médecin de Java*, 1859 (also as *L'Île de Feu*, 1870; *Doctor Basilius*, 1860); *La Maison de Glace*, 1860 (*The Russian Gipsy*, 1860); *Le Père la Ruine*, 1860 (*Père la Ruine*, 1905); *La San-Felice*, 1864-1865 (*The Lovely Lady Hamilton*, 1903); *Le Comte de Moret*, 1866 (*The Count of Moret*, 1868); *La Terreur prussienne*, 1867 (*The Prussian Terror*, 1915); *Les Blancs et les Bleus*, 1867-1868; *The Romances of Alexander Dumas*, 1893-1897 (60 volumes); *The Novels of Alexandre Dumas*, 1903-1911 (56 volumes).

Other literary forms

Other novels are attributed to Alexandre Dumas, *père*, which recent scholarship, such as that by Douglas Munro, Gilbert Sigaux, and Charles Samaran, credits more to his collaborators. Of the many editions of Dumas' works, the standard edition, *Oeuvres complètes* (1846-1877), in 301 volumes by Calmann-Lévy, is not always authoritative. The most recent and best editions of the novels are those in *Oeuvres d'Alexandre Dumas* (1962-1967; 38 volumes), published by Éditions Rencontre, with excellent introductions to the novels by Sigaux. Munro lists at least fifteen English editions of Dumas prior to 1910, and countless others have appeared since. *The Romances of Alexander Dumas*, published by Little, Brown and Co., has been updated several times. Virtually all of Dumas' novels are available in English and many other languages.

Dumas also wrote many plays, several in collaboration with other authors and a number based on his novels. A total of sixty-six are generally ascribed to him, among them *Henri III et sa cour* (1829; *Catherine of Cleves*, 1832; also as *Henry III and His Court*, 1931); *Christine* (1830); *Kean: Ou, Désordre et génie* (1836; *Edmund Kean*, 1847); *Mademoiselle de Belle-Isle* (1839; *Gabrielle de Belle Isle*, 1842; also as *The Lady of Belle Isle*, 1872); *Un Mariage sous Louis XV* (1841; *A Marriage of Convenience*, 1899); *Les Demoiselles de Saint-Cyr* (1843); and *L'Invitation à la valse* (1857, with Paul Meurice; *Childhood Dreams*, 1881). The plays are available in the *Oeuvres complètes*, occupying twenty-five volumes in the Calmann-Lévy edition. The best contemporary edition (in process) is *Théâtre complet*, edited by Fernande Bassan.

Dumas' other writings include histories, chronicles, memoirs, travel notes, articles, and essays. Among the more interesting of these are "Comment je devins auteur dramatique" ("How I Became a Playwright"); "En Suisse" (in Switzerland); *Quinze Jours au Sinai* (1838; *Impressions of Travel in Egypt and Arabia Petraea*, 1839); *Excursions sur les bords du Rhin* (1841, with Gérard de Nerval; excursions on the banks of the Rhine); *Le Midi de la France* (1841; *Pictures of Travel in the South of France*, 1852); *Le Spéronare* (1842; travels in Italy); *Le Corricolo* (1843; travels in Italy and Sicily); *Mes mémoires* (1852, 1853, 1854-1855; *My Memoirs*, 1907-1909); *Mémoires de Garibaldi* (1860; translation); *Les Garibaldiens* (1861; *The Garibaldians in Sicily*, 1861); *Causeries* (1860); *Histoires de mes bêtes* (1868; *My Pets*, 1909); *Souvenirs dramatiques* (1868; souvenirs of the theater).

Achievements

The Larousse *Grand Dictionnaire du XIX° siècle* of 1870 described Dumas as "a novelist and the most prolific and popular playwright in France." Today his novels are regarded as his most durable achievement; they are known to every Frenchman and to millions of other people through countless translations. Indeed, for innumerable readers, French history takes the form of Dumas' novels, and seventeenth century France is simply the France of the Three Musketeers. Dumas was an indefatigable writer, and his production is impressive by its volume alone: more than one hundred novels, including children's stories and tales. Although Dumas worked with many collaborators, the most famous being Auguste Maquet, Paul Meurice, Hippolyte Augier, Gérard de Nerval, and Auguste Vacquerie, a Dumas novel is readily distinguishable by its structure and style, sparkle, wit, rapid action, and dramatic dialogue.

Dumas' narratives teem with action and suspense; like the works of Eugène Sue, Frédéric Soulié, Honoré de Balzac, and Fyodor Dostoevski, most of Dumas' novels were first published in serial form, appearing in *La Presse*, *Journal des débats*, *Le Siècle*, and *Le Constitutionnel*, and later in his own journals, such as *Le Mousquetaire* and *Le Monte-Cristo*. He thus attracted a tremendous public, and he knew how to keep them anxiously awaiting a continuation. Sometimes he himself was uncertain what direction the plot of a given novel would take, and certain inconsistencies and discrepancies occasionally resulted from the serial format, but these are generally insignificant and surprisingly few in number. Often melodramatic, Dumas' novels nevertheless combine realism with the fantastic. Historical personages in his fiction maintain their role in history yet sparkle with life: the haughty Anne of Austria, the inflexible Richelieu, the independent Louis XIV. Like a careful puppeteer, Dumas never allows the intricate plot to escape him, nor does he resolve it until the end.

As a gifted dramatist, Dumas was above all a master of dialogue. The critic Isabelle Jan has analyzed Dumas' dialogue as the very life's breath of his characters, noting that Dumas succeeded in making even the dumb speak—the mute Noirtier in *The Count of Monte-Cristo*. Dumas' characters communicate by gestures and body language as well as by speech; indeed, in Dumas' fictions even stovepipes and scaffold boards are eloquent. The action in a Dumas novel is carried forward through dialogue; a Dumas plot is not described, it is enacted.

Though Dumas did not possess Balzac's profound analytical intelligence, he shared Balzac's powers of observation. Lacking Victor Hugo's awareness of the abyss and his visionary gift, Dumas nevertheless had Hugo's sparkle and wit. Indeed, both Balzac and Hugo admired Dumas greatly, as did Nerval, one of his collaborators, with whom he shared a taste for the occult and the supernatural. Unlike Stendhal, whose unhappy Julien Sorel was created "for the happy few," yet, like him, a true Romantic in spirit, Dumas wrote for all, proving that the novel could be both popular and memorable.

Biography

On July 24, 1802, Alexandre Dumas was born in Villers-Cotterêts, a suburb of Paris with souvenirs of eighteenth century royalty that was to figure in many of his novels. From his father, Thomas-Alexandre Dumas Davy de la Pailleterie, a general in Napoleon's service who dared to defy the Emperor and hence lost possibilities of future honors, he received an adventurous spirit and a mulatto ancestry. His father died in 1806, and young Alexandre was brought up by his mother with little formal education and a love for the country and its woods. In 1818, Adolphe de Leuven and Amédée de la Ponce began to initiate him into German and Italian, and later into the works of William Shakespeare and a love for the theater.

In 1823, Dumas left Villers-Cotterêts and, with little more than the few coins and letter of introduction (the minimum that d'Artagnan also carried), found a job as a copyist for the future Louis-Philippe through the intermediary of his father's former colleague General Foy. Dumas' passion for women developed alongside his love for the theater, and in 1824, he had a child, Alexandre Dumas, *fils*, by Catherine Labay. Dumas' first successful play, *Henri III and His Court* was played at the Comédie-Française in 1828. Thereafter his plays succeeded one another as rapidly as his liaisons, many with actresses, notably Mélanie Waldor; Mélanie Serre (Belle Krelsamer), the mother of Marie-Alexandrine Dumas; and Ida Ferrier, later his wife. He rapidly became acquainted with the most notable authors and artists, including Balzac, Hugo, Alfred de Vigny, and Eugène Delacroix. In 1831, Dumas officially recognized Alexandre as his son, separating son from mother and beginning a turbulent existence with his son that was to last his entire life.

After Dumas had received the Cross of the Légion d'Honneur and was reconciled with Hugo in 1836 (earlier, Dumas thought that Hugo, whom he regarded as a close friend, had taken portions of *Christine* to use for his own work *Marie Tudor*, 1833), the two of them operated the famous Théâtre de la Renaissance. At this time, historical novels in the manner of Sir Walter Scott became popular in France, and Dumas tried his hand at them. With many collaborators, the most important being Auguste Maquet, Dumas produced a tremendous output of fiction, particularly between 1844 and 1855— so great that Eugène de Mirecourt, in his 1845 "Fabrique de romans: Maison Alexandre Dumas et Cie.," accused Dumas of running a "novel factory." As the result of a lawsuit, Mirecourt was convicted of slander, and Dumas continued to write prodigiously, acquiring an immense fortune and spending his money with equal prodigality. In 1847, he received six hundred guests at the housewarming of his Château de Monte-Cristo, a lavish estate that he was to occupy for little more than a year.

The Revolution of 1848 curtailed Dumas' career as it did Hugo's. The Théâtre Historique, which Dumas had founded principally as a showcase for his own works, closed, and Dumas, like Hugo, went to Belgium in 1851, though Dumas' reasons were less political than financial, for he was pursued by his creditors. After reaching an arrangement with them in 1853, he returned to Paris, where he undertook publication of successive journals, such as *Le Mousquetaire* (1853-1857) and *Le Monte-Cristo* (1857-1860). He traveled extensively, always writing travel impressions of each place visited. In 1860, his liaison with Émilie Cordier led him to Italy and brought him another daughter, Micaëlla; he later visited Germany, Austria, and Russia. Among his many interests was cooking, and in 1869 he undertook a *Grand Dictionnaire de cuisine*, which was completed by Anatole France and published in 1873. In 1870, at the declaration of war, Dumas returned to Paris from the south. After a stroke, he returned to his son's home at Puys, where he died on December 5, 1870. In 1872, his remains were transferred to Villers-Cotterêts, and his fame continued to spread far and wide.

Analysis

Alexandre Dumas arrived at the novel indirectly, through the theater and an apprenticeship with history and chronicles. By the time he turned to the novel in the style of Sir Walter Scott, then intensely popular in France, he had already dealt with historical subjects in his plays and had explored the Hundred Years' War, the French Revolution, and the Napoleonic era in his chronicles. Indeed, one can follow French history from the Middle Ages, though rather incompletely, up to the nineteenth century through Dumas' novels. His most successful cycles are set in the sixteenth century (especially the reign of the Valois), the seventeenth (especially the periods of Richelieu and Mazarin), and the French Revolution, and the novels set in these periods are his best-known works—with the exception of *The Count of Monte-Cristo*, which is not really a historical novel but is rather a social novel or a *roman de moeurs*. His best historical fiction was written in the years from 1843 to

1855. Dumas' novels after 1855 are chiefly concerned with the French Revolution, the Directory, and the nineteenth century, and are less well-known than his earlier works.

Among Dumas' medieval novels are *Otho the Archer*, which evokes a German medieval legend; *Lyderic, Count of Flanders*, set in seventh century Flanders; and *The Bastard of Mauléon*, which covers the period from 1358 to 1369, the earlier part of the Hundred Years' War. Dumas treats the period from 1500 to 1570 in greater detail, in scattered novels from 1843 to 1858. *The Brigand* treats the period from 1497 to 1519 and focuses on the youth of Charles V. *The Two Dianas* and *Ascanio*, written with the collaboration of Meurice, treat the reign of François I and the presence of Benvenuto Cellini at the French court. The two Dianas are Diane de Castro and Diane de Poitiers. *The Page of the Duke of Savoy*, set in the years 1555 to 1559, with an epilogue that takes place in 1580, is a companion to *The Two Dianas*. The final novel of the series, *The Horoscope*, treats the beginning of the reign of François II.

The Valois cycle, which covers the period from August, 1572, to June, 1586, comprises three of the most successful and popular of Dumas' historical romances. *Marguerite de Navarre* treats the period from 1572 to 1575, beginning with the wedding of Marguerite de Valois and Henri de Navarre and focusing on their various romantic intrigues; the novel concludes with the famous Saint Bartholemew's Day Massacre. The second book in the cycle, *Chicot the Jester*, is the most popular and introduces one of Dumas' finest creations: Chicot, a rival of d'Artagnan and similar to him in many ways. The novel covers the period from 1578 to 1579 under Henri III and focuses on the death of Bussy d'Amboise. The last book in the cycle, *The Forty-Five Guardsmen*, covers the years from 1582 to 1584; it tells of the Ligue, the Duc de Guise, and the vengeance of the Duc d'Anjou for Bussy's murder.

Unquestionably Dumas' best-written and most popular cycle, however, is that of d'Artagnan, which covers the period from 1625 to 1673. It includes *The Three Musketeers*, the immortal story of Athos, Porthos, and Aramis, who, together with d'Artagnan, interact in the stories of Richelieu, Louis XIII, Anne of Austria, and the Duke of Buckingham, from 1625 to 1628. *Twenty Years After*, as the title indicates, takes place in 1648 and finds the same characters involved with Anne of Austria and Mazarin, the Fronde, and the Civil War in England. *The Vicomte de Bragelonne*, a lengthy account largely set in the period from 1660 to 1673, focuses less on the musketeers than on Louis XIV, Fouquet, and the Man in the Iron Mask. The intervening years (1628 to 1648) are covered in three less important novels, the best being *The War of the Women*, which deals with the new Fronde of 1648 to 1650.

The century from 1670 to 1770 is the subject of four novels, of which the best known are the companion works *The Chevalier d'Harmental* and *The Regent's Daughter*, both of which deal with the Cellamare conspiracy of 1718.

The Marie Antoinette cycle, often referred to collectively by the title of the first volume, *Memoirs of a Physician*, takes place between 1770 and 1791 and is also a very popular series. The first book in the cycle, written in collaboration with Macquet, covers the period between 1770 and 1774, including the death of Louis XV and the marriage of Marie Antoinette to Louis XVI. *The Queen's Necklace* focuses on the scandal of the Queen's diamond necklace and her love affair with Charny from 1784 to 1786. *Taking the Bastille* covers only four months in 1789, the period of the taking of the Bastille. Finally, *The Countess de Charny* begins in 1789, covers the King's flight to Varennes in 1791 and the destinies of Andrée and Charny, and concludes with the King's execution in 1793. Although the series lacks a strong central character, with the possible exception of Joseph Balsamo, it is important for its emphasis on women.

Five other novels cover the intervening period until 1800, of which *The Whites and the Blues*, showing the influence of the novelist Charles Nodier, is the best known. Six novels treat the Napoleonic period, the Restoration, and the reign of Louis-Philippe. Of these, *Les Mohicans de Paris*, dealing with the revolution under the Restoration in the 1820's, and *Salvator*, its companion, together form Dumas' longest novel; although not his most popular, it is a highly representative work.

In Dumas' many social novels, there are frequent historical excursions; among his finest and most popular works in this genre is *The Count of Monte-Cristo*, which begins with Napoleon's exile at Elba, the Hundred Days, and the second Restoration. In the manner of Balzac, this great novel depicts the greed and selfishness of the Parisian aristocracy and the consuming passion of ambition. Dumas treated racial prejudice in *George*, set in Mauritius, and depicted his own native town in three novels known as the Villers-Cotterêts cycle: *Conscience*, *Catherine Blum*, and *The Wolf Leader*.

In virtually all of his novels, Dumas excels in plot and dialogue. His most successful works blend history or social observation with fantasy, and his plots nearly always involve mystery and intrigue. Usually they concern romantic involvements, yet there are relatively few scenes of romance.

Although Dumas' novels are rich with memorable characters, he does not focus on psychological development. A given character remains essentially the same from the beginning to the end of a work. Despite the disguises and the mysteries that often surround a character's name—even the three musketeers have strange aliases—there is never an aspect of personality that remains to be discovered. Dumas' characters are not inspired by moral idealism; they are usually motivated by ambition, revenge, or simply a love for adventure. Dumas does not instruct, but he also does not distort the great movements of history or of social interaction. He aims principally to entertain, to help his readers forget the world in which they live and to move with his characters into a fantastic world that is sometimes truer to life than reality.

The famous d'Artagnan trilogy, which is made up of *The Three Musketeers*, *Twenty Years After*, and *The Vicomte de Bragelonne*, has three differing basic texts: the first, the original published in *Le Siècle*; the second in pirated Belgian texts; the third published by Baudry; many other versions exist as well. The series is set in the seventeenth century and covers the period from 1625 to 1673, focusing on the events during the period of Richelieu, Mazarin, and Louis XIV. The main characters, and even some secondary ones, have their sources in history, although their interaction with the major historical figures is often imaginary. Dumas' primary source is the *Mémoires de M. d'Artagnan* (1700), a fabricated account of d'Artagnan's life by Gatien de Courtilz de Sandras. The trilogy provides an excellent introduction to Dumas' use of historical sources, his storytelling technique, his dramatic power, and his creation of character.

The Three Musketeers begins in April, 1625, at Meung-sur-Loire, where the Quixote-like d'Artagnan, a young Gascon of eighteen years, is making his way to Paris with a letter of introduction to Monsieur de Tréville, the captain of the King's musketeers. It is here that he meets the Count of Rochefort, Richelieu's right-hand man, and "Milady," a beautiful and mysterious woman whose path will cross his throughout the novel and whose shadow will haunt him for the next twenty years. In Paris, d'Artagnan becomes fast friends with Athos, Porthos, and Aramis, the three musketeers who share his adventures throughout the novel. D'Artagnan falls in love with Constance Bonacieux, his landlord's wife, also a lady-in-waiting to the Queen, Anne of Austria. He thus becomes involved in recovering the Queen's diamond studs, a present from the King that she has unwisely given to her lover, the handsome Duke of Buckingham, Richelieu's rival in both political and amorous intrigue. D'Artagnan falls in love with the bewitching Milady and discovers her criminal past, for which knowledge she begins an inexorable pursuit of him. Meanwhile, the siege of La Rochelle permits the four friends to display their bravery and to develop a plot against Milady, who in a very complex intrigue becomes an agent in Buckingham's assassination. Milady's revenge leads her to poison Constance, and for this final crime she is tried and condemned by the four musketeers and her brother-in-law, Lord de Winter. Since the siege of La Rochelle ends to Richelieu's advantage through the invaluable assistance of the musketeers, d'Artagnan becomes a friend of Richelieu and a lieutenant of the musketeers. Porthos marries his mistress, the widowed Madame Coquenard; Aramis becomes a priest; and Athos, or the Comte de la Fère, after a few more years of military service, retires to his estate in Roussillon.

Twenty Years After, as the title indicates, begins in 1648, twenty years after the conclusion of *The Three Musketeers*; Mazarin is at the helm of the government, and Paris is on the verge of the Fronde, a rebellion of the nobles against the regent. The lives of the four musketeers have been singularly without adventure during the preceding twenty years; d'Artagnan, still a lieutenant in the musketeers, lives with "the fair Madeleine" in Paris; Athos, Comte de la Fère, spends his time bringing up his son, Raoul de Bragelonne; Porthos, now Comte du Vallon and master of three estates, is dissatisfied with his lot and aspires to become a baron; Aramis, formerly a musketeer who aspired to be an abbé, is now the Abbé d'Herblay and longs to be a musketeer again. The four men, now a bit distrustful of one another, are unable to join forces, since Athos and Aramis are *frondeurs* and d'Artagnan and Porthos are cardinalists. They meet on opposite sides in their first encounter with the Duke of Beaufort, who escapes from d'Artagnan. Subsequently in England, during Cromwell's overthrow of Charles I, they find themselves opponents but join in an unsuccessful attempt to save the King. Their efforts in this and other intrigues are thwarted by Mordaunt, Milady's son, who seeks to avenge his mother and finally meets with a violent death at sea. Their united support of Charles I wins the four imprisonment from Mazarin, whom they in turn abduct and coerce into signing certain concessions to the *frondeurs*. At the end, d'Artagnan becomes captain of the musketeers and Porthos, a baron.

The third novel in the series, *Le Vicomte de Bragelonne*, which is twice as long as the two previous novels together, covers the period from 1660 to 1673, from Louis XIV's visit to Blois in 1659 and his marriage to Marie-Thérèse of Spain to the death of d'Artagnan. It has four centers of interest: the restoration of Charles II of England; the love affair of Louis XIV and Louise de la Vallière; the trial of Fouquet; and the famous tale of the Man in the Iron Mask. The musketeers are no longer in the foreground; in fact, they do not even appear in several episodes, and the novel as a whole is more disconnected than its predecessors in the trilogy. The main character, Raoul de Bragelonne (Athos' son), is unconvincing, though Louis XIV in particular emerges as a well-developed figure. Indeed, the historical characters dominate the novel, giving it the quality of a "sweeping pageant," as Richard Stowe describes it.

The d'Artagnan novels, especially *The Three Musketeers*, are Dumas at his best. They include his most successful character portrayals, both the primary historical figures—Richelieu, Mazarin, Anne of Austria, and Louis XIV— and the musketeers, who also have a basis in history. D'Artagnan especially is an immortal creation, partaking at once of Don Quixote, the clown, and Ariel; he is a creature of the air and the night whose age hardly seems to matter and whose sprightly, carefree manner is balanced by his inflexible loyalty to his three musketeer friends and to his masters. The three books in the trilogy, more successfully than any others, combine history and fiction and are perhaps the most popular novels produced in the nineteenth century.

Rivaling the d'Artagnan saga in popularity is *The Count of Monte-Cristo*. Incredible as the adventures of Monte-Cristo may seem, they are based on reality. In 1842, Dumas visited Elba with Prince Jérôme, son of Napoleon's youngest brother, and sailed around the island of Monte-Cristo. Dumas said that he would someday immortalize it. At about the same time, he was approached by Béthune and Plon to write a work entitled "Impressions de voyage dans Paris" (travel impressions in Paris). Béthune and Plon did not want an archeological or scientific work, but rather a novel like Eugène Sue's *Les Mystères de Paris* (1842-1843; *The Mysteries of Paris*, 1843). Dumas found the germ of a plot in "Le diamant et la vengeance," a chapter in *Mémoires tirés des archives de la Police de Paris* (1837-1838) by Jacques Peuchet, referred to by Dumas in his *Causeries* as "État civil du 'Comte de Monte Cristo.'" The main character of *The Count of Monte-Cristo* is based on an unjustly imprisoned shoemaker named François Picaud.

The Count of Monte-Cristo first appeared serially, in *Le Journal des débats*, with the spelling Christo, a spelling also used in the Belgian pirated editions. Unlike Dumas' historical novels, *The Count of Monte-Cristo* is set in contemporary France and, except for short passages relating to Napoleon and Louis XVIII, is almost totally a *roman de moeurs*.

The lengthy novel is divided into three unequal parts—based on the cities in which the action takes place, Marseilles, Rome, and Paris—the last being by far the longest. Part 1 opens in 1815, in Marseilles, where Dumas introduces the attractive first mate of the ship *Pharaon*, Edmond Dantès, soon to be promoted to captain. He is celebrating his impending marriage to his beautiful Catalan sweetheart, Mercédès, when he is suddenly arrested. Earlier, the dying captain of the *Pharaon* had given him a letter to deliver to a Bonapartist group in Paris, and because of this he has been accused of treason by two jealous companions: Danglars, the ship's accountant, and Fernand, Dantès' rival for the hand of Mercédès. Caderousse, a neighbor, learns of the plot against Dantès but remains silent. Villefort, the *procureur du roi*, is sympathetic to Dantès until he discovers that the letter is intended for his father, whose Bonapartist and Girondist political views he despises, seeing them as a threat to his own future. He therefore allows Dantès to be condemned to solitary confinement at the nearby Château d'If. Dantès, resentful and despairing, remains in prison for fourteen years, during which time he makes the acquaintance of the Abbé Faria (a character based on a real person), who instructs Dantès in history, mathematics, and languages and wills him the fabulous treasure which the Abbé has hidden on the island of Monte-Cristo. At the Abbé's death, Dantès changes places with his corpse in the funeral sack, is thrown into the sea, and swims to safety.

Once free, Dantès claims the treasure and learns the whereabouts of his betrayers: Danglars has become a successful banker, while Fernand, after acquiring wealth by betraying Pasha Ali in the Greek revolution, has gained the title of Count de Morcerf and has married Mercédès. Shortly afterward, Dantès, now the Count of Monte-Cristo, assumes the persona of Sinbad the Sailor and entertains the Baron Franz d'Épinay at Monte-Cristo. An atmosphere reminiscent of *The Arabian Nights' Entertainments* dazzles Franz, who hardly knows if what he sees is real or imaginary. Later, Franz, in the company of his friend Albert de Morcerf, the son of Mercédès and Fernand, again meets Monte-Cristo in Rome, where Monte-Cristo saves Morcerf from the kidnaper, Luigi Vampa. Albert invites Monte-Cristo to visit him in Paris, thus introducing part 3.

Part 3 is properly speaking the story of Dantès' vengeance and takes place twenty-three years after he was first imprisoned. Disguised sometimes as Monte-Cristo, sometimes as the Abbé Busoni, sometimes as Lord Wilmore, Dantès dazzles all of Paris by his endless wealth, powerful connections, and enigmatic manner. Meanwhile, he slowly but surely sets the stage for his revenge. Directly attacking no one, he nevertheless brings his four enemies to total ruin by intricate and complex machinations. The greedy Caderousse, who gave silent assent to Dantès' imprisonment, is killed by an anonymous assassin while attempting to rob Monte-Cristo's rich hotel on the Champs-Élysées. Before his death, he learns Monte-Cristo's real identity. Danglars is the next victim; by means of false information, Monte-Cristo succeeds in ruining him financially and exposing his wife's greed and infidelity. Fernand is brought down in turn when Monte-Cristo, with the aid of his adopted daughter, Haydée (the natural daughter of Pasha Ali), brings to light several acts of cowardice of which Fernand was guilty during his army service. Fernand's son Albert challenges Monte-Cristo to a duel, but through the intercession of Mercédès, who recognizes her fiancé of many years before, Albert's life is spared. The last victim is Villefort, whose daughter Valentine is in love with Maximilien Morrel, the son of a shipping master who had aided Dantès and his father long ago. Monte-Cristo encourages Madame de Villefort's greedy efforts to acquire the wealth of Valentine (who is her stepdaughter), and the Villefort family is all but destroyed by the poison Madame de Villefort administers as part of her plan; Valentine herself is an apparent victim. Saved by Monte-Cristo, she is at last reunited with her lover on the island of Monte-Cristo, which Edmond Dantès reveals to the lovers as the site of the treasure he bequeaths to them. He sails off in the distance, his revenge complete. The revenge has also brought about a second transformation in Dantès, for he is now a man who "like Satan, thought himself for an instant equal to God, but now acknowledges, with Christian humility, that God alone possesses supreme power and infinite wisdom."

Major publications other than long fiction

PLAYS: *La Noce et l'enterrement*, 1826; *Henri III et sa cour*, 1829 (*Catherine of Cleves*, 1832; also as *Henry III and His Court*, 1931); *Christine*, 1830; *Antony*, 1831 (English translation, 1931); *Charles VII chez ses grands vassaux*, 1831; *Napoléon Bonaparte*, 1831; *Richard Darlington*, 1831; *Le Mari et la veuve*, 1832; *Teresa*, 1832 (with Auguste Anicet-Bourgeois); *La Tour de Nesle*, 1832 (with Frédéric Gaillardet; English translation, 1906); *Angèle*, 1833; *Cath-*

erine Howard, 1834 (English translation, 1859); *Don Juan de Marana: Ou, La Chute d'un ange*, 1836; *Kean: Ou, Désordre et génie*, 1836 (*Edmund Kean*, 1847); *Caligula*, 1837; *Piquillo*, 1837 (libretto; with Gérard de Nerval); *Paul Jones*, 1838; *L'Alchimiste*, 1839; *Bathilde*, 1839 (with Auguste Maquet); *Léo Burchart*, 1839 (with Gérard de Nerval); *Mademoiselle de Belle-Isle*, 1839 (*Gabrielle de Belle Isle*, 1842; also as *The Lady of Belle Isle*, 1872); *Un Mariage sous Louis XV*, 1841 (*A Marriage of Convenience*, 1899); *Les Demoiselles de Saint-Cyr*, 1843; *Les Mousquetaires*, 1845 (with Auguste Maquet); *Une Fille du Régent*, 1846; *La Reine Margot*, 1847; *Monte-Cristo*, 1848 (with Auguste Maquet); *Le Comte de Morcerf*, 1851 (with Auguste Maquet); *Villefort*, 1851 (with Auguste Maquet); *L'Invitation à la valse*, 1857 (with Paul Meurice; *Childhood Dreams*, 1881); *Le Roman d'Elvire*, 1860 (with Adolphe de Leuven); *Les Blancs et les Bleus*, 1869; *Théâtre complet*, 1974- (Fernande Bassan, editor); *The Great Lover and Other Plays*, 1979.

NONFICTION: *Gaule et France*, 1833 (*The Progress of Democracy*, 1841); *Impressions de voyage*, 1833, 1838, 1841, 1843 (*Travels in Switzerland*, 1958); *La Vendée et Madame*, 1833 (*The Duchess of Berri in La Vendée*, 1833); *Guelfes et Gibelins*, 1836; *Isabel de Bavière*, 1836 (*Isabel of Bavaria*, 1846); *Napoléon*, 1836 (English translation, 1874); *Quinze Jours au Sinai*, 1838 (*Impressions of Travel in Egypt and Arabia Petraea*, 1839); *Crimes célèbres*, 1838-1840 (*Celebrated Crimes*, 1896); *Excursions sur les bords du Rhin*, 1841 (with Gérard de Nerval); *Le Midi de la France*, 1841 (*Pictures of Travel in the South of France*, 1852); *Chroniques du roi Pépin*, 1842 (*Pepin*, 1906); *Jehanne la Pucelle, 1429-1431*, 1842 (*Joan the Heroic Maiden*, 1847); *Le Spéronare*, 1842; *Le Corricolo*, 1843; *Mes mémoires*, 1852, 1853, 1854-1855 (*My Memoirs*, 1907-1909); *Souvenirs de 1830 à 1842*, 1854-1855; *Causeries*, 1860; *Les Garibaldiens*, 1861 (*The Garibaldians in Sicily*, 1861); *Histoires de mes bêtes*, 1868 (*My Pets*, 1909); *Souvenirs dramatiques*, 1868; *Grand Dictionnaire de cuisine*, 1873 (with Anatole France); *On Board the "Emma,"* 1929; *The Road to Monte-Cristo*, 1956.

CHILDREN'S LITERATURE: *La Bouillie de la Comtesse Berthe*, 1845 (*Good Lady Bertha's Honey Broth*, 1846); *Histoire d'un casse-noisette*, 1845 (*Story of a Nutcracker*, 1846); *Le Roi de Bohème*, 1853 (also as *La Jeunesse de Pierrot*, 1854; *When Pierrot Was Young*, 1924); *Le Sifflet enchanté*, 1859 (*The Enchanted Whistle*, 1894).

TRANSLATION: *Mémoires de Garibaldi*, 1860 (of Giuseppe Garibaldi's *Memorie autobiografiche*).

MISCELLANEOUS: *Oeuvres complètes*, 1846-1877 (301 volumes); *Grand Dictionnaire de cuisine*, 1873 (with Anatole France); *Oeuvres d'Alexandre Dumas*, 1962-1967 (38 volumes).

Bibliography
Gorman, Herbert. *The Incredible Marquis*, 1929.

Jan, Isabelle. *Alexandre Dumas, romancier*, 1973.
Maurois, André. *The Titans*, 1957.
Munro, Douglas. *Alexandre Dumas père: A Bibliography of Works Translated into English to 1910*, 1978.
Spurr, H. A. *The Life and Writings of Alexandre Dumas*, 1973.
Stowe, Richard S. *Alexandre Dumas, père*, 1976.

Irma M. Kashuba

MARGUERITE DURAS

Born: Giandinh, Indochina; April 4, 1914

Principal long fiction

Les Impudents, 1943; *La Vie tranquille*, 1944; *Un Barrage contre le Pacifique*, 1950 (*The Sea Wall*, 1952; also as *A Sea of Troubles*, 1953); *Le Marin de Gibraltar*, 1952 (*The Sailor from Gibraltar*, 1966); *Les Petits Chevaux de Tarquinia*, 1953 (*The Little Horses of Tarquinia*, 1960); *Le Square*, 1955 (*The Square*, 1959); *Moderato Cantabile*, 1958 (English translation, 1960); *Dix heures et demie du soir en été*, 1960 (*Ten-Thirty on a Summer Night*, 1962); *L'Après-midi de Monsieur Andesmas*, 1962 (*The Afternoon of Monsieur Andesmas*, 1964); *Le Ravissement de Lol V. Stein*, 1964 (*The Ravishing of Lol Stein*, 1966); *Le Vice-consul*, 1966 (*The Vice-Consul*, 1968); *L'Amante anglaise*, 1967 (English translation, 1968); *Détruire, dit-elle*, 1969 (*Destroy, She Said*, 1970); *Abahn Sabana David*, 1970; *L'Amour*, 1971; *India Song: Texte-théâtre-film*, 1973 (English translation, 1976).

Other literary forms

In addition to her novels (all published by Gallimard, with the exception of *Moderato Cantabile* and *Détruire, dit-elle*, which were published by Minuit, the press favored by the New Novelists), Marguerite Duras has published a collection of short stories, *Des journées entières dans les arbres* (1954), and two short texts, *L'Homme assis dans le couloir* (1980) and *L'Homme atlantique* (1982). A number of her plays have been published in the collections *Théâtre I* (1965) and *Théâtre II* (1968) and, together with *Les Viaducs de la Seine-et-Oise* (1960; *The Viaducts of Seine-et-Oise*, 1967), *L'Amante anglaise* (1968), *L'Éden Cinéma* (1977), and *Le Navire "Night"* (1979), these plays continue to be performed on the French stage, in particular by the Renaud-Barrault Company and the Lucernaire Theatre group, both in Paris. Duras has also adapted two of Henry James's short stories for the stage: "The Aspern Papers" and "The Beast in the Jungle." Since 1969, Duras has turned to filmmaking as her principal activity, perhaps encouraged by the success of her scenario for Alain Resnais' *Hiroshima mon amour* (1959; *Hiroshima mon amour: Text by Marguerite Duras for the Film by Alain Resnais*, 1961). In 1961, she collaborated with Gérard Jarlot on the script for *Une Aussi Longue Absence* (English translation, 1966), directed by Henri Colpi, and, in 1969, she wrote and directed her first film, *Détruire, dit-elle*, avowedly inspired by the May, 1968, revolution. Other films include *Nathalie Granger* (1972), *La Femme du Gange* (1973), *Baxter, Véra Baxter* (1976), *Son nom de Venise dans Calcutta désert* (1976), *Des journées entières dans les arbres* (1976), *Le Camion* (1977), *Aurélia Steiner* (1979), *Agatha: Ou, Les Lectures illisibles* (1982), and

L'Homme atlantique (1982). Duras has evolved a new "hybrid" genre with works such as *India Song*, subtitled *Texte-théâtre-film*, and *Le Navire "Night."* *India Song*, the film, was awarded a special prize for the best film *art et essai* at the Cannes Film Festival in 1975.

Achievements

Marguerite Duras' extensive work in the cinema has generated interest in her novels, which are being read and appreciated by a wide audience. Despite her affinities with the New Novelists, who gained prominence in the 1950's and 1960's (Nathalie Sarraute, Michel Butor, Alain Robbe-Grillet, Claude Simon, and Robert Pinget), Duras steadfastly refrains from aligning herself with any one school of literature. She has a deep concern for human values, and some of her fiction of the early 1970's is definitely marked by the events of May, 1968, which proclaimed an end to excessive governmental control and sought a more egalitarian society. For the most part, however, Duras' novels address political issues indirectly. Her talents as a writer lie in character portrayal, particularly in her studies of female protagonists caught in the imaginative re-creation of a passionate love. In her later works, Duras eschews straightforward analysis of characters' emotions for an allusive style which evokes fantasies and imaginations through a lyric, often fragmented, prose. As a result of numerous interviews in periodicals and on television and through her prodigious output in fiction, drama, and film, Duras has become a highly visible, often controversial, figure on the French literary scene. Her work is gaining recognition abroad as well, and several of her novels have been translated into English.

Biography

Marguerite Duras was born Marguerite Donnadieu on April 4, 1914, in Giandinh, Indochina (now Vietnam), where her parents came to teach from northern France. Her father died when she was young, and her mother undertook the rearing of two sons and a daughter by farming a government land grant. Duras' attachment to her older brother and her ambivalent feelings toward her feisty and domineering mother are sketched in many of the novels but most particularly in *The Sea Wall*. The exotic landscape of Indochina, where Duras attended the *lycée* and took her *baccalauréat* in Vietnamese and French, colors her fiction. She excels at evoking a steamy, although oftentimes suffocating, atmosphere in settings that are rich in sensual vegetation.

In 1931, Duras went to Paris to continue her education, earning a *licence* in law and political science in 1935. A secretary for the Colonial Ministry from 1935 to 1941, she married Robert Antelme, an active member of the Communist Party and author of *L'Espèce humaine* (1947). Her own membership in the Party and her participation in the Resistance movement during World War II bespoke a strong sense of political commitment, which she later rejected. It was during the war that she began to work at Gallimard and to write fiction. Although her first manuscript, "La Famille Taneran," was never published, she was encouraged by Raymond Queneau to continue writing. Divorced from Antelme, Duras met Dionys Mascolo, a fellow Communist and author of a book about the Party; they had a son, Jean. In 1950, Duras was one of a number of intellectuals excommunicated from the French Communist Party. As a result of this experience and, later, the revolution of May, 1968, she has advocated a rejection of all ideology and a negation of bourgeois values and social conventions.

During the 1960's, Duras was a journalist and conducted interviews on French television. In 1963, she achieved notoriety for her exposé of the Ben Barka affair during the Algerian revolt. She has also written articles for *Vogue* magazine and, more recently, has published short texts for feminist publications such as *Sorcières*. Duras lightheartedly satirized her own milieu, the intellectual Saint-Germain-des-Prés area of Paris, in a short story, "Madame Dodin." Her country home in Neauphle-le-Chateau, outside Paris, served as the setting for some of her films.

Analysis

All of Marguerite Duras' novels revolve around the central theme of love, a necessary and impossible passion that is most often addressed in a climate of violence, and left unsatisfied. Several studies of Duras' fiction divide the novels into three groups or periods. The first includes the traditional, auto-biographical novels, often referred to as an American-inspired type of fiction, emulating the Hemingwayesque novel of adventure. These early works set forth most of the themes that are elaborated in subsequent novels. *Les Impudents*, *La Vie tranquille*, and *The Sea Wall* are concerned with young heroines in search of a lover or husband to fill the emptiness of their existence. Passive, lethargic women, they seek incarnation in the other, and their inner void is indistinguishable from the ennui and stagnation of their environment. They must wrench themselves from the domination of a brother or a mother, and, at the novel's conclusion, their success is ambiguous.

The second phase of Duras' novelistic career begins with *The Sailor from Gibraltar*; in this novel and its kin, Duras' protagonists are preoccupied with an unhappy love affair from the past, which they attempt to reenact in the present. Similarly, in the screenplay *Hiroshima mon amour*, the French actress confuses her adolescent affair during World War II with a present, illicit affair in a city that is a constant reminder of a tragic past. In *Ten-Thirty on a Summer Night*, a married couple turns to infidelity in order to mediate their past desires for each other. The wife's encounter with a criminal in a city besieged by violent storms is Duras' indirect affirmation of the destructive aspect of their love. Anne, in *Moderato Cantabile*, reenacts with Chauvin a crime of passion which they have both witnessed at the beginning of the novel. Eros and

Thanatos are clearly linked in these novels, where the re-creation of love provokes desires and fantasies associated with crime, disorder, death, and destruction. In this second group of novels, Duras' style begins to conform to her subject matter. The verbosity of description and the careful delineation of narrative events which marked the earlier works are discarded for a more poetic, allusive style in which characters' motives and incidents of plot are evoked in a gesture or setting and emphasized through repetition. The atmosphere of violence associated with destructive passion begins to affect textual structure and style.

The *Ravishing of Lol Stein* begins a third group of novels. Duras has said of this text that, whereas *Moderato Cantabile* is a finished product, the story of Lol is still in the process of being written. For the most part, Duras' subsequent fiction embodies fragments both of *The Ravishing of Lol Stein* and of her earlier works. Thus, text mirrors content (characters' memory or re-creation of past events), and it becomes clear that protagonists' desires are equated with memory and writing, equally fictitious. The incipient stylistic and structural violence of the second group of novels is accentuated in this third group. Sentences and paragraphs are reduced to lyric fragments of the story, decor is stylized, characters' identities are blurred, chronological time yields to phenomenological duration, and narrative control is abandoned in favor of poetic evocation. What has come to be known as the "India Cycle," comprising *The Ravishing of Lol Stein*, *The Vice-Consul*, *L'Amour*, and *India Song*, is but a series of decanted versions of the same story, one that springs from Duras' childhood and adolescent experiences in French Indochina. In a sense, the story of love and desire is progressively internalized and made to reverberate in its repetitions.

Because of its critical success, *The Sea Wall* marks a turning point in Duras' career as a novelist. Published in 1950, the novel was translated into English in 1952 and was adapted for the screen by René Clément in 1967. Often compared with the fiction of Ernest Hemingway, *The Sea Wall* is a fictionalized account of Duras' experiences in colonial Indochina—the sentimental education of its eighteen-year-old protagonist Suzanne and, to a lesser degree, of her older brother Joseph. It is also the story of the siblings' mother, known as Ma. Like Duras' own mother, Ma is a widowed French teacher who had settled with her husband in the colonial city of Ram, near the Gulf of Siam. Forced to support the children after the death of her husband, she works nights as a piano player at the Éden Cinéma (whence comes the title of Duras' 1978 play) in order to buy a land grant from the French government. Her dreams of establishing a fortune by farming are shattered when she realizes that she, like the other settlers in the area, has been sold an uncultivable tract of land by the corrupt colonial government. The farmland is inundated by the Pacific during the summer rainy season. Ma's story is one of a Herculean, almost ludicrous attempt to hold back the forces of nature by constructing a dam at the ocean's edge. Her revolt against the Pacific and her angry protests against government corruption are evidence of her undaunted and overweaning spirit. Suzanne and Joseph must liberate themselves from their mother's control if they are to pass from adolescence to adulthood.

Most of the novel centers upon Suzanne's relationship with the men who actively court her. The wealthy Monsieur Jo represents release from the hardships of life on the plains and from Joseph and Ma. Suzanne feels nothing for him, but she prostitutes herself in order to satisfy her family's materialistic longings. Passivity characterizes most of Duras' protagonists: Their desires remain lodged in the imagination. Suzanne's concept of love derives from long afternoons watching romantic movies at the Éden Cinéma. A modernday Emma Bovary, Suzanne's interpretation of the stormy, passionate affairs that she sees on the screen is that love is destructive and tinged with violence, a conclusion emblematic of her own repressed desire. Like so many Durasian heroines, Suzanne fantasizes love, and, although she succeeds in working out some of her fantasies in other relationships, particularly with Jean Agosti, her emotional involvement is still characterized by passivity, and she retreats into a bitter stoicism. In the subplot concerning her brother, Joseph turns to women and drink to escape from the quotidian boredom in this desolate outpost. At the novel's end, however, the only true release for the siblings comes with their mother's death.

The exotic Vietnamese landscape is a lush background for this novel of thwarted dreams and repressed sexuality. Duras' descriptions of the tropical forest and the forceful powers of the sea are rich in a feminine sensuality. The spiritual and physical misery of life on the plains, together with the sexual awakening of Suzanne and Joseph, bathe the novel in an atmosphere of morbidity and longing. The theme of desire is firmly implanted in the Durasian corpus, to be picked up and elaborated in succeeding novels. The memories of a harsh yet sensuous childhood spent in Vietnam haunt the author and are reflected in practically everything that she has written. Her talent for dialogue—which sparks her plays and films—is evident in this novel, in which characters seem to talk past one another and in which the revelation of feeling resides in what is left unsaid rather than in what is explicitly stated.

Like *The Sea Wall*, *Moderato Cantabile* is the study of a female protagonist caught in a web of fantasy and repressed desire. Duras' most critically acclaimed novel, *Moderato Cantabile* is a masterpiece of stylistic control and emotional transport. Duras prefers to call this text a poem rather than a novel and refers to it as a "metaphysical adventure organically experienced in a blinding moment of near-imbecility." Clearly, the rational forces of order (the *moderato* principle) in this work are in constant conflict with the disorder of a passionate madness (the *cantabile*) in a poetic evocation of an inner experience. Duras eschews the direct, linear narrative of the first group of novels for a more lyric prose.

The central character, whose inner adventure governs the telling of the tale, is Anne, the wife of a prominent factory owner in an unidentified port town. She encounters Chauvin, an unemployed former worker in her husband's factory, at the scene of a crime of passion: the murder of an unfaithful wife by her madly jealous husband. Duras has indicated that the entire novel— and thus fantasy—was generated from this initial scene, in particular from the morbidly erotic image of the husband licking the blood from his dead wife's face, a strange expression of desire in his eyes. Against this backdrop, Anne Desbaresdes and Chauvin meet almost daily in the café to work out in their imaginations the motivation for the crime. The theme of writing and remembering the past as pure fantasy or desire is accentuated as the novel develops and as the reader realizes that Anne and Chauvin are writing their own story of desire, intertwining inventions of possible motivations for the crime with fragments of their own lives. Self-conscious narration, along with a blurring of events and character psychology, aligns this work with the New Novel.

The story unfolds in a contrapuntal fashion best illustrated by the title; it refers to the weekly piano lesson to which Anne accompanies her free-spirited little boy, who refuses to heed his teacher's injunction to play a sonatina *moderato cantabile*. The sonatina is closely associated with the murder, because the crime (the gunshots and cries of the townspeople) interrupts the piano lesson in the opening scene of the novel. The basic conflict between order and disorder is amplified by the very impossibility of the task imposed upon the child. Oppositions in character and plot (between the disorderly child and the disciplined teacher, the bourgeois wife and the mother-adultress, musical culture and crime) are carried out in a quasi-mathematical fashion. Anne and Chauvin meet five times in the course of nine days in a re-creation of the emotional event which is itself a structure of opposites: The control of ritual alternates with the intoxication of liberated desires. These conflicts are buttressed by contrasting motifs in scenic descriptions. The tale is exploded into fragments of decor that are adumbrated in musical modulations. For example, in chapter 1, the pounding surf is indistinguishable from the woman's cry, the murmuring of the onlookers, and the child's attempt to attain the desired *moderato cantabile* at the piano. Throughout the text, scenic motifs, together with Anne and Chauvin's snatches of conversation, are introduced separately, intertwined, and intensified in an orchestration that leads to the climax of *moderato cantabile* at several different textual levels: the child's glorious rendition of the sonatina as marked, the orgasmic moment of the crime of passion, and finally the verbal consummation of Anne and Chauvin's imagined affair. When Chauvin symbolically kills Anne at the end ("I wish that you were dead"), she accepts it with relief ("So be it"), having worked out, in the realm of fantasy, her desires. The insistence on imagination and the almost fatalistic passivity with which Anne undergoes the ritual of self-negation with Chauvin link her to other Durasian protagonists, victims of a desire which they constantly seek to exorcise but which they are doomed to work out in their imaginations. *Moderato Cantabile*'s power lies in its musical resonance, prompting one critic to refer to this novel as *"Madame Bovary* rewritten by Béla Bartók."

The story of repressed desire that structures the plot of both *The Sea Wall* and *Moderato Cantabile* also informs Duras' 1964 novel, *The Ravishing of Lol Stein*. Like the preceding works, this text excels in character portrayal and evocation of decor; its protagonist, a sensitive but passive young woman who thrives on reliving a thwarted passion, is but another version of Suzanne and Anne. In narrative form, however, *The Ravishing of Lol Stein* goes further than either of the two earlier works in its subversion of traditional novelistic techniques. Conflicting elements of order and disorder, reason and madness, eros and thanatos, narrative control and narrative abdication serve to anchor the text in a series of contradictions. The very title, for example, suggests a dual interpretation of the heroine's predicament; the English title is an unfortunate mistranslation of the French. *Ravissement* is more accurately rendered as "ravishment," which can mean both ecstasy and ravage. This ambiguity recalls the juxtaposition of two contrary worlds implied by the title *Moderato Cantabile*. The contrapuntal technique continues to dominate Duras' style.

The Ravishing of Lol Stein marks a reorientation in Duras' writing; successive works, including those works of the "India Cycle," espouse a more open, less controlled form in a radical portrayal of the negation of self implicit in Duras' treatment of desire. These texts, in particular *The Vice-Consul*, *L'Amour*, *India Song*, and the film *Son nom de Venise dans Calcutta désert*, seem to flow musically from *The Ravishing of Lol Stein*, elaborating in fugue-like fashion its basic themes.

Set in a seaside village referred to as S. Thala, the decor is a stylized reflection of the lush, tropical landscape of Duras' youth in Vietnam. The site is emotionally charged in the novel and haunts the heroine of the story, Lola Valerie Stein, as a reminder of an unrequited love experienced when she was nineteen years old. At that time, she was engaged to be married to Michael Richardson, but, at a ball held at nearby T. Beach, she watched helplessly as her fiancé was seduced by an older, beautifully mysterious woman, Anne-Marie Stretter. In voyeuristic fashion, Lol observes their dance of desire from behind a row of plants. The scene of rejection that opens the novel has the same impact on Lol as the passionate crime that generates the action of *Moderato Cantabile*. It crystallizes Lol's identity in a "lack"; the center of her personality (which, the narrator informs the reader, has always been distant and difficult to grasp) is paradoxically "grounded" in negation and unfulfilled desire. Although she later marries, has children, and leads a "respectable" life, an undercurrent of violent desire threatens to burst forth at any moment. As in the case of Anne Desbaresdes, Lol's passion is triggered by an amorous encounter that is a reliving of the primal scene of triangular desire and exclusion. The alliance of form and content already present in the second group of novels is perfected in the third group. The triangular mediation of desire which serves as catalyst for the plot is underscored by the novel's tripartite division. Part 1 relates Lol's initial rejection and her temporary madness. Part 2 deals with her marriage and espousal of bourgeois values, reflected in an excessive orderliness of manner. In both parts, the style is clean and direct, and the narrative is in the straightforward mode of the third person. In part 3, the breakdown of Lol's compulsive behavior, induced by an affair, is reflected in the narrative style, which becomes rambling and confused. When Lol is seduced by Jacques Hold, the lover of her best friend, Tatiana, she is thrust once again into a triangular situation; part 3 repeats part 1. The revelation, by a sudden intrusion of first-person narration, that the narrator is Jacques Hold and that the reader's perspective on preceding events has been manipulated by an interested character-narrator, casts a different light on the story and accounts for the narrative confusion. Jacques's constant reminders in part 3 that he can only "believe" what happened and that he is "inventing" Lol's story erodes the reader's confidence and underlines the theme of memory as a fictive replay or rewriting of the past. Visually, the text betrays this erosion. Question marks, suppositions, hypothetical formulations, unfinished sentences, and blank spaces on the page convey an abdication of control and the very uncertainty of the text that is being read. Desire as lack is translated both formally and thematically.

Stylistic and narrational violence are complemented by subversive elements in time and place which enhance the portrayal of desire. Part 3, a replay or remembering of part 1 (which is itself a replay of preceding texts), continues the theme-and-variations pattern that characterizes the novels. The continual return to an elusive and illusional past succeeds in collapsing distinctions between past and present—a confusion supported by associations in the setting. Lol's seduction by Jacques Hold in part 3 takes place in a room reminiscent of the ballroom in part 1, to which Jacques and Lol make a pilgrimage. The site is consecrated as a sacred place of desire, like the café to which Anne and Chauvin return to reenact the passionate crime. Ambiguities resulting from confusion of past and present, ballroom and hotel room, occur also in character portrayal. The three female protagonists, Tatiana, Anne-Marie Stretter, and Lol, are variously described by the same characteristics of desire and death. They, like the entire Durasian corpus, take on the attributes of allegory in a progressively stylized and thus universalized story of absolute passion.

The publication of *India Song* in 1973 culminated the "India Cycle" (which includes play and film); indeed, *India Song* is a transparent text through which are filtered the essential themes, characters, and events of Duras' novelistic world. It might be regarded as the allegorical blueprint of all of Duras' pre-

ceding novels, containing them yet transcending them in an increasingly fragmented rendition of what Duras maintains in the preface to *India Song* to be
the essence of her story, "a story of love immobilized in the culminating
moment of passion."

Major publications other than long fiction

SHORT FICTION: *Des journées entières dans les arbres*, 1954; *L'Homme assis
dans le couloir*, 1980; *L'Homme atlantique*, 1982.

PLAYS: *Les Viaducs de la Seine-et-Oise*, 1960 (*The Viaducts of Seine-et-Oise*,
1967); *Les Eaux et forêts*, 1965 (*The Rivers and Forests*, 1965); *Théâtre I*,
1965 (includes *The Rivers and Forests*; *Le Square* [*The Square*, 1975]; *La
Musica* [English translation, 1975]); *Des journées entières dans les arbres*, 1966
(*Days in the Trees*, 1967); *Three Plays* (includes *The Square*; *Days in the Trees*;
The Viaducts of Seine-et-Oise); *Théâtre II*, 1968 (includes *Suzanna Andler*
[English translation, 1975]; *Days in the Trees*; "Yes, peut-etre"; "Le Shaga";
Un Homme est venue une voir); *L'Amante anglaise*, 1968; *L'Éden Cinéma*,
1977; *Le Navire "Night,"* 1979.

SCREENPLAYS: *Hiroshima mon amour*, 1959 (*Hiroshima mon amour: Text
by Marguerite Duras for the Film by Alain Resnais*, 1961); *Une Aussi Longue
Absence*, 1961 (with Gérard Jarlot; English translation, 1966); *Détruire, dit-
elle*, 1969; *Nathalie Granger*, 1972; *La Femme du Gange*, 1973; *India Song:
Texte-théâtre-film*, 1973; *Baxter, Véra Baxter*, 1976; *Des journées entières dans
les arbres*, 1976; *Son nom de Venise dans Calcutta désert*, 1976; *Le Camion*,
1977; *Aurélia Steiner*, 1979; *Agatha: Ou, Les Lectures illisibles*, 1982; *L'Homme
atlantique*, 1982.

Bibliography

Cismaru, Alfred. *Marguerite Duras*, 1971.
Gauthier, Xavière. "La Danse, le Désir," in *Cahiers Renaud-Barrault*. LXXXIX
(October, 1975), pp. 23-32.
Murphy, Carol J. *Alienation and Absence in the Novels of Marguerite Duras*,
1982.
Seylaz, Jean-Luc. *Les Romans de Marguerite Duras: Essai sur une thématique
de la durée*, 1963.
Vircondelet, Alain. *Marguerite Duras: Ou, Le Temps de détruire*, 1972.

Carol J. Murphy

JOSÉ MARIA DE EÇA DE QUEIRÓZ

Born: Póvoa de Varzim, Portugal; November 25, 1845
Died: Paris, France; August 16, 1900

Principal long fiction

O crime do Padre Amaro, 1876, 1880 (*The Sin of Father Amaro*, 1962); *O Primo Basílio*, 1878 (*Dragon's Teeth*, 1889; better known as *Cousin Bazilio*, 1953); *O mandarim*, 1880 (*The Mandarin*, 1965); *A relíquia*, 1887 (*The Relic*, 1925); *Os Maias*, 1888 (*The Maias*, 1965); *A ilustre casa de Ramires*, 1900 (*The Illustrious House of Ramires*, 1968); *A cidade e as serras*, 1901 (*The City and the Mountains*, 1955); *Alves e Cia*, 1925; *A Capital*, 1925; *O Conde de Abranhos*, 1925; *A tragédia da rua das Flores*, 1979, 1980.

Other literary forms

José Maria de Eça de Queiróz' first fictional work was a parody of the romantic "mystery" novel, *O mistério da estrada de Sintra* (1885; the mystery of Sintra Road), which was written in collaboration with his friend Ramalho Ortigão (1836-1915). It is not considered a significant work, although it does present themes which Eça de Queiróz later developed in a serious manner. Complete satisfaction with his texts was an elusive goal; as a result, Eça de Queiróz withheld publication of many works. The posthumously published works, edited by his son, his daughter, and others, are pertinent to the study of the thematic and technical development of Eça de Queiróz' fiction. Several novels were to form a Balzacian "Scenes of Portuguese Life" in conjunction with *The Maias*: *A Capital* (the capital city); *O Conde de Abranhos* (the Count of Abranhos); and *Alves e Cia* (Alves and company). In 1979 and 1980, two different editions of a long suppressed novel were published: *A tragédia da rua das Flores*, (the tragedy of Flores Street); the difficulty in deciphering Eça de Queiróz' handwriting led to great variations in interpretations of words and constructions in the two competing editions. A collection of Eça de Queiróz' short stories was published under the title *Contos* (1902; stories); some of these stories were the seeds for later novels. Eça de Queiróz' journalistic collaborations, his letters and impressions about life abroad, and his personal correspondence have also appeared. A translation into Portuguese of H. Rider Haggard's *King Solomon's Mines* (1885), *As minas de Salomão* (1891), is attributed to Eça de Queiróz and included among his works; it is now believed, however, that the translation was prepared by his sister-in-law and only revised by Eça de Queiróz.

From the 1920's through the early 1970's, Eça de Queiróz' works were published by the Livraria Lello & Irmão of Oporto. Lello's three-volume *Obras de Eça de Queiróz* (1966) is the most complete of the various editions of the author's so-called "complete works." As a result of a lawsuit brought by Eça de Queiróz' heirs against Lello & Irmão and a change in the Portuguese copyright law, many of Eça de Queiróz' works are no longer protected under Portuguese copyright provisions. At present, the principal Portuguese publisher of Eça de Queiróz' work is Editora Livros do Brasil of Lisbon; they have promised faithful new editions of Eça de Queiróz' much-corrupted texts.

Achievements

Eça de Queiróz' adversary stance toward the ultraromantic trend of Portuguese culture was well established prior to the publication of his first novel. Indeed, this stance conditioned the Portuguese critical evaluation and attitude toward his works throughout his lifetime. Eça de Queiróz' early novels were scorned by the national literary establishment as nothing more than poor imitations of the French Naturalists. Violent polemics, charges of plagiarism, and legitimate criticisms of his art resulted. The most significant evaluation of these early works was by the Brazilian writer Joaquim Maria Machado de Assis. Rather than discourage Eça de Queiróz' literary output, these criticisms helped him to become a more sensitive artist.

Eça de Queiróz' wide reading in foreign literatures and philosophy as well as his sojourns abroad provided a reference point for the analysis of Portuguese society and an awareness of the literary art which no other previous Portuguese writer had enjoyed. His fiction not only touched on the situation of Portuguese existence in the late nineteenth century, but it also confronted the more serious question of a Portuguese identity within a European context.

Through his novels, Eça de Queiróz revitalized and brought new depth to all aspects of Portuguese fiction. His creation of a personalized linguistic style is of particular distinction. The most revealing testaments to Eça de Queiróz' significance for Portuguese fiction are the enduring shadow his works have cast over twentieth century writers and the continuous critical attention which he attracts. Although widely read and influential in Brazil, Spain, and Spanish America, his major novels have been translated into English, French, and other languages only within recent years. Eça de Queiróz has won the critical attention of important European and American literary critics, but he has yet to achieve the international recognition that his works so justly merit.

Biography

José Maria de Eça de Queiróz was born out of wedlock on November 25, 1845, in Póvoa de Varzim, a village in northern Portugal. Although his parents, members of the rural upper bourgeoisie, married in 1849, Eça de Queiróz spent his childhood with a nursemaid and later with his paternal grandmother. His illegitimacy was a subtle preoccupation that often surfaced in his personal activities as well as in his fiction. It was not until 1885, the year of his own marriage, that Eça de Queiróz was officially recognized by his parents.

In 1861, Eça de Queiróz began to study law at the University of Coimbra. He also became an active member of the school's literary and theatrical clique.

Through his friendship with the poet-philosopher Antero de Quental (1842-1891), Eça de Queiróz' sociopolitical formation was initiated with readings of Auguste Comte, Pierre Proudhon, Ernest Renan, and a wide acquaintance with French literature. After law school, Eça de Queiróz combined his professional life with his journalistic and literary activities; he wrote for Portuguese newspapers on literary and social questions throughout his life. After a short stint as editor of the political opposition's newspaper in Évora in 1867, Eça de Queiróz returned to Lisbon to begin a diplomatic career. A trip to Egypt in 1869 to attend the opening of the Suez Canal included visits to the Holy Land's sacred shrines.

In Lisbon in 1871, the "Cenacle," Eça de Queiróz' literary circle, launched a series of conferences that proposed revolutionary alternatives to the "backwardness" of Portuguese culture in relationship to the rest of Europe. Inspired in his readings of the social philosophers and the events of the Paris Commune, Eça de Queiróz' conference propounded a realist social ethic for Portuguese literature.

Eça de Queiróz' administrative and diplomatic career was harmoniously combined with his literary pursuits. His brief appointment as town administrator in rural Leiria in 1871 provided material for *The Sin of Father Amaro* and *Cousin Bazilio*. His posting to Havana, Cuba, from 1872 to 1874 brought him into contact with the dire conditions of the "enslaved" Portuguese-Chinese emigrant workers, which he officially protested in *A emigração como força civilizadora* (1979; emigration as a civilizing force). Eça de Queiróz visited the United States but was not impressed by its large cities or its reliance on machines. As Portuguese consul in Newcastle upon Tyne, England, he finished two versions of *The Sin of Father Amaro* and *Cousin Bazilio*, as well as *The Mandarin*. Eça de Queiróz spent his vacations in Portugal, where he maintained strong links with Portuguese traditions and problems and often engaged in polemics over national problems with rabid ultrachauvinists.

In 1885, Eça de Queiróz visited Émile Zola in Paris, and later that year, he married Emília de Resende. In 1887, *The Relic* was published and denied an important literary prize. In 1888, the year that his masterpiece *The Maias* was published, Eça de Queiróz was named Portuguese consul in Paris. His Parisian years were spent as an almost complete social and literary recluse. The Dreyfus Affair caused him great disappointment with the personal, moral, and social levels of his once idealized French society. His prime attention turned toward the future of the Portuguese identity, as evident in *The Illustrious House of Ramires* and *The City and the Mountains*. Eça de Queiróz died in Paris on August 16, 1900.

Analysis

In the course of his novels, José Maria de Eça de Queiróz vividly dissected a society lost in past centuries, oblivious to any contemporary political, social, or cultural ideology. Initially, he censured Portugal's backwardness in *romans à thèse* which presented a rather confused, even naïve, comprehension and literary application of the social theories of Proudhon, the religious doctrines of Renan, and the literary aims of Gustave Flaubert. As he discovered his own literary persona, these influences gradually became secondary.

Several thematic and technical interests are recurrent in Eça de Queiróz' literary voyage from Naturalism and realism to his unique personal style, independent of any literary school. His own parentless childhood is often invoked through numerous characters in odd family situations—orphans, wards, widowers, loners without family—and through the theme of incest. Further, Eça de Queiróz' "presence" in the attributes of his novels' characters appears to be an attempt to examine and resolve the extremes of his own personality: the spirit of a romantic dandy with the mind of a practical realist. Finally, his concern with the Portuguese identity led him to examine repeatedly its traditional components: rural existence, the Roman Catholic tradition, and the national preoccupation with and glorification of past centuries' achievements.

The Sin of Father Amaro and *Cousin Bazilio* are closely related in Eça de Queiróz' early development. Both have a basis in actual events that occurred prior to his arrival as administrator of the city of Leiria. The publication history of *The Sin of Father Amaro* is indicative of the almost maniacal search for an appropriate, personalized style, which Eça de Queiróz pursued and which limited his publications. The original version was serialized in the Lisbon *Revista ocidental* in 1875, when the author was in England, and he entrusted the editing to his friends Ramalho Ortigão and Antero de Quental, but he was rather dissatisfied with their efforts. After the serialization, Eça de Queiróz wrote a "definitive" version with substantially developed characters and preponderant social themes.

Father Amaro is an orphan who, through the graces of "benefactors," is ordained and obtains a desirable parish in Leiria. He becomes enamored of his landlady's daughter, the innocent Amélia, who gives herself to Amaro in a spiritual trance of religious possession. Her pregnancy results in guilt, the murder of the child, and her own death. Unrepentant, Amaro travels on to another parish. The rural existence in general and the role of the corrupt priests of the Church in particular are the targets of Eça de Queiróz' censure. Graphic scenes of sexual encounters and blasphemous presentations of religious activities led to hostile commentaries that branded the novel anticlerical and pornographic. A "completely new, revised, and rewritten edition" appeared in 1880, owing to the influence of Machado de Assis, who wrote a sharp criticism of the "definitive" edition and Eça de Queiróz' second novel, *Cousin Bazilio*.

Set in upper-middle-class Lisbon society, *Cousin Bazilio* was written within a few short months of 1877 and reveals the impact of Flaubert's *Madame*

Bovary (1857; English translation, 1886) on Eça de Queiróz. Luiza is a slightly educated woman living in a world of romantic fantasy. When her husband Jorge goes off on business, she becomes involved in an affair with her Cousin Bazilio, who is on a visit from Paris. Luiza's maid Juliana (one of Eça de Queiróz' finest creations) discovers several discarded love letters from Luiza to Bazilio and decides to blackmail her mistress and thus avenge her unfortunate proletarian life. Juliana dies of a fear-provoked stroke, and Luiza succumbs to "brain fever." As in Eça de Queiróz' first novel, there are lurid sexual encounters and a general attack on the aimless existence of Portuguese women.

The essential criticism of both of these novels was provided in a review by Machado de Assis, which appeared in 1878 in a Rio de Janeiro newspaper. Although Machado de Assis found merits in Eça de Queiróz' writings, he rejected Eça de Queiróz' reliance on the descriptive extremes of the Naturalist school, which, he believed, went against Eça de Queiróz' abilities and artistic aims. He cited Eça de Queiróz' plagiarism of parts of Zola's *La Faute de l'Abbé Mouret* (1875; *Albine: Or, The Abbé's Temptation*, 1882; better known as *The Sin of Father Mouret*, 1904, 1969) in *The Sin of Father Amaro*, and the device of the stolen letters as an awkward plot element which proved detrimental to the character development in *Cousin Bazilio*. Eça de Queiróz made a weak attempt at defending himself in the preface to the 1880 edition of *The Sin of Father Amaro*. A more vituperative self-defense, written at the time, appeared in a posthumously published article, "Idealism and Realism."

These two novels present a remarkable overview of Portuguese society. Eça de Queiróz admirably captured the essential traits of various classes. Indeed, he was at his best as a caricaturist; he produced an inimitable Portuguese type in *Cousin Bazilio*: the much-respected expounder of trite clichés, the Counselor Acácio. The petty intrigues of liberals, monarchists, and republicans that kept Portuguese political society afloat are a continuous source of satire in Eça de Queiróz' novels.

In the important letter/preface to *The Mandarin* (included with the romance since its fifth edition), Eça de Queiróz described his "pointless" dedication to realism and his need as an artist to create fantasy. *The Mandarin* and *The Relic* are two related realizations of this creative need. This flight from the reality of realism was to bring about a major revision of Eça de Queiróz' literary aims and artistic techniques.

Fantasy for Eça de Queiróz was, nevertheless, rooted in reality—his own reality. Thus, Teodoro, the protagonist of *The Mandarin*, has much in common with Eça de Queiróz himself—a harassed bureaucrat living alone in a mediocre Lisbon pensione. The financially attractive Faustian offer to kill a Chinese mandarin leads Teodoro to brief wealth, but then to repentance and a begrudging return to his bourgeois existence. With no direct social criticism and only minimal interest in psychological character development, Eça de

Queiróz was preoccupied with stylistic simplicity and directness. A notable narrative structure appears in *The Mandarin* which Eça de Queiróz employed in many subsequent novels: the antithetic comparison. In *The Mandarin*, two very different worlds are juxtaposed: late nineteenth century Portugal and exotic China.

The Relic involves two principal antitheses: spatial (Portugal and Jerusalem) and chronological (hypocritical nineteenth century Portuguese Roman Catholicism and the mystical origins of Christianity). As a reward for his piousness, Teodorico is sent by his sanctimonious aunt on a pilgrimage to the Holy Land, where, aside from engaging in a series of love affairs, he becomes involved in a vivid dream-voyage to the beginnings of Christianity. The basis for this dream includes not only Eça de Queiróz' remembrances of his trip to Egypt but also the contemporary positivistic attitudes toward religion. Eça de Queiróz achieved a comic satire of religious life; it also attests Eça de Queiróz' ever-growing interest in hagiography.

Eça de Queiróz indicated in the letter/preface to *The Mandarin* that he would begin to pay attention to "fine sentences rather than fine notions." Indeed, linguistic creation and technical originality became his prime concerns. This reorientation is evident in his masterpiece *The Maias*, which was written, reworked, and rewritten over several years.

Aristocratic society is the background for *The Maias*. Three generations of a family representing traditional Portugal and the new and future Portugal are lost in their daily existences. Afonso de Maia had been a respected diplomat with a broad knowledge of European life. His grandson Carlos, a doctor, has all the necessary opportunities but is unable to achieve any goal. He falls passionately in love with Maria Eduarda, who turns out to be his half sister; thus, the family "curse" leads to its ruin. Many brilliant caricatures of Portuguese social life are drawn—the Englishman, the Jewish banker, the homosexual, the ultraromantic poet, and so on. Eça de Queiróz himself is present in the moralizing voice of João da Ega.

The lurid sex scenes and the plot detail of Eça de Queiróz' early Naturalistic novels are no longer present in *The Maias*. Eça de Queiróz attained an admirable psychological depth in characterization and an innovative, almost poetic use of the Portuguese adjective. He employed indirect free discourse here and throughout his remaining novels as a means of diminishing authorial presence.

Neither of Eça de Queiróz' final two novels, *The Illustrious House of Ramires* and *The City and the Mountains*, was completely revised by him prior to his death in 1900, but both reveal the author's continuing concern with the questions of artistic technique and his love for Portugal, conditioned by his realization of its limited future.

In *The Illustrious House of Ramires*, Gonçalo Ramires, the last scion of an ancient Portuguese noble family, is preparing his family history for "political" reasons. The intertwining of the Portuguese past and present results in a series of antitheses of satiric and allegorical proportions. Gonçalo cannot live up to the standards of his ancestors, just as Portugal can no longer be what it was in the past. Eça de Queiróz skillfully manipulates both "historical plots" and thus compares time, space, and characters. Ultimately, he reveals eternal Portuguese qualities: innocence, good-heartedness, nostalgia for the past, all mixed with shades of laziness.

To this list of Portuguese characteristics can be added the "rural inclination," as is evident in *The City and the Mountains.* The antithesis here is between the ultramodern city of Paris and the backwardness of the Portuguese countryside. The city dweller Jacinto resides at 202 Champs Elysées and believes that "Absolute Knowledge × Absolute Power = Absolute Happiness." This formula holds true until all of his gadgets and machines begin to fail. His ennui causes a dreaded return to his native rural Portugal. There, Jacinto discovers the simple pleasures of life and resolves his existence.

For Eça de Queiróz, no doubt, this novel was a resolution of his own reality, or indeed the Portuguese reality: an adventurer in his diplomatic and literary careers, but at heart a "poor man from Póvoa de Varzim."

Major publications other than long fiction

SHORT FICTION: *A correspondência de Fradique Mendes*, 1900; *Contos*, 1902 (includes *O Defunto* [*Our Lady of the Pillar*, 1906]; *José Mathais* [English translation, 1947]; *Perfection*, 1923; *The Sweet Miracle*, 1904); *Cartas inéditas de Fradique mendes e mais páginas esquecidas*, 1928; *The Mandarin and Other Stories*, 1965.

NONFICTION: *Prosas Bárbaras*, 1903; *Cartas de Inglaterra*, 1905 (*Letters from England*, 1970); *Ecos de Paris*, 1905; *Notas contemporâneas*, 1909; *Cartas familiares e bilhetes de Paris*, 1912; *Ultimas páginas*, 1912; *A catástrofe*, 1925; *Correspondência*, 1925; *Cronicas de Londres*, 1944; *Prosas esquecidas*, 1966; *Folhas soltas*, 1966; *A emigração como força civilizadora*, 1979.

MISCELLANEOUS: *Obras completas*, 1948; *Obras de Eça de Queiróz*, 1966.

Bibliography
Coleman, Alexander. *Eça de Queiróz and European Realism*, 1980.
DaCal, Ernesto Guerra. *Lenguaje y estilo de Eça de Queiróz*, 1954.
Demetz, Peter. "Eça de Queiróz as a Literary Critic," in *Comparative Literature*. XIX (Fall, 1967), pp. 289-307.
Girodon, Jean. "Eça de Queiróz et *Madame Bovary*," in *Biblos*. XXV (1949), pp. 210-227.
Medina, João. *Eça político*, 1974.
Steegmuller, Francis. "Introduction," in *The Relic*. 1954.

Irwin Stern

GUSTAVE FLAUBERT

Born: Rouen, France; December 12, 1821
Died: Croisset, France; May 8, 1880

Principal long fiction

Madame Bovary, 1857 (English translation, 1886); *Salammbô*, 1862 (English translation, 1886); *L'Éducation sentimentale*, 1869 (*A Sentimental Education*, 1898); *La Tentation de Saint Antoine*, 1874 (*The Temptation of Saint Anthony*, 1895); *Bouvard et Pécuchet*, 1881 (*Bouvard and Pécuchet*, 1896); *The Complete Works*, 1904 (10 volumes); *Oeuvres complètes*, 1910-1933 (22 volumes); *La Première Éducation sentimentale*, 1963 (written 1843-1845; *The First Sentimental Education*, 1972).

Other literary forms

"The novelist's novelist," as Henry James called him, Gustave Flaubert became an undisputed, if controversial, master of prose fiction in a great age of French prose. Celebrated as the founder of the modern novel, especially in its psychological dimensions, Flaubert published no poetry (if one excepts segments of *The Temptation of Saint Anthony*) but did write a great many dramatic scenarios and fragments, as the manuscript collection at the Rouen library illustrates. Among his early plays is the unpublished "Loys XI" (written in 1838), the last play of his youth; like his later plays, this one clearly demonstrates that, although he was devoted to the drama and infused his novels with dramatic elements and effects, he was not a talented dramatist. Flaubert's *Le Château des coeurs* (1885: *The Castle of Hearts*, 1904), written in 1863 in collaboration with his lifelong friend Louis Bouilhet, is a *féerie*, a play that highlights and relies upon the marvelous to carry it; the play was never produced professionally in Flaubert's lifetime. The one play of his maturity of which he is sole author, a farcical comedy in four acts called *Le Candidat* (1874; *The Candidate*, 1904), lasted for four performances at the Vaudeville in Paris. Although it was fueled by Flaubert's contempt for the Third Republic and the grasping materialism of its bourgeois industrialists— and thus potentially explosive—the play is full of stereotypes. Edmond de Goncourt characterized it as a particularly painful failure, funereal and glacial.

Flaubert's *Correspondance, 1830-1880* (1887-1893)—especially his frequently unamorous love letters to his mistress, Louise Colet, his epistles to George Sand, Maxime Du Camp, Ivan Turgenev, and his notes to a host of friends and literary figures of the era—makes for extraordinarily fascinating reading. André Gide, one of many twentieth century writers who have expressed their debt to Flaubert's letters, wrote that for five years the *Correspondance* was his bedside book. The letters provide a particularly useful picture of the inner Flaubert, his life, his theories about art, and his vocation as a writer. They help form a theoretical canon that explicates his intentions and works in the way the essays of Jean-Paul Sartre, Albert Camus, or Michel Butor serve to gloss their novels. An accomplished and prolific correspondent, Flaubert appears in his letters in ways he does not overtly appear in his fiction. Flaubert's travel book, *Par les champs et par les grèves* (1885; *Over Strand and Field*, 1904), written with Maxime Du Camp, is an account of their walking tour of Touraine and Brittany from May to July, 1847. The *Dictionnaire des idées reçues* (1910, 1913; *Dictionary of Accepted Ideas*, 1954), most likely an object of the copying efforts of Bouvard and Pécuchet in the projected second volume of his last and unfinished novel, occupied Flaubert from at least 1850 as a possible anthology of idiocy (*un sottisier*), compendium of foolish conventional opinion, and monument to error.

Apart from his novels, Flaubert's greatest contributions to literature and those upon which a major portion of his fame rests are contained in the volume *Trois Contes* (1877; *Three Tales*, 1903). These three stories, "Un Coeur simple" ("A Simple Heart"), "La Légende de Saint Julien l'Hospitalier" ("The Legend of St. Julian, Hospitaler"), and "Hérodias," reflect many of Flaubert's historical interests, artistic preoccupations, and themes and are major products of his fully mature artistry.

Achievements

"If all high things have their martyrs," wrote Flaubert's English contemporary, Walter Pater, "Gustave Flaubert might perhaps rank as the martyr of literary style" (*Appreciations*, 1889). Flaubert's great and unquestionable achievement as founder and master of the modern novel lies precisely in his perfection of a literary style that seeks to capture the essential unity of idea and form, a style that seeks, before all, *le mot juste*, a style that, in Pater's (and later T. S. Eliot's) phrase, involves a natural economy "between a relative, somewhere in the world of thought, and its correlative, somewhere in the world of language." This style uses elements of composition functionally and emphasizes the more formal dimensions of the novel; in Flaubert's hands, the novel achieves a beauty of form and a power that relate it to the other arts. Flaubert's influence extends to such of his contemporaries and near-contemporaries as Guy de Maupassant, Pater, and James, to writers such as Gide and Oscar Wilde, and to such recent and contemporary writers as Butor and Sartre. Sartre's study of Flaubert, *L'Idiot de la famille* (1971-1972), stands as a forceful witness to his lengthy engagement with Flaubert's life, meaning, and place in the intellectual life of subsequent generations. No one writing in French can fail to reckon with Flaubert; no one writing in English should fail to do so.

One public distinction accorded Flaubert in his lifetime was one his father had received in 1839 for his work in medicine. On the strength of his writing, especially for *Madame Bovary*, and in part because it attracted the notice of

Princess Mathilde and opened the court to him, Flaubert was named Chevalier de la Légion d'Honneur in 1866. In his *Dictionary of Accepted Ideas*, he writes of this title: "Make fun of it, but covet it. When you obtain it, always say it was unsolicited."

The most complete collection of Flaubert's works is the twenty-two volume Conard edition, issued in Paris. His manuscripts are in many locations but principally in the Bibliothèque Nationale (Paris), the Bibliothèque Historique de la Ville de Paris, the Collection Louvenjoul (Chantilly), and the Bibliothèque Municipale (Rouen).

Biography

Born on December 12, 1821, at the Hôtel-Dieu in Rouen, Gustave Flaubert was the fifth of six children and the fourth son of Dr. Achille Cléophas Flaubert, director of Rouen's hospital and founder of its medical school, and Caroline (Fleuriot) Flaubert, herself the daughter of a physician. Only three of the Flaubert children survived infancy: Achille, the eldest (who later became a physician and replaced his father as master of Rouen's hospital), Gustave, and a sister, Caroline, who was Gustave's junior by two and a half years and who died in childbirth at the age of twenty-one. Flaubert's early and prolonged associations with examining rooms, surgeries, dissecting rooms, and the medical scientists who used them left clear marks upon his thought and fiction. His formal education began at the age of nine at Rouen's Collège Royal; there he came under the strong influence of Pierre-Adolphe Chéruel, a disciple of the historian Jules Michelet. An avid student of history, young Flaubert won several prizes for historical essays in the course of pursuing the *baccalauréat*, which was awarded to him in 1840.

In some sense, Flaubert's own sentimental education began at the age of fourteen, when he met Madame Maurice Schlésinger (Elisa Foucault), the wife of a music editor, during a family summer vacation at Trouville. Elisa, who was then twenty-six, became for him an ideal of the beloved but inaccessible woman, the object of unrequited (and unexpressed) love. With great acuity, Enid Starkie asserts that in this first meeting with Elisa, "Flaubert experienced the illumination which permanently fixed the pattern of his emotional life." The beautiful and elusive Madame Arnoux of *A Sentimental Education* is modeled upon Madame Schlésinger.

Upon his graduation from Rouen's *lycée*, Flaubert traveled to the south of France and to Corsica before taking up intermittent study of the law in Paris, study that ended in 1844 with his first major attack of epilepsy. This attack did not merely render him an invalid for several months; it profoundly altered the course of his life. During this illness, Dr. Flaubert bought a house outside Rouen at Croisset and moved his family there; in this house, facing the Seine, "the Hermit of Croisset" was to write some of the greatest fiction in the French language. The year 1846 marked Flaubert's decision to remain permanently at Croisset: In January, his father died; in March, his sister, Caroline, died giving birth to a daughter; and he and the only household he would ever have, his mother and his infant niece, took up domestic life together at Croisset.

Somewhat later in 1846, another event took place that would alter Flaubert's life: On July 28, he met Louise Colet, who became his mistress from 1846 to 1848 and again from 1851 to 1854. This passionate, often stormy, and finally disastrous relationship occasioned some of Flaubert's most important letters. It is arguable that after the first rupture between them (1848), he again pursued her in 1851 to study at first hand the Romantic obsessions he would dissect in *Madame Bovary*—that is, at best, a partial explanation of his intense attraction to her. His self-enforced rustication, away from Paris, away from Louise, led to an irrevocable break in 1854.

Flaubert was not, however, simply the Hermit, as several writers have portrayed him. Croisset remained his primary residence and his place to engage in serious writing over the years, but he also moved about a great deal. In 1847, he and Maxime Du Camp made their celebrated walking tour of Brittany; early in 1848, Flaubert was an eyewitness to the revolutionary fighting at Paris' Palais-Royal; from November, 1849, through July, 1851, he journeyed, mainly with Du Camp, throughout the Middle East, Greece, and Italy. With the publication of *Madame Bovary*, Flaubert entered and fully enjoyed Parisian life, dividing his time between Paris and Croisset from 1856 to his death in 1880.

Early in 1857, *Madame Bovary* caused one of the few great public events of Flaubert's life: He was prosecuted on charges of obscenity and blasphemy. The result was the Napoleonic equivalent of a Scotch verdict, with the ruling that the charges were "not proven." After the notoriety of the trial, the remainder of Flaubert's life was spent in comparative quiet, interspersed with some romantic liaisons, some hard financial times through the improvidence of his niece's husband, and, most of all, the work of producing more remarkable fiction. Flaubert was still at work on *Bouvard and Pécuchet* when he died at Croisset of a cerebral hemorrhage on May 8, 1880.

Analysis

Long the subject of a large and still increasing volume of literary criticism and debate, the novels of Gustave Flaubert are susceptible to a variety of approaches. Classified as a realist, his works deprecated by some of his contemporaries as supreme examples of the excesses to which novelistic realism was prone, Flaubert refused to consider himself an advocate of something he so hated—reality. The psychological realism of *Madame Bovary*, for example, as noted by Charles Baudelaire in an early review, clearly strikes a new note in the development of the novel and is one of Flaubert's major contributions to the genre. This realism is, nevertheless, tempered by some elements of

Romanticism, even though Flaubert regarded Romanticism not as an intellectual or artistic doctrine to be prized but as a disease. One objective of the Romantic generation of the 1830's, *épater le bourgeois* (to shock the middle class), surely seems to be at work in Flaubert's fiction; just as surely, the manner of accomplishing this artistic task has little in common with the many Romantic efforts of the age. In one of the earliest studies of Flaubert, Guy de Maupassant hailed Flaubert as an advocate of impersonality in art, and Flaubert's method of composition as well as numerous letters seem to bear out this notion. Conversely, while he could write, for example, that there was nothing of himself, his sentiments, or his life in *Madame Bovary*, he could still exclaim, "Madame Bovary, c'est moi!" (I am Madame Bovary!).

Flaubert's intentions, then, and the circumstances of his life have figured significantly in the interpretation and evaluation of his fiction. One useful way of thinking about his work as a writer and the writing he produced is to consider his life and work spent in the service of art, a demanding art that provided a refuge from the world of ordinary provincial and urban affairs, an art that helped him reorder experience into the image of objective reality without sacrificing all the Romantic traits he had developed in his youth. One primary Romantic element in the novels is the sense of disillusionment attendant upon the recognition that Romantic ideals themselves are untenable. This sense is usually dominant in the endings of Flaubert's novels, endings that are supremely important in adjusting the reader's perspective. Such Romantic aspects of his novels are usually overlooked—understandably so, because the restrained language, seemingly objective tone, and intense scrutiny of personality overshadow other elements. It has been said that Flaubert, a Romantic by nature, became a realist and a classicist by discipline.

Having turned his hand to writing at an early age, Flaubert was thirty-five when he published his masterpiece, *Madame Bovary*, a novel that has been variously interpreted and characterized. For every just claim that Flaubert undertook this novel to purge himself of the Romantic disease, there are equally cogent claims that the work is a Romantic novel, though different in kind from its predecessors. Emma Bovary is surely the victim of her own Romanticism and, like the legions of Romantic heroes and heroines, is one who longs for absolutes and seeks after something that either does not exist or exists but imperfectly. Her aspirations are completely out of proportion to her capacities and her situation in life. Thus, while *Madame Bovary* may be seen as a literary tour de force that makes superb use of organization and of great virtuosity in the handling of structure and text, it remains essentially a novel that both eschews the received objective of entertainment and sets forth an argumentative analysis of society as that society encourages Emma's folly, blames her for it, and triumphs over it.

The work is divided into three unequal parts that correspond to the three stages of the lives of Emma and her husband Charles. Before turning to the story itself, however, it is essential to look closely at the novel's title: Flaubert called the novel not *Emma Bovary* but *Madame Bovary*. The emphases upon her married name, upon the marriage itself, upon her role as wife (and as mother) are paramount: They are the very things that she will betray and that, in her betrayal, will precipitate her ruin. Moreover, Emma can have no place in the work separate from Charles: One particularly important clue to the nature of the work is the narrative device that opens the novel and then disappears as the objective narrator replaces the first voice that the reader hears. This voice belongs to one of Charles's young classmates at the *lycée*, a classmate who begins casually enough ("We were in class") and who then talks about Charles, his provenance, and his inauspicious beginnings, including having to write the conjugation of *ridiculus sum* twenty times. The idea that Charles is, in fact, ridiculous remains central to the novel, a novel that does not end with Emma's death but with his. Shortly before his death, Charles makes what the narrator considers his one great statement in life; speaking to Rodolphe Boulanger, Emma's first seducer, Charles says: "It is the fault of fate." This statement sums up Charles's inability to understand and to act, the foolishness of his perception of life, and the conventionality of its expression in clichés. The work also ends with the factual statement that the monumental stupidity of another character, Homais, the town chemist, has at last gained proper recognition: Homais has received the Croix de la Légion d'Honneur.

The first of the novel's three segments introduces Charles in a sort of choric prologue to this tragedy of dreams. In what Enid Starkie calls a duet between Charles and Emma, Flaubert presents each of the characters in a series of tableaux that leads the reader through the romance of courtship and the marriage of Charles and Emma, and also to Emma's disillusionment with the unexciting marriage. This section ends, symbolically, with the Bovarys' move from Tostes to Yonville, with the news that Emma is pregnant, and with her burning her now dessicated, tattered wedding bouquet. Each of these occasions, like the rest of the events in the novel, is presented in a detached, declarative, unsentimental manner.

Part 2 consists of another series of tableaux featuring a platonic but potentially passionate relationship between Emma and Léon Dupuis and her carefully plotted seduction by Rodolphe. Indeed, by the time Rodolphe appears, Emma has so languished at Yonville and has so nourished fleshly lusts and acquisitive passions that she is ready for an affair. Having yielded to Rodolphe, she continues to respond to him in an aggressively positive way, especially once Charles's stupidity, matched only by the ignorance of Homais, has led to the crippling of the boy Hippolyte and the consequent diminution of Charles in her eyes and of her, by association, in the eyes of the bourgeoisie of Yonville. Just when she thinks she will finally be free of the tedium of Yonville and the boredom of her marriage to Charles by fleeing with Rodolphe,

Rodolphe not only fails to take her away but also flees himself, to avoid what he rightly perceives as her possessive nature: Having captured her, his first thought is how to become free of her.

In the novel's final section, Emma has irretrievably abandoned herself to her Romantic notions of how her life ought to be lived, the high passion of her affair with Léon, the possession of fine things, and the indulgence of her whims; she assumes an inexhaustible supply of funds to support her new style. Predictably, her affair with Léon and her neglect of Charles and their daughter, Berthe, bring her to moral bankruptcy, while her constant borrowing and signing of promissory notes bring her and Charles to financial bankruptcy. In the end, she cannot pay, cannot tap Rodolphe or Léon or anyone with sufficient funds who will not exact her favors in return for the money. Having lived beyond her means in many senses, she chooses an excruciatingly painful death by arsenical poisoning. Charles, the physician, is helpless for a second time when death claims his wife, yet so involved is he with her existence that his interest for readers barely survives hers: His own end is a necessary consequence of hers.

Flaubert's second novel, *Salammbô*, is unsettling, entirely different from his first; it is arguably the cruelest novel of the nineteenth century. In a letter to the celebrated critic Charles-Augustin Sainte-Beuve, Flaubert said he wanted "to fix a mirage by applying to antiquity the methods of the modern novel." The mirage he fixes is ancient Carthage, in a novel that has been called both Romantic and anti-Romantic and that, like many of his works, contains both elements. *Salammbô* is a work of picturesque barbarity and gratuitous violence; it is an unrelieved, pathological compendium of atrocities that the Marquis de Sade would have enjoyed thoroughly. Neither a "historical novel," a novel of "historical reconstruction" (as Jules Michelet, Augustin Thierry, and other nineteenth century writers defined the genre), nor a psychological novel like his first one, *Salammbô* is a great Parnassian epic that should be judged more as a poem than as a novel. In its last chapters, the nightmarish mirage becomes a surrealistic vision, what Maurice Nadeau calls "a hallucination described in cold blood."

Flaubert achieves these nightmarish effects through his full and objective descriptions of brutality and through his emphasis on the unreality of the landscape, an emphasis achieved through the use of lapidary objects and architecture. These techniques are prime contributions to what Victor Brombert calls an "epic of immobility." The motif of predation, in which birds and animals of prey become recurrent metaphors and evolve into symbols, coalesces with the lapidary metaphors to help create an absolute sense of dehumanization. This sense is never far from the novel's surface and is constantly reinforced by other recurrent elements: the all-pervasive themes of mutilation and self-mutilation, obsessions with disease, the ravages of hunger and thirst, and cannibalism and vampirism. All of these elements and more combine to produce an overwhelming sense of disgust with things as they are. The story progresses from the colorful opening revels, in which the priestess Salammbô appears on the tower high above the exotic garden in which the mercenaries hold their feast, through Mathô's theft and Salammbô's recovery of the sacred veil of Tanit, to the horrific destruction of Mathô, to the somewhat unexpected but internally logical statement that the story has been told to explain how the priestess came to die for having touched Tanit's veil. Throughout this bizarre tale of the revolt of a mercenary army that the Carthaginians employed in the wars with Rome, there is no character who approaches full humanity. The exaltations of place over person, of the animalistic and supernatural dimensions over ordinary human existence, of solid objects over all, lead the reader less toward any sympathy with the characters than to either impassiveness or revulsion. Salammbô herself is one more beautiful object among many beautiful objects, and, through her death, she achieves oneness with the gorgeous artifacts that surround her. An overblown exotic fantasy of gargantuan proportions, the work may also be read as a parable of waste, futility, decadence, and inhumanity that has direct application not only to the highly stylized Carthaginian world but also to the bourgeois France of Flaubert's own time.

In *A Sentimental Education*, an ironic self-portrait of the artist as a young man, Flaubert's life and times are both at the core and on the surface. Frédéric Moreau, like his creator, is part of a generation of young intellectuals in revolt against the bourgeois mediocrity that surrounds them; in sympathy with the Bohemian life, they are in love with love and passionately in love with passion. Also like his creator, Frédéric conceives an inordinate passion for an older, married woman, a love that cannot be requited. When Flaubert wrote this second version of *A Sentimental Education*, he had already changed from a youthful, aspiring law student more interested in being an aspiring writer to an accomplished and widely recognized novelist. His first attempt to write the story of his generation, the earlier version of *A Sentimental Education* (written 1843-1845 and published in 1963 as *The First Sentimental Education*), underwent considerable revision; the celebration of Romanticism and the enthusiasms and sufferings of youth in the first version are replaced by irony and detached and sardonic realism in the second. What remains constant is the notion that life has cheated the characters by replacing their illusions with reality. The great exception is Madame Arnoux: Surely there are lapses when the reader is allowed to see or at least divine her limitations, but in general she is depicted as the apotheosis of both internal and external beauty. Frédéric shares some of the nobility that attaches to Madame Arnoux's character simply because his love for her remains the fixed star of his existence. Otherwise, he is little better than the rest of the odd characters who populate the novel and whose counterparts lived in Flaubert's France.

One of the novel's primary themes is selling—and, in some sense, selling out. From Monsieur Arnoux to Monsieur Dambreuse to Husonnet to Deslauriers, the notion of selling one's wares and oneself is a constant, and the theme of prostitution, literal and figurative, permeates the work. Both the demimonde of Rosanette and the fashionable world of Madame Dambreuse share the same principle, or lack of it, of barter and bargaining. Closely related to this theme is that of betrayal, which exists on every level and in every character (again, with the exception of Madame Arnoux). Both themes work together to form the basis of Frédéric's education.

That education is a series of initiations—into Bohemia, high society, finance, and politics—in which Frédéric discovers cheapened ideals, infidelity, and lost innocence; in short, he finds that reality is antithetical to his Romantic vision of the world. In more than one sense, Frédéric's education is truly sentimental. At the novel's close, for example, Frédéric and Deslauriers meet and agree that the best time they ever had was a frustrated adolescent visit to a provincial bordello; in this agreement, the replacement of the present with a nostalgic desire to recapture the past, Flaubert demonstrates the extent to which the sentimental Frédéric has not been fully educated, as evidenced by the tenacity with which he grasps at the few Romantic notions left him.

The transition from *A Sentimental Education* to *The Temptation of Saint Anthony* is an abrupt one, even though the latter was in progress almost as long as the former, possibly longer if one reads "Smarh" (written 1839) and other juvenilia as a prelude to it. Both antedate *Madame Bovary* in Flaubert's consciousness and are filled with the elemental novelistic matter he continually reshaped and refined; both very diverse works seem to have held his attention simultaneously over a long period of time. His tale of Saint Anthony as "Smarh" went through three successive versions (1846-1849, 1856, 1870) before he finally published it as *The Temptation of Saint Anthony* in 1874. When he read the first version to Maxime Du Camp and Louis Bouilhet, they advised him to burn it, because the Romanticism it exemplified was out of fashion. When Flaubert published part of the work in 1856, Charles Baudelaire accorded it enthusiastic praise. It was still, in 1856, a provisional work; Flaubert struggled on with it, intent upon finding the optimum form into which he could pour the myriad ideas, emotions, and suggestions that the legend of Saint Anthony evoked for him.

Like its predecessors, the final version is a "pandemonic prose poem," in Victor Brombert's phrase, that blends dramatic fragments, monologues, proems, and epic conventions. Ostensibly the story of a hermit tempted by the world, the flesh, and the Devil, it is a work of Romantic decadence that explores and exploits such topics as human sexuality, integrity and bad faith, and the credos and desires of Romanticism as those topics relate to the subject of Saint Athanasius's hagiography and to Everyman. It has a particular relevance to Flaubert's own psyche, what Charles Baudelaire called the secret chamber of Flaubert's mind, as tensions between orgy and asceticism, worldly and mystical perspectives, and reality and illusion are played out in the text. A poetic novel of some eroticism, it is firmly imbued with a hatred of the flesh as well as with an unwillingness to part with it. A work that asks fundamental questions about the nature of life, moral choice, and ethical action, it is finally on the side of death. At the bottom of this work, as in much of Flaubert's writing, there exists a disturbing and thoroughly Romantic longing for oblivion; this longing informs and colors Anthony's reactions to most situations and to himself.

The novel is replete with allusions to theological controversies, historic persons and events, and mythological, mystical, and religious lore that strike modern readers, as they struck Flaubert's contemporaries, as bewildering. Enid Starkie is not alone in judging the novel as largely unreadable without fairly large amounts of specialized knowledge. For example, its seven parts or chapters suggest to Michel Butor a pattern based on an analysis of the Seven Deadly Sins, but that scheme does not fit exactly; it is possible that the mystical associations of the number seven are all that Flaubert intended. In any case, the general reader has only limited access to the novel.

In his last and unfinished novel, *Bouvard and Pécuchet*, Flaubert continued his analysis of the human condition and the human psyche by rendering a nearly perfect double portrait of human stupidity particularized in his two bourgeois antiheroes. The first meeting of two copy clerks on a deserted boulevard on a hot Parisian afternoon in 1838 marks the beginning of an extraordinary friendship. Bouvard soon receives a small but sufficient legacy, and, after a gap of three years, Pécuchet retires from his work: They are now poised for a lifelong venture in retirement in the country place they had sought for the intervening three years. The rest of their story takes place in Chavignoles, Normandy, where they set up as country gentlemen—without, however, having any clear idea of what that may involve. Their rural adventures uniformly end in disaster and are predicated mainly upon ignorance and the perfect confidence that if one reads the great books of direction, one will succeed. Disregarding the experience of those around them, the citified bunglers draw down ruin upon their garden, farm, produce, and livestock. Their bungling does not end there.

Each new failure drives them further into abstruse research: Instead of becoming apprentices or hiring well-qualified, honest masters, they plunge themselves into a regressive quest after first principles. Their failed attempt at canning, for example, leads them to chemistry, then medicine, archaeology, and the study of evolutionary theory: They come, encyclopedically, a very long way from learning the right way to can vegetables. This pattern of regression away from ordinary life and the daily attention it requires is one they follow throughout the novel. The unbalanced quest for first principles leads them to study history and literature in general; in this quest after the past, they overlook the fact that their present is quickly disintegrating.

Some critics find in the novel's last chapters an increasingly sympathetic presentation of the pair. As their disillusionment—with sex, politics, religion, education, and the law—becomes complete, they seem to emerge as objects of pity as well as of irony. Given the importance Flaubert attached to the endings of his works, it is particularly unfortunate that his last novel remains unfinished. In the face of their abysmal failure, the two old men take up copying, the task they had worked at in Paris; what they copy, the matter of a proposed second volume for the novel, is not fully known, although some hints exist. The copying of words, words of others, and the interjection of their own comments serve as a fitting occupation for Flaubert's characters. Throughout his own career as a writer/copier, Flaubert had consistently stressed the necessity of the right words, the classical, disciplined finish that frequently captured his own regret, and presumably would capture the regrets of Bouvard and Pécuchet, that, after all, things did not work out well. To the last, even in his bitter exposition of Rousseauism, the Enlightenment, and encyclopedism, he was never free of the regret for lost illusions.

Major publications other than long fiction
SHORT FICTION: *Trois Contes*, 1877 (*Three Tales*, 1903).
PLAYS: *Le Candidat*, 1874 (*The Candidate*, 1904); *Le Château des coeurs*, 1885 (with Louis Bouilhet, written 1863; *The Castle of Hearts*, 1904).
NONFICTION: *Par les champs et par les grèves*, 1885 (with Maxime Du Camp; *Over Strand and Field*, 1904); *Correspondance, 1830-1880*, 1887-1893; *Dictionnaire des idées reçues*, 1910, 1913 (*Dictionary of Accepted Ideas*, 1954).
MISCELLANEOUS: *The Complete Works*, 1904 (10 volumes); *Oeuvres complètes*, 1910-1933 (22 volumes).

Bibliography
Bart, Benjamin F. *Flaubert*, 1967.
Brombert, Victor. *Flaubert, par lui-même*, 1971.
_____ . *The Novels of Flaubert*, 1966.
Conlon, John J. "The Martyr of Style: Gustave Flaubert," in *Walter Pater and the French Tradition*, 1982.
Cortland, Peter. *A Reader's Guide to Flaubert*, 1968.
Culler, Jonathan. *Flaubert: The Uses of Uncertainty*, 1974.
Diamond, Marie J. *Flaubert: The Problem of Aesthetic Discontinuity*, 1975.
Kenner, Hugh. *Flaubert, Joyce and Beckett: The Stoic Comedians*, 1962.
Nadeau, Maurice. *The Greatness of Flaubert*, 1972. Translated by Barbara Bray.
Sarte, Jean-Paul. *The Family Idiot: Gustave Flaubert, 1821-1857*, 1981 (volume 1, partial translation).
_____ . *L'Idiot de la famille: Gustave Flaubert, 1821-1857*, 1971-1972.
Starkie, Enid. *Flaubert: The Making of the Master*, 1967-1971.

Steegmuller, Francis. *Flaubert and Madame Bovary*, 1939.
Tillet, Margaret G. *On Reading Flaubert*, 1961.

John J. Conlon

THEODOR FONTANE

Born: Neuruppin, Prussia; December 30, 1819
Died: Berlin, Germany; September 20, 1898

Principal long fiction

Vor dem Sturm, 1878; *L'Adultera*, 1882; *Schach von Wuthenow*, 1883 (*A Man of Honor: Schach von Wuthenow*, 1975); *Cécile*, 1887; *Irrungen, Wirrungen*, 1888 (*Trials and Tribulations*, 1917; also as *A Suitable Match*, 1968); *Stine*, 1890 (English translation, 1969); *Unwiederbringlich*, 1892 (*Beyond Recall*, 1964); *Frau Jenny Treibel*, 1893 (*Jenny Treibel*, 1976); *Effi Briest*, 1895 (English translation, 1914, 1962); *Die Poggenpuhls*, 1896; *Der Stechlin*, 1898; *Sämtliche Werke*, 1959-1975 (24 volumes).

Other literary forms

In addition to the novels mentioned above, Theodor Fontane's works include numerous poems, novellas, theater reviews, travel journals, autobiographical writings, four volumes of letters, and essays on literature, history, and art. This extremely prolific writer was a journalist for many years before he was able to devote himself mainly to belles lettres.

Achievements

When considering Fontane's writing, one thinks not only of nineteenth century Prussia, of her landscapes and cityscapes, of her people—particularly the declining gentry, the prosperous upper-middle class, the faithful servants—but also of the emerging working class. Beginning with his *Wanderungen durch die Mark Brandenburg* (journeys through Mark Brandenburg, which appeared between 1865 and 1882) and culminating in his major novels, Fontane painted a fascinating social panorama of his age.

Biography

Henri Theodor Fontane was born on December 30, 1819, in Neuruppin. Both of his parents were of French descent, part of the French Huguenot colony that had existed in Prussia since the Edict of Potsdam of 1685. Fontane's father was a pharmacist. During the first year of his marriage, he acquired a well-established pharmacy in Neuruppin. He was not, however, a good businessman, and he lost considerable amounts of money at the gambling table. In 1827, the elder Fontane sold his pharmacy in Neuruppin and purchased another in Swinemünde. The Fontane family then moved to Swinemünde, a port town that was much livelier than Neuruppin. For Fontane, Swinemünde was always imbued with a certain poetic quality, and he transmuted it into the setting of a few of his works. He attended the *gymnasium* (academic high school) in Neuruppin for a few years, but eventually he switched to a vocational school in Berlin and, in 1836, was apprenticed to a pharmacy there. During those years, his father's fortunes went from bad to worse, and his parents eventually separated.

His father's financial failures meant that, from a very young age, Fontane had to rely almost exclusively on his own resources in order to make a living. While still an apprentice in the pharmacy in Berlin, he wrote poems and novellas, a few of which were published. In April, 1844, he began his one-year military service. During the summer of the same year, he was given leave in order to accompany a friend on a trip to England. He was fascinated by that country and particularly by the city of London. He resolved to find a way of living in England for several years.

In 1847, Fontane received his license as a "first-class pharmacist," but he never practiced his profession in any consistent manner. He became active in a few literary societies in Berlin and received several assignments as a journalist. In 1850, he married Emilie Rouanet-Kummer, to whom he had been engaged for five years. In 1851, their first son was born, and the struggle for day-to-day survival intensified.

In 1852, Fontane was sent to London for several months, as a correspondent for the *Preussische Zeitung*. After his return, he published *Ein Sommer in London* (1854; a summer in London), a collection of essays that are full of his admiration for British history and society and for the country's wealth. Fontane did not, however, hesitate to criticize the prevailing materialism and social injustice. His summer in London in 1852 and his knowledge of the English language and of British institutions were important factors when the Prussian government chose a press agent to be sent to London to present its views on world affairs to the British press.

In 1855, Fontane was posted to London for more than three years and, for the first time in his life, had a comfortable income. These years in England were very important to his development: They were a fruitful period of learning, of absorbing a foreign culture, and of contrasting it to his own. Toward the end of his assignment in England, Fontane went on a journey to Scotland, treading in the footsteps of Ossian and Sir Walter Scott. Shortly after his return to Berlin, he published a very personal account of his journey to Scotland: *Jenseits des Tweed* (1860; *Across the Tweed*, 1965), which received favorable critical reviews. More important, Fontane's work on *Across the Tweed* led to a number of insights, comparisons, and transmutations which were to find their way into *Wanderungen durch die Mark Brandenburg*, in which his monumental depiction of the landscape, the towns, the people, and the history of Mark Brandenburg was to set the stage for his novels and novellas.

In 1860, Fontane joined the editorial staff of the conservative *Kreuzzeitung*, not out of political conviction but in order to have a regular income. Ten years later, he was finally able to break "the chain on which my daily bread dangles." In 1870, he was appointed theater critic of the prestigious (and liberal) *Vossische Zeitung*, with which he remained associated until 1890. Except for a brief internment by the French during the Franco-Prussian War (Fontane had served as a war correspondent), the last third of his life was relatively free of anxiety. Most of his time was devoted to writing, and he was increasingly recognized as a major literary voice. In 1894, when most of his major works (but not his two greatest novels) had been published, he was awarded an honorary doctorate by the University of Berlin. He was held in esteem by the adherents of Naturalism, though their emerging literary form was quite unlike his own. Fontane died on September 20, 1898, apparently from a stroke. One of the papers found on his desk was a list of those people who were to receive copies of his just-published masterpiece, *Der Stechlin*.

Analysis

Theodor Fontane's novels may be divided into three cateories, according to their subject matter: first, novels dealing with the conflicts arising from class distinctions, frequently involving a young nobleman and a girl from the lower classes; second, novels about marriage, in all cases involving adultery; and third, vast epic panoramas of Prussian society with diffuse plots, skillfully depicted settings, and carefully nuanced utterances by large numbers of characters. This third category includes Fontane's earliest novel, *Vor dem Sturm*, and his final masterpiece, *Der Stechlin*.

Turning to a detailed consideration of the first category, one should look first at *A Suitable Match* and *Stine*. The plot of *A Suitable Match* centers on a love affair between Botho von Rienäcker, an officer of the Prussian nobility, and Lene, a seamstress. Botho is eventually induced by family considerations to marry a rich young woman of his own class. Lene also gets married to an honest man, a pietist recently returned from America. Fontane uses this simple plot to create realistic yet subtle portraits, not only of the two protagonists but also of the two social strata that they represent.

Particularly notable in the novel is Fontane's treatment of dialogue. The first two chapters take place in and around a nursery and vegetable farm where Lene, her mother, and Mr. and Mrs. Dörr (the owners of the nursery) live. It is early summer, and "Baron Botho" often visits Lene and spends parts of his evenings in Mrs. Dörr's kitchen, drinking apple cider and conversing with his friends. In these conversations, the characters reveal themselves not only as individuals but also as types who share their attitudes and circumstances with many other members of their class. The conversations in Mrs. Dörr's kitchen are juxtaposed to the one among Botho, his uncle, and another young nobleman. They meet in an exclusive Berlin restaurant (whose decor is as carefully described as Mrs. Dörr's kitchen), they drink Chablis, and most of their conversation is concerned with contemporary society and politics. Only at one point does Botho's uncle touch upon the critical issue at hand—when he says that Botho is "practically committed" ("Du bist doch so gut wie gebunden"). This incident is a good example of Fontane's seemingly effortless artistry, because, later on, during a moment of supreme happiness, Lene ties a bunch of flowers with a strand of her own hair. As she gives the flowers to Botho, she uses almost the same words "Now you are tied [committed to me]" ("Nun bist du gebunden"). The irony of the matter is that Botho *is* committed to marry a young noblewoman, and when his mother insists that he honor that commitment, he obeys. When a fellow officer asks Botho for his advice in a similar matter, Botho stoutly defends the existing class distinctions and advises his friend to terminate his relationship with the young bourgeoise in question. A few years later, however—when he decides to burn a packet of letters that Lene had once written to him, as well as the withered bunch of flowers—he realizes that he still is and always will be "tied" to her.

In *A Suitable Match*, existing social conventions are portrayed as of paramount importance. When they conflict with individual happiness, Botho's happiness must be subordinated to them. The fact that life goes on passably well is adumbrated by Mrs. Dörr in the first chapter. This fact is also demonstrated through the pietist's account of his first meeting with Lene and through the narrator's account of Botho's marriage.

The conflict between social conventions and personal happiness is accentuated and rendered more poignant by the tragic conclusion of *Stine*. The main plot of this novel concerns a love affair between a young girl of the working class and a young count. Stine and Waldemar (the two young people) meet during a supper party arranged by Stine's sister Pauline but paid for by Pauline's lover, an aging count who is Waldemar's uncle. Pauline's way of life—specifically, her total financial dependence on the Count—constitutes an important secondary action of this novel. Accounts of Pauline's present and past life are skillfully interwoven in the narration, and the reader learns that she is a widow with a dependent child who simply cannot make ends meet without the Count's financial help—without, in fact, selling herself to him. When Stine first speaks to Waldemar alone, she makes it clear to him that she prefers a life of poverty to the kind of life her sister leads. Later, Waldemar offers to marry her and to emigrate to America with her, but she refuses and explains to him that the difference between their social classes would preclude any kind of permanent happiness for them. Thereupon, Waldemar, who has been unable to obtain his uncle's support for this marriage, commits suicide. Thus, Waldemar dies because all the people who surround him (including his beloved) tell him that a Count cannot marry a working-class girl, that class distinctions are insuperable barriers.

The reader is left with the impression that Waldemar is a victor of sorts, that the old caste system will not survive for long. Contemporary social conventions are attacked, not only by Waldemar but also by the Baron (a friend of Waldemar's uncle to whom Waldemar first turns for help), who says that he is always happy to see someone breaking through the *Krimskrams* (nonsense) of class distinctions. Even Waldemar's uncle admits that "the divine order of the world does not completely correspond to the calendar of the state and to the ranking list of society." He goes even further and states that "at the present time" he and his ilk are still the *beati possidentes* (happy proprietors). He says to Waldemar: "Be a proprietor, and you are in the right. . . . Why deprive ourselves of this possession and . . . conjure up a future which may not benefit anyone, and certainly not us?" Statements such as this one, if read in conjunction with the accounts of Pauline's precarious financial situation, add a considerable dimension of social criticism to the novel. It becomes clear to the reader that the opulence of the nobility is based upon the low wages of the working class and on a total absence of a social security system for these people. It is, of course, no accident that *Stine* was written at a time when a comprehensive social security system was being debated in the Prussian parliament. (The social security law was finally passed in 1889.)

In *Stine* as well as in *A Suitable Match*, politics is deftly subsumed in the actions and in the characterizations. That is not quite the case in *Jenny Treibel*, the most lighthearted work in the first category of Fontane's novels. Again, the representatives of two social classes interact and mingle socially, but they cannot intermarry. In *Jenny Treibel*, however, the obstacle is not the insurmountable barrier of class distinction but the determination of one of the protagonists, Mrs. Jenny Treibel, a successful social climber. In her youth, she had been poor and idealistic and had had an affair with an equally poor and idealistic high school teacher named Schmidt. She had left him and married an industrialist. When the novel opens, Jenny rules over a substantial villa, over her husband, who is only a *Kommerzienrat* but who has higher political ambitions, and over her somewhat spineless son Leopold, who works in his father's firm. Jenny's older son has already married a suitably rich young woman from Hamburg. The other social circle consists mainly of Mr. Schmidt, his vivacious and intelligent daughter Corinna, and his nephew, Marcell. During a supper party, Corinna flirts with the visiting British businessman, but only in order to attract Leopold's attention. On the way home, she admits to Marcell that she intends to marry Leopold and live a life of luxury, come what may. Marcell is despondent because he loves her and hopes to marry her. Nevertheless, during an outing with both families and some mutual friends, Corinna contrives a sort of engagement to Leopold.

Leaving aside Mr. Treibel's ill-starred political maneuvers, the comedy has two high points, both involving Jenny. In one encounter, she forbids Leopold to marry Corinna, and he refuses to obey her. In the other one, she tries to dissuade Corinna from her endeavor, and the latter refuses to relinquish her "rights" to Leopold. Yet, Jenny wins in the end: Her daughter-in-law conveniently has a sister who will receive a considerable dowry. Jenny invites this young woman to spend a few weeks in her house, and Leopold must at least be polite to her. Meanwhile, he writes letters to Corinna every day, assuring her of his love and steadfastness, but he does not go to see her. Some two weeks later, Marcell receives a tenured appointment as a teacher and is thus able to get married. At this point, Corinna is more than tired of Leopold's letters and more than ready to accept Marcell. The strength of the novel lies in the indulgent irony with which the various characters are depicted and the loving attention paid to details, life-styles, food and drink, and nuances of speech. The novel's subject matter is aptly summed up by Corinna when she says that she was not allowed to marry Leopold because she did not have a dowry that would have doubled the Treibels' assets. Such subject matter may be trivial, but Fontane's artistry in presenting it makes the novel a first-rate comedy of manners.

Fontane's first three novels about marriage and adultery (*L'Adultera*, *Cécile*, and *Beyond Recall*) are uneven in artistic quality. They may be regarded as essentially preparatory to his undisputed masterpiece, *Effi Briest*. The plot of this latter work is based on an anecdote, "a story of adultery like a hundred others," and it is quite simple: Effi von Briest, the seventeen-year-old daughter of a family of the lower nobility, marries Geert von Innstetten, a member of the same social class, thirty-eight years of age. He is a civil servant stationed in the remote seaside town of Kessin. Kessin is a dull place: With one or two exceptions, the townspeople do not measure up to Effi's social and educational levels, and the members of the country gentry in the neighboring estates are narrow-minded and bigoted and receive her coolly. Innstetten tries his best to be attentive to her, but he also has to devote considerable time and effort to his duties and his career. After a year or so, Effi gives birth to a daughter, but even this happy event does not alter the essentially tranquil and boring quality of her life in Kessin. Then Major von Crampas is stationed there, and he brings some life into the town. He organizes amateur theatrical productions in which Effi and other local notables perform. Effi knows that Crampas is a notorious ladies' man, and she sees through him quite easily. Yet, out of boredom, nonchalance, or frivolity, she allows herself to be seduced by him. Her affair with Crampas, with its attendant problems of secrecy and dissembling, does not bring her much joy. She is therefore relieved when Innstetten informs her that he has been promoted and will be transferred to Berlin. The Innstettens move into a suitably elegant apartment in the capital and begin leading the kind of social life that befits members of the upper classes. Effi becomes a society lady and is quite happy. Crampas is forgotten. Then, after almost seven years after their arrival, Innstetten accidentally discovers a packet of letters that Crampas had written to his wife. Innstetten challenges Crampas to a duel and kills him. He then banishes Effi from his home. She lives in a small apartment in Berlin, financially supported by her parents but forbidden to go to their home and shunned by all members of high society. After three years of this kind of life, she is finally allowed to see her daughter, but the child has been completely turned against her and only parrots words drilled into her by her father or her governess. Effi is so upset by this encounter with her child that she has a complete nervous breakdown. Severely ill, she is finally allowed to return to her parents' home. There she spends a few months in a trancelike kind of happiness, almost beatific, and finally dies.

Effi's fate, as sketched above, certainly produces a certain amount of empathy in the reader, but the real interest of the novel lies in the more general conflict between the concepts of personal happiness and social conventions. Many of the characters in *Effi Briest* are thwarted in their pursuit of happiness by a complex set of rules and regulations, which are presented by the narrator in such a manner as to question their validity. The novel contains a wealth of well-drawn characters, and they are carefully orchestrated to express this crucial problem. The problem arises early in the novel, when Effi meets the various members of the country gentry around Kessin. They are drawn as a stiff, prissy, and bigoted lot, and the reader is prompted to ask himself how much happier they could be and how much happier they could make an intelligent and lively young woman like Effi if they were a little warmer, more natural, and more forthcoming. Juxtaposed to these dull and hidebound characters is the figure of Roswitha, Effi's faithful servant. She is a simple, humane person who does not hesitate to demonstrate such deeply felt emotions as grief, love, and compassion. While Effi's mother is prompted by her concern for the norms of society to forbid her sinful daughter to enter her parental home, Roswitha stays with her in very humble circumstances and remains her servant and companion until the end.

This and similar criticisms of social conventions may be regarded as inferential; they may be discerned from a close consideration of plot and characterization. There is, however, at least one protagonist who undergoes a development to the point where he overtly and consciously attacks contemporary social conventions. After Innstetten has discovered the incriminating letters, he has a long conversation with a colleague, whom he asks to act as a second in the duel. The colleague tries to dissuade Innstetten from the duel, particularly in view of the fact that Effi's adultery occurred almost seven years earlier, but Innstetten retorts:

> I have thought it all over. A man is not just an individual, he belongs to a whole, and we must always pay attention to the whole, we are absolutely dependent on it. If I could manage to live in isolation, I could ignore the matter . . . but that . . . society-something [*Gesellschafts-Etwas*] which tyrannizes us does not ask about charm or love or statutes of limitations. I have no choice. I must.

At this point in the narration, Innstetten follows the dictates of the "society-something" and proceeds to kill Crampas. His and Crampas' seconds notify the authorities, and everything is in perfect legal order. On his way back to Berlin, however, Innstetten begins to have his doubts. He remembers the way Crampas looked at him during his dying moments, and he tells himself that he did not kill him out of hatred, which would at least have been a human emotion, but because of a "concept, a made-up story, a comedy almost." Yet he says to himself, "I must now continue the comedy, and must send Effi away and ruin her, and myself along with her." It is this "must," this obedience to man-made codes of behavior, no matter how much one doubts their validity, that brings grief and sometimes catastrophe upon many of Fontane's characters. In Innstetten's case, it takes three years of solitary suffering on his part and a moving letter from Roswitha (who begs him to send Effi her favorite old dog) for him to realize that "culture and honor" and "all this nonsense" are the cause of his and Effi's suffering.

It is the supreme irony of this novel that Effi, shortly before her death, expresses her conviction that her husband, in all of his cruelty, has treated her justly. It should be noted that the opposing views reached by the two protagonists are expressed by them, not by the narrator (who intrudes almost nowhere in the novel). In a brief epilogue that is set one month after Effi's death, her mother expresses doubts whether she and her husband gave Effi the right kind of education and whether Effi might not have been too young to marry. Her husband gives his standard response: "That leads us too far afield." In the final analysis, this evasive answer must be given to the question regarding Fontane's own stand on the problem of personal happiness versus social conventions. He raises many questions; he allows some of his major characters to attack contemporary codes of behavior, but those characters who infringe upon them are punished.

Fontane's "Prussian," or historical, novels are vast panoramas of the entire Prussian society. One of them takes place in the period of 1812 to 1813 and the other one in the late 1890's. Walter Müller-Seidel has described *Vor dem Sturm* as the best historical novel written in Germany in the nineteenth century. Fontane himself described his intentions as follows: ". . . to introduce a large number of characters from Mark Brandenburg from the winter 1812-1813 [and] to depict the manner in which the great feeling which was born then . . . affected various kinds of people." The "great feeling" was the joy and relief that the Prussian people felt at Napoleon's defeat in Russia in 1812 and the anticipation that Prussia would soon be free of French domination and occupation. (Prussia had previously been defeated by the French and forced into an alliance with them against Russia.)

In the novel, as the demoralized remnants of the defeated French army move westward into Prussia, the Prussian king still respects his pact with Napoleon, but the members of the nobility urge him and his government to attack the French and to rid the fatherland of them. This political aspect constitutes one strand of this long (seven-hundred-page) and diffuse novel: Several members of the rural gentry organize a militia and attempt unsuccessfully to drive the French out of Frankfurt an der Oder. Several other strands of the action concern the relationships between two noble houses, their plans for intermarriage, and the disparate destinies of the young people in question. In addition, the novel abounds in vivid depictions of contemporary literary life, of members of the middle and peasant classes, and it even contains a breathtaking account of the battle of Borodino, which is at the same time a moving antiwar text. Obviously, this overabundance of material does not make for a tightly constructed plot, but toward the end of the novel, a unifying tenor does emerge—namely, the renewal of society. It is surely no accident that Lewin von Vitzewitz, the young heir to the manor of Hohen-Vietz, marries Marie, the daughter of a traveling circus artist. Lewin's father welcomes her into his family just as Lewin is about to leave for the war of liberation against the French. The timing of these two events seems to symbolize a juncture between the renewal of the Vitzewitz dynasty and that of the entire country. All in all, the various strands of the action, the vivid descriptions, and the loving care expended on each detail add up to a fascinating panorama of Prussian society at a crucial point in its history.

Turning to *Der Stechlin*, Fontane's last work, it may be well to quote from a letter of his in which he described his work to a Berlin publisher: "At the end an old man dies and two young people marry; that is more or less all that happens in five-hundred pages." Fontane's description of his novel is accurate as far as the paucity of the action is concerned, but it is misleading when one considers the abundance of symbolism and political and moral thought that the work contains. For the most part, the novel is set in the village of Stechlin and in the manor house of the same name, which is inhabited by Dubslaw von Stechlin, a retired major in his sixties. The marriage alluded to above is the one between Dubslaw's son Woldemar and Armgard von Barby, the daughter of a retired diplomat living in Berlin. This marriage solves Dubslaw's one major problem: Armgard's dowry will permit Woldemar to repay a mortgage that his father had to take on the manor, and the necessary repairs will be made. As a result, the material base for the continued existence of the Stechlin dynasty in its accustomed style would seem to be assured.

The many questions raised in the novel, however, go far beyond the material base of the Stechlin estate. Throughout the work, there are conversations and discussions about the role of the nobility and about the social contract between various segments of the population, as well as about the individual's relationship to society. The novel encompasses a vast political spectrum, and the reader becomes acquainted with supporters of the three main political parties—namely, the Conservatives, the Progressives, and the Social Democrats. As usual with Fontane, it is difficult to discern his own sympathies, but on the basis of the unequivocally positive characterization accorded to Pastor

Lorenzen (the village pastor and Woldemar's mentor), it seems safe to say that the views he expresses are very close to the ones the author reached in his old age. Some of Lorenzen's statements, while a little dated now, bear rereading and rethinking even late in the twentieth century. Consider, for example, his definition of the modern age:

> The main contrast between the modern and the old [ways of life] consists of the fact that human beings are no longer placed in their positions on the basis of their birth. . . . Previously one was a lord of a manor or a weaver of linen for three-hundred years; now every weaver can one day be the lord of a manor.

This statement is as relevant, and as debatable, in our day as it was in Fontane's time. Some of Lorenzen's and Dubslaw's other discussions sound even more relevant to our time, particularly the one about the pollution caused by a chemical plant in their county and Dubslaw's proposal that the workers, instead of working there, should each till half an acre of land, which the state should give them. Lest it appear that *Der Stechlin* consists only of dry political or philosophical treatises, it should be pointed out that all of these serious thoughts are presented with light irony, that the interlocutors are depicted with all of their human foibles, and that none of them is presented as a villain. In this way, an air of lightheartedness and serenity pervades the whole work. Upon some reflection, Lorenzen's, Dubslaw's, and Melusine's concerns for their contemporaries emerge as age-old universal concerns—namely, man's care for his fellowman. Thus, in his last work, Fontane's thoughts transcended his previous preoccupation with individual happiness vis-à-vis social conventions to encompass a profound reflection on the question of collective well-being.

Major publications other than long fiction
NONFICTION: *Ein Sommer in London*, 1854; *Jenseits des Tweed*, 1860 (*Across the Tweed*, 1965); *Wanderungen durch die Mark Brandenburg*, 1865-1882. MISCELLANEOUS: *Sämtliche Werke*, 1959-1975 (24 volumes).

Bibliography
Cary, J. R. *Antithesis as a Principle of Structure and Technique in the Novels of Theodor Fontane*, 1954.
Demetz, P. *Formen des Realismus: Theodor Fontane*, 1964.
Hayes, C. N. *Symbol and Correlative in Theodor Fontane's Fiction*, 1967.
Müller-Seidel, W. "Fontane: *Der Stechlin*," in *Der deutsche Roman*, 1963. Edited by Benno von Wiese.
_____ . *Theodor Fontane: Soziale Romankunst in Deutschland*, 1975.

Nürnberger, H. *Theodor Fontane in Selbstzeugnissen und Bilddokumenten*, 1968.
Stern, J. P. *Realism and Tolerance: Theodor Fontane*, 1964.

Franz P. Haberl

ANATOLE FRANCE
Jacques-Anatole-François Thibault

Born: Paris, France; April 16, 1844
Died: Paris, France; October 12, 1924

Principal long fiction

Le Crime de Sylvestre Bonnard, 1881 (*The Crime of Sylvestre Bonnard*, 1890); *Les Désirs de Jean Servien*, 1882 (*The Aspirations of Jean Servien*, 1912); *Thaïs*, 1890 (English translation, 1891); *La Rôtisserie de la Reine Pédauque*, 1893 (*At the Sign of the Reine Pédauque*, 1912); *Le Lys rouge*, 1894 (*The Red Lily*, 1898); *L'Histoire contemporaine*, 1897-1901 (*Contemporary History*, 1910-1922; includes *L'Orme du mail*, 1897 [*The Elm Tree on the Mall*, 1910]; *Le Mannequin d'osier*, 1897 [*The Wicker Work Woman*, 1910]; *L'Anneau d'améthyste*, 1899 [*The Amethyst Ring*, 1919]; *Monsieur Bergeret à Paris*, 1901 [*Monsieur Bergeret in Paris*, 1922]); *Histoire comique*, 1903 (*A Mummer's Tale*, 1921); *L'Île des pingouins*, 1908 (*Penguin Island*, 1914); *Les Dieux ont soif*, 1912 (*The Gods Are Athirst*, 1913); *La Révolte des anges*, 1914 (*The Revolt of the Angels*, 1914); *The Complete Works*, 1908-1928 (21 volumes); *Oeuvres complètes*, 1925-1935 (25 volumes).

Other literary forms

Of the twenty-five volumes which make up the standard French edition of the complete works of Anatole France, more than fifteen are given over to one form or another of prose fiction: ten novels (thirteen if one counts the tetralogy, *Contemporary History*, as four separate novels), ten collections of short stories, and four volumes of fictionalized autobiography. The remainder of the twenty-five-volume set exhibits a startling variety of literary forms: poetry, theater, biography, history, literary criticism, philosophy, journalism, and polemical writings. France's first publication was a book-length critical study of the French Romantic poet Alfred de Vigny (1868), after which he published two volumes of his own poetry, one containing lyric poems, the other a play in verse, and several long narrative poems. In the 1880's and 1890's, he wrote a regular weekly column, mostly about books and the literary world, for a prominent Paris newspaper, *Le Temps*. The best of those columns were republished in five volumes under the title *La Vie littéraire* (1888-1892; *On Life and Letters*, 1911-1914). His major venture into the writing of history was *La Vie de Jeanne d'Arc* (1908; *The Life of Joan of Arc*, 1908), published after a quarter of a century of research. That same year, he published his one original prose work for the theater, *La Comédie de celui qui épousa une femme muette* (1908; *The Man Who Married a Dumb Wife*, 1915), a farce based on a well-known medieval fabliau. His major speeches and occasional writings, on such issues of the times as the Dreyfus Affair, socialism, and pacifism, were collected and published in several volumes under the title *Vers les temps meilleurs* (1906, 1949). Philosophical meditations on human nature and civilization can be found in a volume entitled *Le Jardin d'Épicure* (1894; *The Garden of Epicurus*, 1908), consisting of pieces on general subjects originally written for his weekly newspaper column and not included in the volumes of *On Life and Letters*. One may say, in sum, that Anatole France was the complete man of letters, who tried his hand at just about every form of writing practiced in the literary world of his time. It is nevertheless accurate to say that the writing of fiction so dominated his output, throughout his career, that it constituted his true vocation.

Achievements

The election of Anatole France to the Académie Française in 1896 and his winning of the Nobel Prize for Literature in 1921 were the major public landmarks of the great success and recognition he achieved during his career as a writer, first in his own country and then in the international arena. At the height of his fame, in the early years of the twentieth century, he was widely regarded as France's greatest living author, celebrated for his wit, his wisdom, and his humanitarian vision. The paradoxes of that fame, however, were multiple and heavy with irony: The fame had been an unusually long time in coming (he was nearly fifty years old before he had his first significant success with the public), it was based largely on his association with public events rather than on his genuine but esoteric literary talent, and it lasted only briefly. Indeed, the greatest paradox of his fame was its bewilderingly rapid eclipse after his death. His reputation has still not regained the luster of his glory years, around the turn of the century.

France himself lived long enough to be the saddened witness of a major erosion of his fame in a storm of bitter controversy, which made him an object of both worship and hatred but for purely nonliterary reasons. The truth is that the great fame he enjoyed, during a brief period of his life, was of the public sort, only indirectly occasioned by his writings, which, even at their most popular, appealed to a rather narrowly circumscribed audience. One must separate his fame from his achievements as a writer—which is not to say that his achievements were minor, but only that they were literary and aesthetic, hence accessible to relatively few at any time. As a novelist and short-story writer, France made his mark in the fiction of ideas, and as a literary critic, he established, by personal example, the validity of subjective impressionism as a method. Those are the two major achievements of his career in letters, the accomplishments that have affected literary history. To those literary achievements, one should add a more personal achievement: the creation of a highly distinctive, instantly identifiable style of classic purity and elegance, with subtle rhythms and limpid clarity, which perfectly translated the skeptical and gently ironic view he held of the human condition.

Biography

The only child of a well-established Parisian bookdealer, Anatole France, born Jacques-Anatole-François Thibault, was seemingly predestined to the world of books. His father, Noël-François Thibault, ran the sort of bookshop that was also a gathering place of the literati, who would come not only as customers but also as friends. They would sit and talk with the owner, whom they called by the familiar diminutive "France," an abbreviation of François. Once the son was old enough to help in the shop and participate in the daily conversations, he was naturally called "le jeune France," a custom that suggested to young Anatole the pen name he would choose when he began to write. Shy and unassertive by nature and unprepossessing physically, Anatole matured into an unworldly and bookish young man, easily intimidated by the "real" world and much given to periods of solitude and quiet reverie. In his twenties, he did occasional research and editing chores for the publishers of dictionaries and encyclopedias, having definitely decided against following in his father's footsteps as a bookseller. Eventually, he became a reader of manuscripts for a publisher, wrote articles for ephemeral journals, and took a civil servant's position, working in the Senate Library, all the while using his leisure moments to learn the craft of writing. He was thirty-three, and a published but thoroughly obscure and unknown author, when he overcame his timidity long enough to marry, in 1877. The marriage produced one child, a daughter born in 1881, but was otherwise an unhappy relationship for both sides which ended in a bitter divorce in 1893, after a prolonged separation.

France's unhappy domestic life was the backdrop for his long personal struggle to find his own "voice" and establish himself as a writer. By the 1880's, he had abandoned poetry and was experimenting with different modes of prose fiction, trying both the novel and the short-story forms but attracting very little attention from the reading public. Only after he became the regular literary critic for *Le Temps* and had published a genuinely popular work, the novel *Thaïs*, did he feel securely established enough as a writer to give up his post at the Senate Library. Thereafter, all through the 1890's, his books sold well, and he rose rapidly in public esteem, aided in part by a newfound interest in and involvement with politics and public affairs. In particular, the Dreyfus Affair outraged his sense of justice and galvanized him into public action for the first time in his life. He was then a man in his fifties, and he discovered, a bit to his own surprise, a radical social thinker beneath the placid and conservative exterior he had always presented to the world. During the first years of the new century, he became outspokenly anticlerical and socialistic in his views but was soon plunged into disillusionment when he saw that even victory, as in the Dreyfus Affair, produced little real change in society, and that his own activism served only to make him controversial and the object of vicious attacks, which he found especially painful to endure. This mood of disillusionment drove him to withdraw into himself once more and to give up active involvement in public affairs. His work increasingly concerned the past and took on an unaccustomed satiric edge. The outbreak of World War I tempted him briefly into the public arena once more, to proclaim his pacifist views, but when he was assailed as unpatriotic, he retreated, this time definitively, into the private world of letters. It is perhaps suggestive of the depth of his wounds from the public fray that his literary preoccupations during the final decade of his life were almost exclusively autobiographical. His career as a novelist had effectively ended with the publication of *The Revolt of the Angels* in 1914.

Analysis

The world of books into which Anatole France was born was surely the strongest influence in determining his vocation as a writer, but that influence went far deeper still, for it also determined the kind of writer he would be. Almost all the subjects he chose to write about, in his long career, were derived from or related to books in some way. He was a voracious reader all of his life, and the many books he wrote not only reflect that wide reading but also reveal that what he read was more immediate and more vital to him—more nourishing to his creative imagination, indeed more *real* to him— than the quotidian reality in which he lived. Even when most actively involved in public events, as he was in the years immediately before and immediately after the turn of the century, he tended to approach events as abstractions, dealing with them as intellectual issues, somehow detached from specific occurrences involving specific human beings. This conscious need to convert real events into matter for books can be seen most clearly in the tetralogy that he so pointedly entitled *Contemporary History* and in which he contrived to write about current events as though they were already in the distant past or even the stuff of legend.

Concomitant with his irreducibly bookish view of the world was his almost instinctive taste for storytelling. Whether as reader or as writer, nothing charmed him more than the unfolding of a narrative. Even factual writing— history and biography, for example—he treated as an exercise in storytelling, going so far as to characterize good literary criticism as a kind of novel in which the critic "recounts the adventures of his soul among masterpieces," as he put it in the famous preface to *On Life and Letters*. The art of storytelling was the art he set out to master in his long and difficult apprenticeship, and the storytelling impulse can be identified as the very heart of his vocation as a writer.

To the mind of the man of letters and the instinct of the teller of tales must be added a third characteristic: that of the outlook of the determined skeptic. France trained himself, from an early age, to question everything and to discern the contradictions and ironies in all forms of human behavior, includ- ing his own. He cultivated a perspective of distance and detachment from both people and events, but he learned to temper the bleakness and isolation of such a perspective with feelings of sympathetic recognition of the folly common to all mankind. A subtle blend of pity and irony came to be the hallmark of his view of the affairs of this world, expressed in the tone of gentle mockery with which his celebrated style was impregnated in the works of his maturity. Indeed, all three central characteristics of France—the literary turn of mind, the narrative impulse, and the ironic perspective—can be found in everything he wrote, including the youthful works of poetry, fiction, and literary criticism through which he gradually learned the writer's trade. Those three traits can be seen fully developed for the first time in the novel that won for him his first public recognition, *The Crime of Sylvestre Bonnard*, in 1881.

Published to the accolades of the Académie Française, *The Crime of Sylvestre Bonnard* provided Anatole France with his first taste of success. The improbable hero of the book is an elderly, unworldly scholar and bibliophile who explains, in his own words, in the form of diary entries, how he came to acquire a coveted medieval manuscript and how he rescued a young girl from poverty and oppression. What holds the reader's interest is not the trivial plot but the character of Sylvestre Bonnard, whose naïve narrative style, in his diary, constantly and unwittingly reveals his own bumbling incompetence in dealing with the practical side of life. The reader quickly recognizes as comical the dramatic earnestness with which the simpleminded scholar narrates the only two "adventures" that have ever intruded into his serene existence. The ironic discrepancy between the excited tone of the narrator and the mundane character of the events he narrates is echoed suggestively in the title, which promises a thriller but delivers nothing more violent than a book lover's crime: Having promised to sell his personal library in order to create a dowry for the damsel in distress he has rescued, Sylvestre Bonnard confesses, at the end of the diary, that he had "criminally" withheld from the sale several items with which he could not bear to part.

Perhaps the greatest skill the author displays in this book is that of artfully concealing the inherent sentimentality of the material. The key device of concealment is mockery: Sylvestre Bonnard's interest in old books and manuscripts is magnified, in both incidents, into a grand and criminal passion by a transparently mock-heroic tone. This device distracts and amuses the reader, preventing inopportune reflections about the "fairy-tale" unreality of the happy ending of each incident. It is also true that the eccentric character of Sylvestre Bonnard is charming and that the novelty of a gentle fantasy, published at the height of the popularity of the Naturalistic novel in France, must have struck many readers of the day as a welcome relief. It was for such reasons, no doubt, that the novel enjoyed mild critical acclaim and modest sales in 1881, even as its author, sternly self-critical, recognized its limitations of both form and content and set about immediately trying to do better. What France retained from *The Crime of Sylvestre Bonnard* for future use was the tone of gentle and sympathetic irony about human foibles. In the decade that followed, he experimented with fictionalized autobiography, tales of childhood, and themes borrowed from history or legend, seeking above all a composition that he—and his readers—could recognize as a fully realized work of art. He reached that goal with the publication of *Thaïs* in 1890—his first critical *and* popular success.

The story of Thaïs, the courtesan of Alexandria, has a bookish source, as does most of France's fiction; he changed the legend of Thaïs, however, by giving the central role in the tale to the monk, Paphnuce, whose ambition for saintliness inspires in him the project of converting the notorious actress and prostitute to Christianity. The well-known plot, in which the saintly monk succumbs to sin even as the notorious sinner seeks salvation in piety, is thus, in France's version, seen almost exclusively from the point of view of the monk. The character of Thaïs is developed hardly at all, while the complex motivations of Paphnuce are analyzed and explored in detail. This imbalance in the point of view, however, does not affect the fundamental irony of the story. Thaïs, though superficially presented, is shown clearly to be a seeker of pagan pleasure and prosperity, who yet was influenced in early youth by piety, having been secretly baptized, and whose growing fear of death and damnation happens to make her receptive to the preachings of Paphnuce at that particular time of her life. Paphnuce, on the other hand, has had a long struggle against his own sensuality in trying to live as a monk, and is unaware that his sudden project of converting Thaïs is really prompted by his unconscious but still unruly sensual yearnings. When the two meet, therefore, each is ignorant of the other's true disposition, and Paphnuce, moreover, is ignorant of his own desires. Their encounter is thus fated to be sterile, for by that time, Thaïs is already on her way to salvation, and Paphnuce is proceeding precipitously in the opposite direction. France exploits the irony of their opposing trajectories by making the occasion of their meeting the longest and most concentrated episode in the book. The effect is structural: The book is designed as a triptych, with the shorter first and last segments employed to introduce the protagonists and then to record the ultimate fate of each, while the middle segment, equal in length to the other two combined, examines and analyzes their encounter from every angle and demonstrates the impossibility of any fruitful contact between them, because by that time each is in an unanticipatedly different frame of mind.

The structure of the book is perhaps what critics and public admired most about *Thaïs*. It has a satisfying aesthetic quality which announced that France had mastered the sense of form necessary for the achievement of a work of art. The book's success must also, however, be attributed to the subtle complexity of the ideas the author was able to distill from what is, after all, little more than a mildly indecorous comic anecdote. *Thaïs* is a profound and suggestive exploration of the hidden links between religious feeling and sexual desire and, beyond that, of the intricate and unexpected interplay between pagan and Christian ideals and thought and between worldliness and asceticism as patterns of human behavior. In this novel, characterization and realistic description count for comparatively little, and in spite of the daring subject matter, there is not a hint of prurience. The best effects are achieved by a tasteful and harmonious blend of elegant style, well-proportioned structure, and subtle ideas, all presented with gentle irony through the eyes of an amused and skeptical observer. *Thaïs* remains a delight for the thoughtful and attentive reader, one of France's finest achievements.

At about the same time as *Thaïs* was being composed, France was also diligently exploring the short-story form. Employing similar material from history or legend, he was striving to find the ideal fusion of form and content that would yield a work of art in that genre also, and in some of the stories of the volume entitled *L'Étui de nacre* (1892; *Tales from a Mother of Pearl Casket*, 1896), notably the famous "Procurator of Judea" and "The Juggler of Our Lady," he succeeded as fully as he had for the novel in *Thaïs*. Thereafter, having earned his artistic spurs in both the novel and the short story, France developed his career in both domains, alternating a novel and a volume of short stories with something approaching regularity over the next twenty years. What is notable in the work of those years is the visible effort he made to avoid the facile repetition of past successes, to explore and experiment with new techniques, and to strive to develop and grow as an artist. During the 1890's, for example, he followed the gemlike stories of *Tales from a Mother of Pearl Casket* with a comic fantasy of a novel called *At the Sign of the Reine Pédauque*, then used a trip to Florence, Italy, as inspiration for a volume of short stories, *Le Puits de Sainte-Claire* (1895; *The Well of Saint Clare*, 1909), and a surprisingly conventional love story, *The Red Lily*, appearing in 1894. Those publications confirmed his newly won stature as a major writer and earned for him election to the Académie Française in 1896.

His next project, *Contemporary History*, began as a series of weekly newspaper articles commenting on current events by means of anecdotes and illustrative tales. Soon he began interconnecting the articles by using the same set of characters in each. The articles could have formed the basis for a volume of short stories, but instead, France conceived the notion of weaving selected articles from one year's output into a novel that would record the main events of that year in a kind of fictionalized history. It was a bold experiment, which eventually ran to four volumes and occasioned some brilliant writing and the creation of one truly memorable character, Monsieur Bergeret, a scholar and teacher of a wittily ironic turn of mind, who usually articulated the author's own skeptical view of public events. Some consider *Contemporary History* to be France's finest work, but while it does make unflaggingly entertaining reading, as well as offer a valuable historical record, it may be too randomly structured and too variable in tone to be artistically satisfying for the sophisticated modern reader. It deserves respect, however, both as an interesting experiment in a new kind of fiction and as the inauguration of a new thematic vein in France's work: the overt exploitation of public events, especially politics, in the writing of fiction. The novels and short stories published between 1900 and 1914 are almost all in this new political vein, sometimes seriously polemical, more often comic and satiric. The most widely read work of that period is the amusing and clever *Penguin Island*, which gives a brief and jaundiced view of French history as though it were a history of a society of penguins. The masterpiece of this period, however, and probably the finest of all Anatole France's novels, is his reconstruction of the atmosphere of the French Revolution, called *The Gods Are Athirst*, published in 1912.

France's strong interest in the period of the French Revolution was undoubtedly inspired by his youthful browsing in his father's bookshop, which specialized in that subject. During the 1880's, France began work on a novel about the revolutionary period, but he abandoned it, rearranging some of the completed fragments into short stories that turned up, a few years later, in the collection *Tales from a Mother of Pearl Casket*. By 1910, when he began to work on a new novel of the Revolution, he had been through his own personal "revolution"—involvement in the Dreyfus Affair and public espousal of socialism—only to suffer rapid disillusionment with the way human nature seems inevitably to distort and betray ideals. Something of that disillusionment must have shaped *The Gods Are Athirst*, for it concentrates on the process by which the Reign of Terror developed out of revolutionary zeal for liberty, equality, and fraternity and, by means of the inclusion of a large and varied cast of characters, seeks to depict how daily life was affected by this process. The novel is set in Paris and covers a time span of about two years, from 1792 to 1794.

At the very heart of the novel, France places a struggling young painter, a pupil of Jacques Louis David, whose name is Évariste Gamelin and who, in 1792, is active in the revolutionary committees of his quarter. Gamelin is depicted as a mediocre artist but one who is serious in his devotion both to art and to the humanitarian ideals of the new Republic. His seriousness is a function of his youthful innocence, which is unrelieved by any element of gaiety or humor but which endows him with a capacity for tender feelings of affection or sympathy. Those tender feelings are the noble source of his support for the Revolution, but he gets caught up in complex and emotionally charged events that he is incapable of understanding, and, as a member of a revolutionary tribunal, he unwittingly betrays his own humanitarian principles by voting for the execution of innocent people to satisfy the bloodthirsty mob of spectators. Gamelin thus embodies the book's fundamental and deeply pessimistic theme, which is that even decent individuals and noble ideals will fall victim to the winds of fanaticism. At the ironic end of the novel, Gamelin the terrorist is himself condemned and executed by the Reign of Terror.

Gamelin is surrounded by an array of different types who give magnificent density to the novel's re-creation of the past. Most memorable, perhaps, is Maurice Brotteaux, a neighbor of Gamelin and a former member of the nobility, now earning his living by making puppets to sell in toy shops. Brotteaux is a skeptic and a witty ironist—unmistakably the author's alter ego—who, though not unsympathetic to the Revolution, deplores its decline into fanaticism, consoling himself by reading his ever-present copy of Lucretius' *De rerum natura*. The author's intentional irony in this detail is that the Latin poet's work had the original purpose of explaining nature to his contemporaries without reference to the supernatural, in order thus to liberate his compatriots from their superstitious fear of the gods. As the novel's title suggests, Lucretius' noble project is a futile exercise when the gods thirst for blood. Gamelin's fiancée, the voluptuous Élodie, adds a fascinating psychological element to the novel, for as her lover Gamelin grows more and more savage in his condemnation of his fellow citizens, she is surprised to discover that, her horror of him notwithstanding, her sensual attraction to him intensifies: The more blood there is on his hands, the more uncontrollable her passion becomes.

The novel is masterful in its smooth handling of the welter of significant characters and details, the unobtrusive integration of known historical figures and events into an invented narrative, and the creation of both a sense of inevitable tragedy in the action and the feel of epic grandeur in the composition as a whole. It is an impressively vast canvas the author attempts to encompass here—the greatest and most complex of his career. Although there is, of necessity, much weaving back and forth from setting to setting and from one group of characters to another, the clarity and focus of the narrative line are never blurred, and the careful structure accentuates for the reader the inexorability of the mounting dramatic tension enveloping more and more of the novel's characters. In the manner of a classical tragedy, the novel closes with the return of uneasy calm after the catastrophe and the indication that the dead will be quickly forgotten and that life will go on as before. The final paragraph shows Élodie taking a new lover and employing the same endearments to him as she had used at the start of her affair with Gamelin.

The Gods Are Athirst does not quite attain the majestic historical sweep that a subject such as the French Revolution might be expected to command, perhaps because the figure at its center, Évariste Gamelin, is deliberately not cast in the heroic mold. Yet it is a fine and powerful novel, and its unforgettable images carry their intended message to issues beyond the events described, revealing something fundamentally important about human conduct in any revolution and, indeed, in any group situation subject to the volatile incitements of mob psychology. This brilliant novel, written when the author was nearly seventy, proved to be the artistic culmination of France's long career. The novel that followed it, *The Revolt of the Angels*, is a merry fantasy of anticlerical bent, amusing to read but making no artistic or intellectual claims to importance. It proved, simply, that this veteran teller of tales still had the skill and magic, at seventy, to hold the attention of the reading public.

As a writer of fiction, France has always eluded classification. He showed little interest in the precise observation of daily reality that was the hallmark of his Naturalist contemporaries, nor did he strive to win fame with sensational plotting, flamboyant characters, or studies in spicily abnormal psychology. Though allied, at certain times, with the Parnassians and the Symbolists, he never submitted himself fully to their aesthetic discipline in his own art. He followed his own bent, and because he was so steeped in books and erudition, so unsociable and so fond of solitude, and so little driven by ambition, he tended to cut a strange and solitary figure in the literary world. In both manner and matter, he was really quite unlike anyone else then writing. Probably nothing contributed more to his uniqueness as a writer than his absolute addiction to ideas. The originating inspiration for everything he wrote was neither an event nor a character nor a situation nor even a new literary trick to try out, but ever and always an idea, a concept, an abstraction that he wanted to bring to life by means of a story, a play, or a poem. Even his most conventional novel, *The Red Lily*, seems to be only a routine story of frustrated love and jealousy. What truly animates that novel is the daring concept of feminine independence, which entrenched social attitudes and the habits of male possessiveness in love relationships put out of the reach of even the most lucid and intelligent women, even in that haven of enlightened individualism, Florence. Though not a great novel, *The Red Lily* penetratingly probes an idea that was very advanced for the time: the idea that a woman who conceives the ambition to be a person in her own right, rather than an accessory to someone else's life, faces tragically insuperable obstacles. One can identify a seminal idea of that kind at the very center of the concerns of every novel and every short story France wrote. Ideas are his trademark—not surprisingly, because his literary imagination was so completely grounded in books, rather than in life, and because his carefully maintained view of the world was a skepticism so systematic, and so bathed in irony, that it kept reality at a distance and made the life of the mind virtually the only life he knew. Such a writer is not for everyone, but in spite of the low ebb of his reputation since his death, his audience will never entirely vanish as long as there are those who relish the pleasures of the intellect.

Major publications other than long fiction

SHORT FICTION: *Balthasar*, 1889 (English translation, 1909); *L'Étui de nacre*, 1892 (*Tales from a Mother of Pearl Casket*, 1896); *Le Puits de Sainte-Claire*, 1895 (*The Well of Saint Clare*, 1909); *Crainquebille, Putois, Riquet et plusieurs autres récits profitables*, 1904 (*Crainquebille, Putois, Riquet, and Other Profitable Tales*, 1915); *Les Sept Femmes de la Barbe-Bleue*, 1909 (*The Seven Wives of Bluebeard*, 1920).

PLAYS: *Crainquebille*, 1905 (English translation, 1915); *La Comédie de celui qui épousa une femme muette*, 1908 (*The Man Who Married a Dumb Wife*, 1915).

NONFICTION: *Alfred de Vigny*, 1868; *La Vie littéraire*, 1888-1892 (5 volumes; *On Life and Letters*, 1911-1914); *Le Jardin d'Épicure*, 1894 (*The Garden of Epicurus*, 1908); *Vers les temps meilleurs*, 1906, 1949; *La Vie de Jeanne d'Arc*, 1908 (*The Life of Joan of Arc*, 1908); *Le Génie latin*, 1913 (*The Latin Genius*, 1924); *Sur la voie glorieuse*, 1915.

MISCELLANEOUS: *The Complete Works*, 1908-1928 (21 volumes); *Oeuvres complètes*, 1925-1935 (25 volumes).

Bibliography

Axelrad, Jacob. *Anatole France: A Life Without Illusions*, 1944.

Bresky, Dushan. *The Art of Anatole France*, 1969.

Chevalier, Haakon M. *The Ironic Temper: Anatole France and His Time*, 1932.

Jefferson, Carter. *Anatole France: The Politics of Skepticism*, 1965.

Levaillant, Jean. *Les Aventures du scepticisme: Essai sur l'évolution intellectuelle d'Anatole France*, 1965.

Sachs, Murray. *Anatole France: The Short Stories*, 1974.

Sareil, Jean. *Anatole France et Voltaire*, 1961.

Suffel, Jacques. *Anatole France*, 1946.

Virtanen, Reino. *Anatole France*, 1968.

Murray Sachs

MAX FRISCH

Born: Zurich, Switzerland; May 15, 1911

Principal long fiction

Jürg Reinhart, 1934; *J'adore ce qui me brûle: Oder, Die Schwierigen*, 1943; *Stiller*, 1954 (*I'm Not Stiller*, 1958); *Homo Faber*, 1957 (*Homo Faber: A Report*, 1959); *Mein Name sei Gantenbein*, 1964 (*A Wilderness of Mirrors*, 1965).

Other literary forms

Max Frisch is a versatile writer whose reputation stems from both his dramas and his novels. He has also written diaries, radio plays, short stories, film scenarios, and essays. His essays include discussions of literature, drama, society, architecture, town planning, and travel. There is a six-volume German edition of his works up to 1976, published by Suhrkamp in Frankfurt.

Frisch's drama and his fiction are closely related thematically. In most of his plays, the quest for identity is the central theme. Frisch is critical of the roles that people adopt for themselves or have imposed on them by others: Role-playing, he believes, prevents people from growing and realizing their potential as human beings, a concern that is particularly evident in *Andorra* (1961; English translation, 1964) and *Don Juan: Oder, Die Liebe zur Geometrie* (1953; *Don Juan: Or, The Love of Geometry*, 1967). As in his fiction, Frisch shows in his theater pieces how difficult it is to escape from such roles: However hard his protagonists try, they fail in their attempts to escape, because the social restrictions they face are so overwhelming. Frisch believes that the dramatist has a responsibility to address social and political questions, although he is skeptical that the theater can bring about social change. It can, however, make people more aware. Although most of his plays focus upon personal questions, some directly address such social problems as anti-Semitism and prejudice (*Andorra*) and the moral weakness of the middle class (*Biedermann und die Brandstifter*, 1958; *The Fire Raisers*, 1962; also as *The Firebugs*, 1963). In both his plays and his novels, Frisch sharply criticizes modern society for its hypocrisy, its smugness, and its superficiality—but most of all for the limits it places on the individual.

Achievements

Frisch's international reputation was established in 1954 with the publication of *I'm Not Stiller*, which is still considered his most important work. In 1951, Frisch received a Rockefeller grant to study in the United States. He has been awarded numerous prizes for his works. These include the Georg Büchner Prize and the Zurich Prize in 1958 and the Jerusalem Prize and the Schiller

Prize in 1965. Frisch's dramas are regularly performed in Europe and the United States. In West Germany, Austria, and Switzerland, they are among the most frequently performed dramas by living German-language playwrights. His works have been translated into most European languages and are often best-sellers.

Biography

Max Frisch was born in Zurich on May 15, 1911, the son of a self-taught architect. After attending a *gymnasium* in Zurich between 1924 and 1930, he began studying German literature at the University of Zurich in 1931, at which time he also heard lectures on art history, philosophy, law, and theology. When his father died in 1933, Frisch had to leave the university to earn a living. He became a free-lance journalist and wrote for such newspapers as the *Neue Züricher Zeitung*. In 1933, Frisch traveled to Prague, Budapest, Dalmatia, Istanbul, and Greece, experiences which he used in his first novel, *Jürg Reinhart*. In 1936, thanks to the financial support of a friend, Frisch began to study architecture at the Institute of Technology in Zurich; he was awarded his diploma in 1941. In 1942, he opened his own architect's office in Zurich. The highlight of his architectural career was his winning of a competition to build an open-air swimming pool in the Zurich suburb of Letzigraben, a project that was completed in 1949. In 1948, Frisch became acquainted with Bertolt Brecht, whose theories were to have an important influence on Frisch's drama.

Frisch, an inveterate traveler, wrote in *Tagebuch 1946-1949* (1950; *Sketchbook 1946-1949*, 1977) that we travel for two reasons: to meet people who do not assume that they know us intimately and to reexperience what is possible in life. Frisch has traveled extensively in Europe and the United States and has also visited the Arab countries, Mexico, Cuba, the Soviet Union, Japan, and China. His experiences in the United States and Mexico are reflected especially in the novels *I'm Not Stiller* and *Homo Faber* and the short work *Montauk* (1975; English translation, 1976). Since 1954, when he gave up his architect's office, Frisch has earned his living as a writer. After living in Rome between 1960 and 1965, he returned to Switzerland to live in Tessin.

Analysis

A central theme in Max Frisch's works is the problem of personal identity. The second commandment, "Thou shalt make no graven image," is a key to understanding his works. In an interview with the critic Horst Bienek in 1961, Frisch remarked that people invent plots for their lives, often defending these fictions at great sacrifice. According to Frisch, every "I" that expresses itself is a role. People not only invent roles for themselves but also form images of others; in turn, they suffer from the image others make of them. Adopting a role or being forced into a role by the expectations of others limits a person's possibilities, Frisch believes. Instead of being exciting enigmas, people are reduced to fixed and known entities. Frisch explores the problem of identity within the framework of human relationships, especially marriage. Real love, he believes, leaves room for both partners to grow and change. Most people, however, are guilty of forming images of their partners which cause their relationships to become static and to deteriorate into repetition, the enemy of growth. The story of Philemon and Baucis, as the narrator of *A Wilderness of Mirrors* relates it, portrays not a loving, loyal marriage, as in the legend, but the deadening boredom and triviality of marriage.

In Frisch's works, the individual is caught in a world of restrictions. Society requires that he conform, adopting definite social roles; society functions to preserve the status quo and is hostile to any notion of change. Frisch portrays society as rigid and banal; instead of growth, it offers only repetition and routine. He depicts those who conform to society as smug and self-righteous. Such people rarely question society's values, which, Frisch believes, have often deteriorated into clichés. The focus of Frisch's social criticism is his native Switzerland, but his comments can apply to modern society as a whole. An ideal society, according to Frisch, would allow people the freedom to be themselves, to lead authentic lives.

The protagonist of *I'm Not Stiller* is a man who tries to escape from the role expected of him and acquire a new identity. (The novel opens with the narrator-protagonist asserting defiantly, "I'm not Stiller.") A man named James Larkin White is arrested at the Swiss border because he has a forged United States passport. The Swiss authorities believe that he is the sculptor Anatol Stiller, who disappeared six years previously. They decide to detain him until his identity can be established by court proceedings. In an effort to determine who he really is, his lawyer, Dr. Bohnenblust, tells him to write down the plain, unvarnished truth about his life. The first and longest part of the novel consists of seven notebooks which Stiller/White writes in prison. The novel is written in diary form (a form favored by Frisch) and includes experiences, memories, and fantasies of the narrator-protagonist as well as descriptions of his life in prison. Also included are protocols of the various witnesses, which make Stiller/White aware of how others view him. The epilogue, written by the prosecutor, Rolf, who is sympathetic to Stiller/White, describes his life once he is released.

At the outset, it is clear that White really is Stiller. Six years earlier, Stiller had suddenly become dissatisfied with his life. Longing for a freer existence, he had fled from himself, his marriage, his profession, and his friends to America and Mexico. After failing in an attempt to commit suicide, he returns home, thinking that he is a new person. Even when the authorities confront him with people from his past, he stubbornly denies that he is Stiller. He refuses to be Stiller again—to play the same role with all its imprisoning repetition. A previous attempt to flee from himself by fighting in the Spanish Civil War failed miserably. When his courage was actually tested, he surrendered in a cowardly fashion to the Fascists. Stiller is also disappointed in his artistic talent; it is not by chance that he is a sculptor, one who makes images of others. When Stiller/White is brought from prison to his old atelier, he destroys all of his sculptures, a futile attempt to break with his past.

Stiller's greatest failure, however, is as a husband and lover. Frisch depicts Stiller's painful marriage to the dancer Julika, which is based on a mutual fear of inadequacy. The frigid Julika finds the sexual act distasteful, and Stiller worries about his impotence. Both shy away from close contact with each other; each has formed a rigid image of the other. Julika becomes increasingly narcissistic and withdraws into her dancing—for her, a substitute for life—while Stiller becomes more egocentric. When Stiller is released from prison, they begin their marriage again. Instead of learning from their past, they are fated to make the same mistakes. Because they cannot talk to each other, Julika does not tell Stiller how serious her illness is (she has tuberculosis), and when she dies, Stiller feels responsible for her death. Because he was discontented with his marriage, Stiller had an affair with Sibylle, Rolf's wife, before he fled to North America, yet his fear of impotence also undermined this relationship.

The defense counsel, Dr. Bohnenblust, typifies the philistine mentality from which Stiller fled. Dr. Bohnenblust never questions the values of society, as his long cliché-ridden speech in Stiller's atelier demonstrates. He is hostile to all new ideas. Social conformity and its concomitant safety, security, and comfort are all-important to him. Unlike Stiller, Dr. Bohnenblust does not want to confront himself or his values. He fears such a confrontation, for it would cause the disintegration of his social role. In the figure of Dr. Bohnenblust, Frisch shows that all that society can offer is the comfortable surface of reality, a life of suffocating normality that is detrimental to all growth.

Afraid of such a life, Stiller seeks freedom to be himself in America. Yet the identity he adopts is not his true self but rather what he would like to become. White is a man of action, an adventurer without scruples, the polar opposite of the tormented, weak, reflective Stiller. In prison, Stiller/White spins tales of his American experiences for the gullible jailer Knobel. He tells of murders he supposedly committed, tales of love, passion, and jealousy. These American stories—which are partly fact but mostly fiction—indicate how determined Stiller is to cast off his old identity. Indeed, the stories reveal more about Stiller than do the actual facts of his life, reflecting Frisch's belief that an individual's life is more than the sum of facts.

Stiller fails, however, to escape from his old identity. The court finally declares that White is indeed Stiller, thereby sentencing him to be his old self. The epilogue, related by the prosecutor, depicts Stiller's retreat into the mountains with Julika, Julika's death, and Stiller's loneliness. Forced to accept himself, he has become resigned to his role. He has learned that he cannot escape from his past. The excerpt from Søren Kierkegaard's *Enten-Eller* (1843; *Either/Or*, 1944) which precedes the first part of the novel is an ironic commentary on Stiller's search for identity. Kierkegaard writes that when the passion of freedom awakens in a person, that person chooses his own identity and fights for this possession as if for his happiness, and this fight is his happiness. Yet however hard Stiller fights for his chosen identity, he cannot break free; he is forced to capitulate at the end. His fight to free himself has not brought him happiness.

Frisch's next novel, *Homo Faber*, has as its first-person narrator-protagonist Walter Faber, a fifty-year-old Swiss engineer working for UNESCO. Unlike Stiller, who wants to adopt a new identity, Faber is satisfied with himself until a series of events makes him confront his past life. The novel's subtitle, *A Report*, indicates that Faber intends to present his story objectively and factually; he eventually realizes, however, that facts alone cannot explain his experiences. The action, which lasts about four months, is divided into two parts: "First Stop," which Faber writes when he is ill in Caracas, confined to a hotel room, and "Second Stop," written while he is waiting for an operation for stomach cancer in an Athenian hospital.

Faber (literally, the novel's title means "man the maker") represents modern man, who defines himself according to technology. He wants to be in control, calmly observing and evaluating life rather than participating in it. The predictability of the technological world is his credo. Faber surrounds himself with technological gadgets; lives in the United States, the epitome of technological civilization; and speaks the jargon of technology. He even draws his imagery for nature from technology, at one point likening the tributaries of the Mississippi River, which he sees from a plane, to trickles of molten brass or bronze.

The novel begins with Faber on a professional flight from New York to South America. The plane later develops engine trouble and is forced down in the Tamaulipas Desert. A traveling companion turns out to be Herbert, the brother of an old friend, Joachim, who had married Faber's former girlfriend, Hanna, twenty years ago. To pass the time until they are rescued, they play chess, Faber's favorite game because he can concentrate on the game and not pay attention to the other player. Faber fears becoming involved with others: He dislikes emotions because they are unpredictable. In the desert, without his technological gadgets, Faber feels lost. Because there is no electricity, he cannot use his electric razor; when his beard begins to sprout, he feels as though he is being devoured by nature. Until this point, Faber's world has consisted of routine and predictable events. Faber's rootlessness—the condition of modern man—is shown by the airports, hotels, and traveling that make up his world.

Suddenly and inexplicably, Faber decides to accompany Herbert to visit

Joachim, who oversees a plantation in Guatemala. On their journey to Campeche, Palenque, and Guatemala, they become increasingly engulfed by the jungle. Nature here is uncontrolled and indifferent to man. There is the stench of fertility, blossoming decay, putrefaction, and vultures hovering overhead. When they reach their goal, they find that Joachim has committed suicide. Faber reacts with typical detachment, filming the corpse. The camera is his way of looking at reality; instead of experiencing life directly, he distances himself by means of the camera lens.

Nevertheless, the experiences in the jungle begin to change Faber. When he returns to New York and to his mistress, Ivy, with whom he has only a shallow relationship, he is restless. He decides to go to Europe by sea; on the boat he meets Sabeth, travels with her through Europe, and becomes her lover. He is attracted to her youth and beauty; his relationship with her seems to give him new life. Faber suppresses the mounting evidence that Sabeth is his daughter. He does not know that he has a child. When his relationship with Hanna broke up, she was expecting their child, but there was a tacit agreement that she would have an abortion. Because Faber prides himself on evaluating facts clearly, his self-deception and blindness is particularly ironic. After a night on the beach in Greece, Sabeth is bitten by a viper, falls, and later dies—not from the snakebite but from an undiagnosed skull fracture. In Athens, Faber meets Hanna, whom he has not seen for more than twenty years.

"Second Stop" begins with Faber trying, unsuccessfully, to resume his old life in New York. His experiences with Sabeth have shaken him loose from the sterility of his old life, and he increasingly criticizes the superficiality of the American way of life; the world, he says, is becoming an "Americanized vacuum." When he visits Herbert, who has taken over his brother's place on the plantation, he discovers that Herbert, too, has fallen under the spell of the jungle. Faber then makes a detour to Cuba, where for the first time he becomes alive to sensual beauty, experiencing a kind of euphoria, although he is still observing rather than participating in life. When he returns to Europe, he goes to Düsseldorf to show Joachim's firm the pictures of the latter's death. At this point, Faber becomes aware of the limitations of the camera; he realizes that it can record only the surface of life, because the films give no hint of the stench of Joachim's corpse. Faber moves on to Zurich and finally to Hanna in Athens, where he is hospitalized.

Like Faber, Hanna shies away from personal involvement, as shown by her failed marriages. She wants to be a mother, not a wife and partner. Hanna, however, rejects the technological world. Technology, for her, is the knack of so arranging the world that one does not have to experience it. Life, she says, is not matter and cannot be mastered by technology. Hanna has, however, no positive concept to put in technology's place; instead, she takes refuge in the past, as her profession of piecing together fragments of ancient pottery suggests. Like Faber, she is divorced from life and is one-sided and egocentric. Throughout the novel, the predictable world of technology is challenged. Faber always relies on statistics to explain events, yet statistics fail him. He quotes statistics to show the improbability of a plane crash, for example, but his plane is forced down; he quotes statistics to show how good his chances are for surviving the operation, but the outcome is not promising. Statistics do not help Faber understand and experience life. In fact, technology as a whole is not as reliable as Faber has assumed. Planes break down; his razor does not work; and, most strikingly, when Faber has to rush Sabeth to the hospital to be treated for the snakebite, technology deserts him altogether and he is forced to use a donkey cart.

Chance plays a large role in the novel, further undermining Faber's belief in the predictability of the technological world. Faber's chance meeting with Herbert, for example, initiates his journey into the past. By chance he meets Sabeth, which results in his incestuous affair with his own daughter. The Oedipus myth of incest and blindness in the novel underscores the element of chance, suggesting the impossibility of controlling life through reason. The novel's story ends in Athens, the cradle of Western civilization—an ironic reminder of how modern technological man has divorced himself from his roots.

Although the novel does not end with Faber's death, the imagery used in the novel indicates that the operation is unsuccessful. In the jungle, the waiting vultures and the cycle of birth, decay, and death show the transience of man's existence. The Mayan ruins in the jungle suggest not only personal death but the decline of whole civilizations as well. Faber's two meetings with his former professor foreshadow his own demise. The professor's face seems like a death's head, grotesque and emaciated. Later, Faber is shocked by his own emaciated appearance. When Faber is in Rome with Sabeth, they lie on a tomb on the Via Appia; when Faber is taking a bath in Hanna's apartment, the bathtub resembles a sarcophagus. All this imagery of decay, decline, and death mocks the technologist's hope, as Hanna says, of trying to live without death.

Faber's approaching death is, however, especially bitter because he has learned that his overvaluation of technology has prevented him from experiencing life. The man of action has become a man of reflection who is aware of beauty, sensuality, and nature and is ready to make personal commitments. On the threshold of a new way of life, he dies.

The narrator-protagonist of *A Wilderness of Mirrors* is anonymous. All that the reader knows about him is that he loves a woman who has left him. To try to come to terms with his situation, the narrator creates a variety of fictions; he hopes to find an identity for himself that will help him articulate his experience. For a while, he identifies with the various roles he creates, but then he discards them. Whereas in *I'm Not Stiller*, Stiller/White pretends that his American stories are fact, the narrator of *A Wilderness of Mirrors* presents his creations unequivocally as fiction (he constantly repeats "I imagine"). During the course of the novel, the narrator varies the roles he has created and constantly shifts his position between them. The novel, which has no continuous narrative or clear-cut divisions, consists of a number of stories and variations on the themes of love, marriage, jealousy, and identity.

The identities that the narrator invents are those of the art historian Enderlin, who seduces the actress Lila; Gantenbein, Lila's second husband; and Svoboda, Lila's first husband. The narrator imagines Enderlin undergoing an identity crisis: He has reached the pinnacle of success by being appointed to Harvard; at this moment, however, he suddenly loses confidence in his academic role and believes that he has become the prisoner of other people's expectations of him. Instead of accepting the appointment, he retreats into another role, that of a sick man. Like Faber, Enderlin is wary of personal involvement. Through him, the narrator tries on the role of the detached lover. In fact, Enderlin describes his seduction of Lila as if a stranger, and not he, were seducing her. The narrator imagines Gantenbein playing the role of a blind man. Gantenbein even procures the necessary official documents to prove that he is blind and uses a stick and glasses, the blind man's props. Paradoxically, he pretends to be blind in order to see things clearly. Because people believe he is blind (even when he plays his part badly), they pretend to be what they would like to be, while Gantenbein can see them as they really are. Eventually this role dissatisfies him, however, as it is based on deceit. His supposed blindness allows him to give Lila her freedom—he can pretend not to see her affair with Enderlin. During the novel, however, he is unable to keep his role of the detached, ironic observer; he becomes tormented with jealousy and confesses to Lila that he is not blind. The third role, Svoboda, is never a serious possibility for the narrator. Unlike Enderlin and Gantenbein, the architect Svoboda is a man of action, in the habit, like Faber, of controlling his environment. He is able to accept the breakdown of his marriage.

The importance of role-playing is stressed throughout the novel. In all three roles, the narrator creates models of possible human relationships, trying to find an answer for his own failed relationship. He discards each of the roles because none fits his own experience. The narrator also tells of a *Pechvogel* (an unlucky fellow) who is dogged by bad luck. When he wins a lottery, he begins to doubt himself, and his role threatens to disintegrate. Fortunately for him, he loses his winnings and can thus keep his role intact. Another example of role-playing is seen in the ambassador, who suddenly becomes aware that he is not the man people think he is. He decides to continue playing his role, keeping his knowledge of his real self secret. Unlike Enderlin, the ambassador does not collapse because of his new awareness.

Throughout the novel, Frisch shows that human experience and values are too complex to be explained by statistics or facts. The world, however, sees the individual only in terms of biographical data which do not reveal the whole truth about a person. Frisch believes that biography should include not only what a person has done but also what he might have done; not only what he was or is but also what he might have been or might still become. The barman, to whom the narrator is talking, thinks that biography consists only of facts. The narrator, however, is fascinated not by what he did but what he might have done. He relates a story about meeting a German in the Alps during the war; he was convinced that the German was a spy. What he might have done (push the man over a cliff) is more vivid to him than what he actually did (accept an apple and watch the man descend).

During the novel, the narrator tries on various roles like clothes, to see if they will fit. The fictions he invents, he remarks, are sketches for an ego. Unlike the desperate search for identity in *I'm Not Stiller*, however, the tone of *A Wilderness of Mirrors* is more ironic and cheerful. The conclusion, while it remains open, is more optimistic than in the previous novels. Whereas Stiller is condemned to be himself and Faber is dying, the narrator's last words here, as he sits comfortably eating and drinking in Italy on a warm September day, are "I like life."

As he states in *A Wilderness of Mirrors*, Frisch believes that human life is fulfilled or goes wrong in the individual ego, nowhere else. This explains his protest against the mask people assume by choice or are forced to assume by society, which limits their potential to lead fulfilling lives. Most of Frisch's protagonists who suffer a crisis of identity fail to live more fully. They encounter too many societal restrictions which imprison them in routine and prevent them from freeing themselves. Frisch's works address perennial human problems of identity, love, and death. They successfully capture the anxiety of people who are alienated from their partners, from their friends, from their professions, from the society in which they live—but most of all from themselves.

Major publications other than long fiction

SHORT FICTION: *Bin: Oder, Die Reise nach Peking*, 1945; *Wilhelm Tell für die Schule*, 1971; *Montauk*, 1975 (English translation, 1976); *Der Mensch erscheint im Holozän*, 1979 (*Man in the Holocene*, 1980); *Blaubart*, 1982 (*Bluebeard: A Tale*, 1983).

PLAYS: *Santa Cruz*, 1944; *Nun singen sie wieder*, 1945 (*Now They Sing Again*, 1972); *Die Chinesische Mauer*, 1946 (*The Chinese Wall*, 1961); *Als der Krieg zu Ende war*, 1948 (*When the War Was Over*, 1967); *Graf Öderland*, 1951 (*A Public Prosecutor Is Sick of It All*, 1973); *Don Juan: Oder, Die Liebe zur Geometrie*, 1953 (*Don Juan: Or, The Love of Geometry*, 1967); *Biedermann und die Brandstifter*, 1958 (*The Fire Raisers*, 1962; also as *The Firebugs*, 1963); *Die grosse Wut des Philipp Hotz*, 1958 (*Philipp Hotz's Fury*, 1962); *Andorra*, 1961 (English translation, 1964); *Biografie*, 1967 (*Biography*, 1969);

Triptychon: Drei szenische Bilder, 1978.

NONFICTION: *Tagebuch 1946-1949*, 1950 (*Sketchbook 1946-1949*, 1977); *Tagebuch 1966-1971*, 1972 (*Sketchbook 1966-1971*, 1974); *Frisch: Kritik, Thesen, Analysen*, 1977.

MISCELLANEOUS: *Gesammelte Werke in zeitlicher Folge*, 1976.

Bibliography
Bänziger, Hans. *Frisch und Dürrenmatt*, 1971.
Beckermann, Thomas, ed. *Über Max Frisch*, 1971.
Bienek, Horst. "Werkstattgespräch mit Max Frisch," in *Werstattgespräch mit Schriftstellern*, 1962.
Butler, Michael. *The Novels of Max Frisch*, 1976.
Knapp, Gerhard P., ed. *Max Frisch: Aspekte des Prosawerks*, 1978.
Schmitz, Walter, ed. *Über Max Frisch II*, 1976.
Weisstein, Ulrich. *Max Frisch*, 1967.

Jennifer Michaels

CARLOS FUENTES

Born: Panama City, Panama; November 11, 1928

Principal long fiction
La región más transparente, 1958 (*Where the Air Is Clear*, 1960); *Las buenas conciencias*, 1959 (*The Good Conscience*, 1961): *Aura*, 1962 (English translation, 1965); *La muerte de Artemio Cruz*, 1962 (*The Death of Artemio Cruz*, 1964); *Cambio de piel*, 1967 (*A Change of Skin*, 1968); *Zona sagrada*, 1967 (*Holy Place*, 1972); *Cumpleaños*, 1969; *Terra nostra*, 1975 (English translation, 1976); *La cabeza de la hidra*, 1978 (*The Hydra Head*, 1978); *Una familia lejana*, 1980 (*Distant Relations*, 1982).

Other literary forms
In addition to his work as a novelist, Carlos Fuentes has cultivated short fiction throughout his career. His earliest work was a collection of short stories, *Los días enmascarados* (1954; the masked days); this volume and subsequent collections such as *Cantar de ciegos* (1964; songs of the blind) and *Agua quemada* (1981; *Burnt Water*, 1981) have been critically acclaimed. (*Burnt Water*, Fuentes' first short-story collection to be translated into English, contains stories published in earlier collections as well as in *Agua quemada*.) The subjects of these stories are reminiscent of his novels. They are set in contemporary Mexico and are characterized by social and psychological realism. Several stories feature the interpenetration of the real and the fantastic, so much a part of the author's longer fiction.

Fuentes has also written several plays. In 1970, he published *El tuerto es rey* (the blind man is king) and *Todos los gatos son pardos* (all cats are gray). This latter work dramatizes the author's fascination with the subject of the Conquest of Mexico and portrays Hernán Cortés and other historical figures. *Orchids in the Moonlight*, which premiered at Harvard University in 1982, is Fuentes' first play produced in the United States.

Achievements
Fuentes is known the world over as one of Latin America's premier novelists and intellectuals. He has earned this reputation through involvement in international affairs and prodigious creative activity. Fuentes has produced a broad spectrum of literary works in several genres which convey a sense of Mexican life, past and present. The image of Mexico has been projected by means of extremely varied treatments in his works, from the historical and legendary backgrounds of the Conquest in *Terra nostra* to the analysis of contemporary social reality and the profound aftershocks of the Mexican Revolution in *The Death of Artemio Cruz*. While Fuentes has manifested his concern for the

historical and social realities of Mexico, he has also experimented with fantastic fiction in his short stories and the novella *Aura*, and he has evoked the voluptuousness of decadent settings in *Holy Place*. In view of Fuentes' achievements in capturing and imagining the myriad faces of Mexican reality, it is hardly any wonder that his literary production must be analyzed from several critical stances. Fuentes has resisted any narrow categorization of his work with the dictum: "Don't classify me. Read Me!" Fuentes is one of Latin America's most popular novelists, and his works are eagerly awaited by critics. He is considered to be on the same level with such luminaries of Latin American literature as Mario Vargas Llosa and Gabriel García Márquez in his desire to produce the "total novel," which epitomizes the aspirations and experiences of humankind.

Fuentes has been in the forefront of Mexican letters for decades. As a young writer in the 1950's, he was a cofounder of the prestigious *Revista mexicana de literatura* (Mexican literary review). In 1972, he was elected to the Colegio Nacional of Mexico. He was fellow at the Woodrow Wilson Center for Scholars in 1974. From 1975 to 1977, Fuentes served as Mexican ambassador to France. Fuentes has also received the Villarrutia Prize, Mexico's most important literary award, for *Terra nostra*. Harvard University awarded Fuentes an honorary doctorate in 1983.

Biography

Even though Carlos Fuentes likes to describe himself as a product of "petit bourgeois stock," there is nothing common about him. His father was a diplomat, an attaché to the Mexican legation, when he was born. At the age of four, Fuentes learned English in Washington D.C., where his father served as counselor of the Mexican Embassy. Oddly enough, the dawning of Fuentes' consciousness of Mexico occurred in the United States. He credits his father with having created a fantasy of his homeland, a "non-existent country invented in order to nourish the imagination of yet another land of fiction, a land of Oz with a green cactus road." As a teenager, Fuentes began to travel on his own. He studied the politics, economics, and society of Spanish America, and he developed a sympathy for socialism which he has fervently maintained ever since. Fuentes' interest in socialism blossomed in Chile, especially after learning about Pablo Neruda, whose poetry had already become the anthem of the working man.

While living in Santiago, Fuentes attended The Grange, the Chilean capital's bilingual British school, where he cultivated an appreciation of classical and modern writers. While enrolled there, he began to think about becoming a writer, he has recalled, in order to "show himself that his Mexican identity was real." He started to read the Spanish masters of the Golden Age, and he contributed short stories, written in Spanish, to school magazines. After a six-month stay in Buenos Aires, where he read the great works of Argentine literature, he finally returned to Mexico. As a young but mature man, imbued from afar with the myths of his homeland, Fuentes was finally struck by the contrasts between Mexico and more urbane centers of civilization where he had lived. The Mexico that has become the background of his fiction is a land which still bears the scars of the Mexican Revolution, where the promises of progress clash head-on with the problems of an impoverished indigenous population, and where tangible reality is forever overshadowed by the persistence of the past.

Now that he has developed an ample body of writing on modern Mexico, Fuentes, a combative essayist and crusader against Hispanic dependency upon foreign interests, has, at times, trained his sights on the United States. On numerous occasions, he has criticized American military and economic involvement in Latin America, and like many other writers from Latin America, he has suffered accordingly. To prevent him from visiting the United States, the Immigration Service branded Fuentes an "undesirable alien"—a ban eventually lifted in response to aroused public opinion. Fuentes has become a spokesman for the preservation of Mexican—and, by extension, Latin American—cultural diversity, arguing the need for an alternative to the choices offered by the world's two superpowers. He has advocated the coexistence of ancient and modern, indigenous and imported traditions in the Hispanic world as an antidote to powerful foreign influences.

Mexican President Luis Echeverría rewarded Fuentes' interest in improving Mexico's international relations by naming him ambassador to France, 1975 to 1977. Since retiring from his diplomatic post, Fuentes has lived in the United States, where he is in great demand on university campuses and at professional meetings as an eminent scholar and stimulating lecturer.

Analysis

Few confrontations in history have been more dramatic or devastating than that between Cortés and Moctezuma. When the Conquistador, Cortés, met the Aztec monarch, Moctezuma, two calendars, two worldviews, and two psychologies collided. The Aztec's cyclic concept of catastrophism which held that the earth and its creatures must die and be reborn every fifty-two years came into direct conflict with the European vision of a linear time and the notion of progress. The Machiavellian Spaniard was perceived by the Aztecs as a god who had returned to his homeland from the East as prophesied in native mythology. On the other hand, Cortés, with fine irony, depicted Moctezuma as a simple and naïve man torn by the workings of superstition, a man whose initiative and aggression against a potential enemy were blocked first by shock and then by curiosity about the mortal who was to become his master.

Remote as they seem, these events from sixteenth century Mexico serve as a background for the works of one of modern Mexico's most prolific and

honored writers, Carlos Fuentes. Fuentes claims kinship to both great patri-
archs of Mexico's past from a biological and cultural standpoint, and the key
to their relationship is the notion of diverse worlds in collision which characterized the Conquest and which the modern Mexican has assimilated in his
works. To survey the Mexico of Carlos Fuentes is to come in contact with a
land of dizzying contrasts and violent conflicts. Fuentes' Mexico is a timeless
realm where the steamy and violent past of indigenous Tenochtitlán is evident
in a sleazy and materialistic Mexico City built upon the ruins of ancient
temples.

As a theoretician of the modern Latin American novel, Fuentes has advocated such marvelous juxtapositions in fiction. For Fuentes, the novel's continued life depends upon a new concept of reality which accommodates a
mythic substratum beneath everyday experience. The reader of Fuentes' novels observes a complex Mexican reality in which the barrier between past and
present has eroded.

Fuentes' reorganization of time is the principal structural element of his
masterpiece, *Terra nostra*. This massive, Byzantine work, an ambitious blend
of history and fiction, is indeed nothing less than a compendium of Western
civilization, from the Creation to the Apocalypse. In a narrower sense, the
focus of the work is Hispanic civilization and the historical background of the
epoch of discovery and conquest. In keeping with Fuentes' goals for fiction,
the work succeeds in erasing temporal and spatial boundaries and becomes
a Mexican *Finnegans Wake* (James Joyce, 1939)—timeless, circular, and
meticulously constructed.

In the formal divisions of the work, Fuentes places the reader at the center
of a maelstrom of times and places. The novel is divided into three sections,
"The Old World," "The New World," and "The Next World." Within "The
Old World," time abruptly shifts from twentieth century Paris to sixteenth
century Spain. Fuentes intends this descent into the past to resemble an
excursion into the wellsprings of Hispanic culture. The reader emerges in the
Spain of Philip II, the monarch who built the Escorial. The erection in this
novel of the mausoleum by El Señor, the embodiment of the Spanish monarch,
is a metaphor of Philip's (and, by extension, Spain's) mad obsession with
halting the passage of time. It is here that El Señor holes up and futilely
resists change.

The futility of this scheme surfaces in the second part of the novel, which
chronicles the discovery and conquest of the New World. The promise of new
lands and a new vision of time fire the imagination of the Old World. "The
Ancient," an indigenous patriarch reminiscent of Moctezuma, captures this
vision in his retelling of a tribal legend:

Between life and death there is no destiny except memory. Memory weaves the destiny
of the world. Men perish. Suns succeed suns. Cities fall. Power passes from hand to hand.

Princes collapse along with the crumbling stone of their palaces abandoned to the fury of fire, tempest and invading jungle. One time ends and another begins. Only memory keeps death alive, and those who must die know it. The end of memory is the end of the world.

This new reckoning of time is an embodiment of perpetual change which threatens the stagnation of the Old World in the novel. El Señor, the defender of temporal paralysis, recoils at the threat in the last part of the novel and ultimately fails to freeze Hispanic tradition within the confines of the sixteenth century. His decree that the New World, with its nonlinear passage of time, does not exist is repudiated in an exuberant celebration of change in the novel's conclusion, when the action returns to Paris in the twentieth century.

In addition to the abrupt shifts in time and space which are employed in a particularly radical form in *Terra nostra*, Fuentes exploits throughout his fiction other modern literary techniques, such as hallucinatory imagery, stream of consciousness, interior monologue, and numerous devices adapted from the cinema, including flashback, crosscutting, fades, and multiple points of view. When one considers that the twentieth century is the "Age of Film," it is not surprising that Fuentes' works display a thoroughgoing affinity with cinema. In particular, *Aura, Holy Place, Distant Relations*, and *The Death of Artemio Cruz* reveal that Fuentes' vision of modern Mexico is perceived through the camera's eye.

The theme of *Aura*, one of Fuentes' early novels, is the persistence of the past. Fuentes communicates this theme by means of overlaying, as in cinematographic projections, images of light upon darkness and old identities upon youthful characters. The climax of the story features an astounding and erotic union of personalities as his characters from the twentieth century embody personalities of the nineteenth.

Appropriately enough, the catalyst of this experiment in time is a historian, Felipe Montero. A young man dedicated to preserving the past, Montero's ambition is to sum up the chronicles of the Discoverers and Conquistadors in the New World, but financial need forces him to undertake a more modest project. He agrees to edit and publish the papers of a Mexican general, dead since the turn of the century. Consuelo, the General's widow, orders Felipe to live in the ancestral mansion, and he must even learn to write in the style of the General in order to complete the assignment. Surrounded by relics of the past, then, Felipe is gradually seduced by them. What adds ardor to the historian's undertaking is Felipe's discovery of Aura, Consuelo's young niece and companion. During the course of the novel, Felipe learns that Aura is indeed an "aura" of Consuelo's lost youth, a spiritual emanation of the past who is willed into existence to capture Consuelo's early love for the General.

Through a variety of cinematic techniques such as closeups and montage, Fuentes has the illusion of Aura's presence deceive Montero into believing that she is real. The purpose of this deceit is to render, in a visual way, the author's concept of simultaneity. When Felipe observes how the two women seem to mimic each other at a distance, their separate identities are mirror images of each other. For Fuentes, the two women's divergent personas are surface manifestations of an underlying unity. Fuentes' experiment in cinematic fiction is complete when Felipe stares at Aura's image in photographs from the nineteenth century and discovers his own face superimposed on the image of the General. At the end of the novel, Consuelo has succeeded in uniting past and present in her double identity and in that of Felipe. He now embodies the spirit and flesh of the deceased General.

Fuentes' novel *Distant Relations* carries the cinematic overlaying of past and present one step further than in *Aura*. Fuentes acknowledges his debt to the world of film when he dedicates the novel to the Spanish director Luis Buñuel, with whom he collaborated on a screenplay. In addition to the visual impressions of film in this novel, Fuentes evokes the auditory effect of over-dubbing in the recurrent citation of lines from Jules Supervielle's poem "La Chambre Voisine" (the adjoining room). The poem sets the scene for the juxtaposition of several settings, each with its own temporal reality and cast of characters; Fuentes intertwines the various plots that correspond to the different settings so that the barriers of time and space dissolve.

The title refers to the phenomenon of secret correspondences between people and to their need to bridge the distances that alienate them from one another. The distant relations (or, more literally, "distant family") of the title are a French Count, a Mexican archaeologist, and a wealthy Frenchman. Fuentes suggests the relationship of the latter two in his choice of a common family name, Heredia. The choice is most fortuitous because it refers to the Spanish word *herencia* (inheritance) and more significantly to two poets of the nineteenth century, one French, José Maria de Hérédia, and the other Cuban, José María Heredia, who were cousins. It is curious, then, that Fuentes cites verses from the French Hérédia's *Les Trophées* (1893; English translation, 1897) but makes no reference to the work of the Cuban Heredia (who spent several years of his life in Mexico). An apt reference might have been taken from his narrative poem "En el teocalli de Cholula" (upon the temple at Cholula). Heredia's poem, like Fuentes' novel, features a surrealistic superimposition of realities which leap across the centuries. The narrator of the poem experiences a vivid hallucination of an Aztec human sacrifice which occurred before the arrival of Cortés. Fuentes engages in this kind of novelistic archaeology in *Distant Relations* when the Count's past and that of the two Heredias come together.

A more explicit fascination with film imagery forms the basis for Fuentes' bizarre novel, *Holy Place*. The novel claims that filmmaking creates icons which rival those of classical mythology. One case in point is the charismatic Mexican actress Claudia Nervo. She is depicted as a twentieth century siren who lures men to their doom. Her son, Guillermo (affectionately called "Mito," a name derived from the diminutive Guillermito and which also means "myth"), is neurotically attracted to her as well. More a decadent Des Esseintes from the pages of Joris Karl Huysmans' *À Rebours* (1884, 1903; *Against the Grain*, 1922) than a Ulysses, he surrounds himself with voluptuous furnishings from *la belle époque*. This is his personal "sacred zone," his enchanted grotto and refuge, which he needs as an antidote for his mother's rejection.

In the course of the novel, Fuentes analyzes the thralldom exercised by film images upon spectators and the actors themselves. For example, Guillermo pathetically tries to possess his mother by immersing himself in her old films. In this regard, *Holy Place* deftly captures the hypnotic attraction of films as they create a personal fantasy world for Guillermo, provide an escape from chronological time for him, and indelibly preserve his hallucinatory fantasies in a mythological space.

Perhaps the most striking example of cinema's influence on Fuentes' work, however, is *The Death of Artemio Cruz*. Written early in his career, it is one of his most successful novels from a technical and thematic standpoint and is widely regarded as a seminal work of modern Spanish American literature. The novel owes some of its fragmented temporal structure and much of its theme of the deterioration of modern life to Orson Welles's landmark film *Citizen Kane* (1941). Through the use of such techniques as closeup, flashback, deep focus (a technique which *Citizen Kane* pioneered), crosscutting, and recurrent symbolic motifs, Fuentes' novel matches the visual appeal of Welles's cinematographic masterpiece, and it should be read and understood as a motion picture in prose.

Fuentes has discussed his indebtedness to films in general and to Welles in particular in an interview published in *Paris Review* (volume 23, number 82, Winter, 1981). "I'm a great moviegoer. The greatest day in my life as a child was when I was ten and my father took me to New York City to see the World's Fair and *Citizen Kane*. And that struck me in the middle of my imagination and never left me. Since that moment, I've always lived with the ghost of *Citizen Kane*. There are few other great movies which I am conscious of when I write." Welles's influence on Fuentes can be seen throughout *The Death of Artemio Cruz*, in characterization, themes, and filmic techniques. Artemio Cruz is a Mexican Citizen Kane in several basic respects. Fuentes chronicles his rise from an impoverished childhood on the periphery of Mexican society to the heights of power in Mexico City. The mature Artemio becomes the prime mover of a financial empire with holdings in publishing, real estate, banking, and mining. Similarly, Kane, a New York power broker with interests in mining, publishing, real estate, and manufacturing, traces his origins to a simple family in Colorado. During the course of their lives, both men reverse their beliefs from a proletarian admiration for the common man to an authoritarianism which ultimately destroys their relationships with family and friends. Furthermore, their opportunism and cynicism mirror the moral decay of their times. The degeneration of moral values finds its greatest manifestation in the failure of their respective newspapers to print the truth. In this regard, the most salient feature of their resemblance is their manipulation of the press. Both men, thinly veiled replicas of William Randolph Hearst, are publishers who resort to slander for personal gain and to yellow journalism to support their right-wing political causes.

In addition to the characterization of his protagonist, Fuentes borrows various film techniques from *Citizen Kane*. This adaptation of material from the film adds to the novel's complexity and visual richness. For example, one of the most successful reflections of the film is the novel's tightly knit fabric of fragmentary reminiscences. In *Citizen Kane*, Welles breaks up the linear narrative into overlapping vignettes. Here, newsreel footage and interviews with the people who knew Kane best flesh out the portrait of the vulnerable man behind the image of grandeur. Kane's dying word, "rosebud," forces the editors of the newsreel to discover some unifying quality in Kane's life, and it is the quest for the meaning of "rosebud" that serves as the focus of the film. Artemio's conscious and unconscious alternations between past, present, and future tenses and his strange obsession with his son Lorenzo offer a fragmentary record of his life. By deciphering the mysterious relationship between these fragments, deftly scattered throughout the novel, the reader reconstructs the world of Artemio Cruz.

A particularly striking counterpart to Welles's rosebud motif is the recurrent reference to Lorenzo, Artemio's only son. Artemio repeatedly recalls the scene when he and Lorenzo rode on horseback through the hacienda in Vera Cruz near his birthplace. Lorenzo confesses that he must leave Mexico to fight for the Republican cause in Spain. This is their last time together because, as the reader learns in another fragment, Lorenzo dies in the Civil War. Although the significance of this scene becomes clear only gradually, references to Artemio's last meeting with Lorenzo symbolize a tragic defeat, in the same way as "rosebud" signified Kane's disillusionment and his exile from his family. In Lorenzo, Artemio might have been able to combine his own instinct for survival with his son's idealism to produce a morally correct life; with Lorenzo's death, this opportunity is forever lost. Both Kane and Artemio immerse themselves in painful memories which they masochistically cultivate to the end of their lives.

The novel captures the visual starkness of the film in passages that depict characters and situations through a camera's eye, highlighting grotesque detail and situations through closeups and other pictorial techniques. For example, Welles's stumbling, bloated Charles Foster Kane is mirrored in Artemio Cruz, described as a walking mummy at his last New Year's Eve party. Cruz's fall from greatness—a counterpart to Kane's collapse during the opening scenes of the film—is captured in a clinical description of his decaying body in closeup: ". . . he must sense this odor of dead scales, of vomit and blood; he must look at this caved-in chest, this matted gray beard, these waxy ears, this fluid oozing from his nose, this dry spit on his lips and chin, these wandering eyes that must attempt another glance. . . ."

Fuentes reasserts the cinematographic closeup throughout the novel by means of a tight focus on Cruz in direct descriptions reflected in mirrors. Mirrors and reflections are useful for the narrator to witness his own physical deterioration and for the author to practice his virtuosity in manipulating "camera angles" for special effects. Early in the novel, the prosperous Artemio glances in a storefront window to straighten his tie. What he sees is his reflection, "a man identical to himself but so distant, he also was adjusting his tie, with the same fingers stained with nicotine, the same suit, but colorless." Cruz contemplates his image at a distance, as though he were watching a film of himself. In the reflection—as distant as images on a movie screen—he sees himself surrounded by beggars and vendors whom he ignores. Through this cinematographic technique, Fuentes projects the image of a solitary Artemio Cruz, cast in the mold of Charles Kane, divorced from the common folk and insensitive to their suffering.

Other mirror images in the novel emphasize the theme of alienation and disintegration of the protagonist, particularly in the hospital scenes where Cruz stares at his twin image in the fragmented mirrors of his wife's and daughter's purses. The doubling of Artemio in mirror images has its source in one of the most important scenes in *Citizen Kane*, a scene which associates the multiple images of the protagonist with a corresponding fragmentation of his personality. At the end of the film, after his second wife leaves him, Kane breaks up her bedroom, smashing pictures and china and yanking down her curtains. From the rubble of her belongings he picks up a small glass ball which, when shaken, produces a miniature snowstorm around a white rose. He utters the word "rosebud" and then strolls leisurely from the room, his face empty of turmoil. Kane then passes between two facing mirrors which reflect his image in infinite series. This scene indicates the extent of Kane's deterioration as he seems to put on a mask of indifference and serenity while he feels his inner self tossed about by failure.

Cruz similarly stands between such facing mirrors in a key scene following the longest fragment of the novel, which deals with Artemio's imprisonment during the Mexican Revolution. Captured by Villa's forces, Cruz, Gonzalo Bernal (the brother of the woman Cruz will later marry), and his friend Tobias, a Yaqui Indian, face execution by a firing squad. Cruz alone survives by giving false information to his captors. The mirror scene following this episode sums up Artemio's instinct for survival, the aspect of his personality that has won out over whatever charitable impulses he may have had earlier in his life. Artemio now wears the impassible mask of indifference to others, Kane's frozen persona in the mirrors:

. . . to recognize yourself; to recognize the rest and let them recognize you: and to know
that you oppose each individual, because each individual is yet another obstacle to reach
your goal: you will choose, in order to survive you will choose, you will choose from
among the infinite mirrors one alone, one alone which will reflect you irrevocably, that
will cast a black shadow on the other mirrors, you will shatter them rather than surrender. . . .

Fuentes offsets the tight focus in these mirror closeups with long shots or
general establishing shots elsewhere in the novel. His technique of capturing
several planes of action occurring simultaneously has its origin in the deep
focus of *Citizen Kane*, where this technique is used to juxtapose several
characters and situations which impinge upon one another. Perhaps the most
remarkable example of deep focus shows Charles Kane's parents arranging
for their son's enrollment in a boarding school. Framed by the window in the
center of the screen, the young Charles plays outside in the snow with his
Rosebud sled, oblivious to events indoors before the camera. In a tight shot,
with Charles still in focus, his mother signs the power of attorney which
establishes a trust fund for him and which symbolizes his entry into high
society. Juxtaposed here are the innocent boy and his parents, who prepare
his ticket to the good life. The two planes of action make a harsh visual
statement about power. Charles, seen from a distance, is surrounded and
overwhelmed by his elders and their financial dealings. Later in the film, in
another example of deep focus, a gigantic Kane, in the foreground, dwarfs
all the other characters in the scene, emblematic of his monumental power.
    Fuentes' equivalent of deep focus can be found throughout the novel in
fragments which juxtapose characters and situations. One of these fragments
depicts Artemio's arrival at the hacienda of Gamaliel Bernal. A masterful
juxtaposition of narrative planes focuses on Artemio—the survivor—telling
the family of Gonzalo Bernal how their loved one perished in the Villista
execution. Crosscutting from Artemio's explanation at the dinner table to his
arrival in town and then to his meeting Gamaliel and Catalina Bernal, Fuentes
superimposes several moments in time and space in a single scene. Thus, the
reader sees the conniving Artemio in the foreground as he ingratiates himself
with the Bernal family; in the background, his arrival in Puebla and the rooting
out of information about the Bernals; and in the middle ground, the sump-
tuous furnishings which Artemio will soon possess.
    Here, Fuentes achieves effects of simultaneity that compel the reader/
spectator to superimpose the planes of action and modify each event in the
light of what precedes and what follows it. Such is the effect of other fragments
in the novel which depict Artemio's rise to power after marrying Catalina
and after taking over the hacienda after Gamaliel's death. In a scene that
depicts Artemio's campaign for political office, he and Catalina ride their
buggy through the dusty countryside. They come upon a procession of religious zealots, *penitentes*, who impede their passage. As the narrator describes
the grotesque physical deformities of the *penitentes* and their mortification of

themselves, he juxtaposes their bloody parade to the religious sanctuary with Artemio's exalted and indifferent ride through their seething masses. The various planes of action appear linked for ironic purposes. In the background, the dust of the arid fields mixes the clouds of dust raised by the buggy and that of the *penitentes*. The cinematic impact of this scene rivals that of similar settings in Mariano Azuela's photographic *Los de Abajo* (1916; *The Underdogs*, 1929). In the middle ground, the sincerity of the zealots, symbolized by their bloody footprints, is counterbalanced by the cynicism of Artemio's political campaign, which is motivated by hunger for power alone.

Fuentes has said that in all of his works, he offers Mexicans "a mirror in which they can see how they look, how they act, in a country which is a masked country. . . ." Fuentes offers Mexicans more than a mirror, however, for his fiction cinematically projects the spectacle of Mexican life and history on a broad screen in order to preserve and highlight the past.

Major publications other than long fiction

SHORT FICTION: *Los días enmascarados*, 1954; *Cantar de ciegos*, 1964; *Chac Mool y otros cuentos*, 1973; *Agua quemada*, 1981 (*Burnt Water*, 1981).

PLAYS: *Todos los gatos son pardos*, 1970; *El tuerto es rey*, 1970; *Orchids in the Moonlight*, 1982.

SCREENPLAYS: *El acoso*, 1958 (an adaptation of Alejo Carpentier's *El acoso*, with Luis Buñuel); *Children of Sanchez*, 1961 (an adaptation of Oscar Lewis's *Children of Sanchez*, with Abby Mann); *Pedro Paramo*, 1966; *Tiempo de morir*, 1966: *Los caifanes*, 1967.

NONFICTION: *The Argument of Latin America, Words for North Americans*, 1963; *Paris, la revolución de mayo*, 1968; *El mundo de José Luis Cuevas*, 1969; *La nueva novela hispanoamericana*, 1969; *Casa con dos puertas*, 1970; *Tiempo mexicano*, 1971; *Cervantes: O, La crítica de la lectura*, 1976 (*Cervantes: Or, The Critique of Reading*, 1976).

Bibliography

Brody, Robert, and Charles Rossman, eds. *Carlos Fuentes: A Critical View*, 1982.

Faris, Wendy. *Carlos Fuentes*, 1983.

Guzman, Daniel de. *Carlos Fuentes*, 1972.

Harss, Luis, and Barbara Dohmann. "Carlos Fuentes or the New Heresy," in *Into the Mainstream*, 1967.

Sommers, Joseph. *After the Storm*, 1968.

Howard Fraser

CARLO EMILIO GADDA

Born: Milan, Italy; November 14, 1893
Died: Rome, Italy; May 21, 1973

Principal long fiction
Quer pasticciaccio brutto de via Merulana, 1957 (*That Awful Mess on Via Merulana*, 1965); *La cognizione del dolore*, 1963, 1970 (*Acquainted with Grief*, 1969); *La meccanica*, 1970 (unfinished novella); *Racconto italiano di ignoto del novecento*, 1983 (fragment).

Other literary forms
In addition to the novels listed above, Carlo Emilio Gadda has published several collections of short stories which to date remain untranslated: *La Madonna dei filosofi* (1931; Our Lady of the philosophers); *Il castello di Udine* (1934; the castle of Udine), awarded the Premio Bagutta; *L'Adalgisa* (1944; tales from Milan); and *Novelle dal ducato in fiamme* (1953; stories from the duchy in flames), awarded the Premio Viareggio. Gadda's most important nonfiction writings are *I viaggi la morte* (1958; travels and death), a collection of literary essays, and the anti-Fascist pamphlet *Eros e Priapo* (1967; Eros and Priapus). His war and prison diary, *Giornale di guerra e di prigionia*, first appeared in 1955 and in its definitive form in 1965. Carlo Emilio Gadda has also published many topical articles, essays on public works, architectural engineering, a description of a surgical oration, and even a recipe for cooking risotto, all collected in *Le meraviglie d'Italia* (1939, 1964; the marvels of Italy); a book of fables and aphorisms, *Il primo libro delle favole* (1952; the first book of fables); two comic texts for radio broadcast; a small volume of historical caricatures, dedicated to the memories of Louis XIII, XIV, and XV of France (*I Luigi di Francia*, 1964); and a satiric dialogue entitled *Il guerriero, l'amazzone lo spirito della poesia nel verso immortale del Foscolo* (1967; the warrior, the amazon, and the spirit of poetry in the immortal verses of Ugo Foscolo). Posthumous publications include Gadda's early philosophical notebooks, *Meditazione milanese* (1974; Milanese meditations) and *Le bizze del capitano in congedo e altri racconti* (1981; the extravagances of a captain on leave and other stories), and the fragments of an early novel entitled *Racconto italiano di ignoto del novecento* (1983; an anonymous twentieth century Italian story). Gadda is also the author of numerous, uncollected technical articles which appeared during the thirties in the dailies *Ambrosiano* and *La gazzetta del popolo*.

Achievements
The recognition of Gadda as one of Italy's most important contemporary prose writers came late, when his novel *Acquainted with Grief*, originally

published in serial form in *Letteratura*, a small Florentine literary review, was, in 1963, awarded the prestigious Formentor International Literary Prize. Before then, Gadda was known and admired by a relatively select group of literary critics who praised his work largely for its linguistic eccentricity. The notoriety given to *Acquainted with Grief* called public attention to his earlier writings, especially to *That Awful Mess on Via Merulana*, also previously serialized in *Letteratura*. More important, it caused critics to heed the general significance of his work in relation to the most distinguished manifestations of the European avant-garde. Today, after more than a decade of serious critical study, Gadda is seen to occupy a unique position in the history of Italian literature. At a time when the modern narrative in Italy had found with Italo Svevo, Federigo Tozzi, and the young Alberto Moravia, authors capable of strengthening a comparatively weak national tradition in the novel, Gadda wrote to contest the very idea of narrative, the traditional notions of author and text, and the very institution of literature itself. His revolution strikes so deeply into the core of conventional literary assumptions and practices that only now, in the light of recent developments in criticism, is it possible to take full measure of its importance. During the 1950's and 1960's, the epithets "eccentric," "baroque," and "antiliterary" were used to displace Gadda's work outside what was deemed fixed, legitimate, or proper, linking him to the heritage of the macaronics or pasticheurs, in part, to such renowned outsiders as Teofilo Folengo, François Rabelais, James Joyce, and Louis-Ferdinand Céline, and, more directly, to the indigenous tradition of the Lombard and Piedmontese *Scapigliatura* (Giovanni Faldella, Achille Giovanni Cagna, and Carlo Dossi). Placing Gadda within this tradition helps one set into perspective the elements of caricature, parody, and derision for which his works are noted. It provides, moreover, a general framework for assessing the linguistic inventiveness that makes Gadda an eminently difficult writer.

Biography

Born in 1893, Carlo Emilio Gadda was the oldest of three children. His father, Francesco Ippolito, was a silk weaver by trade who, through his first marriage, became a partner in a prosperous Milanese textile firm. His mother, Adele Lehr, was half-Hungarian. She held a doctorate in letters and philosophy, which enabled her to earn a modest living as a schoolteacher and provide for her children after her husband's death in 1909. What we know of Gadda's life has been filtered in large part through his fiction. His childhood was marked by the financial decline of his family, attributed to his father's imprudent investments and business ventures. In Milan, he attended the Liceo Parini and studied engineering at the Istituto Tecnico Superiore. With the outbreak of World War I, he interrupted his studies to enlist as an officer in the Italian Alpine regiment, saw action on several fronts, including Caporetto, and was taken prisoner. In 1920, Gadda began working as an industrial engineer, traveling to Sardinia and abroad to Argentina and, later, to France, Belgium, and Germany, where he supervised the construction of plants for the production of ammonia. In 1933, Gadda was hired by the Vatican to design and oversee the installation of its electrical power system.

In spite of his scientific background and training, Gadda was never wholly satisfied with his career as an engineer. Philosophy and literature interested him more. In fact, he no sooner began working in industry when he left his job to pursue, at Milan's Accademia Scientifico-Letteraria, a second doctorate in philosophy and wrote under the supervision of philosophers Piero Martinetti and Antonio Banfi, a thesis on Gottfried Leibniz's *Nouveaux Essais sur l'entendement humain* (1765; *Essays Concerning Human Understanding*, 1898). For the most part, Gadda succeeded well in combining his literary and scientific talents, but, in 1940, he broke definitively with his profession and moved to Florence, where, in the company of then more distinguished writers such as Elio Vittorini and Tommaso Landolfi, he dedicated himself totally to writing, completing for *Letteratura* the last two installments of *Acquainted with Grief* and writing his best-known novel, *That Awful Mess on Via Merulana* and parts of *Eros e Priapo*. Ten years later, Gadda moved to Rome to work as a journalist for the Edizioni Radio Italiana. There he lived a modest and secluded life, revising many of his early writings for publication in book form. When Carlo Emilio Gadda died in 1973, he left a rich legacy of texts that have influenced two generations of writers and have brought him fame as one of contemporary Italy's most original, complex, and compelling authors.

Analysis

Carlo Emilio Gadda's fiction originates in his notion of an objectively chaotic and deformed world. Confronted by a reality that resists organization and rational systemization, the writer, according to Gadda's aesthetics, becomes involved in a never-ending process of unraveling and probing into the interminable succession of links uniting facts, circumstances, and experiences. In this perspective, the subject of authorial self loses its once privileged place as an observer, positioned outside the labyrinth of phenomena and thus capable of exercising judgment, of arranging things to form an organic whole and, therefore, of narrating.

Also, in contrast to the modernist aesthetic, the writer, in Gadda's view, cannot reflect the fragmentation of the present by refusing to communicate his personality, by remaining aloof and ironic. Instead, he too is a part of the chaos, a single element or moment in an objective chain that can claim no more than its neutral status as a biological and material presence. In other words, the author for Gadda does not disappear completely in his attempt to produce a thing-centered universe (as is the case with, say Alain Robbe-Grillet), but rather, becomes part of the "game" called "literature."

What is literature for Gadda? Simply, the alter image of reality that produces fictional entities called characters and plots and disposes them for the purpose of creating particular effects. The subject, as part of this game, can only recognize its degraded position, and, in response, try to impose its subjectivity on the reader, knowing full well that the judgments it makes have no special importance, that they are not means of conditioning the reader's comprehension of the fiction, but instead, merely traces of its own devalued presence. Such expressions of authorial subjectivity at times take the form of violent outbursts or tirades against people or actions that conflict with Gadda's innate sense of order and propriety; at times, they become tragic monologues on existence or the comic deformation of characters and events.

If literature mimics reality and if reality is, as Gadda sees it, a disharmonious continuum, the literary work defies unraveling; it can never be explained for it can never be concluded. Furthermore, because literary works are made up of oppositional and coincidental elements, no one work can contain parts that are truly unique to itself, but rather the parts of one work may be transposed to other, different relational systems that are equally as provisional. This idea explains why Gadda's fictional writings are largely unfinished, deprived of denouement and resolution of conflict. It also accounts for why what became *Acquainted with Grief* was originally intended as chapters in *Le meraviglie d'Italia*, then redesigned to include other parts which subsequently appeared in different collections, while two fragments of the official version of the novel are contained in *L'Adalgisa* and a third in *Novelle dal ducato in fiamme*.

From such a notion of the relation of literature to reality, a fundamental aspect of Gadda's work emerges: the artificial, essentially linguistic, nature of literary production, which elicits the functional utilization of language in the search for contradictions and unexpected connections among things. Gadda's emphasis on language is his way of saying that, in the wake of the crisis of ideology, reality *is* language—that the subject matter of literature is historical realities existing as linguistic codes. The writer—he states in an important literary essay, is faced with a specific number of "languages" which correspond to a variety of codes representing different modes of existence and activity. This collection of "codes" makes up, in his judgment, the "empirical," "chaotic," "baroque," and "grotesque" character of the world. To know this reality means to "coordinate" these various languages and to stamp on the process of "coordination" one's own particular seal. For Gadda, coordinating reality entails finding in things one particular element that distinguishes one system from another. It, therefore, denotes focusing on a specific link in a causal chain, magnifying it out of proportion in order to penetrate its essence; in this sense, knowledge and deformation become one and the same thing.

The principal effect of combining and coordinating different linguistic codes is the pastiche. The pastiche suspends meaning by directing the reader's attention to the process of writing and the particular transgression of literary norms it involves. A situation which is inherently tragic or lyric becomes, with the pastiche, comic representation. Even the use of dialect within the context of standard speech, rather than heightening the realistic effect, is only another means of deforming that discourse to achieve comic incongruity. Gadda's two major novels fully embody the aesthetic principles just summarized.

The ideas that make a framework for *Acquainted with Grief* are derived from Gadda's readings of Immanuel Kant and Sigmund Freud. The novel attempts to direct the reader's perception to realities beyond or outside of the world of appearance, particularly to that part of the protagonist's mind behind the phenomenal self which can never directly be known but which influences profoundly the sense of self that is experienced and represented. Also, at its base lies the Freudian conviction that the acceptance of society is one and the same with the repression of guilt. History and historiography—Gadda writes in the work's preface—give a distorted picture of man's inner life; it shows it in tune with the reality principle and blind to the profound violence which affects the human condition. *Acquainted with Grief* is for Gadda, in its most fundamental meaning, a vindication of human history, "cleansed," in his words "of the stutter of reticence and the frank syntax of deception."

The novel consists of a series of fragments or "tracts" and, in both its original and book forms, it is incomplete, although on the inside flap of the volume's jacket, the publisher, speaking for the author, writes that in the missing conclusion, the protagonist's mother, left alone in her villa after her son's departure, is murdered by the agents of the night watchmen's organizations (Nistituó Provinciales de Vigilancia para la Noche), that she dies thinking her son Gonzalo had plotted the horrendous crime. In 1941, Gadda had composed rough drafts of what were to become the novel's final chapters. These fragments, included in the 1970 edition, appear to substantiate the aforementioned outcome. There is, furthermore, evidence, contained in several unpublished notes, that Gadda had intended to write a third and final episode, centered on the police interrogation of Gonzalo.

The novel's action takes place in Maradagàl, a small, imaginary country in South America, situated near Parapagàl, a country of similar size and resources. Close to the city of Pastrufazio, in a modern villa constructed on the highlands, lived the Pirobutirro family which, at the time of the novel's action, was reduced to an old widow whom the people call La Señora and her forty-five-year-old son Gonzalo, who clearly appears as the caricatural reflection of Gadda himself. The whole story, in fact, beginning with its imaginary South American setting in which the people, institutions, geography, and history of early twentieth century Italy (chiefly Lombardy) are easily recognizable, is a kind of autobiographical parody that produces tragicomic deformation. (The family name Pirobutirro, for example, is derived from a type of pear tree, *pere butirro*, that Gadda's father attempted to cultivate at the family's country villa at Longone al Segrino in Brianza.)

Gonzalo is a modern-day misanthrope, extremely jealous of his own privacy and possessions and that of his mother and contemptuous of the outside world, especially of the simple peasant folk whom the Señora charitably supports. He suffers from uneasiness, apprehension, a sense of guilt and unfulfillment, and a general anticipation of danger caused by an undefined image of pain and grief. His manias are for order, silence, and food, and he is obsessed by a wish for death and, allegedly, a desire to kill his mother. He is prone to violent outbursts of rage and long diatribes against anything that appears to intrude on his solitude and sole possession of his mother. In the novel's first part, the Señora appears as a somewhat comic and grotesque figure. She wanders about the house, looking like a bejeweled skeleton in the diamond earrings she cherishes as the last remembrance of past wealth. Gonzalo berates her for her excessive goodness, her need to keep up appearances, and her decision to seek the protection of the night watchmen's organizations, whose members, in Gonzalo's view, are intent on exploiting her fear. In part 2, however, the author's perspective on the mother changes. No longer the grotesque object of Gonzalo's insensitivity and rejection, she stands out as a tragic character and is portrayed with compassion. With the death of her youngest son, she is left hopeless, confined to isolation and emptiness. Images of darkness, death, desolation, and abandonment abound to express in her character an extreme sense of futility, the very same futility that dominates the characterization of her son Gonzalo.

The first edition of *Acquainted with Grief* closes with references to several episodes in Gonzalo's life. The most illuminating from a psychoanalytical standpoint is the time when, enraged because his mother had given him a watch that she had bought from a Russian or Armenian refugee, bursts out "in horrible vituperations" and takes from the wall a portrait of his father and tramples it "as if he were pressing grapes in a vat." The first two fragments included in the 1970 edition tell of a robbery in a nearby villa and how Gonzalo had refused the protection of the night watchmen's organizations. In the final fragment, the reader learns that the Señora has been mortally wounded, "debased"—Gadda writes—"by an evil cause operating in the absurdity of the night." The novel ends with the beginning of an inquest.

Criticism has often brought attention to the fact that the world of *Acquainted with Grief*, although disguised in an imaginary South American setting, is in effect the world of Italian Fascism, and that Gonzalo's numerous spells of verbal aggression are actually directed toward Fascism. It has also been argued that the mother symbolizes Benito Mussolini and Fascism in the affection she displays toward others as a means of coercing them into relationships of dependency. It could even be stated that, generally speaking, Fascism is the novel's principal referent and that Gonzalo's conflicts derive from Fascism's ever-present forms of oppression, as symbolized by the watchmen's organizations and the wall surrounding the villa. Yet, such a political reading of *Acquainted with Grief* falls far short of exhausting the work's total meaning. It tends to ignore the novel's deep psychological structure, the importance of the autobiographical element in seizing the complex patterns of deception and dissemblance that the story embodies.

Gadda began writing his novel *That Awful Mess on Via Merulana* at the peak of the Fascist demagoguery, when Italy had made its disastrous entry into World War II. The catastrophic events of those years caused Gadda to shift his narrative focus from the complex problematic of an individual life lived *in extremis* to the absurdity of human life in general. As in his previous novel, his objectives extend from polemic to benevolent satire, but here the political content is clearly manifested. Yet, the novel is far from being a political work in the strict sense, as are, for example, the stories of Cesare Pavese and Elio Vittorini. Instead, the origins of *That Awful Mess on Via Merulana* are to be located in *Acquainted with Grief*, particularly in Gonzalo's perception of universal guilt. In this respect, the plot of *That Awful Mess on Via Merulana* takes on a special significance because the police investigation at the story's center becomes a vehicle for conveying the guilt of an entire race.

The novel's principal theme is the risk one runs when made the object of inquiry or investigation. The guilty can never be brought to justice because in addition to the perpetrators of the robbery and homicide in Via Merulana, there exist numerous other offenders and criminals, the most evil being the oppressive State, impersonated by the sordid and grotesque figure of its criminal idol Mussolini.

That Awful Mess on Via Merulana follows the action of an elementary detective story. Two crimes are committed in the same apartment house at number 219 Via Merulana in Rome. The first is the theft of some jewels belonging to a certain Countess Menegazzi; the second is the murder of the beautiful Roman gentlewoman Liliana Balducci. Don Ciccio Ingravallo, a friend of the Balduccis, is the detective assigned to the case.

In this novel, more than in his previous work, Gadda shows an exceptional talent for caricature. Don Ciccio, for example, is a typical southern Italian figure: a dilettante philosopher, reflective, sensitive, respectful of ritual, yet somewhat sloppy, and jealous of more charming and handsome men, such as Liliana's cousin Giuliano, whom the detective immediately considers with suspicion. In addition to being a character whose petty jealousies and melancholic disposition set him in polemic contrast to the notion of the ideal Fascist man, Don Ciccio is Gadda's voice in the novel, in that he is continually looking for hidden meanings behind appearances. At a dinner given by Liliana to celebrate her husband's birthday, his inquisitive eye penetrates the Signora's mundane graces to observe that at times she appears to sigh and that her face is full of a strange sadness. He attributes her melancholy to the fact that she has no children. Her presumed sterility, he concludes, causes her to venerate everything that in the least way is associated with maternity. Her mania, he goes on to note, is even more tragic and grotesque when seen in the context of the Fascist myth of fertility and procreation. Don Ciccio's thoughts inspire Gadda to interrupt the flow of the narrative and level a kind of epic satire against Fascism's absurd reverence for maternity. The episode is symptomatic of the entire writing procedure in *That Awful Mess on Via Merulana*, whereby a minimal reference to Fascism brings on literally pages of fierce, comic invective.

The first crime, which takes place shortly after Liliana's dinner party, is of small importance compared to the pastiche it generates and the opportunities it affords for grotesque caricature. An extraordinary example of Gadda's ability for literary parody and comic deformation is his portrayal of the Countess Menegazzi in which he mimics the syntax of Alessandro Manzoni's renowned description of Gertrude in *I promessi sposi* (1840-1842; *The Betrothed*, 1951), creating a picture totally devoid of lyricism or pathos and focusing on the comic absurdity of the human condition as exemplified by this lonely woman who spends her days in a continual state of tormented anxiety.

The presence of physical violence and death also provides a suitable opportunity for Gadda to express his negative vision of life. Here, too, his attitude is one of ironic indifference, which permits his description to become grotesquely comic. The dead body of Liliana at the scene of the crime is open to every sort of disrespect and impiety. Her dress and slip are pulled up and the spectators fix their gaze on her delicately embroidered underwear and the extreme whiteness of her flesh. Only in the next moment do we become aware of the deep wound in her throat. Gadda's description is long and detailed; he examines the body from every possible angle, while the comments of those present are comically abusive.

Liliana's murder turns out to have little meaning when seen from the standpoint of the novel's historical setting, the spring of 1927, when the Fascist regime was promoting an idyllic image of itself, based on tender emotions and familial love. Gadda takes great pleasure in mocking Fascist pretensions for law and order and civil austerity. The prime object of Gadda's polemic is Mussolini, the "Death's Head in a Top Hat," the detective story appears as a pretext for representing the criminality of the State and the uncertainty of human existence in general. In fact, the investigation leads the reader to suspect everyone, while he is certain of nothing, not even the names of the characters. Only with the arrival of Don Corpi, Liliana's confessor who appears at police headquarters to read her will, does the investigation seem to be headed toward solution. The movement, however, begun in search of the stolen jewels, quickly becomes a kind of voyage to the bottom of the earth, where the multiform horrors of the human condition are graphically revealed. The rediscovered jewels stand out in contrast as primordial essences compared to the grotesque world surrounding them. At a certain point, the detective story breaks down. The murder theme, having been put aside for several chapters, returns in the final pages so that a logical connection may be made between the two crimes.

One's first impulse in commenting on *That Awful Mess on Via Merulana* is to view the novel according to the metaliterary directives it embodies, that is, as a process of excavation into nature, of penetrating into some ever more intimate stratum in search of the secret of existence. In this sense, Gadda is a kind of writer-surgeon who cuts through the crust of appearance to scan and probe the sacrosanct recesses of human matter, demonstrating by means of the scientific precision with which he works his absolute power and control. Gadda's fiction abounds with examples of this sort of descriptive process, an explicit instance of which we find at the conclusion of *That Awful Mess on Via Merulana* when the stolen jewels are recovered.

Yet it would be incomplete to see Gadda's objective as simply one of capturing a universe of meanings or the hidden soul of things, whether either to assign to reality a kind of metaphysical transcendence or to produce, naturalistically, a more complete material image of the phenomenon. A closer look at Gadda's novels will show that what the narrator has in fact done is dilate or deform two modes of writing: one which focuses on the object's meanings, the other centered on the lyric, subjective dimension encased in the consciousness of the reader-spectator. The juxtaposition of these highly stylized perspectives carries out a neutralizing function, reducing them to the level of material causes, that is, to the matter and memory of which the event is constructed, devoid of any specific finality.

Keeping in mind the metacritical structure of Gadda's texts and considering them as a discourse on method, one can note that their syntax calls attention primarily to objects and gestures. What counts is the presence of the material components of discourse, which station themselves before the reader, demanding total, undivided attention. The effect of their extreme presence is what Robbe-Grillet has called, in reference to the new novel, "mocking." It is not by accident, then, that Gadda attained his greatest popularity among the more radical exponents of Italy's neo-avant-garde.

At base, the neo-avant-garde, although showing a wide diversity of theoretical positions, posited its experimental methods on the belief that all ideologic representation falsified reality and that the only strategy possible was one of disengagement that produced an art devoid of meaning and messages and whose sole purpose was to restore reality to its nonideologized and dishistoricized intactness. Whether Gadda can truly be considered a forerunner of the neo-avant-garde is not important. His appropriation by writers such as Alberto Arbasino and Raffaele La Capria marked a decisive turning point in his critical fortunes. It meant his inclusion into the European context of experimentalism as the Italian example and thus it heralded a new way of looking at his work. No longer a unique Italian specialty, the great, but difficult, pasticheur stood out precisely on account of the very inaccessibility which, according to traditional narrative standards, relegated him to the sphere of minor writers. His greatness now consisted in the deep, seminal value of his language which, as it expressed an entirely new way of looking at the world, paved the way for the literature of the future.

Major publications other than long fiction

SHORT FICTION: *La Madonna dei filosofi*, 1931; *Il castello di Udine*, 1934; *L'Adalgisa: Disegni milanesi*, 1944; *Il primo libro delle favole*, 1952; *Novelle dal ducato in fiamme*, 1953; *Accoppiamenti giudiziosi*, 1963; *I Luigi di Francia*, 1964; *Le bizze del capitano in congedo e altri racconti*, 1981.

PLAY: *Il guerriero, l'amazzone lo spirito della poesia nel verso immortale del Foscolo*, 1967.

NONFICTION: *Le meraviglie d'Italia*, 1939, 1964; *Giornale di guerra e di prigionia*, 1955, 1965; *I viaggi la morte*, 1958; *Eros e Priapo*, 1967; *Meditazione milanese*, 1974.

Bibliography

Canon, JoAnn. "Notes on Gadda's Critical Essays," in *Canadian Journal of Italian Studies*. V, no. 1-2 (1981-1982), pp. 64-71.

_____ . "The Reader as Detective: Notes on Gadda's *Pasticciaccio*," in *Modern Language Studies*. X, no. 3 (1979), pp. 41-50.

Dombroski, Robert S. *Introduzione allo studio di Carlo Emilio Gadda*, 1974.

_____ . "Moral Commitment and Invention in Gadda's Poetics," in *Rivista di letterature moderne e comparate*. XXV, no. 3 (1972), pp. 210-221.

_____ . "Overcoming Oedipus: Self and Society in *La cognizione del dolore*," in *Modern Language Notes*. XCIX, no. 1 (1984), pp. 125-143.

Ferrero, Ernesto. *Invito alla lettura di C. E. Gadda*, 1972.

Roscioni, Gian Carlo. *La disarmonia prestabilita: studio su Gadda*, 1969.

Robert Dombroski

GABRIEL GARCÍA MÁRQUEZ

Born: Aracataca, Colombia; March 6, 1928

Principal long fiction

La hojarasca, 1955 (novella; *Leaf Storm and Other Stories*, 1972); *El coronel no tiene quien le escriba*, 1961 (novella; *No One Writes to the Colonel and Other Stories*, 1968); *La mala hora*, 1962 (*In Evil Hour*, 1979); *Cien años de soledad*, 1967 (*One Hundred Years of Solitude*, 1970); *El otoño del patriarca*, 1975 (*The Autumn of the Patriarch*, 1975); *Crónica de una muerte anunciada*, 1981 (*Chronicle of a Death Foretold*, 1982).

Other literary forms

In addition to his novels, Gabriel García Márquez has also written short stories, books of conversations, essays on cultural and political subjects, and screenplays. Many of his short stories were published originally in newspapers and all have been collected in volumes in Spanish. His stories have also appeared in *The Atlantic*, *Esquire*, and *The New Yorker*. Almost all of his stories are now available in English with the exception of those written at the beginning of his career, from 1947 to 1955.

Achievements

Since the publication of *One Hundred Years of Solitude* in 1967, García Márquez has had a broad international appeal in both the Hispanic world and beyond. The initial reaction to the Spanish edition, which was first issued in Buenos Aires, was overwhelming: New editions were published at the amazing rate of one a week, as the public and critics alike applauded the Colombian masterpiece. The reaction was similar as translations were published: In France, the novel was proclaimed the best foreign book of 1969; in Italy, it was awarded the Chianchiano Prize (1969); and in the United States, it was named one of the twelve best books of the year (1970). By 1982, *One Hundred Years of Solitude* had been translated into more than twenty-five languages.

The worldwide appeal of García Márquez' masterpiece is widely acknowledged to have been the single most important factor in the extraordinary growth of interest in the Latin American novel. No novelist of the postwar era has had an international influence greater than that of García Márquez; his Magical Realism has given rise to one of the dominant trends in world fiction in the 1970's and the 1980's. The winner of numerous literary honors, including the Neustadt International Prize for Literature in 1972, García Márquez was awarded the world's highest literary accolade, the Nobel Prize, in 1982.

Biography

Gabriel García Márquez was born in Aracataca, near the Caribbean coast of Colombia, on March 6, 1928. His grandparents were more important in his childhood than his parents; he lived with the former the first eight years of his life. García Márquez has emphasized their significance by claiming that nothing interesting has happened to him since his grandfather's death, when he was eight years old. These early years included a heavy dose of history, myth, legend, and traditional oral storytelling. The Aracataca region, which recently had experienced the economic boom of "banana fever," could no longer live off American dollars and dreams of progress; myths and nostalgia were more the staple of young García Márquez' reality. His grandparents' home seemed to nurture this ambience: His grandmother could tell the most incredible tales with naturalness and nonchalance. García Márquez claims that this very naturalness was a key to learning to control the narrative voice in *One Hundred Years of Solitude*. His grandfather's influence was even more important: stories of the wars and fables of Colombia, including tales from the War of a Thousand Days, which much of Colombia, including Aracataca, had experienced at the turn of the century.

García Márquez' parents sent him from the tropical, vibrant coast to the cool and dismal highlands of Bogotá for his secondary education in a private Jesuit school, the National College of Zipaquirá. Neither the frigidness of the Andes nor Bogotá's natives were to his liking, but he was graduated in 1946. He began law studies the following year at the National University in Bogotá. Two key events, coupled with his disinterest in law, made 1947 a more important year for literature than jurisprudence. First, he met Plinio Apuleyo Mendoza, a friend and supporter in the early stages of García Márquez' writing career, and a colleague and collaborator later; in the same year, he published his first story, "La tercera resignación" ("The Third Resignation"), in one of Bogotá's major newspapers, *El Espectador*. Within the next five years, García Márquez published fifteen short stories in Colombian newspapers. In April, 1948, an event occurred which would affect García Márquez' life immediately and, in the course of time, mark an important direction of Colombia's history and fiction for the next twenty years. A liberal populist candidate for the presidency, Jorge Eliécer Gaitán, was assassinated on April 9. This act served as a catalyst for mass violence in Bogotá, civil unrest in much of the country, and civil war in rural areas of Colombia during the next ten years. García Márquez moved back to the coast, taking up residence in Cartagena in May. By then, he had published three stories in *El Espectador*. He began writing as a journalist for Cartagena's newspaper *El Universal* and pursued both his true interest—reading and writing fiction—and the study of law. He was enrolled in the National University of Cartagena from June, 1948, until he finished his third year in 1949.

The period from 1949 to the mid-1950's was important primarily for the modern novels that García Márquez read for the first time and the literary friends he established in Barranquilla, a nearby coastal city to which he moved in 1950; the influence of such writers as William Faulkner, Virginia Woolf, and Franz Kafka was significant, particularly that of Faulkner. Through his journalism and from statements of his close friends of this period, sclars have documented that García Márquez also read works by James Joyce, John Dos Passos, Ernest Hemingway, John Steinbeck and William Saroyan, among others. In 1950, García Márquez began to write for the newspaper *El Heraldo* and to take advantage of the surprisingly cosmopolitan literary life available to him while meeting regularly with the literati of the Happy Bar and La Cueva bar in Barranquilla. The literary father figure of the group was Ramón Vinyes, a Catalonian who stimulated the reading of contemporary world fiction among the young future writers. García Márquez wrote a regular column, "La jirafa," in Barranquilla's newspaper *El Heraldo*. In addition to the short stories he published during this period, García Márquez completed the manuscript for a novel entitled "La casa," an early version of what would become the novella, *Leaf Storm*; the prestigious publishing firm Losada of Buenos Aires rejected the novel. In early 1954, García Márquez' friend Alvaro Mutis convinced him to return to Bogotá to write in *El Espectador*.

The year 1955 was a key turning point in García Márquez' career for several reasons: He published *Leaf Storm*, his first work of long fiction; he gained official recognition as a writer when the Association of Artists and Writers of Bogotá awarded him a prize for his story "Un día después del sábado" ("One Day After Saturday"); in July of that year, *El Espectador* sent him to Geneva on a journalistic mission; the closing of *El Espectador* resulted in a change of the original plans for a short stay in Europe and eventually led to his residence in Paris until 1958.

After moving to Caracas in 1958 and New York in 1961 to work as a correspondent for Cuba's *Prensa latina*, García Márquez lived in Mexico for several years of literary silence. In 1965, the pieces of his culminating work—that is, his previous stories—began to fall into place for the creation of *One Hundred Years of Solitude*. García Márquez had found the key to the creation of the magical reality of Macondo, which had been portrayed only partially in his previous fiction. García Márquez tells of the enthusiasm and excitement involved in the culmination of the novel he had been writing for some twenty years. After its completion and resulting success, García Márquez has enjoyed economic security that enables him to live comfortably in Spain, Mexico, and Colombia, to travel extensively, and to continue writing.

Analysis

Gabriel García Márquez denies that the fictional world which he describes is a world of fantasy. He concludes an article about fantasy and artistic creation in Latin America with the following statement: "Reality is a better writer than we are. Our destiny, and perhaps our glory, is to try to imitate it with humility, and the best that is possible for us." This attitude is present throughout much of García Márquez' writing, and this perception of reality is also reflected in his fiction. A deep-seated strain of antirationality underlies all of his fiction, which deals with Latin American "reality" in broad terms, rejecting the narrow regionalism of his literary fathers. The result is a type of fiction that transcends its regional base, a Faulknerian fiction that one critic of Spanish-American literature, John S. Brushwood, has called "transcendent regionalism." A self-proclaimed admirer of Faulkner, García Márquez has strived toward a transcendent regionalism in nearly all of his works with varying degrees of success. Finally, García Márquez' redefinition of realism implies a faithfulness to a higher truth, a mythical level of reality that a more pedestrian realism cannot comprehend. These three factors—antirationality, transcendent regionalism, and myth—are integral to the aesthetics and universality of García Márquez' fiction.

García Márquez' first published work of long fiction was the novella *Leaf Storm*. Asked in 1982 to judge how the young García Márquez wrote this tale, the mature writer had the following response:

> With passion, because he wrote it quickly, thinking he wouldn't write anything else in his lifetime, that that one was his only opportunity, and so he tried to put in everything he had learned up to then. Especially literary techniques and tricks taken from American and English writers he was reading.

As anyone who reads *Leaf Storm* recognizes immediately, the apprentice writer used techniques from Faulkner. The parallel between *Leaf Storm* and *As I Lay Dying* (1930) in structure and narrative point of view is blatant. The setting is Macondo during approximately the first quarter of the twentieth century, and the action centers on an unnamed doctor, believed to be from France, who had lived in Macondo during this twenty-five-year period and who ultimately committed suicide. All of this is revealed through three narrators who attend the doctor's wake, a nine-year-old boy, his mother, and his grandfather; the multiple points of view involve the reader in a process of discovery. The content of the boy's narration tends to be limited to his immediate situation, revealing primarily what he sees at the wake and how he feels at the moment. The mother's scope is broader; she relates information and anecdotes beyond the immediate circumstance, although limited primarily to her own friends. The grandfather's narration provides a historical account of the doctor's life and Macondo. The effect of this structure is a deeper penetration into the reality of Macondo than either a strictly personal or a strictly historical version would have allowed.

Leaf Storm is a point of departure in establishing elements basic to all of García Márquez' fiction. The underlying antirationality of this structure lies in the fact that effects are often apparent before causes or, in some cases, causes never surface. The reader can never rationally explain, for example, why the town's priest reads from the Bristol Almanac or why the doctor eats grass for dinner. The novel has the formal elements of transcendent regionalism: García Márquez constructs a story of universal thematic scope—death, solitude—on a clearly defined regional base. One reason the novel does not have the universal appeal of his later fiction is the relative ineffectiveness in creating a mythical level of reality. The portrayals of both the doctor and the grandfather make them characters with mythic potential, but neither their characterization nor any other aspect of the novel creates a true sense of myth in *Leaf Storm*. Consequently, *Leaf Storm* is an important, but not totally successful, step in the creation of the Macondo that later will blossom in *One Hundred Years of Solitude*.

The next steps in García Márquez' apprenticeship for the creation of *One Hundred Years of Solitude* were the novella *No One Writes to the Colonel* and the novella or short novel *In Evil Hour*. Both are more firmly based on Colombia's historical reality than most of the writer's later work. This reality is *la violencia*, the period of civil war during the 1950's. *No One Writes to the Colonel* is the story of a stoic retired colonel who waits fifteen years for a pension check that never arrives. Besides the psychological portrayal of this colonel, the characterization and actions of other characters reveal a town suffering from corruption and repression. This backdrop is García Márquez' subtle means of incorporating the social and political realities of life in Colombia during this period. For example, the colonel's son is killed because of his political activism, but this matter never takes the form of direct political denunciation on the part of the author. A traditional omniscient narrator tells this story in a linear fashion.

In Evil Hour also features a controlling omniscient narrator and basically linear development of the story, but here García Márquez employs a juxtaposition of scenes to create a montage effect. Someone puts up placards that undermine the town's stability. These anonymous notes contain personal accusations that lead to conflicts: fights, people moving from the town, and even deaths. The mayor, who had been proud of the control he had established in the town before the appearance of the placards, is forced to repress the town's inhabitants in order to maintain order. García Márquez captures the essence of the fear and distrust that pervaded the national consciousness in Colombia at the time.

The antirationality of these stories functions as the catalyst of the anecdotes. In *No One Writes to the Colonel*, it is the inexplicable hope that the colonel has that he will receive the important letter he awaits. The antirational element in *In Evil Hour* is the presence and effect of the placards. Neither of these phenomena is fully explainable in rational terms, although the reader's speculation is invited. Both works transcend their regional base by capturing universal essences: the hope of the colonel and the fear of the town's inhabitants in *In Evil Hour*. The only element that approaches mythic dimensions is the characterization of the colonel in the first of these two books. "Many years later, as he faced the firing squad, Colonel Aureliano Buendia was to remember that distant afternoon when his father took him to discover ice." These are the opening words of García Márquez' masterpiece, *One Hundred Years of Solitude*. Most readers have found themselves swept from these lines through the discovery of ice, to the firing squad and beyond, unable to forget the enchantment of Macondo and the attractiveness of the novel. As a matter of fact, few critics have passed the opportunity to comment on the possible sources of this very attractiveness. Many have pointed to the author's masterful synthesis of various literary traditions, from the individual biography to the epic. Other critics seem to contradict one another by attributing the novel's attractiveness, on the one hand, to its purely invented reality and, on the other, to its truthful depiction of Colombian history. Many readers are clearly attracted by the humor. In addition, the novel has other interesting characteristics: its people, its fantasy, its plot suspense, its craftsmanship, and its sense of wholeness. It is a novel which is difficult to capture—describe appropriately or analyze—because of the intangible quality of much of the reader's experience. Some critics have found the term "Magic Realism" useful. The term can be helpful in dealing with a novel in which a narrator describes with perfect naturalness a scene in which a character ascends to Heaven or in which no one seems to notice the massacre of thousands of striking workers. Paradoxically, despite the numerous difficulties such a novel presents for the critic, it is not at all difficult to read.

One Hundred Years of Solitude is a family saga which tells the story of five generations of Buendias. It begins with the foundation of Macondo by José Arcadio Buendia and his wife Ursula. Despite their fear that the consummation of their marriage will result in the birth of a child with a pig's tail (there is a family precedent for such an event), José Arcadio Buendia decides to challenge fate to protect his image as a man. A second Macondo is established after José Arcadio Buendia kills a man in the original town. The early years of life in Macondo are primitive, albeit a kind of paradise. Macondo's only contact with the outside world is provided by gypsies who bring items such as the ice and magnets that the inhabitants find amazing. They suffer an insomnia plague that results in the loss of both sleep and memory. Modern civilization finally reaches Macondo, along with its numerous institutions; with the arrival of the national political parties come civil wars caused by their conflicts. The Americans bring economic prosperity and exploitation of the workers on the banana plantations. These intrusions of foreigners and modernity are eliminated by a flood that washes them away and returns Macondo to a state similar to its original paradise. In the end, Macondo is not a paradise, however, but a fiction: a member of the Buendia family deciphers a parchment written in Sanskrit which foretold the entire story of the family and Macondo from beginning to the end—that is, the story of *One Hundred Years of Solitude*. History is the completion of a fiction.

Part of the playfulness in the development of the plot involves following the intricate Buendia family line. The original José Arcadio Buendia engenders two sons, José Arcadio and Aureliano. The latter becomes identified as Colonel Aureliano. All of their offspring also carry similar names—Arcadio, Aureliano José, Jose Arcadio Segundo, and so on—making following the Buendia family line an exercise in futility or a challenging game of identities. The English translation, unlike the original Spanish edition, carries a genealogical chart.

One Hundred Years of Solitude is ostensibly a traditional novel which tells a story in a basically linear fashion. It is also a product of technical mastery by a superb craftsman of fiction. The novel's structure is cyclical, from the internal cycles of events that repeat within the novel to the broader cycle completed with the deciphering of the parchments.

García Márquez' handling of narrative point of view is enormously subtle, although it is managed with deceptive simplicity. On the one hand, the omniscient narrator tells the story with a perspective similar to a child's view of the world. Consequently, this childlike narrator views and describes the world with freshness and innocence, taking for granted the incredible events of Macondo. Conversely, the narrator is surprised and amazed about things that are normally considered ordinary, such as ice or magnets. García Márquez' style is based on a use of hyperbole, a constant source of humor. One of the most hilarious hyperbolic characterizations is of Colonel Aureliano Buendia, whose *machismo* is the target of García Márquez' superb satire.

The antirationality of *One Hundred Years of Solitude* is not only a characteristic, but also a fundamental principle of the entire narrative system. Entrance into the magical world of Macondo is an acceptance of the negation of rationality. It is soon apparent that everything is possible in Macondo. The work's transcendent regionalism can be visualized as a series of concentric circles emanating from Macondo. The circles near the center inscribe a reality of the Caribbean coast and Colombia—both its historical reality and myths. Larger circles contain patterns associated with all of Latin America, such as the tradition of *machismo*. Finally, the novel's connotations are universal; on this level one reads the work as a contemporary novelization of the biblical Creation and other universal patterns, such as the fear of incest that pervades the story.

Perhaps the most important achievement of this novel, however, is its expression of a mythic reality. One aspect of this is mythic time that negates linear time. The repetition of numerous cycles, such as the names of the members of the Buendia family, create this sense of an eternal present. The characterization of Colonel Aureliano Buendia and Ursula makes them characters who function at a mythic level beyond the limits of everyday reality and the capabilities of persons in our everyday world. There is also a biblical level of reading that develops myth from Creation and Original Sin to the apocalyptic ending. García Márquez' creation of a traditional yet fascinating story, his mastery of narrative technique, and his creation of myth make *One Hundred Years of Solitude* not only one of the most important novels from Latin America this century but also a work appreciated by an international readership.

Some critics were disappointed with the appearance of *The Autumn of the Patriarch*. They found neither the accessibility nor the magical world of *One Hundred Years of Solitude*. Judged on its own artistic merit, however, *The Autumn of the Patriarch* is an outstanding novel, marked by the superb craftsmanship and humor characteristic of almost all of García Márquez' work.

Several of the major Latin American writers published novels about dictators in the 1970's. García Márquez' novel deals with a dictator in an unnamed Caribbean nation. The dictator figure is a synthesis of many dictators, historical and fictional. García Márquez had spent many years researching these tyrants. The novel begins with the image of a dictator's corpse rotting in his presidential palace. From the discovery of the corpse by an unidentified narrator within the story, the narrative moves away from the immediate situation to relating events from the dictator's past. His life is bizarre and fantastic, as he is willing to take any measure—including serving one of his generals roasted on a platter—to intimidate others and maintain his power.

Structure and style can present a challenge for readers of *The Autumn of the Patriarch*; its consistently long sentences have caused some readers to question if García Márquez bothered with punctuation at all. In reality, even the length of sentences was carefully controlled in this prose poem. In each chapter, García Márquez uses progressively longer sentences, culminating in the last chapter, which is one sentence. The use of multiple narrative voices within these extensive sentences creates a full portrayal of the pitiful dictator and is a source of much of the novel's humor.

Although it is a relatively minor work in García Márquez' oeuvre, the short novel or novella *Chronicle of a Death Foretold* is an interesting tour de force. The story centers on the assassination of its central character, Santiago Nassar. A pair of brothers kill him to save the honor of their sister, Angela Vicario.

Fascinating occurrences abound in *Chronicle of a Death Foretold*, but perhaps the most incredible of all is the series of events surrounding the assassination itself: Everyone in the town, including Nassar himself, knows that he is going to die. Nevertheless, nothing is done to obstruct the seemingly inevitable series of events leading to his death. The novel consists of five chapters which relate the story in a generally chronological fashion. The time span is quite limited: The first chapter tells the events of the morning of the assassination; the second chapter relates the courtship of Angela Vicario by

Nassar up to the evening of the marriage; the third chapter covers that evening. In the fourth chapter, the narrator moves ahead in time, telling of events after the assassination, such as the autopsy. The last chapter returns to the original chronology, providing the graphic details of the killing the morning after the wedding. García Márquez' major accomplishment in this work is having written a story that maintains the reader's interest despite the fact that its denouement is announced in the first sentence.

The three constants in García Márquez' work are given varied importance, from *Leaf Storm* through *Chronicle of a Death Foretold*. His consistently antirationalist stance is a rejection of modern man's faith in reason. The transcendent regionalism is functional primarily in the fiction of Macondo: *Leaf Storm*, some of the short stories, and *One Hundred Years of Solitude*. All of his work creates mythic characters and patterns, although *One Hundred Years of Solitude* has the most universal resonance. For this reason, it will endure as a classic of Latin American literature.

Major publications other than long fiction
SHORT FICTION: *Los funerales de la Mamá Grande*, 1962; *Isabel viendo llover en Macondo*, 1967 (*Monologue of Isabel Watching It Rain in Macondo*, 1972); *No One Writes to the Colonel and Other Stories*, 1968; *Relato de un náufrago*, 1970; *La increíble y triste historia de la Cándida Eréndira y de su abuela desalmada*, 1972 (*Innocent Erendira and Other Stories*, 1978); *Leaf Storm and Other Stories*, 1972; *El negro que hizo esperar a los ángeles*, 1972; *Ojos de perro azul*, 1972; *Todos los cuentos de Gabriel García Márquez*, 1975.
NONFICTION: *La novela en américa latina: Diálogo*, 1968; *Cuando era feliz e indocumentado*, 1973; *Operación Carlota*, 1977; *Periodismo militante*, 1978; *El olor de la guayaba*, 1982 (*The Smell of Guava*, 1984).

Bibliography
Guibert, Rita. *Seven Voices*, 1973.
Harss, Luis, and Barbara Dohmann. *Into the Mainstream: Conversations with Latin-American Writers*, 1967.
Janes, Regina. *Gabriel García Márquez: Revolutions in Wonderland*, 1981.
McMurray, George R. *Gabriel García Márquez*, 1977.
Vargas Llosa, Mario. *García Márquez: Historia de un deicido*. 1971.

Raymond L. Williams

JEAN GENET

Born: Paris, France; December 19, 1910

Principal long fiction

Notre-Dame des Fleurs, 1944, 1951 (*Our Lady of the Flowers*, 1949); *Miracle de la rose*, 1946, 1951 (*Miracle of the Rose*, 1966); *Pompes funèbres*, 1947, 1953 (*Funeral Rites*, 1968); *Querelle de Brest*, 1947, 1953 (*Querelle of Brest*, 1966); *Oeuvres complètes*, 1952 (4 volumes).

Other literary forms

Jean Genet opened his literary career with a small group of highly personal lyric poems, beginning with "Le Condamné à mort" ("The Man Condemned to Death"). His poems are collected in *Poèmes* (1948).

Genet has published several plays, including *Les Bonnes* (1947; *The Maids*, 1954), *Haute surveillance* (1949; *Deathwatch*, 1954), *Le Balcon* (1956; *The Balcony*, 1957), *Les Nègres* (1958; *The Blacks*, 1960), and *Les Paravents* (1961; *The Screens*, 1962). A so-called autobiography, *Journal du voleur* (1948, 1949; *The Thief's Journal*, 1954), contains probably more allegory than fact, but it remains the only source available covering the early years of Genet's life. His ballet scenario, *'Adame miroir*, was performed by the Ballets Roland Petit, with music by Darius Milhaud, in 1946. Genet's nonfiction includes essays on the philosophy of art, such as "L'Atelier d'Alberto Giacometti" ("Giacometti's Studio") of 1957 and "Le Funambule" ("The Funambulists") of 1958, and essays dealing with dramatic theory, of which the most important by far is the "Lettre à Pauvert sur les bonnes," an open letter to the publisher Jean-Jacques Pauvert written in 1954 including letters to Roger Blin (collected as *Letters to Roger Blin*, 1969) and various prefaces to his own plays. Genet also wrote a series of sociopolitical broadsheets, beginning with "L'Enfant criminel" ("The Child-Criminal") of 1949 and leading to a sequence of pamphlets in defense of the Black Panthers (perhaps epitomized in his "May-Day Speech" of 1968) and of the Palestinian liberation movement.

Achievements

In any attempt to assess Genet's achievement as a novelist, it is essential to separate his qualities as a writer from what might be termed the "sociological" aspect of his subject matter. Though the two interact, in the critical period between 1945 and 1965 it was the nonliterary import of his work that predominated. Genet's name came to be synonymous with the growing demand of the post-World War II generation to read what it wanted to read and to learn the truth about the less palatable aspects of the human condition, regardless of what a paternalistic censorship might decide was good for it.

In this attempt to break through the barriers of what now seems like an antiquated obscurantism but what until less than a generation ago was a powerful and deeply rooted social attitude, Genet did not stand alone. In this respect, he trod in the footsteps of James Joyce and D. H. Lawrence, of Marcel Proust and Jean Cocteau; among his contemporaries, Norman Mailer, Henry Miller, and Vladimir Nabokov were inspired by similar aims. The battle over Lawrence's *Lady Chatterley's Lover* (1928) was fought and won in 1961; behind the writers stood a small group of publishers (Grove Press in New York, Gallimard in Paris, Rowohlt-Verlag in Hamburg, Anthony Blond in London) who were prepared to fight their cases through the courts. In comparison with many of his contemporaries, Genet had one distinct advantage: He wrote in French. French censorship allowed greater latitude to "clandestine" publications (usually in the form of "limited editions," available to subscribers only) than did that of other countries. This same censorship turned a blind eye to books which, although published in France, were in languages other than French (hence the fact that Genet's earliest translator, Bernard Frechtman, lived and worked in Paris). The French magistrates presiding at censorship trials had always at the back of their minds the specter of that guffaw of disbelieving ridicule which still echoes over their predecessors, who, within the space of half a dozen years, had condemned as "immoral" both Gustave Flaubert's *Madame Bovary* (1857; English translation, 1886) and Charles Baudelaire's *Les Fleurs du mal* (1857, 1861, 1868; *Flowers of Evil*, 1909).

As a result, Genet, who never once resorted to anonymity or sought to disguise who or what he was, was able to appear in print with material whose publication would have been inconceivable at that time in other societies or under other conditions. It was at this point that the quality, both of his writing and of his thought, became significant, for it won over to his cause a group of eminent figures who would scarcely have bothered to jeopardize their own reputations by championing a mere "pornographer." Thus, in 1950, when the prestigious firm Gallimard decided to risk publishing Genet's four novels (expurgated remarkably lightly) together with a selection of the early poems, the editors were able to call upon Jean-Paul Sartre, the leading intellectual of his generation, to write an introduction. This introduction, moreover, which appeared in 1952, constitutes what is one of the most significant treatises on ethics that have been written in the present century: *Saint-Genet, comédien et martyr (Saint Genet, Actor and Martyr,* 1963).

French literature from the eighteenth century onward can boast of a long tradition of writers—from Jean-Jacques Rousseau and the Marquis de Sade, by way of Guillaume Apollinaire, to Jean Paulhan, Georges Bataille, and Monique Wittig—who have used the "pornographic" novel (that is, the novel whose principal material resides in the detailed description of extreme and violent forms of sexual experience) not merely to titillate the reader's imagination but for positive and serious purposes of their own. These purposes vary: The intention may be one of self-analysis or of "confession"; it may be a concern with the absolutes of realism; or it may be a matter of denouncing the hypocrisies and the false assumptions by which the majority of "right-thinking people" choose to live. Mystics have been fascinated by the "surreal" quality of erotic experience, but so have anthropologists. The violence of sexual intensity constitutes one of the most readily accessible means of intuiting a dimension of irrational transcendentality; progressively, as European thought has moved toward a climate of materialist rationalism, the attraction of the irrational has grown more powerful. It is perhaps Genet's most significant achievement, in this quasi-sociological domain, to have brought for the first time into the full light of intellectual consciousness the role that "inadmissible" dimensions of experience may play in man's objective assessment of himself. To describe this, in Freudian terms, merely as "beneath the ego lies the id" is to bury it under the colorless abstractions of a Viennese-based scientific observer trained by Jean-Martin Charcot. Genet, in the characters of Divine and Mignon, of Bulkaen and Harcamone, of Jean Decarnin and of the Brothers Querelle, clothes these aspects of the human psyche in flesh and blood, illuminates them with the brilliant and torturous recall of his own experiences, and gives them an unforgettable reality.

Biography

The career of Jean Genet has often been compared to that of his late-medieval predecessor, the thief and poet François Villon. That Genet was a thief is undeniable; the interest lies in how he was transmuted into a poet.

The solid facts concerning Genet's early life are few, because, for reasons that are both literary and personal, he has been at great pains to transmute them into his "legend." Born on December 19, 1910, in a public maternity ward on the rue d'Assas in Paris, the child of a prostitute and an unknown father, Genet was adopted by the Assistance Publique (the national foundling society) and, as soon as he could crawl, was sent off to foster parents in the hill country of Le Morvan, between Dijon and Nevers. There, growing up with a classic sense of insecurity, he took to petty thieving and, by the age of ten, was branded irrevocably as a thief. Many years later, probably under the influence of Sartre's philosophy of Existential choice, he attributed to this critical period of his life a positive significance: His "self" was that which he was for "others"; because, for others, he was a "thief," a thief was what he must necessarily be. How much of this persona is fact and how much is legend is impossible to determine. At all events, by his early teens, Genet found himself confined to a reformatory for juvenile criminals at Mettray, a few miles north of Tours; there, he was subjected to all the most brutal forms of assault and seduction common to establishments of that type. How and when he was released, or escaped, is unknown, as is most of his career during the next ten years or more. He appears, on the one hand, to have developed as a classic layabout—a male prostitute, a skilled pickpocket, a semiskilled shoplifter and a remarkably unskilled burglar (burglary, considered as an exercise in poetic ecstasy, would not lead to the best results). His vagabond existence took him to Spain and then to North Africa, where he developed a feeling of kinship with the Arab victims of colonization that was later to emerge in *The Screens*. On the other hand, and less ostentatiously, he pursued a career as an assiduous autodidact who, on an occasion when he was arrested for stealing a volume of poems by Paul Verlaine, was more concerned with the quality of the poetry than with the commercial value of the book itself.

These two strains—criminality and poetry—would seem to have run together in not uncomfortable harness for a dozen years or more. According to one source, when Genet was sixteen, he worked as guide and companion to a blind poet, René de Buxeuil, from whom he learned at least the rudiments of French prosody, if not also the principles of Charles Maurras' Fascism. Some years later, in 1936 or 1937, he deserted from the Bataillons d'Afrique (the notorious "Bat' d'Af"—the punitive division of the French army in North Africa), after having struck an officer and stolen his suitcases, illegally crossing frontiers in Central Europe and running a racket involving fake or clandestine currency. Yet, in the same period, he taught French literature to the daughter of a leading gynecologist in Brno, Moravia, writing her long letters in which explications of Arthur Rimbaud's "Le Bâteau ivre" ("The Drunken Boat") alternate with laments for the fall of Léon Blum's Front Populaire in June, 1937. His next arrest, in or about 1938, was, according to some authorities, for stealing a car; according to others, it was for forging documents to save Republican refugees from the Spanish Civil War.

Which arrest for which cause led him to the prison at Fresnes in 1942 is again unknown. What is certain is that it was during this period of detention that Genet wrote his first published poem, "The Man Condemned to Death," and also drafted his first novel, *Our Lady of the Flowers*—according to the legend, on stolen brown paper; when the first draft was discovered and confiscated by a warder, Genet simply began all over again.

During this period there was a visitor to the prison at Fresnes named Olga Barbezat. Her husband, Marc Barbezat, owned a small press, L'Arbalète, in Lyons, and his friends included Jean Cocteau, while she herself had for some years been acquainted with Simone de Beauvoir. Genet's manuscripts began to circulate, and it was Cocteau who first acclaimed them as works of genius. When Genet had been released and arrested yet again (the "volume of Verlaine" episode), Cocteau himself appeared among the witnesses in court for the defense, declaring publicly that he considered Genet to be "the greatest writer in France." The outcome is again unknown, but Genet nevertheless continued his dual career as a brilliant writer and an incompetent burglar. Between 1942 and 1946, he appears to have written all four of his novels, as well as *The Thief's Journal* and the plays *Deathwatch* and *The Maids*. *Our Lady of the Flowers* was published in September, 1944, and the other novels appeared in rapid succession over the next four years. Genet's name was becoming known; in 1948, however, he was arrested again, and on that occasion was sentenced to "perpetual preventive detention."

The circumstances of this final appearance of Genet-as-criminal are, as usual, obscure. According to his supporters, he had quixotically taken upon himself the crimes of one of his lovers, Jean de Carnin (the Jean Decarnin of *Funeral Rites*), who had died heroically fighting the Germans during the liberation of Paris some three years earlier. At all events, Genet had powerful backers. On July 16, 1948, the influential newspaper *Combat* addressed an open letter (signed by Sartre, Cocteau, and the literary editors of the paper, Maurice Nadeau and Maurice Saillet) to the President of the Republic, "imploring his clemency on behalf of a very great poet." The President, Vincent Auriol, was convinced, and a free pardon was granted. Since then, Genet has been merely a writer. "I don't steal the way I used to," he told an interviewer from *Playboy* (April, 1964) nearly two decades later. "But I continue to steal, in the sense that I continue to be dishonest with regard to society, which pretends that I am not."

Genet's later work, apart from the three plays *The Balcony*, *The Blacks*, and *The Screens*, all written during the 1950's, is comparatively slight; he has never repeated the great outburst of creativity that took hold of him between 1942 and 1948. His later works include a scattering of film scripts and critical essays in the 1960's, and, more recently, a series of short but searingly controversial articles in defense of the Black Panthers and of the Palestinian terrorists. It is as though, having employed literature to effect his own escape from degradation, he then had little further use for it. In the main, he would seem to have been content simply to be alive.

Analysis

The elements out of which Jean Genet contrives his vision of that haunting and monstrous "other" world, which lies carefully concealed beneath the controlled and rational surface of everydayness, all belong to previously accredited literary traditions; nevertheless, the balance, and consequently the overall impact, is new. The components can be analyzed as follows.

The confession: Both *Our Lady of the Flowers* and *Miracle of the Rose*, at least as much as the *The Thief's Journal*, are basically autobiographical and, in their original (perhaps subconscious) intention, would seem to have been inspired by a desire to *escape*—to escape from the intolerable degradations of existence as a petty criminal, convict, and male prostitute by externalizing these experiences through the rigorous and formal disciplines of prose and poetry, by projecting the self through words into the minds of others, thus making acceptable to them that which, without their connivance and acknowledgment, could not be acceptable to *him*. In one memorable phrase, Genet describes his pilgrimage through literature as "une marche vers l'homme": a progress toward virility—or, perhaps, simply away from dehumanization.

The "normalization" of homosexuality: To the nineteenth century mind, the homosexual was the ultimate social and moral outlaw, the criminal for whom there could exist no forgiveness. Progressively, the last fifty years have seen the weakening of these strictures: The homosexual, in his emotional relationships, is as "normal" as the heterosexual lover, perhaps even more so; because of his previous persecution, he has become almost a "hero of our times." If this attitude is not the most original feature of Genet's work, it nevertheless constitutes a powerful motivation: the concern to portray his own emotions as something as intense and as moving as those of "normal" human beings.

The Existential formation of the self: The intellectual relationship between Sartre and Genet is complex and still awaits analysis; what is clear is that if Genet was not only influenced by Sartre's *L'Être et le néant* (1943; *Being and Nothingness*, 1956) but indeed, according to his own confession, reduced for years to silence by the devastating accuracy of Sartre's psychophilosophical analysis of Genet's creative processes in *Saint-Genet, Actor and Martyr*, Sartre, likewise, at least in *Le Diable et le bon Dieu* (1951; *Lucifer and the Lord*, 1953), acknowledges his debt to Genet. Genet, in fact, takes the Sartrean ontology toward conclusions that Sartre himself hardly dared to explore. If the essence of the self is a void (*un néant*), then it can only "be," either what it *thinks* itself to be (according to Sartre) or what others think it to be (according to Genet). In either case, it can *know* itself to be what it is only in terms of the effectiveness of its actions (Sartre) or by looking at itself in the mirror (Genet). Yet, if I (a negative) look at myself and see my reflection (a positive) in the mirror, then that which is perceived (the inanimate-positive image) is more "real" than the perceiver (the animate-negative). Thus, the image is more "real" than the subject, the fake more "authentic" than the genuine. For Genet, "to be" (this is also a Beckettian theme) is "to be perceived"— especially in the mirror. Hence, Genet's fiction is pervaded by the image of the mirror and of the double—from the early ballet, '*Adame miroir*, to the last of the novels, *Querelle of Brest*, in which the identical twin brothers, Querelle and Robert, constitute an identity only by their absolute reflection of each other.

The reversal of moral values: If the fake is more authentic than the genuine, then, in moral terms also, the evil is more authentic than the good. Genet, brought up as a Catholic believer and profoundly influenced by another Christian believer, Dostoevski, argues as follows: Christ stated that the Kingdom of Heaven is for the humble; no man can *will* himself to be humble, any more than he can will himself to be a saint, without a degree of hypocrisy that destroys both humility and sanctity (this is, in fact, the theme of the play

Deathwatch). Humility, the supreme virtue of the true Christian, can be achieved only involuntarily: One can be truly humble only by being *humiliated*. Consequently, the most truly meritorious acts are those that result in a total rejection or humiliation by the community—for example, murder or treason. The murderer, therefore, or the traitor (or, on a lesser level, the sneak thief) comes closer to achieving "sanctity" than the parson or the social worker. This argument is well summed up in Lawrence's vitriolic parody:

> And the Dostoyevsky lot:
> 'Let me sin my way to Jesus!'—
> And so they sinned themselves off the face of the earth.

Divine of *Our Lady of the Flowers* would agree wholeheartedly.

The attack on the Establishment: Genet's Existential-Dostoevskian reversal of accepted moral values is basically a rationalization of his rejection of *all* values accepted by the French Establishment of his time. That does not mean, in any political sense, that he is a "revolutionary," because "the revolution" (as in *The Balcony*) implies the acceptance of a code of values as rigid as, and perhaps even more intolerant than, those which it claims to replace. In political terms, Genet is an anarchist in the most literal sense: The conformism of the Left is as repugnant to him as the conformism of the Right. Jews, blacks, criminals, Algerians, pimps, prostitutes—these are "his" people, the social outcasts, the "submerged tenth," as unwelcome to one regime as to another. From this point of view, *Funeral Rites*, while one of the weakest of Genet's novels, is at the same time one of his most significant. Ostensibly, its hero is one Jean Decarnin, a stalwart of the Resistance, Genet's lover. Yet no sooner is Decarnin dead than Genet embarks on a paean to all that is Nazi, for Hitler and for the jackbooted SS batallions that had trampled over the fair land of France. If the new Establishment is to be the victorious Resistance, then Genet is as emphatic in his rejection of it as he had been in his rejection of the *grande bourgeoisie* that had preceded it. Michel Leiris once argued that the so-called committed writer can justify his calling only if, like a bullfighter, he *genuinely* exposes himself to danger. Genet accepted the challenge, in a way that Leiris himself, for all of his intelligence, seems scarcely to have envisaged. If Genet rejected the bourgeoisie, it was not so much by writing as by *being* that which no Establishment can accept. Therefore, with deliberate delight, Genet, even when he was an acknowledged poet, continued to be an inefficient burglar: The last of his protests against a society which stole "in a different way."

One of the most intriguing features of the Parisian underworld of criminals, pimps, and prostitutes is its tradition of bestowing upon this unlovely riffraff the most elaborate and frequently the most haunting of poetic nicknames. It is as though the highest form of human aspiration stood guard over the most debased of its activities. This is the paradox which Genet, with his passion for masks and symbols, for those moments of "mystic" revelation in which an object is perceived simultaneously to be itself and not itself, takes as the starting point of his first and, in the opinion of many critics, his best novel. The "magical" name Our Lady of the Flowers (which is also the designation of Filippo Brunelleschi's noble Florence Cathedral), conceals beneath its high sonorities the sordid reality of a moronic adolescent thug, one Adrien Baillon, a former butcher-boy and author of a particularly brutal and senseless murder; "Darling" (Mignon-les-Petits-Pieds) turns out to be a stereotypical muscle-man, pimp, and shoplifter; and "Divine," the hero (or rather, the heroine, for that is how "she" would prefer it), is a transvestite male streetwalker, as are "her" companions of the sidewalk, "Mimosa II" (René Hirsch), "First-Communion" (Antoine Berthollet), and "Lady-Apple" ("Pomme d'Api," or Eugène Marceau), among others: "A host, a long litany of beings who *are* the bright explosion of their names." Half or more of these names have religious connotations, notably that of Divine herself, for surely the most beautiful of masks is that of the Son of God, even if it serves to hide a more-than-Dantesque inferno.

There is no conventional "plot" to *Our Lady of the Flowers*, any more than there is to its successor, *Miracle of the Rose*. Because both of Genet's first two novels are, in part at least, autobiographical (the actual process of writing them was, for their author, a means of liberation, of escape from anonymous degradation, sexual abjection, and possible madness), their structure is as complex as life itself. How Louis Culafroy *became* Divine, how Divine *became* Genet-in-prison, is not told; few things interest Genet less than a coherent narrative in time. The episodes are superimposed on one another, absorbed into one another, so that the beginning is the funeral of Divine and the end is the death of Divine, and both are interwoven with the voice of Genet, who "is" Divine and who is dead and yet alive. The central figure is always Divine, who, in "her" precious dialect of a painted and decaying transvestite, pursues the unending *via dolorosa* laid down for her by her quest for the Absolute.

Divine's most terrifying characteristic is her purity, for hers is a demoniac chastity, born where good and evil meet, the purity of that hell which lies beyond Hell and which consequently drags all those who cannot follow her as far down into the depths as she herself has plunged, toward death and perdition. Her lovers are caught, one by one, in the toils of her "sanctity" and annihilated. Even Our Lady, the "sublime" adolescent strangler, becomes possessed (almost in the biblical sense) with the spirit, or rather with the gestures, of Divine, and confesses to his crime, gratuitously and needlessly— needlessly, in terms of everyday values, but *necessarily* in the context of Divine's world, where the figure has no reality without the image, nor the criminal without his punishment, and where damnation is essential to justify the ways of God to man. Confession is not repentance but defiance without repentance. If God is infinitely high above man exactly to the extent that man is infinitely far below God, then the supreme exaltation and glorification of God lies in *willing* the opposite of God, which is evil, and, with evil, its punishment. Then, and then only, are the two halves joined and the cycle completed.

In place of plot, then, *Our Lady of the Flowers* interweaves variations on a theme; this theme is the relationship between God and his most ignominious creation, man. The vision of God, for that contemporary mystic Genet, owes much to Dostoevski, something to village-church Catholicism, and most of all to post-Freudian anthropology. From Dostoevski comes Genet's obsession with the figure of the *humiliated* Christ—the Christ Who, through His humiliation, bears away the sins of the world—and of the saint who achieves his sanctity through his very degradation. From village Catholicism (albeit oddly distorted) come the Cherubim and the Archangels, the crude plaster statuettes of the Blessèd Virgin working fake miracles. From the anthropologists comes the notion of transgression: the sophisticated equivalent of the taboo. What transforms Genet's antiheroes from subjects of psychiatric case histories, or instances in a criminologist's notebook, into symbols of a metaphysical reality is the fact that they violate not laws, but taboos.

Hence, in *Our Lady of the Flowers*, Genet is interested in crime and in criminals only insofar as they perpetrate a sacrilege, that is, insofar as they violate the laws, not of society, but of that Other Dimension which is God. In one of his allegories, or "parables," Genet sees himself thwarting God. Here lies the key to Genet's attitudes and, furthermore, to the significance of Divine and Darling and Our Lady. They are at death-grips with God, because God offers them sanctity and salvation on *His* terms. They are tempted, but they will not be bullied. They are human beings, and they have one inalienable right: to be what they are. God would take away from them this right, so they defy God. If they are destined for sanctity, they are resolved to achieve it in their own way, not God's. They will plunge headfirst into the mire; their abjection is their dignity; their degradation is their ultimate authenticity. God has sided with society; therefore, God has betrayed them. Not for that, though, will they renounce God's kingdom, but they will get there by diving headforemost into the ditch which reflects the stars—the mirror image of Heaven.

Genet's second novel, *Miracle of the Rose*, contains at least as much, if not more, autobiographical material than the first. In *Our Lady of the Flowers*, both Divine and the child, Culafroy, are semimythical figures, all immediate reality being concealed beneath a golden mask of signs and symbols. In *Miracle of the Rose*, by contrast, Genet speaks in his own name. The "I" who endures (and endows with "magic") the sordid and stultifying brutality of the great prison-fortress of Fontevrault—now redeemed from that function and restored to its former status as a minor château de la Loire—is the same "I" who earlier had been subjected to the vicious cruelty of the reformatory at Mettray, a few miles to the northeast. In neither novel is the material, in any usual sense, "romanticized." The misery and horror, the nightmarish ugliness of the life that Genet describes, is never glossed over. On the contrary, it is portrayed lingeringly in all of its nauseating detail, and the ingenious sadism by which a vengeful society deliberately sets out to reduce its victims to a level considerably below that of animals is, if anything, exaggerated. The signs and the symbols are still present and still serve to transmute prison latrines and punishment blocks into miracles and roses, but the symbolism is rather more self-conscious and therefore more self-revealing. In consequence, the reality underlying these symbols is not concealed as much as it is heightened, given a spiritual or aesthetic significance without ever losing sight of its grim and ugly materiality.

The Central Prison (La Centrale) of Fontevrault is an isolated community cut off from the rest of the world, cruel, intense, superstitious, hierarchical and ascetic—not very different from the medieval abbey, with its dependent monasteries and convents, that had originally occupied the same site. The convicts of the present are simultaneously the monks and lay brothers of the long-dead past, an identification that destroys the intervening barrier of time, thus giving the whole prison a dreamlike and "sacred" quality which Genet discreetly emphasizes by setting the time of his own arrival there late on Christmas Eve: "The prison lived like a cathedral at midnight . . . We belonged to the Middle Ages." Thus Genet establishes the basic structure of *Miracle of the Rose*, which consists in eliminating the "profane" dimension of time by superimposing different fragments of experience-in-time, identifying them and allowing them to interpenetrate so that the reality that survives is outside time altogether.

Undoubtedly, *Miracle of the Rose* owes something to Proust's *À la recherche du temps perdu* (1913-1927; *Remembrance of Things Past*, 1922-1931); it is understandable that Genet, comparing his own childhood with that of the wealthy, spoiled hypochondriacal young Marcel, must have felt a definite sense of alienation. *Miracle of the Rose*, however, differs from the Proustian narrative in its superimposition of a third plane of experience over and above Marcel's levels of time past and time present.

That plane is the plane of the sacred, of existence which is still technically *in* life but, in fact, outside life, space, and time alike—the level of experience that is symbolized by Harcamone. Harcamone, from the mystic solitude of his condemned cell, is already "beyond life"; he lives a "dead life," experiencing the "heartbreaking sweetness of being out of the world before death." Harcamone has, in fact, through his transgression and later through his condemnation, attained that level of sanctity, isolation, and total detachment from profane reality to which Divine aspired yet which he failed to reach— the level at which all miracles are possible. Genet and his convict-lovers,

Bulkaen and Divers, exist simultaneously on two planes, in time and space; Harcamone, on three. Consequently, it is Harcamone who dominates the rest—and not only dominates but, being himself a symbol, gives meaning to all the other symbols which compose the worlds of Fontevrault and of Mettray.

As in *Our Lady of the Flowers*, there is no plot in *Miracle of the Rose*. It is a closely woven, glittering tapestry of memories and of symbols. It is not, however, a Symbolist novel; it is rather, a novel wherein the obsessions of memory fuse into the totality of a significant experience through the multiplicity of symbols with which they are illuminated. Frogs become princes while still remaining frogs. Murderers are changed into roses (Genet, incidentally, dislikes flowers) while still remaining murderers. Harcamone, the murderer, is the Rose of Death, yet the warder he killed was known as "Bois de Rose," recalling the rosewood used for coffins. The rose is head and heart and dex; cut off from its stem, it falls as heavily to the ground as the head beneath the knife of the guillotine; it is mourning, it is mystery, it is passion. It is beauty that symbolizes its mirror-opposite, evil and ugliness; it is paradox, blossoming simultaneously in the profane and sacred worlds. It is the Head of Christ and the Crown of Thorns. It is the Miracle and the symbol of the Miracle; it is profanation, transgression, and ultimately—in Genet's special sense—sanctity.

Once Genet began to outgrow his basically autobiographical inspiration, his novels became less impressive; after *Miracle of the Rose*, it was the drama that was destined to become his true medium of expression. *Funeral Rites*, although it contains many interesting ideas in embryo, is the weakest of his full-length published works. Its technique is uncertain: Deprived of the electrifying impulse given by the memory of his own humiliations, Genet descends to the level of the commonplace novelist struggling with the exigencies of a conventional plot.

By contrast, *Querelle of Brest* is the most technically sophisticated of Genet's novels. It is less lyric, less subjective, less poetic, and perhaps less haunting than *Our Lady of the Flowers*; on the other hand, it has a far more substantial structure, it develops its themes with a persistence in logic (or antilogic) which was missing from the earlier works; it creates a whole new range of characters, symbols, and images to replace the purely personal obsessions of *Our Lady of the Flowers*; finally, in the character of Madame Lysiane, it introduces for the first time a woman who plays an essential part in the development of the plot.

From the outset, Genet's metaphysic was based on the symbol of the mirror. The self had reality only as observed by the other (as image and reflection), but this dual self could be granted authenticity only if apprehended simultaneously by a third source of awareness. Claire and Solange (in *The Maids*) are reflections of each other; their "reality" depends upon Madame, whose consciousness alone can embrace both. In *Querelle of Brest*, this theme of the double is worked out in greater complexity and is pushed toward its inevitable and logical conclusion. What previously was a mirror image is now literally incarnated in the double (Georges Querelle and his identical-twin brother Robert), while the "observers" are equally duplicated (Madame Lysiane and Lieutenant Seblon). To complicate the pattern, both Georges Querelle and Lieutenant Seblon—respectively a seaman and an officer in the French navy—are "doubled" by being both "themselves as they are" and the image or reflection of themselves presented to the world by the uniforms they wear. The double, with all its intricacies of significance in Genet's aesthetic, is the central theme of *Querelle of Brest*.

Genet, to begin, presents a double murder. In the everlasting fogs and granite-veiling mists of the traditional French naval base of Brest, Querelle murders Vic, his messmate, who was his accomplice in smuggling opium past the watchful eyes of the customs officers; perhaps in the same instant, Gil Turko, a young stonemason employed as a construction worker in the dockyard, goaded beyond endurance by the taunting contempt of Théo, a middle-aged fellow construction worker, fills himself with brandy to fire his courage and slashes his enemy's throat with the butt end of a broken bottle. From this moment onward, the two alien destinies begin to coincide—with this difference: Whereas Gil, terrified and hiding from the police in the ruined shell of the ancient galley slaves' prison by the Vieux Port, is the victim, Querelle is the master of his fate, or at least as near master as any mortal can hope to be. Querelle sees in Gil his own reflection, his imitator, his young apprentice who might one day grow up to be the equivalent of himself. He takes care of Gil, feeds him, argues with him, encourages him, secretly exploits him, and finally, for good measure, betrays him to the police. The relationship between Georges Querelle and Gil Turko is, however, only the central relationship in a series of doubles; not only is Georges Querelle doubled by his twin brother Robert, but Madame Lysiane, who loves Robert, also loves Querelle and at most times is unable to distinguish between them. Mario, the Chief of Police in Brest, finds his double in Norbert ("Nono"), the proprietor of the most favored brothel in the dock area, La Féria, and the husband of Madame Lysiane. Even in the absence of character pairs there are mirrors: the great wall mirrors of La Féria, against which a man can lean, propping himself against his own reflection so that he "appears to be propped up against himself."

The arguments of *Querelle of Brest*, both moral and metaphysical, are ingenious, intricate, and awkwardly paradoxical; as usual, they owe much to Dostoevski and something to the Marquis de Sade. Thomas De Quincey, writing "On Murder Considered as One of the Fine Arts," might have learned something from Querelle, just as Querelle might have learned something from Oscar Wilde's "Pen, Pencil and Poison." The outstanding achievement of the novel, however, lies in the way in which structure, plot, argument, and symbols are integrated, forming an imaginative pattern in which every element serves to reinforce the others. The symbol of Querelle's dangerous virility is the granitic, the vertical. Querelle, on the other hand, is flexible and smiling. His symbol is transferred outside himself: It is the ramparts of Brest where he murders Vic; it is the dockyard wall over which the packet of opium must be passed; it is the walls of La Rochelle in Querelle's childhood memories. In the place of roses and angels, Genet is now using a much more abstract, sophisticated, and, in the end, powerful type of symbol. There is a geometrical precision, both of imagery and of argument, in *Querelle of Brest*, which contrasts significantly with the comparative formlessness, the viscosity, and the self-indulgent subjectivity of *Our Lady of the Flowers* or of *Miracle of the Rose*.

In his autobiographical *The Thief's Journal*, Genet refers at one point to his "decision to write pornographic books." As a statement, this is categorical; in any context (not only in that of the 1940's), Genet's novels are unquestionably and deliberately pornographic. There are passages which, even now, are difficult to read without a sickening feeling of disgust: the animality of man is unspeakable, so why speak of it?

In earlier generations, Puritans spoke with similar disgust of the "beastliness" of human appetites. The only difference, compared with Genet, is that they spoke in generalities, allegories, or abstractions. When John Milton's Comus appeared (in *Comus*, 1634), it was in the company of a "rout of monsters, headed like sundry sorts of beasts, but otherwise like men and women, their apparel glistening." The rest of *Comus*, however, is pure poetry; the "rout of monsters" is forgotten. Genet parades before us a similar rout of monsters, but he does not forget about them. Nor, in the last analysis, is he less puritanical than Milton. The exquisite ecstasy of disgust with human sexuality is something that he has known from personal experience; if he chooses to speak of it, it is at least with an authority greater than Milton's. Pushed to its ultimate indignities, pornography becomes puritanism, and puritanical pornography is instinct with poetry. Every word that Genet uses is selected with rigorous and elaborate precision. Divine and her transvestite companions are "the bright explosion [*l'éclaté*] of their names." *L'éclaté* is a rare and precious seventeenth century word, not listed in modern dictionaries, dragged by Genet out of its antique obscurity because it alone possessed the jewellike precision of the poetic nuance he wished to convey. Genet's pornography is poetry of the highest, most rigorous, and most uncompromising order.

Major publications other than long fiction

PLAYS: *Les Bonnes*, 1947 (*The Maids*, 1954); *Haute surveillance*, 1949 (written 1944-1945; *Deathwatch*, 1954); *Le Balcon*, 1956 (*The Balcony*, 1957); *Les Nègres*, 1958 (*The Blacks*, 1960); *Les Paravents*, 1961 (*The Screens*, 1962).

POETRY: *Poèmes*, 1948.

NONFICTION: *Journal du voleur*, 1948, 1949 (*The Thief's Journal*, 1954);
Letters to Roger Blin, 1969.

MISCELLANEOUS: *'Adame miroir*, 1946 (ballet scenario); *Oeuvres complètes*, 1952 (4 volumes; includes poetry).

Bibliography

Aslan, Odette, ed. *Jean Genet: Points de vue critiques, témoignages*, 1973.
Bonnefoy, Claude. *Genet*, 1965.
Brooks, Peter, and Joseph Halpern, eds. *Genet: A Collection of Essays*, 1979.
Coe, Richard N. "Unbalanced Opinions: A Study of Jean Genet and the French Critics," in *Proceedings of the Leeds Philosophical and Literary Society* (Literary and Historical Section). XIV, part 2 (June, 1970), pp. 27-73.
——————. *The Vision of Jean Genet*, 1968.
Driver, T. F. *Jean Genet*, 1966.
Knapp, Bettina. *Jean Genet*, 1968.
Luckow, M. *Die Homosexualität in der literarischen Tradition: Studien zu den Romanen von Genet*, 1962.
McMahon, Joseph H. *The Imagination of Jean Genet*, 1963.
Magnan, Jean-Marie. *Pour un blason de Jean Genet: Un Essai*, 1966.
Naish, Camille. *A Genetic Approach to Structures in the Work of Jean Genet*, 1978.
Sartre, Jean-Paul. *Saint-Genet, Actor and Martyr*, 1963.
Thody, Philip. *Jean Genet: A Study of His Work*, 1968.

Richard N. Coe

ANDRÉ GIDE

Born: Paris, France; November 22, 1869
Died: Paris, France; February 19, 1951

Principal long fiction

L'Immoraliste, 1902 (*The Immoralist*, 1930); *La Porte étroite*, 1909 (*Strait Is the Gate*, 1924); *Les Caves du Vatican*, 1914 (*The Vatican Swindle*, 1925; better known as *Lafcadio's Adventures*, 1927); *La Symphonie pastorale*, 1919 (*The Pastoral Symphony*, 1931); *Les Faux-monnayeurs*, 1925 (*The Counterfeiters*, 1927); *Thésée*, 1946 (*Theseus*, 1950).

Other literary forms

André Gide began his literary career with a number of prose works that defy conventional classification; among them are poetic works in prose, such as *Les Cahiers d'André Walter*((1891; *The Notebooks of André Walter*, 1968) and *Les Nourritures terrestres* (1897; *Fruits of the Earth*, 1949), and the stories *Paludes* (1895; *Marshlands*, 1953) and *Le Prométhée mal enchaîné* (1899; *Prometheus Misbound*, 1953). Although closely related to his development as a novelist, such works are perhaps best described as lyric essays discussing the nature and limits of human freedom. Gide is known also for his *Journal* (1939-1950, 1954; *The Journals of André Gide, 1889-1949*, 1947-1951); several autobiographical volumes, including *Si le grain ne meurt* (1926; *If It Die . . .*, 1935) and *Et nunc manet in te* (1947, 1951; *Madeleine*, 1952); and the travelogues *Voyage au Congo* (1927; *Travels in the Congo*, 1929) and *Retour de l'U.R.S.S.* (1936; *Return from the U.S.S.R.*, 1937). As early as 1899, Gide also applied his talents to the writing of plays; the products of these efforts are rarely performed but were published in English in the collection *My Theater* (1952), a year after the author's death at the age of eighty-one.

Achievements

Despite the relatively small portion of his output that can be classified legitimately as prose fiction, Gide ranks among the most internationally influential French novelists of his time. With the notable exception of Marcel Proust (1871-1922), Gide was the preeminent French novelist of the period between 1900 and 1950, even though he refused to apply the term "novel" to all but one of his extended prose narratives. Although his reputation declined somewhat during the two decades immediately following his death, he is now regarded among the major figures, both as theoretician and as practitioner, in the history of modern prose fiction.

Belonging, along with Proust and the somewhat younger François Mauriac (1885-1970), to the last generation of French writers whose private means released them from the need to earn a living, Gide wrote at first in order to discover and define himself, initially supplying the costs of publication out of his own pocket. Influenced at the beginning of his career by the Decadent and Symbolist movements, Gide's work soon assumed a personal stamp and direction, acquiring universality even as the author sought primarily to find the best possible expression for his own particular concerns. *Fruits of the Earth*, a lyric meditation published in 1897, established Gide's promise as an original writer and a rising literary figure, although it was not until some twenty years later, during and after World War I, that the book would render its author famous (or infamous) for his inspiration (or corruption) of an entire generation of European youth. By that time, Gide's audacious speculations on the nature of freedom and identity had found expression also in the form of extended narratives for which the author adamantly denied the appelation "novel," preferring such recondite (and attention-getting) alternatives as *récit* (tale) or *sotie*, the latter a term for a satiric improvisation performed by French law students during the late Middle Ages.

Such early *récits* as *The Immoralist* and *Strait Is the Gate* established Gide as a master of psychological narrative; *Lafcadio's Adventures*, published in 1914 as a *sotie*, demonstrated Gide's mastery of social satire, with multiple narratives and viewpoints. In *The Pastoral Symphony*, published in 1919, perhaps the most widely read of Gide's prose narratives, he skillfully combined the psychological and satiric strains. It was not, however, until 1925 that Gide saw fit, with *The Counterfeiters*, to publish a book plainly labeled as a "novel" (*roman*). The result was one of the most widely read and influential novels of the decade—indeed, of the entire period between the two world wars and afterward, in view of its considerable effect upon such later developments as the New Novel of the 1950's.

After *The Counterfeiters*, Gide wrote extensively in a variety of genres, although among his later major efforts only *Theseus* might reasonably be considered as extended fiction. Among the first (and oldest) of literary celebrities to be extensively photographed and interviewed, the otherwise reticent Gide spent his later years as an internationally famous literary figure, receiving the Nobel Prize for Literature in 1947, not long after the publication of *Theseus*.

Perhaps correctly identified as a precursor of many significant developments in modern and postmodern fiction, Gide was among the first writers, along with Hermann Hesse (1877-1962), to explore the changing relationships between the individual and society, raising serious epistemological questions with regard to the nature of human identity. He is respected also as a master of prose style in his native language, having perfected a spare, neoclassical sentence that is almost instantly recognizable yet difficult to imitate.

Biography

André Paul Guillaume Gide was born in Paris on November 22, 1869, the only child of Paul Gide (a law professor) and the former Juliette Rondeaux. A shy, introspective boy, inevitably influenced by his parents' severe Protestantism, Gide soon perceived in himself an avid sexuality that would tend toward inversion; as early as the age of seven, he was expelled from school for masturbation and would remain haunted for life by a nagging guilt that he kept trying to neutralize through his various writings. The death of his father in 1880, at the age of forty-seven, added further complication to an already troubled childhood, and Gide would soon undergo treatment for a variety of nervous disorders. Around the age of thirteen, Gide developed a strong, lifelong attachment to his first cousin Madeleine Rondeaux, two years his senior, who became his wife soon after the death of his mother in 1895. Their marriage, although never consummated, was the dominant emotional relationship of Gide's life and ended only with Madeleine's death in 1938 at the age of seventy-one.

Even before his marriage, Gide had begun to emerge as a potential literary figure, thanks in part to a curious work that was written initially with Madeleine in mind. *The Notebooks of André Walter*, privately published in 1891 at the young author's expense, purports to be the diary of a young man, by then deceased, describing his love for one Emmanuèle, under which name Madeleine Rondeaux appears in thin disguise. Although the book failed to sell, it was disseminated within Parisian artistic circles, and Gide continued writing, producing such documents as the Symbolist parable *Le Traité du Narcisse* (1891; "Narcissus," in *The Return of the Prodigal Son*, 1953), the proto-novel *Le Voyage d'Urien* (1893; *Urien's Voyage*, 1964), and the experimental *Paludes*, about a young man who is planning a novel to be called *Paludes*. In 1893, Gide at long last came to terms with his latent homosexuality during the course of a trip to North Africa, the details of which would receive chaste (but, for that time, explicit) fictional treatment in *The Immoralist*. Having for all practical purposes discontinued his formal education after belatedly passing the *baccalauréat* on his second attempt, in 1889, Gide nevertheless continued to develop as a self-taught intellectual, reading widely and participating fully in the vigorous cultural activity then centered in Paris. His first truly significant publication, *Fruits of the Earth*, begun as early as the trip to North Africa, was finished shortly after his marriage to Madeleine but was not published until 1897.

Gide's marriage, discussed at considerable length by numerous commentators as well as by Gide himself, remained a dominant feature of both his life and his work. There is little doubt that his love for Madeleine was as deep and intense as it was otherworldly, firmly rooted in the oddly protective emotion that had overwhelmed him when Madeleine was fifteen and he was two years younger. Like her fictional counterpart, Alissa, in *Strait Is the Gate*, Madeleine had recently discovered her own mother's marital infidelity and was quite undone by what she had learned; André, although little more than a child (and a disturbed child at that), instinctively sought to comfort his cousin. There was thus at the base of their affective relationship a denial of the physical that would never really change. Commentator Thomas Cordle, inspired in part by Denis de Rougemont's landmark essay *L'Amour et l'occident* (1939; *Love in the Western World*, 1983), sees in Gide's love for Madeleine a personification of heretical Catharist doctrine as perpetuated in the Tristan legend; in any case, the nature of Gide's love was such that the prospect of consummation might well have threatened to corrupt its "purity."

Madeleine, for her part, was surely not unaware of her cousin's sexual ambiguities by the time she consented to marry him, after several prior refusals; it is likely, too, that she shared his instinctive horror of the physical, although she appears at one time to have contemplated the possibility of pregnancy and childbirth. In either event, the union appears to have proceeded with relative mutual satisfaction until 1918, when Madeleine, bitter over Gide's apparent homosexual "elopement" with the future film director Marc Allégret (1900-1973), burned all the letters that André had written to her since their adolescence. Gide, claiming those letters to have been the only true record of his life and an irreplaceable personal treasure, decided that Madeleine's spiteful gesture had ruined his career; most of Gide's commentators agree that his career, although not in fact ruined, developed thereafter in a different direction from that it might otherwise have taken. The author's marriage, although not ruined either, remained seriously flawed for the remainder of Madeleine's life. Gide's only child, duly christened Catherine Gide, was born in 1923 to Elizabeth van Rysselberghe, daughter of Gide's close friends Théo and Maria van Rysselberghe. Although Gide claimed both Catherine and his eventual grandchildren, he left no written record of his feelings (if any) toward the mother of his only child.

In 1909, already famous as the author of *The Immoralist* and the well-circulated parable *Le Retour de l'enfant prodigue* (1907; *The Return of the Prodigal Son*, 1953), Gide assumed an active part in the founding of the influential periodical *La Nouvelle Revue française*, along with such other literary figures as Jean Schlumberger (1877-1968) and Henri Ghéon (1875-1944). Soon thereafter, he began work (along with numerous other projects) on the controversial *Corydon* (English translation, 1950), a quasi-Socratic dialogue in defense of homosexuality that would be released privately in 1911, against the advice of Gide's closest friends, and eventually published commercially in 1924. In retrospect, it appears that Gide rather enjoyed controversy, having long (and vociferously) resisted the efforts of several fellow writers to bring him "back into the fold" of the Roman Catholic Church. Because Gide had been reared as a Protestant, there was in fact no question of bringing him "back," as he had never been there; his collected correspondence nevertheless contains a voluminous and vigorous exchange of letters, many of which appeared in print at the time, involving such noted literary contemporaries as the poet Francis Jammes (1868-1938) and the playwright-poet Paul Claudel (1868-1955). Although Gide had abjured his Protestant faith, his writings continued to give evidence of a strong religious sensibility that Claudel and others thought might still be "salvageable." The story is told that Claudel, less than a week after Gide's death in 1951, received a telegram purportedly signed by Gide and claiming, "There is no Hell."

During the 1920's, Gide's penchant for controversy began to acquire political overtones as well, albeit in sporadic and idiosyncratic ways. Ordinarily among the least political of writers, virtually oblivious to the two world wars through which he lived and wrote, Gide nevertheless aroused considerable attention with two well-publicized (and recorded) voyages, the first to colonial Africa and the second, in the mid-1930's, to the Soviet Union. For all of his intelligence, Gide on both occasions appears to have been quite naïve in his expectations; in Chad and the Congo, for example, he was as surprised as he was appalled by the frequent (and flagrant) violation of human rights by the colonial "oppressors." Partly as a result of such observations, Gide in the 1930's began flirting openly with international Communism and was duly courted by the Russians in return; he repeatedly refused, however, to become a Party member, and while touring the Soviet Union as a guest of the Soviet government, he became every bit as disillusioned with the Soviet experiment as he had been by French colonialism a decade earlier in Africa. Still cherishing an ideal of Communism, Gide wrote bitterly of its "failure" in the Soviet Union.

Following his visit to the Soviet Union and the death of Madeleine Gide not long thereafter, Gide effectively retreated from the political scene. Much as he personally deplored the onset of another war and the subsequent collaborationist regime at Vichy, Gide found little place for the war in his writings, preferring instead the sort of inner reflection that had characterized his work from the start. From 1942 until the end of the war, he resided in North Africa, refusing offered passage to London even after North Africa was liberated. It was there, after all, that he had experienced his first great liberations both as person and as writer, and it was there that he would produce his last great *récit*, a reflection on the life and career of Theseus. Honored in 1947 with the Nobel Prize for Literature, Gide remained active with the writing of essays, memoirs, and translations until his death in February, 1951.

Analysis

Although André Gide's career as a published author spanned nearly sixty years, his position in literary history depends primarily on five prose narratives published in the first quarter of the twentieth century. As Gide's reputation rose to prominence, roughly between 1910 and 1920, critics and commentators were quick to discover the author's earlier writings and, in them, the clear annunciation of Gide's mature output. It is likely, however, that without the merited success of *The Immoralist, Strait Is the Gate, Lafcadio's Adventures,* *The Pastoral Symphony,* and *The Counterfeiters,* Gide's earliest writings might well have remained mere literary curiosities of the late Symbolist period. A notable exception might well be *Fruits of the Earth,* a transitional work, which in the years following World War I enjoyed a belated success quite unrelated to that of Gide's other writings. In any case, *The Immoralist* and its successors bear witness to a controlled, mature talent that has few peers in the recent history of French fiction.

With *The Immoralist,* a slim volume of deceptive simplicity, Gide reclaimed for the French tradition a strong foothold in the psychological novel. Skillful psychological narrative had been associated with France as early as the seventeenth century, thanks to Madame de La Fayette and her *La Princesse de Clèves* (1678; *The Princess of Clèves,* 1679), but had recently been pushed aside by the seemingly more urgent claims of realism and Naturalism; it was not until the 1920's and early 1930's that the Belgian Georges Simenon, hailed and admired by Gide, would combine psychological narrative with the strongest legacies of Naturalism. In the meantime, Gide further established his claim with *Strait Is the Gate,* another economical tale, which, although quite different, is in several respects a mirror image of *The Immoralist.* Particularly remarkable in both short novels is the emergence of Gide's mature style—a clear, concise form of expression far removed from his early verbosity yet not without certain affective mannerisms, particularly noticeable in his frequent inversion of adverb and verb; it is quite likely that the proverbial aspect of Gide's style derives at least in part from his frequent reading of the Bible.

Common to Gide's first two *récits* is his skillful use of a somewhat unreliable first-person narrator whose impressions are "corrected" by other narrative or correspondence that is used to frame the text. In both cases, however, Gide is careful not to point to a moral or to intrude himself as narrator within the working of the text. The canvas remains small, perhaps justifying Gide's use of the description *récit* in place of the more ambitious *roman:* In each tale, only two characters are singled out for close attention, with fewer than ten more appearing in the background. *The Immoralist* is the story of the process by which Michel, at once thoughtful and thoughtless, discovers himself, at the cost of his marriage and the life of his wife, Marceline; *Strait Is the Gate,* told mainly by the ineffectual Jérôme, presents the story of Alissa, whose renunciation and sacrifice seem hardly less selfish, in retrospect, than the deliberate indulgence of Michel in *The Immoralist.* More than once during his career, Gide pointed out that the two tales were in fact twins, having formed in his mind at the same time.

With *Lafcadio's Adventures,* Gide broadened his narrative canvas considerably, involving a large cast of frequently outrageous characters in a broad social satire that leaves few sacred cows unmilked. For the first time in his fiction, Gide gives evidence of a perceptive, pervasive sense of humor, which, with some effort and the wisdom of hindsight, has been detected by some critics between the lines of his earlier works. If here, as elsewhere, Gide's stated aim is to disturb the reader, he manages also to entertain, and lavishly so. In his lively evocation of a criminal scheme to extort funds from the faithful in order to "ransom" a Pope who has not in fact been kidnaped, Gide expresses his familiar concerns in a most unfamiliar way; if his main preoccupation remains with the individual, Gide nevertheless gains considerable appeal by placing those individuals against the background of society. Characteristically, however, Gide eschewed the description "novel" even for this effort, preferring the archaic (and exotic) term *sotie*, in part to underscore the *sottise* (stupidity) of most of the characters involved. His true novel, *The Counterfeiters*, moreover, was already in the planning stage, although not to be published until after *The Pastoral Symphony*.

Serving clear notice of the author's ironic intentions as early as its title, *The Pastoral Symphony*, both broadens and deepens the *récit* as Gide had earlier conceived it, presenting the voice of a most unreliable narrator, who nevertheless is presented with sufficient skill not to strain the reader's credulity. Recalling the legend of Oedipus along with that of Pygmalion, *The Pastoral Symphony* presents the testimony of a Protestant pastor who hypocritically overlooks his own motivations as he ministers to the blind foundling Gertrude. Although the sustained images of sight and blindness are likely to appear too obvious in summary, they are extremely well-managed within the story itself, a minor masterpiece of "unreliable" first-person narrative. Here, as in *Strait Is the Gate*, and, later, in *The Counterfeiters*, Gide presents a scathing satire of the Protestant milieu whence he sprang, demonstrating the ill effects of that particular doctrine upon the human spirit. Toward the end of Gide's life, *The Pastoral Symphony* was successfully filmed, with Michèle Morgan in the role of Gertrude.

Late in 1925, already in his middle fifties, Gide at last presented the "novel" that had long occupied his time and energy. Similar in scope to *Lafcadio's Adventures*, its satire softened somewhat by deeper reflection, *The Counterfeiters* proved well worth waiting for, assuring a receptive audience also for Gide's logbook, *Le Journal des faux-monnayeurs* (1926; *Journal of the Counterfeiters*, 1951). Like that of *The Pastoral Symphony*, the title is intended to be understood on several levels; although a band of counterfeiters does, in fact, appear in the novel, the title applies also to nearly all of the adult characters presented in the book, who assume all manner of disguises in order to serve as role models for their understandably disoriented children. It is with the children and adolescents that Gide the novelist is primarily concerned, and they receive his mature sympathy: The adults have all "sold out," in one way or another, leaving the children to fend for themselves. Particularly biting is Gide's satiric portrayal of the Pension Azaïs-Vedel, a seedy Protestant boarding school whose pastor-proprietors, a father and son-in-law, have long since lost the attention and respect of their truly inquiring charges. Through the person of one Édouard, an aspiring novelist approaching middle age, Gide explores the various levels of truth and falsehood not only in life but also in the novel; Édouard, for his part, is planning a volume to be called *Les Faux-monnayeurs*, but one that doubtless will never be written. To his credit, however, Gide in *The Counterfeiters* managed to avoid most of the pitfalls that have awaited his followers in the dubious art of writing a novel about a novelist who is writing a novel. In so doing, moreover, he brought to full expression most of the themes and concerns that preoccupied or haunted him throughout his career. *The Counterfeiters* remains both Gide's masterwork and a landmark in the development of the modern novel.

Gide, in his earliest attempts at writing—intended mainly for himself, his school friends, and his cousin Madeleine—tried to discover and define the nature of a freedom that was felt but not yet experienced. Gide's initial voyage to Africa, in 1893, resulted in an awakening that was psychological and spiritual as well as sexual, inspiring the young would-be author to shake off the bonds imposed by his austere French Protestant upbringing. One of the first concepts to emerge in his quest was that of *disponibilité* (availability). As expressed primarily in *Fruits of the Earth*, Gide's idea of *disponibilité* holds that the individual should keep himself "available" to the full range of potential human experience, for only then can he discover all of himself and conduct himself in a truly sincere and authentic manner. Clearly, Gide as early as 1902 had perceived the possible dangers and advisable limits of such an attitude, for *The Immoralist* is at least in part a cautionary tale about personal freedom pushed thoughtlessly to its extreme. Still, the physical and spiritual flowering of the formerly frail and bookish Michel is not without a certain intentional appeal. Between extremes, Gide appears to be suggesting, even advocating, a self-liberation that stops short of incurring such disastrous consequences as the early death of one's wife. For the purposes of fiction, however, *The Immoralist* is extremely well structured and memorable, involving the decline and failure of Marceline's health in inverse proportion to that of her husband.

Like most of his work published both before and since, *The Immoralist* draws heavily upon the established data of Gide's life; here as elsewhere, however, it would be erroneous to see in the work of fiction a direct transposition of the author's experience. Michel's awakening under the hot sun of North Africa, complete with his sexual initiation by young Arabs, obviously owes much to Gide's own experience; Gide, however, initially discovered Africa before his marriage and not while on his honeymoon. Michel's most important discoveries, however, appear to be not sexual but psychological, as in the memorable scene of the Arab boy Moktir stealing Marceline's scissors. Michel, initially shocked, observes the theft with growing fascination and invents a false tale to tell his wife; only later does he learn from his mysterious friend Ménalque, who hands him the worn and battered scissors, that Moktir, in turn, was aware of being watched. Michel's growing sense of complicity in the reversal of conventional morality constitutes no small part of his newfound freedom; later, upon his return to France, he will conspire with poachers to steal from his own land. Throughout the tale, recounted mainly in the first person by Michel, Gide equates Michel's growing health and strength with his increasing fondness for the wild and elemental; later, when Marceline miscarries and falls ill, the erstwhile near-invalid Michel will prove strangely insensitive to her suffering, claiming that he "got well" all by himself and wondering why she cannot do the same. Still, Michel remains sufficiently attached to Marceline that he will dismiss his "experiment in liberation" as a failure when she ultimately dies.

In *The Immoralist*, as in his later narratives, Gide is particularly concerned to show the negative effects of conventional morality upon the individual; here, however, little mention is made of religion per se, and Gide's concerns are implied rather than directly stated. Clearly, the circumstances of Michel's comfortable bourgeois background are to be seen as stifling, confining, and detrimental to his health; it is not until he breaks away from the security of a precocious academic career (as an archaeologist) that Michel begins to "get well," discovering at the same time what Gide protrays as his authentic self. As in Gide's own case, however, the ties of love remain strong and are less easily dismissed than the constraints of traditional morality.

In *Strait Is the Gate*, conceived around the same time as *The Immoralist*, Gide presents what he sees as the other side of the same coin. Quite unlike Michel, yet with equal intrasigence, Jérôme's cousin Alissa chooses the path of renunciation and self-abnegation, causing some early readers to see in *Strait Is the Gate* a religious or devotional work—indeed, a rebuttal of *The Immoralist*. As in the earlier work, however, ambiguities abound on every page, and it is soon clear that Alissa's "experiment" is hardly more successful or "exemplary" than that of her counterpart Michel; like Michel, indeed, she thoughtlessly contributes to needless human suffering.

Narrated mainly by the callow and ineffectual Jérôme, Alissa's first cousin and sometime fiancé, *Strait Is the Gate* exemplifies and partially satirizes what Cordle has identified as the Catharist dimension of Gide's thought and art. No doubt indebted to the author's life and marriage in certain details, including the age difference and Alissa's discovery of her mother's extramarital affairs, the portrayal of Alissa through Jérôme's love-struck eyes demonstrates a mastery of ironic technique that is all but lacking in *The Immoralist* and finds its strongest expression in *The Pastoral Symphony*. If Alissa indeed suffers from a variety of moral blindness in her adherence to Scripture at the expense of humanity, Jérôme, in turn, suffers from a literal-minded imperceptivity only partially explained by his scholarly training and plans. Perhaps most tellingly, he remains quite unaware of his sensual appeal to Alissa even as he records the effects of that attraction for his potential readers. The latent irony of *Strait Is the Gate* is further enhanced by the inclusion of Alissa's diaries, discovered only posthumously, recording not only her intense feelings toward Jérôme but also her "selfless," determined, and ultimately unsuccessful effort to "marry him off" to her sister Juliette.

Like the love of Gide and Madeleine, the emotion that binds Jérôme and Alissa is clearly "too good for this world," incapable in any case of satisfaction. Although some readers continue to feel that Alissa has given ample proof of sainthood, it is somewhat more likely that she, like Michel of *The Immoralist*, has pushed her inclination to extremes. The reader, although invited to share the excruciating pain of two passionate individuals so hopelessly unable to communicate, might also find occasion to question Alissa's taste in fastening her affections upon a creature as spineless as Jérôme. A stronger Jérôme would render the tale quite implausible, if not impossible, but his limitations spread outward to encompass *Strait Is the Gate* as well, perhaps adding an unintentional note of irony to the book's biblical title.

In *Lafcadio's Adventures*, Gide at last gave free rein to the strong ironic bent that is little more than latent in his earlier efforts; in addition, he added a strong portion of humor that is generally lacking elsewhere in his work, with keen observation that often crosses over into broad caricature. Based presumably upon a true incident recorded in European newspapers during the 1890's, *Lafcadio's Adventures* is nevertheless peopled exclusively with characters that could have sprung only from Gide's increasingly active imagination. Even the names are strange, from the novelist Julius de Baraglioul and his brother-in-law Amédée Fleurissoire to Julius' illegitimate half brother Lafcadio Wluiki; there is also the prostitute Carola, whose surname, Venitequa, means "come here" in Latin. Believers and freethinkers alike are treated with irreverence, portrayed as "crustaceans" whose institutionalized beliefs have stunted and distorted what might have been their true personalities. Here, as in *The Counterfeiters*, Gide clearly adumbrates the same demand for authentic behavior that would later dominate the work of Jean-Paul Sartre (1905-1980); unlike Sartre, however, he is not quite ready to accept the implications of total human freedom. To be sure, he offers a tantalizing portrayal of freedom in the person of the nineteen-year-old Lafcadio, whose illegitimacy purportedly exempts him from the bondage of polite society, yet it is hard even for Gide to condone the now-famous *acte gratuit*, or unmotivated deed, in which Lafcadio, more or less from sheer boredom, pushes the unsuspecting Fleurissoire out the door of a moving train. As in *The Immoralist*, freedom still has its limits, and Lafcadio will find that he has thus murdered the brother of his own sister-in-law. By apparent chance, however, he will go unpunished.

Particularly effective in *Lafcadio's Adventures* is Gide's satiric portrayal of the bourgeois "crustaceans": Julius, unlike Gide, is among the most complacent (and presumably boring) of novelists; Anthime Armand-Dubois, a scientist cast in the mold of Gustave Flaubert's pharmacist Homais, undergoes a sudden conversion to Catholicism that is no less hilarious for being totally sincere. Fleurissoire, the most amiable (if also the most apparently ridiculous) of the three, conserves his goodwill through a harrowing sequence of tortures, only to meet senseless death at the idle hands of Lafcadio; several of Gide's commentators argue with some justice that Fleurissoire may well be the true hero of the book, exhibiting the patience of Job when subjected to similar ordeals. In any event, the fundamental weakness of all three men is their gullibility, reflected in the book's resonant French title, *Les Caves du Vatican*; in French, the word *cave* can refer to the victim of a hoax, similar to the word "mark" in English.

Throughout *Lafcadio's Adventures*, Gide, despite a certain fascination, is careful not to side too closely with the hoaxers, led by the ubiquitous, many-visaged, truly protean Protos. After all, Gide suggests, such parasites can flourish only as long as they find willing victims, and who in his right mind would fork over money to ransom a captive Pope? Only a "crustacean," which further proves the need for increasingly authentic conduct of one's life. Paradoxically, even Lafcadio can exist as he does only in relation to the society he professes to despise; for all of his vaunted freedom, he functions only as the inverted mirror image of respectability, and were respectability to vanish he would vanish too—or change, as do the three "crustaceans" once they have been gulled.

With *The Pastoral Symphony*, Gide returns to the *récit*, investing the form with deeper resonance and insight than are to be found in either *Strait Is the Gate* or *The Immoralist*. As heavily ironic as *Lafcadio's Adventures*, yet tightly controlled within the first-person narrative viewpoint, *The Pastoral Symphony* continues Gide's inquiry into the potentially negative effects, both psychological and social, of organized religion. Significantly, the narrator-protagonist is a Protestant minister, subspecies Calvinist, whose Swiss enclave is hemmed in on all sides by Roman Catholicism. In apparent reaction against Roman Catholic tradition, he has developed a strong personal faith and doctrine based primarily upon the Gospels. In time, however, he has allowed his faith to harden into a crustacean shell that protects him from true introspection as well as from outside influences; thus does he remain hypocritically blind to his true feelings toward Gertrude and insensitive to the needs of his own wife and family.

A dozen years earlier, in 1907, Gide had written the often-reprinted *The Return of the Prodigal Son*, an extended parable or prose poem retelling the tale of the prodigal son. In Gide's version, the prodigal son returns only because he is hungry; although he decides to stay, he inspires his younger brother (a Gidean invention) to leave on the same kind of pagan pilgrimage from which the prodigal has just returned. Intended at least in part as an explanation to his Catholic friends of why he could not join their church, Gide's brief text is interpreted also by some commentators as a concise overview of Catholicism, Protestantism, Judaism, and Muhammadanism. It remains a remarkable text, foreshadowing many of the tensions that were later to animate the action of *The Pastoral Symphony*.

The Pastor, like the prodigal son, instinctively recoils from the restrictions and prohibitions brought to Christianity by the epistles of Saint Paul, preferring instead the good news of love propounded by the Gospels. Unfortunately, he manages to misread the Gospels as shelter for his own hypocrisy, retreating into the shell of his faith when in fact it is his illicit love for Gertrude, and not his Calvinism, that is making his family uneasy. The conflict reaches crisis proportions when the Pastor's son, Jacques, who has been preparing to follow his father into the ministry, finds himself simultaneously attracted to Gertrude and to the Roman Catholic Church; in several telling passages, the wily Pastor attempts to dissuade his son from both attractions by berating his son with Protestant theology; he also attempts to forestall an operation that would restore young Gertrude's eyesight. Gertrude, meanwhile, has become increasingly sensitive to the tensions at work in the Pastor's household and perceives, even before the successful operation, that she poses a threat to the Pastor's marriage, even as she truly loves Jacques. Her *de facto* suicide, presented as a selfless gesture, occurs only after she and Jacques have both been baptized as Roman Catholics; thus does the Pastor conclude that he has "lost" them both.

Given the time of its composition, a number of Gide's commentators have seen in *The Pastoral Symphony* an artistic transposition of the author's own homosexual affair with the young Marc Allégret (whom he later adopted) and his subsequent rupture with Madeleine after she burned his letters. To be sure, the Pastor's marriage is portrayed as dry and loveless, based more on habit than on affection; at one point, the Pastor observes that the only way he can please Amélie is to avoid displeasing her. Still, *The Pastoral Symphony* might also be seen as the least autobiographical of Gide's published novels, relating less to his life than to his sustained preoccupation with religion and its potential pitfalls. In *The Counterfeiters*, albeit on a larger canvas, he continued his inquiry into what he saw as the "inevitable" hypocrisy engendered by Protestant belief.

Reared in the austere and defensive minority environment that was and is French Protestantism, Gide experienced Calvinist guilt at an early age and never really liberated himself from its pervasive clutches. Still, he knew too much, had seen too much, ever to return to the small fold. It is hardly surprising, therefore, that in his first and only "novel" Gide should equate Christianity with Protestantism of a most narrow and unappealing kind. Almost without exception, the troubled adolescents of *The Counterfeiters* are somehow involved with the Pension Azaïs-Vedel, a marginal Protestant boarding school whose precepts are more often honored in the breach than in the observance. Earlier in life, the writer Édouard, in his late thirties at the time of the novel, was both shocked and amazed by the ease with which old Azaïs' solemn pronouncements were shrugged off by his young charges; it was not long, however, before Édouard, hired as a teacher, recognized the students' response as the only reasonable one. Like the Pastor of *The Pastoral Symphony*, both Azaïs and his son-in-law Vedel are steeped in smug hypocrisy, having long since made their private, unrecognized concessions to the demands of human nature. The pupils therefore have little choice but to listen politely, then go and do as they please.

Armand Vedel, grandson of Azaïs, may well be the most potentially corrupt of all the adolescents surveyed in the novel; he is at all events the most jaded. Still seeking further corruption and "adventure," Armand refuses to consult a physician about his possible throat cancer—an affliction that symbolizes the state of his mind. His sisters, meanwhile, have fared hardly better: Rachel, the eldest, has never married and bears upon her shoulders the day-to-day administration of the school, including frequent financial shortfalls; her father, meanwhile, could not care less, blindly believing that "the Lord will provide." Her younger sister Laura, formerly in love with Édouard, who would not marry her although he returned her love, has abandoned her teacher-husband for an affair with the dissolute medical student Vincent Molinier, brother of two pension students who figure prominently in the novel. Now abandoned in turn by Vincent and carrying his child, Laura will eventually be invited to rejoin her husband with promise of forgiveness. Ironically, however, it is Édouard whom she still loves.

Perhaps because of the multiplicity of characters and necessary subplots deemed appropriate to the "novel" as opposed to the more restricted *récit*, *The Counterfeiters* often appears confused in its organization, its disparate parts frequently linked by implausible coincidence or by cumbersome (and uncharacteristic) intervention on the part of the author. In order to allow the reader access to Édouard's unpublished journal, for example, Gide arranges for Édouard to have his suitcase stolen by the runaway Bernard Profitendieu, a friend of Édouard's nephew Olivier Molinier; the reader thus reads the journal, as it were, over the shoulder of Bernard, who is reading it himself and will act upon what he has learned. The journal, meanwhile, intersperses facts with frequent ruminations on the theory of the novel.

As in *Lafcadio's Adventures*, and as befits the title of his "novel," Gide in *The Counterfeiters* appears primarily concerned with the nature of authentic thought and behavior, making fun of middle-aged "crustaceans" or "counterfeiters," whose essence has retreated behind mere form. Édouard's brother-in-law Oscar Molinier, for example, is a veteran womanizer who believes his wife, Pauline, to be quite unaware of his philandering; when a packet of letters from his mistress disappears, he concludes that Pauline has discovered him at last. Pauline, no stranger to her husband's secret life, is even more appalled by the disappearance of the letters, correctly guessing that their youngest son, Georges, has stolen them to use as a form of blackmail. Édouard, Pauline's brother, is thus drawn into several levels of intrigue within the story, and it is his rather inept effort to make sense of his own observations that provides the backbone of the novel-within-a-novel, while Gide himself remains in control. As in his earlier efforts, Gide proves especially skillful at unreliable first-person narration, for Édouard is in his own way every bit as much a counterfeiter as the rest of his contemporaries.

Throughout *The Counterfeiters*, partly because of a more liberal literary climate than obtained at the turn of the century, Gide for the first time in his creative prose speaks freely of homosexual love and attraction, as well as of the autoeroticism that had plagued his own childhood and youth. Édouard, although apparently bisexual, is strongly attracted to boys and men, including his nephew Olivier, who, with Pauline's tacit permission, becomes Édouard's lover after Édouard saves Olivier from an attempted suicide. This sexual ambiguity in Édouard prevents him from providing Laura Douviers-Vedel with the love and affection that she both wants and needs. Nor is Édouard the only practicing homosexual in *The Counterfeiters*; several rungs below him on the moral level stands Count Robert de Passavant, also a writer, who openly seeks to corrupt the young (Olivier Molinier as well as Armand Vedel) and maintains a sporadic sybaritic relationship with the cold, frankly amoral Lilian, also known as Lady Griffith.

Bernard Profitendieu, whose flight from his home opens the action of the novel, remains a pivotal if minor figure throughout all that follows. The reason for his flight is that he has discovered his own illegitimacy, learning that his mother bore him out of wedlock. The discovery provides him with all the ammunition that he seems to need for revolt against the authoritarian figure of Judge Albéric Profitendieu, and for a while Bernard tests and tries to enjoy the "bastardly freedom" of the author's earlier creation Lafcadio (who, according to Gide, was initially supposed to appear in *The Counterfeiters* as well). In time, however, with the approach of true spiritual maturity (symbolized by a rather bizarre supernatural experience), Bernard will return to the Profitendieu household, having grown, developed, and learned more than most of the other characters.

In the person of the diabolic counterfeiter Strouvilhou, aided by his nephew Ghéridanisol and their occasional associate Robert de Passavant, Gide invests the shadowy underworld with an even more sinister presence than that of Protos in *Lafcadio's Adventures*. Strouvilhou, himself a former student at the Pension Azaïs-Vedel, is less a confidence man than a true anarchist, for whom crime serves merely as one possible means to the eventual end of total chaos. Not content with mere counterfeiting, he inspires his young victims to blackmail their parents and consciously engineers the gratuitous suicide of the

troubled young Boris, who has enrolled in the pension to be near his grandfather, Édouard's longtime friend, the elderly musician La Pérouse. As in
Lafcadio's Adventures, however, Gide takes pains to show that the criminal
element, however motivated, can exist only at the expense of a polite society
that is its complaisant, if less than willing, host. If the novelist Édouard
emerges at the end of the novel with the grudging respect of author and reader
alike, it is because he fares better than most at the difficult task of being
honest with himself. Of all the characters, however, it is doubtless Bernard
whose attitude most closely approaches the exemplary.

With the publication of his "novel," Gide doubtless concluded that his
exploration of the novel form was complete. An early commentator, Albert
Guérard, observed that Gide was in fact less a "novelist" than a traditional
French "man of letters" who happened, occasionally, to write novels. Such
an assertion appears to be borne out by subsequent developments in Gide's
career; although unflaggingly active as a writer well into his eighties, Gide
would return only once to the prose narrative form, and then to the *récit* that
he had helped to perfect nearly half a century earlier. *Theseus*, which might
be read as a philosophical tale or meditation in the manner of Voltaire,
provides a fitting capstone to Gide's distinguished if sporadic career as a writer
of narrative prose, restating his habitual concerns about human freedom with
a wisdom that only age could provide. In all likelihood, however, *The Pastoral
Symphony* and *The Counterfeiters* will continue to be regarded as his true
masterpieces.

Major publications other than long fiction

SHORT FICTION: *Paludes*, 1895 (*Marshlands*, 1953); *Le Prométhée mal
enchaîné*, 1899 (*Prometheus Misbound*, 1953).

PLAYS: *Philoctète*, 1899 (*Philoctetes*, 1952); *Le Roi Candaule*, 1901 (*King
Candaules*, 1952); *Saül*, 1903 (English translation, 1952); *Bethsabé*, 1912
(*Bathsheba*, 1952); *My Theater*, 1952.

POETRY: *Les Cahiers d'André Walter*, 1891 (*The Notebooks of André Walter*,
1968); *Le Traité du Narcisse*, 1891 ("Narcissus," in *The Return of the Prodigal
Son*, 1953); *Le Voyage d'Urien*, 1893 (*Urien's Voyage*, 1964); *Les Nourritures
terrestres*, 1897 (*Fruits of the Earth*, 1949); *Le Retour de l'enfant prodigue*,
1907 (*The Return of the Prodigal Son*, 1953); *Les Nouvelles Nourritures*, 1935
(*New Fruits of the Earth*, 1949).

NONFICTION: *Amyntas*, 1906 (English translation, 1958); *Corydon*, 1911,
1924 (English translation, 1950); *Le Journal des faux-monnayeurs*, 1926 (*Journal of the Counterfeiters*, 1951); *Si le grain ne meurt*, 1926 (*If It Die . . .* ,
1935); *Voyage au Congo*, 1927 (*Travels in the Congo*, 1929); *Retour de
l'U.R.S.S.*, 1936 (*Return from the U.S.S.R*, 1937); *Retouches à mon "Retour
de l'U.R.S.S.,"* 1937 (*Afterthoughts on the U.S.S.R.*, 1938); *Journal*, 1939-
1950, 1954 (*The Journals of André Gide, 1889-1949*, 1947-1951); *Et nunc*

manet in te, 1947, 1951 (*Madeleine*, 1952); *Ainsi soit-il: Ou, Les Jeux sont faits*, 1952 (*So Be It: Or, The Chips Are Down*, 1959).

Bibliography
Cordle, Thomas. *André Gide*, 1969.
Fowlie, Wallace. *André Gide: His Life and Art*, 1965.
Freedman, Ralph. *The Lyrical Novel*, 1963.
Peyre, Henri. *The Contemporary French Novel*, 1955.
Starkie, Enid. *André Gide*, 1954.

David B. Parsell

JEAN GIONO

Born: Manosque, France; March 30, 1895
Died: Manosque, France; October 8, 1970

Principal long fiction

Colline, 1929 (*Hill of Destiny*, 1929); *Un de Baumugnes*, 1929 (*Lovers Are Never Losers*, 1931); *Regain*, 1930 (*Harvest*, 1939); *Naissance de l'Odyssée*, 1930; *Le Grand Troupeau*, 1931 (*To the Slaughterhouse*, 1969); *Solitude de la pitié*, 1931; *Jean le bleu*, 1932 (*Blue Boy*, 1946); *Le Serpent d'étoiles*, 1933; *Le Chant du monde*, 1934 (*The Song of the World*, 1937); *Que ma joie demeure*, 1935 (*Joy of Man's Desiring*, 1940); *Batailles dans la montagne*, 1937; *Pour saluer Melville*, 1943; *Un Roi sans divertissement*, 1947; *Noé*, 1947, 1961; *Les Âmes fortes*, 1949; *Mort d'un personnage*, 1949; *Les Grands Chemins*, 1951; *Le Hussard sur le toit*, 1951 (*The Horseman on the Roof*, 1954); *Le Moulin de Pologne*, 1952 (*The Malediction*, 1955); *Le Bonheur Fou*, 1957 (*The Straw Man*, 1959); *Angélo*, 1958 (English translation, 1960); *Deux Cavaliers de l'orage*, 1965 (*Two Riders of the Storm*, 1967).

Other literary forms

Jean Giono is remembered chiefly for his novels. During the 1930's, however, he surfaced briefly as a social theorist with such volumes as *Les Vraies Richesses* (1936; true riches) and *Le Poids du ciel* (1938; the weight of the sky). He also wrote several performed plays, of which the most noteworthy is *La Femme du boulanger* (1942), expanded from an episode in his autobiographical novel *Blue Boy* and filmed by Marcel Pagnol in 1938.

Achievements

Championed early in his career by André Gide and other prominent writers of the time, Jean Giono is the preeminent "regional," or rural, French novelist of the twentieth century; his novels have been compared to those of Thomas Hardy in England and William Faulkner in the United States. In the mid-1930's, Giono acquired a considerable following as a "poet and prophet of the soil," emerging as leader of the agrarian Contadour movement that flourished during the years preceding World War II. Briefly imprisoned both in 1939 and in 1945 for the unshakable pacifist convictions he had developed during his years of service in World War I, Giono fell from favor as a writer, only to rebound spectacularly during the late 1940's and early 1950's with a new documentary style quite different from his earlier modes. In 1953, he received the Prix Monégasque, awarded by the Prince of Monaco for the finest ensemble of works in the French language; the following year, he was elected to the prestigious Académie Goncourt.

Biography

Jean Giono was born in 1895 at Manosque, a rural village in southern France where, except for extended military service during World War I, he would spend his entire life. His father, a cobbler, and his mother, a laundress, had married when they were no longer young, and Jean was their only child. His childhood, recalled in *Blue Boy* and elsewhere, appears to have been a reasonably happy one, although lived close to the poverty line and in close touch with the forces of nature. In 1911, faced with the declining health of his father, Jean cut short his formal education to take a job in the local branch of a national bank; with time out for military service, he would remain with the bank until 1930, when he at last believed himself capable of earning a living from his writings; it was in that year that he bought the house in which he would spend the remaining forty years of his life, and in which he would receive visitors attracted from throughout the world by the increasing success of his writings. In 1920, soon after the death of his father, he married Élise Maurin, who bore him two daughters, Aline in 1926 and Sylvie in 1934.

As early as 1931, with *To the Slaughterhouse*, Giono began to express in his writings the deep and obdurate pacifism that was the result of nearly five years of enlisted service during World War I. With the publication of his "rural epics," notably *The Song of the World* and *Joy of Man's Desiring*, Giono's pacifism gradually fused with his glorification of rustic life to produce the phenomenon of Contadour, a back-to-the-soil movement that anticipated by some thirty years many similar communal experiments in the United States and Western Europe. According to critic and Giono expert Maxwell Smith, the Contadour experience arose more or less by accident when, in the fall of 1935, the number of youthful "pilgrims" to Giono's home in Manosque exceeded the Gionos' capacity for hospitality, and Élise suggested to her husband that he take some of their uninvited guests "for a walk." Knapsacks on backs, Giono and some three dozen of the faithful set off soon thereafter on an extended hike through areas that Giono especially loved or about which he had written. When, after several days, the leader happened to sprain his ankle near the tiny town of Contadour, the group decided that they had found what they had been seeking. Housed at first in a barn, the group later bought land for sheep farming and a permanent residence.

As Smith points out, the true function of the Contadour "pilgrimages," several of which would occur annually until the onset of World War II, was to test the mettle and adaptability of disillusioned urbanites in search of an alternative life-style; in time, the Contadour movement became associated with that of the International Youth Hostels, which completed the task of "resettling" many former city dwellers throughout rural France. During the late 1930's, the Contadour movement published its own quarterly, *Cahiers*, and helped to inspire Giono's social essays of the same period.

With the outbreak of war in 1939, Giono came under severe public censure for his pacifist sentiments and activism and spent two months in prison at Marseilles, from which he was released upon the combined intervention of Gide and the Queen Mother of Belgium. Erroneously suspected of being a Fascist sympathizer, Giono remained purely and simply a pacifist, who saw in all wars the denial and destruction of his strongest personal values. Returning to Manosque, he was again imprisoned at the end of the war, largely for his own protection against reprisals from the far Left, whose sympathizers had gained control of the region following cessation of hostilities; he was also censured and blacklisted for a time by the increasingly Left-leaning Comité National des Écrivains.

Between prison sentences, Giono appears to have spent most of his time and energy on the French translation of Herman Melville's *Moby Dick* (1851), a project begun in the mid-1930's with his longtime friend Lucien Jacques and their British acquaintance Joan Smith. Jacques, a writer, artist, and sometime editor, had helped to publish and publicize some of Giono's earliest writings; the two men were further bound by shared pacifist convictions resulting from service in the previous war, and Jacques had assumed an active part in the Contadour experiment. An unexpected side effect of the translation was the writing and publication of *Pour saluer Melville*, Giono's tribute, in the form of a novel to a writer he had long admired. Bordering closely upon a literary hoax, although intended in utter good faith, *Pour saluer Melville* inserts totally invented characters and incidents between the recorded lines of Melville's life—so convincingly, in fact, that at least one of Melville's descendants would accept the story as authentic.

Once cleared of suspicion after World War II, Giono, by then in his early fifties, returned to the literary scene in full vigor, but in a new and different mode that he himself called *chroniques* (chronicles). As different from his spare early style as from his rural epics of the 1930's, the *chroniques* won for him new admirers while disappointing certain older ones. Historical in context, drawing heavily upon the lives and exploits of Giono's paternal Italian ancestors, the *chroniques* are perhaps as epic in scope as *The Song of the World*, but with new attention paid to the delineation of character, sometimes at the expense of plot. The so-called Hussar Cycle, inaugurated by *The Horseman on the Roof* in 1951, demonstrated Giono's eventual mastery of the new form and brought him honors that only a short time earlier might have been considered unthinkable. Although somewhat disillusioned by the failure of his social thought, dismissing the Contadour movement as a youthful mistake, Giono remained personally optimistic, vigorous, and active as a writer well into his seventies, continuing to welcome the visitors who came from far and wide to see him. Jean Giono died at his home in Manosque in 1970.

Analysis

Almost without exception, Jean Giono's commentators trace the emergence of his early styles to his voracious reading of the Greek classics in translation, a program of self-education and entertainment begun in childhood, to be continued after-hours at the bank. While in school, Giono, like his contemporary Antoine de Saint-Exupéry, had performed poorly in French composition, showing little promise of his eventual career. As Henri Peyre has pointed out, however, Giono had the distinct advantage of acquiring the classics on his own, outside the classroom in a rustic Mediterranean environment not utterly different from that of ancient Greece; in all likelihood, the sights, sounds, and smells were much the same, as were man's perennial contact and struggle with the soil. Indeed, Giono's first attempt at long fiction, not published until subsequent works had made of him a better risk to publishers, was *Naissance de l'Odyssée*, a vigorous, ironic work written "within the margins" of Homer's *Odyssey* (c. 800 B.C.).

Giono first rose to prominence in the late 1920's and early 1930's with the so-called Trilogy of Pan, comprising *Hill of Destiny*, *Lovers Are Never Losers*, and *Harvest*. Giono, later to be succeeded by the Spanish-born dramatist Fernando Arrabal (born 1932), evokes the spirit of Pan to symbolize the forces of nature, with which man often coexists in an uneasy truce. In *Hill of Destiny*, nature quite literally goes "on strike" against human "improvements" wrought upon the land; the elderly Janet is unjustly accused of witchcraft, having acquired the odd gift of communication with nature and having warned his fellow villagers to mend their ways before it is too late. *Lovers Are Never Losers*, by contrast, presents the lyric aspect of Pan, singing the lost-and-found love of Albin for Angèle through the voice of the old peasant Amédée. *Harvest*, later successfully filmed, unites humanity with nature in the marriage of the near-giant Panturle and the itinerant Arsule, who has saved him from drowning; love, although present, is here subordinated to the cycle of the seasons.

As Maxwell Smith observes, Giono in his Trilogy of Pan delighted readers with his seemingly effortless gift for striking, apt, and memorable metaphor, particularly in his descriptions of nature or of the forest fire in *Hill of Destiny*. In *Lovers Are Never Losers*, description is equally vivid, although style and vocabulary are pared down somewhat, to suit the speech patterns of the uneducated peasant narrator. The style of *Harvest* remains restrained if colorful, with seemingly authentic rustic speech. Only in the middle volume, *Lovers Are Never Losers*, does Giono see fit to delineate or "humanize" his characters in a way that makes them memorable; in *Hill of Destiny* and *Harvest*, it is nature itself that dominates, often attaining the stature of a character through the author's vivid descriptions.

Perhaps the most successful of Giono's novels in his earliest mode, *Lovers Are Never Losers* combines his rare evocative power with a sure gift for storytelling. The narrative, although limited in voice and viewpoint to the uneducated old peasant Amédée, is both sensitive and credible in its portrayal of young Albin and his pining love for Angèle, who has been "carried away by a city slicker." Within the context of the tale, Baumugnes is a village whose Huguenot inhabitants, their tongues cut out by religious persecutors, learned to communicate with one another by playing the harmonica; understandably, their descendants, including the unfortunate Albin, have supposedly inherited an uncanny gift for playing that instrument, and Albin's talent stands him in good stead in the rescue of Angèle, long since abandoned by her lover and held captive on her father's farm. Unlikely though the story may sound in summary, *Lovers Are Never Losers* remains a remarkable and memorable narrative, as notable for the deftness of its characterizations as for the economy of its style. Only the city-bred seducer Louis seems closer to caricature than to character, but even that lapse can be seen as credible within the story's rural context.

In 1930, the year that he resigned from the bank and purchased his house, Giono managed also to publish his first-written novel, *Naissance de l'Odyssée*, which would enjoy an even larger printing eight years later, with another publisher. He also began for the first time to put "himself" into his books, with such semiautobiographical novels as *To the Slaughterhouse* and *Blue Boy*. His style in these volumes is increasingly confident and frankly lyric, tending toward exuberance; perhaps his most masterful scene, also a metaphor (as reflected in the original title *Le Grand Troupeau*), shows two old men stampeding sheep through a provincial village; the young shepherds who would normally have done the job have themselves been "stampeded"—to war. Giono's descriptions, worthy of the Greek poets whom he so admired, anticipate the "epic" style that would soon burst forth, full-blown, in *The Song of the World* and *Joy of Man's Desiring*. The style of the meandering, episodic *Blue Boy* is more restrained, although amply supplied with deft similes and metaphors. Representative of the book's tone and content is the doubt of old Franchesc Odripano, on hearing of the Wright brothers' flight, "that anything will really change."

With his epic novels of the middle 1930's, Giono began increasingly to assert the claims of the soil against, and above, those of modern technology. Indeed, the modern world is conspicuous primarily by its absence from his impassioned, vivid storytelling, set in modern times but showing man eternally involved with nature.

In *The Song of the World*, the first, as well as the best-remembered and most durable, of his epic novels, Giono depicts the primordial, archetypal struggle between the peasants Antonio and Matelot, on one side, and the seemingly malevolent mountain tyrant Maudru, on the other; storms and the river, meanwhile, pose at least as powerful a threat to both sides as the opposing sides do to each other. Credible though the incidents may be, little effort is made toward verisimilitude; the author instead aspires to the monumental. Here, both man and nature are writ large, with much of the action taking place at night, in the false shelter of ominous shadows. Giono's choice of title is seconded by Henri Peyre, who observes that Antonio, Matelot, and even the menacing Maudru are "epic heroes not because they accumulate feats in violent battle but because they are the very forces of nature embodied in simple, strong creatures; they echo the song of the world." Reduced to simple plot, the action of *The Song of the World* might well be seen as little more than a feud among peasants. In Giono's capable hands, however, the narrative assumes truly monumental as well as highly memorable proportions, enriched by the author's vivid, resonant vocabulary and a country dweller's homage to the cycle of the seasons.

Joy of Man's Desiring, despite a proliferation of unhappy characters, waxes so lyric in its paean to the rustic life as to have inspired in some critics an unflattering recollection of Jean-Jacques Rousseau and of Voltaire's observation that his notorious contemporary was inviting mankind "to walk upon all fours." Significantly, it was soon after the publication of *Joy of Man's Desiring* that the Contadour movement arose as if spontaneously, although Giono's novels had begun to attract a following as early as 1931, before his epic phase. *Batailles dans la montagne*, published between the two propaganda volumes *Les Vraies Richesses* and *Le Poids du ciel*, is perhaps the most effective of the three "epics" in portraying man's struggle with nature; a small mountain village is doubly threatened with destruction by flood, both from a melting glacier and from a river accidentally dammed by a landslide. Particularly memorable, and epic, is Giono's description of the hero Saint-Jean's anguished quest for dynamite to blow up the dam, in the course of which he is pitted against an enraged bull. Here as elsewhere, Giono excels in his deft, if verbose, evocation of nature, whose phenomena are as beautiful as they are terrifying.

Thanks in part to his enviable mastery of the French language and its vocabulary—a mastery exceeding that of many more sophisticated writers—Giono managed throughout most of his career to avoid accusations of false primitivism as well as of condescension to his characters or audience. Giono was, in fact, a true provincial, a committed son of the soil who was ready and more than willing to meet the rest of the world on its own terms; many another writer, transplanted urbanite as well as native rustic, has tried and failed to achieve the artistic position that Giono was to assume as if by birthright. Despite Giono's occasional vulnerability to charges of being a latter-day Rousseau, the integrity and vigor of his thought and prose quite naturally protected him from the danger of becoming a literary counterpart to "Grandma" Moses or even Norman Rockwell. At worst, the social propaganda of his Contadour period reflects a certain shallowness; happily, though, such weaknesses are absent from the novels written around the same time.

In his postwar novels, collectively known as *chroniques*, Giono moved on to a new, quasi-documentary style of narrative exposition that he claimed to have developed contemporaneously with his epic novels, although the results would not be seen until the late 1940's. The first published novel in the new mode, which appeared in 1947, was *Un Roi sans divertissement*, seen by some observers as a glorified detective story. Consisting of first-person testimony from a variety of participants and witnesses, *Un Roi sans divertissement* deliberately leaves unresolved many of the ambiguities that would be reconciled in a more conventional mystery. Reviewers, although somewhat nonplussed by Giono's seemingly abrupt change of manner, found much to praise in his delineation of character, especially in the case of the protagonist Langlois. *Noé*, published later in the same year, appears to have been the author's favorite among his many novels and was reissued at his own request in 1961; described by Smith and others as a "novelist's novel," *Noé* builds upon the autobiographical foundation of the earlier *Blue Boy* to provide fresh insight into the author's art and craft as characters from his work-in-progress begin to appear in his mind, much in the manner of persons encountered in "real life." In style and content, however, *Noé* is closely related to the *chroniques*, with which it is usually classified.

Between 1949 and 1952, Giono added three major volumes to his series of *chroniques. Les Âmes fortes*, consisting entirely of conversation among three old ladies at a wake, reconstructs in often hair-raising, apparently "realistic" detail a curious tale of envy, fraud, and murder covering the preceding sixty years. *Les Grands Chemins*, likewise dealing with murder and fraud, has generally been deemed less successful. *The Malediction* recalls in grim detail the "family curse" hanging over the head of a certain Julie Coste. The novel was well received, but Giono, in the meantime, had attracted even more critical attention with *The Horseman on the Roof*, published in 1951 and inaugurating what would come to be known as his Hussar Cycle.

A subgrouping of the *chroniques*, Giono's Hussar novels are set against the background of nineteenth century Europe, before the unification of Germany and Italy. Drawing heavily upon his own Italian origins, Giono presents in the Hussar cycle a colorful fresco of tribulation and adventure featuring the carbonaro Angelo Pardi, a character modeled, at least in part, on Giono's own paternal grandfather. In *The Horseman on the Roof*, Giono involves Angelo and other recurring characters in the cholera epidemic of 1838, portraying man's struggle against disease in a chronicle that has been favorably compared to Albert Camus' *La Peste* (1947; *The Plague*, 1948). *The Straw Man* shows Angelo cast as a scapegoat or "straw man" by conspirators during the Italian campaign against Austrian rule in 1848; dismissed by some commentators as an unsuccessful imitation of Stendhal's *La Chartreuse de Parme* (1839; *The Charterhouse of Parma*, 1895), *The Straw Man* was correctly recognized by others as a step in the direction of postmodern fiction; like Alain Robbe-Grillet, Michel Butor, and other "New Novelists" of the 1950's, Giono, in *The Straw Man*, was clearly experimenting with modes of perception and presentation in the novel, questioning established concepts of time and character even as he sought to present a rousing, well-told tale against a historical background.

Different though it may be from Giono's nature epics of the 1930's, the documentary style of the *chroniques*, including the Hussar Cycle, remains strongly rooted in the soil. As in his earliest novels, the landscape in *The Horseman on the Roof* is never far removed from view, even as increasing attention is paid to the delineation and development of character. Although nature is cast in a relatively minor role, Giono's characters are still very much at the mercy of the elements—the cholera epidemic, for example, is similar to the floods, storms, and savage beasts that figure prominently in the earlier novels—which in turn help define both personality and behavior. In the view of some critics, *The Horseman on the Roof* is the finest of Giono's novels.

Set largely in Giono's home town of Manosque as it must have been some sixty years before his birth, the novel takes its rather unusual title from the fact that Angelo Pardi, fleeing for his life after killing an Austrian spy in a duel, is eventually driven to the rooftops in his search for sanctuary; the people of Manosque, superstitious by nature and further maddened by the presence of the plague in their midst, wrongly suspect the fugitive Angelo of having poisoned the town's water supply. Told in a sober, matter-of-fact style somewhat different from Giono's earlier mode, *The Horseman on the Roof* excels also in its portrayal of man's inhumanity to man, as Angelo witnesses innumerable scenes of brutality and violence from the relative sanctuary of his elevated hiding place. As in Camus' *The Plague*, however, the narrative is saved from gloominess by the exemplary behavior of the featured characters. The character of Angelo Pardi, together with that of the Marquise Pauline de Théus, reappeared throughout Giono's subsequent novels, although here they are perhaps at their most memorable. Significantly, it is *The Horseman on the Roof* that appears to have brought to Giono's work, at long last, the double honor of the Prix Monégasque and election to the Académie Goncourt.

Although Giono's reputation declined somewhat in the years following his death, he is still recognized for a singular talent of rare scope and evocative power, perhaps impossible to imitate. As a pacifist inalienably committed to the land and its values, he may also be seen as presaging by some thirty years the "counterculture" of the 1960's, which in turn exerted considerable influence upon the values of the present day.

Major publications other than long fiction

PLAYS: *Lanceurs de graines*, 1932; *Le Bout de la route*, 1937; *La Femme du boulanger*, 1942; *Théâtre*, 1943 (collection); *Voyage en calèche*, 1946.

NONFICTION: *Les Vraies Richesses*, 1936; *Le Poids du ciel*, 1938; *Triomphe de la vie*, 1942; *Voyage en Italie*, 1953; *Notes sur l'affaire Dominici*, 1955; *Le*

Désastre de Pavie, 1963 (*The Battle of Pavia*, 1966).
TRANSLATION: *Moby Dick*, 1939, 1943 (with Lucien Jacques and Joan Smith; of Herman Melville's *Moby Dick*).

Bibliography
Goodrich, N. L. *Giono, Master of Fictional Modes*, 1973.
Peyre, Henri. *French Novelists of Today*, 1967.
Redfern, W. D. *The Private World of Jean Giono*, 1967.
Smith, Maxwell A. *Jean Giono*, 1966.

David B. Parsell

JOSÉ MARÍA GIRONELLA

Born: Darnius, Spain; December 31, 1917

Principal long fiction

Un hombre, 1946 (*Where the Soil Was Shallow*, 1957); *La marea*, 1949; *Los cipreses creen en Dios*, 1953 (*The Cypresses Believe in God*, 1957); *Un millón de muertos*, 1961 (*One Million Dead*, 1963); *Mujer, levántate y anda*, 1962; *Ha estallado la paz*, 1966 (*Peace After War*, 1969); *Condenados a vivir*, 1971.

Other literary forms

José María Gironella's renown springs from the series of panoramic novels that depict the Spanish Civil War, although the author has published in a variety of literary forms. His first work in print was poetry (*Ha llegado el invierno y tú no estás aquí*, 1945), but he quickly abandoned the genre in favor of the novel. *Los fantasmas de mi cerebro* (1959; *Phantoms and Fugitives: Journeys to the Improbable*, 1964; includes translation of *Todos somos fugitivos*) is the documentation of a nervous breakdown in a series of essays. A partial collection of Gironella's short stories appears in *Todos somos fugitivos* (1961). The author has produced travel books—*Personas, ideas, y mares* (1963; persons, ideas, and seas), *El Japón y su duende* (1964; Japan and her ghosts), and *En Asia se muere bajo las estrellas* (1968; in Asia you die under the stars)—along with essays that outline his personal vision in a wide variety of subjects, newspaper articles, literary analyses, criticism, biographical accounts, interviews, and meditations. *China, lágrima innumerable* (1965; China, countless tears) is an expanded essay accompanied by photographs. *Gritos del mar* (1967; shouts from the sea) collects in one volume various articles previously published in periodicals.

Achievements

Gironella has been labeled as a post-Spanish Civil War writer belonging to the realist tradition of nineteenth century literature, a fact which places him in Spain's *generación del 1939*. His novels represent a rupture in the trend toward introspection and intellectualization that existed prior to the Civil War. Gironella is a serious writer who identifies with the common man, desiring to convey through literature his own experiences in life. One is impressed by his sincerity and flexibility, his awe and optimism as he effects his personal ongoing search for knowledge and willingly shares it.

Gironella's major literary success has centered on his personal commitment to explain, through the historical novel, the reality and complexity of the Spanish Civil War (1936-1939); his epic novels *The Cypresses Believe in God* and *One Million Dead*—made both discrete and panoramic through the author's attempt to be objective—have become international best-sellers.

Biography

José María Gironella spent his early life in the northeastern Spanish province of Gerona, the locale of his most successful literature. His childhood desire to enter the priesthood was abandoned primarily because his attitude toward the Church had failed to crystallize. He worked at various unskilled positions until the eve of the Spanish Civil War, at which time he was employed in the Arús Bank in Gerona. During the war, Gironella served on the side of the Nationalists with a battalion of ski soldiers in the Pyrenees mountains. At the conclusion of the conflict, he returned to Gerona. He had already begun to write, and now he nurtured this desire with a position as a newspaper reporter and contributor of articles to various journals.

In 1946, he married his childhood sweetheart, Magda, and won the coveted Nadal Prize with the publication of his first novel. A year later, Gironella and his bride left Spain illegally and began several years of travel throughout Europe. During this time, he published his second novel, and, in 1951, he suffered a nervous breakdown. Gironella freely wrote about his illness while he sought relief at various clinics. The publication of *The Cypresses Believe in God* brought international recognition, and its sequel, *One Million Dead*, was also well received. These works assured for their creator a place in the literary history of Spain. The novelist returned to a residence in his native country, but he has traveled extensively throughout the world while continuing to write.

Analysis

According to José María Gironella, the seed for his mammoth enterprise, to create in novel form an explanation of historical events in contemporary Spain, was planted December 30, 1937. Spain was in its second winter of civil war. Gironella was serving as a ski soldier in the Pyrenees along Spain's border with France when he was approached by a French girl from among the many skiers who frequented the area. Tearing a button from Gironella's uniform as a souvenir, the girl quickly darted away on her skies, but not before inquiring as to the ridiculousness of shooting one's brothers. This incident provoked in the young Spaniard a desire to explain to this girl and the entire world what was occurring in his country. Sixteen years later, with the publication of *The Cypresses Believe in God*, Gironella's effort became a reality. This first work of the series covers the pre-Civil War period, from April, 1931, to July, 1936, and won for its author Spain's national prize for literature in 1953. It is considered to be the author's masterpiece.

The Cypresses Believe in God is an ambitious epic written in the realistic tradition; it neither defends nor condemns, but observes and records, with the attitude that the reader may reach his own conclusions relative to the events that are narrated. To afford continuity to the epic, the author has selected one family, the Alvears, and one location, the city of Gerona, in Catalonia, as representative of all Spanish families and places who contribute to the amalgam of the period which incubates the war. Thus, the Alvears are elevated to a symbolic stature, and Gerona as well becomes a microcosm of the entire country, one in which the reader can view the evolution of those forces that divided Spain into two uncompromising extremes.

Though it is a panoramic work, sociopolitical in intent, *The Cypresses Believe in God* is also the chronicle of a family. Matías Alvear, a Castilian and clerk at the local telegraph office, is married to Carmen Elgazu, a Basque. In the home, there is an atmosphere of mutual respect in spite of the native differences, which are reflected also in the contrasts among the three children. César, given to meditation and spiritual matters, enters the priesthood aided by the urging of his mother. Pilar is sheltered and obedient. Ignacio, a mirror of the author, is both an idealist and a skeptic. He is the protagonist who, like Spain itself, bears the burden of an inner struggle as he searches but continues to doubt during the course of the national conflict. The novel is primarily Ignacio's story, narrating his journey into adulthood and documenting the challenges and growth that are associated with the individual, the family, and the national scene as well.

Upon leaving the seminary, Ignacio determines to experience life as abundantly as possible. He acquires a position at a bank while continuing to work toward a degree in law. Through Ignacio and his association with various individuals, the reader is provided a tour of the culture and institutions of Gerona, the intellectual arguments and positions of all political parties, platforms, and events, in a variety of social environments. Ignacio's cousin, José, representing the voice of the Falange, schools the protagonist in anticlericalism and introduces him into politics. Together, they attend political meetings and discussions. David and Olga Pol allow Ignacio the perspective from the political Left, and they, in turn, instruct Ignacio in their ideology. They escort the protagonist to an overcrowded mental institution and discuss with him the need for social reform. These and other characters serve as representatives of the various social and political points of view.

The fictional episodes of the Alvear family and Ignacio's experiences are interwoven with the historical events surrounding the deterioration of the political crisis. The protagonist becomes romantically involved with the aristocrat Ana María, and while on vacation with his family, he quits school and later returns to the study of law. A schoolmate, Mateo Santos, a leader of the Falange, becomes a major character through his romantic involvement with Pilar. As the threat of war escalates, the Communists, reacting to the execution of a member of the Party, set fire to the cypress forests around Gerona. This action is for Ignacio's brother César a signal of the potential for a godless Spain, as these stately trees symbolize a belief in the deity (hence the title of the novel). This act of violence brings the Falange into political prominence, and the atrocities escalate on both sides. Ignacio's political commitment remains nebulous, although he has developed feelings for Marta de Soria, a Falangist leader. The protagonist passes part of his law examinations, but the political situation forces him to postpone the completion of his studies. His friend, Mateo Santos, who has been detained, is freed and goes into hiding. César is detained also and, despite Ignacio's belated attempt to save his brother, is executed for no good reason. This death, although fulfilling César's desire to achieve martyrdom, demonstrates the chaos that accompanies the violence of the period. The novel closes with César's execution, and the reader, who is not subjected to his moralizing, is nevertheless impressed by the fact that a senseless action has occurred.

The character of Ignacio is a combination of idealism and hope in conflict with doubt and skepticism. He represents a struggle between reason and emotion and is a symbol of two Spains, the struggle between the progressive and the traditional. Inasmuch as Gironella utilizes the protagonist to effect a composite view of the Spain of that period, the character has been assessed as a transparent window, without depth of character or personal convictions, through which one might view the opinions and intrigues that precipitated the war. Indeed, one of the principal shortcomings of the novel is the protagonist's failure to generate a strong personal commitment to anything. Yet the character is artfully drawn and does represent an active force in the novel.

Ignacio and his creator believe that the individual, through his own moral capabilities, will survive over the collective. Each Spaniard will develop a personal interpretation of the war based on his own experiences. It is this personal concept, directed toward the future in the hope of creating a more sensitive and searching national conscience, that distinguishes Gironella. In spite of the tragedy of the war, Gironella teaches that each side may retain its personal dignity and yet recognize the courage and honor of the other.

The epic nature of the novel is enhanced by the artistic integration of historical data with fiction. Thus, the sweeping proportions of *The Cypresses Believe in God* do not diminish the fact that this is a novel about a family. For Gironella, the family is the basic unit of a successful society, and throughout this novel an accounting is made of each of the Alvears. The novel succeeds on both levels, yet the breadth of the work is extensive at the expense of depth. Historical, economic, and political intricacies, as well as family episodes of minor importance, could have been omitted.

One Million Dead narrates the period from July 30, 1936, to April 1, 1939, and purports to provide a panoramic view of the war years. The author portrays the two factions simultaneously and attempts to be as impartial as possible. Gironella evinces a skill for meticulous documentation and verisimilitude, and, as for the preceding volume, he spent years collecting data, interviewing Spanish and foreign participants and witnesses, and searching archives for pertinent newspapers, photographs, and editorials. His personal participation in the conflict contributes to his insight. The title of this novel is intended to stand for the actual number of those who died in the conflict— slightly less than half a million—as well as those who, possessed by hate, destroyed their own souls.

In this novel, the Alvear family continues to occupy center stage, but the setting broadens to include all parts of Spain. The action begins in the cemetery where César has been killed. Ignacio discovers his brother's body and is haunted by the speculation that he might have been able to save him. The incident ignites a criticism of the war by the protagonist, who, with his family, is neutral as the struggle escalates. Ignacio's present sweetheart, Marta de Soria, a Falange activist, escapes to France. She has a short-lived relationship with an Italian soldier who, like many other characters in this volume, introduces an international thread to the fabric of the conflict. As the war proceeds, Ignacio finally enlists in the Nationalist armies as a medical aide. His travels take him to Barcelona and Madrid, where he works in a hospital for the wounded. He also experiences a journey into the Pyrenees, where he meets a group of Nationalist soldiers in a ski patrol. He is awed by the peace that he finds in these mountains. This and many other incidents in the novel reveal the author's autobiographical stamp on the action of the narrative.

Ignacio's mother adopts a homeless orphan whose parents had been killed at Guernica. As the war draws to a close, the various members of the family are drawn again to Gerona. Mateo de Soria also returns, as does his sister, Marta. Together, the family attends the first public mass to be held in Gerona's cathedral in three years. The novel concludes with a quiet scene in which General Francisco Franco, at work in his office in Nationalist headquarters, is informed by an aide that the war is officially over. The General simply responds that it is good and, thanking the aide, returns to his work.

This novel is broader in scope than its predecessor. It narrates the war from the point of view of both factions, not simply from a military perspective; it includes sociological, religious, and political intrigues as well. The author remains apart, detached, as he analyzes each occurrence without judging. This preference for the external and for objective distance does not serve Gironella well in his portrayal of the inner world of his characters. As a result, the vitality of some of the characters in *The Cypresses Believe in God* is fettered in the sequel. The author isolates himself from individuality, though he makes an effort to portray the distinctive souls of the provinces of Spain and to bless his characters with a unique and personal psychological depth. In each case, the author fails, a victim of his need to discover objectively and explain the significance of the Civil War. Although *One Million Dead* does not accommodate the empathy that might unlock the interior world of its characters, it is a systematic, organized analysis of the war. *The Cypresses*

Believe in God has been termed a novel with historical pretensions, whereas *One Million Dead* has been judged a historical work interlaced with fiction. The fictional aspect of the novel is further weakened by the author's tendency to stereotype minor characters and to level certain judgments based on their political affiliations. Communists, for example, are generally portrayed as villains in contrast to the noble efforts of the Falangists. Although Gironella insists on impartiality in his portrayal of the historical and political aspect of his novels, there is a tendency to favor the Nationalist platform. His continual reminder of the strength of the family unit as the key to Spain's hope for the future is a constant reiteration of the Nationalist theme. The victorious Falange is spared severe criticism, although it has been argued that Gironella was required to tread with care to avoid possible censorship. As the novel concludes, General Franco is portrayed, without excessive praise or propaganda, as the hope of Spain's future.

Peace After War—a slow-paced and all-too-predictable sequel to *One Million Dead*—treats the period between 1939 and 1941. Its emphasis is on the reconstruction of Spain under Franco, and the author praises the reforms of the Nationalists while portraying an atmosphere of unity and pride. Reform and greater national liberty through changes instituted by the government are emphasized, while resentment against the regime is kept to a minimum. Gironella demonstrates complete acceptance of Franco's policy and places emphasis once again on the fictional aspects of the work. The Alvears are reunited. Ignacio graduates from the University of Barcelona and assumes a life given more to reflection than to action. His sweetheart, Marta de Soria, devotes her attention to politics, while Ignacio renews his affection for his first love, Ana María. The marriage of Pilar to Mateo Santos assumes a more important position in this novel. Mateo displays a fanatical zeal to sacrifice his life, if necessary, in the fight against Communism. Pilar makes an unsuccessful attempt to dissuade him, but, unable to draw from herself the strength she requires, she withdraws to her family for moral support. Pilar's foil is her cousin, Paz, sensual, alienated from the family because of her leftist politics, but, unlike most of Gironella's protagonists, strong and motivated.

In addition to his Civil War cycle, Gironella has published several other novels, but his reputation ultimately will rest on a single work, *The Cypresses Believe in God*. Although in many respects this novel has dated badly, it retains its historical value as a sweeping portrait of Spain during a crucial period in her history.

Major publications other than long fiction
SHORT FICTION: *Todos somos fugitivos*, 1961 (English translation).
POETRY: *Ha llegado el invierno y tú no estás aquí*, 1945.
NONFICTION: *El novelista ante el mundo*, 1954; *Los fantasmas de mi cerebro*, 1959 (*Phantoms and Fugitives: Journeys to the Improbable*, 1964; includes

translation of *Todos somos fugitivos*); *Personas, ideas, y mares*, 1963; *El Japón y su duende*, 1964; *China, lágrima innumerable*, 1965; *Gritos del mar*, 1967; *Conversaciones con don Juan de Borbon*, 1968; *En Asia se muere bajo las estrellas*, 1968; *El Mediterraneo es un hombre disfrazado de mar*, 1974; *El escandola de Tierra Santa*, 1977.

Bibliography

Alborg, Juan L. *Hora actual de la novela española*, 1959.
Barzun, Jacques. *Classic, Romantic and Modern*, 1961.
Grupp, William J. "J. M. Gironella, Spanish Novelist," in *Kentucky Foreign Language Quarterly*. IV (1957), pp. 129-135.
Perez Minik, Domingo. *Novelistas españoles de los siglos XIX y XX*, 1957.
Schwartz, Ronald. *José María Gironella*, 1972.

Alfred W. Jensen

JOHANN WOLFGANG VON GOETHE

Born: Frankfurt am Main, Germany; August 28, 1749
Died: Weimar, Germany; March 22, 1832

Principal long fiction

Die Leiden des jungen Werthers, 1774 (*The Sorrows of Werter*, 1780; better known as *The Sorrows of Young Werther*, 1902); *Wilhelm Meisters Lehrjahre*, 1795-1796 (*Wilhelm Meister's Apprenticeship*, 1824); *Die Wahlverwandtschaften*, 1809 (*Elective Affinities*, 1872); *Wilhelm Meisters Wanderjahre: Oder, Die Entsagenden*, 1821, 1829 (*Wilhelm Meister's Travels*, 1882); *Works*, 1848-1890 (14 volumes); *Goethes Werke*, 1887-1919 (133 volumes).

Other literary forms

Johann Wolfgang von Goethe was a master in every major literary genre. He published his first book of poetry, *Neue Lieder* (*New Poems*) in 1770. Most of his well-known poems appeared individually in journals and were later collected in his *Works*. Collections of poetry that were published separately include *Epigramme: Venedig 1790* (1796; *Venetian Epigrams*), *Romische Elegien*, 1793 (*Roman Elegies*), *Xenien* (1796, with Friedrich Schiller; *Epigrams*), *Balladen* (1798, with Friedrich Schiller; *Ballads*), *Sonette* (1819; *Sonnets*), and *West-östlicher Divan* (1819, 1827; *West-Eastern Divan*), the translations of which are to be found in *Works*. Many well-known poems appeared in his novels; others were published in his posthumous works.

Goethe's first play, *Götz von Berlichingen mit der eisernen Hand* (*Gortz of Berlichingen with the Iron Hand*, 1799; also as *Goetz of Berlichingen*, 1880) was published in 1773. Many tragedies, comedies, and operettas (or *Singspiele*) followed, the most famous of which are *Clavigo* (1774; English translation, 1798, 1897), *Stella: Ein Schauspiel für Liebende* (1776; *Stella*, 1798), *Iphigenie auf Tauris* (1787; *Iphigenia in Tauris*, 1793), *Egmont* (1788; English translation, 1841), *Torquato Tasso* (1790; English translation, 1827), *Faust: Ein Fragment* (1790), *Die natürliche Tochter* (1804), and *Faust: Eine Tragödie* (1808) and *Faust: Eine Tragödie, zweiter Teil* (1833), which were translated together as *Faust: A Tragedy in Two Parts* (1838).

Goethe also wrote a collection of short fiction, *Unterhaltungen deutscher Ausgewanderten* (1795; *Conversations of German Emigrants*, in *Works*), and a paradigm of the short prose form entitled simply *Novelle* (1826; *Novel*, 1837). Other short stories appeared in his later novels, and he also wrote two verse epics, *Reinecke Fuchs* (1794; *Reinecke the Fox*, 1855) and *Hermann und Dorothea* (1797; *Herman and Dorothea*, 1801); an autobiography, *Aus meinem Leben: Dichtung und Wahrheit* (1811-1814; *Poetry and Truth: The Autobiography*); and essays on literature, art, and science. His letters and diaries in dozens of volumes reveal insights into his life, work, and times.

Achievements

Goethe has been called the last Renaissance man. Not only was he a writer whose work in every literary genre was startlingly new and exemplary for later generations of writers, but he also took great interest in painting, music, botany, geology, physiology, optics, and government, and many of his ideas in these fields of endeavor were novel and seminal.

Goethe belongs to that select group of men, including Homer, Dante, Leonardo da Vinci, Michaelangelo, Miguel de Cervantes, and William Shakespeare, who were able to encompass all aspects of the human condition in their creativity. Goethe's work is universal; it reflects man's sufferings and joys, successes and failures. From his earliest work, Goethe had a concept of what he thought man should be: an active, striving individual not afraid to make errors but dedicated to discovering his capabilities and to perfecting them to the best of his ability. His tragedy, *Faust*, on which he worked for more than fifty years, can be viewed as a summation of his thought, and it belongs among the masterpieces of world literature.

Goethe's influence, like that of Shakespeare, can hardly be measured. He has become a part of German and world culture. Every generation has poets, philosophers, artists, and general readers who look to Goethe as a model, and the volumes that make up the Goethe bibliography attest that influence.

Biography

Johann Wolfgang von Goethe was born August 28, 1749, in Frankfurt am Main. His father, Johann Kaspar Goethe, was a well-to-do nonpracticing lawyer holding the title of Imperial Councilor. His learning and many-sided interests were passed on to the young Goethe. The father was strict, often overbearing, and Goethe was never close to him. Goethe's mother, Katharina Elisabeth (née Textor), the daughter of the mayor, received more of his affection. In Frankfurt, Goethe first made contact with the theater via puppet plays and French troupes. He recorded these impressions vividly in his autobiography, *Poetry and Truth*. From 1765 to 1768, he attended the university in Leipzig, famous for its Enlightenment and Rococo writers, and studied law. There he also studied painting and had the first of his many famous love affairs (this one with Kätchen Schönkopf), which always resulted in beautiful poetry. His not atypical student life was interrupted by a lung hemorrhage, which compelled him to return to Frankfurt. Home again, and sickly, he came under the influence of the pietist and mystic Susanna von Klettenberg, whose teachings can be found in "Bekenntnisse einer schönen Selle" ("Confessions of a Fair Saint"), which constitutes the sixth book of *Wilhelm Meister's Apprenticeship*. Goethe returned to the university in 1770, this time to Strasbourg, where he received his degree in 1771. While in this French-German border city, he met Johann Gottfried Herder, the theologian and critic who, at this time was singing the praises of Shakespeare, Ossian, primitive poetry, and the need for a German literature freed from French influence. Herder's great influence on Goethe is unmistakable and can be seen especially in Goethe's drama *Goetz of Berlichingen* and in a speech commemorating Shakespeare. This university period produced famous poems to Friederike Brion in *Sesenheimer Liederbuch* (1775-1789, 1854; *Sesenheim Songs*). After receiving his degree, Goethe returned to Frankfurt and somewhat grudgingly set up a law practice. The years 1771 to 1775 mark Goethe's *Sturm und Drang* period, years of feverish literary activity. His best-known works from these years are *Goetz of Berlichingen*, the novel *The Sorrows of Young Werther*, and his *Sturm und Drang* lyrics.

In 1775, Duke Karl August invited Goethe to Weimar, and, feeling the need to begin a new "epoch" in his life, Goethe decided to stay in the Thuringian city. Except for numerous trips, he spent the rest of his life in Weimar. This transitional period from the tempestuousness of the *Sturm und Drang* to the restraint of his classical period was marked by an intensive study of nature and the sciences and by numerous court activities. Goethe wrote many minor works in the following decade, and he started or continued several major works which for various reasons he left unfinished. A need for a rebirth, a rejuvenation, drove Goethe to Italy, where he stayed from 1786 to 1788. There he experienced the "noble simplicity and quiet grandeur" (in Adam Oeser and Johann Winckelmann's words) of Roman and Greek art and gained new impetus for his work, completing *Iphigenia in Tauris* and *Egmont*. He chronicled these travels in his *Italienische Reise* (1816, 1817; *Travels in Italy*, 1883), which makes up part of his autobiography. In the decade after his return to Weimar, he took up new scientific endeavors and wrote numerous works, including *Torquato Tasso*, *Venetian Epigrams*, *Roman Elegies*, and *Wilhelm Meister's Apprenticeship*.

The year 1794 marked the beginning of Goethe's friendship with Friedrich Schiller, which proved fruitful for both men. Their shared interests can be seen in *Epigrams*, a collection of satiric distiches, in *Ballads*, and in their insightful two-volume correspondence. The last thirty years of Goethe's life reveal an unflagging productivity. Besides his increasing scientific interests, he wrote his autobiography, the novels *Elective Affinities* and *Wilhelm Meister's Travels*, and the lyric cycle *West-Eastern Divan*, and he succeeded in finishing his lifework, *Faust*. He died at the age of eighty-two on March 22, 1832, and was buried in Weimar next to Schiller.

Analysis

Johann Wolfgang von Goethe's first novel, *The Sorrows of Young Werther*, did for the German novel what his early play *Goetz of Berlichingen* did for German drama—it revolutionized prose writing in German and rescued German literature from a deadening provincialism. The people and places in *The Sorrows of Young Werther* have been so well documented, to a great extent by Goethe himself in his autobiography *Poetry and Truth*, that the reader with biographical knowledge of Goethe has difficulty separating the author from the titular hero Werther. The autobiographical content of the novel has often led to one-sided interpretations that have ignored other important aspects of the work, yet the genesis of the story in Goethe's own experience is impossible to ignore.

After Goethe had finished his law studies in Strasbourg, he returned to his parental home in Frankfurt to pursue, somewhat halfheartedly, a law career. At the behest of his father, Goethe went in May, 1772, to Wetzlar, which still claimed fame as the seat of the Reichskammergericht (supreme court) of the Holy Roman Empire. At a ball in the small town (which becomes one of the central episodes in the novel), Goethe met Lotte Buff, who was unofficially engaged to Johann Christian Kestner, a secretary to the Hanoverian legation. Goethe often visited her at the home of her father, a widower with many children, and he, like Werther, eventually fell in love with her; but Goethe fell in love often and easily, and the intensity of his relationship with Buff has been overemphasized. Goethe's letters to her do not read like Werther's; the identification of Goethe with Werther should not be carried too far. This is not to say that Goethe's emotions for Buff were shallow—his hasty retreat from Wetzlar without even a farewell speaks against this—but Goethe was attracted to married or "taken" women, a not unimportant psychological phenomenon.

After leaving Wetzlar, Goethe visited the popular writer of sentimental novels, Sophie von La Roche, at Ehrenbreitenstein. Here, he fell in love with the author's daughter, Maximiliane, who, like Buff, was engaged to be married. This sensitive situation continued even after Maximiliane's marriage, until her husband, Brentano, put an end to it, nearly a year and a half after Goethe had left Wetzlar. Shortly after leaving Wetzlar, Kestner, who carried on a correspondence with Goethe for many years, wrote to Goethe, describing in great detail the suicide of a young man two years Goethe's senior, Karl Wilhelm Jerusalem, whom Goethe had met. Jerusalem had killed himself over unrequited love for a married woman. Although in *Poetry and Truth* Goethe claims that the Jerusalem incident was the catalyst for *The Sorrows of Young Werther* (a catalyst that took nearly two years to bring about an effect), recent scholarship indicates that it was not until Goethe's affair with Maximiliane that he began to get the idea for the novel. By the time Goethe wrote *The Sorrows of Young Werther*, he was naturally no longer the same man he was two years earlier. He had essentially already left behind many of his *Sturm und Drang* traits, those rebellious Romantic characteristics that modern man so fondly cherishes in his struggle against society and technology. Like his contemporary, Friedrich Maximilian Klinger, Goethe saw the dangers of Romantic excess, and *The Sorrows of Young Werther* can claim to be Goethe's reckoning with his not-too-distant past.

The Sorrows of Young Werther begins (as does Jean-Jacques Rousseau's epistolary novel *Julie: Ou, La Nouvelle Héloïse*, 1761) and ends (as does Samuel Richardson's epistolary novel *Pamela*, 1740-1741) with comments by the editor, who has collected Werther's letters to provide "consolation" for those who feel like Werther. The first letter is dated May 4, 1771, and serves as exposition. Werther has been sent by his mother to find out about an inheritance. He has left behind "the poor Leonore," whom he has abandoned after being attracted to her sister. This often-overlooked fact reveals much about Werther's character and does not present Werther in a favorable light at the beginning of the novel.

Werther is an artist, or at least he claims to be, but he deludes himself. In his second letter (May 10), he writes: "I am so happy, dear friend, so completely immersed in the feeling of a tranquil existence that my art suffers from it. I couldn't draw now, not a line, and have never been a greater painter than at this moment." Werther allows himself to be overwhelmed by his feelings for nature, and he uses these feelings to rationalize his dilettantism.

Werther loses himself in nature, in reveries about an old love, in the patriarchal atmosphere of Homer, and essentially withdraws from society into himself. The letter of June 16, the longest in the novel, describes the ball where Werther meets Lotte. He has been warned that Lotte is engaged to Albert, but that is of little concern to him. His letter is replete with broken thoughts, effusions, and dashes that portray his inner turmoil, and the fact that this letter comes seventeen days after the previous one shows how enthralled he is with his "new" love. Werther imagines the idyllic scene at the end of Oliver Goldsmith's *The Vicar of Wakefield* (1766), a scene which for him must remain unrealized. Lotte serves as a new cathexis; Werther completely loses himself in thoughts of her and does not know "either that it's day or night." His search, his yearning for an idyllic, harmonious life contrasts with his romantic longing for independence.

Werther often compares himself to a child and is very fond of children. He mentions his mother only briefly and his father not at all. He often longs for the innocence of childhood and subconsciously seems to wish that he could be among children for whom Lotte cuts the daily bread. His search for security, for protection, is very childlike, and he looks to Lotte as much for maternal as for sexual affection.

His passing comment about the local preacher's daughter ("I must say I found her not unpleasing"), who again is "taken," underlines his emotional instability. At times, however, Werther is capable of profound thoughts and of analyzing his own problems: "If we once have the power to pull ourselves together, our work will pass briskly through our hands, and we shall find a true pleasure in our activity" (July 1). "Activity" is a key word for Goethe and serves as a means of interpreting the novel. Wilhelm, the recipient of Werther's letters, and Werther's mother admonish him to find some kind of productive activity, which he only ridicules: "Am I not now active, and isn't it basically one and the same whether I count peas or lentils?" (July 20).

Later in the novel, Werther begins to read James Macpherson's skillful forgery, *The Works of Ossian* (1765), in whose stormy and turbulent descriptions of nature he finds his own feelings mirrored. Goethe commented later (August 2, 1829) that Werther read Homer while sane and Ossian after he went mad. The changing style of Werther's letters reflects his inner turmoil. Absent now are the pithy statements; subjectivism has taken over. Again, his friend Wilhelm admonishes him "to get rid of the miserable feeling that must consume all of your powers," but Werther notes in his diary that there is no "appearance of improvement."

Werther's second-longest letter deals with his argument with Albert about suicide (August 12). Werther justifies it, while Albert ridicules it as a tool of a spineless man, and the reader has a presentiment. Only ten days later, Werther writes that he is incapable of doing anything: "I have no imaginative powers, no feeling for nature, and books make me sick." He hopes that a new position will cure him (another important theme in Goethe's works), but the first book closes with his statement: "I see no end to this misery but the grave."

The second book begins one month and ten days after the last letter of book 1 and more than five months after the first letter of the novel. Werther now has the position of secretary to an ambassador, a position that he cannot endure for long. The position does, however, bring about a kind of recovery that enables Werther to see his problem: "nothing is more dangerous than solitude" (October 20). There are now longer intervals between the letters, in which he often vacillates between recognizing his problems and putting the blame on others for them: "And you are all to blame whose twaddle placed this yoke on me and who have prated so much about activity. Activity!" (December 24).

Three months after his arrival, Werther writes Lotte for the first time, and his vocabulary once again is marked by such words as "isolation," "loneliness," and "limitation." Goethe interjects the parallel story of a farmhand, whom Werther had met earlier, whose unrequited love will later lead to murder. Werther identifies so much with this man's fate that he later makes an attempt to save him. This and the parallel motif of a man who worked for Lotte's father, fell in love with Lotte, was driven from the household, and became insane as a result of his unrequited love skillfully mark Werther's decline.

On December 6, about nineteen months after the first letter of the novel, Werther's correspondence ends, and the editor tells how he gathered the material that covers Werther's last days. The editor's longer, analytical sentences contrast sharply with Werther's rhapsodic prose. Like Wilhelm, he speaks of Werther's inactivity: "He seemed to himself justified in his inactivity by all this. . . ," but he also presents material (the very informed source is not given) which shows that Lotte was not totally without blame, that she spurred Werther on somewhat until it was too late. When Werther, at the end of the novel, sends his servant to borrow Albert's pistols for a supposed trip, Lotte reacts in horror; she knows that Werther wants the pistols to shoot himself, yet she does nothing about it, because Werther had visited her against Albert's wishes and she now fears Albert's remonstrations.

The end of the novel is masterful in its succinct style: "At twelve noon he died. . . . At night toward eleven [the steward] had him buried at the spot Werther had chosen. The steward followed the body, and his sons, but Albert found it impossible. People feared for Lotte's life. Workmen carried him. No clergyman escorted him."

Goethe intended to depict in *The Sorrows of Young Werther* the problems of an excessively sensitive soul, showing how unbridled emotions and inactivity could lead to death. He drew from his own life, but he also saw many Werthers around him, as in the figure of the gifted contemporary poet and dramatist Jakob Michael Reinhold Lenz. The influence of the novel was great, but Goethe's intent was widely misunderstood. Young men with romantic hearts saw in the book a justification for excessive emotion and suicide, and they emulated Werther by dressing in the blue coat and yellow vest that he wears in the novel. "Werther fever" was on the rise, and there was even a spate of suicides à la Werther. For this and other reasons, Goethe revised the novel in 1787. Still, Werther became a model for Romantic writers throughout the world, and to this day, his story is the best known among Goethe's works.

Like most of Goethe's mature works, *Wilhelm Meister's Apprenticeship* had a long genesis. Goethe made first mention of this, his second novel, in an entry in his diary dated February 16, 1777, although he probably was working on the novel as early as 1776; it took him nearly twenty years to complete it. To be sure, he had finished a large portion of the novel by 1785, through book 6 and part of book 7, but work on the novel, as with the plays *Iphigenia in Tauris*, *Egmont*, and *Torquato Tasso*, was interrupted by his trip to Italy from 1786 to 1788. Not until his friendship with Friedrich Schiller, who supplied insightful criticism and suggestions, many of which Goethe adopted, did Goethe regain interest and finish the work. The novel Goethe published in 1795 and 1796 was essentially a thorough revision of the earlier version entitled *Wilhelm Meisters Theatralische Sendung* (1911; *Wilhelm Meister's Theatrical Mission*, 1913), the manuscript of which was not discovered until 1910.

Wilhelm Meister's Theatrical Mission is a *Bildungsroman* in both the literal and the figurative sense. The fragment opens with Wilhelm as a boy, and the interesting psychological development of the child, which closely follows Goethe's autobiography, is to a great extent sacrificed in *Wilhelm Meister's Apprenticeship*, which begins with Wilhelm as a young man about to leave the parental home (the few childhood scenes are told in retrospect). In *Wilhelm Meister's Apprenticeship*, the theater loses in importance: *Wilhelm Meister's Theatrical Mission* reflects the ambitions and concerns of a budding dramatist; *Wilhelm Meister's Apprenticeship*, Goethe's ideas on culture and human development. The former follows the pattern woven by Goethe in many of his early poems and dramas about the artist; the latter can no longer be termed "a portrait of the artist as a young man." The theater represents only one step on Wilhelm's path of self-development. The language of the former reads much like Goethe's *Sturm und Drang* prose and is quite different from the stylized, sculptured prose in the latter, which is characteristic of Goethe's prose style after his years in Italy. Many of the ideas and most of the characters, however, were transferred from the early fragment to the novel and merely reshaped to represent the thinking of the mature Goethe.

Thematically, *Wilhelm Meister's Apprenticeship* consists of five parts: home (book 1 and book 2, chapters 1 and 2), Wilhelm's travels as a businessman and his first theatrical encounter (book 2, chapter 3, to book 3, chapter 12), the theatre of Serlo (book 3, chapter 13, to book 5, and book 7, chapter 8), "Confessions of a Fair Saint" (book 6), and the "Society of the Tower" episodes (book 7, chapters 1-7 and 9, and book 8). The linear construction enables the reader to follow the development of Wilhelm from a somewhat naïve, eager young man through his many trials and tribulations to his reception into the Society of the Tower, where he is given an indenture that will guide him in his journeyman years.

At the beginning of the novel, Wilhelm, like many young people, disdains his family's supposed avarice and bourgeois life and views the theater as a means of escape. His mother curses the day she gave him a puppet theater, for she believes his calling to the theater will ruin him physically and morally. Goethe's description of theater life mirrors quite accurately the circumstances and plight of theater groups in Germany in the 1760's and 1770's.

A series of coincidences and misunderstandings involving Wilhelm's lover, Marianne—an actress who, unbeknown to him, is pregnant—causes him to abandon her and resign himself to his father's business. Years pass; Wilhelm despairs over his ability as a writer, which he still believes to be his calling, burns his manuscripts, and seems to dedicate himself diligently to his father's merchant profession. Following the advice of his father and his friend Werner, Wilhelm sets out on a trip to collect some debts owed to his father. As soon as he hears of a theatrical troupe performing in the vicinity where his travels have taken him, the old flame smouldering inside flares up and he is consumed by the idea of the theater. He encounters a motley group of actors and takes up with them.

The two theater episodes help Wilhelm gain insights into himself. At first enthusiastic about pursuing his dream of belonging to an acting troupe, he dedicates body and soul to the theater, which he serves as actor, writer, and director. (These activities reflect Goethe's involvement as writer, actor, and, after 1791, director of the Weimar Theatre.) While at a castle with the troupe, Wilhelm is introduced to the theater of Shakespeare by Jarno, a mysterious figure and a member of the Society of the Tower whose function becomes clear only later. Shakespeare has a profound effect on Wilhelm, as he did on all the German dramatists of the 1770's; Wilhelm's conversations about Shakespeare and *Hamlet* with Serlo, the director of a troupe in a large city of commerce (probably modeled on Hamburg), and with his sister Aurelie, and their subsequent successful performance of the play, form the nucleus of the fourth book. The sections on *Hamlet* do not, however, represent the thinking of the older Goethe, but rather the subjective sentimentality of the *Sturm und Drang* writers. Wilhelm's dissatisfaction with the members of the troupe and the bustle of the city causes him to reflect on the direction he has taken in his life; for the first time, he admires the order and activity of the world of commerce (book 4, chapter 20). Wilhelm still views the theater as a goal, however, writing to his friend Werner, "to develop myself exactly as I am, that was vaguely my wish and my intention from the days of my youth." The German word *(aus)bilden* (to develop, to educate, to cultivate), whose variant is found in *Bildungsroman* is a key word in the novel and appears more than a hundred times. At this point in the novel, Wilhelm knows he must develop himself, but he still falsely views the theater as an end and not as a means.

Toward the end of the fifth book, Wilhelm becomes more and more disillusioned with the theater, and his criticism of it culminates in the declaration in book 7, chapter 8: "I am leaving the theatre to join up with men whose association has to lead me in every sense to a pure and certain activity." The word "activity" (*Tätigkeit*), as in *The Sorrows of Young Werther*, is a key word in Goethe's novels, and it is toward an active, constructive life that Wilhelm must move.

The Society of the Tower makes up most of book 7 and all of book 8. Wilhelm discovers that many of the people who have crossed his path throughout the novel (Jarno, the Abbé, Natalie "the beautiful amazon," the Countess, Friedrich, and others) are connected with the Society and have monitored and guided his development. Wilhelm is now initiated into the secrets of the Society, and the Abbé says: "Your apprenticeship is over, nature has released you" (book 7, chapter 9). Wilhelm discovers that the boy Felix, who has been with him since his days with Serlo, is his son by Marianne, who died in childbirth. He also learns that Mignon and the harp player, those Romantic spirits whom he met while with the first acting troupe, are father and daughter from an incestuous affair. Symbolically, they must die, for they represent an aberrant side of life not compatible with Wilhelm's active, healthy endeavors. (Significantly, and ironically, German Romantic writers and musicians of the early nineteenth century were enraptured with the figure of Mignon and the harp player.)

Wilhelm falls in love with Natalie, who, like the other members of the Society, will play a significant role in the continuation of the novel, *Wilhelm Meister's Travels*. Wilhelm's development, however, is not yet over; the Society will direct him on his next journey, which he will make with his son Felix.

Wilhelm Meister's Apprenticeship is a milestone in the development of the novel as a genre. Not until Charles Dickens did a novelist again weave such an intricate plot. Goethe had literary debts to such writers as Samuel Richardson, Jean-Jacques Rousseau, and Oliver Goldsmith, but he paid them back with interest. His use of different genres within the novel—of letters, songs, and stories within the story—was to have a great influence on the next generation of novelists in England, France, and Russia. In Germany, Goethe made the novel into an art form, a form which, unlike poetry or drama, was able to encompass the breadth of the human condition.

Goethe's third novel, *Elective Affinities*, was first conceived as a novella to be placed in what was later to become his fourth novel, *Wilhelm Meister's Travels*, but the idea became so important to Goethe that he expanded the novella into a novel in what was for him a relatively short period of time; of his novels, *The Sorrows of Young Werther* was written more quickly. Goethe himself said that *Elective Affinities* should be read three times to comprehend its ramifications, and in his diary, he noted that the idea behind the novel was to portray "social relationships and their conflicts in a symbolic way."

Elective Affinities differs from Goethe's other novels in that it focuses attention on a group of people rather than on an individual, as in *The Sorrows of Young Werther* and *Wilhelm Meister's Apprenticeship*. In *Elective Affinities*, Goethe, somewhat like his contemporary, Jane Austen, uses a small group of people as a microcosm to represent the problems of contemporary society.

Elective Affinities begins with what seems to be an idyll. Edward and Charlotte live on a large estate and are arranging it to their tastes. They are both in their second marriage. Having been lovers in their youth who were forced into marriages of convenience, they were able to marry after the deaths of their spouses. Soon, however, flaws begin to appear in the idyllic setting. Edward and Charlotte are designing a new house, a pleasure pavilion (*Lustgebäude*), and, as with most actions in the novel, this one is symbolic: The old house, representing their marriage, is no longer adequate, and the building of the new one is an unconscious admission that their marriage itself is no longer adequate to one or to both of them. Apart from *Faust*, *Elective Affinities* is Goethe's most symbolic work, and attention must be paid to every object—the plane trees, the church, water, the paths, headaches, and so on—for symbolic meaning blended into the novel in a masterful way.

The stagnation of the marriage becomes clear when Edward wants to invite his old friend, the Captain, who has fallen on hard times, to come live with them. Charlotte, who is by far more perceptive than Edward, fears this move. She knows that a third person will change their lives, but whereas she is completely happy and satisfied in her activity (*Tätigkeit*), Edward is a dilettante who needs the "active" Captain to stimulate him. The narrator, whose function in *Elective Affinities* is generally to analyze the characters and their relationships objectively rather than to admonish, as in *The Sorrows of Young Werther*, comments that before the arrival of the Captain, Edward and Charlotte had had less conversation than usual, because they had disagreed over the building of the park: "Thus daily Charlotte felt lonelier."

The Captain arrives, and Charlotte decides to have Ottilie, the orphaned daughter of an old friend, brought from the boarding school which she attends with Luciane, Charlotte's daughter from her first marriage; thus, the tragic constellation is complete. One day, the four of them are together when the Captain begins speaking of elective affinities, the tendency in chemistry for particles to break up and form new combinations. Edward, who misconstrues nearly everything, comments that these relationships become interesting only when they cause separations (*Scheidungen*—in German also meaning "divorces"), and he makes the analogy (quite unaware, consciously at least, of its implications) that Charlotte represents A, he himself B, the Captain C, and Ottilie D: When A and B break up, and C and D likewise, they form the new unions of AD and BC. Edward's casual talk disturbs Charlotte, who recognizes in it his subconscious yearning.

The new pairs are indeed gradually formed. Charlotte finds with the Captain new "activity" which she no longer shares with Edward, and Edward delights in being with Ottilie, with whom he shares a childlike nature. The names of the characters are themselves significant: Edward's real name, "Otto" (which is also the Captain's first name), "Charlotte," and "Ottilie" all have the same root, showing symbolically the close affinity among them. The action of the first part pinnacles in a scene of psychological adultery. Edward visits Charlotte's bedroom one night after "a strange mix-up took place in his soul," and during intercourse, he thinks of Ottilie while Charlotte thinks of the Captain. Upon waking, Edward has a presentiment and considers what he has done a crime. Thereafter the thought of Ottilie consumes him, just as Lotte's image consumed Werther.

Elective Affinities, like most of Goethe's later works, contains the theme of renunciation (*Entsagung*), and it could, in fact, justifiably carry the subtitle of *Wilhelm Meister's Travels: Oder, Die Entsagenden* (or those who renounce). Charlotte learns to renounce the Captain; Edward does not renounce, nor does Ottilie at this point in the novel. The Captain leaves, and when Edward learns that Charlotte is pregnant, he flees to seek his end in a war of which he has no real understanding, just as he does not understand most things in his life.

The first half of the second part deals with how Charlotte and Ottilie lead their lives during the absence of Edward and the Captain. Ottilie, even though she still longs for Edward, matures, and this maturation process can be followed in her diary, excerpts from which occasionally break the narrative flow of the novel. At times, it is hard to believe that Ottilie, who had difficulties in school, can actually understand the pithy statements she copies into her diary. Readers of Goethe are inclined to view Ottilie as an authorial mouthpiece in these passages, just as the aphorisms in "Makarien's Archive," at the end of *Wilhelm Meister's Travels*, serve to represent Goethe's thinking. Ottilie's diary also prepares the reader for her renunciation of Edward and for her belief that it is wrong to break up the marriage of Edward and Charlotte. When the baby, which has Ottilie's eyes and the Captain's facial features, is born (conceived on the night of psychological adultery), Ottilie begins to sublimate her love for Edward into a pseudo-mother-love for the child.

In *Elective Affinities*, Goethe assimilates, as in his other novels, a variety of literary genres. Ottilie's diary has already been mentioned; particularly striking is the function of the novella, "The Strange Neighbor Children," which is integrated into the novel. The children in the novella parallel to a certain degree the characters in the novel, but the novella, based on events in the Captain's past, has a happy ending (despite the parallel symbols of water and drowning), unlike the novel.

One day, Ottilie takes the baby to the lake, where she is suddenly surprised by Edward. Edward has returned from the war ever more intent on having Ottilie. He has met with the Captain (who is now a major, perhaps through advancement in the same war in which Edward fought) and has convinced him, even though the Captain hesitated at first, that Charlotte and he should divorce and that the Major should marry Charlotte and raise the baby. Ottilie resists Edward's proposal that they marry, saying that Charlotte must decide their fate. In her confusion, she hurries, after parting from Edward, to a skiff, loses her balance, and drops the baby into the lake. By the time she retrieves it, it is dead.

Despite the tragic loss, Charlotte agrees to a divorce. Ottilie, however, has learned to "renounce." She resolves to be a teacher and to return to the boarding school, where she can be "active." Edward surprises her on her journey back to the school and gets her to return to the estate. During their brief meeting at an inn, however, Ottilie does not say a word; she refuses to express her love for Edward, realizing that the only escape for her is in death. Her maturation and new convictions become apparent when they return to the estate and she places Charlotte's and Edward's hands together. She continues not to speak and resolves to starve herself to death. Edward soon follows her in death, and the two are buried side by side.

Wilhelm Meister's Travels belongs to that group of Goethe's later works (in poetry, *West-Eastern Divan*, and in drama, *Faust*) which are characteristic of his *Altersstil* (mature style) and which are not easily accessible. Goethe himself recognized the difficulty of his last novel; he admitted (February 17, 1827) that it could not have been written earlier. In a conversation six years before this admission (June 8, 1821), he cited the problem which readers would have with the novel: "Everything is really to be taken symbolically, and everywhere there is something else hidden behind it. Every solution to a problem is a new problem." The absence of plot; the interspersed novellas, poems, letters, aphorisms, dramatic dialogue, and technical discussions of various trades; and the often obscure wisdom of the aged Goethe make for difficult reading, but when the novel is read in the context of Goethe's later works and his worldview, its seemingly vague symbols become clearer.

Goethe formed the conception of *Wilhelm Meister's Travels* as soon as he finished its companion piece, *Wilhelm Meister's Apprenticeship*, but actual work on the novel did not begin until 1807, and it was not completed for more than twenty years. The novel fuses materials of two kinds: the novellas, written mostly between 1807 and 1818, which in style and content differ from the framework, and the framework itself, most of which was completed later. A first version appeared in 1821 and was then thoroughly revised for the second version in 1829. The novellas present vignettes of the human condition, the vicissitudes of human existence, and are moralistic in that they reinforce the teachings implicit in the novel's framework; almost all of them deal with the problem of passion. The title of the novel itself is bipartite: *Wilhelm Meister's Travels* indicates a continuation, however loosely, of *Wilhelm Meister's Apprenticeship*; the subtitle, *Die Entsagenden* (those who renounce), mirrors the philosophy of the Society which directs the protagonist.

The Society of the Tower has given Wilhelm rules which dictate his travels: He cannot stay longer than three days under one roof; when he leaves a place, he must travel at least one German mile (approximately five miles); and he cannot return to the same place for more than a year. The novel begins with Wilhelm and his son Felix journeying through the mountains. Goethe immediately introduces the symbolic figures of Joseph, a carpenter, and Maria, his wife, who live in an abandoned monastery and offer Wilhelm shelter. Goethe's ideas on religion are encapsulated in this segment, both symbolically (the ruins of the monastery and Joseph's work on it) and explicitly (in conversations between Wilhelm and Joseph). The theme of the family recurs throughout the novel, and this "first family" serves as a model.

Continuing on his wanderings, Wilhelm meets Montan, the Jarno of *Wilhelm Meister's Apprenticeship*. Like many of the characters in the novel, Montan/Jarno is one who has "renounced," and he later fulfills a utilitarian function in the new society; his métier is geology, hence his name. The characters in the novel who will later make up the Society have professions that represent the vast and varied interests of Goethe: astronomy, weaving, geology, botany, and so on.

Wilhelm and Felix come to the house of the "Uncle" (*der Oheim*), where they meet Hersilie, with whom Felix falls in love. Felix's love for Hersilie depicts the impetuous and immature side of love. His handling of the situation parallels to a great extent Wilhelm's amorous adventures in *Wilhelm Meister's Apprenticeship* and is juxtaposed to the maturity of the now older and wiser Wilhelm. Wilhelm also meets at the Uncle's house Juliette and Leonardo. Leonardo has been away to educate himself, has overcome the many obstacles of impetuous youth, and is now returning to his Uncle's to take up new activities. The Uncle owns vast tracts of land in America, which Leonardo will inherit. The Society also possesses large landholdings in America, and Leonardo plans to join them to found colonies in the new land for those people of the mountain regions whose skills are being replaced by the machines of the Industrial Revolution. (This utopian vision of America runs throughout German literature and can be seen even today in the novels of several young Austrian writers and German filmmakers.)

Wilhelm visits the castle of Aunt Makarie, whose nebulous figure seems to shed guiding light over the Society's proceedings. Her pithy advice and aphorisms allow Goethe to express his wisdom on every subject of interest to him. Makarie is the example *par excellence* of one who has renounced. She is confined to a chair, but her wisdom and guidance are sought by everyone. Wilhelm then comes to the Pedagogical Province, where he leaves Felix to be educated while he continues his journey. The Pedagogical Province is a strict, almost totalitarian educational system (with overtones from Plato, Rousseau, and Johann Heinrich Pestalozzi) where young people are rigorously trained to serve a function in society. Every aspect of the student's life is dictated, and at first, Felix, again as a figure of youth whose passions must be controlled, is hesitant, but he does conform. The idea behind the Province is that man can attain the highest that he is capable of reaching. Some of the Province's pupils will emigrate to America with the Society.

Wilhelm later comes to that mountainous region whose inhabitants are threatened by the Industrial Revolution. There he meets a group planning to emigrate to America, and he begins practicing the profession he has chosen in order to be a useful member of society, namely, that of a doctor. Book 3 contains long passages on technical aspects of spinning and weaving, the society's plans for colonies in America and in Europe, and finally a meeting of the emigrants at Markarie's castle. Here some of the principal characters from *Wilhelm Meister's Apprenticeship* come together; they now all have a useful profession, a function in the new society: Friedrich, because of his good memory, is a copyist; the frivolous Philine has become, somewhat incredulously, an expert, selfless seamstress; and the Abbé is a teacher.

The novel ends as it began, symbolically. As Wilhelm travels upriver to join Felix, who is now several years older, a horse with rider plunges into the river. It is Felix, who has recently visited Hersilie on a mission of love, was rejected, and was riding grief-stricken when his horse fell into the river. Wilhelm saves his son by opening a vein—he has now completed his education; several years before, a similar incident had occurred in Wilhelm's life, but he was untrained and had to watch a fisher-boy die. Wilhelm will now join Natalie and the Society.

Wilhelm Meister's Travels is not a psychological study of man and society such as *Elective Affinities*; rather, it is a receptacle into which Goethe poured the wisdom gathered over a long life. It contains some of his most profound thoughts on man, society, literature, art, music, and the sciences. It also contains the vision of *Faust*: The central themes of activity and renunciation help define man's purpose on earth and his function in society—an unusual optimism for a writer in his eightieth year.

Major publications other than long fiction

SHORT FICTION: *Unterhaltungen deutscher Ausgewanderten*, 1795 (*Conversations of German Emigrants*); *Novelle*, 1826 (*Novel*, 1837).

PLAYS: *Götz von Berlichingen mit der eisernen Hand*, 1773 (*Gortz of Berlichingen with the Iron Hand*, 1799; also as *Goetz of Berlichingen*, 1880); *Clavigo*, 1774 (English translation, 1798, 1897); *Götter, Helden, und Wieland*, 1774 (*Gods, Heroes, and Wieland*); *Erwin und Elmire*, 1775 (libretto; *Erwin and Elmire*); *Claudine von Villa Bella*, 1776 (libretto; *Claudine of Villa Bella*); *Die Geschwister*, 1776 (*The Brother and Sister*); *Stella: Ein Schauspiel für Liebende*, 1776 (*Stella*, 1798); *Proserpina: Ein Monodrama*, 1778 (*Proserpina: A Monodrama*); *Die Fischerinn*, 1782 (*The Fisherwoman*); *Die Mitschuldigen*, 1787 (written 1768; *The Fellow-Culprits*); *Iphigenie auf Tauris*, 1787 (*Iphigenia in Tauris*, 1793); *Der Triumph der Empfindsamkeit*, 1787 (*The Triumph of Sensitivity*); *Egmont*, 1788 (English translation, 1841); *Faust: Ein Fragment*, 1790; *Jery und Bätely*, 1790 (*Jerry and Bätely*); *Scherz, Lust, und Rache*, 1790 (*Jest, Pleasure, and Revenge*); *Torquato Tasso*, 1790 (English translation, 1827); *Der Gross-Cophta*, 1792 (*The Grand Cophta*); *Der Bürgergeneral*, 1793 (*The Citizen General*); *Die Aufgeregten*, 1794 (*The Agitated*); *Die natürliche Tochter*, 1804; *Die Laune des Verliebten*, 1806 (written 1767; *The Wayward Lover*); *Faust: Eine Tragödie*, 1808 (in *Faust: A Tragedy in Two Parts*, 1838); *Pandora*, 1808 (English translation); *Des Epimenides Erwachen*, 1815 (*The Waking of Epimenides*); *Faust: Eine Tragödie, zweiter Teil*, 1833 (*Faust: A Tragedy in Two Parts*, 1838; includes first part, of 1808).

POETRY: *Neue Lieder*, 1770 (*New Poems*); *Sesenheimer Liederbuch*, 1775-1789, 1854 (*Sesenheim Songs*); *Romische Elegien*, 1793 (*Roman Elegies*); *Reinecke Fuchs*, 1794 (*Reinecke the Fox*, 1855); *Epigramme: Venedig 1790*, 1796 (*Venetian Epigrams*); *Xenien*, 1796 (with Friedrich Schiller; *Epigrams*); *Hermann und Dorothea*, 1797 (*Herman and Dorothea*, 1801); *Balladen*, 1798 (with Friedrich Schiller; *Ballads*); *Neueste Gedichte*, 1800 (*Newest Poems*); *Gedichte*, 1812, 1815 (*Poems*); *Sonette*, 1819 (*Sonnets*); *West-östlicher Divan*, 1819, 1827 (*West-Eastern Divan*).

NONFICTION: *Von deutscher Baukunst*, 1773 (*On German Architecture*);

Versuch die Metamorphose der Pflanzen zu erklären, 1790 (*The Metamorphosis of Plants*); *Beyträge zur Optik,* 1791, 1792 (*Contributions to Optics*); *Zur Farbenlehre,* 1810 (*Theory of Colors*); *Aus meinem Leben: Dichtung und Wahrheit,* 1811-1814 (*Poetry and Truth: The Autobiography*); *Italienische Reise,* 1816, 1817 (*Travels in Italy,* 1883); *Compagne in Frankreich 1792,* 1822 (*Campaign in France in the Year 1792*); *Die Belagerung von Mainz 1793,* 1822 (*The Siege of Mainz in the Year 1793*); *Essays on Art,* 1845; *Goethe on Art,* 1980. MISCELLANEOUS: *Works,* 1848-1890 (14 volumes; includes all of his poetry and much of his prose); *Goethes Werke,* 1887-1919 (133 volumes).

Bibliography

Atkins, Stuart Pratt. "Johann Caspar Lavater and Goethe: Problems of Psychology and Theology in *Die Leiden des jungen Werthers,*" in *PMLA.* LXIII (1948), pp. 520-576.

——————— ."*Die Wahlverwandtschaften:* Novel of German Classicism," in *German Quarterly.* LIII (1981), pp. 1-45.

Blackall, Eric A. *Goethe and the Novel,* 1976.

Bruford, W. H. "Goethe's *Wilhelm Meister* as a Picture and a Criticism of Society," in *Publications of the English Goethe Society,* 1933.

Clark, Robert T. "The Metamorphosis of Character in *Die Wahlverwandtschaften,*" in *Germanic Review.* XXIX (1954), pp. 243-253.

——————— . "The Psychological Framework of Goethe's *Werther,*" in *Journal of English and Germanic Philology.* XLVI (1947), pp. 273-278.

Diamond, William. "Wilhelm Meister's Interpretation of *Hamlet,*" in *Modern Philology.* XXIII (1926/1927), pp. 89-101.

Fairley, Barker. *A Study of Goethe,* 1947.

Graham, Ilse. *Goethe: Portrait of the Artist,* 1976.

Hatfield, Henry C. "Towards the Interpretation of *Die Wahlverwandtschaften,*" in *Germanic Review.* XXIII (1948), pp. 104-114.

Long, O. W. "English and American Imitations of Goethe's *Werther,*" in *Men, Myths and Movements in German Literature,* 1931.

Maurer, K. W. "Goethe's *Elective Affinities,*" in *Modern Language Review.* XLII (1947), pp. 343-352.

Muenzer, Clark S. "Eduard and Rhetoric: Characterization and Narrative Strategy in Goethe's *Die Wahlverwandtschaften,*" in *Modern Language Notes.* XCIV (1979), pp. 493-509.

Reiss, Hans. "Die Leiden des jungen Werther: A Reconsideration," in *Modern Language Quarterly.* XX (1959), pp. 81-96.

——————— . *Goethe's Novels,* 1969.

Rose, William. "The Historical Background of Goethe's *Werther,*" in *Men, Myths and Movements in German Literature,* 1931.

Vietor, Karl. *Goethe the Poet,* 1949.

Kim Vivian

NIKOLAI GOGOL

Born: Sorochintsy, Russia; March 31, 1809
Died: Moscow, Russia; March 4, 1852

Principal long fiction

Taras Bulba, 1835 (as short story), 1842 (revised as a novel; English translation, 1886); *Myortvye dushi*, part 1, 1842; part 2, 1855 (*Dead Souls*, 1887).

Other literary forms

Nikolai Gogol was the author of many short stories, most of which belong to two cycles: the "Ukrainian cycle" and the later "Petersburg cycle." He wrote two plays, *Revizoz* (1836; *The Inspector General*, 1892) and *Zhenit'ba* (1842; *Marriage*, 1927), as well as a great deal of nonfiction, much of it collected in *Arabeski* (1835; *Arabesques*, 1982) and *Vybrannye mesta iz perepiski s druzyami* (1847; *Selected Passages from Correspondence with Friends*, 1969), Gogol's *Polnoe sobranie sochinenii* (1940-1952; collected works), which includes unfinished works and drafts, as well as his voluminous correspondence, fills fourteen volumes. All of Gogol's finished works, but not his drafts or correspondence, are available in English translation.

Achievements

Gogol's first collection of short stories, *Vechera na khutore bliz Dikanki*, (1831, 1832; *Evenings on a Farm near Dikanka*, 1926), made him famous, and his second collection, *Mirgorod* (1835; English translation, 1928), highlighted by *Taras Bulba*, established his reputation as Russia's leading prose writer. While Gogol's early stories, set in the Ukraine, are for the most part conventionally Romantic, his later Petersburg cycle of short stories, among which "Zapiski sumasshedshego" ("Diary of a Madman") and "Shinel" ("The Overcoat") are among the best known, marks the beginning of Russian critical realism. Gogol's two comedies are both classics and are as popular on the stage (and screen) today as they were in Gogol's lifetime. His novel *Dead Souls* is rivaled only by Leo Tolstoy's *Voyna i mir* (1865-1869; *War and Peace*, 1886) as the greatest prose work of Russian literature. Russian prose fiction is routinely divided into two schools: the Pushkinian, which is objective, matter-of-fact, and sparing in its use of verbal devices; and the Gogolian, which is artful, ornamental, and exuberant in its use of ambiguity, irony, pathos, and a variety of figures and tropes usually associated with poetry. Tolstoy and Ivan Turgenev belong to the Pushkinian school, Fyodor Dostoevski to the Gogolian. In his historical, critical, and moral essays, but especially in *Selected Passages from Correspondence with Friends*, Gogol established many of the principles of Russian conservative thought, anticipating the ideas of such writers as Dostoevski and Apollon Grigoriev.

Biography

Nikolai Vasilyevich Gogol, the son of a country squire, was born and educated in the Ukraine. Russian was to him a foreign language which he mastered while attending secondary school in Nezhin, also in the Ukraine. After his graduation in 1828, Gogol went to Saint Petersburg, where he joined the civil service. His first literary effort, "Hans Küchelgarten" (1829), a sentimental idyll in blank verse, was a failure, but his prose fiction immediately attracted attention. After the success of *Evenings on a Farm near Dikanka*, Gogol decided to devote himself entirely to his literary career. He briefly taught medieval history at Saint Petersburg University (1834-1835) and thereafter lived the life of a free-lance writer and journalist, frequently supported by wealthy patrons. The first night of *The Inspector General* at the Aleksandrinsky Theater in Saint Petersburg on April 19, 1836, attended and applauded by Czar Nicholas I, was a huge success, but it also elicited vehement attacks by the reactionary press, enraged by Gogol's spirited satire of corruption and stupidity in the provincial administration, and Gogol decided to go abroad to escape the controversy.

From 1836 to 1848, Gogol lived abroad, mostly in Rome, returning to Russia for brief periods only. The year 1842 marked the high point of Gogol's career with the appearance of part 1 of *Dead Souls* and the publication of a four-volume set of collected works, which contained some new work, in particular the great short story "The Overcoat." After 1842, Gogol continued to work on part 2 of *Dead Souls*, but he was now increasingly preoccupied with questions of religion and morality. His book, *Selected Passages from Correspondence with Friends*, actually a collection of essays in which Gogol defended traditional religious and moral values as well as the social status quo (including the institution of serfdom), caused a storm of protest, as liberals felt that it was flagrantly and evilly reactionary, while even many conservatives considered it to be unctuous and self-righteous.

Sorely hurt by the unfavorable reception of his book, Gogol almost entirely withdrew from literature. He returned to Russia for good in 1848 and spent the rest of his life in religious exercise and meditation. Shortly before his death, caused by excessive fasting and utter exhaustion, Gogol burned the final version of part 2 of *Dead Souls*. An earlier version was later discovered and published in 1855.

Analysis

The cover of the first edition of *Dead Souls*, designed by Nikolai Gogol himself, reads: "*The Adventures of Chichikov or Dead Souls*. A Poem by N. Gogol. 1842." "The Adventures of Chichikov" is in the smallest print, "Dead Souls" is better than twice that size, and "A Poem" is twice again the size of "Dead Souls." The word "or" is barely legible. The fact that "The Adventures of Chichikov" was inserted at the insistence of the censor, who felt that "Dead

Souls" alone smacked of blasphemy, accounts for one-half of this typograph-
ical irregularity. The fact that "A Poem" (Russian *poema*, which usually
designates an epic poem in verse) dominates the cover of a prose work which
at first glance is anything but "poetic" also had its reasons, as will be seen.

The plot structure of *Dead Souls* is simple. Chichikov, a middle-aged gentleman of decent appearance and pleasing manners, travels through the Russian
provinces on what seems a mysterious quest: He buys up "dead souls," meaning serfs who have died since the last census but are still listed on the tax
rolls until the next census. Along the way, he meets various types of Russian
land- and serf-owners: the sugary and insipid Manilov; the widow Korobochka, ignorant and superstitious but an efficient manager of her farm; the
dashing Nozdryov, a braggart, liar, and cardsharp; the brutish but shrewd
Sobakevich; and the sordid miser Plyushkin. Having returned to the nearby
provincial capital to obtain legal title to his four-hundred-odd "souls," Chichikov soon comes under a cloud of suspicion and quickly leaves town. Only
at this stage does the reader learn about Chichikov's past and the secret of
the dead souls. A civil-service official, Chichikov had twice reached the threshold of prosperity through cleverly devised depredations of the state treasury,
but each time he had been foiled at the last moment. After his second fiasco,
he had been allowed to resign with only a small sum saved from the clutches
of his auditors. Undaunted, he had conceived yet another scheme: He would
buy up a substantial number of "dead souls," mortgage them at the highest
rate available, and disappear with the cash.

The plot of part 1 takes the story only this far. In what is extant of part 2,
Chichikov is seen not only trying to buy more dead souls but also getting
involved in other nefarious schemes. It also develops, however, that Chichikov
is not happy with his sordid and insecure existence and that he dreams of an
honest and virtuous life. He would be willing to mend his ways if he could
only find a proper mentor who would give him the right start. There is reason
to believe that Gogol planned to describe Chichikov's regeneration and return
to the path of righteousness in part 3. The whole plot thus follows the pattern
of a picaresque novel, and many details of *Dead Souls* are, in fact, compatible
with this genre, which was well established in Russian literature even before
Gogol's day.

Actually, part 1 of *Dead Souls* is many other things besides a picaresque
novel: a humorous novel after the fashion of Charles Dickens' *Pickwick Papers*
(1838), with which it was immediately compared by the critics; a social satire
attacking the corruption and inefficiency of the imperial administration and
the crudity and mental torpor of the landed gentry; a moral sermon in the
form of grotesque character sketches; and, above all, an epic of Russia's
abjection and hoped-for redemption. The characters of part 2, while copies,
in a way, of those encountered in part 1, have redeeming traits and strike
the reader as human beings rather than as caricatures. The landowner Ten-

tetnikov, in particular, is clearly a prototype of Oblomov, the hero of Ivan Goncharov's immortal novel of that title (1859), and, altogether, part 2 of *Dead Souls* is a big step in the direction of the Russian realist novel of the 1850's and 1860's. The following observations apply to part 1, unless otherwise indicated.

The structure of *Dead Souls* is dominated by the road, as the work begins with a description of Chichikov's arrival at an inn of an unidentified provincial capital and ends with him back on the road, with several intervening episodes in which the hero is seen on his way to his next encounter with a potential purveyor of dead souls. Chichikov's tippling coachman, Selifan, and his three-horse carriage (Russian, *troika*) are often foregrounded in Gogol's narrative, and one of the three horses, the lazy and stubborn piebald, has become one of the best-known "characters" in all Russian fiction. The celebrated *troika* passage concludes part 1. Some critics, such as Vladimir Nabokov, have seen "the whole first volume of *Dead Souls* as a closed circle whirling on its axle and blurring the spokes, with the theme of the wheel cropping up at each new revolution on round Chichikov's part."

When Chichikov is not on the road, the narrative becomes a mirror, as each new character is reflected in Chichikov's mind, with the assistance of the omniscient narrator's observations and elucidations. One contemporary critic said that reading *Dead Souls* was like walking down a hotel corridor, opening one door after another—and staring at another human monster each time.

The road and the mirror by no means exhaust Gogol's narrative attitudes. *Dead Souls* features some philosophical discussions on a variety of topics; many short narrative vignettes, such as when Chichikov dreamily imagines what some of his freshly acquired dead souls may have been like in life; an inserted novella, "The Tale of Captain Kopeikin," told by the local post-master, who suspects that Chichikov is in fact the legendary outlaw Captain Kopeikin; repeated apostrophes to the reader, discussing the work itself and the course to be taken in continuing it; and last but not least, Gogol's much debated lyric digressions. Altogether, while there is some dialogue in *Dead Souls*, the narrator's voice dominates throughout. In fact, the narrative may be described as the free flow of the narrator's stream of consciousness, drifting from observation to observation, image to image, and thought to thought. It is often propelled by purely verbal associations. A common instance of the latter is the so-called realized metaphor, such as when a vendor of hot mead, whose large red face is likened to a copper samovar, is referred to as "the samovar"; when Chichikov, threatened with bodily harm by an enraged Noz-dryov and likened to a fortress under siege, suddenly becomes "the fortress"; or when the bearlike Sobakevich is casually identified as a "fair sized bear" in the role of landowner. It is also verbal legerdemain which eventually turns Sobakevich's whole estate into an extension of its owner: "Every object, every chair in Sobakevich's house seemed to proclaim: 'I, too, am Sobakevich!'"

Hyperbole is another device characteristic of Gogol's style. Throughout *Dead Souls*, grotesque distortions and exaggerations are presented as a matter of course—for example, when the scratching of the clerks' pens at the office where Chichikov seals his purchase of dead souls is likened to "the sound of several carts loaded with brushweed and driven through a forest piled with dead leaves a yard deep." Often the hyperbole is ironic, such as when the attire of local ladies is reported to be "of such fashionable pastel shades that one could not even give their names, to such a degree had the refinement of taste attained!"

A sure sign of the author's own point of view surfaces in frequent literary allusions and several passages in which Gogol digresses to discuss the theory of fiction—for example, the famous disquisition, introducing chapter 7, on the distinction between the writer who idealizes life and the writer who chooses to deal with real life. Gogol, who fancies himself to be a realist, wryly observes that "the judgment of his time does not recognize that much spiritual depth is required to throw light upon a picture taken from a despised stratum of life, and to exalt it into a pearl of creative art" but feels "destined by some wondrous power to go hand in hand with his heroes, to contemplate life in its entirety, life rushing past in all its enormity, amid laughter perceptible to the world and through tears that are unperceived by and unknown to it!" The phrases "to exalt it into a pearl of creative art" and "amid laughter perceptible to the world and through tears that are unperceived by and unknown to it" have become common Russian usage, along with many others in *Dead Souls*.

Dead Souls is studded with many outright digressions. It must be kept in mind, though, that the mid-nineteenth century novel was routinely used as a catchall for miscellaneous didactic, philosophical, critical, scholarly, and lyric pieces which were often only superficially, if at all, integrated into the texture of the novel. Still, the number and nature of digressions in *Dead Souls* are exceptional even by the standards of a *roman feuilleton* of the 1840's. According to Victor Erlich, there are two basic types of digressions in *Dead Souls*: "the lateral darts and the upward flights." The former are excursions into a great variety of aspects of Russian life, keenly observed, sharply focused, and always lively and colorful. For example, having observed that Sobakevich's head looks quite like a pumpkin, Gogol, in one of his many "Homeric similes," veers off into a village idyll about a peasant lad strumming a balalaika made from a pumpkin, to win the heart of a "snowy-breasted and snowy-necked Maiden."

Gogol's upward flights are of a quite different order. They permit his imagination to escape the prosaic reality of Chichikov's experience and allow him to become a poet who takes a lofty view of Russia and her destiny. In several of these passages, Gogol's imagination becomes quite literally airborne. One of them, at the conclusion of chapter 5, begins with a lofty aerial panorama:

"Even as an incomputable host of churches, of monasteries, with cupolas, bulbous domes, and crosses, is scattered all over holy and devout Russia, so does an incomputable multitude of tribes, generations, peoples swarm, flaunt their motley and scurry across the face of the earth." It ends in a rousing paean to "the Russian word which, like no other in the world, would burst out so, from out the very heart, which would seethe so and quiver and flutter so much like a living thing."

Early in chapter 11, Gogol produces another marvelous panoramic vision of Russia, apostrophized in the famous passage, "Russia, Russia! I behold thee—from my alien, beautiful, far-off vantage point I behold thee." (Gogol wrote most of *Dead Souls* while living in Italy.) The conclusion of this, the final chapter of part 1 then brings the most famous lines of prose in all of Russian literature, the *troika* passage in which a speeding three-horse carriage is elevated to a symbol of Russia's historical destiny. The intensity and plenitude of life and emotion in these and other airborne lyric passages stand in stark contrast to the drab pygmy world which is otherwise dominant in *Dead Souls*. These lyric digressions were challenged as incongruous and unnecessary even by some contemporary critics who, as do many critics today, failed to realize that Gogol's is a dual vision of manic-depressive intensity.

As a *poema* (epic poem), *Dead Souls* is a work which Gogol perceived as the poetic expression of an important religious-philosophical conception, that is, something of the order of Dante's *The Divine Comedy* (c. 1320) or John Milton's *Paradise Lost* (1667, 1674). Incidentally, there is one rather inconsequential allusion to Dante in chapter 7, where one reads that a Collegiate Registrar "served our friends even as Virgil at one time had served Dante, and guided them to the Presence." Immediately after the appearance of *Dead Souls*, critics were split into two camps: those who, like Konstantin Aksakov, greeted the work as the Russian national epopee, found numerous Homeric traits in it, and perceived it as a true incarnation of the Russian spirit in all of its depth and plenitude, and those who, like Nikolai Polevoi and Osip Senkovsky, saw it as merely an entertaining, though rather banal and in places pretentious, humorous novel. The latter group—which included even the great critic Vissarion Belinsky, who otherwise felt that *Dead Souls* was a perfect quintessence of Russian life—found Gogol's attempts at philosophizing and solemn pathos merely pompous and false. There is no agreement in this matter to this day. Nevertheless, several passages in part 1, the whole drift of part 2, and a number of quite unequivocal statements made by Gogol in his correspondence (in *Selected Passages from Correspondence with Friends* and in his posthumous "Author's Confession") all suggest that Gogol did indeed perceive *Dead Souls* as a *Divine Comedy* of the Russian soul, with part 1 its *Inferno*, part 2 its *Purgatory*, and part 3 its *Paradise*.

How, then, is part 1 in fact an *Inferno*, a Russian Hell? It is set in a Hades of dead souls, of humans who lead a shadowy phantom existence bereft of any real meaning or direction. Thus, it must be understood that in the Romantic philosophy of Gogol's time, the "normal" existence of a European philistine was routinely called "illusory," "unreal," and even "ghostly," while the ideal quest of the artist or philosopher was considered "substantial," "real," and "truly alive." As Andrey Bely demonstrated most convincingly, all of part 1 is dominated by what he calls "the figure of fiction." Whatever is said or believed to be true is from beginning to end a fiction, as unreal as Chichikov's financial transactions. For example, when the good people of N. begin to suspect that something is wrong with Chichikov, some of them believe that he plans to abduct the Governor's daughter, others conjecture that he is really Captain Kopeikin, a highway robber of legendary fame, and some actually suspect that he is Napoleon escaped from his island exile, but nobody investigates his motive for buying dead souls. As Bely also demonstrated, even time and space in *Dead Souls* are fictitious: The text will not even allow one to determine the season of the year; Chichikov's itinerary, if methodically checked, is physically impossible, and so on. Behind the figure of fiction, there looms large the message that all earthly experience and wisdom are in fact illusory, as Gogol makes explicit in a philosophical digression found in chapter 10.

In this shadowy world of fiction there exist two kinds of dead souls. There are the dead serfs who are sold and mortgaged and who, in the process, acquire a real semblance of life. Mrs. Korobochka, as soon as she has understood that Chichikov is willing to pay her some money for her dead serfs, is afraid that he may underpay her and somewhat timidly suggests that "maybe I'll find some use for them in my own household." Sobakevich, who haggles about the price of each dead soul, insists on eloquently describing their skls and virtues, as though it really mattered. Chichikov himself firmly rejects an offer by the local authorities to provide him with a police escort for the souls he has purchased, asserting that "his peasants are all of eminently quiet disposition." The same night, however, when he returns home from a party thrown by the local police chief to honor the new owner of four hundred souls, he actually orders Selifan "to gather all the resettled peasants, so he can personally make a roll call of them." Selifan and Petrushka, Chichikov's lackey, barely manage to get their master to bed.

The humanitarian message behind all of this is obvious: How could a person who finds the buying and selling of dead souls "fantastic" and "absurd" have the effrontery to find the same business transactions involving living souls perfectly normal? This message applies not only to Russia in the age of serfdom (which ended only in 1861—that is, at about the same time formal slavery ended in the United States) but also to any situation in which human beings are reduced to their social or economic function.

The other dead souls are the landowners and government officials whom we meet in *Dead Souls*. As the critic Vasily Rozanov observed, the peculiar thing about Gogolian characters is that they have no souls; they have habits and appetites but no deeper human emotions or ideal strivings. This inevitably deprives them of their humanity and renders them two-dimensional personifications of their vices—caricatures. Sobakevich is a very shrewd talking bear. Nozdryov is so utterly worthless that he appears to be a mere appendage of his extraordinarily handsome, thick, and pitch-black sideburns, thinned out a bit from time to time, when their owner is caught cheating at cards and suffers a whisker pulling. Plyushkin's stony miserliness has deprived him of all feeling and has turned him, a rich landowner, into a beggar and an outcast of society. *Dead Souls* has many such caricatures, which have been likened to Brueghelian grotesque paintings. This analogy applies to the following passage in chapter 11, for example: "The clerks in the Treasury were especially distinguished for their unprepossessing and unsightly appearance. Some had faces for all the world like badly baked bread: one cheek would be all puffed out to one side, the chin slanting off to the other, the upper lip blown up into a big blister that, to top it all off, had burst."

As early as 1842, the critic Stepan Shevyrev suggested that *Dead Souls* represented a mad world, thus following an ancient literary and cultural tradition (which today is often referred to as that of the "carnival"). The massive absurdities, *non sequiturs*, and simply plain foolishness throughout the whole text could, for Gogol and for many of his readers, have only one message: That which poses for "real life" is in fact nothing but a ludicrous farce. The basic course of Gogol's imagination is that of a descent into a world of ridiculous, banal, and vile "nonbeing," from which it will from time to time rise to the heights of noble and inspired "being."

While *Dead Souls* is unquestionably Gogol's masterpiece, his only other work of long fiction, *Taras Bulba*, is not without interest. The 1835 version of *Taras Bulba* is a historical novella; the 1842 version, almost twice as long and thus novel sized, has many digressions and is at once more realistic and more Gothic, but also more patriotic, moralizing, and bigoted. The plot is essentially the same in both versions.

Taras Bulba is a Ukrainian Cossack leader, so proud of his two fine sons recently back from school in Kiev that he foments war against the hated Poles, so that Ostap and Andriy can prove their manhood in battle. The Cossacks are initially successful, and the Poles are driven back to the fortress city of Dubno. The Cossacks lay siege to it, and the city seems ready to fall when Andriy is lured to the city by a messenger from a beautiful Polish maiden with whom he had fallen in love as a student in Kiev. Blinded by her promises of love, Andriy turns traitor. The Cossacks' fortunes now take a turn for the worse. They are hard-pressed by a Polish relief force. On the battlefield, Taras meets Andriy (now a Polish officer), orders him to dismount, and shoots him. The Cossacks, however, are defeated, and Ostap is taken prisoner. Old Taras makes his way to Warsaw, hoping to save him, but can only witness his son's execution. Having returned to the Ukraine, Bulba becomes one of the leaders of yet another Cossack uprising against the King of Poland. When peace is made, Bulba alone refuses to honor it. He continues to wreak havoc on the Poles all over the Ukraine but is finally captured by superior Polish forces. He dies at the stake, prophesying the coming of a Russian czar against whom no power on earth will stand.

There is little historical verity in *Taras Bulba*. Different details found in the text point to the fifteenth, sixteenth, and seventeenth centuries as the time of its action. It is thus an epic synthesis of the struggle of the Orthodox Ukraine to retain its independence from Catholic Poland. The battle scenes are patterned after Vergil and Homer, and there are many conventional epic traits throughout, such as scores of brief scenes of single combat, catalogs of warriors' names, extended Homeric similes, orations, and, of course, Bulba's solemn prophecy. Taras Bulba is a tragic hero who expiates his hubris with the loss of his sons and his own terrible death.

The earlier version of *Taras Bulba* serves mostly the glorification of the wild, carefree life at the Cossack army camp. In the later version, this truly inspired hymn to male freedom is obscured by a message of Russian nationalism, Orthodox bigotry, and nostalgia for a glorious past that never was. The novel features almost incessant baiting of Poles and Jews. Gogol's view of the war is a wholly unrealistic and romantic one: We are told of "the enchanting music of bullets and swords" and so on. From a literary viewpoint, *Taras Bulba* is a peculiar mixture of the historical novel in the manner of Sir Walter Scott and the Gothic tale. The narrator stations himself above his hero, gently faulting him on some of his uncivilized traits, such as the excessive stock Bulba puts in his drinking prowess or his maltreatment of his long-suffering wife. Rather often, however, the narrator descends to the manner of the folktale. His language swings wildly from coarse humor and naturalistic grotesque to solemn oratory and lyric digressions. There are scenes of unspeakable atrocities, reported with relish, but also some wonderful poems in prose, such as the well-known description of the Ukrainian steppe in the second chapter.

Altogether, *Taras Bulba* contains some brilliant writing but also some glaring faults. It immediately became a classic, and soon enough a school text, inasmuch as its jingoism met with the approval of the Czar—and eventually of Soviet school administrators. Several film versions, Russian as well as Western, exist.

Although Gogol's production of fiction was quite small by nineteenth century standards, both his novels and his short stories have had an extraordinary influence on the development of Russian prose—an influence that is still potent in the late twentieth century, as witnessed by the works of Andrei Sinyavsky and other writers of the Third Emigration.

Major publications other than long fiction

SHORT FICTION: *Vechera na khutore bliz Dikanki*, volume 1, 1831; volume 2, 1832 (*Evenings on a Farm near Dikanka*, 1926); *Mirgorod*, 1835 (English translation, 1928).

PLAYS: *Revizoz*, 1836 (*The Inspector General*, 1892); *Zhenit'ba*, 1842 (*Marriage*, 1927).

NONFICTION: *Arabeski*, 1835 (*Arabesques*, 1982); *Vybrannye mesta iz perepiski s druzyami*, 1847 (*Selected Passages from Correspondence with Friends*, 1969); *Letters of Nikolai Gogol*, 1967.

MISCELLANEOUS: *The Collected Works*, 1922-1927 (6 volumes); *Polnoe sobranie sochinenii*, 1940-1952 (14 volumes); *The Collected Tales and Plays of Nikolai Gogol*, 1964.

Bibliography

Erlich, Victor. *Gogol*, 1969.

Fanger, Donald L. *The Creation of Nikolai Gogol*, 1979.

Frantz, Philip. *Gogol: A Bibliography*, 1983.

Gippius, V. V. *Gogol*, 1981.

Maguire, Robert A., ed. *Gogol from the Twentieth Century: Eleven Essays*, 1974.

Nabokov, Vladimir. *Nikolai Gogol*, 1944.

Setchkarev, Vsevolod. *Gogol: His Life and Works*, 1965.

Victor Terras

WITOLD GOMBROWICZ

Born: Małoszyce, Poland; August 4, 1904
Died: Vence, France; July 24, 1969

Principal long fiction
Ferdydurke, 1937 (English translation, 1961); *Opetani*, 1939 (unfinished; *Possessed: Or, The Secret of Myslotch*, 1981); *Trans-Atlantyk*, 1953; *Pornografia*, 1960 (English translation, 1966); *Kosmos*, 1965 (*Cosmos*, 1966); *Dzieł zebrane*, 1969-1977 (11 volumes).

Other literary forms
In addition to his four principal novels, Witold Gombrowicz was the author of three equally important plays and the monumental three-volume *Dziennik* (1957, 1962, 1966; diary), which represents a unique blend of intimate diary, fiction, and literary or philosophical essay. His literary debut was a 1933 collection of short stories (reedited in an enlarged version in 1957); the genre of the short story, however, appears as marginal in his output. The same is true of literary criticism, which he cultivated most intensely in the 1930's, returning to it only occasionally in the later decades. Throughout his life, he was characteristically preoccupied with commenting upon and explaining his own work; in addition to *Dziennik*, such a self-explanatory purpose is served, more or less directly, by a book-length interview conducted by Dominique de Roux, *Rozmowy z Gombrowiczem* (conversations with Gombrowicz; actually, the writer's own confession published in guise of an interview; translated as *A Kind of Testament*, 1973) and by an autobiographical book *Wspomnienia polskie: Wędrówki po Argentynie* (Polish reminiscences: wanderings through Argentina), published posthumously in 1977.

Achievements
The story of Gombrowicz's literary career presents a striking contrast between his nearly lifelong isolation as a writer and the international fame enjoyed by his works since the 1960's. Today he is universally considered one of the major European novelists and playwrights of the twentieth century, a towering figure in modern Polish literature; his works have been translated into many foreign languages and have occasioned numerous critical analyses. All of this, however, including the coveted Formentor Prize in 1967, came only toward the end of his life, after the sixty-year-old Gombrowicz moved back to Europe from his Argentinian retreat, where he had spent twenty-four years, known only to a handful of his Argentinian admirers and to his enthusiasts in Poland.
    The Polish reception of Gombrowicz appears as another paradox. Although his work, as that of an émigré writer, has been steadfastly banned by the Communist regime (with the exception of a brief interval in 1957-1958), it

has always been known in Poland's intellectual circles thanks to the wide circulation of émigré editions. Oddly enough, since the writer's death, it has become possible in Poland to stage his plays and publish critical monographs on his work, although his books are still banned. This bizarre situation results from the fact that Polish authorities apparently have political objections to certain passages of Gombrowicz's diary; the writer specified in his last will that his work not be reprinted in Poland unless in its entirety. In spite of the difficulties that Polish readers face in obtaining copies of his books, Gombrowicz's reputation in his homeland grows as steadily as it does abroad; his work has exerted a particularly strong influence on the development of recent Polish fiction, drama, and criticism.

Biography

Witold Gombrowicz's life falls into two main phases, separated by his decision in September, 1939, to stay in Argentina, where he was caught by the outbreak of World War II in Europe. He was born in 1904 into the family of a landed proprietor-turned-industrialist; in 1911, his family moved from a country manor in southern Poland to Warsaw. The most rebellious and whimsical child in his family, Gombrowicz nevertheless was graduated from high school and, in 1922, acceding to his father's wish, began to study law at Warsaw University. After he was graduated in 1927, he continued his studies in Paris but soon returned to Poland, where his unorthodox views made it impossible for him to find a job as a lawyer. In all probability, this professional failure hastened his decision to devote himself entirely to writing. In 1933, his first book, a collection of short stories under the provocative title *Pamiętnik z okresu dojrzewania* (a memoir written in puberty), was published to rather skeptical reviews which generally dismissed the book as "immature." Nevertheless, Gombrowicz quickly won recognition in the circles of young writers. By the mid-1930's, he was already enjoying a moderate fame as a colorful personality and fascinating *causeur* as well as an insightful literary critic. It was, however, his first novel, *Ferdydurke*, that became a genuine event of Polish literary life; published in 1937, it provoked a heated critical debate on avant-garde tendencies in modern Polish prose. Before the war, Gombrowicz managed to publish in magazines and journals three more short stories, his first play, *Iwona, księżniczka Burgunda* (1938; *Princess Ivona*, 1969), and an unfinished novel, *Possessed: Or, The Secret of Myslotch*, a Gothic parody that was published pseudonymously as a newspaper series.

By a strange twist of fortune, only a few weeks before the German invasion of Poland, Gombrowicz took part in a trip of a group of young writers to Argentina. While in Buenos Aires, he learned about the outbreak of war and decided not to return. The first Argentinian years, while offering him inner freedom by cutting off all of his ties and obligations, were also extremely difficult, marked by isolation and financial hardship. To make his living, he took a poorly paid job as a clerk in a Polish bank in Buenos Aires. At the same time, he stubbornly continued his writing and after some time gained recognition—not so much among Polish émigrés, though, as among young Argentinian writers. He returned to the literary scene in 1953 with the novel *Trans-Atlantyk* and the play *Ślub* (*The Marriage*, 1969), issued jointly in a single volume by the émigré publishing house Institut Littéraire in Paris. Also in 1953, he began to publish fragments of his diary in the Institut Littéraire's monthly, *Kultura*. The publication of *Trans-Atlantyk*, a novel dealing satirically with the notion of traditional Polish patriotism, was met with vitriolic attacks from the conservative segment of the émigré community. On the other hand, after 1957-1958, when four books by Gombrowicz had been published in Poland during the short-lived political "thaw," he became almost a cult object for many young writers and critics, who enthusiastically welcomed everything avant-garde and unorthodox after the years of Socialist Realist boredom.

Between 1957 and 1966, Gombrowicz published, through the Institut Littéraire, the rest of his most important books written in exile: two novels, *Pornografia* and *Cosmos*, and the diary in three volumes, the last of which also included his third play, *Operetka* (1966; *Operetta*, 1971). Meanwhile, in 1963, he received a grant from the Rockefeller Foundation and left for Europe. After some time spent in West Berlin (this stay as well as some of Gombrowicz's public statements made him a victim of vicious attacks in the official media in Poland), he moved to Paris and finally settled with his young French wife in the small town of Vence in Southern France. The last years of his life were marked by his rapidly growing international fame as well as by his deteriorating health. He died in Vence in 1969, after a long struggle with illness.

Analysis

Seemingly nonsensical and capricious, Witold Gombrowicz's work is revealed, on a closer look, to be based on an amazingly consistent and complex philosophical system, as original as it is profound. Regardless of genre, the writer explores throughout his works the fundamental notions and antinomies which underlie his vision of the human world; in a sense, his novels are modern versions of the philosophical parable, although they are far from being didactic.

What can be called the basic existential experience of Gombrowicz is his awareness of man's solitude and helplessness in confrontation with the powerful pressure of culture—if "culture" is understood in a Freudian sense, as a collective superego that stifles the authentic impulses of the human self. Accordingly, the chief antinomy of Gombrowicz's philosophical system is the omnipresent conflict between the solitary individual and the rest of the human world; the individual's natural need is to remain free, independent, spontaneous, unique, whereas the outside world crams him into the schematic frames of that which is socially and culturally acceptable.

This conviction would appear as not particularly original (in fact, it would seem a mere continuation of the argument of Jean-Jacques Rousseau and the Romantics) were it not for the fact that Gombrowicz immediately counterpoises it with its exact opposite. He is equally aware that, contrary to his need to remain free and unique, the individual also feels constantly the fear of isolation and desires to affirm himself through contacts with other people, through his reflection in the eyes of others. This contradiction is particularly dominant in the case of an artist or writer: He wishes to reveal his individual uniqueness to the audience, but in order to reach the latter and be understood, he has to resort to a "language" of approved convention, which, in turn, destroys his uniqueness. In other words, each manifestation of the artist's freedom-seeking self means his imprisonment in a rigid scheme of finished shapes—and thus, it means his death as an artist.

The situation of an artist, however, is considered by Gombrowicz as only one particularly dramatic version of a more universal paradox of human existence as such. In his view, every individual lives his life in constant suspension between two ideals: "Divinity" and "Youth." Divinity can be understood as Fullness, Completeness, Perfection; Youth is synonymous with Unfulfillment, Spontaneity, Freedom. In yet other terms, the opposition of Divinity versus Youth equals that of Form versus Chaos. The main characters in Gombrowicz's fiction (more often than not, fictional impersonations of himself and his own neurotic obsessions) are always torn between their striving for Form on the one hand and Chaos on the other; or the plot consists in a clash between characters symbolizing Form and those symbolizing Chaos (significantly, the motif of a duel or fight is frequently used in crucial scenes).

This basic opposition takes on many specific shapes. The struggle between Form and Chaos may reveal itself, for example, in its sociological version, in which Aristocracy (or higher classes in general) represents the complete, perfect Form, while Peasantry (or lower classes in general) stands for spontaneous, chaotic Youth. It may also be illustrated by the inequality of civilizations—Western civilization is, in this respect, a symbol of Form, while the "second-rate," "immature" civilizations of countries such as Poland represent Chaos. Finally, the tension between the extremes of Form and Chaos can also be demonstrated on the level of individuals; here, the already shaped personality of an adult is another version of Form, while the still-developing personality of a child or teenager is a symbolic image of Chaos. It is evident that all possible embodiments of the opposition between Form and Chaos have a common denominator in the concept of inequality; each opposed pair can be interpreted as a case of Superiority confronted with Inferiority. According to Gombrowicz, the essence of human existence lies in the fact that the individual strives all of his or her life for Superiority and Form but in fact is not really attracted by these values, since their ultimate attainment would be tantamount to death. Therefore, the individual secretly desires Inferiority and Chaos, because only these extremes offer a chance of freedom. Yet, on the other hand, the ultimate attainment of this other goal would mean isolation, lack of communication, impossibility of affirming one's self-image through its reflection in the eyes of others. In the final analysis, the conflict is insoluble.

It can be, however, partly overcome and contained, if not fully resolved, by artistic creativity. Gombrowicz, as noted above, views the artist as someone who experiences the existential antinomy in a particularly acute way, but the artist has, at the same time, a certain advantage that nobody else has. Even though he cannot avoid the use of Form—if he did, he would not be under-stood—he can at least be aware of the artificial nature of Form and, as a consequence, he can be free to *play* with it. To play with Form means, in practice, to use it consciously and to make it "visible" instead of concealing it. Accordingly, Gombrowicz's own works are filled with deliberately intro-duced literary conventions which the reader can recognize instantly—the conventions of the mystery novel, operetta, family chronicle, traditional oral tale, Shakespearean historical drama, or novel of the life of the upper classes. At the same time, the personality of the narrator is usually multilayered: He exists within the world presented by his narration, but he can also at any given moment rise above that reality and his own narration to comment on them, or rise even higher to comment on his own comment, and so forth; in other words, he plays not merely with the conventions of literary genres and styles but also with the very convention of literary discourse.

All of his ambiguity considered, the narrator's point of view in Gombro-wicz's novels is, however, stable in one specific sense: As a rule, he represents the author, if not fully identifying himself with Gombrowicz (even to the point of assuming the latter's name). Likewise, the time of the novel's action is always, or at least seems to be, historically specified, and it usually coincides with various phases of Gombrowicz's own life. What is particularly meaningful is the place of the novel's action, usually a single and rather limited setting; the narration more often than not begins with the moment of the narrator's arrival in a certain place new to him, which he must then explore and com-prehend. In the course of such exploration, the narrator is usually confronted with a problem that he is supposed to solve, and thus the next phases of action develop conspicuously along the lines of the traditional detective story or novel of adventure.

What seems to be particularly characteristic of Gombrowicz is that his narrator's relationship with the reality presented is twofold. On the one hand, it is a reality that oppresses him, poses problems to solve, forces him to assume a certain stance or adopt a certain behavior. On the other hand, it is, simultaneously, the narrator himself who attempts to shape reality, to stage and direct events, to manipulate other characters, to impose some sense upon the world that surrounds him. Accordingly, two basic models of fictional plot coexist with each other in Gombrowicz's novels—the model of an *investigation* (in which reality appears to the narrator as a problem to solve) and the model of a *stage-setting* (in which the narrator becomes an active manipulator of reality).

All of this is additionally complicated by the fact that the world presented in Gombrowicz's fiction consists not only of facts, persons, objects, and their mutual relations, but also of *words*, their sounds and their meanings. Words not only serve here as a means to tell the story but also assume, as it were, an independent existence. This particular aspect of Gombrowicz's artistic play has for its object the tension between the order of facts and the order of words, between the meaning of a related situation and the meaning of specific words or expressions in which the situation is related; one can never be sure whether the action will follow the former or the latter semantic line. Sometimes, for example, a word that is central to a specific situation is foregrounded by constant repetition and other stylistic devices to such an extent that it, so to speak, proliferates and begins to function as an independent Form imposed on the Chaos of reality.

This is particularly noticeable in Gombrowicz's first and most famous work of long fiction, *Ferdydurke*, which has been perhaps artistically surpassed by his later novels, yet still remains the most exemplary illustration of his philosophy, his vision of society, his idea of narration, and his use of language. The attacks against this novel from both the Right and the Left in the late 1930's seem, in a sense, understandable, since the novel ridicules all ideologies or, more generally, all socially sanctioned attitudes, conventions, or Forms. *Ferdydurke* falls into three sharply divided parts, each of which is preceded by a brief essay or parable. At the outset of the story, the reader meets the narrator (and, at the same time, the main character of the whole novel), a man in his thirties who, like Gombrowicz himself, has published his first book and has been massacred by the critics as an immature and irresponsible youngster. The narrator is torn between his desire to achieve maturity and social acceptance (that is, any Form) and his dislike for various specific Forms which have been imposed on him by others and which he cannot accept as his authentic self. What, actually, is his "authentic" Form? To find an answer, he embarks upon writing another book. Here, however, something unexpected occurs: A certain Professor Pimko, an old-fashioned high school teacher, arrives and literally kidnaps the narrator to put him back in school, as if he were still a teenager.

The subsequent three parts of the novel put the narrator-turned-teenager into three different locales, each of which represents a different kind of petrified, inauthentic Form. After the school sequence, the narrator is placed by Pimko as a subtenant in the house of Mr. and Mrs. Youthful, a middle-aged couple imprisoned, as it were, within their own idea of what is "modern" and "progressive"; finally, he finds himself in a countryside manor where the conservative social distinctions between the upper class and the "boors" are still very much alive. In none of these three places—the school, the "modern" household, the traditional manor—can the narrator feel fully identified with the Form that prevails there, nor can he find an authentic Form of his own. Each of the three plots sooner or later develops into the narrator's attempts to manipulate the people who surround him, which in turn leads each time to a conflict culminating in a grotesque brawl and the narrator's escape. The conflict between Form and Chaos, shown simultaneously in its cultural, social, civilizational, generational, and sexual dimensions, cannot possibly be resolved—escape is the only solution. Even that, however, proves futile: In the final scene, the escaping narrator winds up in the company of his hosts' young daughter and thus unwillingly contributes to the triumph of yet another hollow Form—the romantic stereotype of lovers' elopement.

In his subsequent novels, Gombrowicz continued to explore the fundamental problem of Form versus Chaos, illustrating it with even more intricate fictional plots. *Trans-Atlantyk*, a novel ostensibly based on the author's 1939 Argentinian defection, dissects Form in its specific version of patriotic stereotype, while the extreme of Chaos, Freedom, and Youth is identified with a refusal to conform to such a stereotype. There is, perhaps, no other work by Gombrowicz in which language, style, and literary convention would play such a crucial role: A twentieth century story is told here in the masterfully parodied style of an oral tale spoken by a seventeenth century Old Polish nobleman.

In *Pornografia*, the relationship between Form and Chaos, Divinity and Youth, takes on the shape of a perverse story of a young couple whose love is "stage-set" and "directed" by a pair of older men—all of this against the social and political background of Nazi-occupied Poland. Gombrowicz's last novel, *Cosmos*, is his most metaphysical, although, like everything he wrote, it also reveals his powerful *vis comica* and penchant for the grotesque. The central problem here is nothing less than the nature of external reality as reflected in human consciousness. Is meaning immanent, or is it merely imposed on reality by the human mind? Gombrowicz asks this question by structuring his novel once again upon the model of an investigation and by parodistically referring in its style and construction to the conventions of the mystery story. Like the rest of Gombrowicz's work, *Cosmos* can be read as a mad piece of nonsensical tomfoolery—but it can also be read as a profound philosophical treatise on the most excruciating conflicts of human existence.

Major publications other than long fiction

SHORT FICTION: *Pamiętnik z okresu dojrzewania*, 1933; *Bakakaj*, 1957 (includes *Pamiętnik z okresu dojrzewania* and other stories).

PLAYS: *Iwona, księżniczka Burgunda*, 1938 (*Princess Ivona*, 1969); *Ślub*, 1953 (*The Marriage*, 1969); *Operetka*, 1966 (*Operetta*, 1971).

NONFICTION: *Dziennik*, 1957, 1962, 1966; *Sur Dante: Glose*, 1968; *Rozmowy z Gombrowiczem*, 1969 (*A Kind of Testament*, 1973); *Varia*, 1973; *Wspomnienia polskie: Wędrówki po Argentynie*, 1977.
MISCELLANEOUS: *Dzieła zebrane*, 1969-1977 (11 volumes).

Bibliography
Bondy, F., and C. Jelenski. *Witold Gombrowicz*, 1978.
Georgin, R. *Gombrowicz*, 1977.
Jarzębski, J. *Gra w Gombrowicza*, 1982.
Kępiński, T. *Witold Gombrowicz i świat jego młodości*, 1974.
Roux, Dominique de. *Gombrowicz*, 1971.
Thompson, E. M. *Witold Gombrowicz*, 1979.
Volle, J. *Gombrowicz, Bourreau-Martyr*, 1972.
Wyskiel, W. *Witold Gombrowicz: Twórczość literacka*, 1975.

Stanisław Barańczak

IVAN GONCHAROV

Born: Simbirsk, Russia; June 18, 1812
Died: Saint Petersburg, Russia; September 27, 1891

Principal long fiction

Obyknovennaya istoriya, 1847 (*A Common Story*, 1894); *Oblomov*, 1859 (English translation, 1915); *Obryv*, 1869 (*The Precipice*, 1916).

Other literary forms

Ivan Goncharov's early stories and poems, considered mediocre by the author himself as well as the public, have long been out of print. Goncharov's first significant piece was the sketch "Ivan Savich Podzhabrin," available in *Sobranie sochinenii* (1883, 1888, 1952; collected works). Still widely published and read is the travelogue *Fregat Pallada* (1858; *The Voyage of the Frigate Pallada*, 1965). During the final two decades of his life, Goncharov concentrated on critical essays, reminiscences, and polemical articles. "Mil'yon terzaniy" (1872), his analysis of Aleksandr Griboyedov's *Gore ot uma* (1825, 1831; English translation, 1857), and his autobiographical memoir "Luchshe pozdno, chem nikogda" (1879; better late than never) continue to enjoy limited circulation among literary specialists.

Achievements

Goncharov's novels mark the transition from Russian Romanticism to a much more realistic worldview. They appeared at a time when sociological criteria dominated analysis and when authors were expected to address the injustices of Russian life. The critic Nikolay Dobrolyubov derived the term Oblomovism from Goncharov's most famous novel, using it to denote the physical and mental sluggishness of Russia's backward country gentry. Thus, Goncharov is credited with exposing a harmful national type: the spendthrift serf-holding landowner who contributed nothing to the national economy and resisted progress for fear of destroying his carefree existence. By presenting this type in his rather ordinary surroundings and endeavors, stripped of the Romantic aura with which Alexander Pushkin's classical and Mikhail Lermontov's Romantic verse had imbued him, Goncharov gained renown as a critical realist. While all three of his novels remain popular classics in his homeland, only *Oblomov* has found a wide readership and critical acclaim abroad. Emphasis on that work has caused modern Western scholars to value Goncharov as highly for his artful psychological portraits of stunted adults adrift in a changing world as for his sociological contribution. *Oblomov*'s "return to the womb" predates Sigmund Freud by several decades. On the artistic level, Goncharov far transcends the realistic label often applied to him. His talent for transforming an endlessly mundane provincial existence into a delicate poetic network of pre-Petrine Russian values set standards for the budding Russian novel; his stream-of-consciousness approach points ahead to James Joyce and Marcel Proust. Goncharov has firmly established a place for himself within the genre of the modern psychological novel.

Biography

Ivan Aleksandrovich Goncharov, born June 18, 1812, grew up in remote Simbirsk (now Ulyanovsk) on a country estate of the type featured in his novels. After losing his merchant father at age seven, he was reared in the old tradition by his strong-willed mother and her landowning companion. This heritage of easygoing manor life and progressive mercantile activity characterizes Goncharov's own outlook and that of his major fictional characters. Encouraged to follow in his father's footsteps, he languished for eight years in a school of commerce without graduating. From 1831 to 1834, he attended Moscow University, without taking an active part in the famous philosophical student circles of the time. Instead, he entered the literary world as a tutor in the culturally sophisticated Maikov family, using this experience to produce his first poems and stories.

Goncharov's rise to fame was slow, and he was trapped in a civil-service career spanning more than thirty years, almost half of which was spent uneventfully as a translator in the Finance Ministry. Goncharov's private existence turned out to be equally monotonous. Although he was attracted to a number of women, his courtships were not successful, and he never married. The frustrations of his relationships with women are prominently mirrored in all three novels.

The success of his first novel, *A Common Story*, did not alleviate Goncharov's self-doubt, and he remained fettered to extraliterary activity. A worldwide sailing tour on behalf of the Trade Ministry in the 1850's yielded material for his travel sketches. The same period brought an appointment to the literary censorship board, a result of Alexander II's relaxed attitude. Goncharov followed a middle-of-the-road philosophy in this post, often enraging progressive writers, whose harsh judgments of conservative ideals he would not accept. He secured his own literary fame with *Oblomov* but felt too insecure to devote himself exclusively to literature. After a brief try at editing the official newspaper *Severnaya pchela* in the 1860's, he returned to a censorial post in the influental Press Council. His civic duties earned for him the Order of Vladimir, third class, prior to retirement in 1868.

Meanwhile, his mental state had gradually deteriorated. Ivan Turgenev's literary success easily eclipsed that of Goncharov, and when the former's *Dvoryanskoe gnezdo* (1859; *Liza: Or, "A Nest of Nobles,"* 1869; better known as *A Nest of Gentlefolk,* 1959) superseded *Oblomov* in critical acclaim, Goncharov accused his rival of plagiarism. Arbitration found Turgenev innocent, and the writers reconciled, but in private, the increasingly neurotic Goncharov continued the accusations, venting on Turgenev all the frustrations of his own unsatisfactory existence. Philosophically, Goncharov moved from a modestly progressive stance to a firm defense of the traditional values of the landed gentry. These sentiments found expression in *The Precipice*, in which moral regeneration is embedded in the unchanging order of provincial Russia. Goncharov died on September 27, 1891, a stranger to the swiftly moving social currents of the latter part of the century. His later published works chronicle his artistic decline. A complete recluse, he burned his letters and manuscripts. He spent his final days not unlike his major hero Oblomov, in a Saint Petersburg flat, looked after by a kindly widow and her children.

Analysis

"My life began flickering out from the very first moment I became conscious of myself." Thus Ilya Oblomov explains his arrested development to his successful business friend, Stolz, who is making a last try to rouse Oblomov from his fatal lethargy, and thus Ivan Goncharov points the reader to the cause of Oblomov's inertia: his childhood in a sleepy, backward manor house, attended by an army of serfs, every moment structured to reinforce an existence of indolently blissful inactivity, a paradise to which the adult strives all of his life to return. Oblomov's failure as a man and his search for a surrogate childhood in a simple Saint Petersburg family fit perfectly the scheme of the psychological novel. From this perspective, the seemingly typical Russian landowner Oblomov becomes a universal figure, and the old-fashioned Russian village becomes merely background. Such a perspective, however, has its drawbacks. If one considers *Oblomov* apart from Goncharov's other novels, as is often the case in the West, the wider artistic sweep of his fiction is neglected. Each of his novels gives expression to a different facet of the contradictions encountered by the Russian patriarchal order as it confronted sociopolitical reform. Goncharov's characters can be said to embody the two warring dominant philosophies of nineteenth century Russia: Slavophilism and Westernization. The author's own struggle between these two opposing forces is cast into sharp focus in the novels, as his progress-oriented mind gradually loses ground to his tradition-loving, Slavophile heart.

Neither Goncharov's personal dissatisfactions nor his conservative turn impair his stature as an accomplished novelist. The expert use of several literary devices contributes to this renown. There is, first of all, his power of observation, the ability to create such a lifelike image of an ordinary event through accumulation of detail that his scenes are compared to Flemish interiors. Auctorial ambiguity also enriches the narrative. The first two novels conceptually demonstrate the advantages of a progressive economy and the futility of perpetuating serfdom, but Goncharov presents a dying way of life with such a wealth of attractive imagery that social indifference, indeed exploitation, infantilism, and stagnation, are turned into a languidly cozy, almost noble way of life, feeding on nostalgia and winning sympathy for its prejudices. No less impressive is Goncharov's skill in suggesting the delusions of the regressive personality. Oblomov's insecure psyche reshapes his ordinary village into a harmless, safe refuge, smoothing craggy mountains into gentle hillocks, swift rivers into murmuring brooks, extremes of climate into eternally pleasant weather, passions into lethargy. Readers are scarcely aware that the descriptions are no longer objective, but the distortions of a frightened mind. Finally, Goncharov excels in drawing exquisite female portraits; his women also symbolize the synthesis between the old and new. In *A Common Story*, Lizaveta is able to balance the contradictory forces which pull the male characters into adversary position; in *Oblomov*, Olga combines the best of old Russia, its cultural heritage, with an inquisitive mind and an active personality; in *The Precipice*, Vera eventually unites the positive features of her patriarchal upbringing with the progressive forces of a commercially enterprising spouse.

In his final novel, Goncharov's moralizing instincts undermine his mastery of style, as didactic elements intrude too explicitly. The author's own estrangement from the present and his nostalgia for a less complex existence color his perceptions. His slow-paced upbringing, his later insecurities, his realization that progress was necessary, his struggle between old and new, and his final withdrawal from society are the building blocks of all of his works. He delicately managed to balance these elements before yielding to his own preferences.

The unstinting praise of Russia's foremost social critic, Vissarion Belinsky, assured the success of *A Common Story* the moment it appeared in the literary journal *Sovremennik*. Ironically, the work was hailed as an exposé of the degenerate gentry class and a call for modernization. Critics and readers alike noted only the main character Alexander Aduev's final acceptance of Saint Petersburg's progressive life-style, not his mentor-uncle's disillusionment with it. They also overlooked the author's cautious suggestion that the city's competitive utilitarianism was no more satisfying than the monotony of the backward village.

This misperception attests Goncharov's balancing skill. Alexander is lured from his peaceful, idyllic estate, lovingly presented in the fragrance of its lilacs, berries, bushes, and forests, by visions of cosmopolitan dazzle. Once he is taken in hand by a "new man," his coldly efficient, philistine Uncle Peter, one disappointment succeeds another. Like an early Oblomov, Alexander adjusts only superficially, never able to integrate his rustic values with Saint Petersburg's diverse phenomena. Like a young Goncharov, Alexander blunders from one unsuccessful love affair to another. His literary endeavors, characterized by overblown sentimental clichés, are equally fruitless. Despite all efforts by Peter, he turns into a rather ridiculous figure, an out-of-place relic in the bustling city. Goncharov's ambiguous attitude, however, gives enough scope to elicit a measure of pity from the reader, to mark the young man's discomforts and his inability to cope. Peter's young wife, Lizaveta, compassionately brings out Alexander's positive traits. When all attempts at acclimatization end in failure, he returns to his quiet country home and recovers his bearings. Yet the lessons of the city are not lost. At a distance, its hectic multiplicity develops into a fair alternative to the boring idyll of the placid province. In the end, Alexander sets out for Saint Petersburg once more, cured of his romantic expectations, determined to copy his uncle's career through realistic adaptation and lowered sights. His success is presented in the epilogue. He parallels Peter faithfully: fat and balding, engaged to a young heiress, adjusted, mature, eager for progressive endeavors.

While this conclusion heartened liberal critics, Goncharov's reservations are apparent in the incompletely dramatized and therefore unconvincing psychological transformation of Alexander. The artistically unmotivated ending causes a change of focus. The carefully developed juxtaposition of old versus new, village versus city, Slavophile versus Westernizer assumes the outline of a *Bildungsroman*. Peter and Alexander represent two stages of identical development. Alexander's romantic striving mirrors Peter's own youthful immaturity, while Peter's rational, mature stage serves as a marker for Alexander's similar destiny. At the moment of Alexander's arrival at that stage, Peter's dry and joyless stance casts doubt on the wisdom of these very accomplishments, foreshadowing eventual disillusionment for his nephew. The general inattention to this downbeat element is a result of the shortage of bourgeois heroes in Russian literature. The Romantic characters of Pushkin, Lermontov, and the early Turgenev are immobile, purposeless, and contemptuous of practical activity. Liberal critics had long called for a positively depicted, businesslike nobleman, and they accepted Alexander in his final guise enthusiastically as such. The careful reader is left questioning both men's aspirations and sharing Lizaveta's wistful awareness that Saint Petersburg's progress is far from ideal. The alternative of seeking that ideal in Russia's past surfaces only in Goncharov's later works, although the absence of a critical stand against serfdom and landowner privileges already serves to modify the seeming victory of Westernization.

Turgenev's popular *A Nest of Gentlefolk* threatened to overshadow *Oblomov*, which was first printed in *Otechestvennye zapiski*, until Dobrolyubov's 1859 article "Chto takoyo Oblomovshchina?" ("What Is Oblomovism?") swiftly drew national attention to the work. Following Dobrolyubov's cue, most readers and succeeding generations saw in the hero's inertia the psychological consequence of total dependence on serf labor. By lavishing endless pages on the harmful effects of Oblomovism and the virtues of Stolz, a Western-influenced business type, Goncharov seemed to strike a forceful blow at the roots of Russia's economic and social evils. Oblomov appears as the epitome of the superfluous nobleman, the lazy, alienated dreamer who cannot adjust to change or find a place for himself in the present. Different embodiments of this type exist in Pushkin's Onegin, Lermontov's Pechorin, and Turgenev's Rudin. Oblomov differs from these characters in that he rejects even the search for an alternative, preferring instead the never-changing ways of his childhood Oblomovka. The location of this estate on the Asian border aptly suggests the Oriental fatalism and circular philosophy which represent Oblomov's and, by extension, Russia's Eastern Tartar heritage. The hero's Oriental dressing gown, serving as his security blanket and finally his shroud, is an equally fitting symbol.

The reader is initiated into all the details of Russian provincial backwardness through Oblomov's lengthy dream of his sleepy backwater. The dream, a thematic outline of the work and its centerpiece, had been published separately as a sort of overture as early as 1849. The finished novel shows the deadening effect of this "blessed spot" on those who cannot free themselves from the dependencies it fosters. Little Ilya was born a normal child, willing to experiment, to rough it, to develop. The atmosphere of Oblomovka snuffed out all of these inclinations. Tradition stipulates that a Russian gentleman sit, surrounded by hordes of serfs who attend to his every whim, that he eat and doze most of the day, phlegmatically observe the seasonal and ecclesiastical rituals, ignore any attempt at change, be it literacy or postal service, and hope that the waves of Peter the Great's Westernizing reforms never reach his quiet hamlet. Inevitably, they do reach Oblomovka, and the product of its upbringing must serve his term in Saint Petersburg. The innumerable ways in which the transplanted Oblomov manages to ignore the city's reality take up a good portion of the narrative. Each failure on the realistic plane is paralleled by a success on the imaginary level, which always features a happy Oblomov in a paradisiacal Oblomovka. Eventually, Oblomov gains a questionable victory. A motherly widow's shabby lodging transforms itself into a blissful surrogate of Oblomovka for the by-now infantile hero. He has returned to the womb and lives out a short but happy span, until mental stagnation and greedy overeating end his life.

Two people try their best to save him. First Stolz, the half-German entrepreneur, as lean as an English racehorse where Oblomov is fat and flabby, uses reason and intellectual appeal to convince Oblomov to change. Then Olga, already adapted to a modern intelligentsia but preserving a deep love for Russia's cultural past, lures him with promises of selfless love. Sexually aroused, Oblomov briefly responds to her, but when he finds that Olga also demands intellectual arousal, constant mental awareness, he takes flight. The equally dull-witted widow offers both maternal and mistress services without the necessity of mental effort.

Stolz and Olga, who eventually marry, represent the best of traditional Russia fused with the best of imported progressive behavior. Stolz is an improved version of Peter Aduev. The latter's negative traits and final pessimistic outlook have been replaced by Stolz's cheerfulness and compassion.

Even here, however, the author's descriptive talents hover lovingly over the blubbery Oblomov—over his dreams, his reflections, his blunders—while Stolz comes across as artificial and wooden, the victim of uninspired portrayal. Olga, who loves and appreciates Oblomov's values, is a more credible figure, and it is she who embodies and carries into the future the reconciliation of the conflict. In some respects, she acts as Goncharov's mouthpiece. Her dissatisfactions, even with the faultless Stolz, echo the author's own inability to believe fully in the spiritual benefits of a forward-moving Russia.

Goncharov had no such reservations when it came to praising the charms of Oblomovka. Its oneness with nature renders each inhabitant a paragon of virtue. No passionate outbursts or personal animosities mar the peacefulness. Serfs are not slaves, but content to be reflections of their masters. Their sloth and their ample participation in all the feasting, indulged by benevolent owners, help to deplete Oblomovka's reserves. When this slothful behavior is transplanted to Saint Petersburg in the person of Oblomov's loyal valet Zakhar, it loses much of its bucolic enchantment, yet the touching interdependence of master and servant redeems the ineptness. It was simply impossible for Goncharov to carry to its logical conclusion his commonsense understanding that radical Slavophilism would result in national stagnation and regression.

Goncharov's unwillingness to endow his progressive characters with the vitality necessary to make them convincing and interesting asserts itself more fully in his last major work, *The Precipice*. It appeared in *Vestnik Evropy* at a time when emancipation was a fact, when Alexander II's liberalism gave wide scope to social commentators, when literature closely echoed the *Zeitgeist* of reform. Goncharov's liberal representative is the political exile Volokhov, who, like Turgenev's nihilist Bazarov, spreads unrest in a deeply conservative village. Volokhov's positive qualities are quickly neutralized by his seduction of a virtuous country woman, Vera, who naïvely tries to straighten him out. Vera is also a link to the other male principal, Raisky, a Saint Petersburg intellectual, who has failed to find a purpose in life and returns to his country estate in search of a footing. It is easy to see in him yet another embodiment of Goncharov's favorite type: the neurotic male whose interests, convictions, and common sense pull him toward reform but whose temperament and deep-seated impulses chain him to the past. In each of these split personalities, Goncharov's own schism finds expression. As before, he reserves the best of his descriptive talents for the backwoods, symbolized by the figure of the grandmother. It is in this traditional setting that the abused Vera finds regeneration and mental recovery; it is the rural past which bequeaths stability, sanity, and direction for the future.

Goncharov had once again drawn an exquisite cameo of old Russia, once again contrasted the conflicting values of old and new, once again pictured an artistically masterful "homecoming." Despite the popularity of the somewhat meandering work, Goncharov's point of view drew heavy moral indignation. Liberal critics were quick to point out that Goncharov had come down on the side of rural conservatism, that he favored the Slavophiles. Obviously and painfully out of step with the tenor of the time, and psychologically unable and unwilling to recapture his artistic independence, Goncharov withdrew. His subsequent writings did not approach the stature of his novels.

Goncharov's significance in the development of the Russian novel and Russian intellectual history remains great. He brought to life the characters of old Russia, with a style peculiarly his own, at a time when that patriarchal order began to disintegrate. In his portraits of Slavophiles and Westernizers, he elaborated on the dominant conflict of mid-century Russia. He was the first Russian author to integrate psychological complexities successfully and expertly into his plots, and thereby he created universal types.

Major publications other than long fiction

SHORT FICTION: "Ivan Savich Podzhabrin," 1848; "Slugi starogo veka," 1888.

NONFICTION: *Fregat Pallada*, 1858 (*The Voyage of the Frigate Pallada*, 1965; "Mil'yon terzaniy," 1872; "Luchshe pozdno, chem nikogda," 1879; "V universitete," 1887; "Na rodine," 1888; "Neobyknovennaya istoriya," 1924.

MISCELLANEOUS: *Sobranie sochinenii*, 1883, 1888, 1952 (8 volumes).

Bibliography

Ehre, Milton. *Oblomov and His Creator: The Life and Art of Ivan Goncharov*, 1973.

Lavrin, Janko. *Goncharov*, 1954.

Lyngstad, Alexandra, and Sverre Lyngstad. *Ivan Goncharov*, 1971.

Moser, Charles. *Anti-Nihilism in the Russian Novel of the 1860's*, 1964.

Prutskov, N. I. *Masterstvo Goncharova-romanista*, 1962.

Reeve, F. D. *The Russian Novel*, 1966.

Margot K. Frank

EDMOND DE GONCOURT and JULES DE GONCOURT

Edmond de Goncourt

Born: Nancy, France; May 26, 1822
Died: Champrosay, France; July 16, 1896

Jules de Goncourt

Born: Paris, France; December 17, 1830
Died: Anteuil, France; June 20, 1870

Principal long fiction

En 18 . . , 1851; *Charles Demailly*, 1860; *Soeur Philomène*, 1861 (*Sister Philomène*, 1890); *Renée Mauperin*, 1864 (English translation, 1888); *Germinie Lacerteux*, 1865 (English translation, 1887); *Manette Salomon*, 1867; *Madame Gervaisais*, 1869. By Edmond alone: *La Fille Élisa*, 1877 (*Elisa: The Story of a Prostitute*, 1959); *Les Frères Zemganno*, 1879 (*The Zemganno Brothers*, 1886); *La Faustin*, 1882 (English translation, 1882); *Chérie*, 1884; *Oeuvres complètes*, 1922-1937 (41 volumes).

Other literary forms

Edmond and Jules de Goncourt began their writing career with minutely detailed studies of the eighteenth century on such subjects as the French Revolution, art, and women. They wrote several plays, although without achieving any great success on the stage. Their talent for documentation and observation can best be seen in their famous *Journal: Mémoires de la vie littéraire* (1887-1896, 1956-1959), which preserves an unparalleled view of social and literary life in nineteenth century France. After his brother's death, Edmond continued the *Journal* by himself and also published studies on Japanese art.

Achievements

The Goncourt brothers excelled at depicting the manners and morals of contemporary French society, both in their *Journal* and in their novels, which, at times, resemble sociological studies. They were among the first to describe realistically the unfortunate lives of the lower classes of society. The realism of the Goncourts was an important precursor of Émile Zola's Naturalism.

As historians, the Goncourts produced studies of eighteenth century painting that are still read by students of art history. In their *Journal* is preserved an irreplaceable chronicle of their own period in French history. Their most concrete achievement was the establishment of the Académie Goncourt, whose members still award an annual prize for literary excellence.

Biography

Edmond-Louis-Antoine and Jules-Alfred Huot de Goncourt were the sons of a cavalry officer in Napoleon's Imperial Army and the grandsons of Antoine Huot de Goncourt, deputy of the National Assembly of 1789. They were, respectively, the eldest and the youngest child of Annette-Cécile Guérin and Marc-Pierre Huot de Goncourt. Edmond was born in Nancy on May 26, 1822, but the family moved to Paris shortly thereafter. Jules was born in Paris on December 17, 1830. Their father died four years later, leaving the boys and their mother in modest financial circumstances which nevertheless permitted the boys to attend school until both had passed the *baccalauréat* examination. Edmond began to study law in 1841 but, for financial reasons, left his studies in 1847 to take a minor position in the Treasury.

When their mother died in 1848, they inherited a limited income, but one which spared them the necessity of working for a living and allowed them to devote themselves to art. Jules had recently finished his studies, and, once their financial affairs were in order, the brothers decided to hike to southern France while considering what direction their lives should take. They both sketched and kept a diary of their travels, in which they tried to capture the landscape in words as it would appear in a painting. Later, they viewed this trip as the turning point at which they became men of letters instead of artists, but on their return to Paris, they both continued to paint while collaborating on several inconsequential one-act plays and contributing essays on art criticism to contemporary reviews.

During this period, they also wrote their first novel, *En 18 . .*, which suffered the misfortune of appearing on December 2, 1851, the very day of Napoleon III's *coup d'état*. (Fate was not kind to the Goncourts with their publication dates: *La Faustin* was issued on the morning of Léon Gambetta's downfall, and the seventh volume of the *Journal* on the day of Sadi Carnot's assassination.) The publisher of *En 18 . .* refused to advertise it, for fear that the new regime would see in the title an allusion to Napoleon I's eighteenth of Brumaire (the French Republican Calendar's equivalent of November 9, 1799).

In 1851, their cousin, the Comte de Villedeuil, decided to found a weekly review of literature and the arts and offered editorial positions to Edmond and Jules. The first issue of *L'Éclair* appeared in January, 1852, but soon gave way to *Le Paris*, a review intended for a broader audience and to which the brothers continued to make literary contributions. Through these periodicals, the Goncourts met many personalities in literary and artistic circles, such as Gavarni, Nadar, and Théodore de Banville. The brothers were arrested on one occasion for having quoted some slightly erotic verse in an article. They were eventually acquitted of the charge of committing "an outrage against public morality," but the shock hastened their departure from the world of journalism.

Between 1859 and 1870, the Goncourts published monographs on eighteenth century painters, which were later collected in a single volume, *L'Art au XVIIIe siècle* (1859-1875; *French Eighteenth Century Painters*, 1948). They also wrote on the social history of the eighteenth century, publishing works of a more intimate nature than the official political histories. At the same time, they kept their *Journal* faithfully, recording the lives of their circle of literary and artistic friends. The salon of Princess Mathilde Bonaparte figures prominently, for example, as well as their friendships with Gustave Flaubert, Émile Zola, Guy de Maupassant, and Alphonse Daudet.

The two decades between 1850 and 1870 were marked by regular publications of novels and historical works and by a brief return to the theater in 1865, when their first major play, *Henriette Maréchal* (1865), was produced by the Comédie-Française. The opening night provoked a hostile demonstration by students from the Latin Quarter, not because of the play itself, which was rather conventional, but because of the Goncourts' anti-Republican sympathies and their friendship with Princess Mathilde. After several performances, the audiences became more calm, but then the Imperial censors decided to ban the play. It was Jules's theory that the Empress Eugénie had acted out of dislike for Princess Mathilde. In any case, the play, caught between the Republican opposition and the Imperial regime, was withdrawn by the end of its first month.

In 1868, the brothers moved to the Paris suburb of Auteuil because of Jules's declining health. They managed to continue work on *Madame Gervaisais*, for which they had prepared during trips to Italy in 1856 and 1867. The novel was published in 1869, but the brothers were not pleased with it. Their melancholy deepened when their friend Charles-Augustin Sainte-Beuve, the influential critic, did not review the novel at all. During that summer, they traveled gloomily, until finally, in September, they focused all of their energy on writing a biography of Gavarni, who had died in 1866.

On January 19, 1870, Jules made his last entry in the *Journal*. He began to lose his ability to spell, to recognize objects, and finally, to speak. He died on June 20, 1870, at the age of thirty-nine. Thus came to an end the remarkably close professional and emotional partnership between Jules and Edmond de Goncourt.

In the summer of 1870, however, the Franco-Prussian War overwhelmed Edmond's private sorrow. He had continued making entries in the *Journal* in a desultory way, but the man of letters was now revitalized by a desire to chronicle first the illusion of victory and then the disintegration of defeat. By the time the Germans had laid siege to Paris, Edmond had taken on the responsibility of reporting the afflictions of war, the nightmarish reality beneath the collective self-deception of his compatriots. During the turmoil of the Commune, Edmond's house in Auteuil was bombarded, and he witnessed the death of *communards* at the barricades. These events resulted in some of the best-written and most vivid accounts in the *Journal*.

The last decades of Edmond's life were entirely devoted to literature. He wrote new novels and saw early ones adapted to the stage. Literary friendships were cultivated during regular evenings in his *grenier* (attic). The perpetuation of the Goncourts' name was ensured through the establishment of the Académie Goncourt. Edmond's will of 1874 set up a board of directors who would award an annual prize for a promising new literary talent. The first directors were chosen by Edmond himself from among the best writers of the day who represented new directions in literature—and who would *not* become members of the Académie Française. The directors began their work upon Edmond's death in 1896 and awarded their first prize in 1903.

Analysis

In the second half of the nineteenth century, intellectual analysis became the driving force behind the art of fiction in France. In reaction to Romanticism, the new generation produced the realism of Gustave Flaubert and of Edmond and Jules de Goncourt. Although no novel by the Goncourts can be compared to Flaubert's *Madame Bovary* (1857), the Goncourt brothers are credited with producing the precursors of the great works of Naturalism by Émile Zola. For these writers, the novel became a kind of critical commentary on human society and especially on the social structure of the Second Empire. The Goncourts tended to focus on the plight of a single individual, analyzing the hereditary and environmental factors which contribute to the particular conflict at the heart of each novel.

Charles Demailly, written nearly a decade after *En 18 . . .*, was the first of the Goncourts' novels to receive serious critical attention. The hero, Charles Demailly, is a journalist for a newspaper called *Le Scandale*. Attempting to keep his personal integrity intact, he isolates himself from his cronies and writes a serious novel. At the same time, he marries an actress, Marthe, who turns out to be stupid and cruel and who destroys him with the help of a colleague in journalism who is jealous of Charles's literary success. Marthe's betrayal causes Charles to go mad, and he ends up in an asylum.

As might be expected, the novel was not favorably received by journalist-critics at the time. As would nearly always be the case, the characters were closely modeled on acquaintances of the Goncourts, but in *Charles Demailly* the emphasis is on venal journalism; writers of quality are omitted. A typical flaw is the lack of a plot line to blend the disparate scenes.

It was the Goncourts' next novel that brought their first critical success. In *Sister Philomène*, the Goncourts left their own familiar world of arts and letters to write of a nursing sister who falls in love with an intern. To research the setting of their novel, the Goncourts spent several days in the hospital in Rouen, to which they gained entry through Flaubert, whose father was a doctor. The result was a novel in which life in a hospital—reactions of the patients, conversations among the interns, visits of the chief surgeon—creates an absorbing, somber atmosphere.

The publication of *Sister Philomène* coincided with the vogue for realism, and as a result it received praise as a study from life. The realist writers were heavily influenced by the work of Hippolyte Taine, who held that an individual can be explained by his race, his moment in history, and his milieu. Thus, the novel begins with a lengthy section showing how the girl, Marie Gaucher, is reared and how her temperament, social class, and upbringing cause her to become the nurse, Sister Philomène. The Goncourts were always fascinated by the interplay of illusion and reality in human lives, and here the theme appears in the portrait of the idealistic young nurse beginning to perceive the realities of her new profession.

The first scene in the hospital takes place at night, when the nurses make their rounds by candlelight. The play of darkness and light underscores Philomène's confusion between a romanticized view of her profession (bringing light and life to the suffering) and the inescapable realities of pain and death. This passage demonstrates the Goncourts' artistry in description, for unlike some extreme advocates of realism, they believed that flat documentation must be illuminated by a fine writing style and artistic effects. In time, their characteristic style became known as *écriture artiste* (artistic writing).

Philomène's beloved is a young doctor, Barnier, who conceals a sensitive soul beneath a gruff, even crude, exterior. He finds the ideal love he seeks in his relationship with Sister Philomène. This love contrasts with the disillusion he encounters when obliged to operate on a former mistress, Romaine. She had remained for him a symbol of youthful love but now appears in a "fallen" state, having been injured during an orgy. Nevertheless, when his surgical skill cannot save Romaine, Barnier is in anguish. In a moment of madness, he embraces Philomène with passion, then commits suicide out of guilt and despair.

Sister Philomène demonstrates that the Goncourts had learned how to manage the form of the novel, providing credible motivations for their characters against a realistic setting. They had also proved capable of leaving their own world to examine a strange, even disagreeable, milieu in a way that has been called "pre-Naturalistic."

For their next novel, the brothers wished to study an entire social class, that of the modern bourgeoisie during the Second Empire. The novel was to have analyzed that middle class held in contempt by artists and writers of the time for its love of money, lack of taste, and naïve belief in "progress." The initial plan was modified when the Goncourts became friends with Louis and Blanche Passy. Jules admired Blanche to the extent of wishing to make her the heroine of a novel, and thus *Renée Mauperin* became the story of an intelligent, lively girl at odds with the conventions of her bourgeois family.

Most of the novel is a study of the bourgeoisie, for which Renée serves as a foil and a victim. The premise is that Renée has been educated by her doting father to think for herself and to see through the dull pretensions of her social class. It is not surprising, then, that she refuses all offers of marriage to the shallow young men her despairing mother finds as suitors. The central situation of the novel, however, deals with Renée's social-climbing, eminently proper brother, Henri, and his machinations to marry the wealthy daughter of his mistress.

This situation violates Renée's sense of honor, especially when Henri gives up his family name, at the request of his future father-in-law, to take on a noble one. The new name is supposed to have been extinct, but a last survivor appears, having been notified by Renée. When the aristocrat kills the arriviste in a duel, Renée falls ill of a heart disease and dies.

The novel scores some points against the pretensions of conventional society, especially in the portraits of Renée's older brother and sister. Henri is clearly an unscrupulous, but superficially correct, young man. The implication of his social success is that he is a typical bourgeois type, ambitious for money and power. The sister, Madame Davarande, has accepted society's values entirely and without question. She spells her name in the aristocratic fashion, "d'Avarande," and seeks moral guidance from a fashionable priest, who "makes God seem *chic*."

Renée's spiritual and physical drama, which dominates the final chapters of the novel, is considerably less engrossing. After her shock at having indirectly caused her brother's death, Renée is taken to the country, where her lively, impertinent personality fades with her health. Furthermore, her illness is not medically believable, but resembles a literary death from a broken heart. Even the psychological motivation is unsound, because her brother is portrayed as insufferably unworthy of her love. Even so, in her refusal to compromise with the social system, Renée deflates its shallow, vulgar pretensions and reveals the vacuous posing at its heart.

Germinie Lacerteux, generally considered to be the Goncourts' finest work, is a study of the class that serves the bourgeoisie. It is the story of a servant girl whose character and upbringing lead her to debauchery, theft, sickness, and death. The character Germinie is based on the Goncourts' own servant, Rose Malingre, who had been an ideal servant to them from the time of Jules's infancy. When she died, bills began to arrive from her creditors revealing a sordid double life. She had stolen from her employers to support her lover and had even given birth to a child, managing to conceal her pregnancy. When the infant died, she sank into a life of frantic sexual promiscuity and alcoholism. The pneumonia and pleurisy that ended her life were contracted while she stood all night in the rain watching the house where her lover entertained another woman. The Goncourts, who had tended her faithfully during her illness, were astounded, although part of Rose's success in deceiving them was no doubt the result of their aristocratic myopia with regard to the lower classes. For them, Rose was a beloved servant, but not quite a whole and authentic individual.

The preface to *Germinie Lacerteux* proclaims the desire of the authors to seek the truth in fiction. The novel they offer the public represents a serious social inquiry, undertaken with scientific methods of analysis and psychological investigation. In *Germinie Lacerteux*, the Goncourts showed themselves to be in the vanguard of the enthusiasm for science that marked the decades of positivism. In comparing the work of the novelist to scientific work, they directly anticipated Naturalism.

The resounding call, in the preface, for the common people to have their own novel certainly laid down a principle for future novelists that led to a broadening social representation in the novel. *Germinie Lacerteux*, however, provides a voyeuristic tour of the lower classes for aristocratic and middle-class readers. In this work, the brothers depict the sordid byways of vice and pathology and thus serve as observers and collectors of what is ugly, morbid, and repulsive.

The intention of the Goncourts was not to show a debauched hypocrite masking her nature beneath a proper maid's exterior. They wished to make her degeneration the logical and inescapable outcome of her social background and individual temperament. Thus, the novel begins with an exposition of her early childhood, peasant origins, the death of her parents, and the necessity of joining her sisters in Paris. Germinie is abused and raped in her first jobs and finally finds a tranquil home as maid to an elderly spinster, Mademoiselle de Varandeuil, who lives in genteel poverty.

To this point, Germinie has been the passive victim of society's exploitation, but now her own temperament (which, the misogynistic brothers imply, is typically feminine) begins to emerge. "Like all women," she needs to confide, to love, and to have a child. Unfortunately, Germinie is a guileless innocent when it comes to judging human nature, and her first friend and lover, a mother and son, respectively, take ruthless advantage of the love that comes to obsess Germinie.

Germinie has a child and is briefly happy until the infant dies, whereupon her degradation accelerates under the impetus of her insatiable and uncontrollable desires. At the same time, however, she remains devoted to her mistress. Even as she steals to pay her lover, Germinie is tormented by the possibility that her secret life may be revealed to Mademoiselle de Varandeuil. In the end, Germinie suffers the death of Rose Malingre and is buried in an unmarked pauper's grave.

The Goncourts' next two novels both follow the pattern of isolation and disintegration established in *Renée Mauperin* and *Germinie Lacerteux*. *Manette Salomon* is the story of a brilliant artist, Coriolis, who takes as his mistress the beautiful, exotic model Manette Salomon. When Manette becomes a mother, the drive of her maternal instinct overwhelms and destroys the artist's fragile creative genius. The novel's anti-Semitism and misogyny make it unpalatable reading today, for Coriolis weakens progressively as Manette alienates his Gentile friends. In *Madame Gervaisais*, the last novel the brothers wrote together, it is the heroine's extreme religious mysticism that isolates her from all but her brutal, perverse confessor, Father Sibilla.

The Goncourts based *Madame Gervaisais* on the religious conversion of their aunt, Nephtalie Lebas de Gourmont, whose anticlerical husband considered her to have gone nearly mad after a visit to Rome. The purpose of the text was to demonstrate how the combination of milieu and character could lead to a religious crisis in even an educated woman; this premise was supported by the brothers' belief that all women have an emotional need for religion.

The novel was not well received, in part because Father Sibilla preaches a twisted philosophy that causes the heroine to renounce her own child. The psychological motivation of the heroine is unconvincing, and her extreme isolation results in a work bereft of action and dialogue. It is a disappointing end to the collaboration of the two brothers.

After Jules's death, Edmond returned to fiction writing with a novel they had prepared together, *Elisa: The Story of a Prostitute*, but which displays a heavily sociological style, no doubt attributable to the absence of Jules's lighter touch. This novel recalls *Germinie Lacerteux* in its depiction of the depths of society. In this case, the brothers also wished to expose the horrors of incarceration in a women's prison and especially of the "Auburn system," under which inmates were kept in total silence. Finally, they wished to be strictly faithful to social reality, believing that literary portrayals of prostitutes were often sentimentalized.

As had been the usual practice of the brothers, Edmond chose to focus on one individual rather than to paint a social panorama. The novel opens in the courtroom where Elisa is condemned to death for the murder of a soldier, after which it reverts to her childhood to show how heredity and environment formed the young girl. In those days, midwives were closely linked to prostitutes in the social system, so Elisa drifts easily from the home of her mother, exhausted by that profession, into a life of prostitution.

Being too lazy to learn any other kind of work, Elisa is made to bear part of the responsibility for her plight, but the focus begins to shift to demonstrate how a young prostitute is victimized by society. As Elisa drifts from one bordello to another, she gradually loses her individuality as well as control over her own destiny. Feeling helpless, she begins to hate all men, and at last, degraded and dehumanized, she stabs a young soldier to death. Although for the reader her act is perfectly well motivated, the jury can only condemn it as an unjustifiable murder. Elisa's sentence is commuted to life imprisonment, and in prison her mind disintegrates under the rule of silence. She dies, a victim of a hypocritical penal system and social injustice. The pattern of progressive isolation is entirely appropriate to the subject.

Edmond's next novel was, in a sense, a tribute to his brother Jules. *The Zemganno Brothers* tells of two brothers, Gianni and Nello, who perform together in a traveling circus. Many of the biographical details are drawn from the Goncourts' own lives. The two acrobats seem almost to become one as they perform, until their act is sabotaged and the younger brother breaks his legs. They are forced to become violinists for the circus, an end nearly as tragic as death.

Aside from the psychological insights into the relationship between Edmond and Jules, *The Zemganno Brothers* gives full play to the theme of illusion and reality. The motif of the mask, both literal and figurative, intrigued Edmond profoundly, especially the notion that an illusion can reveal a truth. The circus world obviously provides an ideal setting for such a theme, and in the novel, Nello is perplexed when his circus persona seems to absorb the real man. *The Zemganno Brothers*, psychologically complex and sociologically accurate, deserves to be better known.

With his interest in worlds of illusion, it is no surprise that Edmond should have written *La Faustin*, the life of an actress. Based on the life of Rachel (the stage name of Élisa Félix), the inspired tragedienne, *La Faustin* tells of a famous actress at the Comédie-Française whose greatest role is Phèdre. She does not achieve brilliance, however, until she experiences a great passion of her own. When this passion—her lover—dies, La Faustin cannot keep from imitating his agonized grimace, thus revealing that for her, the mask of the actress has become the only reality.

With his last work, *Chérie*, Edmond attempted to depict the life of fashionable society in a series of vignettes centered on a young girl, spoiled by her grandfather. Unwilling to conform to popular standards of fiction, Edmond failed to breathe life into a subject that had already been dealt with successfully by Zola. *Chérie* is, nevertheless, typical of even the best of the Goncourts' novels in its lack of plot in the traditional sense. Analysis and sociological documentation dominate their creations, revealing their pessimistic view of human nature and social institutions. In an age of positive belief in progress, they could see only a static reality beneath an optimistic illusion. For them, the only human progress was toward death.

It is this very obsession with reality, however, that makes the Goncourts' novels compelling documents of their age. Ultimately, their achievement in fiction lies in their search for the truth in all realms of society and in their insistence on being historians and sociologists as much as novelists.

Major publications other than long fiction

PLAYS: *Henriette Maréchal*, 1865; *La Patrie en danger*, 1873; *À bas le progrès*, 1893.

NONFICTION: *Histoire de la société française pendant la Révolution*, 1854;

Histoire de la société française pendant le Directoire, 1855; *Sophie Arnould*, 1857; *Histoire de Marie Antoinette*, 1858; *L'Art au XVIIIe siècle*, 1859-1875 (*French Eighteenth Century Painters*, 1948); *Les Maîtresses de Louis XV*, 1860; *La Femme au XVIIIe siècle*, 1862 (*The Women in the Eighteenth Century*, 1927); *Gavarni*, 1869; *Journal: Mémoires de la vie littéraire*, 1887-1896, 1956-1959; *Outamaro*, 1891; *Hokousai*, 1896; *The Goncourt Journals (1851-1870)*, 1937, 1958.

MISCELLANEOUS: *Oeuvres complètes*, 1922-1937 (41 volumes).

Bibliography

Auerbach, Erich. *Mimesis: The Representation of Reality in Western Literature*, 1953.

Billy, André. *The Goncourt Brothers*, 1960.

Grant, R. B. *The Goncourt Brothers*, 1973.

Richard, Jean-Pierre. *Littérature et sensation*, 1954.

Ullman, Stephen. *Style in the French Novel*, 1957.

Jan St. Martin

MAXIM GORKY
Aleksey Maksimovich Peshkov

Born: Nizhny-Novgorod, Russia; March 28, 1868
Died: Moscow, U.S.S.R.; June 18, 1936

Principal long fiction

Goremyka Pavel, 1894 (novella; *Orphan Paul*, 1946); *Foma Gordeyev*, 1899 (English translation, 1901); *Troye*, 1901 (*Three of Them*, 1902); *Mat*, 1906 (*The Mother*, 1906); *Ispoved*, 1908 (*A Confession*, 1910); *Zhizn Matveya Kozhemyakina*, 1910 (*The Life of Matvei Kozhemyakin*, 1959); *Delo Artomonovykh*, 1925 (*Decadence*, 1927; also as *The Artomonov Business*, 1948); *Zhizn Klima Samgina*, 1927-1936 (*The Life of Klim Samgin*, 1930-1938; includes *The Bystander*, 1930; *The Magnet*, 1931; *Other Fires*, 1933; *The Specter*, 1938).

Other literary forms

Maxim Gorky wrote a total of fifteen plays, only three of which were staged during his lifetime: *Na dne* (1902; *The Lower Depths*, 1906), *Vassa Zheleznova* (1910, 1935; English translation, 1945), and *Yegor Bulychov i drugiye* (1931; *Yegor Bulichoff and Others*, 1937). His other plays include *Meshchane* (1901; *The Smug Citizens*, 1906), *Dachniki* (1905; *Summer Folk*, 1905), *Deti solntsa* (1905; *Children of the Sun*, 1906), *Varvary* (1905; *Barbarians*, 1945), *Vragi* (1906; *Enemies*, 1945), *Chudaki* (1910; *Queer People*, 1945), *Zykovy* (1914; *The Zykovs*, 1945), *Starik* (1919; *The Judge*, 1924; also as *Old Man*, 1956), *Falshivaya moneta* (1926; the counterfeit coin), and *Dostigayev i drugiye* (1933; *Dostigaeff and the Others*, 1937). All are available in Russian in the thirty-volume *Polnoe sobranie sochinenii* (1949-1955; complete works) and in English in *Seven Plays* (1945), *Five Plays* (1956), and *Plays* (1975).

Gorky wrote about three hundred short stories. Among the most important are "Makar Chudra" (1892), "Chelkash" (1895; "Tchelkash"), "Starukha Izergil" (1895; "The Old Woman Izergil"), "Malva" (1897; English translation), "V stepi" (1897; "In the Steppe"), "Dvadtsat'shest' i odna" (1899; "Twenty-six Men and a Girl"), "Pesnya o burevestnike" (1901; "Song of the Stormy Petrel"), "Pesnya o sokole" (1908; "Song of the Falcon"), and the collections *Po Rusi* (1913, 1917; *Through Russia*, 1921) and *Skazki ob Italii* (1923; tales of Italy). A two-volume collection of his stories, *Ocherki i rasskazy*, was first published in Russian in 1898, the second volume appearing in 1925. The short stories are available in the collected works; some of the best of them are available in English in *Selected Short Stories* (1970), introduced by Stefan Zweig.

Among Gorky's numerous essays and articles, the most important "O Karamazovshchine" (1913; "On Karamazovism"), "Revolyutsia i kultura" (1917; "Revolution and Culture"), *Vladimir Ilich Lenin* (1924; *V. I. Lenin*, 1931), and "O meshchanstve" (1929; "On the Petty Bourgeois Mentality"). The collection *Untimely Thoughts: Essays on Revolution, Culture, and the Bolsheviks* (1968) includes many of these essays in English translation.

Achievements

Hailed by Soviet critics as a true proletarian writer and the model of Socialist Realism, Gorky is one of the few authors to see his native town renamed for him. Many schools, institutes, universities, and theaters bear his name, as does one of the main streets in Moscow. These honors, says Helen Muchnic, result from the fact that Gorky, along with Vladimir Ilich Lenin and Joseph Stalin, "shaped and disseminated the country's official philosophy." Stalin admired Gorky greatly, awarding him the coveted Order of Lenin. As chairman of the All-Union Congress of the Soviet Writers in 1934, Gorky delivered an address in which he defined Socialist Realism, a doctrine that unfortunately was to be interpreted in a manner different from what he intended or practiced; the *Soviet Encyclopedia* (1949-1958) calls him "the father of Soviet literature . . . the founder of the literature of Socialist Realism."

Although Gorky's novels are not among the best in Russian literature, they did inaugurate a new type of writing, revealing to the world a new Russia. In contrast to the countless *fin de siècle* evocations of the tormented Russian soul, with their gallery of superfluous men, Gorky offered a new hero, the proletarian, the revolutionary, such as Pavel Vlassov and his mother Pelagea Nilovna in the poorly constructed but ever-popular *The Mother*. Indeed, Richard Hare argues that even today *The Mother* is the prototype for the socially tendentious novel in the Soviet Union, with its crude but determined effort to look into the dynamism of social change in Russia.

Gorky's highest artistic achievements, however, are his literary portraits; the best, says Muchnic, are those which he drew from life, especially of Leo Tolstoy and Anton Chekhov. Also notable is Gorky's affectionate portrait of his grandmother. Gorky had a strong visual sense, the gift of astute observation, and the ability to translate these insights into sparkling dialogue. He created an entire portrait gallery of vignettes, most of which can be traced to people he met in his endless wanderings through Russia and abroad.

The child of a lower-middle-class family that faced rapid impoverishment, a self-taught student, a young man whose universities were the towns along the Volga and the steamers that made their way along its mighty waters, Gorky was nevertheless sympathetic to culture. He devoured books voraciously and indiscriminately and encouraged others to study. From 1918 to 1921, not wholly in favor with the new regime, he worked tirelessly to save writers and intellectuals from starvation and from censorship. He befriended the Serapion Brothers (a group of young Russian writers formed in 1921) and later Mikhail Sholokhov, always encouraging solid scholarship.

Estimates of Gorky even now depend on political ideology, for he is closely associated with the Revolution. His vision, however, is broader than that of any political movement. He repeats often in his autobiographical works his dismay at the ignorance of people and their lack of desire for a better life, and he felt keenly the injustice done to the innocent. His writing is permeated by the desire to bring people from slavery to freedom, to build a good life; he believed in the power of human beings to change their world. Courageous, generous, and devoted to the public good, Gorky was timid, lacking in self-confidence, and infinitely modest. His commitment to social justice is unquestionable. These qualities may be what Chekhov had in mind when he said that Gorky's works might be forgotten, but that Gorky the man would never be.

Biography

Maxim Gorky, champion of the poor and the downtrodden, was born Aleksey Maksimovich Peshkov in Nizhny-Novgorod (a town that has borne the name Gorky since 1932), on March 28, 1868. His father, who died three years later from cholera, was a joiner-upholsterer and later a shipping agent; his mother's family, the Kashirins, were owners of a dyeing establishment. After his father's death, Gorky's mother left young Gorky to be reared by her parents, with whom he lived until the age of eleven, when his recently remarried mother died. Gorky recounts his childhood experiences in brilliant anecdotes and dialogue in his autobiographical *Detstvo* (1913; *My Childhood*, 1915). The influence of his grandparents was great: His grandfather was a brutal, narrowly religious man, while his grandmother was gentle and pious; her own peculiar version of a benevolent God, sharply in contrast to the harsh religiosity of her husband, marked the impressionable child.

The frequent wanderers in Gorky's works are a reflection of his own experience. In 1879, his grandfather sent him "into the world." He went first to the family of his grandmother's sister's son, Valentin Sergeyev, to whom he was apprenticed as a draftsman. Gorky hated the snobbishness and avarice of this bourgeois family, which became the prototype of the Gordeyevs and the Artomonovs in his fiction. For the next ten years, he filled many other minor posts, from messboy on a Volga steamer to icon painter, reading when and where he could. Other than an idealistic admiration for a neighbor whom he named "Queen Margot," there were few bright spots in this period, which he describes in *V lyudyakh* (1916; *In the World*, 1917).

In 1889, after an unsuccessful suicide attempt which left him with a permanently weakened lung, Gorky met the Populist revolutionary Mikhail Romas, who helped him to clarify his confused ideas. At the same time, his acquaintance with the writer Vladimir Korolenko aided his literary development, as Tolstoy and Chekhov were to do in later years. In 1892, Gorky published his first story, "Makar Chudra," assuming at that time the pen name Maxim Gorky, meaning "the bitter one," a reflection of his painful childhood.

Gorky wandered through Russia, wrote, and began a series of unsuccessful romantic involvements, first with Olga Kaminskaya, an older woman of some sophistication, with whom he lived from 1892 to 1894, and then with Ekaterina Pavlovna Volzhina, a proofreader on the newspaper for which he was working. Gorky married Volzhina in 1896, and she became the mother of his two children, Maxim and Ekaterina. Imprisoned several times, Gorky was seldom free of police surveillance. In 1899, he became literary editor of the Marxist newspaper *Zhizn* and directed his attentions to the problems of social injustice.

In 1905, Gorky's violent protests of government brutality in suppressing the workers' demonstrations on Bloody Sunday once again brought him imprisonment, this time in the Peter-Paul Fortress. By then, however, Gorky was famous, and celebrities all over Europe and America protested the sentence. Upon his release, he once again began to travel, both for political reasons and for his health. He visited New York, which he called "the city of the yellow devil," in 1906, where he attacked America for its inequalities and America attacked him for the immorality of his relationship with Maria Fyodorovna Andreyeva, an actress of the celebrated Moscow Art Theater. After six months in the United States, he spent seven years in Italy, settling in Capri, where his Villa Serafina became a center of pilgrimage for all revolutionaries, including Lenin.

Gorky returned to Russia in 1913. When the Revolution broke out in 1917, he was not at first among its wholehearted supporters, although he served on many committees, working especially to safeguard culture. In 1921, for reasons of health, he went to Sorrento, Italy, where he spent his time writing. Although he made periodic visits to his homeland beginning in 1928, it was not until 1932 that he returned to the Soviet Union for good; in that same year, Stalin awarded him the Order of Lenin. In 1934, he was elected chairman of the All-Union Congress of Soviet Writers; during this period, he became increasingly active in cultural policymaking. Although he continued to write, he produced nothing noteworthy; his four-novel cycle *The Life of Klim Samgin*, the last volume of which he did not live to complete, is an artistic failure. Gorky's death in 1936 was surrounded by mysterious circumstances, although official autopsy reports attribute it to tuberculosis and influenza.

Analysis

Although Soviet critics tend to exalt the realism of Maxim Gorky's works, D. S. Mirsky said that Gorky never wrote a good novel or a good play, while Tolstoy remarked that Gorky's novels are inferior to his stories and that his plays are even worse than his novels. Maintaining that Gorky's "tremendous heroic emotions ring false," Tolstoy criticized Gorky's lack of sense of proportion, as Chekhov had noted Gorky's lack of restraint. It is obvious that Gorky did not know how to limit his stories, that he piles up details along with extraneous dialogue. His narrative technique consists in recounting the life story of a single protagonist or the saga of a family. His narratives are always linear, often proceeding from birth to death; the main character yearns for a new life and struggles with a stagnant environment, sometimes experiencing flashes of light. Thus, the typical Gorky novel is a tireless and often tiresome documentary on a single theme.

Gorky's weak narrative technique is counterbalanced by excellent characterization. True, he is guilty of oversimplification—his characters are types rather than individuals, figures from a modern morality play—but he introduced into Russian fiction a wide range of figures from many different walks of life rarely or never treated by earlier novelists. Though not highly individualized, Gorky's characterizations are vivid and convincing, imbued with his own energy.

Gorky sees people as social organisms, and therefore he is especially conscious of their role in society. He was particularly familiar with the merchant class or the *meshchane*, because he grew up among them, in the Kashirin and Sergeev households. They form some of his most successful portraits, representing not only the petty bourgeoisie but also the barge owners, grain dealers, mill owners, and textile manufacturers, the Gordeyevs, Artomonovs, and Kozhemyakins. Gorky represents them as self-centered individualists, characterized by envy, malice, self-righteousness, avarice, and intellectual and spiritual torpor. Their decadence is symbolic of the malady that ravages prerevolutionary Russia.

In contrast to the merchants are the lonely and downtrodden, not always idealized as in the novels of Fyodor Dostoevski but presented, rather, as the ignorant victims of society and its lethargic sycophants. The corrupt and indifferent town of Okurov in *The Life of Matvei Kozhemyakin* symbolizes Russia's decadence, as do the thieves and vagabonds of Kazan, the flophouse of *The Lower Depths*, and the orgies of the theology students in the houses of prostitution. More Dostoevskian are the *bosyaki*, the barefoot tramps, such as Chelkash and Makar Chudra, who are the heralds of the future. Along with them, yet very different in spirit, is the revolutionary intelligentsia, the new heroes created by Gorky. They are Pelagea Nilovna, the "mother," her son Pavel and his friends, Mansurova in *The Life of Matvei Kozhemyakin*, and Derenkov and Romas in Gorky's own life; it is for such characters that Gorky is exalted by the Soviets, though to foreign readers they are usually the least attractive.

Gorky's best characters are presented without excessive ideological trappings. They range from his saintly grandmother, Akulina Kashirina, perhaps his most unforgettable character, to Queen Margot, the idol with clay feet. They include Smoury, the cook on the steamer, who first encouraged Gorky to read, and many other simple people whom Gorky was to meet, "kind, solitary, and broken off from life." They also take the form of figures such as the merchant Ignat Gordeyev, the image of the Volga, vital, seething, creative, generous, and resolute.

Most of Gorky's women are victims of violence, beaten by their husbands and unappreciated by their families, such as Natasha Artomonova and Saveli Kozhemyakin's wife, whom he beats to death. Love in Gorky's novels is either accompanied by violence and brutality or idealized, as in Queen Margot or Tanya in the story "Twenty-six Men and a Girl." It ranges from tender devotion in *The Mother* to drunken orgies on Foma Gordeyev's Volga steamer. Gorky's own experience of love was unhappy, and he was ill at ease when portraying sexual scenes. Even his coarsely erotic scenes seem to be tinged with a moralizing intent.

Against a background of resplendent nature, the Volga, the sea, or the steppe, Gorky depicts the eruptions of violence and brutality, the orgies and the squalor, the pain and the harshness which, says Muchnic, are at the heart of his work. One has only to read the opening pages of *My Childhood* to feel its force. His own weight of harsh experience impelled him to force others to look at the bestiality which he saw rampant in Russia and to urge them to exterminate it. Ever the champion of social justice, Gorky felt the need to fight ignorance, cruelty, and exploitation.

Gorky's first and best novel, *Foma Gordeyev*, is set along the banks of the Volga, a region well-known to the author. It is the story of the Volga merchants, represented here by the Gordeyev and Mayakin families. Rich, greedy, and passionate, both families represent the iron will and the domination of the merchant class. Gorky's merchants are of peasant origin, unsophisticated and uneducated. In Foma's revolt, Gorky shows the decay of society at the turn of the century and the impending Revolution, as yet only dimly anticipated.

Foma, the only son of Ignat Gordeyev, a self-made barge owner and one of Gorky's richest character sketches, is brought up by his godfather and his father's business colleague, Yakov Mayakin, whose family has owned the local rope works for generations. Foma shows no talent for or interest in business and, after his father's death, wastes his money on debauchery, drink, and wanton destruction. At first dimly attracted to Lyubov Mayakina, he is unable to conform to her educated tastes, and she, in obedience to her father's wishes, marries the respectable and highly Europeanized Afrikan Smolin. Foma continues his wild rebellion, actually a search for self and meaning, not unlike that of Mikhail Lermontov's Pechorin. Finally institutionalized for apparent insanity, Foma becomes an enlightened vagabond.

Foma Gordeyev follows the storyline generally adopted by Gorky: the life story of the hero from birth to a crisis. Although it is weak in plot and characterization, it is readable, especially powerful in its evocation of the Volga, the elemental force that intoxicated the wealthy Ignat. Ignat is a finished portrait of the boisterous, dynamic businessman Gorky knew so well—vital, creative and resolute. He is one of Gorky's most sympathetic portraits, along with Yakov Mayakin, who shows the characteristic traits of the Russian merchant that go back to the sixteenth century *Domostroy* (a book on social conduct). Foma, though not so well drawn, represents the rift in generations and the universally disturbed mood that pervaded Russia on the eve of the abortive Revolution of 1905. The whole novel attempts to assess the flaws in the capitalistic system, and thus is very modern in spirit.

The Mother, written while Gorky was in America after the 1905 Revolution, reflects his disillusionment with both czarist and capitalistic social structures and his desire "to sustain the failing spirit of opposition to the dark and threatening forces of life." It was published first in English, in 1906, by *Appleton's Magazine* in New York, and then in Russian in Berlin. It became the symbol of the revolutionary cause and was widely read and acclaimed, even after the Revolution, as a model of the Socialist novel. Translated into many languages, it became the basis for other novels and plays, such as Bertolt Brecht's *Mutter Courage und ihre Kinder* (1941; *Mother Courage and Her Children*, 1948). As a novel, it is one of Gorky's weakest in characterization and plot, yet its optimistic message and accessible style have assured its continuing popularity.

Written in the third person, through the eyes of the courageous mother, Pelagea Nilovna Vlassova, the novel relates her encounter with the Social Democratic Party, inspired by her son Pavel. Pelagea suffered mistreatment from her husband and seems destined to continue in the same path with her son until his "conversion" to socialism. Pavel becomes a champion of the proletarian cause, the acknowledged leader of a small group of fellow revolutionaries who study forbidden books and distribute literature among the factory workers in their village. After Pavel's arrest, the illiterate Pelagea continues Pavel's work, stealthily distributing pamphlets and becoming a mother to the other members of the group: Sasha, who is secretly in love with Pavel; the "God-builder" Rybin; Andrei, the charming and humorous *kholokol*; the misanthropic Vesovshchikov; and the openhearted urban intellectual Nikolai. Pavel's release from prison is immediately followed by his bold leadership in the May Day demonstration, for which he is again imprisoned. The mother's work becomes more daring and widespread as she passes to other villages like the holy wanderers so common in Gorky's early work. After Pavel's condemnation to exile in Siberia, Pelagea herself is arrested as she prepares to distribute the speech her son made prior to his sentence.

The best portrait in this weak novel is that of the mother, the only character to show psychological development. Yet Pelagea passes from one type of religious fervor to another, and her Socialist convictions are simply the transferral of her Orthodox beliefs to the kingdom of this world. Even the revolutionaries invoke Christ and compare their work to his. The austere Pavel remains remote and unconvincing, while maternal love is the dominant force in the affectionate and almost mystical Pelagea.

Written in 1924 and 1925 while Gorky was living abroad in Sorrento, Italy,

The Artomonov Business is a retrospective novel on the causes of the 1917 Revolution. Encompassing three generations and covering the period from 1863 to 1917, it has a much broader base than most of Gorky's works. Although here, as elsewhere, Gorky fills his narrative with extraneous detail, he draws many convincing portraits of the demoralized merchant class at the turn of the century. Frank M. Borras singles out Gorky's interweaving of the historical theme with the characters' personal destinies as one of the merits of the novel.

Ilya Artomonov is the patriarch of the family, a passionate and dynamic freed serf who establishes a linen factory in the sleepy town of Dryomov. His son Pyotr inherits his father's sensuality but not his business skill, and the narrative of his debauchery and indifference to his workers occupies the greater part of the novel. The Artomonov family also includes the more businesslike and adaptable Aleksei and the hunchback Nikita, who becomes a monk though he has lost his faith in God. The women in the novel occupy a secondary and passive role, existing mainly for the sensual gratification of the men, both attracting and repelling them.

Pyotr has two sons and two daughters. The eldest son, Ilya, leaves home to study and, as in Chekhov's stories, becomes an unseen presence, presumably joining the revolutionary Social Democratic Party. Yakov, the second son, is a sensualist, indifferent to business, and is killed by revolutionaries as he escapes in fear of them. Miron, Aleksei's son, though physically weak, shows, like his father, an aptitude for commerce. Yet none is strong enough to save the family's ailing business, weakened by the corruption and indifference of its managers.

Gorky's symbolism is evident in his characterization of Tikhon Vialov (the quiet one), an enigmatic ditchdigger, gardener, and ubiquitous servant of the Artomonov family. It is Tikhon who at the very end of the story proclaims the Revolution, calling for revenge for the injustices that he has suffered at the hands of the Artomonovs. Quite obviously he symbolizes the proletariat, victim of the bourgeoisie. Aside from Tikhon, Gorky emphasizes much less the oppression of the workers than the empty, selfish, and superfluous lives of the factory owners.

Alternating wild episodes of debauchery, cruelty, and murder with scenes of boredom and superfluous dialogue, *The Artomonov Business* is both a modern novel and a return to Dostoevskian melodrama. Gorky had planned to write the novel as early as 1909 but was advised by Lenin to wait for the Revolution, which would be its logical conclusion. This story of the progressive deterioration of a family is also a profound study in the consequences of the failure of human relationships.

Gorky's finest prose work is unquestionably his autobiographical trilogy, which recounts in somewhat idealized form the first twenty-four years of his life. Like Tolstoy, who in his *Detstvo* (1852; *Childhood*, 1886) had written a psychological study of every child, Gorky wished to write a universal work—

not about himself, but "about that narrow, stifling impression in which the Russian used to, and indeed, still does live." The first volume of Gorky's trilogy, *My Childhood*, first appeared in serial form in 1912 and 1913 in the newspaper *Russkoe slovo*; the second volume, *In the World*, was written in 1914 and serialized in 1915 and 1916; and the final volume, *Moi universitety* (*My Universities*, 1923), based partly on previous sketches, appeared in *Krasnaya nov*, in 1923.

Of the three parts, *My Childhood* is universally acknowledged as the best. It portrays the progressive impoverishment of a middle-class merchant family, the Kashirins, seen through the perceptive eyes of a child. This theme was later to mark many of Gorky's novels, notably *Foma Gordeyev* and *The Artomonov Business* though the causes of the family's decline are not identical in each case. Gorky relates his experiences from the age of three to the age of eleven, beginning with his father's death in 1871 and ending with his mother's death in 1879, whereupon his grandfather sent him "into the world." The story is marked by vivid portraits of his faintly remembered yet idealized father; his widowed and remarried mother, who never succeeded in establishing a bond with her son; and especially of his maternal grandparents, with whom he passed his childhood. Grandfather Vasili Kashirin is authoritarian, rigid, and uncompromising, yet his authority wanes with his fortune. Grandmother Akulina, on the other hand, is portrayed with great affection, and she emerges as a *nyanya* in the tradition of Pushkin's Arina Rodionovna or Tolstoy's Natalya Savishna. Her confident, childlike attitude toward God reflects her affection for all human beings, and she is the greatest inspiration and resource of the young Aleksei.

Although *In the World* covers only the period from Gorky's eleventh to his sixteenth year, it is less cohesive and concise than *My Childhood*, for it lacks a center of interest. Gorky describes his various employments during this period, beginning with his apprenticeship as a draftsman to the elder son of his grandmother's sister, Matryona Sergeeva, mistress of a self-righteous, indolent, avaricious household. After leaving this unattractive family, Gorky moved rapidly from place to place; the portraits of the people and groups he meets are brief and usually depressing, their downtrodden condition seemingly irremediable. His only salvation is in books, and a neighbor who provides his supply becomes idealized as Queen Margot, only to disappoint him when he finds her in the arms of her lover. On the whole, Aleksei's impression of life is its injustice, the ignorance of its people, and their lack of desire for a better life, yet he preserves an unquenchable thirst for both learning and enlightenment.

My Universities, probably the least popular part of the trilogy, nevertheless has greater unity and focus than the second part. Aleksei first describes his three-year sojourn at Kazan, where he hoped to enter the university; this period ended with his attempted suicide in 1887. The second part recounts a brief three-month encounter with the Populist group of Mikhail Romas, marked by Aleksei's recovery of his mental equilibrium and the clarification of his ideas through the influence of Romas, who, along with the gentle baker Derenkov, is one of the few positive figures in the entire work. As Gorky discovers his vocation to be a writer, he concludes with his "tragicomic love affair" with Olga Kaminskaya and the influence of Korolenko on his career.

Gorky's autobiography is a gripping work, opening with the juxtaposition of his father's death, his brother's birth, and his mother's agony. The entire trilogy is a succession of masterful portraits, brief but convincing. Gorky's recollections are essentially visual, with penetrating descriptions ranging from the domes of Nizhny-Novgorod to the reopened grave of his decaying mother. Ideas occupy only a small place in the work, yet Gorky's preoccupation with injustice, his desire for truth, and his passion for learning dominate every scene. Although Gorky presents an idealized portrait of himself and a dismal picture of his surroundings, his work reveals his own character and the spirit of Russia on the eve of the Revolution.

Gorky was less a man of ideas and reason than one of instinct and emotion. His best works are based upon intuition and observation. His truth and reality are humanistic, not metaphysical; they deal with the useful and the practical. Unlike Honoré de Balzac, whom he admired, Gorky did not succeed in investing the sordid with mystery or the petty with grandeur. He wrote a literature of the moment, "loud but not intense," as Muchnic describes it. It is, however, a literature of the people and for the people, accessible and genuine. Although some of his works are monotonous to today's Western reader, and no doubt to the Soviet reader as well, at their best they are honest portrayals of people, inspiring confidence in man's power to change the world.

Major publications other than long fiction

SHORT FICTION: "Makar Chudra," 1892; "Chelkash," 1895 ("Tchelkash"); "Starukha Izergil," 1895 ("The Old Woman Izergil"); "Malva," 1897 (English translation); "V stepi," 1897 ("In the Steppe"); *Ocherki i rasskazy*, 1898-1925 (2 volumes); "Dvadtsat'shest' i odna," 1899 ("Twenty-six Men and a Girl"); "Pesnya o burevestnike," 1901 ("Song of the Stormy Petrel"); "Pesnya o sokole," 1908 ("Song of the Falcon"); *Rozhdenie cheloveka*, 1912; *Po Rusi*, 1913, 1917 (*Through Russia*, 1921); *Tales of Two Countries*, 1914; *Stories from the Steppe*, 1918; *Skazki ob Italii*, 1923; *Vospominaniya*, 1924; *Selected Short Stories*, 1959, 1974; *Selected Short Stories*, 1970 (with an introduction by Stefan Zweig); *A Book of Short Stories*, 1973.

PLAYS: *Meshchane*, 1901 (*The Smug Citizens*, 1906); *Na dne*, 1902 (*The Lower Depths*, 1906); *Dachniki*, 1905 (*Summer Folk*, 1905); *Deti solntsa*, 1905 (*Children of the Sun*, 1906); *Varvary*, 1905 (*Barbarians*, 1945); *Vragi*, 1906 (*Enemies*, 1945); *Chudaki*, 1910 (*Queer People*, 1945); *Vassa Zheleznova*, 1910, 1935 (English translation, 1945); *Zykovy*, 1914 (*The Zykovs*, 1945);

Starik, 1919 (*The Judge*, 1924; also as *Old Man*, 1956); *Falshivaya moneta*, 1926; *Yegor Bulychov i drugiye*, 1931 (*Yegor Bulichoff and Others*, 1937); *Dostigayev i drugiye*, 1933 (*Dostigaeff and the Others*, 1937); *Seven Plays*, 1945; *Five Plays*, 1956; *Plays*, 1975.

NONFICTION: *Detstvo*, 1913 (*My Childhood*, 1915); "O Karamazovshchine," 1913 ("On Karamazovism"); *V lyudyakh*, 1916 (*In the World*, 1917); "Revolyutsia i kultura," 1917 ("Revolution and Culture"); *Vozpominaniya o Lev Nikolayeviche Tolstoi*, 1919 (*Reminiscences of Lev Nikolaevich Tolstoy*, 1920); *Moi universitety*, 1923 (*My Universities*, 1923); *Vladimir Ilich Lenin*, 1924 (*V. I. Lenin*, 1931); "O meshchanstve," 1929 ("On the Petty Bourgeois Mentality"); *Reminiscences of Tolstoy, Chekhov and Andreyev*, 1949; *Untimely Thoughts: Essays on Revolution, Culture, and the Bolsheviks*, 1968.

MISCELLANEOUS: *Polnoe sobranie sochinenii*, 1949-1955 (30 volumes); *Polnoe sobranie sochinenii*, 1968-1976 (25 volumes); *Collected Works of Maxim Gorky*, 1979-1981 (8 volumes).

Bibliography
Bialik, Boris Aronovich. *O Gorkom*, 1947.
Borras, Frank M. *Maxim Gorky the Writer*, 1967.
Gourfinkel, Nina. *Gorky*, 1960.
Habermann, Gerhard E. *Maksim Gorky*, 1971.
Hare, Richard. *Maxim Gorky*, 1962.
Kastorski, S. *Stati o Gorkom*, 1953.
Levin, Dan. *Stormy Petrel*, 1967.
Muchnic, Helen. *From Gorky to Pasternak*, 1961.

Irma M. Kashuba

GÜNTER GRASS

Born: Gdańsk, Poland; October 16, 1927

Principal long fiction

Die Blechtrommel, 1959 (*The Tin Drum*, 1961); *Katz und Maus*, 1961 (*Cat and Mouse*, 1963); *Hundejahre*, 1963 (*Dog Years*, 1965); *Örtlich betäubt*, 1969 (*Local Anaesthetic*, 1969); *Aus dem Tagebuch einer Schnecke*, 1972 (*From the Diary of a Snail*, 1973); *Der Butt*, 1977 (*The Flounder*, 1978); *Das Treffen in Telgte*, 1979 (*The Meeting at Telgte*, 1981); *Danziger Trilogie*, 1980 (includes *Die Blechtrommel*; *Katz und Maus*; *Hundejahre*); *Kopfgeburten: Oder, Die Deutschen sterben aus* 1980 (*Headbirths: Or, The Germans Are Dying Out*, 1982).

Other literary forms

Although Günter Grass achieved fame and critical acclaim as a novelist, he has by no means limited his literary creativity to that genre. In fact, the author first attracted attention—albeit of a limited nature—as a playwright and a poet. In 1954, his one-act play in the absurdist vein, *Noch zehn Minuten bis Buffalo* (*Only Ten Minutes to Buffalo*, 1967), was staged, and in 1956, Grass's first collection of poetry, *Die Vorzüge der Windhühner* (the advantages of windfowl), was published. There is no exact correspondence between the German editions of Grass's plays and those in English translation. Six plays have been collected in *Theaterspiele* (1970; pieces for the theater), including *Only Ten Minutes to Buffalo*, *Hochwasser* (1963; *Flood*, 1967), *Onkel, Onkel* (1965; *Mister, Mister*, 1967), and *Die bösen Köche* (1961; *The Wicked Cooks*, 1967); the English versions of these plays have been published in *Four Plays* (1967), whereas *Die Plebejer proben den Aufstand* (1966; *The Plebeians Rehearse the Uprising*, 1966) and *Davor* (1974; *Max*, 1972) were published independently in English translations.

Grass's collected poems in *Gesammelte Gedichte* (1971) include the previously published volumes *Die Vorzüge der Windhühner*, *Gleisdreieck* (1960; rail interchange), and *Ausgefragt* (1967; *New Poems*, 1968). Selections from the first two collections are available in translation in *Selected Poems* (1966); the small collection *Poems of Günter Grass* (1969) incorporates both *Selected Poems* and *New Poems*. *Poems of Günter Grass* is also available as a bilingual edition under the title *In the Egg and Other Poems* (1977); *Mariazuehren, Hommageàmarie, Inmarypraise* (1973) was published as a trilingual edition, as the title indicates. The collection entitled *Liebe geprüft* (1974; love tested) is a bibliophile edition.

As in Grass's plays, one may discern in his poems a gradual departure from his earlier playfulness and an increasing concern with political and social problems. Poetry continues to be a vital aspect of the author's creativity; this fact is clearly evidenced by the numerous poems that have been integrated into the voluminous novel *The Flounder*.

There is also a considerable body of writings that originated as a result of Grass's political involvement and, to a lesser extent, his commitment to his craft. These speeches, essays, open letters, and other comments have been printed in the following major collections: *Über das Selbstverständliche* (1968; partially translated in *Speak Out!*, 1969), *Über meinen Lehrer Döblin und andere Vorträge* (1968; about my teacher Döblin and other essays), *Der Bürger und seine Stimme* (1974; the citizen and his voice), *Denkzettel* (1978; lessons to remember), *Aufsätze zur Literatur* (1980; essays on literature), and *Widerstand lernen: Politische Gegenreden 1980-1983* (1984; learning how to resist: political rebuttals). Many of the concerns that Grass voiced in his political writing are also reflected in his fiction.

Achievements

Günter Grass has long been acknowledged as a novelist of international stature—a rank he achieved with the publication of *The Tin Drum*, his first novel, whose English version appeared in 1961 in Great Britain and two years later in the United States. Although Grass has continued to publish at a fairly steady pace and to produce works of challenging complexity—notably *The Flounder—The Tin Drum* continues to be his most widely acclaimed work. The American novelist John Irving, for example, wrote in *Saturday Review* (March, 1982) that the novel "has not been surpassed, it is the greatest novel by a living author." Irving continued by claiming that "you can't be well-read today if you haven't read him. Günter Grass is simply the most original and versatile writer alive."

Although Grass is not held in such high esteem by all critics, his formidable stature is acknowledged, if grudgingly, by most serious students of literature. There are several reasons that Grass has remained in the center of public attention. To begin with, Grass aroused topical interest by his chronicling of Germany's Nazi past—if from an idiosyncratic narrative point of view. The surface realism of *The Tin Drum*, for example, is mingled with elements of the fantastic, grotesque, and comical that require the reader to reexamine his preconceived notions not only about the period in question but also about the very nature of reality itself. Second, despite Grass's underlying view of history as ultimately meaningless and his perception of human existence as bordering on the absurd, his major works do convey a sense of commitment and responsibility that challenge the reader. Third, Grass has never confined himself to the proverbial ivory tower of the artist—quite the opposite. He has repeatedly stated that his responsibility as both a citizen and a writer demand his active involvement in politics, and he has acted according to his professed belief. Periodically, critics claim to have discerned a diminishing of

Grass's creativity as a result of his participation in election campaigns in support of the Social Democratic Party, but so far Grass has succeeded in proving his critics wrong; after each spate of intense political activity, he has inevitably returned to literary pursuits.

Today, Grass is generally acknowledged as the "author who put postwar German literature back in the world market" (*Newsweek*, May 24, 1965). His fiction displays a virtuosity of language practically unparalleled in contemporary letters, and although the Nobel Prize for Literature has as yet eluded him, he has received numerous domestic as well as foreign literary awards, among them the prestigious prize of Gruppe 47 (in 1958). In 1980, the film version of *The Tin Drum*, based on the screenplay by Grass and director Volker Schlöndorff, was nominated for an Academy Award in the foreign film category; the film also received several international prizes.

Biography

Günter Wilhelm Grass was born October 16, 1927, in the city of Gdańsk (called Danzig in German), then a Free State. Both the social milieu of the lower-middle class in which he grew up—Grass's father was a grocer—and the ethnically mixed marriage of his parents (his father was a German; his mother was of Cassubian or Kashubian—that is, Slavic—origin) proved to be lasting influences. After attending school in Danzig, which in 1939 had been annexed by the Third Reich, Grass, then still a teenager, was drafted into the army during the final phase of World War II. In 1945, he was wounded and subsequently taken captive by the American forces. After a brief period of imprisonment, he began to work in a potash mine and then became a stonemason's apprentice in Düsseldorf in the Rhineland. From this period of 1946 to 1947 dates Grass's beginning awareness of Nazi atrocities as well as his first exposure to postwar politics. He was attracted to the pragmatism of the Social Democrats, who tended to prefer the achievement of tangible results in the social realm to blind adherence to ideology.

Although Grass, a self-professed autodidact, eschewed the continuation of his formal education, which had been interrupted by the war, he did enroll at the Düsseldorf and Berlin academies of art (1948-1951 and 1953-1956) to study sculpture under various teachers. In 1954, he married Anna Schwarz, a ballet student from Switzerland; the marriage eventually ended in divorce, and Grass remarried in 1979.

During the middle and late 1950's, Grass gradually began to attract attention as a writer. In his first phase of literary activity, from approximately 1955 to 1959, he wrote primarily short prose pieces, poetry, and absurdist or poetic plays. In 1955, he was awarded a prize for his lyrics by the Suddeutsche Rundfunk (South German radio network); in the same year, he established contact with Gruppe 47, the most influential association of writers, publishers, and critics in postwar Germany, and in 1958, he was awarded that group's coveted prize. Grass's first collection of poetry, *Die Vorzüge der Windhühner*, was published in 1956; meanwhile, he had gone to live in Paris, where he worked on his novel *The Tin Drum*; its publication in 1959 propelled him to instant fame—or, owing to allegedly obscene and blasphemous passages in the novel, infamy.

Thus, the year 1959 marks the beginning of the second phase in Grass's career, which was characterized by an outburst of creative energy that the author has not been able to duplicate. In two-year intervals, from 1959 to 1963, the works of *Danziger Trilogie* (Danzig trilogy) were published; this trilogy was responsible for establishing Grass as one of the leading contemporary writers of fiction.

Grass's involvement in politics began as early as 1961. In that year, he provided material for the speeches of Social Democrat Willy Brandt, then mayor of West Berlin, who ran for chancellor of the Federal Republic. Only in 1965, however, did Grass actively campaign on behalf of the Social Democrats by delivering speeches in more than fifty cities. During this third phase of his career, Grass became a public figure whose celebrity, or notoriety, extended far beyond the literary scene. Grass's works from this period reflect his political commitment. The play *The Plebeians Rehearse the Uprising* takes issue with Bertolt Brecht's alleged preference for the aesthetic experience of revolutionary theater when faced with a potential revolutionary situation in East Germany. The novel *Local Anaesthetic* and the play *Max* explore the alternatives for political action available to those younger Germans of the postwar generation who opposed the Vietnam War.

The year 1972 marks the beginning of a fourth phase in Grass's development as a writer. *From the Diary of the Snail*, an account of the author's participation in the 1969 election campaign that ended in Willy Brandt's election as chancellor, harks back to the themes of *Danziger Trilogie* but employs a new narrative perspective. During the early and middle 1970's, Grass refrained from extensive political involvement and devoted his energies to the completion of his great historical novel *The Flounder*, which was followed by two shorter narratives, *The Meeting at Telgte* and *Headbirths: Or, The Germans Are Dying Out*.

Grass's unequivocal and vociferous engagement in the peace movement since 1979, the year of the NATO decision to deploy medium-range nuclear missiles in Western Europe, marks a fifth stage in his development. The author is no longer content to confine himself to grass-roots politics in the Federal Republic; on the contrary, owing to his exposure to problems of a global nature—particularly those of Third World countries—during his extensive travels, Grass feels compelled to speak out on a host of issues, from the nuclear arms race to the environment. Grass, however, has not abandoned literature in favor of politics; his announcement that he is working on a new novel is evidence of his continuing efforts to practice his craft.

Analysis

Although Günter Grass's novel *The Tin Drum* forms the first part of *Danziger Trilogie* and shares some characters, events, and themes with *Cat and Mouse* and *Dog Years*, the novel was conceived independently and can be discussed without explicit reference to the other two works. Nevertheless, it should be noted that the title of the trilogy reflects the extraordinary significance of Günter Grass's birthplace for his fiction. In fact, this significance has been compared to that of Dublin for James Joyce or Yoknapatawpha County for William Faulkner. Owing to political developments after World War II, Grass was forced to sever his ties with his place of birth forever: Danzig became the Polish Gdańsk, a city that the author was able to visit repeatedly but that was no longer the predominantly German-speaking Danzig.

Hence, the very act of narration is an evocation of the past, a resurrection from oblivion. Grass, however, is concerned neither with nostalgic memories nor with mourning the lost city; rather, he wants to keep alive in the collective memory the reasons for the loss of Danzig. These reasons are to be sought in history—more specifically, in the Nazi period. In *The Tin Drum*, Grass sets out to elucidate these reasons—albeit from a highly unconventional narrative perspective.

Oskar, the narrator of *The Tin Drum*, is the inmate of an insane asylum in postwar West Germany—a fact that he freely admits in the very first sentence of the novel. Instead of endeavoring to offer his readers an explanation for his confinement—the reason, his implication in a murder, is only gradually revealed in the course of the novel—Oskar reverses the normal order of things by declaring his hospital bed to be his sanctuary and refuge that protects him from the outside world. Oskar's position as an unapologetic outsider tends to disorient the reader and force him to assume a critical attitude.

Oskar's memoirs, written during his confinement, are a record both of his family's history, which began in Danzig around the turn of the century, and of political history. Thus, the three books of the novel depict the prewar period, the war itself, and the postwar period through 1954—the year in which Oskar turns thirty and completes his narration. As aids in his efforts to evoke the past and make history come alive, the narrator uses his tin drum—the instrument that gave the novel its name—and the family photograph album.

Although the novel is realistic in the sense that it provides exact details relating to the topography of Danzig, the speech patterns of various social groups, the milieu of the lower-middle class, the chronology of historical events, and so on, fantastic and supernatural elements are by no means absent. In fact, they are introduced, somewhat in the manner of Franz Kafka's *Die Verwandlung* (1915; *Metamorphosis*, 1936), almost casually. Thus, Oskar's mental faculties are said to be fully developed at birth. Confronted with the unpleasant realization that return to the safety of the womb is impossible, on his third birthday Oskar opts for the second-best solution—that is, to stop growing. He camouflages this willful act by injuring himself in a way that provides a medical explanation for his retarded physical development.

Without a doubt, Oskar's refusal to grow up is a protest against the world of adults in general and the narrow petit bourgeois sphere of his parents in particular. His diminutive size affords Oskar the possibility of observing the adults in their intimate moments—hence the sexually explicit passages that aroused controversy when the novel was published. Oskar, however, is not a mere voyeur. True, he has a keen eye for the triangular relationship that exists between his mother and his two "presumable" fathers, Matzerath, the German, and Bronski, the Pole, but the outsider Oskar also recognizes clearly the drift toward Nazism in Danzig with its attendant evils, such as the beginning persecution of the Jews.

Even though Oskar is an opponent of Nazism, he rarely uses his supernatural faculties—his evocative, spellbinding drumming and his ability to shatter glass with his voice—for acts of outright opposition. Admittedly, he does disrupt a Nazi rally by magically transforming the martial music of the drums and fifes into waltzes and the Charleston; conversely, Oskar employs his artistic abilities to contribute to the war effort by entertaining the German troops in France. Moreover, in some instances, Oskar's shattering of glass seems to be inspired by a desire for wanton destruction rather than by an aroused conscience.

Ultimately, Oskar's role remains somewhat ambivalent. His professed complicity in the deaths of Bronski and Matzerath, for example, appears less serious when these deaths are viewed as an inevitable consequence of his presumable fathers' actions. When the amorous but cowardly Bronski deserts the defenders of the Polish post office in Danzig at the outbreak of World War II, Oskar leads him back to the besieged building; as a consequence, Bronski is executed by the Germans. Amiable Matzerath, who has become a member of the Nazi Party, is killed at the end of World War II by the Soviets, who have invaded Danzig; Oskar contributes to his demise by handing him the Party badge that Matzerath is desperately trying to get rid of.

The fates of Bronski and Matzerath demonstrate that Grass poses the question of the individual's responsibility for his actions, regardless of his station in life. This question also applies to Oskar himself—who, in fact, seriously ponders it at a decisive juncture in his life that coincides with the historical juncture constituted by the end of World War II. At Matzerath's funeral, Oskar, who in 1945 has turned twenty-one and attained majority, decides to grow and to assume his proper place in the adult world. Neither Maria, Matzerath's second wife, nor her son Kurth accept Oskar very enthusiastically as a husband and father substitute, however, and despite his belated growth, Oskar does not develop into a physically normal adult; he never achieves normal height and is disfigured by a hunchback. Thus, he remains a conspicuous outsider in postwar West German society; his attempts to start afresh and to assume responsibility have essentially failed. Oskar's failure is shared by an entire society that is only too eager to forget the past and savor the blessings of the economic miracle. Although Oskar, who has resumed his artistic drumming, keeps the past alive in the face of the general tendency to suppress it, he must acknowledge his complicity in the evil of the times, his standing aside while others acted. Its parodistic, comical, grotesque, picaresque, and mythical dimensions notwithstanding, in the final analysis, the telling of the story, which results in the novel, is the artist Oskar's way of atoning for his failure to conduct himself as a responsible citizen.

The first-person narrator of *Cat and Mouse*, Pilenz, resembles Oskar in that he is compelled by guilt to tell the story of his ambivalent relationship with "the great Mahlke," a youth in wartime Danzig whom he both admires and envies. Mahlke seeks to divert attention from his excessively protuberant Adam's apple by accomplishing uncommon feats—among them an extended masturbation scene—that cannot be matched by his classmates. When Mahlke has become a highly decorated war hero, he gradually begins to realize that his youthful idealism has been misused. As an AWOL, he endeavors to hide on a sunken Polish navy vessel, but he perishes in the attempt as a result of Pilenz's lack of support, amounting to a betrayal. Somewhat in the manner of Oskar, Pilenz survives the war in order to be able to tell of his own failure and the martyrdom of Mahlke.

In the complex novel *Dog Years*, Matern, one of the three narrators, is induced by the chief of the "authors' collective" to revive the Danzig Nazi past in writing—although Matern is endeavoring to suppress it and even engages in acts of revenge against those people who were implicated in unsavory acts that he himself committed. One may note in concluding discussion of *Danziger Trilogie* that Grass uses in these novels a retrospective narrative approach which draws attention to the time of World War II as well as the prewar period in order to trace its remnants in postwar society. Grass's adoption of such a perspective rested on the assumption that history was of vital significance in the consciousness of the reading public of the 1950's and early 1960's. Even if Grass interpreted history in a remarkably idiosyncratic fashion, he did not tamper with historical facts and events. After the transitional novel *From the Diary of a Snail*, however, Grass wrote three narratives—for all practical purposes, a second trilogy—in which history assumes a new dimension.

In *The Flounder*, *The Meeting at Telgte*, and *Headbirths: Or, The Germans Are Dying Out*, there is a closer correspondence between author and narrator than in *Danziger Trilogie*. This close correspondence enables Grass to transcend the chronological and spatial boundaries imposed upon a fictional first-person narrator and to give free rein to his exuberant and whimsical imagination. Here, history becomes raw material to be reshaped and reinvented by the author, who provides alternative versions that challenge presumably established facts. Such imaginative reinterpretation of history is designed to counteract the reader's tendency to regard history as an inevitable and ultimately meaningless process that absolves him from the responsibility of participating in it.

Grass's new approach can be most clearly seen in *The Flounder*, a novel set in Danzig but employing a vastly expanded time frame. Amassing information from the most diverse fields of extant knowledge, Grass uses this encyclopedic material to buttress his plausible account of the antagonistic relationship of the sexes from the Neolithic Age to the 1970's. In particular, Grass follows literary history fairly closely in developing his central conceit— the alleged former existence of a second version of the fairy tale "The Fisherman and His Wife," by the Brothers Grimm. The narrator, who closely resembles the present-day author Grass but has also assumed the identity of male figures in past centuries, avers that in contrast to the version printed by the Brothers Grimm, the lost second version showed an overweening, prideful male instead of a female falling prey to hubris. Because the predominantly male fairy-tale collectors of the Romantic age, foremost among them the Grimms, perceived the second version to be a potential threat to the patriarchal order, they burned it. Although the narrator was not a participant in the burning, his pervasive guilt as a male who has contributed to the exploitation of women throughout the centuries impels him to reconstruct the alternative version, which depicts woman in a favorable light.

While mindful of and sympathetic toward women in general (they are chiefly represented in their vital function as food-providing cooks), the narrator/author warns of the excesses in which the extreme fringe of the women's liberation movement is wont to indulge. On the one hand, the women's tribunal puts the mythical, omniscient Flounder of fairy-tale renown, after whom the novel is named, on trial as the embodiment of the male principle; on the other hand, the radical feminists accept the Flounder's help in their efforts to establish their domination over men. In view of the continuing antagonism of the sexes, the novel suggests a synthesis that does not seek to derive the ideological justification for the male or female cause from one version of the fairy tale only; rather, as an old woman had told one of the fairy-tale collectors, who had inquired about the "correct" version, both versions taken together would yield a viable solution.

The Meeting at Telgte offers annother instance of Grass's imaginative re-creation of history and his exploration of alternative possibilities. In this narrative, a fictitious meeting of famous and lesser-known writers takes place in 1647, at the end of the Thirty Years' War. The writers' conference proceeds according to the rituals of Gruppe 47; like their twentieth century colleagues, the seventeenth century poets try to resurrect literature from the rubble caused by a devastating war—thereby demonstrating that literature will continue to flourish even in perilous times.

In a similar vein, *Headbirths: Or, The Germans Are Dying Out*, Grass's literary contribution to the election campaign of 1980, is concerned with the place of literature in society, the relationship of art and politics, and the function of the writer. Grass addresses a wide variety of topics; as the title suggests, he also playfully speculates on the possibility of the Germans' dying out on account of their low birthrate—thus projecting history into the future. His central theme, however, is of a literary nature—that is, how to ensure the survival of literature and, for that matter, life itself, in a world that is threatened by the nuclear arms race and other undesirable results of rampant technological progress. To characterize the magnitude of the task ahead, Grass discards the metaphor of the snail, symbol of slow progress, that he had used in *From the Diary of a Snail*; instead, he employs the myth of Sisyphus as derived from Albert Camus. Only Sisyphean labors, Grass avers, will be able to prevent the advent of the Orwellian state in the 1980's.

Thus, *Headbirths*—a work whose mood ranges from dire gloom about the future to playful irony—attempts a fusion of two seemingly antithetical themes that have increasingly occupied Grass in recent years. Without a doubt, the author will continue to define, articulate, elucidate, and reshape the function of literature in the modern world as well as the role of the individual, and notably that of the writer, in the political process. It remains to be seen, however, whether the literary transformation of these concerns will eventually result in works that invite comparison with the best of Grass's fiction.

Major publications other than long fiction

PLAYS: *Noch zehn Minuten bis Buffalo*, 1954, 1958 (*Only Ten Minutes to Buffalo*, 1967); *Die bösen Köche*, 1961 (*The Wicked Cooks*); *Hochwasser*, 1963 (*Flood*); *Onkel, Onkel*, 1965 (*Mister, Mister*); *Die Plebejer proben den Aufstand*, 1966 (*The Plebeians Rehearse the Uprising*, 1966); *Four Plays*, 1967 (includes *Only Ten Minutes to Buffalo*; *The Wicked Cooks*; *Flood*; *Mister, Mister*); *Theaterspiele*, 1970 (includes *Noch zehn Minuten bis Buffalo*; *Hochwasser*; *Onkel, Onkel*; *Die bösen Köche*); *Davor*, 1974 (*Max*, 1972).

POETRY: *Die Vorzüge der Windhühner*, 1956; *Gleisdreieck*, 1960; *Selected Poems*, 1966 (includes poems from *Die Vorzüge der Windhühner* and *Gleisdreieck*); *Ausgefragt*, 1967 (*New Poems*, 1968); *Poems of Günter Grass*, 1969; (includes *Selected Poems* and *New Poems*; also in a bilingual edition as *In the Egg and Other Poems*, 1977); *Gesammelte Gedichte*, 1971 (includes *Die Vorzüge der Windhühner*; *Gleisdreieck*); *Mariazuehren, Hommageàmarie, Inmarypraise*, 1973 (trilingual edition); *Liebe geprüft*, 1974.

NONFICTION: *Über das Selbstverständliche*, 1968 (*Speak Out!*, 1969, partial translation); *Über meinen Lehrer Döblin und andere Vorträge*, 1968; *Der Bürger und seine Stimme*, 1974; *Denkzettel*, 1978; *Aufsätze zur Literatur*, 1980; *Widerstand lernen: Politische Gegenreden 1980-1983*, 1984.

Bibliography

Cunliffe, W. Gordon. *Günter Grass*, 1969.

Diller, Edward. *A Mythic Journey: Günter Grass's "Tin Drum,"* 1974.

Hollington, Michael. *Günter Grass: The Writer in a Pluralistic Society*, 1980.

Irving, John. "Günter Grass: King of the Toy Merchants," in *Saturday Review*. IX, no.3 (March, 1982), pp. 57-60.

Leonard, Irène. *Günter Grass*, 1974.

Mews, Siegfried, ed. *"The Fisherman and His Wife": Günter Grass's "The Flounder" in Critical Perspective*, 1983.

Miles, Keith. *Günter Grass*, 1975.

Neuhaus, Volker. *Günter Grass*, 1979.

Reddick, John. *The "Danzig Trilogy" of Günter Grass*, 1975.

Siegfried Mews

JULIEN GREEN

Born: Paris, France; September 6, 1900

Principal long fiction

Mont-Cinère, 1926 (*Avarice House*, 1927); *Adrienne Mesurat*, 1927 (*The Closed Garden*, 1928); *Léviathan*, 1929 (*The Dark Journey*, 1929); *L'Autre Sommeil*, 1931; *Épaves*, 1932 (*The Strange River*, 1932); *Le Visionnaire*, 1934 (*The Dreamer*, 1934); *Minuit*, 1936 (*Midnight*, 1936); *Varouna*, 1940 (*Then Shall the Dust Return*, 1941); *Si j'étais vous*, 1947 (*If I Were You*, 1949); *Moïra*, 1950 (*Moira*, 1951); *Le Malfaiteur*, 1955 (*The Transgressor*, 1957); *Chaque Homme dans sa nuit*, 1960 (*Each in His Darkness*, 1961); *L'Autre*, 1971 (*The Other One*, 1973); *Le Mauvais Lieu*, 1977.

Other literary forms

Julien Green first drew critical attention in the late 1920's as a writer of short fiction ("Le Voyageur sur la terre," "Les Clefs de la mort") before attempting the longer narratives that have since become his forte. Today, Green is almost as well-known for his autobiographical works as for his novels. His *Journal*, begun in 1928, has thus far appeared in nine volumes published between 1938 and 1972; a second series, begun in 1963 and collectively entitled *Autobiographie*, is more personal and frankly confessional in tone: *Partir avant le jour* (1963; *To Leave Before Dawn*, 1967), *Mille Chemins ouverts* (1964), *Terre lointaine* (1966), and *Jeunesse* (1974). An additional volume, *Memories of Happy Days* (1942), was written and published in English during Green's self-imposed wartime exile in the United States.

Encouraged by Louis Jouvet to try his hand at writing plays, Green achieved moderate success as a playwright with *Sud* (1953; *South*, 1955), *L'Ennemi* (1954), and *L'Ombre* (1956), but he soon concluded that his true skills were those of a novelist. In any case, Green's plays are seldom performed and are of interest mainly to readers already familiar with his novels.

Achievements

In 1971, shortly after publication of his novel *The Other One*, Julien Green became, at the age of seventy, the first foreigner ever elected to membership in the Académie Française; his election brought sudden and considerable attention to a long, distinguished, but insufficiently appreciated literary career. Green, born in France to American parents, had been writing and publishing novels in French since the age of twenty-five, attracting rather more critical attention in France than in the United States, despite the availability of his work in English translation. Even in France, however, his novels have not received extensive critical notice, owing in part to the fact that his work tends to resist classification.

Encouraged by the success of his earliest writings, Green lost little time in developing a characteristic mode of expression, alternately mystical and sensual, often both at once. Many critics, as if willfully blind to the erotic dimension of Green's work, sought to classify him as a "Catholic" writer in the tradition of Georges Bernanos and François Mauriac; others, focusing on the oppressive atmosphere pervading many of his novels, sought to place Green closer to the Gothic tradition. Neither classification is quite accurate, yet it was not until after Green's autobiography began to appear in 1963 that reassessment of his novels began in earnest.

Using a clear, ornament-free style that has been described as classical, Green quickly involves his readers in the solitary lives of tortured characters obsessed with the need to escape. Often, the compulsion toward escape leads to violence, madness, or death; when it does not, it produces an implied "leap of faith" which is not, however, totally satisfying to those who would see Green as a religious writer in the Catholic tradition. Even in those rare cases in which solutions are offered, it is still the problems that dominate the consciousness of author and reader alike. Endowed with keen powers of observation, Green excels in the portrayal of psychological anguish that any thoughtful reader can understand, even if he or she does not share it.

The publication of Green's autobiography beginning in the 1960's permitted at last a "demystification" of the novels—in Green's case, more help than hindrance. In the light of Green's frankness, many of the tortures undergone by his characters stood revealed as artistic transpositions of the author's own private anguish as he sought to reconcile his spiritual aspirations with a growing awareness of his homosexual tendencies. Far from detracting from the power of Green's novels, such disclosures shed valuable light upon his life in art, allowing critics and casual readers alike to appreciate the true nature of Green's novelistic achievement. Whatever their source, Green's novels remain powerful portraits of alienation and estrangement unmatched in contemporary French or American literature.

Biography

Julien Hartridge Green was born in Paris on September 6, 1900, the youngest of eight children. His father, Edward Moon Green of Virginia, had since 1895 served as European agent of the Southern Cotton Seed Oil Company. Green's mother, the former Mary Hartridge of Savannah, Georgia, dominated her son's early life with a curious blend of love and Puritan guilt; her death in 1914, instead of liberating the young Green from the tyranny of her moods and ideas, seems rather to have increased her hold upon his developing conscience. Green grew to manhood torn between a strong, if repressed, sensuality and a mystical desire for sainthood, often equally strong. Converted to Catholicism within a year after his mother's death, he seriously considered

Critical Survey of Long Fiction

entering a monastic order but deferred his plans for the duration of World War I. In 1917, he served as an ambulance driver, first for the American Field Service and later for the Red Cross; the following year, still (as he remained) an American citizen, he obtained a commission in the French army by first enlisting in the Foreign Legion. Demobilized in 1919, he returned to Paris and soon renounced his monastic vocation, a loss that caused him considerable anguish.

Unable to decide on a career, he accepted with some reluctance the offer of a Hartridge uncle to finance his education at the University of Virginia. Enrolled as a "special student," Green read widely in literature, religion, and sociology; in 1921, after two years in residence, he was appointed an assistant professor of French. Still homesick for his native France, more at ease in French than in English, Green returned to Paris in 1922 to study art, gradually discovering instead his vocation as a writer and attracting the attention of such influential literary figures as Jacques de Lacretelle and Gaston Gallimard. By the age of twenty-five, already an established author with a growing reputation, Green had found his lifework.

During his thirties, Green read widely in mysticism and Oriental religions. Returning to the Catholic Church as early as 1939, Green was soon thereafter obliged to leave Paris by the onset of another world war. After the fall of France in 1940, he moved to the United States for the duration, teaching at various colleges and universities before and after brief service as a language instructor in the United States Army. Returning to Paris in September, 1945, he remained there, pursuing the life and career of a French man of letters.

Analysis

Educated primarily in the French tradition, Julien Green brings to his novels a distinctly French concern for the presentation and development of character. Whether his novels are set in France, the United States, or elsewhere, his characters are observed and portrayed with the psychological precision that has characterized French fiction from Madame de La Fayette down through Honoré de Balzac and Gustave Flaubert to Marcel Proust. With critical and seemingly pitiless exactitude, Green takes the reader inside his characters to show their thought and motivations, achieving considerable identification even when the characters tend toward violence or madness. On the surface, few of Green's characters would appear to invite identification on the part of the reader; they tend to be misfits of one sort or another, haunted by strange fears and insecurities. It is Green's singular talent, however, to present them and their thoughts in such a way that they seem almost instantly plausible and authentic, and to hold the reader's interest in what will happen to them. Life, as particularized in Green's characters, emerges as both threat and promise, most often as a trap set for the unwary.

Typically, Green's protagonists, often female with one surviving and insensitive parent, find themselves trapped in an existence that they can neither tolerate nor understand; not infrequently, they contribute to their own misfortune through a stubborn refusal to express themselves. Even so, the reader senses that to speak their minds would render them vulnerable to even greater assaults from a hostile environment. Locked within themselves, they suffer all the tortures of an earthly hell from which they yearn to escape. In his autobiography, Green observes that a feeling of imprisonment was a recurring childhood nightmare; in his novels, the theme is enlarged to archetypal proportions, assuming the authority of fable. Green's characters, for all their particularities, emerge as highly convincing exemplars of the human condition.

Escape, for all of its apparent promise, offers no relief to the suffering of Green's characters. Adrienne Mesurat, among the most convincing of Green's early heroines, gradually retreats into madness once she has achieved through an act of violence the freedom for which she has longed; Paul Guéret, the ill-favored viewpoint character of *The Dark Journey*, strikes and disfigures the young woman whose attentions he has sought, thereafter becoming a fugitive. Manuel, the title character of *The Dreamer*, retreats from the undesirable world into a fictional universe of his own making, only to die soon thereafter. Elisabeth, the protagonist of *Midnight*, seeks to escape with her lover, only to be killed with him in a fall. Clearly, the oppressive atmosphere that stifles Green's characters is internal as well as external; like Adrienne Mesurat, they remain imprisoned even when they are free to come and go as they please. Even in the later novels, such as *The Other One*, death is frequently the only means of escape available.

The power of Green's novels derives in no small measure from the author's skill in providing motivation for the behavior of his characters. In the case of Adrienne Mesurat, for example, Green quickly and convincingly shows normal desire stifled by silence until it becomes first an obsession, then true madness. Philippe Cléry, the main viewpoint character of *The Strange River*, passes the age of thirty before being obliged to examine his life; thereafter, he becomes most convincingly self-conscious, questioning his every move in an authentically ineffectual way. Sympathetic or not (and most are not), Green's characters are inescapably human and believable, commanding the reader's identification; although they seem to exist in a world of their own, they are unmistakably drawn from life, the products of Green's keen powers of observation.

It is possible, that, had Green not been reared in a time less tolerant than the twentieth century, his novels might never have come into being. Arguably, Green's expression has responded somewhat to the temper of the times, dealing more and more openly with homosexual attraction in such novels as *The Transgressor*; indeed, by the time Green wrote and published his autobiography in the 1960's, his revelations seemed less scandalous than timely and enlightening. The restraint that helped to shape his earlier works was in a sense no longer necessary. It seems likely, moreover, that the writing of the autobiographical volumes lessened the sense of creative urgency that marks the best of Green's earlier writing. In fact, Green's later novels (*Le Mauvais Lieu* in particular), while still holding the reader's attention, cover little new ground and move perilously close to self-parody.

Green's second novel, *The Closed Garden*, written and published within a year after the success of *Avarice House*, ranks among his best and is perhaps the most memorable. Refreshingly normal at the start of the novel, eighteen-year-old Adrienne quickly erodes into madness and amnesia as a result of the stifling circumstances of her life. Recently out of school (the time is 1908), she lives in a provincial French town with her retired father and her thirty-five-year-old spinster sister, Germaine. A chronic invalid whose illness their autocratic father refuses even to recognize, Germaine rules over Adrienne with the authority of a mother but with none of the attendant love. As in Green's *Avarice House*, kinship is no guarantee of understanding or even friendship; indeed, the family emerges as perhaps the most inimical and threatening of human institutions. Using heavy irony, Green shows Adrienne's daily interaction with her hostile relatives; the reader, privy to Adrienne's innermost thoughts, looks on with horror as she is repeatedly unable to express them.

At the start of the novel, Adrienne is looking with healthy scorn at a group of family portraits to which she inwardly refers as "the cemetery," concluding with some satisfaction that her own features place her on the "strong" side of the family. Dressed as a servant, she is doing the family housework, exhibiting physical strength by moving heavy furniture with ease. It is precisely such apparent strength that will soon prove to be her undoing, as it turns inward upon herself, accomplishing in several weeks a deterioration that otherwise might take years. Deprived of normal human companionship, Adrienne becomes infatuated with a neighboring physician, Dr. Maurecourt, whom she has seen but once; such adolescent passion, harmless enough at face value, functions rather in Green's universe as an instrument of destruction. Adrienne, unable to confide to her father or sister the relatively innocent causes of her slightly irregular behavior, retreats further and further into her fantasy with each new demand for an explanation.

Steadfastly refusing to name the object of her secret passion, she soon finds herself literally locked up in the house, forbidden to leave but still dreaming of escape. Ironically, it is the nearly bedridden Germaine, rather than the healthy Adrienne, who in fact does manage to escape the father's tyranny, sneaking out of the house with Adrienne's help in order to seek refuge in a convent near Paris. Germaine's departure triggers a rare and violent dispute between Adrienne and her father, who reveals that he, like Germaine, has guessed the identity of Adrienne's lover. Overcome with shame and grief, Adrienne runs toward her father and pushes him downstairs; she is never quite sure whether she intended to kill him. In any case, he dies, and although Adrienne is never formally charged with his murder, she is eventually convicted of the crime by the tribunal of malicious gossip. Indeed, the entire village soon takes on the sinister aspect of Adrienne's now-absent family, hemming her within a circle of watchful and accusing eyes.

A brief attempt at leaving the village finds Adrienne drifting aimlessly from one provincial town to another, beset by nightmares as she sleeps fitfully in seedy hotels, imagining that she is being watched. Returning home to live among her tormentors, she falls physically ill; Dr. Maurecourt is summoned, and at the end of a lengthy and difficult conversation, she blurts out her unrequited love for him. Maurecourt, a frail widower of forty-five, is understandably nonplussed; with genuine compassion, he explains to Adrienne that he is mortally ill, having hardly more than a year left to live, while she, Adrienne, has her whole life ahead of her. For all practical purposes, though, Adrienne's life is as good as over; she again leaves the house, intending to escape but succeeding only in wandering aimlessly about the town until she is found suffering from amnesia.

Like other novels and plays of the period—John O'Hara's *Appointment in Samarra* (1934) and Jean Cocteau's *La Machine infernale* (1934; *The Infernal Machine*, 1936) come readily to mind—*The Closed Garden* is the carefully recorded history of what can happen to a human life and mind when everything possible goes wrong. Subjected to torture such as might be inflicted upon a steel rod in laboratory tests, Adrienne's mind eventually snaps. Until very near the end, however, Adrienne remains painfully lucid, aware of all that is happening to her yet powerless to stop it. Unlike such characters as O'Hara's Julian English and Cocteau's Oedipus, Adrienne seems singularly undeserving of her cruel fate; neither arrogant nor thoughtless, she seems to have been chosen almost at random by unseen forces bent upon destroying her for no good reason.

The Dark Journey, Green's third novel, breaks new ground in presenting several viewpoint characters and a number of interlocking subplots. Each of the main characters, reminiscent of Balzac's provincial "monomaniacs," is governed and identified by a ruling passion, much as Adrienne Mesurat is governed by her passion for the helpless Dr. Maurecourt. The main viewpoint character, whose life provides a link among the others, is one Paul Guéret, an ill-favored and unhappily married man in his thirties who is obsessed by his passion for the young and attractive Angèle. A rather typical Green heroine, Angèle has been thrust by circumstances into a thankless and sordid existence from which she longs to escape, presumably in the loving company of a young man her own age. A laundress by day, she moonlights by sleeping with various gentlemen who frequent the restaurant owned and operated by the insatiably curious Madame Londe. In a sense, Angèle is less prostitute than spy, engaged by Madame Londe to supply her with useful information concerning the gentlemen's private lives. Guéret, to his consternation, is excluded from Angèle's regular clientele because he is simply not interesting enough, either as a person or because of his station in life, to warrant Madame Londe's interest. Angèle, meanwhile, is flattered and at least amused by Guéret's awkward attentions, even if she cannot bring herself to return his love in kind.

Guéret, driven nearly to distraction by Angèle's flirtatiousness and inaccessibility, becomes increasingly obsessed with his need to possess the girl, and before long his obsession leads to violence. First, after a long and painful struggle to scale the wall of Angéle's building, he breaks into her room, only to find that she is not there. The next day, unable to tolerate her taunting behavior, he beats her up and goes into hiding, leaving her for dead on a riverbank. Angèle survives, although disfigured for life. Guéret, meanwhile, is in fact guilty of murder, having bludgeoned to death an old man who stumbled upon his hiding place. After several months as a fugitive, he is given asylum by the bored and sadistic Eva Grosgeorge, mother of a boy he once tutored. Eventually, Madame Grosgeorge tires of Guéret and denounces him to the police against the protestations of Angèle, still convalescent, who does her best to rescue him. Unsuccessful, Angèle lapses into a dreamlike state and, like Adrienne Mesurat before her, wanders about town in what she thinks is an attempt to escape; delirious, she dies of exposure soon after being brought back to her room. Madame Grosgeorge, meanwhile, having shot herself melodramatically at the moment of Guéret's arrest, is expected to survive.

The Dark Journey differs from Green's earlier novels in both the depth and the scope of its character development. Although both Guéret and Angèle show clear lines of descent from Green's earlier protagonists, such characters as Madame Londe and the Grosgeorge couple bear witness to a broadening of Green's psychological and social observation; Eva Grosgeorge, in particular, is a most convincing grotesque, the bored and self-indulgent younger wife of a rather bovine industrialist. Guéret, the misfit, serves unwittingly as the link between these various social types, whose paths would otherwise be unlikely to cross. As elsewhere in Green's work, interpersonal love is shown to be an unattainable illusion. Guéret's passion for Angèle, among the more normal obsessions portrayed in the book, is doomed by its own intensity. Angèle, meanwhile, is too lost in her own romantic fantasies to see beyond Guéret's ugliness to her own genuine feelings toward him until it is too late for them both.

Less sensational in subject matter and in treatment than *The Closed Garden* or *The Dark Journey*, Green's fifth novel, *The Strange River*, remains one of his least known; nevertheless, it ranks among his best. Nearly devoid of external action or incident, *The Strange River* presents social and psychological analysis of rare accuracy and power, approaching Flaubert's ambition to write a book about "nothing." To a far greater degree than in *The Dark Journey*, Green reveals his seldom-used gifts as a social satirist, here portraying in painful detail the empty existence of the idle rich. *The Strange River* is, moreover, the only one of Green's fifteen novels to be set in Paris, where he himself resides.

As in *The Dark Journey*, Green derives considerable effect in *The Strange River* from the presentation of multiple viewpoints, primarily those of Philippe Cléry and his sister-in-law, Eliane, but not excluding that of Philippe's wife, Henriette. Philippe, rich through inheritance, suffers in his own ineffectual way the double torture of being superfluous and knowing it. As titular head of a mining company about which he knows nothing and cares even less, he need only appear (and remain silent) at monthly meetings in order to do all that society expects of him. The rest of the time, he is free to remain in his elegant apartment (he owns the building) or go for long walks dressed as the gentleman he is. At thirty-one, he is aware that his marriage has long since become as meaningless and hollow as his professional title; Henriette goes out on the town without him nearly every evening and has taken a lower-class lover to occupy the rest of her time. Their only child, ten-year-old Robert, spends most of the year out of sight and mind in boarding school; his rare presence during school vacations, when he has nowhere else to go, proves irritating to his parents and aunt, as they have no idea what to say to him. Philippe, meanwhile, unless he is out walking, usually finds himself in the company of Henriette's elder sister, Eliane, who secretly loves Philippe even as she comes to despise him for what he is.

Against such a background of silence and mistrust, Green sketches in the private thoughts and feelings of his characters, expressing the pain of existence in all of its contingency. The plot of *The Strange River*, such as it is, turns upon an incident that Philippe thinks he may have witnessed in the course of one of his long walks: A middle-aged, shabbily dressed couple appeared to be struggling on the banks of the Seine, and the woman may or may not have called out to Philippe for help. In any case, Philippe went on his way, not consulting the police until hours later. As the novel proceeds, the incident often returns to haunt Philippe with its implications.

Anticipating by some twenty-five years the central incident of Albert Camus' *La Chute* (1956; *The Fall*, 1957), Philippe's experience disrupts the balance of a previously unexamined life; Philippe, however, is already too weak to do much of anything with what he has learned about himself. For months after the incident, he scans the papers for reports of bodies fished from the Seine; at length he finds one, and it is quite likely that he was in fact witness to a murder. In the meantime, another of his nocturnal walks has provided him with further evidence of his own cowardice; accosted by a stranger, he hands over his billfold at the merest threat of violence. Attending a monthly board meeting, he impulsively takes the floor and resigns his post, to the astonishment of his sister-in-law and wife, who fear that he has lost his mind; his life, however, goes on pretty much as before, closely observed by the lovesick spinster Eliane. Like Adrienne Mesurat, Eliane is both powerless and lucid in her unrequited love, increasingly attached to Philippe even as she begins to deduce his guilty secret concerning the couple on the riverbank.

Unlike all but one of Green's other novels (*L'Autre Sommeil*), *The Strange River* is open-ended, leaving the main characters with much of their lives yet before them. The action is not resolved in violence, as in *The Dark Journey*, or in madness, as in the case of Adrienne Mesurat. Philippe, of course, is too weak to do much of anything except worry about himself.

Not until *The Transgressor*, written a quarter of a century later, did Green again try his hand at the sort of social satire so successfully managed in *The Strange River*; despite his skill in such portrayal, it is clear that Greene's true interest lies elsewhere, deep within the conscience of the individual. *The Strange River* is thus in a sense a happy accident; Green, in order to probe the inmost thoughts of a Philippe Cléry, had first to invent Philippe and place him against a social backround. The result is a most satisfying work, rather different from Green's other novels but thoroughly successful in accomplishing what it sets out to do.

For a period after *The Strange River*, Green's novels tended increasingly toward fantasy, taking place in a real or fancied dreamworld fashioned by individual characters. It is perhaps no accident that these novels, atypical of Green's work taken as a whole, were written during the time of Green's estrangement from Catholicism, when he was reading extensively in mysticism and Oriental religions. Reconciled with the Church in 1939, Green was soon thereafter to leave France and his career as a novelist for the duration of World War II. *Moira*, the first of Green's true postwar novels, returns to the familiar psychological ground of his earliest work, going even further in its portrayal of the conflict between the mystical and the sensual.

Returning to the time and setting of his American university experience, Green presents in *Moira* the thoughts and behavior of one Joseph Day, a Fundamentalist rustic who is even more of an outsider to the university life than Green himself must have been. Joseph is at odds with the school from the first day of his enrollment, horrified by the license and corruption that he sees all around him. His landlady, Mrs. Dare, smokes cigarettes and wears makeup, and his classmates discuss freely their relations with the opposite sex. His missionary zeal fueled by a truly violent temperament to match his red hair, Joseph seeks to save the souls of those around him; thus inclined, he is quite unable to see either himself or his fellows as human beings. Derisively nicknamed "the avenging angel," he burns with a white heat, quite unaware of the eroticism at its source. Early on, he unwittingly rebuffs the homosexual advances of a young art student, who later commits suicide as a result; meanwhile, Joseph feels mysteriously drawn to the elegant, aristocratic

Praileau, who has made fun of Joseph's red hair. Challenging Praileau to a fight, Joseph is so overcome by an excess of clearly sexual frenzy that he nearly kills the young man, who tells him that he is a potential murderer.

Unable to reconcile his Protestant faith with his increasingly violent feelings and behavior, Joseph confides in a fellow ministerial candidate, David Laird, whose vocation is both stronger and less temperamental than Joseph's own. David, however sympathetic, is quite unprepared to deal with the problems of his tortured friend, who proceeds toward the date with destiny suggested in the book's title. Moira, it seems, is also the name of Mrs. Dare's adopted daughter, a licentious young woman who emerges as almost a caricature of the flapper. Even before he meets the girl, Joseph is scandalized by all that he has heard about her; even so, he is quite unprepared for her taunting, loose-mouthed treatment of him. Another apparent homosexual, Killigrew, tries and fails to get close to Joseph. Joseph does, however, vividly recall Killigrew's description of Moira as a she-monster whenever thoughts of the girl invade his daydreams. At length, Joseph, having changed lodgings, returns to his room to find Moira planted there as part of a prank perpetrated upon the "avenging angel" by his classmates. Moira, of course, is a most willing accessory, her vanity piqued by the one man, Joseph, who has proved resistant to her rather blatant charms. By the time the planned seduction occurs, it is Moira, not Joseph, who believes herself to have fallen in love. In the morning, however, Joseph strangles Moira in a fit of remorse over what they have done. After burying the girl's body without incident, he twice considers the possibility of escape but finally turns himself in to the police, who have sought him for questioning.

Despite a plot almost too tightly rigged to seem quite plausible, *Moira* ranks with the best of Green's earlier novels, showing considerable development in the depth and scope of his literary art. As in *The Dark Journey* and *The Strange River*, Green shows himself to be a shrewd and discerning observer of society and its distinctions. Characteristically, however, he remains concerned primarily with the inner workings of the human mind and emotions, and the variety of characters portrayed in *Moira* affords him ample opportunity to display his talents. Freed from taboos (both internal and external) against the depiction of homosexuality in literature, Green in *Moira* seemed to be moving toward a new, mature frankness of expression. Unfortunately, the novels that he has written since, however explicit, fail to match *Moira* either in suggestive power or in tightness of construction. The first novel of Green's "mature" period thus remains quite probably its best.

Major publications other than long fiction
SHORT FICTION: *Le Voyageur sur la terre*, 1930 (*Christine, and Other Stories*, 1930).
PLAYS: *Sud*, 1953 (*South*, 1955); *L'Ennemi*, 1954; *L'Ombre*, 1956.

NONFICTION: *Journal*, 1938-1972 (9 volumes); *Memories of Happy Days*, 1942; *Partir avant le jour*, 1963 (*To Leave Before Dawn*, 1967); *Mille Chemins ouverts*, 1964; *Terre lointaine*, 1966; *Jeunesse*, 1974.

Bibliography
Brodin, Pierre. *Julien Green*, 1957.
Burne, Glenn S. *Julien Green*, 1972.
Dunaway, John M. *The Metamorphoses of the Self: The Mystic, the Sensualist and the Artist in the Works of Julien Green*, 1978.
Kostis, Nicholas. *The Exorcism of Sex and Death in Julien Green's Novels*, 1973.
Rose, Marilyn Gaddis. *Julien Green: Gallic-American Novelist*, 1971.

David B. Parsell

HANS JAKOB CHRISTOFFEL VON GRIMMELSHAUSEN

Born: Gelnhausen, Germany; March 17, 1621(?)
Died: Renchen, Germany; August 17, 1676

Principal long fiction

Der keusche Joseph, 1666; *Der abenteuerliche Simplicissimus*, 1669 (*The Adventurous Simplicissimus*, 1912); *Die Continuatio*, 1669 (*The Continuation*, 1965; selections); *Dietwald und Amelinde*, 1670; *Lebensbeschreibung der Ertzbetrügerin und Landstörtzerin Courasche*, 1670 (*Courage: The Adventuress*, 1964); *Der seltsame Springinsfeld*, 1670; *Proximus und Lympida*, 1672; *Das wunderbarliche Vogelsnest I*, 1672; *Das wunderbarliche Vogelsnest II*, 1675 (*The False Messiah*, 1964).

Other literary forms

Almost everything that Hans Jakob Christoffel von Grimmelshausen wrote falls into the category of narrative fiction. One exception is a series of annual almanacs published between 1671 and 1675. In addition to this series, Grimmelshausen produced a special type of almanac entitled *Des Abenteuerlichen Simplicissimi Ewig-währender Calender* (1671; the adventurous Simplicissimus' perpetual calendar). None of the almanacs constitutes a work of major importance, but they remain of interest to literary scholars because they contain a vast amount of information pertaining to the popular culture of the Baroque era. In *Der Abenteuerlichen Simplicissimi Ewig-währender Calender*, moreover, there is an extensive dialogue between an astrologer and the protagonist of *The Adventurous Simplicissimus* that sheds light on certain aspects of the novel's structure. One may also find Grimmelshausen's views on a variety of mundane and spiritual matters in the twenty discussions in the two volumes of *Der satyrische Pilgram* (1666, 1667; the satiric pilgrim). Although Grimmelshausen wrote but few poems, most of which appear within the context of his novels, his poetry is of a high order, and selections from it are frequently included in anthologies of German verse.

Achievements

Grimmelshausen's *The Adventurous Simplicissimus* is undoubtedly the greatest German novel of the seventeenth century. The work proved to be an immediate popular success, albeit not a critical one, when it was published in 1669, and Grimmelshausen extended the story by issuing a separately bound continuation in the same year. *The Continuation* was eventually incorporated into later printings of *The Adventurous Simplicissimus*, where it now supplements the five books into which the original novel was divided. Public demand, moreover, led Grimmelshausen to write a number of other sequels over the next few years. Of these continuations, *Courage: The Adventuress*, *Der selt-*

same Springinsfeld (the rare Springinsfeld), and the two sections of *Das wunderbarliche Vogelsnest* are particularly important. *The Adventurous Simplicissimus* and its sequels are today referred to collectively as the "Simplician cycle." What distinguishes these writings from the standard German fiction of that era is the fact that they give the reader a vivid and realistic picture of the devastation caused by the Thirty Years' War and the demoralization of the country in its aftermath. The only other novelist to write anything in a similar vein was Johann Michael Moscherosch, whose *Wunderliche und warhafftige Gesichte Philanders von Sittewald* (1643; the strange and true visions of Philander von Sittewald) contains, as one of its four parts, a section entitled "Soldaten Leben" (soldier's life) that foreshadows *The Adventurous Simplicissimus* in presenting a graphic account of the disasters of war.

The literary Establishment in Germany during the Baroque period favored the more aristocratic genres, such as the heroic-gallant and historical-political novels, and condemned *The Adventurous Simplicissimus* for its crudity. Eager for critical acclaim, Grimmelshausen attempted to write in the style of courtly literature and produced a pair of tedious novels, *Dietwald und Amelinde* and *Proximus und Lympida*, that embodied this alien aesthetic. These works are, however, of little interest to the modern reader; only the Simplician cycle has survived the test of time. Much of the literary distinction of *The Adventurous Simplicissimus* stems from the ingenious way that Grimmelshausen adapted the form of the picaresque novel to make it serve as a vehicle for religious content. Some critics even go as far as to refer to the novel as antipicaresque. Unlike the usual picaresque novel, there is genuine character development in *The Adventurous Simplicissimus*. Many literary historians, for this reason, regard Grimmelshausen's masterwork as a forerunner of both the *Bildungsroman* (the novel of education) and the *Entwicklungsroman* (the novel of development).

Biography

The author of *The Adventurous Simplicissimus* could trace his descent back to a line of landed nobility that had established itself in Thuringia during the Middle Ages. In the course of the sixteenth century, however, the family gradually became impoverished, to the point that the author's paternal grandfather, Melchior Christoffel, was forced to take up the occupation of baker and innkeeper in Gelnhausen, a predominately Lutheran town located in Hesse not far from Hanau, and even stopped using his noble surname. It was in Gelnhausen that Hans Jakob Christoffel von Grimmelshausen was born. On the basis of autobiographical remarks to be found in one of his almanacs, the year of his birth appears to be either 1621 or 1622, although subsequent scholarship places the date at or near March 17, 1621. His father, Johannes Christoffel, died a few years later, and his mother, Gertraud, soon moved from Gelnhausen to nearby Frankfurt in order to remarry, leaving her six-year-old son in the care of her father-in-law. The relationship between Melchior and his grandson was full of affection, and the character of the kindly grandfather was later depicted in fictional form in the person of the elderly hermit who plays a key role in the early part of *The Adventurous Simplicissimus*.

For six or seven years, young Grimmelshausen attended the only school in Gelnhausen, receiving, in addition to a thorough indoctrination into the Lutheran faith, extensive instruction in both music and Latin. In 1634, when he was about thirteen years of age, Gelnhausen was sacked by Croatian soldiers serving in the Imperial army. Many of the town's inhabitants, including Grimmelshausen himself, sought refuge in the city of Hanau in order to enjoy the protection of the Swedish garrison stationed there. A month or so later, Grimmelshausen was captured by Croatian soldiers as he was playing outside the walls of Hanau. His period of captivity under the Croatians was relatively brief; he soon fell into the hands of Protestant units composed of Hessians and was pressed into their service. What happened to Grimmelshausen while he was with the Hessians is uncertain, but in 1636, at age fifteen, he found himself part of a cavalry unit in the Imperial army that was besieging the Protestant fortress of Magdeburg. He continued to serve as both a light cavalryman and a musketeer in various Catholic armies for the next few years, eventually receiving an appointment as Regimental Secretary to Count Hans Reinhard von Schauenburg, the commander of the Imperial stronghold of Offenburg (a city near the Rhine River to the east of Strasbourg). In 1648, the year in which the Peace of Westphalia was signed, Grimmelshausen left his post with Schauenburg and served with the Bavarian army in some of the final campaigns of the war. He was discharged from military service the following year at about the age of twenty-eight, after having spent some fifteen years in the company of men at war.

On August 30, 1649, Grimmelshausen married Katharina Henninger, the daughter of an officer who had served in Schauenburg's regiment. That the wedding ceremony was performed by a priest is proof of the bridegroom's formal membership in the Roman Catholic Church at the time of his marriage. Precisely when his conversion to Catholicism occurred, however, remains an unresolved issue. The marital union turned out to be a happy one, and Katharina was to bear him ten children over the next two decades. A week after the wedding ceremony, Grimmelshausen assumed the duties of a steward on the estate of Count Schauenburg outside the village of Gaisbach near Oberkirch. He left the employ of Schauenburg in 1660 and from 1662 to 1665 worked in a similar position at the summer residence of a Strasbourg physician. After a brief period as the proprietor of an inn in Gelnhausen called The Silver Star, Grimmelshausen accepted an appointment from the Bishop of Strasbourg to serve as *Schultheiss* (mayor) in the Black Forest village of Renchen. He continued to occupy that office for the remaining nine years of his life. His last three years proved to be quite trying for him, owing to the warfare between French and Imperial forces that had engulfed the area. At one point in this conflict, he was obliged to resume military service for a time. Grimmelshausen died in Renchen on August 17, 1676, survived by his wife and six of their children.

Grimmelshausen's literary career did not begin until he was nearly forty. In 1659, he published a German-language version of a French translation of Francis Godwin's *The Man in the Moon: Or, A Discourse of a Voyage Thither by Domingo Gonsales, the Speedy Messenger* (1638). The next year, Grimmelshausen published two satiric dream-visions of his own, but his first significant works—*Der satyrische Pilgram I* and *Der keusche Joseph* (the chaste Joseph)—appeared later. It was, however, only after he became Mayor of Renchen that Grimmelshausen became truly productive. In addition to publishing *The Adventurous Simplicissimus* and its sequels while at Renchen, he tried his hand at writing aristocratic fiction such as *Dietwald und Amelinde* and *Proximus und Lympida*. Except for these two heroic-gallant novels, which were published under his own name, Grimmelshausen made it a practice to conceal his authorship of fictional works by using pseudonyms that were anagrams of his full name. *The Adventurous Simplicissimus*, for example, was published under the pseudonym "Samuel Greifnson von Hirschfeld." He also used eight other pseudonyms. It was not, in fact, until the middle of the nineteenth century, when interest in Baroque literature revived, that German literary scholars were able to establish the identity of the author of *The Adventurous Simplicissimus*.

Analysis

In keeping with the traditional form of the picaresque novel, Hans Jakob Christoffel von Grimmelshausen's *The Adventurous Simplicissimus* is written from the first-person point of view, and the events it relates are presented as autobiography. The protagonist narrates his life history from boyhood to early manhood against the background of the Thirty Years' War and its aftermath. The contents of the novel are highly episodic and often anecdotal in character. Even though supernatural incidents occur with some frequency, most of the narrative is realistic in tone. There is, in fact, much gross physical detail depicting the sexual escapades of the hero as well as the acts of brutality committed by combatants serving on both sides of this savage conflict. Like many other creative spirits of the Baroque era, the author of the Simplician cycle was preoccupied with opposition and contradiction. *The Adventurous Simplicissimus* is frequently described as contrapuntal in its contrast of dualities such as innocence and experience, civilian and military, Catholic and Protestant, and spiritual and mundane. Another prominent feature of the novel is its allegorical character. Although far less didactic than John Bunyan's *The Pilgrim's Progress* (1678, 1684), *The Adventurous Simplicissimus* is likewise an account of the journey of a human soul through the perils of a sinful world in a quest for salvation.

Of the various autobiographical parallels in *The Adventurous Simplicissimus*, the protagonist's conversion to Roman Catholicism is certainly the most controversial. Many scholars suspect that Grimmelshausen's own adherence to this creed was purely a matter of expediency. There is clearly much evidence in the novel to corroborate this opinion. At one point midway through the third book, Simplicius Simplicissimus informs a Protestant clergyman with whom he is debating the merits of competing Christian denominations that the doctrinal differences which separate these sects have nothing to do with the essence of Christianity. When Simplicius does finally convert to Catholicism, moreover, it is out of fear of the Devil rather than from any conviction in the absolute truth of Catholic theology.

In all likelihood, however, Grimmelshausen's impatience with doctrinal disputes manifests itself most emphatically in the visionary exhortations of the madman who believed himself to be the great god Jupiter. In one of the opening chapters of the third book, "Jupiter" prophesies that Germany will one day play host to a national leader who will unify Europe under German hegemony and convene a church council to resolve all theological differences. After that, the prophet goes on to declare, anyone who continues to foster religious dissension will do so only on pain of death. In the light of twentieth century historical experience, the idealism that inspired this utopian vision has too much in common with the goals of the Third Reich to elicit any degree of sympathy from contemporary readers of *The Adventurous Simplicissimus*.

Grimmelshausen's ardent desire to see religious unity restored to his homeland was a direct response to the horrendous suffering that he witnessed during the course of the Thirty Years' War. This conflict, which lasted from 1618 to 1648, had its origin in the tensions between Catholic and Protestant rulers within the Holy Roman Empire of the German nation. Although the kingdom of Bohemia was traditionally part of the domain of the Habsburg emperors in Vienna, the Bohemian nobility struck a blow for religious freedom by choosing a German prince of the Calvinist faith as their king. Imperial forces soon reestablished Habsburg control over Bohemia, but their subsequent attempt to extend Catholic domination over other areas in Germany provoked a Protestant reaction on both a national and an international level. Before long, Denmark and Sweden sent in troops to aid the beleaguered Protestant states within Germany.

The Emperor's chief German ally was Bavaria, but he was also able to draw upon forces from satellite areas such as Croatia. France, despite its formal allegiance to Catholicism, consistently supported the Protestant cause out of fear that a Habsburg victory would pose a threat to its national interests and eventually intervened militarily in order to ensure continued sectarian division among the German states. The religious character of the conflict was thus diluted by political considerations. The German nobility, for its part, was likewise motivated by dynastic and property concerns. Grimmelshausen's own bitterness toward his country's rulers finds full expression in the assertion made by the prophet Jupiter, in which the promised German hero is described as depriving the nobility of its hereditary privileges altogether and instituting a parliamentary government whose membership will be composed of the two wisest men summoned from each town in all of Germany.

Grimmelshausen's masterwork begins with a motif that later was popular among the Romantics: The child who comes to be known as Simplicius Simplicissimus is described as having been reared in total isolation from society on a farm in a forest region known as the Spessart. His putative parents are indifferent to his education, and he therefore grows up as a simpleton who spends most of his time tending to the needs of livestock. His greatest joy is to play the bagpipes, the sound of which, he is told, will scare off the wolves that might attack the sheep under his care. At the age of ten, the boy is forced to flee for safety into a nearby forest in order to escape from a band of marauding soldiers who were plundering the farmstead and who were sure to abduct him if he fell into their hands. To his good fortune, a hermit living in the forest befriends him. It is this hermit who names him "Simplicius" and attempts to educate him. Among other things, the hermit teaches him to read and write; he also succeeds in transforming the boy into a pious Christian. This tutelage comes to an abrupt end after two years, upon the death of the hermit. Utterly distraught, Simplicius wanders about aimlessly until he is captured by a group of soldiers and taken to the city of Hanau, which at that time was a Protestant stronghold under the control of Swedish forces.

The governor of the fortress is James Ramsay, a Scottish soldier of fortune in the service of the Swedish crown and the sole historical personage to appear in Grimmelshausen's novel. It is soon determined that the hermit who had come to the boy's aid was Ramsay's brother-in-law, an entirely fictional character whose surname is reported to be Sternfels von Fuchshaim and who at one time held the military rank of captain. This nobleman, already sickened by the war, decided to renounce the world altogether after his pregnant wife, Susanna, disappeared amid the turmoil of battle. Much later in the novel, Simplicius, during a visit to a spa near Strasbourg, encounters the peasant who reared him as a child and learns from him that the hermit and Susanna were his true parents. The peasant and his wife had assisted Susanna in the process of childbirth and had decided to adopt the baby after the mother died as a consequence of the dire circumstances surrounding the delivery. Ramsay, of course, has no knowledge of the fact that Simplicius is his nephew, but he takes an immediate liking to the boy and decides to make him his page. This partiality toward Simplicius, we are led to believe, may stem from the striking resemblance that the youth bears to his mother, the governor's sister.

Shortly after Simplicius becomes a page, a commissioner representing the

Swedish war council comes to inspect the garrison of Hanau. The boy is therefore required to have a family name in order to answer properly during the roll call, and it is the governor himself who proposes that he be called "Simplicius Simplicissimus" because of his extreme innocence. Totally unfamiliar with the ways of the world, Simplicius is continually appalled by the un-Christian behavior of the men whom he encounters in the garrison. He proves to be so inept as a page, moreover, that the governor finally decides to make him a court jester. A scheme is thereupon concocted to derange the boy's mind in order to render him an even better buffoon than he already is. A clergyman who was a friend of the hermit discovers the plot and forewarns Simplicius of the ordeal that lies ahead. The next night, Simplicius is abducted by four men dressed like devils and is subjected to several unnerving experiences calculated to deprive him of his reason. Following the clergyman's advice, he feigns madness and allows himself to be cast in the role of fool. Despite the indignity of having to wear a costume that makes him resemble a calf, Simplicius finds the life of a court jester much to his liking; he not only is well fed but also is able to express his unconventional thoughts quite freely. Misfortune, however, soon strikes again. A raiding party composed of Croatian soldiers who were part of the Imperial army captures Simplicius during one of his frequent strolls outside the walls of the fortress and compels him to become a stableboy for their cavalry troop.

Highly dissatisfied with his new masters, Simplicius escapes from the Croatian cavalry unit at the first opportunity and takes to stealing food from peasant homesteads in order to survive. While in a forest, he comes upon a large knapsack containing some provisions and a purse within which is a large sum of gold coins. After consuming the food, he conceals the gold coins on his person by cleverly sewing them into his clothing. Shortly thereafter, he comes upon a witches' Sabbath being held in a wooded area and is obliged to participate. By invoking the Lord's name, however, he manages to cause the entire gathering to disappear and finds himself flying through the air immediately. When he finally descends, Simplicius discovers that he has been supernaturally transported to an open field near Magdeburg, a city which at that time was under siege by Imperial forces. The colonel in charge of the Imperial camp to which Simplicius is eventually taken decides to keep him on as a fool after hearing the boy's story. Simplicius is, however, provided with a tutor named Ulrich Herzbruder to further his education. The tutor's son, who bears the same name as his father, becomes a steadfast friend of Simplicius. The younger Herzbruder wishes to become the colonel's secretary, a position already held by a villainous character named Olivier. In order to eliminate this threat to his position, Olivier plants evidence to make it appear that the tutor's son has stolen a valuable object from the colonel. The younger Herzbruder, now in total disgrace, would like to be able to purchase an honorable discharge from the Imperial army, and Simplicius comes to the rescue by providing his friend with the necessary sum. A short while after his son's departure, the elder Herzbruder is senselessly killed by an officer who has taken offense at a prophecy concerning his fate that was made by the clairvoyant tutor.

As Simplicius matures, he advances in rank from stableboy to dragoon and finally to elite cavalryman. Simplicius becomes part of a group of horsemen whose task it is to obtain supplies by foraging through the countryside around the Westphalian city of Soest. Military units of that day customarily lived off the land while campaigning. Dressed in the distinctive green attire of a hunter, Simplicius achieves great renown for his courage and resourcefulness and soon acquires the title of "Huntsman of Soest." Simplicius considers the rich to be fair game, but he takes great pains never to exploit the poor. It is during this phase of his military career that Simplicius encounters the madman who believes himself to be Jupiter. Another major episode which occurs at this point involves the entrapment of a villain who, dressed in a habit similar to the one worn by Simplicius, seeks to trade on his reputation as the Huntsman of Soest and has been perpetrating great crimes on the civilian populace under that disguise. The imposter is eventually captured, but when Simplicius sees how terrified the man is, he decides to spare his life. Simplicius' companions, however, insist on forcing the man to perform a degrading act involving animals and scratch up his face before releasing him. Even though there is a bright moon on this particular night, Simplicius inexplicably fails to recognize the culprit as his erstwhile companion Olivier. Not until he encounters Olivier years later does Simplicius become aware of the identity of the imposter.

While conducting raids, Simplicius usually manages to divert much of the looted treasure to his personal coffer in the hope that this wealth might someday help him achieve his ambition to rise to the rank of officer and perhaps even to be made a member of the nobility itself. After some time, he takes this treasure to Cologne and leaves it with a merchant for safekeeping. Returning from Cologne, Simplicius is captured by Swedish forces and taken to their headquarters in Lippstadt. When the commander learns that his prisoner is the renowned Huntsman of Soest, he proposes to make him an officer in his own battalion. The offer is respectfully declined, but the captive is nevertheless granted complete freedom to move inside and outside the city after pledging not to attempt to escape. During the next six months, Simplicius devotes much time to improving his mastery of firearms and fencing, as well as to reading historical works, heroic fiction, and manuals of love. He also womanizes on a grand scale and is soon the father-to-be of several offspring. His courtship of a retired officer's daughter, however, is a case of true love. When her father catches them in bed together—although a physical union has not been consummated and the entire incident appears to have been calculated to force Simplicius into marriage—Simplicius agrees to marry the girl. Despite the coercive character of the marriage, Simplicius is so pleased with his new situation that he agrees to become an officer in the Swedish army, and he is permitted to go to Cologne for the purpose of retrieving his fortune. The lovers, however, are destined never to see each other again. Only after the passage of many years is Simplicius able to return to the region and inquire about the fate of his bride of one month. He then learns that his wife died soon after giving birth to a male child and that the boy has been adopted by his sister-in-law and her husband. Simplicius, whose physical appearance has so altered over the years that he is not even recognized, deems it not in the best interests of the child to disrupt this arrangement and therefore decides not to reveal his identity as the child's father.

The journey from Lippstadt to Cologne proves uneventful, but once in the city, Simplicius discovers that he is unable to retrieve his treasure. The merchant to whom he entrusted his money has declared himself bankrupt and left the country. A local attorney, however, volunteers to help Simplicius recover the money. Because the legal process promises to be a protracted one, Simplicius, in order to earn enough wages to meet his living expenses, agrees to drive two noblemen to Paris in the attorney's coach. As soon as the party arrives at its destination, the coach and horses are confiscated by the authorities to settle an outstanding debt owed by the attorney, and Simplicius thus finds himself stranded in the French capital. Forced to live by hook or crook, he eventually becomes a male prostitute. Known locally as "Monsieur Beau Alman," Simplicius is in great demand among well-born Parisian ladies and soon accumulates sufficient funds to enable him to return to Germany. On the way back, he suffers from an attack of smallpox which leaves his face permanently disfigured. He is, moreover, robbed of all of his money while undergoing treatment for the affliction and can find no other means of paying for his traveling expenses than to become an itinerant medicine man. Soon after he arrives in his homeland, Simplicius encounters a freebooter who turns out to be Olivier, the nemesis of the younger Herzbruder. Despite his antipathy for Olivier, he enters into a partnership with him and agrees to participate in acts of brigandage. On one of their expeditions, they are attacked by a group of six soldiers. Olivier is slain in the encounter after he kills two of them, and Simplicius is left to dispatch the other four on his own. In this way, the prophecy of the elder Herzbruder, to the effect that Simplicius would avenge the death of Olivier, is fulfilled.

Simplicius soon meets the younger Herzbruder himself and decides to accompany his good friend on a pilgrimage to the shrine of Our Lady of Einsiedeln in Switzerland. There he witnesses an exorcism and becomes so frightened of the Devil that he immediately converts to the Catholic faith. Returning to Germany, Simplicius succeeds, with the assistance of Herzbruder, in obtaining a commission as captain in the Imperial forces. His service in this new rank is, however, a brief one. His company's first engagement with the enemy ends in defeat, and Herzbruder's testicles are shot off as well.

Simplicius gives up his commission in order to take care of Herzbruder, who by now is also paralyzed from the waist down. The two friends settle down at a spa near Strasbourg, and while Herzbruder is undergoing treatment, Simplicius visits Cologne and then goes on to Lippstadt. There he learns of his wife's death and, deeply saddened by the news, returns to the spa in time to witness Herzbruder's death. Before long he runs into his foster father, Melchior, whom he recognizes by the enormous wart in the middle of his forehead, and learns the true identity of his parents. His baptismal name, moreover, proves to have been Melchior Sternfels von Fuchsheim. (This is another anagram of the author's own name.) Simplicius decides to marry a woman that he previously met at the spa, and to make her happy he buys the farm where she was born as their new homestead. His wife, who among other serious shortcomings is guilty of infidelity, gives birth to a baby that looks exactly like one of the hired hands. Both his wife and the child die soon after, from alcohol-related causes.

A widower once again, Simplicius has his foster parents move in with him and turns the management of his estate over to them. In this way, he is free to devote his time to study and meditation. Some local peasants tell him about an unusual body of water called the Mummelsee, located atop one of the highest mountains in the region. His curiosity whetted, Simplicius goes to the lake and makes contact with the water sprites that inhabit it. Their prince takes him on a journey to the center of the earth through the waters of the bottomless lake and endeavors to instruct him in religion and philosophy. After being given a tour of the subterranean realm, Simplicius is returned to the earth's surface, and he once again consecrates himself to his studies.

Swedish forces, however, overrun the region, and their colonel offers to make him a lieutenant colonel under his command. Simplicius accepts and accompanies the colonel to Livonia for the purpose of recruiting a new regiment. The project fails, and the two men go on to Moscow in the hope of obtaining high military positions in the Russian army. After many adventures in Russia and Asia, Simplicius returns to Germany to find that the war has ended; he decides to renounce the world by becoming a hermit and living in a high mountain range that is part of the Black Forest.

Much of what Simplicius learns about life in the course of the novel is foreshadowed in a dream that he has shortly after the death of his hermit mentor. He dreams that all of the trees in the forest in which he dwells are magically transformed into hierarchical symbols of society. At the top of each tree sits a cavalier and below him are branches consisting of groups of soldiers neatly divided according to rank. There is a constant effort among these individuals to rise to higher branches where they would be able to receive greater exposure to rain and sunshine. The roots of the trees are made up of common people—craftsmen and peasants whose labors support the entire social order. At one point in the dream, the forest merges into a single tree on top of which sits the war god, Mars.

In the course of the novel, Simplicius plays several roles in this hierarchy, but at every level the motive forces are lust, greed, and social ambition. Having spent his boyhood in a state of extreme innocence, Simplicius must experience the full measure of the baseness of society before he can bring himself to renounce worldly vanities for a life of piety. When he informs his foster father of his intention to join a community of Hungarian Anabaptists whose simple life-style he has come to admire, Melchior cautions Simplicius to remember that there are no honest men. Simplicius thereupon makes his decision to forgo human companionship entirely and to commune with God in the solitude of the forests. The novel ends with a lengthy adieu to the world that is taken verbatim from a German translation of a work by the Spanish moralist Antonio de Guevara. Grimmelshausen lays the ground for a continuation of Simplicius' story by having his protagonist remark: "Whether I will be able to persevere to the end, as my blessed father did, remains to be seen."

The Continuation (or book 6 of *The Adventurous Simplicissimus*) begins with Simplicius reporting how his ardor for the life of an anchorite gradually diminished after a few months. He therefore sets out on a pilgrimage to the holy places at Loretto and Rome. After unexpectedly coming into possession of some gold coins, Simplicius persuades himself to go on to Jerusalem as well, but he is captured by robbers in Egypt while en route to Palestine. These robbers exhibit him as a wild man until he is rescued by a party of Europeans. The Middle East has in the meantime become engulfed in war, and Simplicius therefore decides to return to Europe in a large Portuguese galleon via the Cape of Good Hope. Somewhere in the vicinity of Madagascar, the vessel is wrecked in a storm, and only Simplicius and the ship's carpenter manage to reach the shores of a nearby island. The island proves to be uninhabited but bountiful. Before long, an Abyssinian woman drifts ashore in a box and volunteers to become their cook. She promptly connives with the carpenter to kill Simplicius. The Lord causes her to disappear, however, when Simplicius makes the Sign of the Cross over his food and asks for divine blessing. The two men are then reconciled, but the carpenter dies an early death as a consequence of his addiction to palm wine. Simplicius resumes the contemplative life of a hermit and finally attains peace of mind. When a Dutch sea captain stops at the island and offers to take Simplicius back to Europe, the offer is declined. Before the captain departs, Simplicius presents him with some palm fronds on which he has recorded his life story; the sea captain later publishes these writings. The memoirs of Simplicius thus come to a formal end.

The Continuation is, for the most part, a worthy supplement to the five books of the original edition of *The Adventurous Simplicissimus*. The effect of the narrative is to intensify the inner struggle experienced by the protagonist in his quest to achieve spiritual salvation. The episode on the island was, incidentally, in no way inspired by Daniel Defoe's *Robinson Crusoe* (1719), a work that first made its appearance fifty years later. An earlier English prototype for Grimmelshausen's "Robinsonade" may, however, be found in the widely translated novel by Henry Nevil entitled *The Isle of Pines* (1618).

The next two sequels to *The Adventurous Simplicissimus* are *Courage: The Adventuress* and *Der seltsame Springinsfeld*. Both Courage and Springinsfeld are characters who make brief appearances in *The Adventurous Simplicissimus*. Although Grimmelshausen never referred to her by a specific name in the earlier work, Courage turns out to be one of the women of easy virtue with whom Simplicius amused himself from time to time at the spa in the Black Forest when he was caring for the younger Herzbruder. After Simplicius had married for the second time, Courage left a baby at his doorstep, along with a written message identifying Simplicius as the father of her illegitimate child. In *Courage*, she confesses that the child was not hers at all but that of her maid, who had exchanged sexual favors with an unknown gentleman for a modest sum of money. It is clear that Courage made her allegation against Simplicius out of pure spite for his having jilted her and that her sole intent was to cause problems for her former lover, both with the authorities and with his wife.

Courage's own story begins in 1620, in Bohemia, when she is a thirteen-year-old girl named Libuschka, and ends fifty years later, when she is part of a Gypsy band whose chieftain is her husband. Over this time span, she manages to marry five army officers and a musketeer, as well as to engage in sex for pleasure and profit with a multitude of other men. She acquires the nickname "Courage" after inadvertently using this term in reference to her genitalia. Modern readers have become familiar with this captivating character through Bertolt Brecht's chronicle play *Mutter Courage und ihre Kinder* (1939; *Mother Courage and Her Children*, 1941). Brecht, however, uses the nickname in its literal sense, to convey the notion of his character's personal tenacity in overcoming adversity.

The episode in Grimmelshausen's novel which serves as the point of departure for Brecht's play occurs when Courage becomes a camp follower who peddles provisions to soldiers. To assist her with the sutlery, Courage enlists the services of a callow youth who is madly in love with her; she promptly calls him "Springinsfeld." Best translated as "Jump-into-the-Field," the name is derived from the opening words of the first command given to him by Courage and is intended to remind him of his subordinate position in both their commercial and their sexual relationships. Under Courage's tutelage, Springinsfeld develops into an accomplished rogue in his own right, but she decides to rid herself of his company after he takes to assaulting her in his sleep, even though he is deeply apologetic once awake. It is after his separation from Courage that Springinsfeld joins Simplicius and his band of marauders in the forests of Soest. Later in life, he encounters an unemployed secretary in the guest room of an inn, to whom he dictates his autobiography. It is this purported narrative that Grimmelshausen published under the title of *Der seltsame Springinsfeld*.

One item of information contained in *Der seltsame Springinsfeld* pertains to the identity of the man who fathered the baby boy whom Courage's maid has borne out of wedlock. It comes to light that the unknown gentleman who has made her pregnant is Simplicius himself. By placing this child at his doorstep, Courage has unintentionally done him a great favor, because he would otherwise never have had the pleasure of rearing a child of his own. Her malicious attempt to spite Simplicius, therefore, brings forth the opposite effect. In the final chapters of *Der seltsame Springinsfeld*, a magical bird's nest that has the power to render a person invisible comes into the possession of the protagonist and his young wife. The nest soon passes into the hands of a young soldier, who happens to kill Springinsfeld's wife while attempting to arrest her for a series of thefts committed while her spouse was away on military duty. Springinsfeld likewise meets with misfortune, losing a leg in battle. Upon his return from the wars, the penniless widower is granted permission to spend his remaining years on Simplicius' farmstead. The further adventures of the young soldier who killed Springinsfeld's wife are related in part 1 of *Das wunderbarliche Vogelsnest* (the magical bird's nest). His ownership of the nest provides him with an unparalleled opportunity to pry into private affairs and to discover the evil that lies behind mankind's façade of civility. The situation is thus remarkably similar to the one depicted in Alain-René Lesage's *Le Diable boiteux* (1707; *The Devil upon Two Sticks*, 1708). Possession of the nest changes hands for a third time after the young soldier attempts to destroy the object that he has come to regard as an instrument of Satan. The new owner is a young merchant whose experiences are described in part 2. Neither part of *Das wunderbarliche Vogelsnest* appears to have any direct connection with the other works in the Simplician cycle. In his preface to part 2, however, Grimmelshausen insists that both are essential components of the total saga. Regardless of their relationship to the rest of the opus, the two parts of *Der wunderbarliche Vogelsnest* succeed in enlarging our picture of life in seventeenth century Gemany. Grimmelshausen, it should never be forgotten, was the only German writer of that century who fully appreciated the literary value of the contemporary scene.

Major publications other than long fiction
NONFICTION: *Der satyrische Pilgram I*, 1666; *Der satyrische Pilgram II*, 1667; *Des Abenteuerlichen Simplicissimi Ewig-währender Calender*, 1671; *Der Bart-Krieg*, 1673; *Der teutsche Michael*, 1673.

Bibliography
Hayens, Kenneth C. *Grimmelshausen*, 1932.

Negus, Kenneth. *Grimmelshausen*, 1974.
Wagener, Hans. *The German Baroque Novel*, 1973.

Victor Anthony Rudowski

KNUT HAMSUN
Knut Pedersen

Born: Lom, Norway; August 4, 1859
Died: Nørholm, Norway; February 19, 1952

Principal long fiction

Den gådefulde, 1877; *Bjørger*, 1878; *Sult*, 1890 (*Hunger*, 1899); *Mysterier*, 1892 (*Mysteries*, 1927); *Ny jord*, 1893 (*Shallow Soil*, 1914); *Redaktør Lynge*, 1893; *Pan*, 1894 (English translation, 1920); *Victoria*, 1898 (English translation, 1929); *Sværmere*, 1904 (*Dreamers*, 1921); *Under høststjærnen*, 1906 (*Under the Autumn Star*); *Benoni*, 1908 (English translation, 1925); *Rosa*, 1908 (English translation, 1926); *En vandrer spiller med sordin*, 1909 (*A Wanderer Plays on Muted Strings*); *Den siste glæde*, 1912 (*Look Back on Happiness*, 1940); *Børn av tiden*, 1913 (*Children of the Age*, 1924); *Segelfoss by*, 1915 (*Segelfoss Town*, 1925); *Markens grøde*, 1917 (*Growth of the Soil*, 1920); *Konerne ved vandposten*, 1920 (*The Women at the Pump*, 1928); *Wanderers*, 1922 (includes *Under the Autumn Star* and *A Wanderer Plays on Muted Strings*); *Siste kapitel*, 1923 (*Chapter the Last*, 1929); *Landstrykere*, 1927 (*Vagabonds*, 1930; also as *Wayfarers*, 1981); *August*, 1930 (English translation, 1931); *Men livet lever*, 1933 (*The Road Leads On*, 1934); *Ringen sluttet*, 1936 (*The Ring Is Closed*, 1937).

Other literary forms

Although he always considered the novel his strongest genre, Knut Hamsun also wrote plays, poetry, and expository prose. *Fra det moderne Amerikas aandsliv* (1889; *The Spiritual Life of Modern America*, 1969) is an impudent but witty survey of social and cultural conditions in the United States; Hamsun later repudiated it and would not allow it to be reprinted. Some of the poems in *Det vilde kor* (1904; the wild chorus) are among the best written in Norway during the period. Hamsun was a rather weak dramatist, although his trilogy, comprising *Ved rigets port* (1895; at the gate of the kingdom), *Livets spil* (1896; the game of life), and *Aftenrøde* (1898; the red of evening), is interesting as a drama of ideas. His memoir *På gjengrodde stier* (1949; *On Overgrown Paths*, 1967), written when he was nearly ninety years old, is one of his finest books.

Achievements

During his long career as a writer, Knut Hamsun was well-known and highly regarded not only in his native Norway but also in the rest of Scandinavia, Continental Europe, and the English-speaking world. He was one of the first to introduce the modern psychological novel into Scandinavian literature; his *Hunger* is a classic example of the genre. Later, he created works in which analysis of the development of society played an equally important role; one of them, a celebration of agrarian values entitled *Growth of the Soil*, earned for him the Nobel Prize for Literature in 1920.

Because he was accused of collaborating with the Germans during World War II, Hamsun suffered a period of neglect in the postwar years. This is no longer the case; both Norwegian and foreign critics now consider him his country's greatest novelist. He appeals both to a general audience and to academic critics; a number of his novels have recently been reissued in new English translations, and his works are frequently taught in literature courses in both Scandinavia and America.

Biography

Knut Hamsun was born Knut Pedersen on August 4, 1859, at the farm Garmotræet in the district of Lom, Norway. His father, Peder Pedersen, was a tailor and small farmer, and Hamsun's mother, Tora, was also of peasant stock. In 1863, Pedersen moved with his family to Hamarøy in Nordland, Norway, where he settled on his brother-in-law's farm, Hamsund, from which Hamsun later took the name by which he is known.

Hamsun's earliest childhood years were happy ones. The happiness came to an end, however, when at the age of nine he was sent to live with his maternal uncle, a wealthy landowner and merchant. Hamsun's parents were not happy with this arrangement either; it was only when heavy financial pressure was brought to bear on them they would agree to it. The uncle needed Hamsun's labor, and the boy had many experiences which later were of use to him in his art, although he was harshly treated.

Hamsun was released in 1873 and began a long career of odd jobs. He first clerked in several country stores, after which he became an itinerant peddler, then a shoemaker's apprentice, and even a sheriff's deputy. He also worked as a country schoolmaster, for which he was qualified by his native intelligence and masterful penmanship.

Hamsun did not read widely during this period of his life, but he had become familiar with the peasant tales of his countryman, Bjørnstjerne Bjørnson, and in 1877, when Hamsun was only eighteen years old, he published his first book, a naïve love story entitled *Den gådefulde* (the riddle). This youthful work is significant only as the first version of what was to become one of Hamsun's most persistent motifs—namely, a relationship between a lower-class man and an upper-class woman. In the beautiful and lyric novel *Victoria*, this motif became the main theme.

The year 1878 saw the publication of another youthful tale, *Bjørger*. Hamsun's early writings enabled him to obtain the support of a wealthy merchant, and he was able to concentrate fully on the task of becoming a poet of note. To this end, he produced a manuscript and traveled to Copenhagen, where he offered it to Scandinavia's best-known publisher, Hegel of Gyldendal. To his dismay, his manuscript was rejected, and he spent a difficult winter in the city of Kristiania, Norway. The experiences of this winter, as well as later, similar ones, provided him with the material for his novel *Hunger*, which in 1890 gave him his breakthrough as a writer.

Prior to the publication of *Hunger*, however, Hamsun spent several years in America. During two separate stays, he again worked in a variety of jobs, but in addition he read widely in both European and American literature. He also lectured to Norwegian immigrants on literary and cultural topics. In 1888, after his final return from America, he lived in Copenhagen, where he anonymously published the first chapter of *Hunger* in a periodical. This made him a talked-about figure in literary circles even though his identity was known by but a few. The following year, he gave a series of lectures about America in Copenhagen's Student Society; these lectures were published as *The Spiritual Life of Modern America* later in the same year.

After the publication of *Hunger*, a ground-breaking psychological novel, Hamsun wrote an article in 1890 in which he outlined the basic principles employed in its composition. This article, entitled "Fra det ubevidste sjæleliv" ("From the Unconscious Life of the Mind"), became the genesis of a series of lectures held in a number of Norwegian cities and towns during the year 1891. Hamsun attacked earlier Norwegian literature for being concerned with social conditions rather than with the mental life of the exceptional individual; he maintained that this made it dull.

The 1890's were very productive years for Hamsun, during which he wrote such significant novels as *Mysteries*, *Pan*, and *Victoria*. He enjoyed his growing reputation and traveled much, in both Scandinavia and Europe. He longed for more stability in his life, however, and hoped that that would be the result of his marriage to Bergljot Bech, whom he met in 1897 and married in 1898. The experience of meeting her lies behind the beautiful love story told in his novel *Victoria*, published in the same year. The couple's expectations were not fulfilled, however, and the marriage was dissolved in 1906.

During the years following the divorce, Hamsun wrote a number of works in which the protagonist is a middle-aged wanderer whose experiences and musings on existence constitute the subject of the books. Such novels as *Under the Autumn Star* and *A Wanderer Plays on Muted Strings* are not regarded as among Hamsun's best, but they are important for what they tell about his artistic development. After the author's marriage to the young actress Marie Andersen in 1909, however, his books took a different turn.

In his lectures on literature delivered in 1891, Hamsun had distanced himself from what he considered the dull social literature of his contemporaries, opting for a kind of fiction that would explore the exceptional consciousness. After his second marriage, however, he began to write books which, in a sense, mediate between these opposing standpoints, emphasizing unusual men in their social setting. *Children of the Age* and its sequel, *Segelfoss Town*, are such books; the protagonists are exceptional men, yet at the same time, Hamsun analyzes the workings of society. In *Segelfoss Town*, for example, the values embodied in the aristocratic Willatz Holmsen give way to those of the modern entrepreneur Tobias Holmengraa, and Hamsun appears to place himself in opposition to all that is new in both intellectual and material culture.

In 1911, Hamsun had bought the farm Skogheim in Hamarøy in northern Norway, where he lived as a farmer and writer. In 1917, he sold this farm and moved to the southern part of the country; the farm had, however, fulfilled its mission: The year 1917 also saw the publication of Hamsun's best-known book, the novel *Growth of the Soil*, for which he received the Nobel Prize in 1920. The book tells the story of a man who goes into the northern Norwegian wilderness, clears land for a farm, and rears a family in close contact with nature. It has been regarded as a hymn both to agrarian life and to the traditional values that Hamsun had espoused in *Children of the Age* and *Segelfoss Town*.

After the publication of *Growth of the Soil*, Hamsun began searching for a new and permanent home. Eventually, he settled at the farm Nørholm, where he lived for the rest of his life. He continued as a combination of writer and farmer, and he improved the farm greatly. During this period, he also published two more novels, *The Women at the Pump* and *Chapter the Last*.

The mid-1920's was a difficult time for Hamsun. He worked hard but feared that his creative powers had begun to fail him. During the winter of 1926, he availed himself of the services of a psychiatrist, and in the fall, he began one of his finest works, the novel *Vagabonds*, which was published the following year. The book is the first volume of a trilogy; the other two volumes are entitled *August* and *The Road Leads On*. The trilogy tells about the adventures of a certain August, a dreamer and eccentric, and how his actions influence the lives of people who, were it not for him, could have possessed the stability that he is lacking. The novels continue that investigation of modern society which is so prominent in *Children of the Age* and *Segelfoss Town*. The connection between these earlier books and the trilogy has been made obvious by the fact that the action in *The Road Leads On* moves from Polden, the isolated north Norwegian community, which is the setting of the trilogy's first two volumes, to Segelfoss, where characters from *Children of the Age* and *Segelfoss Town* are again encountered. *The Road Leads On* can thus be viewed as the concluding volume of two separate trilogies, both of which treat social conditions during a period of transition.

At the time of the conclusion of his August trilogy, Hamsun was a man well into his seventies. His hearing was failing, and his energies had suffered that decline which normally comes with age. He produced only one more novel, *The Ring Is Closed*, and would probably have remained relatively silent were it not for political developments in both Europe and Norway. Hamsun had always been an admirer of Germany and German culture at the same time that he detested the British. After the German invasion of Norway and the flight to England of King Haakon and his cabinet, Hamsun supported the collaborationist government headed by Vidkun Quisling and encouraged Norwegian soldiers not to fight against the invaders. After the war, he was arrested and tried. In the course of the trial, his mental condition was examined, and he was found not to be senile, but to have permanently impaired mental faculties. He was nevertheless convicted of treason and heavily fined, the result of which was that he was left a financially ruined man. After the trial, he published the poignant memoir *On Overgrown Paths*, which abundantly demonstrated that his mental faculties were anything but impaired.

Hamsun's final years were quiet ones. By tacit agreement, no critical attention was paid to his work, and he had nothing further to say. The author died on his farm on February 19, 1952.

Analysis

Knut Hamsun the novelist can be viewed as an outsider who writes about outsiders. Originating in a family that by any standard must be considered poor, Hamsun was keenly aware of the difference between himself and those who possessed power and prestige in society. Power and its opposite, powerlessness, are therefore important themes in his work.

Several of Hamsun's early novels, such as *Hunger* and *Pan*, are narrated in the first person, and their first-person protagonists have character traits and experiences that appear to have been modeled on Hamsun's own. The later novels are without exception narrated in the third person, but that does not mean that the autobiographical content is less. In addition, one can always trust the narrators in the later works to represent Hamsun's own views, while unreliability is a feature of some of the early narrators.

The author's interest in the character of the outsider manifests itself in the careful attention that is paid to individual psychology in the early novels, as well as in the interest in the exceptional individual's relation to society and social forces, especially those of social change, which is found in the later works. The early Hamsun hero, who is often an artist or an artistlike figure, attempts to overcome his powerlessness either through his ability to inspire love in a woman of higher social standing or through his art or both. The typical hero of the later works is either the victim of social change or an embodiment of that which is new in modern social and economic life. In the latter case, he is either somewhat of a charlatan, like Tobias Holmengraa in *Segelfoss Town*, or a dreamer and maker of a multitude of stillborn projects, like August of *Vagabonds* and the other two volumes of the August trilogy. Common to all of Hamsun's protagonists is their essential difference from the average person. This difference can be positive or negative, but it always makes for a character whom the reader will find interesting.

Hamsun's earliest novel of significance, *Hunger*, has as its setting Kristiania (now Oslo), a city where Hamsun had had many unhappy experiences. The greater number of his later novels are set in northern Norway, where the author had lived most of his childhood and youth and where he spent a significant part of his manhood. Most of the action in these novels also takes place in the period of Hamsun's youth, the 1870's and the early 1880's. There is therefore good reason to regard his fiction as fundamentally autobiographical. He never tired of writing about the experiences of his youth, on which he reflected throughout his long career as a novelist.

Hunger, Hamsun's first novel of any importance, was also the first modern psychological novel in Norwegian literature. It is the story of a young writer of exceptional sensibility who, stripped of all of his property and without any secure means of support, is about to succumb to starvation in Norway's capital city of Kristiania. This first-person novel is highly autobiographical; Hamsun had experienced the same degree of destitution on several occasions, most notably in the winter of 1886. Such experiences were surely not unusual among artists at the time; the importance of *Hunger* lies not in its subject matter but rather in the manner in which the author deals with it.

The total narrated time of the novel is two months. The narration is, however, concentrated on four periods during which the narrator suffers greatly from hunger; the author does not appear to be interested in the three periods of time between them when the protagonist seems to live a relatively normal life. The narrator is clearly an individual who earlier was somewhat better off economically, but no reasons for the decline of his fortune are given. Only a few details concerning his identity are mentioned, and these details do not even include his name.

The novel also has but little action in the traditional sense. With the exception of the story of a few attempts made by the narrator to secure employment, as well as the tale of a brief encounter with a lady of the middle class, the text is almost exclusively made up of reports of the narrator's mental life during periods of extreme hunger.

The stream-of-consciousness technique employed by Hamsun is effective in portraying the strange workings of the mind while in an altered state resulting from a lack of nourishment. The reader is given access both to the perceptions, moods, and strange ideas of the narrator and to his reflections on his own state of consciousness. The narrator perceives himself as an artist, and his chief concern is twofold: on the one hand, to prevent his hunger from negatively affecting those sensibilities which make him capable of producing art and, on the other hand, to utilize his unpleasant experiences in his art. The narrator's strong tendency toward self-observation can be viewed both as a means of making sure that the demands of his body do not conquer his mental or artistic needs and as part of his artistic project, the gathering of material for the novel which the reader has before him.

Hamsun is interested not in the physical effects of starvation per se, but only in its consequences for the mind. This attitude stands in direct opposition to the prevailing trends in Scandinavian literature at the time. A case in point is Arne Garborg's novel *Bondestudentar* (1883; students from the country), in which the protagonist, like the narrator in *Hunger*, suffers from starvation in the city of Kristiania. The difference is that, unlike Hamsun, Garborg portrays only the physical and social consequences of hunger. In contrast, the attitude of Hamsun's narrator toward his hunger could indeed be termed one of experimentation.

It is a question, however, whether Hamsun the artist was as exclusively concerned with the mental side of life as he claimed to be in his 1891 lectures. The narrator's attention to a mysterious young woman of the middle class does not seem to originate in any specific interest in art, but rather in a concern with the social position that can be won by a successful artist or by a young man who has success in any endeavor. The narrator-protagonist in *Hunger*, like his creator Hamsun, can also be regarded as a practical man for whom art is a means of social advancement at least as much as an end in itself.

In *Hunger*, Hamsun's autobiographical tendencies manifest themselves both in his choice of subject matter and in the location of the action. In *Pan*, the story occurs at a fictional place in northern Norway called Sirilund, but the social milieu is the same as that which Hamsun had known so well in his youth. In this novel, the theme of art is subservient to that of love, but the social function of love in *Pan* is similar to that of art in *Hunger*.

Unlike the narrative situation of *Hunger*, that of *Pan* is quite complex. The novel consists of two parts, the main text and a brief epilogue entitled "Glahn's Death." Both the text proper and the epilogue are narrated in the first person, but while the main part of the book is narrated by its protagonist, a lieutenant named Thomas Glahn, the epilogue is narrated by his hunting companion and killer, a man whose name is not given.

The main story takes place during the summer months of the year 1855. Lieutenant Glahn is an outsider who has obtained leave from his commission and who is now leading a rather primitive life as a hunter and fisherman in a cabin near the trading post Sirilund. Tired of urban life and incapable of getting along well according to the norms of cultured society, he has immersed himself in nature, attempting to live as part of it. His intermediary position between nature and culture is symbolized by the fact that his cabin is located where the forest meets the fields surrounding Sirilund. In narrating the story, Glahn tells both about the external events of his life in nature and about his reflections on his existence, and from his story, it would appear that he is entirely successful in his attempts to live as an integral part of the natural world. It is clear, however, that he is far too reflective to lay claim to a natural existence entirely unmediated by culture. This and other signs of unreliability are of great significance to any interpretation of the book.

During visits to the trading post at Sirilund, Glahn meets the young Edvarda, the daughter of the post's owner, the trader Mack. Glahn falls in love with Edvarda, who—because of her father's wealth—is his social superior. A love-hate relationship develops between the two, and each tortures the other in turn.

Glahn's love for Edvarda is not an end in itself, however, but rather a means to social advancement. Glahn would simply like to inherit Mack's position of wealth, power, and prestige by marrying his only daughter. Edvarda, on her part, sees in Glahn an opportunity to get away from Sirilund. Glahn's true intentions are revealed by the fact that he has an affair with a young woman named Eva, the wife of a local blacksmith, as soon as he discovers that Mack uses her to satisfy his erotic needs. For Glahn, the affair is little more than a way symbolically to assume Mack's social position, but when the trader discovers it, he punishes them by having Eva killed and by forcing Glahn to leave the place.

Glahn tells the story two years later. The outward reason for his telling the story at this time is that he has just received a message from Edvarda, who is now married to another man. That Glahn writes down the story establishes as a fact, however, something that is at best implied in the text, namely that Glahn must also be regarded as an artist. It is necessary to be aware of that when the epilogue, "Glahn's Death," is considered.

The epilogue bears the date 1861, which places its narration four years after the telling of the main part of the story. There is, however, no indication of how much time has passed between the events themselves and the telling of them.

The story in the epilogue is about how Glahn causes the unnamed narrator to take his life by making him jealous and taunting him. Glahn apparently wants to die, and this desire has at least in part been brought about by another letter from Edvarda, who cannot forget him. Glahn's killer writes down the story ostensibly in order to make it clear to the dead man's family that there is no longer any need to inquire about his whereabouts through newspaper advertisements. He seems to be unaware that by so doing, he incriminates himself.

The signs of unreliability that can be found in the main portion of the novel, however, together with the curious narrative situation in the epilogue, make it reasonable to suspect that the narrator of the epilogue is indeed Glahn himself, who has simply made up the story of his death as a final attempt to inflict pain on Edvarda. This interpretation is quite reasonable in view of the fact that when Edvarda learns of Glahn's supposed death, as it is told in Hamsun's later novel *Rosa*, it indeed causes her much grief.

Pan is one of Hamsun's most complex novels. Many critics regard it as his finest work from the 1890's, and some claim that it is his masterpiece. It clearly sets forth Hamsun's view of the relationship between power, love, and the artistic temperament.

Published in 1915, *Segelfoss Town* stands in the middle of Hamsun's oeuvre. A continuation of *Children of the Age*, which appeared two years earlier, it is also composed in such a manner that it can be read as a separate work. If its criticism of contemporary society is to be evaluated, however, it is helpful to have some familiarity with the earlier work.

Segelfoss is a small community in northern Norway, consisting mainly of a flour mill and the large estate from which the community has derived its name. For generations, the farm and the mill have been owned by the Holmsen family, which by its inherited wealth and benevolent aristocracy has lent order and stability to the community. In *Children of the Age*, however, it is learned that business has been going poorly for the Holmsens, and when an opportunity to sell the flour mill arises, its owner eagerly accepts.

The new owner is Tobias Holmengraa, a local boy of peasant stock who has accumulated a fortune by means of rather mysterious dealings while abroad. Holmengraa is, within Hamsun's artistic universe, a relation of both the protagonist of *Hunger* and Thomas Glahn, the chief difference being that Holmengraa has both the imagination and the financial wherewithal to attempt to realize his social daydream. Once in the possession of the flour mill, he creates a new age for Segelfoss, which may now rightfully refer to itself as a town. There is an abundance of employment and, consequently, money to be had; a trader, a distant relative of Holmengraa, is asked to come and set up a store; a telegraph station is established; and both a lawyer and a doctor arrive.

Thus, new centers of power are created. The most obvious one is Holmengraa's business, but the store also becomes a means to the accumulation of wealth, especially when Theodor, the son of the original owner, takes over after his father. Through his portrayal of social and economic change, Hamsun analyzes the process by which the old and semifeudal social order vanishes and is replaced by a twentieth century social reality. He strongly voices his distrust of the new, mainly through the character Baardsen, the telegraphist, who is also a musician, somewhat of a philosopher, and a drunkard. A character who is split and divided, he is by far the most interesting figure in the book; in the end, he takes his own life, unable to bear the tension in his existence.

The third-person narrator also allows his voice to be heard directly. What he finds most objectionable in modern life is the absence of respect for authority, especially that of the employer, the new money-based economy, and the fact that talented young people leave the class into which they have been born and through education degenerate into clergymen, doctors, and lawyers. The view that is advanced by the author is thus a totally reactionary one, one that Hamsun later, unfortunately, did not distinguish from the ideology of the Nazi Party and that eventually caused his treason during World War II.

Segelfoss Town, however, is much more than a reactionary tract. If justice is to be done to it as a work of art, it must also be read as a novel about life in all of its variety. In the end, Holmengraa goes bankrupt as a result of his emphasis on the outward show of wealth and his lack of sound business practices; the flour mill is shut down; and the future becomes uncertain for the many workers who have depended on this entrepreneur and charlatan. The disaster is not a victory for Hamsun's reactionary views, however, but rather one for the inhabitants of Segelfoss, who despite economic misfortune find a way to get by. Life itself continues independent of the fates of individuals.

Hamsun had used *Segelfoss Town* as a means of voicing his distrust of the development of modern society. In *Growth of the Soil*, he expressed the same norms, but he attempted to prescribe a positive remedy for social ills by giving his public an example worthy of emulation. His rhetorical success is perhaps most clearly indicated by the fact that the novel earned for him the Nobel Prize in 1920.

The protagonist of *Growth of the Soil* is Isak Sellanraa, a man without a past but also without any of the cultural baggage of contemporary life. One day, he is walking through the wilderness somewhere in northern Norway, searching for a place to settle down and make a home for himself, his situation not unlike that of many Norwegian emigrants to America. The American immigrant pioneer was a well-known figure in Norway; Hamsun used the comparison in order to point out that breaking new soil in one's own land is better than emigrating.

The first part of the book details the growth of Isak's farm as he clears the land, builds shelter, and acquires both farm animals and a wife, Inger. The qualitative difference between the man and his wife is indicated by the fact that he has been given the name of an Old Testament patriarch, while her name, Inger, is a common one. Inger is an entirely ordinary person; she casts her lot with the antisocial Isak only because she has a harelip and is therefore unable to find a husband in any other way. Inger is possessed by fear that one of her children will inherit her defect, which indeed happens to her third baby, a girl. Knowing the suffering that is in store for the infant, Inger kills her, later confesses her crime, and is sent to prison for five years.

During this time, she has an operation on her lip, is educated in modern life, and, in Hamsun's view, is spoiled by civilization. When she returns, she is no longer satisfied with the simple life of the farm. This division in Isak's family is then extended to the children; one of his two sons remains a solid young man, while the other is sent to town and is finally fit for nothing but emigration to America.

While Isak is struggling to maintain his (and Hamsun's) values in his home, civilization closes in on the farm, both through the arrival of more settlers and through the discovery of copper ore in a nearby mountain, which leads to the establishment of a mine. The catalyst in this development is a curious character named Geissler, who is a carrier of both Hamsun's values and their opposites. Geissler makes *Growth of the Soil* a complex novel whose value system is perhaps not as clear as it has traditionally been thought to be, and this lack of univocality is indicated by his referring to himself as "the fog" in an important monologue at the end of the book.

Growth of the Soil is undoubtedly Hamsun's most widely read novel. Seductive in both rhetoric and style, the novel makes it difficult for the reader to maintain a proper distance from the author's norms. As a work of art, it is splendid; its values, however, like those of *Segelfoss Town*, are some of those which later led Hamsun to embrace the Nazi ideology.

The first volume of a trilogy and the most significant novel from Hamsun's later years, *Vagabonds* is set mainly in northern Norway. It is centered on a community named Polden, similar to Segelfoss but much smaller. There is, for example, no social or economic leader on the order of a Holmsen or even a Holmengraa. In the novel, the Polden environment is significant as a laboratory for the social change that Hamsun so thoroughly despises, but it is also important as the background for one of Hamsun's most tragic characters and for one of his most comical ones.

The tragic character is Edevart, who as a young boy has one of his decisive experiences in the first few pages of the book. During the wintertime, when all the adult males in the community are away at the Lofoten fisheries, Polden is visited by two foreign-looking confidence men who, by appealing to the inhabitants' need for adventure, succeed in tricking them out of whatever small amounts of money they have. Edevart, who at first is taken in by them but then sees through their sham, thus receives his initiation into the deceit and hollowness of the world. As a result, he loses both some of his innocence and much of that innate faith which, if shielded from the attacks of the world, would have aided him in living a life of happiness and satisfaction. This episode is an important one, for it presents Hamsun's thesis that modern civilization is essentially a similar kind of confidence game, albeit on a grander scale, and that its effects on people are similar to those of the strangers on Edevart.

Edevart has another important experience a few years later, when as a young man he encounters a woman named Lovise Magrete Doppen, with whom he falls deeply in love and who initiates him sexually. Shortly thereafter, Lovise Magrete accompanies her husband, an ex-convict who was in jail when Edevart met her, to America. This man, like one of Isak's sons in *Growth of the Soil*, is so depraved that he is fit for nothing but emigration. This experience causes Edevart to lose his trust in the power of love, much as his experience with the confidence men had caused him to lose faith in people. As a result, Edevart becomes a "vagabond in love."

These and similar experiences lead to Edevart's complete demoralization. Dishonesty takes the place of his original honesty, restlessness replaces his sense of belonging in Polden, and dissatisfaction takes the place of his ability to be happy in limited circumstances. The fundamental cause of Edevart's moral decline, however, is not a defect in his personality but the changes that society is undergoing. They include the capitalization of agriculture, the process of industrialization, and the change to a monetary economy, all of which Hamsun opposes. Edevart's development parallels that of society at large.

Hamsun's views, however, are somewhat equivocal. The ambiguity is expressed mainly through the character August, who is only one of two important figures in *Vagabonds* but the clear protagonist of the trilogy of which the novel is the first volume. August has no close relatives; like Tobias Holmengraa in *Segelfoss Town*, he has spent a number of years abroad, and, like Tobias, August is a dreamer. In both *Vagabonds* and the trilogy as a whole, he is an embodiment of the social forces to which Hamsun is opposed. One would, therefore, expect that August should be portrayed as a villain of the highest order, but that is not the case. The author is charmed by him, admires him, and causes the reader to share that admiration. At the same time, Hamsun is critical of what August represents. August therefore expresses Hamsun's ambivalent attitude toward those forces in society which he so soundly condemns. This might be taken as an indication that the author's values are confused, but it could also simply mean that Hamsun, in the final analysis, views life as more complex than any theory or ideology. His tendency to cling to an ideology is, however, present in *Vagabonds* as well as in *Growth of the Soil* and *Segelfoss Town*.

To many present-day readers, Hamsun will seem like a reactionary writer whose values are out of touch with the modern world. There is a fundamental irony in this, as the charge is similar to that which he, in his youth, leveled against his immediate predecessors in Norwegian literature. Even though today's critics thus will find little to admire in Hamsun's value system, his books nevertheless have the power to charm new generations of readers. Hamsun is a master of his craft, of rhetoric, and of style, and he is therefore a true artist whose books attract readers not because of but in spite of some of the values they express.

Major publications other than long fiction

SHORT FICTION: *Siesta*, 1897; *Kratskog*, 1903; *Stridende liv*, 1905.

PLAYS: *Ved rigets port*, 1895; *Livets spil*, 1896; *Aftenrøde*, 1898; *Munken Vendt*, 1902; *Dronning Tamara*, 1903; *Livet ivold*, 1910 (*In the Grip of Life*, 1924).

POETRY: *Det vilde kor*, 1904.

NONFICTION: *Fra det moderne Amerikas aandsliv*, 1889 (*The Spiritual Life of Modern America*, 1969); *I æventyrland*, 1903; *På gjengrodde stier*, 1949 (*On Overgrown Paths*, 1967).

Bibliography

Buttry, Dolores. "Knut Hamsun and the 'Rousseauian Soul,'" in *Scandina-*

vica. XIX (November, 1980), pp. 121-150.

McFarlane, J. W. "The Whisper of the Blood: A Study of Knut Hamsun's Early Novels," in *PMLA*. LXXI (September, 1956), pp. 563-594.

Naess, Harald. *Knut Hamsun og Amerika*, 1969.

Sehmsdorf, Henning K. "Knut Hamsun's *Pan*: Myth and Symbol," in *Edda*. LXXIV (1974), pp. 345-393.

Simpson, Allen. "Knut Hamsun's Anti-Semitism," in *Edda*. LXXVII (1977), pp. 273-293.

Turco, Alfred, Jr. "Knut Hamsun's *Pan* and the Riddle of 'Glahn's Death,'" in *Scandinavica*. XIX (May, 1980), pp. 13-29.

Unruh, Kathryn I. "The Long Dark Summer in Segelfoss Town," in *Edda*. LXXVII (1977), pp. 263-272.

Jan Sjåvik

PETER HANDKE

Born: Griffen, Austria; December 6, 1942

Principal long fiction

Die Hornissen, 1966; *Der Hausierer*, 1967; *Die Angst des Tormanns beim Elfmeter*, 1970 (*The Goalie's Anxiety at the Penalty Kick*, 1972); *Der kurze Brief zum langen Abschied*, 1972 (*Short Letter, Long Farewell*, 1974); *Wunschloses Unglück*, 1972 (*A Sorrow Beyond Dreams*, 1974); *Die Stunde der wahren Empfindung*, 1975 (*A Moment of True Feeling*, 1977); *Die linkshändige Frau*, 1976 (*The Left-Handed Woman*, 1978); *Das Gewicht der Welt*, 1977 (*The Weight of the World*, 1983); *Langsame Heimkehr*, 1979 (*The Long Way Around*); *Die Lehre der Sainte-Victoire*, 1980 (*The Lesson of Mont-Sainte-Victoire*); *Kindergeschichte*, 1981 (*Child Story*); *Die Geschichte des Bleistifts*, 1982; *Der Chinese des Schmerzes*, 1983; *Slow Homecoming* (includes *The Long Way Around*, *The Lesson of Mont-Sainte-Victoire*, and *Child Story*).

Other literary forms

Peter Handke made his debut on the German stage with the drama *Publikumsbeschimpfung* (1966; *Offending the Audience*, 1969). His subsequent dramatic works include *Hilferufe* (1967; *Calling for Help*, 1971), *Kaspar* (1968; English translation, 1969), *Das Mündel will Vormund sein* (1969; *My Foot My Tutor*, 1971), *Quodlibet* (1970; English translation, 1976), *Der Ritt über den Bodensee*, 1971 (*The Ride Across Lake Constance*, 1973), *Die Unvernünftigen sterben aus* (1973; *They Are Dying Out*, 1977), and *Über die Dörfer* (1981; across the villages). After publishing several radio plays in the early 1970's, Handke wrote a film script, *Chronik der laufenden Ereignisse* (1971; chronicle of occurring events), which he also produced, and a television script, *Falsche Bewegung* (1975; wrong move). An early collection of short stories, *Begrüssung des Aufsichtsrats* (1967; saluting the trustees), should also be noted. Handke's best-known collection of poetry is *Die Innenwelt der Aussenwelt der Innenwelt* (1969; the inner world of the outer world of the inner world); it gives poetic expression to his recurring concern with language as its phrases, in their description of the outer world, simultaneously reflect the inner world or consciousness of the author and vice versa. These concerns have also been raised in several of Handke's critical essays, notably *Ich bin ein Bewohner des Elfenbeinturms* (1972; I am an inhabitant of the ivory tower).

Achievements

With the sudden and unprecedented advent of Handke on the German literary scene in 1966, the era of postwar German literature, which had tried to come to terms with World War II and the Nazi past, reached its conclusion.

Handke is the representative of a new generation of German writers for whom the Federal Republic of Germany constitutes the societal reality that furnishes the material and the conflicts that inform their works. Born in Austria, then reared in East Berlin for some years before returning to Austria, Handke regards the new Germany with the eyes of an outsider who nevertheless possesses an insider's intimate knowledge of his subject. Handke's stance as an outsider is reflected in his disregard for social problems, unless they reflect his primary concern for language: In the midst of the student revolts of the late 1960's, he became one of the first writers in West Germany to emphasize that changes in the political realities of the new republic would not come about through protest resolutions or political manifestos but rather through the exact use of the word, the honesty of literary expression, and the truth of fiction (as Manfred Durzak notes). The majority of Handke's West German fellow writers recognized the validity of his claim only after the fall of Willy Brandt as Chancellor in 1974.

Handke's outsider's attempts at registering West German societal developments and their effects upon the individual are in some ways mirrored on a larger and certainly less intellectual scale by frequent media attempts in West Germany today in which the social and economic ills of that society are blamed on America, from which they have supposedly been imported. In contrast, Handke traces the ills that afflict his characters to the larger ills of West German society. Under these circumstances, it becomes noteworthy that in two of his novels, *Short Letter, Long Farewell* and *The Long Way Around*, Handke has depicted America's untouched nature as regenerative, offering the possibility of spiritual rebirth for his protagonists. Such a special relationship with America is perhaps connected to the fact that Handke's own birth as an author of prominence took place in the United States rather than in Germany. In Princeton in early 1966, at the conference of the West German writers' group, Gruppe 47, Handke was suddenly pushed into the limelight not so much for his literary production—which was just getting under way— as for his attacks upon the production of the German literary Establishment at that time. The young outsider Handke had recently had his first novel, *Die Hornissen* (the hornets), accepted by the renowned German publishers Suhrkamp Verlag, under whose auspices he was more or less incidentally invited to participate at the conference. There, he immediately affronted the German literary Establishment, proclaiming that their writings were characterized by a sterile descriptive tedium and a total disregard for the dimension most essential to literary realization—namely, language itself. During the next few years, Handke wrote in almost every genre imaginable, while his theme remained always the same. In his prose, his drama, and his poetry, his mission was to question the value of life in a modern age of directed mass communication, whose net of linguistic standards had entangled the individual, leaving him no room for self-expression. Literature should, therefore, make the individual conscious of himself again. Handke perceived a metareality beyond the barriers of language, and only the perception of this reality would render the material character of language obvious.

The intensity of Handke's metaphysical search led to his second creative phase, in the early 1970's, when the author's private life began to play an ever-increasing role in his prose. Several critics have termed this "autobiographical" phase Handke's most fruitful and accomplished period; during these years, he wrote his best-known novels, *The Goalie's Anxiety at the Penalty Kick*, *Short Letter, Long Farewell*, and *A Sorrow Beyond Dreams*.

In his more recent prose and drama, written after the late 1970's, Handke's ego seems to have attained a somewhat inflated stature of "well-practiced narcissism," as one critic has observed. Handke exhibits the visionary zeal of a religious prophet in such novels as *The Long Way Around* and *The Lesson of Mont-Sainte-Victoire*. Similar tendencies are obvious in his two diaries, *The Weight of the World* and *Die Geschichte des Bleistifts* (the story of the pencil). The latter diary, however, in contrast to the earlier one, does transcend the entirely private sphere, aiming for universality similar to that of Johann Wolfgang von Goethe's *Maximen und Reflexionen* (1833; *Maxims and Reflections*) and *Zur Farbenlehre* (1810; *Theory of Colors*). Durzak has quoted Handke as having uttered in this context, "I don't aspire to being a star, but a figure with certain mystical intentions. . .I would not mind that at all." It should be noted that Handke has won most of the prestigious literary awards available to German-language writers.

Biography

Peter Handke's early literary revolt against all repressive systems of rules and social customs and against the experience of daily dependency and dull coercive repetition is certainly linked to his birth and upbringing in a poor working-class environment. His birthplace, Griffen, in the province of Carinthia, Austria, lies about twenty-five miles northeast of Klagenfurt, the only sizable city in the region, and only a few miles from the border with Yugoslavia. Handke's maternal grandfather, of Slovak descent, was a peasant and carpenter; his mother, the fourth of five children, worked as a dishwasher, maid, and cook during the war and became pregnant with Handke by a German soldier, a bank clerk in civilian life, who was already married. Before Handke's birth, his mother married another German soldier, Bruno Handke, in civilian life a streetcar conductor in Berlin. In 1944, Maria Handke moved to Berlin with her son to await her husband's return from the war. For some time after 1945, Handke's stepfather continued to work as a streetcar conductor in Berlin, until in 1948 he moved his family to Griffen, where he found employment with Maria's father. The stepfather's alcoholism, the cramped quarters—the family, by then numbering six, shared two attic rooms—and the backwardness of the region became increasingly oppressive for the young

Handke. After attending the local elementary school, he finally escaped from his hated stepfather and the confines of home by entering a parochial boarding school near Klagenfurt.

At the parochial school, the quiet and serious-minded Handke remained isolated from his fellow pupils. His superior intelligence allowed him to catch up on a year's work in Latin within a short time, and to become the best student in class. His German teacher recognized his writing talent and encouraged him to publish his first short stories in the school newspaper. Through this teacher, Handke became acquainted with the works of Thomas Wolfe and William Faulkner, among others. Handke, however, soon felt the pressure of conformity at this school, with its expressed purpose of preparing young men for the priesthood, and he changed schools once more, to attend the *gymnasium* in Klagenfurt, from which he was graduated in 1961. Apparently his former teacher advised Handke upon graduation to enter law school, so that the young man might have enough time to pursue his love for writing and reflection. He entered the University of Graz, where he soon came into contact with an avant-garde group of young writers. He was able to publish in their literary magazine, and in 1963 a short story by Handke was broadcast over a regional radio station.

In Graz, Handke met the actress Libgart Schwarz, whom he married soon afterward. Their daughter, Amina, was born in 1969, and in 1972 Handke and his wife separated; Amina continued to live with him. Handke's marriage and divorce and his daughter Amina respectively form the autobiographical cores of the novels *Short Letter, Long Farewell* and *Child Story*. In November, 1971, Handke's mother committed suicide. Handke apparently was deeply shaken by her death; it rekindled long-suppressed memories of his own childhood and of his mother's life of constant stricture and monotony, from which she could free herself only through voluntary death. Within a few months, Handke wrote *A Sorrow Beyond Dreams*, which several critics consider to be his best work.

Repeated moves and frequent travel characterized Handke's life in the decade after 1965. His spectacular appearance at the 1966 conference of Gruppe 47 had launched his career as a serious and financially independent writer, and he quit law school after having passed several preliminary examinations with distinction. His travels led him to Romania, to Yugoslavia, and, in 1971, on a second trip through the United States. During that decade, he moved several times: In 1966, he left Graz for Düsseldorf; in 1968, he moved to Berlin; in 1969, to Paris; in 1971, to Cologne; in 1972, to Kronberg (outside Frankfurt). In 1975, Handke moved back to Paris, thereafter living in Salzburg, the setting for *Der Chinese des Schmerzes* (the Chinese of pain).

Analysis

"Every story distracts me from my real story. Through its fiction it makes me forget myself and my situation. It makes me forget the world." With this statement from his artistic credo, *Ich bin ein Bewohner des Elfenbeinturms*, Peter Handke demonstrated not only the intent of his writing but also his relationship to the art of fiction. For the author Handke and for his reader, the familiar fictional methods of describing the world are no longer valid, since their familiarity is evidence that they are not descriptions of the world itself, but rather copies of other descriptions. Such copies cannot render any new insights; it is the primary function of genuine literature to break open all seemingly finite concepts of the world. The familiarity with and acceptance of the customary methods of description render society incapable of sensing that it is not the world which is being described but rather the method of description, which finally becomes completely automated in a "trivial realism," in advertising and modern mass communication.

Handke's purpose in writing is to gain clarity about himself, to get to know himself, to learn what he does wrong, what he says without thinking, what he says automatically. His goal is to become more attentive and to make other people so—to become more sensitive, more exact in his communication with other people. Improved communication becomes possible through a close investigation of the vehicle of communication itself—namely, language. Handke's method in his investigation is to observe how he, as an individual, continually grows into a linguistic "adulthood" through an increasing awareness of his encounters with the everyday world, with its commonplaces, its extraordinary situations, its images, and particularly its words. The idea of such a "naïve" or natural perception of the world is not altogether new. Friedrich Schiller, in his philosophical essay "Über naive und sentimentalische Dichtung" (1796; "On Naïve and Sentimental Poetry"), had already defined a "naïve poet" as one for whom "language, as if by inner necessity, springs forth from reflection and is so much one with that reflection, that even under the wrappings of the word its sense appears as if unclothed." Similarly, for Handke, as Durzak has observed,

> The images of the perceptible world are not quoted metaphorically via comparisons, which would necessitate a homogeneous and objective system of reality perception anyhow. Rather, they are the immediate internal expressions of the observing ego and can only be comprehended in their pictorial logic from the perspective of the observing ego. The ego has, so to speak, turned its inside out.

As these objects of the outside world become in the true sense of the word "literal" in the mind, they can be expressed only through the words assigned to them. Their power as signature diminishes, however, as soon as the true reality behind the words is forgotten. Handke's argumentation is indebted to the philosophy of Ludwig Wittgenstein, who postulated that language can never be employed as an instrument in the search for truth, since reality itself is obstructed by the tautological fiction of language.

For Handke it therefore becomes essential to transcend the signature character to reach the real object. This can be accomplished by making the reader conscious of the mere signature character of the word and thereby emphasizing the actual reality behind it. Handke renders the signature character of a given word, phrase, or even story obvious through the conscious—perhaps self-conscious—use of language, syntax, and plot structure. These become the "material" through which the individual gains access to the "real reality" beyond. This "real reality" no longer requires the invention of a fable in the traditional sense; as a matter of fact, such fiction obviously hampers access to it. Handke is concerned with the transmission of experiences, linguistic and nonlinguistic, and for this purpose a conventional story is no longer needed. He concedes that literature might lose some of its "entertainment value" through this method, but through it, the reader gains the "real" aspect of each individual sentence, and the individual word in a sentence, once the obstructive fable is stripped away.

Handke's first two novels, *Die Hornissen* and *Der Hausierer* (the peddler), illustrate his theoretical position. They are novels without plots, becoming—in the case of *Die Hornissen*—linguistic exercises which bore the reader to the level of exhaustion, as one critic remarked. *Die Hornissen* represents the creative process of writing a novel rather than the end result of that process. The narrator acts out the perennial dilemma of the writer, who must make choices at all times and who does not—as the reader might imagine from the finished product—have firm control over the action and the characters of the story which he unfolds. Thus, there is no continuity of plot in *Die Hornissen*; instead, there is continuous vacillation between descriptions and explanations, fantasies and dreams. This novel is a writer's confession about the difficulties encountered during his work. Such difficulties can be illustrated only through a plot which the narrator is attempting more or less successfully to construct; thus, there is the trace of a conventional story in *Die Hornissen*. The novel is about two brothers, or perhaps three. One of them has become blind while searching for the second one. A war may have had some influence upon his blindness. On a Sunday, much later, the blind brother awakens and is reminded of his absent brother by something that remains rather vague in his mind. The periodic arrival of the local commuter bus seems to be important for the blind man, who shares a house with his father and his second wife. The Sunday events are reminiscent of events during the war. Shortly before the end of the novel, there is a hint at a possible connection among all of these disjointed elements. The blind narrator thinks of a book, possibly with the title *Die Hornissen*, which he once read. He vaguely remembers some of the events in the book, while he has forgotten particulars. The events still remembered begin to change and become superimposed on events from the present.

Handke had observed that a method of description can be used only once before its repetition becomes the description of the method rather than that of the world, and his second novel, *Der Hausierer*, was an attempt to salvage and revivify a method made moribund by repetition. In it, Handke begins with the perception that the detective story has a plot structure which is always the same, with the same descriptive clichés of murder, death, fear and fright, pursuit and torture. By making his readers conscious of the signature character of these clichés, he wanted to show the true human emotions of fear and pain behind them. *Der Hausierer*, with its barren attempt at making "real reality" perceptible behind a huge inventory of detective-story clichés, has been deemed Handke's most monumental failure in novel-writing to date.

Some early critics thought that this failure, as well as possible difficulties in discovering constantly new descriptive methods, might have forced Handke back into a more conventional narrative stance in his third novel, *The Goalie's Anxiety at the Penalty Kick*. The novel indeed possesses a continuously unfolding plot, clearly defined characters, and a recognizable setting and time frame. Nevertheless, Handke did not abandon his original intention of discovering metaperspectives for himself and his readers. Rather than focusing on language, his investigation this time concentrates on the reliability of psychological causality as it is conventionally depicted in literature. The leitmotif of the novel is the false interpretation of a gesture by the protagonist, Josef Bloch—an "insignificant" event that sets in motion everything which happens thereafter. By describing Bloch's reaction, Handke again questions the validity of a "signature."

A construction worker who was once a well-known soccer goalie, Josef Bloch thinks that he has been fired from his job. Nothing has been said to him to indicate his termination; Bloch has interpreted as a sign of his dismissal the fact that only the foreman looked up from his lunch when Bloch entered the workers' shack, while the other workers continued eating. Out of work, Bloch roams the streets and frequents cheap restaurants and movie houses. He sleeps with a movie usherette, Gerda, whom he chokes to death the following morning. He flees to a small border village to hide out with a former acquaintance, Herta, an innkeeper. The police have no leads in the murder case, yet Bloch's reactions and observations of his surroundings are those of a hunted man. He interprets every event in the village—a missing child who accidentally drowned, inquisitive policemen, customs officials on guard—as connected to him alone. The novel's last scene shows a soccer field, where Bloch asks a bystander to observe the game from the perspective of the goalie, for a change, rather than from that of the players. Bloch's whole life by now has assumed the typical reactive attitude of a goalie defending against a penalty kick, who must try to anticipate the direction in which the opposing player will kick the ball. A comparison to Franz Kafka's *Die Verwandlung* (1915; *Metamorphosis*, 1936) seems to offer itself, as Bloch also undergoes an inner metamorphosis and loses contact with his environment. Handke has stated that it was his intention to portray a protagonist for whom the environment proceeded to turn into a "signature" as a consequence of a single event—namely, the murder: "A schizophrenic interprets every event as alluding to himself. This is the principle behind the story, yet the process is not applied to a schizophrenic, but rather to a 'normal' protagonist." *The Goalie's Anxiety at the Penalty Kick* became a best-seller in Germany shortly after its publication, and it established Handke's reputation in the United States as one of the foremost modern German-language writers.

In 1972, Handke published two novels, *Short Letter, Long Farewell* and *A Sorrow Beyond Dreams*, regarded by many critics as his finest works. The detective-story cliché of the pursuit, which Handke had used in *The Goalie's Anxiety at the Penalty Kick*, is varied once more in *Short Letter, Long Farewell*. The narrator is at once the victim and the detective-observer of the pursuit. The adoption of first-person narrative in this novel as well as in *A Sorrow Beyond Dreams* is significant. Handke's earlier linguistic experimentation, which he had largely overcome in *The Goalie's Anxiety at the Penalty Kick*, was abandoned altogether to make room for the author-narrator's ego and its relationship to the surrounding world. Destabilizing events in Handke's personal life contributed to this new perspective; in an interview, he stated that these events had led to an expansion of his definition of himself. His mother's death, the birth of his daughter, and the protracted proceedings surrounding his divorce from his wife brought on the realization that the automatisms of life itself were as unreliable as the linguistic ones had been found to be. The autobiographical component would be overstated, however, if one were to assume that these events triggered the writing of the two novels in order simply to free the author from his emotional distress. Rather, they are—in a more general sense—"biographical materializations of problems having arisen from human communication per se, which the author now scrutinized from his own experiences," as Durzak suggests. Indeed, Handke has asserted that he had planned the writing of a *Bildungsroman*, a label frequently applied to *Short Letter, Long Farewell*, for almost ten years prior to its date of publication. Also, the novel does remain a typical Handke product, because, in contrast to the traditional novel of education, it educates its author rather than the protagonist.

The author-narrator, no longer merely Handke's abstract alter ego sifting through possible literary methods and models, has become a concrete and discernible individual in his appeal to himself to know and experience more of the world per se in order to reach his goal of cognition. Handke's former protest against stagnant literary conventions has thus given way to his attempt to find the communicative possibilities inherent in his own earlier models. In *Short Letter, Long Farewell*, Handke has gone forward another step in his quest for truth, now seeking the moral veracity of his own writing. The narrator asserts at the end that "all this has really happened," which is, of course, not true in a factual sense, since Handke never really met the film-maker John Ford, as depicted in the last scene of the novel. The "real happening" has taken place inside the author-narrator. Repeated statements in the work indicate that Handke had by then separated himself completely from his earlier linguistic experiments as purely evasive maneuvers, in order to come to terms with his literary environment.

The assessment of a nonliterary and very real environment, which Bloch had attempted unsuccessfully in *The Goalie's Anxiety at the Penalty Kick*, is taken up by the narrator-author of *Short Letter, Long Farewell*, who has traveled to America in search of a new self. The firm ground of his prior existence has begun to sway during the separation from his wife. The fears of his childhood as well as present anxieties and threats must be raised from the subconscious to the level of consciousness. Only then can the narrator, at long last, free himself from them, bid them good-bye, and achieve a new sense of life without fear. The stations of his journey through America become the symbolic backdrop for his gradual liberation. Time and space form a curious congruity in the novel, as the narrator travels from east to west. America's geographic east-west progression in time from infancy to maturity becomes the larger reflection upon the narrator's development, as in St. Louis he separates from his traveling companion Claire and her daughter Benedictine. (Their names are certainly symbolic as well.) The child, through her sudden outbreaks of fright, has helped him to comprehend his own childhood fears. A happily married couple in St. Louis serves as a foil in the narrator's assessment of his ended marriage. After these events, he can embark upon his journey to the new frontiers of America and his own life.

The novel is divided into two parts, entitled "Short Letter" and "Long Farewell," both of which are prefaced by a quote from a *Bildungsroman*. The first part is prefaced by a passage from *Anton Reiser* (1785-1790), by Karl Philipp Moritz, an eighteenth century writer and companion of Goethe. The book, written in the form of an autobiographical account, was of great historical importance to the development of psychological fiction, as it entered the innermost depths of the soul and at the same time attempted to be an objective sociocritical and pedagogical account of the age, thereby combining the two prominent currents of Pietism and Enlightenment thought. The relevance of *Anton Reiser* for Handke becomes obvious in its protagonist's disrupted relationship to his environment. He—like Handke's unnamed narrator—draws his sole understanding of his environment from the books which he reads during his journey. The loneliness, estrangement, and fear of Anton Reiser are shared by Handke's traveler in the first part. The second part, "Long Farewell," is prefaced by a quotation from the Swiss writer Gottfried Keller's *Der grüne Heinrich* (1854-1855; *Green Henry*, 1960), in which the protagonist does finally achieve the elusive union between himself and his environment, between the inner world and the outer world.

Short Letter, Long Farewell is the story of an unnamed Austrian first-person narrator who is being pursued by his estranged wife, Judith. He has arrived in America, endowed with sufficient financial means to undertake what might be referred to ironically as the customary nineteenth century *Bildungsreise* (educational journey)—with the typical Handke twist that it is a *Bildungsreise* in reverse, from Europe to America. In Providence, Rhode Island, he receives a letter from Judith advising him not to look for her, as it "would not be nice" to find her. He travels back to New York, on to Washington, and then to a small town in Pennsylvania, where he is joined by Claire and Benedictine, with whom he continues to the Midwest. From St. Louis, he sets off by himself to Arizona and finally to Oregon: Pursuer and pursued meet at Oregon's Hay Stack Rock. Its enormous granite form, standing alone in the midst of the ocean but at the same time in harmonious union with its natural environment, becomes the backdrop for their encounter, as the narrator faces Judith's pointed gun. Together, Judith and the narrator travel on to California to meet John Ford. Ford's film *Young Mr. Lincoln* (1939) had touched the narrator's inner sense of reality, as the people on the screen prefigured those he would soon meet. Like them, he desires to be fully present in body and mind, an equal moving among equals, carried along by their motion yet free to be himself.

A Sorrow Beyond Dreams replaces the utopian hopefulness of America with a provincial Austrian remembrance of the past, dictated by the finality of death. Handke's mother, who, at the age of fifty-one, lay down to swallow a whole prescription of sleeping pills, bore little resemblance to the young and spirited woman of thirty years earlier. Again, quotations preface the novel, this time by Bob Dylan ("He not busy being born is busy dying") and mystery writer Patricia Highsmith ("Dusk was falling quickly. It was just after 7 P.M., and the month was October"). The quotation of Highsmith is meant to evoke the tone of her novels, which are not tied to spectacular events or extraordinary characters and seem to eschew judgmental statements. Handke's often expressed aversion for characterizing, and thereby judging and degrading, the individual prevails in the *Erzählung* (short narrative). Nevertheless, the author seems to reach far beyond the customary emotional detachment from his earlier and also his later protagonists. *A Sorrow Beyond Dreams* may be considered Handke's first work to strike an emotional chord. In it, as June Schlueter has observed, "the intellectual coldness of the earlier novels gives way to a deeply personal retelling of his mother's life and death."

The metalevel of the narrative, as in *Short Letter, Long Farewell*, remains the differentiated investigation of the author-narrator's ability to perceive his environment as well as an analysis of these perceptions themselves. Thus, the narrator is again the focal point. He explicitly notes the dangerous tendency among abstractions and formulations to grow independent of the person for whose characterization they were created. Consequently, a chain reaction of phrases and sentences sets itself in motion, "as in a dream, a literary ritual in which the life of the individual functions merely as the triggering occasion. Two dangers—the mere realistic retelling of events on the one hand, and the painless disappearance of a person in poetic sentences on the other—these retard my writing." As in his early revolutionary statement at Princeton, Handke thus cautions himself in *A Sorrow Beyond Dreams* against the sterile descriptive tedium of simply retailing a plot, in which he would either permit life itself to tell the story, thereby rendering it without interest to anyone outside his immediate family, or bury the story under an overpowering aesthetic superstructure that would choke it in meaningless poetic formalism.

Handke first had to overcome the stunned perplexity which he felt at reading the obituary notice in the *Kärntner Volkszeitung*. The notice turned his mother's death into a statistic without any further human implication whatsoever. His narration takes its departure from this printed notice: "In the village of A. (G. township), a housewife, aged 51, committed suicide on Friday night by taking an overdose of sleeping pills." Even beyond her death, this woman has thus been denied her existence as an individual. The author-narrator becomes the "remembering and formulating machine" which will restore to his mother what is rightfully hers, at the same time departing, as in *Short Letter, Long Farewell*, on a voyage into his own childhood, which he begins to see in a different light through the description of his mother's life. Two continuous impediments seem to have stifled his mother's attempts at individuation: the socially conditioned, material limitations during her youth, exemplified in the description of the grandfather, and her individually motivated depressions, which she felt as a result of the growing automatisms of her particular life as a woman, for whom a palm reading at the county fair, which was to reveal the future, was nothing but a cruel joke. Handke quotes a rhyme which the girls in her village chanted about the stations in a woman's life: "Tired/ Exhausted/ Sick/ Dying/ Dead."

As the son begins to study at the university, he introduces her to literature: "She read every book as a description of her own life, felt revitalized, learned to speak about herself . . . and so I gradually found out details about her life." Different from those in *Short Letter, Long Farewell*, Maria Handke's visions gleaned from books are only those of the past, making obvious to her the fact that she has no future. Having led his mother to the Tree of Knowledge, the son has become the tempter in the Garden of Eden and therefore is, at least in part, responsible for her death.

A Sorrow Beyond Dreams was Handke's second attempt to "describe the political circumstances as part of an individual story, to connect the individual with the general events." At the same time, the author could reach into himself within a concrete and historically verifiable context instead of his usual private method. This has made *A Sorrow Beyond Dreams* his most lucid and most successful work to date.

In *A Moment of True Feeling* and *The Left-Handed Woman*, Handke made two renewed attempts at reaching a higher level of feeling beyond the usual literary clichés. Yet in the same measure in which he strove to depict these truer feelings, he seems to have missed his mark because of an increasing abandonment of a concretely discernible narrative. *A Moment of True Feeling* has been labeled "an angry act of regression," and *The Left-Handed Woman* "as closed as an oyster, a sign- and signal-labyrinth similar to the universe of a schizophrenic, in which language no longer serves the purpose of communicating, but rather to encode communication."

The diary *The Weight of the World* is the harbinger of Handke's new perception of the world during the 1980's. German critics have been divided in their response to this work; some have seen it as an "inventory of [Handke's] delusions of grandeur," a "trite game of hide-and-go-seek with notes arbitrarily strung together," while others have regarded it as an expansion of Handke's earlier efforts to overcome the shortfalls and deficiencies of language on a higher and more sophisticated level. Peter Pütz states that *The Weight of the World* is Handke's most radical attempt "to note, catalogue and thus preserve all appearances, experiences and acts of consciousness" in a preselective state, when their value has not yet been conditioned by human judgments. Everything should be freed from the superfluous value which humans attach to it, permitting a fresh assessment of the world's net weight.

Handke widens the focus from singular things, perceptions, and feelings and the intended preservation of their individual weight in his next novel, *The Long Way Around*. There, he strives to uncover the connection between all things as well as their salutary harmony. During his slow homecoming to Europe from the snowy loneliness of Alaska via California and New York, Valentin Sorger, the protagonist of the novel, rediscovers nature as the new essence of reality. In California, Sorger had lost his sense of space under the impact of his return to civilization; in a New York coffee shop, he regains the consciousness of his "earthen form" and subsequently regards his return to Europe as the beginning of a prophetic revelation. There exists an immediate connection between natural things, which phantasy must uncover or—more skeptically—to which Sorger "must apply his own lie." Glimpses of such nature revelations can be found in Handke's earlier novels—for example, in the heaving cypress tree in *Short Letter, Long Farewell* and in the chestnut-tree leaf in *A Moment of True Feeling*. In *The Long Way Around* and *The Lesson of Mont-Sainte-Victoire*, these revelations of nature become the essence of reality altogether.

In *The Lesson of Mont-Sainte-Victoire*, a narrative situated somewhere between a short story and an essay, the protagonist of the trilogy has returned to Europe. The narrative perspective has changed from the third to the first person to allow Handke to supply the theoretical supplement for the trilogy that comprises *The Long Way Around*, *The Lesson of Mont-Sainte-Victoire*, and the dramatic poem *Über die Dörfer*. Biblical allusions abound, as well as references to Goethe's *Zur Farbenlehre* and Friedrich von Schlegel's *Universalpoesie*, in which artistic endeavor overcomes the boundaries between writing and painting, poetry and philosophy, and also between present and past, fact and phantasy. Nature, as revealed in art, becomes the author's weapon against the "calcified Federal Republic which has grown more and more evil" and against the raw brutality of a madly barking dog along the narrator's path. Mont-Sainte-Victoire, near the southern French city of Aix-en-Provence, was painted repeatedly by Paul Cézanne during his most creative years after 1870. In these paintings, the narrator perceives the perfect synthesis between the eternal and the transitory, between nature and human endeavor. As the narrator climbs the mountain for a second time, "the realm of the words" lies suddenly open before him, "with the Great Spirit of The Form." He senses the structure of all things in himself as the ready substance of the works which he will write. His future works will be devoted to the metamorphosis of nature into art and the salvation of those things threatened by the world of man.

Handke's attempt in *Child Story* to repeat the delicate balance of the inner with the outer world, which he had achieved in *A Sorrow Beyond Dreams*, met with mixed reactions from the critics. The narrator's daughter begins to loosen her bonds with him at the age of ten or eleven, and he reflects on her influence on him and his writing during the decade of their lives together. In the spirit of *The Lesson of Mont-Sainte-Victoire*, the novel is Handke's attempt at saving the endangered daughter and eternalizing her. Some critics have noted the "insurmountable ego-stylization" in the novel and have criticized Handke for turning his daughter into a marketable commodity; others interpret the book as Handke's successful redemption from the "almost choking solipsism" that he had displayed in *The Lesson of Mont-Sainte-Victoire* and *The Long Way Around*. His *Der Chinese des Schmerzes* seem to indicate Handke's return to the messianic stance of those two novels, in this case filtered through the classical restraint of a first-person narrator who is a teacher of Greek and Latin; his name, Loser, might be translated as "the listener." Loser goes further than the protagonists of Handke's earlier novels in his attempts to preserve that which is in danger. He removes language from nature by destroying election posters and slogans which have been attached to trees, and in the second part of the novel, he intervenes decisively by hurling a stone and thereby killing a swastika painter who has desecrated a mountain. "The mountain must remain empty," he triumphs over the murdered man. A circle in Handke's work seems to close with Andreas Loser, a teacher of classical languages and an etymologist whose favorite work is Vergil's *Georgics* (c. 37-29 B.C.).

Throughout Handke's novels, the unusually close bond between author and work seems to have been both a source of strength and a liability. Handke's early questioning of the automatisms of postwar German literature—and consequently the automatisms of life altogether—required the undetached participation of the author in his works, for Handke, like the schizophrenic whom he mentions in his discussion of *The Goalie's Anxiety at the Penalty Kick*, needed to interpret every event as alluding to him and him alone. Such a schizophrenic stance made Handke the outsider from the start, and it has led almost automatically to some of the narcissistic excesses in his recent novels, in which he has begun to regard himself as an isolated seer who can save himself and the world from the forces of these automatisms through an intense, more direct, and somewhat mystical kinship with nature, as it had already been advocated by his nineteenth century compatriot, the Austrian novelist Adalbert Stifter. Such prophetic visions have naturally antagonized some of Handke's critics, who see him as having moved dangerously close to a Nazi *Blut und Boden Romantik* (blood and earth romanticism).

Major publications other than long fiction
SHORT FICTION: *Begrüssung des Aufsichtsrats*, 1967.
PLAYS: *Publikumsbeschimpfung*, 1966 (*Offending the Audience*, 1969); *Hilferufe*, 1967 (*Calling for Help*, 1971); *Kaspar*, 1968 (English translation, 1969); *Kaspar and Other Plays*, 1969; *Das Mündel will Vormund sein*, 1969 (*My Foot My Tutor*, 1971); *Quodlibet*, 1970 (English translation, 1976); *Der Ritt über den Bodensee*, 1971 (*The Ride Across Lake Constance*, 1973); *Chronik der laufenden Ereignisse*, 1971 (film script); *Die Unvernünftigen sterben aus*, 1973 (*They Are Dying Out*, 1977); *Falsche Bewegung*, 1975 (television script); *The Ride Across Lake Constance and Other Plays*, 1976; *Über die Dörfer*, 1981.
POETRY: *Die Innenwelt der Aussenwelt der Innenwelt*, 1969.
NONFICTION: *Ich bin ein Bewohner des Elfenbeinturms*, 1972.

Bibliography
Durzak, Manfred. *Peter Handke und die deutsche Gegenwartsliteratur*, 1982.
Mixner, Manfred. *Peter Handke*, 1977.
Rorrison, Hugh. "The 'Grazer Gruppe,' Peter Handke and Wolfgang Bauer," in *Modern Austrian Writing: Literature and Society After 1945*, 1980. Edited by Alan Best and Hans Wolfschütz.
Scharang, Michael. *Über Peter Handke*, 1972.
Schleuter, June. *The Plays and Novels of Peter Handke*, 1981.

Klaus Hanson

JAROSLAV HAŠEK

Born: Prague, Bohemia; April 30, 1883
Died: Lipnice, Czechoslovakia; January 2, 1923

Principal long fiction

Osudy dobrého vojáka Švejka ve světove války, 1921-1923 (4 volumes; *The Good Soldier Schweik*, 1930; also as *The Good Soldier Švejk and His Fortunes in the World War*, 1973).

Other literary forms

Apart from his single masterpiece, Jaroslav Hašek wrote more than twelve hundred short stories, *feuilletons*, and articles, the best of which were published in a collection translated by Cecil Parrott, *The Red Commissar: Including Further Adventures of the Good Soldier Švejk and Other Stories* (1981).

Achievements

Hašek was too controversial to be accepted as a great writer in his time. His great unfinished masterpiece, *The Good Soldier Schweik*, sharply divided critics into those who rejected him (most of the literary establishment) and those who understood the originality and comic genius of the novel. Among the latter belonged Max Brod, the biographer of Franz Kafka, and Ivan Olbracht, a noted novelist. Indeed, the biggest spurt toward the worldwide renown of the novel came from Prague's German community following Grete Rainer's German translation in 1926. The novel then established its reputation in Europe as an antimilitarist satire and as a great comic novel. A film version of the novel, *Der brave Soldat Schwejk (The Good Soldier Schweik*, 1963), was produced in Germany in 1960.

The main achievement of Hašek lies in combining two kinds of satire: on the one hand, topical, historical, political satire of the Austro-Hungarian military machinery; on the other, satire of human nature. This satire is communicated through a unique and sometimes enigmatic character, Josef Schweik, whose stories manifest a distillation of popular wisdom used as a weapon against the inimical environment.

Hašek's influence on the subsequent development of Czech prose has been overwhelming and not always salutary. Hašek's humor at its most subtle is inimitable and wholly his own: Superficial adaptations fall flat. Hašek's book does not have a rival in its genre in this century; the closest equivalent (though distant in time and in its concept of comedy) might be H. J. C. von Grimmelshausen's *Der abenteurliche Simplicissimus* (1669; *The Adventurous Simplicissimus*, 1912). The appearance of direct descendants of *The Good Soldier Schweik* (as in Bertolt Brecht's 1957 play, *Schwejk im zweiten Weltkrieg*) and indirect traces in the works of satirists as diverse as Joseph Heller (in his

Catch-22, 1961) and Vladimir Voinovich (in his Chonkin books) reveal the
enduring influence of Hašek's masterpiece.

Biography

Jaroslav Hašek's life and Jaroslav Hašek's legend are difficult to disentangle.
He was a Bohemian, a hoaxer, a joker, and a very irresponsible man. His
exaggerations, embellishments, and mystifications make the few testimonials
by his friends suspect. Even the little that is verifiable about him does not
make him look too good: He was by turns an anarchist, a monarchist, and a
Communist; he was a bigamist who, like his father, died an alcoholic.

Hašek was only thirteen when his father died and, because of the family's
poverty, he had to work in a chemist's shop. He returned to school and was
admitted to a commercial academy, where he appears to have acquitted himself very well indeed. On account of his good record, he obtained a position
in a bank but was unable to keep his job and started to write short *feuilletons*.
His journalistic activity fell short of supplying him with steady or sufficient
income and only encouraged his Bohemian proclivities.

In 1906, Hašek joined the anarchist movement and met Jarmila Mayerová,
with whom he fell deeply in love. Jarmila thought that she could influence
him to abandon his vagabond life; she had a great willingness to understand
him, although her middle-class parents were hoping she would marry a more
respectable man. Hašek's involvement with anarchism and his reluctance to
lead a different life postponed the wedding until 1910, a good year for his
literary production as well: He wrote and published seventy-five stories.

The following year, 1911, he published the first stories about the good
soldier Schweik. While this prototype of Schweik bears some resemblance to
the end product, it is but a rough sketch: The humor seems forced, despite
the occasional dash of genuine comedy.

After Jarmila bore him a son, in 1912, Hašek resumed his Bohemian existence, becoming so alienated from society that he refused to register his
residence, as was required by law, preferring instead to spend a few days at
a time with some of his friends, often disappearing from Prague with common
vagabonds. At the same time, he continued to write stories prolifically, living
a rather carefree life until 1915, at which time he was drafted into the Austrian
army.

World War I was the key experience of Hašek's life, and it would be fair
to say that it changed him for the better. Surprisingly, though he was to turn
his experience in the Austrian army into a masterpiece of satire that suggests
lifelong military involvement, Hašek remained an Austrian soldier for only
a few months; he was taken prisoner in September, 1915, by the Russians,
after the latter's sudden counterattack. It is rather the larger view of the war
as seen from the prisoner-of-war camp that shaped his thinking. More important still, the most enigmatic part of Hašek's life, his involvement in the

Russian Civil War, must also have added to his violent outburst against militarism present in his masterpiece.

The enigma of Hašek's participation rests in the apparent fact that Hašek managed for the duration of his participation in the Civil War in Russia to change himself into a teetotaler and a committed Communist who advanced the cause by, among other activities, his journalistic propaganda among the foreign troops of the Red Army in Ufa and later in Siberia. It is not altogether clear how strong his commitment was throughout his stay, but after the Communist victory, he returned to Prague with a Russian wife, resuming his irresponsible life-style and ignoring Communist Party orders to work as an agitator in a mining district.

Hašek's return was ignominious. He was, after all, a deserter from the Czechoslovak Legion that fought the Bolsheviks in the Russian Civil War. He was not prosecuted on account of the amnesty proclaimed after the establishment of the Republic of Czechoslovakia in 1918, and he also was not prosecuted for bigamy, but that still did not change the minds of those who considered him a traitor. He found it very hard to adapt to the new circumstances, but his Russian wife demanded that he try to make money one way or another, and it was then that Hašek decided to attempt to write a long novel; the result was his masterpiece.

Hašek could not find a publisher for the first volume of the projected four and published it privately. It was a success, and the remaining volumes were eagerly accepted by a publisher. Having started the novel in 1921, Hašek continued writing until his death in 1923. He had bought a modest cottage in Lipnice on the Sázava River, and while it was a good move to go to Lipnice and to concentrate on writing, his health was not improved, for he continued drinking, which aggravated his illness and hastened his death.

The success that Hašek lived to enjoy was only a faint portent of the world fame that came to his masterpiece a few years after his death, yet it is doubtful whether even this would have surprised him.

Analysis

Jaroslav Hašek's *The Good Soldier Schweik* had its genesis in 1911, the time of the publication of the first of his Schweik stories; in a broader sense, his preparation for the work included his whole conscious life. One way to look at his masterpiece is to see it as a compendium of almost three hundred stories told by Schweik or other characters.

The type of story that one finds in the novel is usually likened to a "pub story" (*die Gasthausgeschichte*). It is of anecdotal construction and is often produced as an illustration of some thought, as support for some opinion, or, apologetically, as justification of a certain kind of behavior. There is, however, one important modification in Hašek's story that sets it apart from a common anecdote. A successful anecdote is characterized by a construction in which the "story" moves swiftly toward its "point," with minimal hindrance and no digressions. Not so in Hašek's tale. With Hašek, it is the digression, the often irrelevant detail, the play on words, the humorous inventiveness that is characteristic.

The fact that the novel is a collection of so many stories has no effect on its unity. Most of the stories come from the main character, Schweik, and they always serve to illustrate a particular point of the main and rather skeletal plot. The plot itself can be summarized briefly: Josef Schweik, who has been making a living by selling dogs whose pedigrees he often forged and who has been certified by the military as an imbecile, is drafted in World War I and transported to the front. Schweik never sees combat, since the writing of the fourth volume, which would have taken him to the front line, was interrupted by Hašek's death. It is to Hašek's credit that he could flesh out this austere plot with vivacity and excitement, mostly derived from humor surrounding the main character, Schweik, coming either from the descriptions of Schweik's activities or from the stories Schweik and other characters recount.

Another integrating element of the novel is satire. *The Good Soldier Schweik* is a satiric novel, perhaps the greatest satiric novel written in the twentieth century. The subgenre in which it could be classified is that of antimilitarist satire, though it is mixed with another type of satire: the satire of human nature, or misanthropic satire. The success of the novel can be attributed to the mixture of these two kinds of satire; one type strengthens the other, and vice versa.

Hašek's salvos against the high and mighty are more pronounced and more numerous than his excursions into misanthropic satire, wherein the little guy becomes a target as well. This notwithstanding, it would be a grave mistake to portray Hašek as a champion of the downtrodden—he is far too cynical for that. Nevertheless, this is precisely what the literary establishment in Czechoslovakia and other Communist countries has done. By their account, Hašek is an "exemplary novelist of the proletariat, despite occasional ideological errors." While Hašek's political sympathies might support this view, a close reading of his novel does nothing of the sort. On the contrary, as the famous Czech novelist Milan Kundera has suggested, it is Hašek's "blasphemy"—that is, his misanthropic satire—that is often overlooked and deserves to be studied and noticed more.

The Austro-Hungarian Empire is no more; it was already gone at the time of the writing of the novel. This means that the satiric attacks aimed at the Empire, the court, and so on were even then less important to the author than the catalog of stupidity that he found flourishing in the military milieu.

It is the atmosphere of the crisis, of the war, of tremendous stress on the individual that reveals best the real qualities of human beings. The novel also evokes the mood of disillusionment following the terrible clash of the idealistic expectations of the nineteenth century with the reality of mass murder engineered on a gigantic scale by World War I.

One should not forget that the great formative period of Hašek's life was spent in revolutionary Russia, where he witnessed the blood, famine, and pestilence of the new Leviathan; this, too, may have contributed to his doubts about the ability of humans to order their affairs rationally, or bring about true freedom, as he, when he was a young anarchist, once envisioned it.

Hašek was a natural comic; his comic genius is apparent in the many stories that he wrote for the papers in his youth. He always found it easy to laugh at the world, to look at the comical side, resolutely rejecting the serious approach to life, refusing the responsibility often asked of him. In addition to this proven natural comic ability, however, it is possible to witness in his fiction the development of a sophisticated artist.

The true value of the art that Hašek's comedy represents can easily be measured by comparing Hašek's novel with two previous attempts to write about Schweik. In none of the stories written in 1911 or in 1917 does one encounter the ambiguous and accomplished raconteur and trickster Schweik of the great novel. All of these attempts seem heavy-handed; they lack the highly successful amalgam of two kinds of satires, the political and the misanthropic, achieved only in Hašek's masterpiece.

While the public success of the novel was immediate, critical acclaim came slowly, but when it arrived, it elevated Hašek to the first rank of comic geniuses. Critics have acknowledged the ambiguities in Hašek's work and the disturbing question of his misanthropy, but these have been judged of lesser importance when compared to the significance of Hašek's inventiveness, his imagination, and his playful exploitation of language for the purposes of comedy. It is fair to say that at best, Hašek's comedy transcends the narrowly partisan limits that are suggested in some of his more heavy-handed writing and takes its rightful place next to Miguel de Cervantes and François Rabelais in literature, and Molière and Charlie Chaplin in the broader area of the art of comedy.

Major publications other than long fiction
SHORT FICTION: *Dobrý voják Švejk a jiné podivné historky*, 1912.
POETRY: *Májove výkřiky*, 1903.
MISCELLANEOUS: *The Red Commissar: Including Further Adventures of the Good Soldier Švejk and Other Stories*, 1981.

Bibliography
Frynta, Emanuel. *Hašek, the Creator of Švejk*, 1965.
Parrott, Cecil. *The Bad Bohemian: A Life of Jaroslav Hašek*, 1978.
——————— . *Jaroslav Hašek: A Study of 'Švejk' and the Short Stories*, 1982.

Peter Petro

ALFRED HAUGE

Born: Stjernarøy, Norway; October 17, 1915

Principal long fiction

Septemberfrost, 1941; *Tuntreet blør*, 1942; *Storm over Siglarholmen*, 1945; *Ropet*, 1946; *Året har ingen vår*, 1948; *Fossen og bålet*, 1949; *Vegen til det døde paradiset*, 1951; *Ingen kjenner dagen*, 1955; *Kvinner på Galgebakken*, 1958; *Cleng Peerson*, 1961-1965 (includes *Hundevakt*, 1961; *Landkjenning*, 1964; *Ankerfeste*, 1965; abridged English translation of *Cleng Peerson*, 1975); *Mysterium*, 1967; *Legenden om Svein og Maria*, 1968; *Perlemorstrand*, 1974; *Leviathan*, 1979 (includes "Forvandling").

Other literary forms

Although known primarily as a novelist, Alfred Hauge has also produced works of short prose, poetry, drama, and nonfiction. Much of his short prose and nonfiction originally appeared in the daily newspaper *Stavanger aftenblad*, where he has been employed as a cultural correspondent for more than thirty years. In conjunction with the research for his trilogy about Cleng Peerson, the father of Norwegian emigration to America, he traced the movement of the immigrants across the American continent, and two books, *Gå vest—* (1963; go west) and *Gjennom Amerika i emigrantspor* (1975; through America in the footsteps of the emigrants), resulted from these travels. Later came *Sannferdig saga om Cleng Peerson* (1982; the true saga of Cleng Peerson), which is a factual presentation of the results of Hauge's research and which was published by the Norwegian Society of Texas on the bicentennial of Peerson's birth, May 17, 1982. Two other important volumes of nonfiction are Hauge's autobiographical *Barndom* (1975; childhood) and *Ungdom* (1977; youth).

Hauge has also used the Cleng Peerson material dramatically in his play *Cleng Peerson: Utvandring* (1968; Cleng Peerson: emigration), but on the whole he has given relatively little attention to drama. Poetry is more important to him; his first collection, entitled *Skyer i drift over vårgrønt land* (1945; clouds drifting over land green in spring), sold well but was not a critical success. In 1970 came *Det evige sekund* (the eternal second), the third volume in Hauge's hitherto unfinished *magnum opus*, the Utstein Monastery Cycle.

Achievements

Hauge occupies a singular position in contemporary Norwegian literature. One of its ablest novelists, he has been inventive both thematically and formally. It is even more remarkable that he has reached his qualitative high at an age when many writers are in decline. His novel *Mysterium* (mystery), the first volume in his Utstein Monastery Cycle, is clearly one of the very finest works of post-World War II literature in Norway, and the yet unfinished series to which he has contributed *Perlemorstrand* (a shore made of mother-of-pearl) and *Leviathan* may equal it in significance.

The author is even better known for his emigrant novels. His trilogy about Cleng Peerson was translated into English and published in a two-volume, abridged edition in 1975 as part of the sesquicentennial celebration of Norwegian emigration to the United States. It is Hauge's later novels, however, which stand as his greatest artistic achievement.

Biography

Alfred Hauge was born on October 17, 1915, the oldest child of Kolbein Andersson Hauge and Marianne Rasmusdotter Auglend. His mother's family came from the Jæren district, south of Stavanger, Norway; his father's family lived at Stjernarøy, an island to the northeast, where Hauge grew up. Both sides of the family were farmers. The area is one of the strongholds of popular pietistic religiosity in Norway, and Hauge early accepted the religious ideas that were present in his surroundings.

Having received his basic education in the public schools at home, Hauge traveled to Bryne, Jæren, at the age of fifteen to attend a college preparatory school for young people of rural origin. He later transferred to a similar school at Voss, east of Bergen, where, in addition to other academic subjects, he was able to receive instruction in Greek. In 1935, he entered the University of Oslo in order to study theology. In 1937, however, he gave up theology and entered a teacher's college, from which he was graduated two years later. He first worked as a teacher at a folk high school, then as a literary consultant for a publishing house, and from 1953 as a cultural correspondent for the daily paper *Stavanger aftenblad*. He married Kirsten Væhle on July 27, 1940.

Hauge's literary debut took place in 1941, when he published *Septemberfrost* (the frost of September), a historical novel with a message of encouragement to people in occupied Norway. Then came several novels in which the author drew on his intimate knowledge of life in western Norway; their main value lies in their faithful portrayal of a local community at a time of transition from the old agrarian social order to a twentieth century society. Two novels from this period, *Ropet* (the call) and *Ingen kjenner dagen* (nobody knows the day), also treat the conflict between religious and artistic demands so keenly felt by the author.

Hauge became internationally known for his *Cleng Peerson*, a trilogy based on the life of the man who has been called the father of Norwegian emigration to America. Then came the novel *Mysterium*, the first volume of his hitherto unfinished Utstein Monastery Cycle, which also includes the poetry collection *Det evige sekund* and the novels *Legenden om Svein og Maria* (the legend of Svein and Maria), *Perlemorstrand*, and *Leviathan*.

Hauge appears still to be at his best as a writer; he is at work on an additional Utstein Monastery volume and is planning a book concerning Norwegian emigration to New Zealand.

Analysis

Alfred Hauge's main concern as a writer is to deepen his understanding of the human soul. The philosophical content in his novels is therefore substantial, but that does not mean that his works are removed from the real world. His early books are firmly anchored in the sociological reality that he knew from his own upbringing. The Cleng Peerson trilogy succeeds admirably in re-creating both the Norwegian surroundings of the emigrants and the new world they encountered in America. *Perlemorstrand* and *Leviathan* both draw on the author's intimate knowledge of life in western Norway in the early part of the twentieth century.

The sociological and historical material found in Hauge's books is, however, subordinate to his real concerns. A religious and existential humanist, Hauge asks both the question of how man should act toward other human beings and how he should relate to the divine. Above all, Hauge considers how man can achieve the greatest personal growth through full participation in life. His tentative answers are informed both by his nondogmatic Christian faith and by the results of his self-analysis, which is influenced by Jungian thought. Hauge's literary works clearly show that his personal quest for understanding has been a strenuous one.

The personal nature of Hauge's works is reflected in their form. The early novels were written primarily in the third person, but most of his later books are narrated from the first-person point of view. In *Cleng Peerson*, the narrator is the aged Cleng, who relates the story of his life in terms of a never-ending search for understanding of both self and others. In *Mysterium, Perlemorstrand*, and *Leviathan*, the narrator is formally identical with the author. It is, however, in the later novels that Hauge's innovative narrative technique most forcefully strikes the reader.

Written during a period of some twenty-five years, the trilogy about Cleng Peerson required considerable research and other formal preparation. Its main theme is man's quest for liberty. Through the story of Cleng's personal search for understanding, Hauge describes the striving for that personal freedom which comes only as a result of a man's being at peace with himself through self-knowledge. Through his portrayal of the emigration movement, Hauge describes people's search for religious, political, and economic liberty.

In the first volume of the trilogy, *Hundevakt* (midwatch), Cleng tells the story of his childhood, youth, and early manhood. The book begins with the young child's attempt to sail to the sun in a small boat. This voyage serves as an illustration of the individual's search for wholeness; according to Jungian thought, the sun is a symbol of both the integrated self and man's unity with the divine. The young Cleng is largely unsuccessful in his quest, however, for he is both a scoundrel among men and a sinner before his God. While basically well-meaning, he is unable to distinguish fact from fiction and often tells tall tales, a practice which has a disastrous effect on his associates.

During the Napoleonic wars, Cleng and a number of other Norwegians spend several years on board British prison ships. Some of them become Quakers, and after their return to Norway they are severely persecuted by the civil and religious authorities. One of their options is to emigrate to America, and although not formally a member of the group, Cleng is sent off as a scout. Upon his return, he characteristically exaggerates the virtues of the new land. The second volume of the trilogy, *Landkjenning* (landfall), tells of the trials the emigrants undergo and for which Cleng is to a large extent responsible. This novel and the third one, *Ankerfeste* (anchorage), tell the story of early Norwegian emigration in both broad outline and significant detail. The economic hardships are shown, but Hauge's focus is on the emigrants' striving for religious development. Removed from the authority of the Norwegian State Church, they fall prey to all manner of religious enthusiasms, the most dangerous of which, from Cleng's point of view at least, seems to be Mormonism. The men and women who join the various sects are all searching for spiritual wholeness. So is Cleng, who even goes as far as to seek it by chemical means. Through a substance derived from mushrooms, he is initiated into an ancient religious mystery by the Indian chief Shabbona, and the result is that he finally gains a measure of self-knowledge. While in the altered state of consciousness brought on by the drug, he has a vision of himself sitting on a throne like a god, while a figure who looks like both a medieval fool and a rooster (but who, at the same time, is Cleng himself) is dancing around the throne. Cleng thus learns that throughout his life he has worshiped only himself and that his various attempts at charitable acts have been a part of this self-worship. This is a haunting scene which, slightly varied, returns in Hauge's next novel, *Mysterium*.

At the end of the trilogy, Cleng has obtained a modicum of serenity. On the whole, however, his quest for self-knowledge and integration of the personality has failed. Because he did not reach his human potential, he is fundamentally a tragic figure.

Cleng Peerson's development constitutes a partially failed, partially successful process of individuation which is portrayed against the backdrop of the early Norwegian emigration to America. The protagonist in *Mysterium* also undergoes a process of individuation, but in his case the historical and sociological backdrop is almost entirely lacking. *Mysterium* therefore strikes some readers as rather abstract.

When the novel was first published, it was particularly the narrative technique which surprised the reviewers. The first-person narrator, who is formally identical with the author, repeatedly addresses the reader, discusses the novel's characters and their actions "with" him, and even invites him to finish the work (the last sentence in the book ends with a colon, and the reader is asked to fill in two names). The novel also has little action in the traditional sense. A victim of amnesia named Victor arrives at a place that can be identified as Utstein Monastery in western Norway. There he meets a Greek professor of archaeology named Hermes Oneiropompos. Victor is searching for his lost memory so that he might know where to find his wife and daughter.

The illusion of reality is completely shattered, however, when Victor and the professor begin exploring some tunnels and caverns under the monastery. It soon becomes apparent that their wanderings are actually taking place in the hidden recesses of Victor's unconscious. These experiences are also supplemented by reports of dreams that Victor has between his trips with Oneiropompos. The text thus takes on the appearance of a psychiatrist's journal; Victor is the patient and Oneiropompos (whose name means "he who guides through dreams"), the analyst. Victor finally comes out of the amnesia, remembering that he left his wife and lost his memory at a time when she was in the midst of a sudden attack of pain caused by a malignant brain tumor. He is now ready to return to her and to face the effects that her illness will have on their life together.

In the course of the analysis, it becomes clear that Victor's nervous breakdown with its accompanying amnesia occurred not only because of his inability to tolerate the sight of his wife's suffering but also because her impending death forcefully reminded him of the fact that he, too, must die. His awareness of his concern for self in the face of his wife's crisis causes him to feel deeply ashamed. This feeling manifests itself in a series of three dreams which emphasize the tension between appearance and reality, as well as in a scene during the first journey through the subterranean vaults. In this scene, which is reminiscent of a similar one toward the end of *Cleng Peerson*, Victor sees himself sitting on a throne as a god, and a figure which is half himself and half turkey is dancing around the throne.

Throughout *Mysterium*, Hauge encourages the reader to compare himself to Victor and to search his own soul in order to determine if he possesses the human qualities of empathy, tenderness, and the ability to sustain others through suffering, which Victor is partly lacking. Victor's process of individuation advances in the course of the novel; through archetypal symbolism, Hauge attempts to engage not only the reader's intellect but also his unconscious. *Mysterium* thus becomes a kind of Jungian *Bildungsroman* in that it attempts to further the reader's process of individuation by portraying that of its main character.

Hauge's question of how to achieve an integrated self is one which is typical of existential humanism. The answer, which also has strong religious overtones, is to be found in the most important symbol in the novel—namely, a rotating cross to which human beings have been fastened. The cross is a symbol of suffering, but through its rotation it takes on the appearance of a sun, the Jungian symbol of both the unity of the self and the divine, which is also central to *Cleng Peerson*. The author's message is that man can both achieve unity of the self and move closer to the divine by passing through suffering and by actively identifying with the suffering of others, thus helping them bear their burdens.

Mysterium and the two novels that will be dealt with in this section belong to Hauge's Utstein Monastery Cycle, a group of thematically related works that stress the need to develop the quintessentially human qualities of empathy, tenderness, and the ability to accompany others through suffering. *Perlemorstrand* and *Leviathan* constitute a subgroup within the cycle, "Århundre" (century). The theme of these two books is similar to that of *Mysterium*, but in the later works, Hauge includes a historical-philosophical dimension that is not present in the earlier book. This philosophy of history informs his choice of narrative technique and is expressed in mythic fashion in a prose poem, "Forvandling" (metamorphosis), which is found both in the author's poetry collection *Det evige sekund* and in *Leviathan*.

"Forvandling" relates the story of a young nobleman and a woman of the people who have a beautiful daughter named Iselin. At the age of five, however, she is suddenly changed into an ugly monster. The parents seek means by which the process can be reversed, but Iselin becomes more monstrous each time another remedy is applied. She finally returns to her normal state, however, and accepts a suitor's proposal of marriage. In the ensuing marriage ceremony, which takes place in church, the groom is called Isidor Saeculum XX, and the bride is called Iselin Saeculum XV. The two are wed but are immediately changed into the fragrance of roses and blood. At the same time, the life processes of their parents are reversed; they gradually become two newborn infants. The priest then christens the father Isidor Saeculum XXI and the mother Iselin Saeculum XVI.

On one level, this prose poem deals with parenthood and the commitment of parents to a child who must pass through much mental and physical suffering. On the historical-philosophical level, however, Hauge allegorically expresses his view that the fifteenth century and the twentieth century are basically similar, in that both can be characterized as periods of fundamental change in social conditions.

The fifteenth century brought about the historical situation in which the Reformation later took place, and the concomitant religious and political upheavals caused people to lose their spiritual bearings. The result was growing fear and superstition; figuratively, because Saeculum XVI was the result of Saeculum XV, the events of Saeculum XXI will be the result of the actions of Saeculum XX, which have caused the present generation to lose the firmer spiritual foundation of the past.

With the exception of the participants in the myth described in "Forvandling," the characters in both *Perlemorstrand* and *Leviathan* are squarely anchored in a historical and social reality, as both novels are set on a small island which appears to have been modeled on the one where Hauge was reared. The main character is Bodvar Staup, and the first-person narrator, who is virtually identical to Hauge, is one of Bodvar's childhood friends. In *Perlemorstrand*, which the author/narrator says was written during the months of September and October, 1973, the narrator primarily tells the story of Bodvar's childhood during the decade of 1920 to 1930. The events of the period are thus seen from the perspective of a contemporary observer who was then a child and who at the time of writing is a man well past the middle of his life. There is an additional temporal level, however, for the narrator also tells about a period that he and Bodvar spent together at Utstein Monastery during the month of June, 1973. At this time, they often talked about the events of their common childhood. The narrator is thus able to give the reader access to Bodvar's own childhood memories, and the author's use of several temporal levels enables him to create a panorama of the twentieth century.

The story of Bodvar Staup is brief. He grows up together with his first cousin and foster brother, Mons, and the two are rivals for the love of their common aunt and stepmother. Bodvar, who before his father's remarriage had the upper hand in his relationship with Mons, sees that he is no longer favored and becomes intensely jealous. The narration on the first temporal level ends when Bodvar brings Mons and another of their aunts, Tina, to a drinking bout at the home of a questionable character named Kid Skarvaskjer. The two boys and Tina get drunk, but Bodvar leaves before completely losing control. While both Mons and Tina are in a stupor, Tina is raped by Kid, who then leaves the island. Mons awakens, sees the bloody Tina, believes that he has committed the crime, and takes his own life.

Bodvar, who believes that he is responsible for his brother's death, has a nervous breakdown. He spends some time in a mental institution but continues to feel a desperate need to atone by taking upon himself the suffering of others. The narration on the second temporal level, or the month of June, 1973, ends with one of Bodvar's numerous failures to remove suffering from other people.

In *Leviathan*, Bodvar's story is continued on three temporal levels corresponding to those of the previous novel: a level of remembered experience spanning the years from 1930 to 1970; a second level, when Bodvar and the narrator are together at Utstein Monastery in the summer of 1981 (note that the book was published in 1979); and the time when the story is being written down by the author/narrator, in January, 1979. The burden of the story is Bodvar's continued search for atonement and his repeated failures, until he recognizes his fundamental megalomania and understands that he cannot free others from suffering, but only assist them in enduring it. Bodvar's path therefore leads from a state of wholeness felt in his earliest childhood, through his fratricidal experience and its attendant schizoid state, then back to a state of inner unity and peace. The mother-of-pearl image, which also refers to the womb, serves as the most important image of wholeness, and the shore made of mother-of-pearl becomes symbolic of the goal of the process of individuation. The sea monster, Leviathan, stands for the forces that prevent man from reaching his spiritual destination. In *Leviathan*, the monster appears in the shape of a sea serpent, a giant whale that is being trapped and killed, and a shipwrecked oil tanker. The forces that inhibit man's spiritual progress can thus be identified as primarily fear and greed. The twentieth century is dominated by the latter.

Both *Perlemorstrand* and *Leviathan* are similar to *Mysterium* in that Hauge frequently addresses the reader directly, much as Cleng Peerson, as narrator of the trilogy, addresses his inscribed reader. Hauge thus breaks down the illusion of reality that he has so skillfully created and is able to communicate with his readers through both their reason and their emotions. Through his archetypal imagery, he also attempts to reach the reader's unconscious. His sophisticated narrative technique serves as the vehicle for a simple yet important message: Even though man finds himself in an often-hostile world, he must not neglect the cultivation of the quintessential qualities which define him as a human being. Indeed, the need to develop maturity and wholeness is Hauge's perennial theme.

Major publications other than long fiction
SHORT FICTION: *Det lyse fastland*, 1965; *Fotspor gjennom årstider*, 1969; *Landskap*, 1972; *Fabelskip*, 1974.
PLAYS: *Cleng Peerson: Utvandring*, 1968; *Morten Kruse*, 1975.
POETRY: *Skyer i drift over vårgrønt land*, 1945; *Det evige sekund*, 1970 (includes "Forvandling"); *Hafrsfjord: Kvad ved fest*, 1975; *Evangelium*, 1977.
NONFICTION: *Gå vest—*, 1963; *Barndom*, 1975; *Gjennom Amerika i emigrantspor*, 1975; *Ungdom*, 1977; *Sannferdig saga om Cleng Peerson*, 1982.

Bibliography
Flatin, Kjetil. "The Rising Sun and the Lark on the Quilt: Quest and Defiance in Alfred Hauge's *Cleng Peerson* Trilogy," in *Proceedings of the Pacific Northwest Conference on Foreign Languages*. XXVII (1976), pp. 133-136.
Sjåvik, Jan. "Alfred Hauge's Utstein Monastery Cycle," in *World Literature Today*. LVI (1982), pp. 54-57.

Jan Sjåvik

ANNE HÉBERT

Born: Sainte Catherine de Fossambault, Canada; August 1, 1916

Principal long fiction

Les Chambres de bois, 1958 (*The Silent Rooms*, 1974); *Kamouraska*, 1970 (English translation, 1973); *Les Enfants du sabbat*, 1975 (*Children of the Black Sabbath*, 1977); *Héloïse*, 1980; *Les Fous de Bassan*, 1982 (*In the Shadow of the Wind*, 1984).

Other literary forms

In addition to her novels, Anne Hébert has explored the forms of poetry, short story, and drama. While the novels, for the most part, have been works of her mature years, the poems and stories began appearing simultaously in magazines and newspapers when the author was in her early twenties. These early poetic works are gathered in *Les Songes en équilibre* (1942), whose themes and short line free verse prefigure the more successful *Le Tombeau des rois* (1953; *The Tomb of the Kings*, 1967) and *Le Torrent*, (1950, 1963, 1965; *The Torrent*, 1973), a short-story collection which, in its final form includes stories written from 1939 to 1963, some, like "The Torrent," previously published in truncated versions. Both *The Torrent* and *Les Songes en équilibre* include juvenilia, but the more finished stories and poems in these collections are beautiful and provocative. The short stories focus on social inequities and the individual suffering they produce. "Un Grand Mariage" ("A Grand Marriage"), "Le Printemps de Catherine" ("Springtime for Catherine"), and "La Mort de Stella" ("The Death of Stella") deal with the effects of material poverty: an ambitious young man who is on the rise from his indigent beginnings to wealth while betraying his true love; a despised drudge who finds freedom in the chaos of war that destroys those with belongings to protect; and the death scene of a tubercular mother of a young family, cast out from society by the guilt of her own suffering. While some are simplistic in their development of plot and character, all have the intensity that Hébert later brought to her novels, and "The Death of Stella" and "The Torrent" in particular are narratively complex works, drawing characters whose impact on the reader is strong. The shifts of time frame and narrative voice, through change of character speaking or through change in the mental state of that character, prefigure the later development of these devices in the novels.

Eleven years after *Les Songes en équilibre*, Hébert published *The Tomb of the Kings*, which was later reissued with the theoretical essay "Poésie, solitude rompue" ("Poetry, Broken Solitude"), and a new verse collection *Mystère de la parole* (Mystery of the Verb) in *Poèmes* (1960; *Poems*, 1975). *The Tomb of the Kings* has been studied extensively as a poetic unit, each individual poem working in harmony to produce a spare, taut, poetic universe, devoid of ornament. The ultimate fears of solitude and death are faced in these verses, in mirrors where deadly shades cling to the reflection ("Vie de Châ-teau"; "Chateau Life"), where hands are planted in the garden, waiting for a flower or the flight of a bird ("Nos Mains au jardin"; "Our Hands in the Garden"), where, in the title poem, the narrator takes her heart on her fist "comme un faucon aveugle," (like a blind falcon) and descends into the tomb of the kings. If the final note of *The Tomb of the Kings* is hope after utter desolation, that hope is expanded in *Mystery of the Verb*, where all aspects of life are offered for celebration in verse lines grown to paragraph length. Although she has published major poems since this volume appeared, no collection of them has been made, and *The Tomb of the Kings* remains the most fully realized of Hébert's verse works. Her novels often incorporate themes, images, and whole lines from her poems and may be said to put into practice the hope for salvation through words advanced in the verse.

Hébert's drama, collected in *Le Temps sauvage, La Mercière assassinée, Les Invités au procès: Théâtre* (1967), is overburdened thematically and not often performed. All three of her plays are poetically intense at times, albeit unevenly. *Les Invités au procès* is a quasi-religious mystery play, with its introduction of semiallegorical figures and use of characters transformed by death. *La Mercière assassinée* is a curious combination of detective thriller with poetic investigation of solitude and death. The mechanical framework is that of the detective story: A young Canadian journalist on vacation in France stumbles into a local murder mystery, has some farcical exchanges with various local types (the lady innkeeper, the elderly noblewoman, and so on), and eventually solves the mystery. Hébert also includes a character, Achille, who is a sort of poet and prophet, commenting on and predicting the action of the play in necessarily obscure verses. The themes of social injustice, the suffering of a young servant at the hands of jealous young nobles, the role of time and solitude, and the fear of death are all explored, but the mixing of styles severely hampers the success of the drama.

Le Temps sauvage is Hébert's most consistent play in tone and plot, pre-senting a family isolated from society by the fierce will of the mother, Agnès, a disappointed woman who seeks her success in her maternity, the only path of development open for her within the terms of Quebecois culture. The addition of an orphaned niece to the closed circle leads to its explosion as each individual is catalyzed into examination of his own adult hopes and needs, escaping from the enforced perpetual childhood which preserved the mother's triumphant role. Although the Church is presented as a repressive social force, this play gives us the novelty of a priest in a positive role, a rare exception to Hébert's general anticlericalism.

Hébert's plays are significant to the readers of her novels chiefly for their development of themes which the novels later treat: death, the return of the dead, individual isolation from the community, and the individual's struggle to redeem himself from the paralyzing force of the past.

Achievements

Hébert has reached a position of eminence among Canadian writers through her work both as a poet and a novelist. The numerous literary prizes which she has won in both roles have brought her a modest share of international fame among French-language writers, while guaranteeing her place in the foreground of Canadian literary circles as a representative of her native province. Her position as a classic French Canadian writer was already guaranteed by her early successes in poetry and the short story. She received the Prix David of the secretariat of Quebec province in 1942 for *Les Songes en équilibre*. It was *Kamouraska*, her second published novel, however, which brought her talents to world attention. A best-seller, translated into many languages, winning the prestigious Prix des Libraires de France in 1971, *Kamouraska* was also made into a motion picture.

The subsequent publication of three more novels confirmed Hébert's commitment to the genre, which she has endowed with many of the characteristics of her verse. The novels are painstakingly polished and poetic in their use of language. The emotional atmosphere, as in her poems, is highly charged. Her characteristic choices of theme in both genres are death and the isolation of the individual, embellished by a certain fascination with the supernatural. Her novels are distinguished by an innovative format in which time and states of consciousness are layered and confused, narrators change, and often lurid subject matter is transformed by the novelist's touch.

All of Hébert's novels are set in Quebec province or in France, particularly Paris. Both settings are given peculiar symbolic weight in the individual narratives, while in no way confining those narratives to restricted local interest. The distinctive situation of Quebec province, where an English-speaking minority government and an extremely conservative Catholic clergy combine to create an isolating and repressive environment, is evoked within the examination of the fictional characters and their isolation from their world; it is not in itself the overriding theme of the novel.

Hébert appeals to a diverse readership, with her poetic attention to language, her intelligent exploitation of the formal possibilities of the new novel, and her treatment of themes both romatic enough for a broad audience and controversial enough to win a strong feminist following.

Biography

Anne Hébert was born in the small summer home of her parents in Sainte Catherine de Fossambault, a country village in Quebec province. The oldest of four children, she enjoyed a close relationship with parents who were both intelligent and cultivated. The family's principal residence was in the city of

Quebec, where her father, Maurice Hébert, pursued his career as a bureaucrat in the provincial government. Maurice Hébert was also an essayist and poet of some note, who wrote literary criticism of local interest and was a member of the honorific Royal Society of Canada. He is known to have been particularly insistent on correct usage of the French tongue—an issue which assumes such a weight of importance in the population of French Canada. Both parents were interested in nature, but Hébert's mother is said to have been her particular guide to the forest and streams which surrounded their summer home. The summers spent at Sainte Catherine de Fossambault also brought Anne Hébert into close contact with her cousin Hector de Saint-Denys Garneau (1912-1943), four years her senior, who was destined to be a prominent poet, one of the first in his regional tradition to write in modern form and an initiator of the new dynamic of Quebecois verse. His illness and premature death of heart disease, after the cold reception given his innovative verse by the conservative literary Establishment in Quebec, made him a symbolic, tragic figure.

Hébert's formal education was largely accomplished at home, under the supervision of her parents, with short stays in several Catholic girls' schools in Quebec. She has said that it was her father's pride in her early poetic production (he copied her poems in a pocket notebook and carried them with him to show to friends) that gave Hébert her first encouragement as a writer. Her verses and short stories began to appear in print in various magazines and newspapers in 1939, and her first collection of poems, *Les Songes en équilibre*, appeared in 1942. This volume, now regarded as a promising bit of juvenilia, won the Prix David and gathered very favorable notice for its graceful treatment in spare, free verse of themes of filial love, religious fervor, and the vocation of the poet. In many ways, her verses are reminiscent of those of Saint-Denys Garneau. Her next major publication, *The Tomb of the Kings*, while still written in short-line free verse, is much more intense and tightly knit and shows a new preoccupation with death, perhaps in part inspired by the deaths of Saint-Denys Garneau and her own younger sister Marie, in 1952.

Hébert worked for Radio Canada and the National Film Board from 1950 to 1954, writing scripts for various short features; probably her best-known work in this medium is the lyric text she wrote to accompany a short feature on the life of Saint-Denys Garneau, which did not appear until 1960. In 1954, she received a grant from the Royal Society of Canada, one of the first of a series of awards and stipends which enabled her to devote herself full-time to her literary career. She used her newfound independence to leave the close-knit Quebec society and establish herself in Paris. Her subsequent novels and verse have been published by the Parisian publishing house Seuil, a significant point for a French-Canadian writer, since it indicates not only acceptance by the larger French-speaking community but also the desire to seek such acceptance, rather than remaining within the familiar circles of Quebecois writers and publishers.

In 1958, Seuil published Hébert's first novel, *The Silent Rooms*, a critical success which won for her the Prix France-Canada and the Prix Duvernay of the Société Saint-Jean-Baptiste in Quebec. In the same year, her murder-mystery drama *La Mercière assassinée* was produced on Canadian television. The year 1960 was marked both by her father's death and the publication of *Poems* by Seuil, as well as the first appearance of "La Traduction, dialogue entre le traducteur et l'auteur" in collaboration with Frank R. Scott; the release of *Saint-Denys Garneau* by the National Film Board of Canada; and election to membership in the Royal Society of Canada, an honor earlier accorded her father. *Poems* was enthusiastically received and has since inspired many academic critical studies, uniting as it does two very different poetic styles together with the important essay "Poetry, Broken Solitude," a highly personal venture into poetics. *The Tomb of the Kings* explored the kingdoms of solitude and death with surgically spare, short-line free verse. *Mystery of the Verb* is written in *versets*—a poetic form especially associated with Paul Claudel and also with Hébert's fellow Quebecois, Rina Lasnier—where the verse line is expanded sometimes to several printed lines, roughly corresponding to the expression of an entire thought or the duration of a breath. In "Poetry, Broken Solitude" and *Mystery of the Verb*, Hébert emphasizes the poet's power to build a new world and the obligation to redeem the old world, in a sense, through words (the *Parole* of the title in French). This was, however, to be Hébert's last major collection of verse, although several significant single poems have been published since.

In 1961-1962, Hébert received a grant from the Conseil des Arts. The second, augmented edition of *The Torrent* appeared in 1963, published at her own expense; it was later reissued by Seuil in 1965, further evidence of her acceptance in the larger French-speaking world. In 1967, Hébert received the Prix Molson, and *Théâtre*, a collection of three plays was published. In her fifties, she had received a great deal of critical praise, attained a position as a major poet in her own country and attracted a certain amount of attention in the worldwide French community. The publication of *Kamouraska* in 1970 brought her fame as a best-selling novelist. In 1971, she received the Prix des Libraires de France for *Kamouraska*, an event widely reported and celebrated in her native Quebec. Subsequent years have seen the publication of *Children of the Black Sabbath*, *Héloïse*, and *In the Shadow of the Wind*, winner of the prestigious Prix Femina.

Hébert has written a number of newspaper and journal articles in Quebec speaking of the role of literature; one cannot ignore the significance of her position as a major French-Canadian author during a period when writing in French is a political act. Some authors have turned to the Montrealais dialect "joual" and other regional variants of French to emphasize their identification with their homeland, but Hébert chooses to write within the impeccable French so prized by her father (although individual characters, in particular the parents of *Children of the Black Sabbath* and the servant girl Amélie Caron of *Kamouraska*, speak in dialect). Her residence in France echoes this rejection of deep politicization of her writing, but her choice of themes and locations important in the literature of Quebec, as well as her continued identification with its literary life make her a participant in a dynamic, changing world. As Saint-Denys Garneau became a symbol of the martyrdom of the poet, Anne Hébert has become a symbol of hope, of the vibrant life of words beyond suffering and solitude. *The Tomb of the Kings*, in its descent into death at the hands of old kings, ending with a hope of dawn, followed by the exuberant *Mystery of the Verb*, has been interpreted as the call to new life for a province languishing under the tyranny of old traditions and forms. The success of her later prose work may be seen as the fulfillment of this poetic challenge.

Analysis

The reader of Anne Hébert's poetry and prose will recognize a kinship of theme and language among the different works. *Héloïse* opens with a verse from "En guise de fête" ("A Kind of Feast," from *The Tomb of the Kings*). Its ironic refrain is repeated as the order of the fictional world collapses: "Le monde est en ordre/ Les morts dessous/ Les vivants dessus." ("The world is in order/ The dead below/ The living above.") Olivia de la Haute Mer (Olivia of the High Sea), the ghost of the murdered Olivia Atkins, returns to float with the tides off Griffins Creek, in *In the Shadow of the Wind*, quoting another poem from *The Tomb of the Kings*: "Il y a certainement Quelqu'un" ("There is certainly Someone . . ."). More than the practice of direct quotation, however, the continued exploration of common themes binds the novels to the poems.

The title poem of *The Tomb of the Kings* best outlines one major theme of Hébert's work, that of the child/woman victim or sacrifice. Such a figure is to be found in all of her novels, as either a major or a minor character. Catherine, of *The Silent Rooms* is brought to the point of death by her husband's pursuit of an aesthetic of immobility and silence. In *Kamouraska*, Élizabeth d'Aulnières leaves the feminine cocoon of her aunts' home to marry a young "seigneur," Antoine Tassy, who proves violently abusive, threatening her with death, until he himself is murdered by her lover. In *Children of the Black Sabbath*, the sacrificial figure is Sister Julie, Lady of the Precious Blood, victim and sacrifice for her parents, adepts of the Black Mass, and the later victim of cruelties at the hands of the Mother Superior and Chaplain of her convent. In these three cases, the victim finally escapes from her tormentors and in fact, may be said to retaliate: Catherine leaves Michel in utter solitude; Antoine Tassy is murdered by his childhood friend, now the lover of his wife;

and the nuns of Sister Julie's convent suffer numerous troubles from her malice. In *Héloïse*, however, there is no escape for the young lovers, Bernard and Christine, who are victimized by a pair of vampires, their life and love crushed. Nora and Olivia, the double victims of *In the Shadow of the Wind*, are cousins whose fathers were brothers, their mothers sisters. As they flower into beauty, they absorb the life of the entire community. When they are murdered together at the hands of their cousin, Stevens Brown, their bodies thrown into the sea, their death is the death of the community and their status as victim is doubled with the victimization of other women: an aunt who hangs herself that same summer, never having truly lived; the mother of Olivia, who died of tuberculosis after harvesting the potato crop in freezing weather; the aging cousin abused and abandoned by her young lover.

Yet the toll of victims rises even higher, for the violent Antoine Tassy, Michel, and Stevens Brown, grown men that they are, are all abused children, with the echo of fear ringing in their ears. In *Kamouraska*, Élizabeth d'Aulnières is told by her mother-in-law, the old Madame Tassy, to ignore her husband's drunken rages, that his father had done the same. The lover of Élizabeth, Dr. Nelson, recalls Antoine as a schoolboy, his face always drowned in tears, turning to Nelson as his friend in a solitude otherwise complete.

When Stevens Brown kills Nora, then rapes and kills Olivia, he is convinced that the wild wind of a storm drowns out their screams: The wind is within his mind, the storm his own rage at a childhood of beatings by his father. François, of "The Torrent," is also an abused child, rendered deaf by a beating from his mother, La Grande Claudine. He hears only the roaring of the torrent, as Stevens hears the stormy ocean. Stevens has an idiot brother, an elemental creature named Perceval, who incarnates François' rage and batters La Grande Claudine to death. For both François and Stevens, love of women is poisoned by their tormented boyhood; they can feel desire but do not love. François takes a wandering woman, whom he names Amica, into his home and bed, but she becomes a nightmare presence to him, intruder in his solitude, long before she steals his money and leaves. Stevens seduces and sleeps with his cousin's widow, Maureen, then leaves her with taunts about her age after reawakening her as a sexual being. He brutally murders Nora and Olivia who consciously and unconsciously returned his desire. Both François and Stevens eventually commit suicide, François in the waters of the torrent, Stevens with pills stolen from a hospital.

It is a petrification that is responsible for the evil in François and Stevens, caught forever by the trauma of their childhood suffering. In *The Silent Rooms*, Michel and Lia, noble-born but abused children grown into abusive adults, are caught in their own rigidity of family heredity and aesthetic preference. So, too, the vampires of *Héloïse* are still clad in the style of their youth, still using the artifacts of the nineteeth century. Héloïse quotes the last line of Baudelaire's sonnet "La Beauté" in acknowledging her need to destroy Bernard to preserve her own immortality, but the first line of the poem "Je suis belle, ô mortels, comme un rêve de pierre," ("I am beautiful, O mortals, like a dream of stone") expresses the aesthetic of immobility espoused by Michel, toyed with by Bernard, the hatred of life with its strong odors, colors, and movement.

In both *The Silent Rooms* and *Héloïse*, meals of rice and white fish symbolize the imprisonment of the living by a dead aesthetic, palates too weak to accept the strong savor of life. The near escape of Christine (one cannot ignore the significance of her sacrificial name) and Bernard from the vampires involves a trip to the open marketplace and the preparation of a highly flavored meal of rabbit in mustard sauce. Catherine's decision to break with Michel revolves around a similar trip to the market with her lover, Bruno, and the preparation of a dinner "plein d'odeurs" (full of scents), with "petits citrons amers, des oursins violets, des baies sauvages" (little sour lemons, violet sea urchins, wild bay).

The forces of evil, petrification, and death are shown by Hébert not only on an individual scale but also on the broader scale of institutions and society, within which the individual is a victim of rituals and codes, isolated from himself and others. In *Kamouraska*, Élizabeth is presented as vibrantly female, overflowing with sexual energy, pregnant twice within the first year of her first marriage. When this marriage fails, there is no possibility—within the rules of her community—for this energy to be expressed. Her lover is an alien to the society, an American isolated from his own culture by his father's political rigidity (a Royalist who stayed in America after the Revolution), isolated from that of Quebec by his recent arrival, his accented French, the fact that he was a convert to Catholicism. The death of Antoine Tassy, a sacrifice to the demands of society (for Élizabeth must be a widow before she can marry her lover), is a bloody catastrophe in which Dr. Nelson expresses his elemental maleness, his dominance of the other, but utterly fails in all practical aspects of crime, leaving a trail of blood all the way to the American border. Élizabeth, abandoned by her lover, becomes a prisoner of society in a stricter sense; imprisoned, tried, and freed on technical grounds, she redeems her virtue by her exemplary life as wife of the insignificant Jerome Rolland, bearing him eight children to add to her first three. Her maternity is the one expression of her sexuality. Her outer person is a perfect, unchanging shell; her inner self is haunted by the images of her youth, when she was truly alive. It is the recurrence of these memories in her dreams that gives flesh to her story. It is significant that the story is set in Quebec province in the 1840's, a place and period where society's repression of the individual has maximum force.

Children of the Black Sabbath, also set in Quebec province, again invokes the repressive powers of the society in the isolation and sacrifice of the individual. The parents of Julie and Joseph are outcasts from society by choice;

they are the witch and her master, practitioners of the Black Mass, but the congregation they gather from the cities and surrounding countryside are the pitiful citizens of a society where dancing is forbidden, where Prohibition reigns, where the Great Depression of the 1930's is in force. The Black Mass frees its celebrants from society's restrictions; they indulge in sexual license, they gorge on the sacrificial pig, they dance and drink moonshine. To this extent, the Satanic pair are liberators, but they are also rigidly held within a ritual code, the mother defined by her long lineage of wives and mothers of Satan, and the abuse of Julie by her parents is defined within this tradition of evil: She is raped by her father, her body used as the altar on which the Communion bread of the Black Mass is baked.

Later, she enters a convent and encounters a parallel ritual, similarly petri-fied and rigid, and equally evil in its abuse of the individual in the name of the ultimate Victim and Sacrifice. She undergoes torture at the hands of the Mother Superior and Chaplain, who try the entire surface of her body with a needle in search of a witch's spot that feels no pain. The spot they find is the scar left by burns suffered during the Black Mass. Liturgical Latin is used by Hébert in *Children of the Black Sabbath* to frame Sister Julie's flight from the "real" world of her convent life to the delirious memories of her childhood, with their increasingly powerful call for her to abandon her amnesia and take up the succession of her mother's race. It is the moral sclerosis of the Church, where women serve the Holy Father as the witches serve Satan, that produces the horrible suffering, not only of Sister Julie, but also of the other nuns in the convent, (exemplified by the nuns dying in the infirmary when the Mother Superior orders their medication discontinued). The ultimate sin, the killing of a newborn child, is committed not by Sister Julie, who escapes with her shadowy lover, but by the Mother Superior, anxious to escape a scandal, thus preserving the respectability of her order at the expense of Christian spirit.

As Latin phrases frame the action in *Children of the Black Sabbath*, biblical references introduce the characters of *In the Shadow of the Wind*, characters that are caught in the double isolation of an English-speaking community, exiled like Dr. Nelson through political rigidity following the American Rev-olution to French-speaking Canada, surviving through the years as a micro-cosm of a "chosen people" within the body of another "chosen people." The first narrative voice in this novel is given to Pastor Nicholas Jones, speaking in 1982 and re-creating two hundred years of his community, only to see it vanish in the recollection of the summer of 1936 when Nora and Olivia Atkins were murdered. Pastor Nicholas, childless, is a failed patriarch. He longs for sons, yet the only genealogy he can establish is a reversed one; he engenders his own ancestors in framing a history of Griffins Creek. As narrator, he lusts after his nubile nieces, Nora and Olivia, focusing the attention of the reader on them and on their cousin, Stevens Brown, who replaces Nicholas as nar-rator through letters written to a friend in Florida, the antithesis of Griffins

Creek. Stevens has returned only for the summer from a self-imposed exile. At the moment of his return, he takes a panoramic survey of the town: He sees his grandfather as a tree from whose branches all the life of the village springs in the numerous descendants, legitimate and bastard, which people it. Yet both the pastor and Stevens feel the power of Felicity Brown, their mother and grandmother, an enigmatic figure, half sea animal (much is made of the identification *mère/mer*), profoundly female, who dominates her grandchildren.

The sexual tension created by the burgeoning of Nora and Olivia Atkins, within the context of an institutional morality which allows no outlet to sexuality except that of marriage and childrearing, is more than Nicholas or Stevens can bear: Nicholas attempts to molest Nora and is observed by the idiot Perceval, who later screams out at the barn dance when he sees his uncle hover over and leer at the girls. Stevens goes a step further to rape and murder on the last night of the summer. Nicholas' barren wife responds to the unspoken passions of the barn dance with suicide, yet she was never really "alive" and her death has little impact. The death of the Atkins girls destroys the "chosen people" to whom they belonged.

In both *Children of the Black Sabbath* and *In the Shadow of the Wind*, the violence of the individual is part of the violence of the immediate society which in its turn is framed by the worldwide violence of World War II. Sister Julie's brother Joseph escapes from his family in taking up the uniform of the Canadian armed forces; her supposed psychic violence reaches out to cause his death in battle. Stevens Brown, after being acquitted of murder, also leaves Canada to fight in Europe. He reacts psychotically to combat and spends his postwar life in a psychiatric hospital until his escape allows him to write a final "letter" and give his own account of the night of the murders. The institutionalized murders of wartime trigger unbearable memories of the personal murders of his own past.

If the outer society of the Quebec-based novels acts as an alienating force by the strength of its repressions of the individual, the novels set in Paris show no such repression. *The Silent Rooms* works exclusively on an individual basis—that is, each character is defined and limited within his own history, his own aesthetic choices. In *Héloïse*, the city seems indifferent to the drama of the characters; the throngs that pass through the Métro and down the boulevard Saint Michel simply do not notice that there are vampires in their midst. Bernard, who gives up poetry for the financial promise of law school, is a failed Orpheus, the Parisian Métro the Stygian realm which he must wander. His nemesis, Héloïse, can sit and drink a vial of his blood on the curb of Saint Michel Fountain and pass unremarked among the generation of young drug abusers and social outcasts gathered there. There is no rescue for the beautiful Christine, who, in her dancer's grace, combines body and soul in perfect harmony. Her husband's weakness marks them both as victims of the living dead. While the untouched modern apartment that Christine had longed to live in and make her own can be described in a few words, Hébert devotes pages of lush description to the nineteenth century gem which "waits" for and devours the young couple, a confusion of colors, a profusion of art motifs (including a painting of Orpheus and the animals), crowded to the point of suffocation yet empty, even as the Métro is crowded with people yet empty of humanity.

The Quebec novels are arguably richer as a group than the Paris novels; they treat the central theme of individual alienation through themes such as the influence of society, the repressive nature of the Church, the impact of World War II on the colony of a principal power, the alienation of the speaker of one language within a society of another tongue, all subjects proper to the French-Canadian novel, but with an emotional climate peculiar to Hébert's work. It is in the emotional intensity of her work that Hébert offers her words as an effort at redemption of the very world of evil which she lays before us. In the poem "Le Tombeau des Rois" ("The Tomb of the Kings"), the young victim, seven times drunk and crushed by the dead kings, is still a hopeful figure, facing the dawn, "les morts hors de moi, assassinés" ("The dead outside of me, assassinated"). Other poems, especially those of *Mystery of the Verb* celebrate in detail the poet's power to name and redeem the world, to justify the living and the dead. One of the post-*Poems* verses, "Noël," evokes war and death and the suffering of the innocent in juxtaposition with the Christmas promise of joy, a promise encrusted with the traditions of the centuries. The poet must be the compassionate searcher for knowledge, panning for gold, washing the words "Coeur. Tendresse. Larmes." ("Heart. Tenderness. Tears."), which are "les plus perdus, les plus galvaudés, les plus traînés, les plus trahis," ("the most lost, the most muddled, the most dragged about, the worst betrayed"), in order to renew them and to begin again with nativity and morning. The infant God born of this search is the Word, the beginning of a new world.

Anne Hébert's novels, as they explore the realms of death and terror mapped out in her poems, continue the effort to name the unnamable, to break down the forces of repression and cruelty which freeze the human heart in living death. It is the beauty of her language, the prose poems to be found within the bleakness of a work such as *In the Shadow of the Wind*, which give hope and purpose to her work, where love and life are so seldom attained and so much desired.

Major publications other than long fiction

SHORT FICTION: *Le Torrent*, 1950, 1963, 1965 (*The Torrent*, 1973).

PLAYS: *Saint-Denys Garneau*, 1960 (film script); *Le Temps sauvage*, 1963; *Le Temps sauvage, La Mercière assassinée, Les Invités au procès: Théâtre*, 1967.

POETRY: *Les Songes en équilibre*, 1942; *Le Tombeau des rois*, 1953 (*The Tomb of the Kings*, 1967); *Poèmes*, 1960 (*Poems*, 1975; includes *Le Tombeau des rois* [*The Tomb of the Kings*]; the theoretical essay "Poésie, solitude rompue" ["Poetry, Broken Solitude"]; and a verse collection *Mystère de la parole* [*Mystery of the Verb*]).

NONFICTION: *Dialogue sur la traduction: À propos du "Tombeau des rois,"* 1970 (with Frank R. Scott).

Bibliography

Boak, Denis. "Kamouraska, Kamouraska!" in *Essays in French Literature.* (November, 1977), pp. 69-104.

Brazeau, J. R. *An Outline of Contemporary French-Canadian Literature*, 1972.

Lemieux, Pierre Hervé. *Entre songe et parole: Structure du "Tombeau des rois" d'Anne Hébert*, 1978.

Major, Jean-Louis. *Anne Hébert et le miracle de la parole*, 1976.

Russell, Delbert W. *Anne Hébert*, 1983.

Theriault, Serge A. *La Quête d'équilibre dans l'oeuvre romanesque d'Anne Hébert*, 1980.

Anne W. Sienkewicz

VERNER VON HEIDENSTAM

Born: Olshammar, Sweden; July 6, 1859
Died: Övralid, Sweden; May 20, 1940

Principal long fiction
Endymion, 1889; *Hans Alienus*, 1892; *Karolinerna*, 1897-1898 (*A King and His Campaigners*, 1902; better known as *The Charles Men*, 1920); *Heliga Birgittas pilgrimsfärd*, 1901; *Folkungaträdet*, 1905-1907 (*The Tree of the Folkungs*, 1925).

Other literary forms
Bonniers has published Verner von Heidenstam's collected works in twenty-three volumes. In addition to the novels listed above, they include volumes of poetry: *Vallfart och vandringsår* (1888; pilgrimage and wander-years), *Dikter* (1895; poems), *Nya dikter* (1915; new poems); collections of short stories: *Sankt Göran och draken* (1900; Saint George and the dragon), *Skogen susar* (1904; the woods whisper); essays: *Renässans* (1889; Renaissance), *Pepitas bröllop* (1890, with Oscar Levertin; Pepita's wedding), *Modern Barbarism* (1894), *Klassicitet och germanism* (1898; the classical and the Germanic), *Tankar och tekningar* (1899; thoughts and drawings), *Dagar och händelser* (1909; days and events), *Proletärfilosofiens upplösning och fall* (1911; the decline and fall of the philosophy of the proletariat), *Vad vilja vi?* (1914; what do we want?); autobiographical writings: *Från Col di Tenda till Blocksberg* (1888; from Col di Tenda to Blocksberg); and a history textbook: *Svenskarna och deras hövdingar* (1908-1910; *The Swedes and Their Chieftains*, 1925). In addition, the following volumes of essays and poetry were published posthumously: *När kastanjerna blommade* (1941; when the chestnut trees bloomed), *Tankar och utkast* (1941; thoughts and plans), *Sista dikter* (1942; last poems), and *Fragment och aforismer* (1959; fragments and aphorisms).

Achievements
In 1916, Verner von Heidenstam was awarded the Nobel Prize for Literature, which bore the apt inscription: "The leader of a new era in our literature." Beginning with his first book of poems, *Vallfart och vandringsår*, in 1888, and continuing until the publication of *Nya dikter* in 1915, Heidenstam challenged the literary trends of his time. He rebelled against the bleak world-view and confining aesthetics of Naturalism in his early works and was responsible for ushering in the new poetry of the 1890's. First and foremost a poet, Heidenstam embraced the creative power of the imagination above any attempt in his writing simply to imitate everyday life. His rejection of Naturalism did not, however, take him to opposite extremes: Decadence, or art for art's sake, was not an answer for Heidenstam. He tried to blend realism and the

inspired creations of the imagination. Disgusted by the pessimism in the writing of his contemporaries, Heidenstam increasingly turned to the past to find a cultural heritage and a set of values powerful enough to launch a new national literature. His three historical novels and *Nya dikter* succeeded in doing so.

The Swedes recognized Heidenstam's important role in revitalizing their national literature. Besides the Nobel Prize, Heidenstam received several other honors, including membership in the Swedish Academy in 1912 and an honorary doctorate from the Royal Institute of Technology in Stockholm in 1909. It is important to point out, however, that Heidenstam's cultural nationalism does not have at its core a narrow chauvinism. Heidenstam's frame of reference, ultimately, is a classical humanism, based on the love of ideals, beauty, and the creative powers of the human mind.

Biography

Carl Gustaf Verner von Heidenstam was born at the family manor, Olshammar, Sweden, on July 6, 1859. He was the only child of Nils Gustaf von Heidenstam, chief engineer for the Royal Coast Guard, and his wife, Magdalena Charlotta Rütterskiöld. The family lived in Stockholm, where Verner attended the prominent Beskowska School. He spent his summers at Olshammar, where his vivid imagination was nurtured by his grandmother and several other women of the household. During these early years, Heidenstam developed a love for Lake Vättern and the Tiveden landscape, a feeling for the land and its history which he never lost. Because both his health and his academic performance were poor, Heidenstam was taken out of school and sent south to travel. From 1876 to 1878, he toured southern Europe, Egypt, Palestine, Syria, and Greece, recording his impressions in drawings and paintings. These impressions later found expression in the striking vividness and immediacy of the settings in his early works.

In 1879, Heidenstam settled in Rome to become a painter, but he spent an increasing amount of time writing poetry. Against his father's wishes, he married a childhood friend, Emilia Uggla, in 1880, causing a break between father and son. Heidenstam spent the next several years in middle and southern Europe, studying, painting, and writing—striving to find his own artistic form. In 1884, he made contact with August Strindberg, at that time living in Switzerland, and the two men began an intense and inspiring series of discussions on all topics, particularly literature and politics. Although Heidenstam presented himself as a radical, his first published volume of poetry, *Vallfart och vandringsår*, with its colorful Eastern exoticism, had little in common with the doctrines of Naturalism which Strindberg, at that time, championed.

Heidenstam returned to Sweden in 1887 and was reconciled with his father who, terminally ill, killed himself the next year. Back in Sweden, the new head of his family, Heidenstam concentrated on his writing. The debut volume of poetry, *Vallfart och vandringsår*, was published in 1888. In *Renässans* and *Pepitas bröllop*, Heidenstam developed his theories about art, rejecting the Naturalism and documentary realism of the 1880's and instead embracing the power of the imagination and love of beauty.

In the late 1890's, Heidenstam wrote increasingly about the issue of cultural nationalism. In both his essays and his creative literature, Heidenstam attempted to define and express the Swedish national character. Mining Swedish history, Heidenstam focused on Charles XII (in *The Charles Men*), Birgitta (in *Heliga Birgittas pilgrimsfärd*), and Folke Filbyter (in *The Tree of the Folkungs*) to explore in historical novels the circumstances and temperament which formed and best expressed the Swedish character. Reacting against the materialism of his day and fearing the influence of foreign countries such as the United States on traditional Swedish social and cultural values, Heidenstam lectured and wrote to raise the Swedes' consciousness about their history and cultural heritage. He interrupted a planned series of historical novels to research and write a history textbook, *The Swedes and Their Chieftains*, from 1908 to 1910, a project which exhausted him and apparently drained his creative resources. Although he continued to write essays after completing the text, Heidenstam, with one brilliant exception, *Nya dikter*, was never again able to concentrate his creative powers. Some poems, memoirs, and essays were published posthumously, and many were fragments.

While Heidenstam's literary productivity ended in 1915, he lived until 1940. After three failed marriages, to Emilia Uggla (1880-1893), Olga Widberg (1896-1903), and Anna Sjöberg (1903-1906), Heidenstam spent the last decades of his life in a successful relationship with Kate Bang. After 1915, Heidenstam began another period of travel, revisiting the Riviera, Switzerland, and Italy, as well as spending several years in Denmark. In 1925, he retired to Övralid, an estate he built overlooking Lake Vättern. He made occasional public appearances (for example, to speak before the Swedish Academy), but for the most part, he lived his last years secluded at Övralid. He died on May 20, 1940, after several years of worsening senility. He is buried at Övralid; his former home is now a museum.

Analysis

Verner von Heidenstam came of age as a writer when he organized and defined his thoughts about literature in *Renässans* and *Pepitas bröllop*. These essays stimulated a new literary and cultural movement in Sweden, one which rejected the doctrines and methodology of Naturalism and the philosophical pessimism which Heidenstam saw as its product. Heidenstam called for a new national literature, developing out of and expressing the Swedish national character. Its impulse was to come from Swedish sources, particularly Esaias Tegnér and Victor Rydberg, along with the classical idealism of Johann Wolfgang von Goethe and Friedrich Schiller, and was to unite realism with the "subjective . . . the imagination, the sense of the beautiful." In *Pepitas bröllop*, Heidenstam asks if Mephistopheles and Peer Gynt do not exist with the same intense reality as some of the shadows we talk to on the streetcorner. "It is not only the purely concrete that comprises reality!"

For Heidenstam, the creative powers of the imagination—not the ability to imitate everyday life—was the essence of artistic expression. Heidenstam placed his faith in the insight of the poet; his gifts are more lyric than narrative. His career as a poet began with the publication of *Vallfart och vandringsår*; the work which marks the beginning of Heidenstam's mature period is also a collection of poems, *Dikter*; and *Nya dikter*, perhaps his greatest work, ends his literary production. Between the two volumes of poetry which mark his mature period, however, Heidenstam wrote three historical novels, *The Charles Men*, *Heliga Birgittas pilgrimsfärd*, and *The Tree of the Folkungs*, works which rank Heidenstam among major historical novelists. Historical fiction provided the form Heidenstam needed to express his ideas and offer an alternative to the pessimism and decadence he saw as characteristic of the literature of his time. By writing about the past, Heidenstam believed, he could revitalize traditional values and illustrate aspects of the Swedish national character that he hoped would lead to a humanism based on classical ideals.

Heidenstam's first work, the collection of poems *Vallfart och vandringsår*, added a fresh, vivid, exotic flavor to Swedish poetry. Not only did Heidenstam draw on his travels to provide an exotic setting for many of his poems, but the lively tone and dynamic, colorful imagery, as well as the themes glorifying youth, beauty, and pleasures of the moment, were a shocking antidote to readers accustomed to the darker settings and themes of Naturalism. Heidenstam's first novel, *Endymion*, worked similar ground; the reader enters a world of harems, baths, Bedouin caravans, and bazaars. Although viewed from a foreigner's perspective, the scenes have vitality because they are seen through the eyes of a sensitive, receptive protagonist. Heidenstam depicts the decline of Arabic culture, and with it the life-spirit which had characterized that ancient culture. Although some critics dismissed Heidenstam's first prose work as a travel book disguised as a novel, "a romanticized Baedeker," Heidenstam raises the issues of cultural nationalism and the tragic role of national heroes which he later successfully developed in his major novels.

Hans Alienus is a more original book, interesting for its insights into Heidenstam's evolving philosophy, but a chaotic blend of verse and prose—more a book of thoughts than a successfully wrought novel. The protagonist, Hans Alienus, is a stranger in his own time, searching for an ideal image of humanity, a meaning for which he can live. He travels freely through time and space, studying, experiencing, and ultimately rejecting the life philosophies he encounters in places ranging from the Vatican to the court of Sardanapalus to Hades. The last section of the book, strongly autobiographical, finds Hans

Alienus in Sweden, reconciled with his father and embracing a belief in beauty and the imagination. The father, however, takes his own life, and the novel ends with Hans Alienus isolated, resigned, and wanting to die.

Despite the novel's obvious autobiographical elements, Heidenstam, fortunately, moved beyond the despair and spiritual bankruptcy which defeat Hans Alienus. In his remaining novels, he turned to the history of the Swedish nation to discover and illustrate those values and beliefs with which to face life and give it meaning.

In his desire to create a new literature based on Sweden's cultural heritage, Heidenstam looked to the historical past to find subjects capable of infusing a literary national consciousness. In the figure of Charles XII, Heidenstam found a character whose complexity and stature could express the Swedish national character. Heidenstam read diaries and original documents to gain an accurate sense of the period about which he was writing, but his most important source was Anders Fryxell's history of Charles XII and the men who served under him. Heidenstam's reliance on historical sources, however, was to provide a framework and background for his sketches of the King and of the fates of individual Swedes on campaign during the long war years. These characters, representative of the Swedish people, were depicted in what Heidenstam believed was the building block of historical fiction, the revealing anecdote. The novelist, Heidenstam argues, must select anecdotes of dramatic power and arrange them in an order which most effectively expresses the conception of the novel as a unified whole.

Unity, however, is not easily achieved, as *The Charles Men* demonstrates. Its structure is a series of short stories, much like that of Sherwood Anderson's *Winesburg, Ohio* (1919) or Ernest Hemingway's *In Our Time* (1924, 1925); all three works are complete in themselves but provide a composite of a central character—George Willard for Anderson, Nick Adams for Hemingway, and, in Heidenstam's work, Charles XII—and one other significant composite "character," for Heidenstam: the Swedish people. Though the stories illuminate the character of Charles XII and provide insight into the moral dilemma he faces, they are not essential parts of an organic whole; they can stand by themselves, and, indeed, some were published several years before they reappeared as chapters in *The Charles Men*. The structure does, however, emphasize Heidenstam's strength as a writer. Instead of a detailed, sweeping historical narrative, Heidenstam gives his readers the individual event, striking and immediate, without rhetorical or interpretive comment. He wastes no words, using the means of the poet to provide meaning—symbol, image, suggestion. Fredrik Böök, coeditor with Kate Bang of Heidenstam's collected works, has likened Heidenstam's style to a "monumental fresco," an epic style with limited use of detail whereby even the decorative is simplified and concentrated.

Heidenstam chose to write about a time in history when the nation was a major power led by a king who gained an international reputation. *The Charles Men*, however, is not a glorification or a romanticized interpretation of Sweden's role in shaping European history. Heidenstam's emphasis is on the defeat of the King and the nation. Charles XII is a complex character, and the reader senses Heidenstam's ambivalent attitude toward his hero. Charles XII is shown as cold and indifferent to other people's suffering; much of the time he is lost in a world of his own thoughts, melancholy and isolated even when surrounded by his men. On the other hand, he is also courageous, leading his soldiers on the battlefield and commanding their loyalty to the bitter end. He is driven by his convictions and willingly sacrifices his men, the country's resources, and ultimately himself in his mission to keep Sweden undivided. Though some of his people question whether the King is not tempting God, a soldier answers, after Charles has been shot: "He believed in the righteousness of his own conduct. Such defiance God forgives. Such defiance even men forgive."

Heidenstam's portrait of Charles XII assumes tragic overtones. The King and his men are doomed to defeat, but, as Heidenstam has written, war can shape brave and stable personalities, "even mold new life in an entire people." The Charles men, hungry, cold, besieged, and imprisoned, are transformed from selfish, weak individuals to self-sacrificing, dutiful men. In Heidenstam's fiction, defeat can be ennobling; greatness can arise out of terrible suffering and self-sacrifice.

Heidenstam continued his examination of the heroic character under stress in *Heliga Birgittas pilgrimsfärd*, a transitional novel published between his two major prose works. Again the setting is historical, the fourteenth century, and the novel focuses on one of Sweden's most famous figures. The concerns coming under Heidenstam's scrutiny are mainly religious ones, as opposed to the military and political concerns which are primary in *The Charles Men*. In both works, however, Heidenstam is less interested in the broad sweep of historical circumstances than he is in depicting the psychic tensions and pressures they impose on the consciences of his heroes. For Birgitta, the conflicts are between her "call" and her life as a sexual woman, mother, and wife; between her desire for Christian humility and her selfishness and unyielding pride. Her fanaticism makes her insensitive, even brutal, in her treatment of her children—and herself. She is compared to an octopus, consuming those who come within her reach while "her devilish eyes are directed upward toward the stars." Like Charles, she willingly sacrifices all to follow steadfastly her own will. Heidenstam suggests that an unyielding drive and self-sacrifice are necessary for greatness. *Heliga Birgittas pilgrimsfärd* does delineate, however, as Alrik Gustafson has demonstrated in his study of Heidenstam's works, a new and evolving conception of the tragic hero. Birgitta finds purity and fulfillment in her faith because she transforms her fanaticism through humility and resignation. She discovers that aggressive zealousness can do evil even when she most desires to do good: "So is it Thy meaning that also they who most intensely burn with desire to serve Thy love and righteousness shall do evil. . . ." The human condition, she finally recognizes, is both good and evil; resigned to her own imperfections, she can empathize with the feelings of others and become truly humane.

In his last novel, *The Tree of the Folkungs*, Heidenstam returned to the foundation of the Swedish state itself. Part 1 of the novel is set at the end of the Viking period, when Christian worship is slowly replacing heathen beliefs and landowners wield political power. Heidenstam follows our knowledge of the basic history of that period, but because that knowledge is sketchy at best, his imagination is given free reign as he transforms names in historical documents into passionate, ambitious human beings. The founder of the Folkungs is Folke Filbyter, a Viking chieftain, who decides to acquire land and domestic animals at home instead of plunder abroad. Folke is a coarse, hulking man, interested in only one thing beyond his physical needs—the accumulation of wealth. He has no regard for social rules or law; in fact, he sends his thralls to rob people on the roads, and he becomes a blood brother with an outlaw. He even kidnaps his neighbor's daughter after his son's request to marry her has been rejected by the neighbor's family. It is upon such suspicious beginnings that the Swedish state is founded.

Nevertheless, Heidenstam is able to make Folke sympathetic at the end of part 1. Folke grows to love his grandson; after the boy has been kidnaped by a Christian preacher, the reader can feel Folke's anguish as he scours the country looking for the boy. Decades later, Folke finds him, an earl in the King's service, but the old man is told to keep quiet about the Earl's questionable background. Folke, the patriarch, is rejected by his own sons and grandson because he has no culture, no beliefs, no conscience.

In one lifetime, Swedish society has undergone vast changes: Folke's offspring belong to a rising nobility who will establish the central power of the Folkungs. Paganism is being suppressed: The sacred grove of the heathens is burned by young Christian priests in the King's retinue. Weary, displaced, a man left behind by the times, Folke cannot win the love in his sons' hearts. Nevertheless, he feels no bitterness; indeed, he is proud of his sons. As the young Folkungs ride off, dreaming of their destiny, Folke assumes a tragic grandeur when he opens his veins and prepares for a house sacrifice, faithful to his own customs and resigned to his fate.

Part 2 takes up the story of the Folkung family two hundred years after Folke Filbyter's death. The Folkungs have consolidated their power. Through the characterizations of two brothers, Valdemar and Magnus, Heidenstam is able to explore what qualities of leadership are necessary to establish effective social and political order. The brothers end up fighting for the crown because Valdemar is indifferent about his duties as a ruler. He seeks the pleasures of the moment, much like the characters in Heidenstam's early fiction, but such irresponsibility is fatal for a leader. His brother Magnus fills the power vacuum.

The state is unified under Magnus' rule. Laws are codified and enforced; ties with the Church are strengthened; a state army of knights is trained and mobilized. Despite his success as a temporal leader, however, Magnus is an anguished man, torn by internal conflicts. He feels guilty about imprisoning his brother and usurping Valdemar's power, yet, as a politician and leader, Magnus recognizes the necessity of having done so. He is both selfish and hypocritical, but he is also motivated by a real desire to establish order and justice.

A tortured spirit like Heidenstam's other heroes, Magnus is not able to find happiness. His personal compromises, however, do not overshadow the fact that he has molded a nation striving for peace and a more just society. Heidenstam suggests that his heroes are a mixture of good and evil, possessed of both virtues and vices, and that these heroes reflect the character of the nation as a whole. Though Heidenstam shows Magnus as flawed, one can take heart in the fact that civilization has made great strides from Folke Filbyter's day to Magnus Folkung's: In his last novel, Heidenstam offers the hope of progress.

Major publications other than long fiction
SHORT FICTION: *Sankt Göran och draken*, 1900; *Skogen susar*, 1904.

POETRY: *Vallfart och vandringsår*, 1888; *Dikter*, 1895; *Nya dikter*, 1915; *Sweden's Laureate: Selected Poems of Verner von Heidenstam*, 1919; *Sista dikter*, 1942; *Fragment och aforismer*, 1959.

NONFICTION: *Från Col di Tenda till Blocksberg*, 1888; *Renässans*, 1889; *Pepitas bröllop*, 1890 (with Oscar Levertin); *Modern Barbarism*, 1894; *Klassicitet och germanism*, 1898; *Tankar och tekningar*, 1899; *Svenskarna och deras hövdingar*, 1908-1910 (*The Swedes and Their Chieftains*, 1925); *Dagar och händelser*, 1909; *Proletärfilosofiens upplösning och fall*, 1911; *Vad vilja vi?*, 1914; *När kastanjerna blommade*, 1941; *Tankar och utkast*, 1941.

MISCELLANEOUS: *Samlade skrifter*, 1909-1949 (23 volumes).

Bibliography
Axberger, Gunnar. *Diktaren och elden*, 1959.
Björck, Staffan. *Verner von Heidenstam*, 1947.
Böök, Fredrik. *Verner von Heidenstam*, 1945, 1946.
Gustafson, Alrik. *A History of Scandinavian Literature*, 1961.
_____ . *Six Scandinavian Novelists*, 1940.
Rossel, Sven H. *A History of Scandinavian Literature, 1870-1980*, 1982.

Christer L. Mossberg

HERMANN HESSE

Born: Calw, Germany; July 2, 1877
Died: Montagnola, Switzerland; August 9, 1962

Principal long fiction

Peter Camenzind, 1904 (English translation, 1961); *Unterm Rad*, 1906 (*The Prodigy*, 1957; also as *Beneath the Wheel*, 1968); *Gertrud*, 1910 (English translation, 1955); *Rosshalde*, 1914 (English translation, 1970); *Knulp: Drei Geschichten aus dem Leben Knulps*, 1915 (*Knulp: Three Tales from the Life of Knulp*, 1971); *Demian*, 1919 (English translation, 1923); *Klingsor*, 1920 (*Klingsor's Last Summer*, 1970; includes the three novellas "Klein und Wagner," "Kinderseele," and "Klingsors letzter Sommer"); *Siddhartha*, 1922 (English translation, 1951); *Der Steppenwolf*, 1927 (*Steppenwolf*, 1929); *Narziss und Goldmund*, 1930 (*Death and the Lover*, 1932; also as *Narcissus and Goldmund*, 1968); *Die Morgenlandfahrt*, 1932 (*The Journey to the East*, 1956); *Das Glasperlenspiel*, 1943 (*Magister Ludi*, 1949; also as *The Glass Bead Game*, 1969).

Other literary forms

In 1899, Hermann Hesse published a collection of his poems under the title *Romantische Lieder* (romantic songs), and this was to be the first volume of a truly prodigious literary output. In addition to his longer prose works, Hesse wrote several volumes of poems, fairy tales, and short prose pieces. Hesse was also a prolific letter writer and reviewer: In the course of his lifetime, he reviewed more than 2,500 books, and his correspondence fills many volumes. Hesse's essays, which typically express pacifist views or a humanitarian identification with all mankind, have appeared both as separate volumes and as a part of his massive collected works.

Achievements

By the beginning of World War I, Hesse had become, in the German-speaking countries of Europe, a solid literary success. His poems, prose vignettes, and novels sold well, and he was tantamount to a habit with German readers by 1914. At the outbreak of the war, however, this situation soon changed in Germany, the result primarily of Hesse's outspoken disparagement of militarism and chauvinism. After the war, Hesse once again became a popular author, especially among younger readers, but this popularity lasted only until the advent of National Socialism, and in 1939, Hesse was officially placed on the list of banned authors, having long since been vilified as a "Jew lover" and unpatriotic draft dodger (from 1890 to 1924, Hesse was a German, not a Swiss, citizen). Throughout and despite this ebb and flow of critical celebration, Hesse continued to write.

After World War II, Hesse was once again sought after—personally and as a writer—as one who could offer moral guidance to a spiritually bankrupt and physically crippled Germany. He became, almost overnight, a celebrity, and was awarded a series of literary prizes, including the Goethe Prize and the Nobel Prize for Literature, both in 1946. Although some still voiced doubts about Hesse as a writer and insisted he was not of the stature of a Thomas Mann, a Bertolt Brecht, or a Franz Kafka, Hesse's popularity in Germany lasted until about 1960, when it rapidly declined. It was at that time, paradoxically enough, that an international "Hessemania" took hold, a kind of exuberant reverence which was particularly strong among disaffected young people in countries as disparate as Sweden, Japan, and the United States. In America alone, more than ten million copies of Hesse's works were sold between 1960 and 1970 (when the Hesse wave crested), a literary phenomenon without precedent. Whatever reservations one may have about Hesse, it is a fact that he remains the most widely read German author of all time.

Biography

Hermann Hesse was born on July 2, 1877, in Calw, Germany, the son of Johannes Hesse, a Baltic-born Pietist missionary, and Marie Hesse (née Gundert), the oldest daughter of the missionary and scholar of Indic languages Hermann Gundert. From 1881 to 1886, Hesse lived with his parents in Basel, Switzerland, where his father taught at the Basel Mission School, but in 1886, Hesse returned to Calw to attend elementary school. During the academic year 1890-1891, Hesse was a pupil at the Göppingen Latin school, where he prepared to take the rigorous state examinations for entrance to one of Württemberg's four church schools. He passed, and in fall of 1891 he was sent to the seminary in Maulbronn. There the young Hesse was desperately unhappy, and after seven months, he fled from the institution, resolving to be "either a writer or nothing at all." After a suicide attempt in June of 1892, Hesse was sent for a few months to a home for retarded children in Stetten. Promising better behavior, Hesse was sent in November to the *gymnasium* in Cannstatt; once again he ran away, however, and this episode concluded Hesse's formal education.

From 1895 to 1898, Hesse worked as an apprentice in a Tübingen bookstore owned by J. J. Heckenhauer, and from 1899 to 1903, he was employed as a stock clerk in a rare-book store in Basel; it was during the latter years that Hesse began to write in earnest. When his articles and reviews began to appear in the *Allgemeine schweizer Zeitung*, he achieved some measure of local success, which was a great source of encouragement to him. Volumes of poems were published in 1899 and 1902, and by the time *Peter Camenzind* was published in 1904, Hesse had "arrived" as a writer. In this same year, Hesse married his first wife, Maria Bernoulli, a member of an old Basel academic family. The couple moved to an idyllic peasant house in Gaienhofen on Lake Constance, where Hesse worked on his novels, painted, and continued his career as a free-lance contributor to numerous journals and newspapers. Hesse's sons Bruno, Heiner, and Martin were all born at Gaienhofen between 1905 and 1911. By the latter year, however, Hesse was restless and felt the need to travel to India with his artist friend Hans Sturzenegger; this journey was to have a profound influence on Hesse for the rest of his life.

From the outbreak of World War I through 1919, Hesse's pacifist articles appeared in German, Swiss, and Austrian newspapers. In 1915, Hesse suffered a nervous breakdown and underwent psychotherapy with J. B. Lang, a student of C. G. Jung, in Sonnmatt near Lucerne. In 1919, he moved to Montagnola, Ticino, in part to escape the memories of Gaienhofen and his first marriage, which ended with his wife's institutionalization. He lived in Montagnola in the Casa Camuzzi until 1931. A writer's block of some eighteen months precipitated therapy once again, this time with Jung himself, in Küsnacht near Zurich. In 1924, Hesse became a Swiss citizen and married Ruth Wenger, the daughter of a writer; at her request, the unhappy union ended in divorce in 1927. In 1931, Hesse married the art historian Ninon Dolbin. The couple moved into a house on the Collina d'Oro with lifetime right of occupancy; this marriage, at last, was a happy one. From 1939 to 1945, Hesse's works were proscribed in Germany, but in 1946, publication of his works was resumed by Suhrkamp, and it was in this year that Hesse received the Goethe Prize and the Nobel Prize. In 1955, Hesse was awarded the Peace Prize of the German Booksellers' Association, and in 1956, a Hermann Hesse Prize was established by the state of Baden-Württemberg. Hesse died at Montagnola on August 9, 1962.

Analysis

Despite a literary career which, if measured by quantity of literary output or by size of readership, was enormously successful, Hermann Hesse has not been numbered among the luminaries of twentieth century German literature. There are two primary reasons for this critical assessment: First, Hesse's prose is simply too readable and discursive to be considered profound; second, Hesse's limited and recurring themes remain, in their many novelistic permutations, rather juvenile and solipsistic in nature. This may well explain the fact that Hesse's readership has always been primarily a young one.

Hesse was among the first European writers to undergo psychoanalysis, and it was his fascination with the self which, from the beginning to the end of his literary career, was to remain the wellspring of his inspiration. Hesse's interior life became the stuff of his fiction, and it is this "private mythology" (Hesse's term) which is the organizing principle of his novels. It is in this sense that Hesse is a "psychological" writer, and it has often been pointed out in Hesse scholarship that, to a rare degree and perhaps in too facile a manner, the link between personal life and literary work is transparent. As

Christopher Middleton has observed, Hesse can be characterized as a literary "acrobat of self-exploration," one who oscillates between self-esteem and self-disgust, often with an implicit moralizing intent. Hesse is an essentially confessional writer, an inveterate and somewhat didactic self-anatomizer.

The narrative scheme of all of Hesse's novels is essentially triadic: A protagonist's character and background are carefully presented; the disillusioned main character chooses to break with his setting and/or former self in search of a new identity or individuation (Hesse's protagonists are invariably males); the experiment results in a prodigal's return or in a successful forging of deeper inroads into the self, sometimes even in the adoption of an almost new personality.

Demian, published in 1919, was Hesse's sixth novel, but it can be considered his first major one. It was preceded by the following less distinguished works: *Peter Camenzind*, the story of a Swiss village lad who leaves his native surroundings in search of inner peace and who, after much meandering and a variety of experiences, returns to his ailing father and accepts a village way of life; *Beneath the Wheel*, a somewhat stock *Schulroman*, or school novel, which depicts the extreme authoritarianism, inhumanity, and pressures of a typical German secondary school of the time; *Gertrud*, a *Künstlerroman* (a genre which arose in German literature in the late eighteenth century—the term used to designate any novel with an artist as its protagonist) treating the tribulations of a physically handicapped composer; *Rosshalde*, an autobiographical novel reflecting the breakup of Hesse's marriage to Maria Bernoulli, who suffered from a progressive mental illness; and finally *Knulp*, a novel in three parts which marks the culmination of Hesse's Romantic phase and which narrates the picaresque life and death of its central character.

Demian, Hesse's first postwar novel, incorporates Hesse's reaction to World War I as well as his psychoanalysis during 1916 and 1917. Both of these experiences had led Hesse to a fundamental reassessment of his life, and this revaluation finds expression in the *Bildungsroman*, which chronicles (in a first-person narrative) the youth of Emil Sinclair. At the outset of the novel, Sinclair becomes acutely conscious of the essential duality of life, a polarity he notes in the disparity between the safe, moral, ordered world of his home and the dynamic, cruel world outside. The latter is represented by the bully Franz Kromer, from whom Sinclair is rescued by a new boy at school, Max Demian. Demian alleviates Sinclair's moral confusion by telling him of the god Abraxas, in whom good and evil are fused and who represents the highest moral order. Demian also emphasizes the decline of European civilization, predicts its impending doom, and anticipates the advent of a regeneration of the world. With the outbreak of war in 1914, Demian's prophecy comes true. Both Demian and Sinclair are called up, and the latter is wounded. He is brought to a field hospital, where he has a final encounter with Demian, who lies dying; Sinclair is then separated from his mentor forever, but he believes himself to be the inheritor of his friend's personality.

Considered as a whole, therefore, the division of the novel is tripartite: Sinclair goes from a state of initial "light," of childhood innocence and security, to a period of "dark," of doubt and inner torment, to a final internal synthesis of the two antipodes. The novel is somewhat fraught with symbols which are intended to underscore the universality of this sequence; one of the book's central dream-images is elucidated in a manner which succinctly captures the dynamics of any process of individuation: "The bird fights its way out of the egg. The egg is the world. Who would be born must first destroy a world." Demian is Sinclair's shaman for this process of destruction (Socrates used the word *daimon* to describe the admonishing inner spirit), a process which Hesse imbues with tension by mixing Nietzschean thought, Christian terminology, and a religious, often parablelike tone. At the end of the novel, Sinclair has internalized Demian, much as the Church Fathers and later Christian authors admonished their readers to internalize Christ. Emil Sinclair is, therefore, now a missionary of the new gospel of Demian (read: Hesse)—namely, that one must be willing to suffer the progressive alienation and pain which result from shedding traditional or inherited strictures and definitions, a necessary divestiture which will ultimately make possible a rejuvenation, an authentic sense of self-identity.

Siddhartha, Hesse's second major novel and arguably his best-known work, took nearly four years to complete. *Siddhartha* is the product both of Hesse's trip to India in 1911 and of his lifelong fascination with that country's philosophy and religion. At the same time, however, it would be an oversimplification to state (as some critics have done) that this novel is a paean to Indic philosophy or Eastern mysticism, since the implicit admonition of the work is that one must seek one's own way in life and not simply adhere to a prescribed system or path.

The plot of *Siddhartha* exhibits the essential tripartite structure of all of Hesse's works, two-section and twelve-chapter divisions notwithstanding: The Brahman's son Siddhartha (whose name means "he who has achieved his aim") leaves his paternal home, has the requisite educative experiences of a *Bildungsroman* protagonist, and finally achieves peace. What makes *Siddhartha* such an atypical and successful "novel of education" are its Eastern setting and its complementary stylistic features, the latter signifying a level of technical originality and subtlety Hesse was never again to achieve. Feeling restless, Siddhartha forsakes his home and the teachings of Brahmanism and, with his friend Govinda, becomes a total ascetic. Still unsatisfied, he considers the teachings of Buddha but ultimately departs from him, leaving Govinda behind. As an alternative to his previous existence, Siddhartha seeks a life of the senses; the courtesan Kamala teaches him the art of love, and he acquires a great deal of wealth. After a time, however, he comes to feel that this surfeit of sensual pleasures is robbing him of his soul, and he takes sudden leave of this life and of Kamala, unaware that she is pregnant. In despair and on the verge of suicide, he encounters the wise ferryman Vasudeva, from whom he learns "the secrets of the river," the simultaneity, unity, and time-lessness of all that is:

> This stone is stone: it is also animal, it is also God, it is also Buddha. I love and venerate it not because it might someday become this or that—but because it has long been all these things and always will be.

After Siddhartha has spent twelve years at the river, Kamala unexpectedly arrives with their son, whereupon she is bitten by a snake and dies. Siddhartha's love and teaching are rejected by his son—just as Siddhartha himself rejected his father many years earlier—but the protagonist overcomes his anguish and loss with the help of the river. Vasudeva dies, Siddhartha becomes the ferryman in his place, and the narrative concludes with the reunion of Siddhartha and Govinda.

Like *Demian*, *Siddhartha* is meant to carry universal implications. The protagonists in both novels are stylized figures whose lives and personalities are only episodically sketched, since what was important to Hesse was less their individuality as literary personae than what they embodied. Both stories possess only a modicum of realistic narrative, and both central figures represent the path of individuality which, Hesse was convinced, must be chosen by all self-seekers. Demian's Abraxas and Siddhartha's river are simply narrative means to this end, symbols of the conflux of opposites, the harmony one experiences with self and all existence in a heightened state of self-awareness. As Hesse stated in his diary of 1920, "Nirvana, as I understand it, is the liberating step back behind the *principium individuationis*." Artistically, however, *Demian* and *Siddhartha* are very different. Unlike *Demian*—and indeed, unlike the several major novels of Hesse to follow—*Siddhartha* maintains a stylistic simplicity and an extraordinary harmony of form and substance which Hesse was never again to capture. The book's initial paragraph reveals, even in translation, much of the stylistic genius of *Siddhartha*:

> In the shade of the house, in the sun of the river bank by the boats, in the shade of the Sal forest, in the shade of the fig tree Siddhartha grew up, the handsome son of the Brahman, the young falcon, along with Govinda, his friend, the son of the Brahman.

The paratactic repetitions—incantatory, alliterative, and often threefold in nature—give the work an almost liturgical quality which is consonant with the novel's theme and setting and which exerts a subliminal but obviously well-calculated effect on the reader. Hesse's following work was to be a radical departure in terms of both style and narrative tack.

Steppenwolf, published in 1927, is certainly Hesse's most unorthodox novel, one which Mann compared to James Joyce's *Ulysses* (1922) and André Gide's *Les Faux-monnayeurs* (1925; *The Counterfeiters*, 1927) in experimental daring. Like these novels, Hesse's work met with a great deal of criticism, a fact which is easily explained in the light of the demands which these narratives place on their readers. Although it is in places essentially surrealistic and is hence somewhat difficult to recapitulate adequately, *Steppenwolf* does evidence Hesse's typical three-part structure: a preliminary or introductory segment; a somewhat realistic central section; and a final part chronicling the protagonist's experiences in a "Magic Theater."

An unnamed and self-described "bourgeois, orderly person" functions as the author of an introduction to the reflections of Harry Haller, whose first-person jottings he is editing. This editor also articulates the two poles of existence, the inner tension of Harry Haller, namely, his fundamental dichotomy as both "wolf" and "bourgeois." The schizophrenic protagonist, a scholarly aesthete and conformist by day but at night an outsider who despises society and its values, describes himself as a living dualism: "I don't know why it is, but I—the homeless Steppenwolf and lonely hater of the petty bourgeois world—I always live in proper middle-class houses." Haller's ruminations on his rootless existence are interrupted, however, by the interjection of a "Tract of the Steppenwolf," a booklet which he has mysteriously acquired while on one of his frequent nocturnal walks. This tract, prefaced by the motto "only for madmen," distinguishes between three levels of existence: that of the Bourgeois; that of the Immortals (the highest plane, which transcends all polarities); and that of the Steppenwolf, a level midway between the first two. In describing a particular Steppenwolf called Harry, the document suggests that he abandon polarity as a life-ordering principle and simply affirm all that is as good, and do so with "a sublime wisdom that can only be realized through humor." Harry Haller is unable to comply, however, and he soon takes up with several sympathizers. Hermine, an oracular prostitute, and Pablo, a drug-using saxophone player, show Haller that there are others of his ilk who choose not to conform to society and yet are happy among themselves. Finally, Harry enters into the "Magic Theater" alluded to in the "Tract" and announced earlier in the novel as well. In this penny arcade of the mind, he sheds the final vestiges of his bourgeois personality by means of a series of surreal, drug-induced experiences. The novel concludes on a note of cautious optimism, with Haller projecting that he will someday "play the game of figures better," that he will someday "learn how to laugh."

As Hesse made obvious by the choice of Harry Haller as his protagonist's name, *Steppenwolf* is a highly autobiographical work. Haller's physiognomy, habits, and tastes are Hesse's, as is his basic psychological dilemma. Hesse at the time of the novel's composition was a fifty-year-old man looking inward and outward with little satisfaction. This accounts for the self-laceration as well as the cultural pessimism of *Steppenwolf*, and such disharmony and negativity reflect an inner relapse on the part of the author of the placid *Siddhartha*. Whether Hesse himself indulged in the erotic and chemical adventures of his protagonist is not known and, ultimately, is of little consequence. Certain, however, is the fact that Hesse suffered a good deal of censure as a result of these elements of the book, a fact which distressed him greatly and which caused him to compose and publish in 1928 a poetic postlude to the novel, entitled *Krisis*, a candid personal account of his intention in writing *Steppenwolf* and an assessment of the literary realization of this intention.

Like those of many of Hesse's novels, the ending of *Steppenwolf* is abrupt and unsatisfactory. The concept of humor as a tool for rising above inner and outer tensions seems an inadequate solution for Haller's problems, and one senses, that this is a very forced conclusion. This feeling is reinforced as well by the amazing formal pendulations of Hesse's novels: *Demian* employs psychological symbolism, *Siddhartha* utilizes psychological exoticism, and *Steppenwolf* uses psychological fantasy and even hallucination in order to delineate the same essential problems (How does one arrive at any true self-definition? How is one to reconcile inner polarities, the flesh and the spirit? What is the artist's place in society?) via a variety of expressive modes. If the endings are often truncated or lacking in aesthetic closure, it is because these individual "fragments of a long confession" (Hesse's phrase) represent only one phase, one segment of a process which was to continue. It is no surprise, therefore, that Hesse chose in his next novel yet another narrative format with which to allegorize his dualistic dilemmas.

Much like *Siddhartha*, *Narcissus and Goldmund* can be viewed as a lull following a storm. Hesse himself described *Narcissus and Goldmund* as an essentially escapist tale, and it is the novel about which his critics are most divided. Joseph Mileck, for example, considers it Hesse's finest work, whereas Theodore Ziolkowski flatly states that it is his "most imperfect" work; many critics find the story cloying and regard the novel as a whole as highbrow kitsch.

The names of the two protagonists are symbolic: Narcissus represents the world of the spirit—in this case, the medieval monastery—and is a prototype of the introverted, reflective, self-preoccupied individual; Goldmund (golden mouth) is an artistic extrovert who personifies the world of nature, of the flesh. Hesse once again presents the reader with types rather than with flesh-and-blood characters. Narcissus is the mentor of Goldmund in a monastic school called Mariabronn, but it soon becomes evident that the latter is rather unsuited for a celibate life. He leaves the monastery and leads a life replete with varied experiences and love affairs, all of which lead him closer to his artistic crystallization of the "pole of nature," exemplified in his mind by the image of his mother and eventually by Eve, the "primal mother."

Related to these love-thematics is the stark reality and insuperable dominance of death, which Goldmund seeks to conquer by love. Both protagonists discuss the topic of death and confront it, each in his own manner: Narcissus seeks to exist in a timeless realm of the spirit which in itself is a preparation for death, while Goldmund, hearing in his heart but dreading "the wild song of death," abandons himself to life and love. Sensing this to be an unsatisfactory *modus vivendi* in the light of the transitory nature of everything human, yet unable to accept Narcissus' way as his own, Goldmund eventually discovers in art his answer to death: "When, as artists, we create images or, as thinkers, seek laws and formulate thoughts, we do so in order to save something from the Great Dance of Death, to establish something that has a longer duration than we ourselves." Goldmund dies in peace, having returned to the monastery not as an ascetic, but as an artist.

The underlying idea or conception of art personified in Goldmund is Hesse's own, at least in that it represents his personal ideal. That this ideal is in essence a Romantic one is clear if one outlines the narrative trellis on which the Goldmund character is strung: He represents the vital vagrant who, by dint of a wealth of contacts and experiences, is impelled (if only temporarily) to recede from the din of life in order to internalize, incubate, and finally express what he has encountered in the Orphic creation of a new and timeless work of art. It is in a certain sense true, therefore, that the Hesse who published from 1898 to 1930 never went beyond Romanticism, beyond this conception of the self as the font of meaning and progenitor of all art. This explains as well why realistic fiction was of little importance to Hesse; if literary art is conceived of as an array of self-reflecting mirrors, then exterior reality can be of only secondary or even tertiary significance. It is to Hesse's credit that he came to see that such self-preoccupation was tantamount to irresponsible self-paralysis, and that this *l'art pour l'art* approach was abandoned in his final novel.

Shortly after Hesse's *Narcissus and Goldmund*, his *The Journey to the East* appeared in 1932. The novel is another experiment in narrative technique and setting and is perhaps the most esoteric of Hesse's works. In many ways, this story of "H. H."—of his acceptance into an Order, his participation in a "journey to the East," and his defection and eventual return to the fold—prefigures the dynamics and thematics of Hesse's final novel, *The Glass Bead Game*, published in 1943. The latter took eleven years to compose and is considered by many critics to be Hesse's most substantive novel, his *magnum opus*, which recapitulates but also modifies all that preceded it.

The Glass Bead Game is a modified *Bildungsroman* about Josef Knecht, whose surname means "servant," and is seen by some critics as Hesse's response to the quintessential German novels of education, Johann Wolfgang von Goethe's Wilhelm Meister novels (the surname meaning "master"). Hesse's novel contains three chief divisions: an introduction describing the history of the "glass bead game," characterized as "the quintessence of intellectuality and art, the sublime cult, the *unio mystica* of all separate members of the *universitas litterarum"*; the middle section, which outlines the life of Josef Knecht; and finally an appendix, consisting of some of Knecht's supposed posthumous papers. The novel is set in the twenty-fourth century in a "pedagogical province" called Castalia, in which, in at least quasi-monastic fashion, an elite group dedicates itself to the life of the spirit and the highly developed glass bead game. The latter has evolved in the course of time from a relatively simple game played on an abacus frame into a complex interdisciplinary exercise combining quantitative and theoretical knowledge from various disciplines with symbology and meditation. Knecht becomes a master gameplayer, the *magister ludi* and head of the Order. Gradually, however, inspired partly by his conversations with a brilliant Benedictine monk by the name of Pater Jakobus and partly by his own nagging feelings of responsibility to the world at large, Knecht's reservations about Castalia and its life of utter aestheticism grow to the point that he resigns his post and leaves the rarefied realm he seemed destined from his very youth to lead. Three days after doing so, however, he drowns by accident in an icy mountain lake.

Hesse's final novel is many interesting things, not the least of which is a very clever *roman à clef* whose name-games and onomastics can occupy one inclined to puzzle over them for some time. More significantly, however, the work represents a personal breakthrough for Hesse, since in Knecht one is at last presented with a Hessean protagonist who attempts to overcome his paralytic self-enclosure and accept some notion of social responsibility. Theodore Ziolkowski has suggested that this gesture, represented clearly by Knecht's decision to leave Castalia and commit himself to something practical, was not Hesse's original intention, but that the imminent outbreak of war forced Hesse to abandon his initial literary and aesthetic ideal while writing the second section of the novel. This is more than plausible, and it would explain as well the book's narrative shift regarding the depiction of Castalia.

A stylistic comparison of *The Glass Bead Game* with Hesse's earlier works reveals that language has been given less attention in this final novel, the result in part of the work's heavy freight of theoretical and philosophical ideas (ranging from a theory of music to intellectual concerns of various kinds). Indeed, Josef Knecht is even less a flesh-and-blood persona than Hesse's customary protagonists.

As to the glass bead game itself—described in length but always in somewhat nebulous terms—it appears clear that it symbolizes the attempt on the part of some to achieve an integrated synthesis of what is good or salvageable from the fragmented debris of modern civilization. In this respect, Hesse's last novel marks a fitting conclusion to a lifelong quest for spiritual wholeness.

Major publications other than long fiction

SHORT FICTION: *Eine Stunde hinter Mitternacht*, 1889; *Hinterlassene Schriften und Gedichte von Hermann Lauscher*, 1901; *Diesseits: Erzählungen*, 1907;

Nachbarn: Erzählungen, 1908; *Umwege: Erzählungen*, 1912; *Aus Indien*, 1913; *Am Weg*, 1915; *Schön ist die Jugend*, 1916; *Märchen*, 1919 (*Strange News from Another Star, and Other Tales*, 1972); *Piktors Verwandlungen: Ein Märchen*, 1925; *Die Nürnberger Reise*, 1927; *Kleine Welt: Erzählungen*, 1933; *Stunden im Garten: Eine Idylle*, 1936; *Traumfährte: Neue Erzählungen und Märchen*, 1945 (*The War Goes On*, 1971); *Beschwörungen*, 1955.

POETRY: *Romantische Lieder*, 1899; *Unterwegs: Gedichte*, 1911; *Musik des Einsamen: Neue Gedichte*, 1915; *Gedichte des Malers*, 1920; *Krisis*, 1928; *Trost der Nacht: Neue Gedichte*, 1929; *Neue Gedichte*, 1937; *Späte Gedichte*, 1946; *Poems*, 1970.

NONFICTION: *Boccaccio*, 1904; *Franz von Assisi*, 1904; *Zarathustras Wiederkehr: Ein Wort an die deutsche Jugend von einem Deutschen*, 1919; *Ein Blick ins Chaos*, 1920; *Betrachtungen*, 1928; *Kleine Betrachtungen*, 1941; *Krieg und Frieden: Betrachtungen zu Krieg und Politik seit dem Jahr 1914*, 1946 (*If the War Goes On*, 1971); *Hermann Hesse: Essays*, 1970.

Bibliography

Boulby, Mark. *Hermann Hesse: His Mind and Art*, 1967.

Freedman, Ralph. *Hermann Hesse: Pilgrim of Crisis, a Biography*, 1978.

Mileck, Joseph. *Hermann Hesse: Biography and Bibliography*, 1977 (2 volumes).

_____ . *Hermann Hesse and His Critics*, 1958.

Seidlin, Oscar. "Hermann Hesse: The Exorcism of the Demon," in *Symposium*. IV (1950), pp. 325-348.

Ziolkowski, Theodore. *Hermann Hesse*, 1966.

_____ . *The Novels of Hermann Hesse: A Study in Theme and Structure*, 1965.

N. J. Meyerhofer

E. T. A. HOFFMANN

Born: Königsberg, Germany; January 24, 1776
Died: Berlin, Germany; June 25, 1822

Principal long fiction

Die Elixiere des Teufels: Nachgelassene Papiere des Bruders Medardus, eines Kapuziners, 1815-1816 (*The Devil's Elixirs: From the Posthumous Papers of Brother Medardus, a Capuchin Friar*, 1824); *Lebensansichten des Katers Murr, nebst fragmentarischer Biographie des Kapellmeisters Johannes Kreisler in zufälligen Makulaturblättern*, 1820-1822 (*The Life and Opinions of Kater Murr, with the Fragmentary Biography of Kapellmeister Johannes Kreisler on Random Sheets of Scrap Paper*, 1907).

Other literary forms

For most of his life, E. T. A. Hoffmann cherished the hope that he would one day be remembered as a composer, and it was only late in his career as an artist that literary preoccupations began to outweigh his interest in music. By the time of his death, Hoffmann had, nevertheless, produced a considerable literary oeuvre that included two novels and more than seventy tales. Hoffmann gathered most of the tales into three collections. He published the first under the title *Fantasiestücke in Callots Manier* (1814-1815; fantasy pieces in the style of Callot). Included in it are Hoffmann's important first story, "Ritter Gluck: Eine Erinnerung aus dem Jahr 1809" ("Ritter Gluck"), as well as his most famous fairy tale, "Der goldene Topf: Ein Märchen aus der neuen Zeit" ("The Golden Flower Pot"). Hoffmann's second collection, *Nachtstücke* (1817; night pieces), contains his most ghostly, even ghoulish, creations. Its opening story, "Der Sandmann" ("The Sandman"), still served Sigmund Freud in 1919 as a case study of man's sense of the uncanny. Into the four volumes of *Die Serapionsbrüder* (1819-1821; *The Serapion Brethren*, 1886-1892), Hoffmann incorporated "Rat Krespel" ("Councillor Krespel"), "Die Bergwerke zu Falun" ("The Mines of Falun"), and—immortalized by Peter Ilich Tchaikovsky in 1892 as *The Nutcracker Suite*—the fairy tale "Nussknacker und Mausekönig" ("Nutcracker and the King of Mice"). The first detective story in European literature and Hoffmann's most popular tale during his lifetime, "Das Fräulein von Scudéri" ("Mademoiselle de Scudéri") also appeared in *The Serapion Brethren*.

During the last three years of his life, Hoffmann wrote three lengthy, complex tales in which he tried to achieve a unique blend of fairy tale, social satire, and aesthetic speculation: *Klein Zaches, genannt Zinnober* (1819; *Little Zaches, Surnamed Zinnober*, 1971), *Prinzessin Brambilla: Ein Capriccio nach Jakob Callot* (1821; *Princess Brambilla: A "Capriccio" in the Style of Jacques Callot*, 1971), and *Meister Floh: Ein Märchen in sieben Abenteuern zweier*

Freunde (1822; *Master Flea: A Fairy Tale in Seven Adventures of Two Friends*, 1826). Hoffmann's letters and diaries have been published in the four-volume *Tagebücher* (1971).

Achievements

In his own day, Hoffmann became a successful writer in a remarkably short time. His ghost and horror stories were received with favor by the critics and with enthusiasm by the general reading public. Still, few would have considered Hoffmann to be more than an admittedly original and masterful entertainer. With his mixture of the miraculous, the fantastic, and the horrible, he clearly catered to his generation's fascination with the occult, his readers' thirst for the thrill of a spine-chilling story.

After Hoffmann's death, his reputation diminished rapidly and was finally destroyed by a formidable opponent from abroad. In 1827, Sir Walter Scott published a scathing attack against the excessive employment of supernatural elements in fiction entitled *On the Supernatural in Fictitious Composition: Works of Hoffmann*. Using the works of Hoffmann to make his point, he concluded that only an opium-inflamed mind could have conceived such frightful chimeras. Scott's assault on Hoffmann's reputation proved fatal, because Johann Wolfgang von Goethe then made it his personal responsibility to recommend Scott's indictment of the unsavory Hoffmann to the sane sensibilities of his German compatriots.

That Hoffmann's writings survived this Olympian disapproval is largely the result of their success in France. Though none of Hoffmann's works had been translated into a foreign language during his life, French translations of several of his tales shortly after his death were quickly followed by a veritable Hoffmann vogue among France's most distinguished writers. Honoré de Balzac and Charles Baudelaire showed themselves to be greatly impressed, and in 1836, Gérard de Nerval summarized the French conception of Germany's literary pantheon by speaking of Germany as the land of Friedrich Schiller, Goethe, and Hoffmann. Stimulated by the French, enthusiasm for Hoffmann caught fire in Russia as well. Indeed, there is no major Russian writer of the nineteenth century—from Alexander Pushkin and Nikolai Gogol to Fyodor Dostoevski and Leo Tolstoy—who did not acknowledge Hoffmann's impact on his work.

In the Anglo-Saxon world, by contrast, Scott's article squelched whatever interest there might have been in the achievements of Hoffmann. Still, as if by an ironic twist, it is in that world that Hoffmann doubtless found his most congenial successor, Edgar Allan Poe. The precise nature and extent of Hoffmann's influence on Poe, have, however, remained a much-debated and apparently elusive issue among literary historians.

Hoffmann would certainly have derived special gratification from the fact that, while his own musical compositions did not bring him fame, composers throughout the nineteenth century set his literary inspirations to music. Thus, for a wide and international audience, Hoffmann's name is often linked, if not identified, with the names of his greatest musical admirers. Robert Schumann's *Kreisleriana* (1838; eight fantasies for keyboard devoted to Kreisler, the hero of Hoffmann's second novel), Jacques Offenbach's opera *Les Contes d'Hoffmann* (1881; *The Tales of Hoffmann*), and Tchaikovsky's ballet *The Nutcracker Suite* are only the best known of many musical offerings to the genius of Hoffmann.

In the twentieth century, Hoffmann has finally emerged, even in Germany, as one of that country's most brilliant writers of fiction. He has become especially valued as a fearless explorer of the labyrinthine qualities of the human psyche in its desperate search for inner order in the face of instinctual lust and aggression. Hoffmann's works are definitely casting their spell again, though more than ever before the reader often feels ambivalent about what is charm and what is curse within that spell's obsessive power.

Biography

Ernst Theodor Wilhelm Hoffmann—who in later life replaced his third baptismal name with Amadeus, in honor of Wolfgang Amadeus Mozart—was born in Königsberg, then the capital of East Prussia, now part of the Soviet Union. The disastrous marriage between his father, an alcoholic lawyer, and his mother, a mentally unstable recluse, was dissolved when Hoffmann was only three years old. He subsequently grew up under the pedantic tutelage of a bachelor uncle. The precocious boy spent a loveless and lonely childhood from which only his instructions in music and painting provided some much-needed relief.

At the age of sixteen, Hoffmann enrolled as a student of law at the University of Königsberg. Three years later, he passed his examinations with great distinction. He thereupon joined the legal branch of Prussia's civil service and was employed in various capacities in Glogau (1796-1798), Berlin (1798-1800), Posen (1800-1802), Plock (1802-1804), and Warsaw (1804-1806). All through these years, Hoffmann combined a punctilious execution of his official duties with an increasing interest in music, as well as a wild bachelor existence in which the consumption of alcohol played an increasingly significant part. Hoffmann's marriage in 1802 to Michalina Rohrer, the daughter of a minor Polish civil servant, was entered into almost casually and seems to have been of little consequence to Hoffmann for the rest of his life.

It was in Warsaw that Hoffmann seriously started to cultivate a second career as composer and conductor. When, in 1806, the collapse of Prussia's Polish empire under the Napoleonic onslaught deprived him of his position and livelihood in Warsaw, he decided to embark on a musical career as a new profession. For more than a year, he tried to establish himself in Berlin, an impossible task, as it turned out, in the defeated and impoverished capital of

Prussia. He finally accepted a position as music director at the theater and opera house of Bamberg, a small town in northeastern Bavaria.

Hoffmann began his career in music with great expectations and, in spite of an almost immediate disenchantment with the new occupation, remained in Bamberg for four and a half years, supplementing his frequently uncertain income by giving music lessons to members of patrician families in town. His hopeless passion for the gifted vocal student Julia Marc was to become the most embittering experience of his stay. In 1813, Hoffmann joined an opera company that traveled between Leipzig and Dresden, yet this change only caused his professional frustrations to reach new heights. When, therefore, an influential friend, Theodor Gottlieb von Hippel, managed to have him reinstated in Prussia's legal service in 1814, Hoffmann eagerly jumped at the chance. He returned to his beloved Berlin, where he was to reside until his death in 1822.

In 1814, Hoffmann was thirty-eight years old. Until that time, little in his life suggested that during the eight years left to him he was to become one of the most prominent writers of his age. In the preceding ten years, he had made a concerted effort to establish himself as a composer. By 1814, the list of his compositions included several operas, two masses, and one symphony, as well as a considerable quantity of vocal and instrumental music, yet it was only with the publication of his first collection of tales, during the same year, that Hoffmann finally gained the recognition that had eluded him in all of his musical productivity. Hoffmann, obviously exhilarated by the experience of success, set out to write with single-minded fervor. Publishers sought him out, and so did the literary salons of Berlin. The publishers Hoffmann tried to satisfy; the literary salons, however, he more and more regularly exchanged for the wine cellar of Lutter and Wegener, where he and his alter ego, the famous actor Ludwig Devrient, drank themselves into states of fantastic exaltation.

In spite of his private excesses, Hoffmann's professional career—he was to become vice president of the Supreme Court of Prussia—and literary career proceeded with unimpeded speed until his body gave way under the triple strain. In 1821, Hoffmann began to suffer from a rapidly advancing paralysis, perhaps the result of a syphilitic infection. Writing—finally dictating—at a feverish pace, Hoffmann died several months later, at the age of forty-six.

Analysis

E. T. A. Hoffmann's literary work constitutes a compelling and insightful expression of the prevailing anxieties of a deeply unsettled age. The rational improvement of the private self and the enforced stability of the social self were severely shaken by the upheavals of the French Revolution and the rise of Napoleon's will to power. The heroes of this restless time revealed to the perceptive observer unexpectedly atavistic passions compared to which all existing social and ethical norms proved exceedingly insubstantial. People came to the realization that they had hardly known themselves to that point and that it was critical for them to learn more about what was asserting itself so menacingly in their lives. Interest in marginal, even pathological, states of the mind—in hypnosis, telepathy, magnetism, somnambulism, dreams, and trances—became a widespread obsession. In its wake, there arose the specter of a human existence threatened from within by chaotic instincts and threatened from without by capricious turns of events.

Probably more than any other writer of his time, Hoffmann delved into the vicissitudes that the defenseless psyche undergoes as it finds itself in the grip of conflicting demands that it can neither adjudicate nor deny. To introduce the reader to the torture chambers of the mind, Hoffmann employed an arsenal of literary devices that his audience knew well from Gothic horror stories. Madness, witchery, cloak-and-dagger intrigues, secret passageways, mysterious doubles, incest, rape, and human sacrifice follow one another with baffling speed in mystifying plots that disorient the reader until he no longer can tell what is real and what is imagined, what is mere wish and what is accomplished fact.

In *The Devil's Elixirs*, the plot of which was clearly inspired by Matthew Gregory Lewis' Gothic novel *Ambrosio: Or, The Monk* (1795), the Capuchin friar Medardus recounts the story of his rebellious flight from the monastery and his repentant return to it. Medardus is born within the precincts of a monastery, grows up in the vicinity of a nunnery, and promptly resolves to live a religious life himself. After having become an extraordinarily successful preacher at his monastery, he suddenly experiences a breakdown of his rhetorical abilities and is desperate for a cure from the mysterious ailment. He knows that among the monastery's sacred relics there is preserved a flask filled with a potent elixir which the Devil had once offered to the hermit Saint Anthony during his temptations in the desert. Medardus takes a draught from the flask, finds his powers restored, but also senses new and ominous passions rushing through his veins. Medardus' superior, concerned about the peace of the monastic community, soon finds himself forced to send the agitated and arrogant monk on a mission to Rome.

From the moment Medardus leaves the monastery, the reader is hard put to assess the actual nature of the monk's frenzied adventures. Torn between contradictory desires, Medardus' personality repeatedly breaks apart, integral elements battling one another as life-size enemies. Presented with a chance to assume another identity—which in fact appeals to everything he has suppressed during his years as a monk—Medardus wantonly enters an adulterous affair with a Baroness while, at the same time, falling in love with her angelic stepdaughter, Aurelie. The resulting emotional turmoil culminates in a scene of horror in which Medardus poisons the Baroness and tries to rape Aurelie. Momentarily exorcised from his evil self by the enormity of the crime, he hurries away in frantic fear of his own passions.

After further wanderings, Medardus meets Aurelie again. This time, he is determined to court her with genuine love and devotion, yet the demoniac compulsion to subjugate and destroy the love he awakens never completely leaves him. On their wedding day, the indomitable strain in Medardus' soul flares up with renewed ferocity. As he sees his alter ego carted off to execution, he refuses to let it die, rejects Aurelie and everything noble in himself, and runs off, his satanic double on his back, until rage and frustration deprive him of his senses. Several months later, Medardus revives, finding himself in an Italian insane asylum. He proceeds to submit his body to a rigorous course of penance and, after many additional adventures, returns to the monastery from which he had set out. He arrives the day before Aurelie is to take her religious vows in a nearby convent. Overwhelmed by the coincidence, Medardus feels rent apart again. He claims Aurelie for himself and slays her on the steps of the altar. Having thus destroyed the object of his passion, Medardus is at last free to reject the call of instinct and to reenter the tranquillity of monastic life.

The Devil's Elixirs can be read on at least two levels. Late in the novel, the reader is told that the main characters are, unbeknown to themselves, members of one family which for several generations has lived under a curse resulting from a sacrilege committed by one of its ancestors. That curse can be laid to rest only if the remaining members of the family renounce earthly love and thus mark the family for extinction. Medardus and Aurelie, the last of the unholy clan, embrace the necessary self-denial and break the chain of sin and guilt. The notion of an inherited curse was the stock-in-trade of the Gothic novel. The introduction of supernatural agencies allowed authors to explain the many otherwise inexplicable coincidences needed to sustain the suspense of their stories. The real impact of *The Devil's Elixirs*, therefore, does not arise from Hoffmann's belated revelations about Medardus' guilt-ridden family but rather from his relentless depiction of a man's fearful struggle with instincts that lie, in stubborn and hostile cynicism, beyond the reach of his moral self.

Medardus, of course, does put an end to the curse, not only for his family but also for his own troubled self. *The Devil's Elixirs*, after all, is his auto-biography; it contains his retrospective creation of a continuous self and signals a significant victory over his chaotic past. The success with which Medardus has managed to construct—from the fragmented impulses of his psyche—the notion of a responsible personality shows that he has established for himself a basis for moral behavior. Still, he has stabilized his personality at a high price: the exclusion of all instinct, the truncating of his very life. Secure as Medardus' self now might be, a unified self it is not, and no amount of Catholic pageantry can disguise the pessimism of that conclusion.

Hoffmann's second novel, *The Life and Opinions of Kater Murr*, remained a fragment, a fact which—considering the less than convincing end of *The Devil's Elixirs*—rather enhances its effectiveness. In contrast to *The Devil's Elixirs*, which in spite of its confusing plot followed the traditional technique of a chronological narration, *The Life and Opinions of Kater Murr* surprises the reader with one of the most amusingly original structures in German literature. The novel is composed of two distinct narratives bewilderingly conflated: the autobiography of a tomcat (Murr) and the biography of a musician (Kreisler). Murr, so the editor apologizes, had, while writing his memoirs, torn up the biography of Kreisler in order to use its pages as writing pad and blotting paper. When Murr had his work published, the printer mistakenly thought the sheets from Kreisler's life to be part of the tomcat's autobiography, so that in the finished product two very dissimilar stories interrupt each other with maddening regularity.

In Murr's account, Hoffmann parodies the educational novel, the *Bildungsroman*, of his day. Murr, a smugly egotistical tomcat, pompously details the stages by which he planned to advance himself in the world. With all the naïveté of his inflated ego, he tells how he first embarked on an academic career, then felt free to pursue romantic love, became involved in the political arena, and finally aspired to be recognized as a true gentleman. At the end, the reader is informed that the splendid cat has unfortunately died, a fate common to those who achieve too much at too early an age.

That Murr's penmanship at least left much to be desired might be gathered from the fact that about two-thirds of all pages in the book were apparently needed as blotting paper. These pages tell of the life of Johannes Kreisler. The story opens at the small court of Sieghartsweiler, where for some time now the former mistress of Prince Irenäus has spun an intrigue that is to lead to a marriage between Irenäus' half-witted son Ignaz and her own daughter, the beautiful and sensitive Julia.

The plot gets under way as the eccentric musician Kreisler joins the tedious life at the miniature court. He soon is asked to give Julia and Hedwiga, Prince Irenäus' only daughter, music lessons, and the two girls are quickly attracted to Kreisler by the strange powers that his curiously extravagant behavior reveals. Their idyllic association is destroyed by the news that Hedwiga is to marry the handsome but unscrupulous Prince Hektor. Hektor, assured that in time he will possess Hedwiga, promptly sets out to seduce Julia. For a while, Kreisler manages to foil Hektor's plans, until an attempt on Kreisler's life forces the musician to flee from court. He takes up residence in a nearby Benedictine abbey and there resumes work as composer and music director. Unfortunately, Kreisler has barely achieved peace in his new surroundings when an urgent letter from Sieghartsweiler implores him to return to court, where a double wedding between Hektor and Hedwiga, Ignaz and Julia is about to take place. Whether Kreisler was able to prevent this impending misfortune remains unclear as the novel breaks off in the middle of a sentence.

Throughout the story, evidence accumulates suggesting that Kreisler, whose identity is the central mystery of the plot, may well be the victim of a long-standing court intrigue. Yet the attraction that Kreisler's character exerts seems to depend even less on the unraveling of a web of fateful family relations than did the account of the friar Medardus. What the torn-out pages of Kreisler's biography tell about the torn-up life of its hero, no clandestine schemes could possibly bind together. Kreisler's existential rootlessness is ultimately the result not of clever machinations from without but of his own self-lacerating quest for human perfection in a petty environment. Sheltering a highly idealistic and highly vulnerable personality behind masks of cynicism and eccentricity, Kreisler is plagued by the sudden shifts of an artistic vision that shows the trivial to be sublime as often as it shows the sublime to be trivial. Thus barred from any consistent perspective on world or self, he is forced to vacillate between ecstatic joy and despondent frustration: ecstatic joy at the world's grandeur, despondent frustration at its inevitable depreciation at the hands of unresponsive men. In contrast to Medardus, who could still reconstruct his divided will from the secure vision of an undisputed faith, Kreisler's divided perception finds no such security; even his monastic retreat offers him hardly more than a brief respite from his self-tormented life.

It would, nevertheless, be inaccurate to think of *The Life and Opinions of Kater Murr* as a thoroughly pessimistic novel. It must not be forgotten that Hoffmann chained Kreisler's volatile idealism to the pedestrian common sense of the tomcat Murr. If the musician unmasks the cat's vain shallowness, Murr, too, provides a mocking mirror for Kreisler's pursuit of perfection at the Lilliputian court of Sieghartsweiler. How serious Hoffmann was about seeing the perspectives of the conformist animal and of the nonconformist artist as complementary becomes clear when Murr ends his memoirs with the remark that henceforth he will live with a new master, the concertmaster Kreisler.

Murr's death, of course, leaves it to the reader to imagine what the unlikely companions could have meant to each other. For Hoffmann, the outcome of their partnership cannot be in doubt. Whenever people admit to being part self-serving cat and part self-effacing idealist, self-irony—the tolerant smile at one's own incongruous personality—will turn the menace of a divided ego into the promise of a healthily deflated, less commanding but also less aggressive self. Although Hoffmann's creatures have not yet attained their creator's humorous wisdom, the reader understands and is invited to rise to its challenge.

Major publications other than long fiction

SHORT FICTION: *Fantasiestücke in Callots Manier*, 1814-1815; *Nachtstücke*, 1817; *Klein Zaches, genannt Zinnober*, 1819 (*Little Zaches, Surnamed Zinnober*, 1971); *Die Serapionsbrüder*, 1819-1821 (4 volumes; *The Serapion Brethren*, 1886-1892); *Prinzessin Brambilla: Ein Capriccio nach Jakob Callot*, 1821 (*Princess Brambilla: A "Capriccio" in the Style of Jacques Callot*, 1971);

Meister Floh: Ein Märchen in sieben Abenteuern zweier Freunde, 1822 (*Master Flea: A Fairy Tale in Seven Adventures of Two Friends*, 1826); *Four Tales*, 1962; *The Best Tales of Hoffmann*, 1967; *Selected Writings of E. T. A. Hoffmann*, 1969.

NONFICTION: *Briefwechsel*, 1967-1969 (3 volumes; correspondence); *Tagebücher*, 1971 (diaries, 4 volumes); *Selected Letters*, 1977.

MUSICAL COMPOSITIONS: *Liebe und Eifersucht: Oper*, 1807; *Trois Canzonettes*, 1808; *Arlequinn: Ballett*, 1811; *Musikalische Werke*, 1922-1927.

Bibliography
Blackall, Eric A. "The Divided Self: Hoffmann," in *The Novels of the German Romantics*, 1983.
Daemmrich, Horst S. *The Shattered Self: E. T. A. Hoffmann's Tragic Vision*, 1973.
Hewett-Thayer, Harvey W. *Hoffmann: Author of the Tales*, 1948.
Negus, Kenneth. *E. T. A. Hoffmann's Other World*, 1965.
Reddick, John. "E. T. A. Hoffmann," in *German Men of Letters*, 1969.
Taylor, Ronald. *Hoffmann*, 1963.

Joachim Scholz

VICTOR HUGO

Born: Besançon, France; February 26, 1802
Died: Paris, France; May 22, 1885

Principal long fiction

Han d'Islande, 1823 (*Hans of Iceland,* 1845); *Bug-Jargal,* 1826 (*The Noble Rival,* 1845); *Le Dernier Jour d'un condamné,* 1829 (*The Last Day of a Condemned,* 1840); *Notre-Dame de Paris,* 1831 (*The Hunchback of Notre Dame,* 1833); *Claude Gueux,* 1834; *Les Misérables,* 1862 (English translation, 1862); *Les Travailleurs de la mer,* 1866 (*The Toilers of the Sea,* 1866); *L'Homme qui rit,* 1869 (*The Man Who Laughs,* 1869); *Quatre-vingt-treize,* 1874 (*Ninety-three,* 1874).

Other literary forms

Victor Hugo dominates the nineteenth century in France both by the length of his writing career and by the diversity of his work. Indeed, it is difficult to think of a literary form he did not employ. Lyric, satiric, and epic poetry; drama in verse and prose; political polemic and social criticism—all are found in his oeuvre. His early plays and poetry made him a leader of the Romantic movement. His political writing includes the publication of a newspaper, *L'Événement,* in 1851, which contributed to his exile from the Second Empire. During his exile, he wrote vehement criticism of Napoleon III, and then his visionary works of poetry. His poetic genius ranged from light verse to profound epics; his prose works include accounts of his travels and literary criticism as well as fiction.

Achievements

The complete works of Victor Hugo constitute more nearly a legend than an achievement. In poetry, he had become a national institution by the end of his life. He was a member of the Académie Française, an officer of the Légion d'Honneur, and a Peer of France under the monarchy of Louis-Philippe. When he died, he was accorded the singular honor of lying in state beneath the Arc de Triomphe before his burial in the Panthéon.

During his lifetime, Hugo's novels accounted for much of his popularity with the public. Both sentimental and dramatic, they were an excellent vehicle for spreading his humanitarian ideas among large numbers of people. His two most famous novels are *The Hunchback of Notre Dame* and *Les Misérables.* The former is an example of dramatic historical romance, inspired in France by the novels of Sir Walter Scott. It is said to have created interest in and ensured the architectural preservation of the Notre Dame cathedral in Paris. It is also a study in Romanticism, with its evocation of the dark force of fate and the intricate intertwining of the grotesque and the sublime.

Les Misérables testifies to Hugo's optimistic faith in humanitarian principles and social progress. The intricate and elaborate plot confronts both social injustice and indifference. It is typical of many nineteenth century attitudes in its emphasis on education, charity, and love as powerful forces in saving the unfortunte creatures of the lower classes from becoming hardened criminals. *Les Misérables* is a novel on an epic scale both in its historical tableaux and as the story of a human soul. Thus, even though Hugo's achievements in the novel are of a lesser scale than his poetry and drama, they are enduring and worthy monuments to the author and to his century.

Biography

Victor-Marie Hugo was born in Besançon in 1802, the third son of Joseph-Léopold-Sigisbert Hugo and Sophie-Françoise Trébuchet. His father had been born in Nancy and his mother in Nantes. They met in the Vendée, where Léopold Hugo was serving in the Napoleonic army. His military career kept the family on the move, and it was during Major Hugo's tour of duty with the Army of the Rhine that Victor-Marie was born in Besançon.

Léopold and Sophie did not have a happy marriage, and after the birth of their third son, they were frequently separated. By 1808, Léopold had been promoted to general and was made a count in Napoleon's Empire. During one reunion of Hugo's parents, Victor and his brothers joined General Hugo in Spain, a land that fascinated Victor and left its mark on his poetic imagination.

In spite of their father's desire that they should study for entrance to the École Polytechnique, Victor and his next older brother, Eugène, spent their free time writing poetry, hoping to emulate their master, François René de Chateaubriand. In 1817, Victor won the first official recognition of his talent by winning an honorable mention in a poetry competition sponsored by the Académie Française. Because he was only fifteen, the secretary of the Académie asked to meet him, and the press displayed an interest in the young poet.

Eugène and Victor received permission from their father to study law in 1818 and left their boarding school to live with their mother in Paris. Sophie encouraged them in their ambition to become writers and never insisted that they attend lectures or study for examinations. Victor continued to receive recognition for his poems, and the brothers founded a review, *Le Conservateur littéraire*, in 1819. Unfortunately, the two brothers also shared a passion for the same young woman, Adèle Foucher. In love as well as in poetry, Eugène took second place to his younger brother. Adèle and Victor were betrothed after the death of Madame Hugo, who had opposed the marriage. The wedding took place in 1822. At the wedding feast, Eugène went insane and spent nearly all the rest of his life in institutions.

Hugo's early publications were favorably received by the avant-garde of Romanticism, and by 1824, Hugo was a dominant personality in Charles

Nodier's *cénacle*, a group of Romantic poets united in their struggle against the rules of French classicism. The year 1824 also marked the birth of Léopoldine, the Hugos' second child and the first to survive infancy. She was always to have a special place in her father's heart. In 1827, the Hugos had another child, Charles.

The Hugos were acquainted with many of those writers and artists who are now considered to be major figures in the Romantic movement, among them Alexandre Dumas, *père*, Alfred de Vigny, and Eugène Delacroix. The sculptor David d'Anger recorded Hugo's youthful appearance on a medallion. (Decades later, Auguste Rodin would also preserve his impression of the aged poet.) The influential critic Charles-Augustin Sainte-Beuve also became a frequent visitor to the Hugos' apartment.

Momentum was building for the Romantic movement, and in December, 1827, Hugo published a play, *Cromwell* (English translation, 1896), whose preface became the manifesto of the young Romantics. Two years later, *Hernani* (1830; English translation, 1830) would provide the battleground between Romanticism and classicism. In the meantime, General Hugo had died in 1828, and a son, François-Victor, had been born to Victor and Adèle.

The famous "battle of *Hernani*" at its premiere on January 10, 1830, was an outcry against outmoded conventions in every form of art. Artists sympathetic to Romanticism had been recruited from the Latin Quarter in support of Hugo's play, which breaks the rules of versification as well as the three unities of classical drama (time, place, and action). They engaged in a battle for modern artistic freedom against the "authorities" of the past. *Hernani* therefore had political significance as well: The restoration of the Bourbons was in its final months.

Stormy performances continued at the Théâtre-Français for several months, and by the end, the tyranny of classicism had been demolished. In addition to artistic freedom for all, *Hernani* brought financial well-being to the Hugos. It also brought Sainte-Beuve increasingly into their family circle, where he kept Adèle company while Hugo was distracted by the *Hernani* affair.

In July of 1830, Victor and Adèle's last child, Adèle, came into the world to the sound of the shots of the July Revolution, which deposed Charles X, the last Bourbon "King of France." The new monarch was Louis-Philippe of the Orléans branch of the royal family, who called himself "King of the French." There was now a deep attachment between Madame Hugo and Sainte-Beuve. Although Adèle and Victor were never to separate, their marriage had become a platonic companionship.

In 1832, the Hugos moved to the Place Royale (now called the Place des Vosges), to the home that was to become the Victor Hugo museum in Paris. Scarcely a year passed without a publication by Hugo. By that time, he was able to command enormous sums for his work in comparison with other authors of his day. He was already becoming a legend, with disciples rather than friends. His ambition had always been fierce, and he was beginning to portray himself as a bard, a seer with powers to guide all France. Only in his family life was he suffering from less than complete success.

At the time, *Lucrèce Borgia* (1833; *Lucretia Borgia*, 1842) was in rehearsal, and among the cast was a lovely young actress, Juliette Drouet. Soon after opening night, she and Hugo became lovers, and they remained so for many years. Juliette had not been a brilliant actress, but she abandoned what might have been a moderately successful career to live the rest of her life in seclusion and devotion to Hugo. In *Les Chants du crépuscule* (1835; *Songs of Twilight*, 1836), Hugo included thirteen poems to Juliette and three to Adèle, expressing the deep affection he still felt for his wife.

Critics were beginning to snipe at Hugo for what seemed to be shallow emotions and facile expressions. (Sainte-Beuve deplored Hugo's lack of taste, but Sainte-Beuve was hardly a disinterested critic.) The fashion for Hugo seemed to be somewhat on the wane, although adverse criticism did not inhibit the flow of his writing. The publication of *Les Rayons et les ombres* (1840) marked the end of one phase of Hugo's poetry. The splendor of the language and the music in his verse as well as the visual imagery were richer than ever, but Hugo was still criticized for lacking genuine emotion. He had by this time decided, however, to devote himself to his political ambitions.

He was determined to become a Peer of France, having been made an officer of the Légion d'Honneur several years before. In order to obtain a peerage, a man of letters had to be a member of the Académie Française. After presenting himself for the fifth time, he was elected to the Académie in 1841, and in the spring of 1845 he was named a Peer of France, a status that protected him from arrest the following summer, when police found him *flagrante delicto* with the wife of Auguste Biard. Léonie Biard was sent to the Saint-Lazare prison, but Hugo's cordial relations with King Louis-Philippe helped calm the scandal, and Léonie retired to a convent for a short while before resuming her affair with Hugo.

An event of much deeper emotional impact had occurred in 1843, when Hugo's eldest daughter, Léopoldine, had married Charles Vacquerie. Hugo had found it difficult to be separated from his child, who went to live in Le Havre. That summer, in July, he paid a brief visit to the young couple before leaving on a journey with Juliette. In early September, while traveling, Hugo read in a newspaper that Léopoldine and Charles had been drowned in a boating accident several days before. Grief-stricken, Hugo was also beset by guilt at having left his family for a trip with his mistress. He published nothing more for nine years.

Eventually, the political events of 1848 eclipsed Hugo's complex relationship with his wife and two mistresses. During the Revolution of 1848, Louis-Philippe was forced to abdicate. The monarchy was rejected outright by the provisional government under the leadership of the Romantic poet Alphonse de Lamartine. The peerage was also abolished, and although Hugo sought political office, he was generally considered to be too dramatic and rhetorical to be of practical use in government. More than a few of his contemporary politicians viewed him as a self-interested opportunist. He seems to have longed for the glory of being a statesman without the necessary political sense.

On June 24, 1848, militant insurgents had occupied the Hugo apartment on the Place Royal. The family had fled, and Adèle had refused to live there again. One of the first visitors to their new apartment was Louis-Napoleon Bonaparte, nephew of Napoleon I. He was seeking Hugo's support of his candidacy for president of the new republic. Thereafter, Louis-Napoleon was endorsed in Hugo's newspaper, *L'Événement*, which he had founded that summer and which was edited and published by his sons.

Louis-Napoleon became President in December of 1848, but he did not long remain on good terms with Hugo. Hugo and *L'Événement* increasingly took leftist political positons, while the new government moved toward the right. Freedom of the press was increasingly limited, and, in 1851, both of Hugo's sons were imprisoned for violating restrictions on the press and for showing disrespect to the government.

It was in this year that Juliette and Léonie attempted to force Hugo to choose between them. In the end, politics resolved the conflict. On December 2, 1851, Louis-Napoleon dissolved the National Assembly and declared himself Prince-President for ten years. When Hugo learned of the *coup d'état*, he attempted to organize some resistance. There was shooting in the streets of Paris. Juliette is given credit for saving him from violence. She hid him successfully while a false passport was prepared, and on December 11, he took the train to Brussels in disguise and under a false name. Juliette followed him into exile.

From exile, the pen was Hugo's only political weapon, and he wrote *Napoléon le petit* (1852; *Napoleon the Little*, 1852) and *Histoire d'un crime* (1877; *The History of a Crime*, 1877-1878). Having been authorized to stay in Belgium for only three months, Hugo made plans to move to Jersey, one of the Channel Islands. His family joined him, and Juliette took rooms nearby. He began work on *Les Châtiments* (1853), poems inspired by anger and pride. France remained his preoccupation while he was in exile. Indeed, it has been said that exile renewed Hugo's career. Certainly, his fame suffered neither from his banishment nor from the tone of righteous indignation with which he could thus proclaim his contempt for the Empire of Napoleon III.

There was a group of militant exiles on the island, and when, in 1855, they attacked Queen Victoria in their newspaper for visiting Napoleon III, Jersey officials informed them that they would have to leave. The Hugos moved to Guernsey, where they eventually purchased Hauteville House. At about the same time, in the spring of 1856, *Les Contemplations* was published, marking Hugo's reappearance as a lyric poet. Juliette moved to a nearby house that she called Hauteville-Féerie, where the lawn was inscribed with flowers forming a bright "V H." Although Hugo's prestige benefited immensely from his exile, his family suffered from their isolation, especially his daughter Adèle, who was in her early twenties. Eventually, she followed an army officer, Albert Pinson, to Canada, convinced that they would marry. After nine years of erratic, senseless wandering, she was brought home to end her life in a mental institution.

For her father, exile was a time to write. The first two volumes of *La Légende des siècles* (1859; *The Legend of the Centuries*, 1894) was followed by *The Toilers of the Sea* and *The Man Who Laughs*, among other works. In 1859, Napoleon III offered amnesty to Republican exiles, but Hugo refused to accept it, preferring the grandeur of defiance and martyrdom on his rocky island.

After Adèle's flight, the island became intolerable for Madame Hugo. In 1865, she left for Brussels with the younger son, François-Victor, and spent most of her time there during the remainder of Hugo's exile. In his isolation, Hugo continued his work.

On the occasion of the Paris International Exposition in 1867, the imperial censors permitted a revival of *Hernani* at the Théâtre-Français. Adèle traveled to Paris to witness the great success of the play and the adulation of her husband. Another visitor to the Paris Exposition would be instrumental in ending Hugo's self-imposed banishment. Otto von Bismarck came to Paris ostensibly on a state visit from Prussia but secretly taking the measure of French armaments. Adèle died in Brussels the following year. Her sons accompanied her body to its grave in France; Hugo stopped at the French border and soon returned to Guernsey with Juliette.

One of Hugo's dreams had always been a United States of Europe, and in 1869, he presided over the congress of the International League for Peace and Freedom in Lausanne. Early in 1870, he was honored by the Second Empire with a revival of *Lucretia Borgia* and a recitation of his poetry before the Emperor by Sarah Bernhardt. On July 14 of that year, the poet planted an acorn at Hauteville House. The future tree was dedicated to "the United States of Europe." By the following day, France and Prussia were at war.

The Franco-Prussian War brought an end to the Second Empire and to Hugo's nineteen years of exile. He returned in time to participate in the siege of Paris and to witness the cataclysmic events of the Commune. His own politics, however, although idealistically liberal and Republican, did not mesh with any political group in a practical way. He refused several minor offices that were offered to him by the new government and resigned after only a month as an elected deputy for Paris to the new National Assembly.

The following years were marked by family sorrows. Soon following Hugo's resignation from active politics, his elder son, Charles, died of an apoplectic stroke. Hugo was to remain devoted to his son's widow, Alice, and to his grandchildren, Jeanne and Georges. In 1872, Adèle was brought home from Barbados, insane. The following year, his younger son, François-Victor, died of tuberculosis. Only the faithful Juliette remained as a companion to Hugo in his old age.

He continued to write unceasingly in Paris, but in 1878 he suffered a stroke. This virtually brought his writing to an end, although works he had written earlier continued to be published. On his birthday in 1881, the Republic organized elaborate festivities in his honor, including a procession of admirers who passed beneath his window for hours. In May, the main part of the avenue d'Eylau was rechristened the avenue Victor-Hugo.

Juliette died in May of 1883. On his birthday in 1885, Hugo received tributes from all quarters as a venerated symbol of the French spirit. He became seriously ill in May, suffering from a lesion of the heart and congestion of the lungs. He died on May 22, 1885. Hugo's funeral was a national ceremony, the coffin lying in state beneath the Arc de Triomphe. He was the only Frenchman to be so honored before the Unknown Soldier after World War I. While Napoleon III lay buried in exile, the remains of Victor Hugo were ceremoniously interred in the Panthéon, France's shrine to her great men of letters.

Analysis

The earliest published full-length fiction by Victor Hugo was *Hans of Iceland*, begun when he was eighteen years old, although not published until three years later. In part a tribute to Adèle Foucher, who was to become his wife, it is a convoluted Gothic romance in which it is not clear where the author is being serious and where he is deliberately creating a parody of the popular Gothic genre. It is worthwhile to begin with this youthful work, however, because it contains many themes and images that were to remain important in Hugo's work throughout his life. The characters in *Hans of Iceland* are archetypes rather than psychologically realistic figures. In a sense, it is unfair to criticize Hugo for a lack of complexity in his characterizations, because he is a creator of myths and legends—his genius does not lie in the realm of the realistic novel. This is the reason his talent as a novelist is eclipsed by the other great novelists of his century, Stendhal, Honoré de Balzac, Gustave Flaubert, and Émile Zola. Hugo's last novels were written after Flaubert's *Madame Bovary* (1857) and after Zola's first Naturalistic novels, yet Hugo's late books remain closer in tone to *Hans of Iceland* than to any contemporary novel.

It is thus more useful to consider *Hans of Iceland* as a romance, following the patterns of myths and legends, rather than as a novel with claims to psychological and historical realism. Although tenuously based on historical fact, set in seventeenth century Norway, the plot of *Hans of Iceland* closely resembles that of the traditional quest. The hero, Ordener Guldenlew (Golden

Lion), disguises his noble birth and sets out to rescue his beloved, the pure maiden Ethel, from the evil forces that imprison her with her father, Jean Schumaker, Count Griffenfeld. Ordener's adventures take him through dark and fearsome settings where he must overcome the monster Hans of Iceland, a mysterious being who, although a man, possesses demoniac powers and beastly desires.

As in traditional romance, the characters in *Hans of Iceland* are all good or evil, like black and white pieces in a chess game. Ethel's father is the good former grand chancellor who has been imprisoned for some years after having been unjustly accused of treason. His counterpart is the wicked Count d'Ahlefeld, who, with the treacherous Countess, is responsible for Schumaker's downfall. Their son Frédéric is Ordener's rival for Ethel's love. The most treacherous villain is the Count's adviser, Musdoemon, who turns out to be Frédéric's real father. Opposed to everyone, good or evil, is the man-demon Hans of Iceland, who haunts the land by dark of night, leaving the marks of his clawlike nails on his victims.

Ordener's quest begins in the morgue, where he seeks a box that had been in the possession of a military officer killed by Hans. The box contains documents proving Schumaker's innocence. Believing it to be in Hans's possession, Ordener sets off through storms and danger to recover the box.

As the adventure progresses, Hugo begins to reveal his personal preoccupations and thus to depart from the traditional romance. Hans's ambiguous nature, grotesque as he is, has some unsettling sympathetic qualities. One begins to feel, as the story progresses and as the social villains become more devious and nefarious, that Hans, the social outcast, is morally superior in spite of his diabolically glowing eyes and his tendency to crunch human bones. Hugo appears to suggest the Romantic noble savage beneath a diabolic exterior. Because Ordener is a strangely passive hero, who fails to slay Hans or even to find the box, the reader's interest is transferred to Hans. In this monster with redeeming human qualities, it is not difficult to see the prefiguration of later grotesques such as Quasimodo.

The social commentary that is constant in Hugo's narratives has its beginning here in the figure of Musdoemon, the true evil figure of the work. This adviser to the aristocracy, whose name reveals that he has the soul of a rat, betrays everyone until he is at last himself betrayed and hanged. The executioner turns out to be his brother, delighted to have revenge for Musdoemon's treachery toward him years before.

At one point, Musdoemon tricks a group of miners (the good common people) into rebelling against the King in Schumaker's name. Ordener finds himself in the midst of the angry mob as they battle the king's troops. Hans attacks both sides, increasing the confusion and slaughter. Later, at the trial of the rebels on charges of treason, Ordener takes full responsibility, thus diverting blame from Schumaker. Given the choice of execution or marriage to the daughter of the wicked d'Ahlefeld, he chooses death. He and Ethel are married in his cell and are saved by the chance discovery of the documents. Hans gives himself up and dies by his own hand.

By comparing *Hans of Iceland* with another early novel, *The Noble Rival*, the reader can trace the preoccupations that led to *The Hunchback of Notre Dame* and *Les Misérables*. *The Noble Rival* is the story of a slave revolt in Santo Domingo. The hero of the title is a slave as well as the spiritually noble leader of his people. The Romantic hero is Léopold, a Frenchman visiting his uncle's plantation. Like Ordener, Léopold is pure but essentially passive. The heroic energy belongs to the outcast from society, Bug-Jargal. In both novels, Hugo's sympathy for the "people" is apparent. The miners and the slaves point directly to the commoners of Paris in *The Hunchback of Notre Dame*.

At the center of *The Hunchback of Notre Dame* is the theme of fatality, a word which the author imagines to have been inscribed on the wall of one of the cathedral towers as the Greek *anankè*. The cathedral is the focus of the novel, as it was the heart of medieval Paris. It is a spiritual center with an ambiguous demoniac-grotesque spirit within. Claude Frollo, the priest, is consumed by lust for a Gypsy girl, Esmeralda. Quasimodo, the bellringer, a hunchback frighteningly deformed, is elevated by his pure love for Esmeralda, whom he attempts to save from the pernicious Frollo. In an image central to the novel and to Hugo's entire work, Frollo watches a spider and a fly caught in its web. The web, however, stretches across a pane of glass so that even if the fly should manage to escape, it will only hurl itself against the invisible barrier in its flight toward the sun. The priest will be the spider to Esmeralda, but also the fly, caught in the trap of his own consuming desire. All the characters risk entrapment in the web prepared for them by fate. Even if they somehow break free of the web, the glass will block escape until death releases them from earthly concerns.

Esmeralda believes she can "fly to the sun" in the person of the handsome military captain Phoebus, but he is interested in her only in an earthly way. Frollo's destructive passion leads him to set a trap for Esmeralda. For a fee, Phoebus agrees to hide Frollo where he can watch a rendezvous between Phoebus and Esmeralda. Unable to contain himself, the priest leaves his hiding place, stabs Phoebus, and leaves. Esmeralda is, of course, accused of the crime.

Quasimodo saves her from execution and gives her sanctuary in the cathedral, but she is betrayed again by Frollo, who orders her to choose between him and the gallows. Like the fly, Esmeralda tears herself away from the priest to collapse at the foot of the gibbet. Phoebus, who did not die of his wound, remains indifferent to her plight, but Quasimodo pushes Frollo to his death from the tower of Notre Dame as the priest gloats over Esmeralda's execution. Quasimodo, the grotesque, gains in moral stature throughout the novel, just as Frollo falls from grace. Two years later, a deformed skeleton is found in a burial vault beside that of the virtuous Esmeralda.

The Hunchback of Notre Dame and *Les Misérables* are justly Hugo's most famous novels because they combine the exposition of his social ideas with an aesthetically unified structure. By contrast, *The Last Day of a Condemned*, written in 1829, is basically a social treatise on the horrors of prison life. In the same way, *Claude Gueux*, a short work of 1834, protests against the death penalty. In both works, the writer speaks out against society's injustice to man, but it was with *Les Misérables* that the reformer's voice spoke most effectively.

Les Misérables tells of the spiritual journey of Jean Valjean, a poor but honorable man, driven in desperation to steal a loaf of bread to feed his widowed sister and her children. Sent to prison, he becomes an embittered, morally deformed creature until he is redeemed by his love for the orphan girl Cosette. The plot of the novel is quite complex, as Jean rises to respectability and descends again several times. This is true because, as a convict, he must live under an assumed name. His spiritual voyage will not end until he can stand once more as Jean Valjean. His name suggests the French verb *valoir*, "to be worth." Thus, Jean must become worthy of Jean; he cannot have value under a counterfeit name.

His first reappearance as a respectable bourgeois is as Monsieur Madeleine, Mayor of Montreuil-sur-Mer. He is soon called upon, however, to reveal his true identity in order to save another from life imprisonment for having been identified as Jean Valjean, parole breaker. He descends into society's underworld, eluding capture by his nemesis, the policeman Javert. In Hugo's works, the way down is always the way up to salvation. Just as Ordener descended into the mines, *Jean* must now pass through a valley (*Val*) in order to save *Jean*. Here, as in *The Hunchback of Notre Dame*, moral superiority is to be found among the lowly.

In order to save himself, Jean must be the savior of others. He begins by rescuing Cosette from her wicked foster parents. Later, he will save Javert from insurrectionists. His greatest test, however, will be that of saving Marius, the man Cosette loves and who will separate Jean from the girl who is his paradise. This episode is the famous flight through the sewers of Paris, a true descent into the underworld, whence Jean Valjean is reborn, his soul transfigured, clear, and serene. He still has one more trial to endure, that of regaining his own name, which, through a misunderstanding, brings a painful estrangement from Cosette and Marius. He begins to die but is reconciled with his children at the last moment and leaves this life with a soul radiantly transformed.

Les Misérables was written partly in exile, and certain episodes begin to show a preference for images of water. *The Toilers of the Sea*, written on Guernsey in 1864 and 1865, is a novel dominated by the sea. The text originally included an introductory section entitled "L'Archipel de la Manche" ("The Archipelago of the English Channel"), which Hugo's editor persuaded him to publish separately at a later date (1883). The two parts reveal that Hugo has separated sociology from fiction. It would seem that, at odds with the predominant novelistic style of his time, Hugo preferred not to communicate his social philosophy through the imagery and structure of his novels. Thus, the prologue contains Hugo's doctrine of social progress and his analysis of the geology, customs, and language of the Channel Islands. The larger section that became the published novel is once again the story of a solitary quest.

The hero, Gilliatt, is a fisherman who lives a simple, rather ordinary life with his elderly mother on the island of Guernsey. In their house, they keep a marriage chest containing a trousseau for Gilliatt's future bride. Gilliatt loves Déruchette, niece of Mess Lethierry, inventor of the steamboat *Durande* with which he has made his fortune in commerce. When the villain, Clubin, steals Lethierry's money and wrecks his steamer, Gilliatt's adventures begin.

Like the king of myth or legend, Lethierry offers his niece's hand in marriage to whomever can salvage the *Durande*. Gilliatt sets out upon the sea. Ominously missing are the magical beasts or mysterious beings who normally appear to assist the hero as he sets off. Even Ordener, for example, had a guide, Benignus Spiagudry, at the beginning of his quest. It is entirely unaided that Gilliatt leaves shore.

He now faces nature and the unknown, completely cut off from human society. He survives a titanic struggle for the ship against the hurricane forces of nature, but he must still descend into an underwater grotto, where he is seized by a hideous octopus. Gilliatt is, in Hugo's words, "the fly of that spider." The language of the passage makes it clear that in freeing himself from the octopus, Gilliatt frees himself from evil.

Exhausted, Gilliatt prays, then sleeps. When he wakes, the sea is calm. He returns to land a savior, bringing the engine of the ship as well as the stolen money. When he learns that Déruchette wishes to marry another, he gives her his own marriage chest and leaves to die in the rising tide. *The Toilers of the Sea* is considered by many to be the finest and purest expression of Hugo's mythic vision.

Almost immediately after *The Toilers of the Sea*, Hugo turned his attention back to history. In 1866, he began work on the first novel of what he intended to be a trilogy focusing in turn on aristocracy, monarchy, and democracy. The first, *The Man Who Laughs*, is set in England after 1688; the second would have taken place in prerevolutionary France; and the third is *Ninety-three*, a vision of France after 1789. The role of fate is diminished in these last two novels, because Hugo wished to emphasize man's conscience and free will in a social and political context.

In *The Man Who Laughs*, the disfigured hero, Gwynplaine, chooses to leave his humble earthly paradise when he learns that he had been born to the aristocracy. Predictably, the way up leads to Gwynplaine's downfall. Noble society is a hellish labyrinth (another type of web), from which Gwynplaine barely manages to escape. A wolf named Homo helps him find his lost love again, a blind girl named Déa. When she dies, Gwynplaine finds salvation by letting himself sink beneath the water of the Thames.

Hugo's vivid portrayal of a demoniac aristocratic society justified the cause of the French Revolution in 1789, preparing the way for his vision of an egalitarian future as described in his last novel, *Ninety-three*. By choosing to write about 1793 instead of the fall of the Bastille, Hugo was attempting to deal with the Terror, which he considered to have deformed the original ideals of the Revolution.

Rather than the familiar love interest, Hugo has placed the characters Michelle Fléchard and her three children at the center of the novel. In Hugo, kindness to children can redeem almost any amount of wickedness. The monstrous Hans of Iceland, for example, was partially excused because he was avenging the death of his son. It is therefore not surprising to find that each faction in the Revolution is tested and judged according to its treatment of Michelle and her children.

The extreme positions in the violent political clash are represented by the Marquis de Lantenac, the Royalist leader, and his counterpart, Cimourdain, a former priest and fanatic revolutionary. Both men are inflexible and coldly logical in their courageous devotion to their beliefs. The violent excesses of both sides are depicted as demoniac no matter how noble the cause. Human charity and benign moderation are represented in Gauvain, a general in the revolutionary army. He is Lantenac's nephew and the former pupil of Cimourdain. He is clearly also the spokesman for Hugo's point of view.

In the course of events, Lantenac redeems his inhumanity by rescuing Michelle's children from a burning tower. He is now Gauvain's prisoner and should be sent to the guillotine. Gauvain's humanity, however, responds to Lantenac's act of self-sacrifice, and Gauvain arranges for him to escape. It is now Cimourdain's turn, but he remains loyal to his principles, condemning to death his beloved disciple. Before his execution, Gauvain expounds his (Hugo's) idealistic social philosophy in a dialogue with Cimourdin's pragmatic view of a disciplined society based on strict justice.

In this final novel, Hugo's desire to express his visionary ideology overwhelms his talents as a novelist. At the age of seventy, he had become the prophet of a transfigured social order of the future. He would create no more of his compelling fictional worlds. It was time for Hugo the creator of legends to assume the legendary stature of his final decade.

Major publications other than long fiction

PLAYS: *Cromwell*, 1827 (English translation, 1896); *Amy Robsart*, 1828 (English translation, 1895); *Hernani*, 1830 (English translation, 1830); *Marion de Lorme*, 1831 (English translation, 1895); *Le Roi s'amuse*, 1832 (*The King's Fool*, 1842); *Lucrèce Borgia*, 1833 (*Lucretia Borgia*, 1842); *Marie Tudor*, 1833 (English translation, 1895); *Angelo*, 1835 (English translation, 1880); *Esmeralda*, 1836 (English translation, 1890); *Ruy Blas*, 1838 (English translation, 1890); *Les Burgraves*, 1843 (*The Burgraves*, 1896); *Torquemada*, 1882 (English translation, 1896).

POETRY: *Odes et poésies diverses*, 1822, 1823; *Nouvelles Odes*, 1824; *Odes et ballades*, 1826; *Les Orientales*, 1829 (*Les Orientales: Or, Eastern Lyrics*, 1879); *Les Feuilles d'automne*, 1831; *Les Chants du crépuscule*, 1835 (*Songs of Twilight*, 1836); *Les Voix intérieures*, 1837; *Les Rayons et les ombres*, 1840; *Les Châtiments*, 1853; *Les Contemplations*, 1856; *La Légende des siècles*, 1859-1883 (5 volumes; *The Legend of the Centuries*, 1894); *Les Chansons des rues et des bois*, 1865; *L'Année terrible*, 1872; *L'Art d'être grand-père*, 1877; *Le Pape*, 1878; *La Pitié suprême*, 1879; *L'Âne*, 1880; *Les Quatre vents de l'esprit*, 1881; *The Literary Life and Poetical Works of Victor Hugo*, 1883; *La Fin de Satan*, 1886; *Toute la lyre*, 1888; *Dieu*, 1891; *Les Années funestes*, 1896; *Poems from Victor Hugo*, 1901; *Dernière Gerbe*, 1902; *Poems*, 1902; *The Poems of Victor Hugo*, 1906; *Océan*, 1942.

NONFICTION: *Littérature et philosophie mêlées*, 1834; *Le Rhin*, 1842 (*The Rhine*, 1843); *Napoléon le petit*, 1852 (*Napoleon the Little*, 1852); *William Shakespeare*, 1864 (English translation, 1864); *Actes et paroles*, 1875-1876; *Histoire d'un crime*, 1877 (*The History of a Crime*, 1877-1878); *Religions et religion*, 1880; *Le Théâtre en liberté*, 1886; *Choses vues*, 1887 (*Things Seen*, 1887); *En voyage: Alpes et Pyrénées*, 1890 (*The Alps and Pyrenees*, 1898); *France et Belgique*, 1892; *Correspondance*, 1896-1898.

MISCELLANEOUS: *Oeuvres complètes*, 1880-1892 (57 volumes); *Victor Hugo's Works*, 1892 (30 volumes); *Works*, 1907 (10 volumes).

Bibliography

Gayer, Foster Erwin. *The Titan: Victor Hugo*, 1955.
Grant, Elliott M. *The Career of Victor Hugo*, 1945.
Grant, Richard B. *The Perilous Quest*, 1968.
Houston, John Porter. *Victor Hugo*, 1974.
Maurois, André. *Olympio*, 1956.
Piroué, Georges. *Victor Hugo romancier*, 1964.

Jan St. Martin

JORIS-KARL HUYSMANS

Born: Paris, France; February 5, 1848
Died: Paris, France; May 12, 1907

Principal long fiction

Marthe: Histoire d'une fille, 1876 (*Marthe: Story of a Prostitute*, 1927); *Les Soeurs Vatard*, 1879; *En ménage*, 1881 (*Living Together*, 1969); *À vau-l'eau*, 1882 (novella; *Down Stream*, 1927); *À rebours*, 1884 (*Against the Grain*, 1922); *En rade*, 1887; *Un Dilemme*, 1887; *Là-bas*, 1891 (*Down There*, 1924; better known as *Là-Bas*, 1972); *En route*, 1895 (English translation, 1896); *Là Cathédrale*, 1898 (*The Cathedral*, 1898); *L'Oblat*, 1903 (*The Oblate*, 1924); *Oeuvres complètes*, 1928-1934 (23 volumes).

Other literary forms

Although writing fiction was the prime vocation of Joris-Karl Huysmans throughout his active career of some thirty years, his novels were regularly interspersed with other kinds of writing, mostly journalistic and, during his final decade, primarily religious. His first publication was not a novel but a collection of short journalistic pieces written in the lyric style of Charles Baudelaire's prose poems: *Le Drageoir aux épices* (1874; *A Dish of Spices*, 1927). Six years later, he published a larger collection of the same kind of writing, this time under a more descriptive and prosaic title, *Croquis parisiens* (1880; *Parisian Sketches*, 1962). Neither collection of prose poems added significantly to his reputation, but when he turned his hand to art criticism, he was quickly noticed for his discernment in spotting the best work of the new Impressionist school. His studies of Impressionism appeared in book form in 1883, under the title *L'Art moderne*. Later, he would publish another collection of articles on art and architecture, *Certains* (1889), and in 1905, toward the end of his life, an expression of his interest in religious art, under the title *Trois Primitifs* (three primitives). His other nonfictional writings on religious subjects include the hagiographical *Sainte Lydwine de Schiedam* (1901; *St. Lydwine of Schiedam*, 1923) and a book about the meaning of the shrine at Lourdes, *Les Foules de Lourdes* (1906; *The Crowds of Lourdes*, 1925). For most of his career, he contributed articles to a variety of journals, on a variety of subjects—book reviews, drama criticism, social analysis, religious architecture—but very little of that work was collected and published in book form. On the other hand, several volumes of his correspondence with various public figures, literary and other, have been published.

Achievements

Huysmans was too eccentric, in his person, in his interests, and in his literary activity, ever to be at the center of the intellectual life of his times. Yet, from his position on the periphery, he was able to contribute at least three notable achievements to his age, all of which were influential long after his death. The first achievement was his early championing of the controversial art of the Impressionists. His ability to explain what they were doing and to identify their aesthetic accomplishments helped the Impressionists to achieve wide public recognition as major artists and helped the public of the 1880's to appreciate their work. Huysmans was not their only champion in the earliest days of the school—his friend Émile Zola had championed their cause even earlier than Huysmans had—but he had the great merit of expounding their artistic principles with clarity and perceptiveness, thereby also preparing a receptive public for other movements in the arts which grew out of Impressionism: Symbolism, Surrealism, and primitivism. Two literary achievements can be added to his accomplishments as an art critic, both of which have clear lines of affinity with the ideas about painting that he advocated. His most lasting literary achievement was to have created two masterpieces that served his generation as models of what could be done in fiction by the literary equivalents of the Impressionist movement, known variously as Symbolism, Decadence, or modernism. One of these masterpieces, the novel *Against the Grain*, which has been called "the breviary of Decadence," opened the domain of fiction to the expression of strange new forms of human sensibility. Its haunting influence on experimental fiction continues to the present day. Huysmans' other masterpiece, *Là-Bas*, demonstrated that the extremes of religious sensibility, Satanism and mysticism, could provide suitable matter for a novel whose goal was to analyze the temper of modern man. In order to extend the range of subject matter available to the novelist, Huysmans found himself creating a new prose style that could express those areas of human experience which transcend observable reality. The creation of this new style was his third significant achievement. While the arcane vocabulary, contorted syntax, and nervous rhythms that characterized this particular new style were too idiosyncratic to have inspired much emulation, their very newness constituted a significant literary achievement for Huysmans, primarily because his example helped to shatter the realistic mold in which the art of French prose had long been encased. He demonstrated that the capabilities of prose were richer than those of the classic clarity that had always been the pride of the French man of letters.

Biography

The roots of Joris-Karl Huysmans' eccentric character and interests are not to be found in the prosaic surface details of his biography. Born in Paris, the only son of a thoroughly bourgeois couple, Huysmans entered government service when he was eighteen and held a position in the Ministry of the Interior for more than thirty years. By the time he retired from that post, at the age of fifty, he had become an established author whose books had sold well enough to make him economically independent. He had never married, had relatively few friends, and had played little public role in the literary or political controversies of the times. He died at the age of fifty-nine, after a prolonged battle with cancer.

Beneath this uneventful surface of a civil servant's life, however, a private existence of increasing alienation and anguished search for meaning had developed, and the evolution of those personal feelings had found its natural expression in the literary activity which had been the most vital part of Huysmans' life since early manhood, although it had been pursued as an afterhours avocation. One may surmise that his feelings of alienation from his world were partly inherited: His father was a Dutch lithographer who had come to Paris in search of work when he was about thirty years of age, had married a Parisian, and, having been unsuccessful at his trade and unhappy in his marriage, had died at the age of forty-one, a lonely and embittered man. When Huysmans' mother remarried, within months of his father's death, the boy, not yet ten years old, must have experienced the kind of shock of insecurity and alienation that can last a lifetime. One symbolic expression he gave to those feelings was his insistence, when he began to publish his works, on changing his name from the French Charles-Marie-Georges, with which he had been baptized, to the Dutch Joris-Karl, perhaps in order to proclaim his self-willed alien status in the Parisian literary world and his sympathy with his father's fate. Throughout his literary career, he seemed to make it a point to be visibly outside the literary mainstream, both in his choice of subject matter and in his choice of friends. That he was centrally preoccupied with the question of the meaning of his own existence is dramatically evident in that all of his works of fiction are transparently autobiographical and trace his private odyssey from disillusionment with reality to Decadent aestheticism and on to the extremes of spiritual crisis and religious conversion. Even the eccentric style he cultivated in his novels seemed to express both his alienation—by its rejection of what is most typically French in the language—and the anguish of his search for personal meaning—by its often painfully contorted forms. Loneliness and suffering, often by his own choice, were the hallmarks of Huysmans' literary career and, indeed, of his entire life.

Analysis

Joris-Karl Huysmans' career as a novelist falls, almost too neatly, into three distinct phases, each lasting about one decade, but those three phases—Naturalistic, Decadent, and religious—are so startlingly different from one another that traditional literary historians have usually found little underlying unity in his development and much that seems arbitrary and even willfully eccentric. It is perhaps this impatiently unsympathetic reaction to his work and his personality that accounts for the common tendency to relegate Huysmans to the role of a minor curiosity in the history of the novel. With the perspective of time, however, one can recognize more readily that Huysmans evolved quite comprehensibly as a writer, in accordance with the forces at work in and around him. Although it is true that his work, as a whole, falls well short of greatness, at its best it is worthy of serious attention and is significant in the history of literary ideas and aesthetics.

The special quality of Huysmans' sensibility and imagination determined the apparently erratic course of his evolution as a novelist and imprinted on his career whatever unity it can be shown to possess. Because he was intellectually insecure and lacked confidence in his own literary formation, he was easily influenced at the start of his career by more assertive personalities. That is why his early works strike the informed reader as derivative in both theme and approach, resulting, as they clearly do, from his acquaintance with such figures as Edmond de Goncourt, Zola, Gustave Flaubert, and Guy de Maupassant. If Huysmans was almost porously subject to outside influences, his way of internalizing those influences was certainly unique. He invariably and instinctively responded to these influences in terms of his inner needs, converting every theme into a device for exploring his private psyche and taking every approach to its extreme limits.

Thus, in his first work of fiction, *Marthe*, which depicts the life of a prostitute, Huysmans showed the influence of his literary friends by his choice of subject matter—the portrayal of the humble and the downtrodden—but consciously cast the subject in an extreme, therefore new, form, by focusing on the relatively new social phenomenon of the government-licensed prostitute living in a brothel. When he heard, however, that his friend Edmond de Goncourt had hit upon the very same subject for his next novel, he hastened to get his work into print at his own expense in order to be the first to treat the subject. *Marthe* does, indeed, have the distinction of being the first work of fiction to treat the precise phenomenon of the licensed prostitute, but it is a poor novel, and it attracted few readers. Its most interesting aspect for the modern reader, moreover, is not the depiction of Marthe and her grim life of degradation but the account of her relationship with Léo, a young poet and journalist who falls in love with her and tries unsuccessfully to win her away from the life of degradation into which circumstances have forced her. The psychology of Léo is more probingly and more convincingly presented than is the psychology of Marthe, doubtless because Huysmans used his subject as a pretext to examine and try to comprehend his own first sentimental involvement as a young man. Léo is the first in a long series of characters in Huysmans' fiction that are based on the author himself. In the case of *Marthe*, the character Léo is simply the means by which Huysmans contrived to make his Naturalistic subject something profoundly personal.

The same process occurred with Huysmans' next novel, *Les Soeurs Vatard*, a Naturalistic subject ostensibly focused on the fate of two working-class sisters who find it impossible to attain happiness in their lives, even though one chooses the path of vice and the other the path of virtue. The two sisters command less of the author's attention, however, than do the relationships they enter—namely, that of the older sister with a painter and that of the younger sister with a sensitive and timid young man who works in the same shop with her. The two suitors patently represent two aspects of Huysmans' own character, and the failure of both relationships, which proves to be the central concern of this novel, is presented more from the point of view of the male characters than from that of the sisters. The novel was probably inspired by Zola's *L'Assommoir* (1877; English translation, 1879) and is dedicated to him, but Huysmans departed sufficiently from Zola's Naturalistic principles to have turned it into another exploration of his personal inability to establish a successful relationship with a woman. He had set out to examine a certain social milieu and had ended by analyzing a private problem instead. This personalized approach became more overt in Huysmans' next novel, *Living Together*, which featured the painter of *Les Soeurs Vatard* and one of his friends, a writer, as exemplary cases of the incompatibility of art and domestic life.

In retrospect, these first three novels, none of which succeeded as a work of art, can be understood as Huysmans' apprenticeship to the novel. The result of this apprenticeship was the discovery of his own voice and a clearer focus on the only subjects that really interested him: the exploration of himself and of his frustrating private search for happiness and meaning in life. Both the personal voice and the personal subject find full artistic expression for the first time in the short novel, or novella, *Downstream*, which he published in 1882.

The novel's French title, *À vau-l'eau*, means, literally, "as the water wills" and is a figurative colloquialism suggesting a passive drift to destruction and evoking the image of flotsam carried away by a current. The title alludes to the life of the book's pathetic central figure, Jean Folantin, who is shown in his middle years to be the prisoner of a dreary daily routine, hardly distinguishable from death. Born in poor circumstances and unable to obtain an education, he is forced, at an early age, into a clerical post that affords no opportunity for advancement and pays too little to enable him to enjoy any personal comfort in his life, let alone to support a family. As the book begins, Folantin has arrived at middle age, a lonely bachelor suffering from chronic indigestion who has so reduced his aspirations in life that his central preoccupation has become finding a way to get his daily meals without suffering. He has long since ceased to take any interest in his work, and he has no social or sentimental life outside his office. The bitter emptiness of his existence is epitomized by the recollection that the one woman whose company he had ever really enjoyed, in his youth, had given him a venereal disease.

The heart of the novel is an account of the last futile gestures he makes toward creating some comfort or pleasure for himself before finally resigning himself to his fate. Having found all restaurants within his means intolerable, he is excited to learn of a place that will contract to deliver edible meals to his apartment at an affordable price. He even redecorates his apartment in anticipation of a new threshold of contentment to be enjoyed. After the first few digestible meals, however, the quality of the food abruptly declines. His dream shattered, he is thrown back on the mercy of the infamous restaurants. In need of social contact, he seeks out an old friend, but they have a miserable evening together, beginning with a bad meal and finishing with a painful evening at the theater (the play, which he remembers having enjoyed in his youth, turns out to be boring as well as poorly acted). In the narrative's final scene, Folantin goes into a restaurant at a late hour, hoping to be the only customer so that he can at least enjoy some peace and quiet to make up for the bad food. Instead, a prostitute comes in, sits down with him, and cajoles him into paying for her meal. He spends the night with her, for which she charges him an outrageous sum. This experience proves to be the last straw. Recognizing that every attempt he has made to increase his pleasure or comfort in life has only made things worse, he decides that, henceforth, he must abandon all such efforts and let his life drift passively, *à vau-l'eau*, offering no resistance to events because no matter what he does, "only the worst will happen." Those are the last words of the book—"seul le pire arrive"—and they represent Jean Folantin's bitter summation of life.

In spite of the utter absence of exciting characters or events, *Down Stream* is a curiously moving novel—by implication, a relentless and haunting study of frustration and futility in the life of the anonymous masses of mankind. The subject matter is part of the very material used by the Naturalists for their novels and short stories. Huysmans, however, made the Naturalistic subject his own—first, by creating the protagonist unmistakably in his own image, and second, by conceiving of the most extreme form in which the subject could be expressed. It would be difficult to imagine a drearier or a more hopeless failure of an existence than that of Jean Folantin, yet Huysmans manages to persuade the reader that so extreme a case is, nevertheless, the true image of man's fate. It is true that Folantin reflects, at the end, that nothing good can ever happen to "those who have no money," but the novel should not be mistaken for an analysis of the economics of poverty. It concerns, rather, the human condition. Almost as though he wished to underscore that point, Huysmans deliberately made the equally frustrated protagonist of his next novel a person of wealth and position: the decadent duke, Jean des Esseintes.

Published in 1884, *Against the Grain* scandalized the public of the day and promptly took its place as the breviary of the Decadents because it seemed to be a catalog of the aesthetic values advocated by that late nineteenth century coterie. With even less plot than *Down Stream* and with only one character of consequence, *Against the Grain* is one of the strangest compositions ever to bear the label "novel." The central figure, Duke Jean des Esseintes, is the last of his line, sickly and hypersensitive, representing the ultimate decay into which a once-noble family has fallen. In order to flee the real world, he sells the family estate and purchases a small, secluded cottage whose interior he transforms into the most artificial environment imaginable, with exotic colors on the walls, rare carpeting on the floors, a collection of books dominated by the authors of the Latin decadence, phantasmagoric paintings, and eccentric furnishings of all kinds. Most windows are covered so that little light is admitted and day cannot always be distinguished from night. Certain rooms are kept almost hermetically sealed, lighted only by candles. In this way, des Esseintes attempts to create an environment designed to flatter his refined taste and sensitivity and to be as little like the outside world as possible. He even eats breakfast in the evening and dinner at dawn, sleeping during the daylight hours, in order to experience life in a pattern opposite to, or "against the grain" of, the natural order. Most of the novel is devoted to descriptions of the different ways des Esseintes invents to transform his environment and provide himself with constantly changing sensual experiences. After a year of living out his fantasies in this way, des Esseintes becomes dangerously ill and is forced to give up his sanctuary and return to Paris for medical care, recognizing that his attempt to flee the real world and inhabit an environment of his own creation is a failure—in fact, an impossibility.

Because there is no action to narrate and no interpersonal relationships to analyze, Huysmans has contrived to hold the reader's attention with a nervous and curiously ornate style designed to make all of des Esseintes' strange experiments come vividly to life. The style is indeed arresting, at least in the first chapters, and some of the scenes described are hauntingly unforgettable in their bizarre details, such as the tortoise whose jewel-inlaid shell allows the play of light to create a constantly shifting pattern of color in the room or the account of des Esseintes' experiment with an array of liqueur-dispensing containers that allow him to create a veritable symphony of subtly contrasting taste sensations by rearranging the order in which he sips from the collection of bottles and by mixing the contents in different ways. Eventually, however, in spite of the inventive style, these exotic orgies of sight, sound, smell, and taste pall, for the book consists of nothing else. The repetition causes boredom to set in for the reader, as it does for des Esseintes himself.

Against the Grain is certainly Huysmans' most famous book, a remarkable achievement of sustained fantasy. Much of the fame of the novel results from its curiosity value. The effete and eccentric character of des Esseintes, and the eerie quality of his escapist fantasies, exert an undeniable power of fascination by themselves. The evident identification of des Esseintes with Huysmans himself, moreover, gives *Against the Grain* some of the titillating appeal of a scandalous confession, which seems to reveal the tormented soul of its author. Like *Down Stream*, *Against the Grain* offers a highly personal vision of man's earthly condition, expressed in the form of an extreme case, on the outer edges of human possibility. Those characteristics are, as already noted, always the central features of Huysmans' creative imagination. For such a sensationally revealing self-portrait, there will doubtless always be an audience.

Writing *Against the Grain* left Huysmans emotionally drained. Three years went by before he began another novel, and that new project proved to be only a temporary haven for him—as its title, *En rade* (at anchor), suggests—rather than a continuation of his spiritual odyssey. *En rade*, published in 1887, describes the futile attempt of a middle-aged Parisian couple to get away from their creditors during a period of financial difficulty by moving out to the country. They are so dismayed by the venal and predatory behavior of the peasants who surround them that they conclude it will be more comfortable to return to Paris and face their creditors. A similar tone of world-weariness informs the short novel *Un Dilemme*, which offered a glimpse of the sordid moral values that characterized the urban middle class.

Those two works of social criticism, so lacking in spirit and conviction, seem to mark a period of hesitation and self-searching on Huysmans' part, as though he were contemplating a return to the principles of Naturalism but seemed unconvinced of the validity of those principles. Whatever the explanation, these two works are the least personal of all Huysmans' compositions, containing no characters that can be clearly identified as based on aspects of his own personality. That the issue of the validity of Naturalistic principles may have been his underlying concern in these two works is strongly suggested by the opening pages of the work that followed them, the novel *Là-Bas*, in which Huysmans returned to the theme of his own painful spiritual odyssey. In those opening pages, he introduces his new protagonist, a novelist named Durtal, earnestly discussing with his friend des Hermies the value of Naturalism as a literary theory. In this discussion, it is des Hermies, a medical doctor who has rejected his profession's scientific pretensions, who denounces Naturalism for its crassly materialistic outlook, while Durtal defends its accomplishments in rendering the real world artistically. Durtal quickly concedes that Naturalism *is* materialistic, and that its glaring failure has been an inability to deal with the nonmaterial aspects of human life, the spiritual side of man. Durtal concludes the discussion by suggesting that Naturalism has been valuable but, having gone as far as it is capable, has outlived its usefulness and must be replaced by a kind of "spiritual Naturalism," which will treat matters outside the realm of materialistic Naturalism.

This conversation about literature is a daring opening stratagem for a novel, but it works well as an expository device, introducing the character of the protagonist effectively and revealing the depth of his central concern, which is to confront the supernatural both in his professional and in his personal life. *Là-Bas* tells two interrelated stories: Durtal's struggle to write a book about the notorious and enigmatic Gilles de Rais (a contemporary of Joan of Arc who, late in his life, engaged in necromancy and the kidnaping and murdering of children) and, as a consequence of research into the life of Gilles de Rais, Durtal's involvement with Satanism and with the diabolic Madame Chantelouve, who is, briefly, his mistress. Both professionally and personally, Durtal is pursuing the theme of the supernatural in its most extreme form, the worship of Satan. Studying the historical figure of the cruel Gilles de Rais, and attending a Black Mass in the company of Madame Chantelouve, Durtal journeys "down there" to spend his season in hell, immersing himself totally in the world of Satanism. The immersion results, however, not in spiritual peace or satisfaction but in horror and revulsion. The novel ends, symbolically, with the simultaneous completion of the book on Gilles de Rais and the termination of the affair with Madame Chantelouve, leaving Durtal ready for the one remaining path to the resolution of his own spiritual crisis: conversion to Christianity.

Là-Bas is Huysmans' finest novel. The vivid characters, well-integrated structure, and dramatic intensity of the action all seize the imagination of the reader, satisfy aesthetic expectations, and haunt the memory long afterward. In the character of Durtal, Huysmans created his ideal fictional protagonist, the perfect vehicle for expressing his central concern as a novelist from that time onward, namely, to describe the road to spiritual peace. The odyssey is completed in three novels, all of which have Durtal as protagonist but none of which attains the blend of artistic skill and dramatic intensity that makes *Là-Bas* so impressive a work of art. Those three novels, *En route*, *The Cathedral*, and *The Oblate*, appearing over a period of a decade, recount Durtal's (and Huysmans') conversion to Catholicism, his retreat to Chartres and its cathedral, and his embrace of the monastic life. At that stage in his career, Huysmans no longer made any pretense at invention, allowing his novels, rather, to be undisguisedly autobiographical in nature. If the last three novels make for slow and tedious reading, it is perhaps because the source of Huysmans' creative energy, the tortured emotions of his own inner being, had dried up. Once his spiritual crisis had been resolved, it seems, his imagination lost its driving force—an account of the coming of spiritual peace only infrequently has the same power as an account of spiritual torment.

Huysmans must be regarded as a minor figure in French literary history, the eccentric representative of a minor segment of the literary world at the end of the nineteenth century, the small band of spiritually troubled Decadents, among whom he was clearly a leading spokesman. It is not, however, his advocacy of any particular literary theory that gives Huysmans his enduring place in the history of the novel. Rather, it is the highly personal character of his fiction that attracts and fascinates. Huysmans clearly wrote out of inner necessity, using his creative imagination as a form of self-therapy. His novels are, at bottom, one long, painful, and occasionally lurid personal confession. Taken together, his best works afford precious insight not only into the strange personality of Huysmans himself, but also into a disturbing mental state characteristic of a significant portion of France's intelligentsia during the final decades of the nineteenth century. Because of what he tells us about himself and about his age, Huysmans will always have a small, but devoted—and fascinated—readership.

Major publications other than long fiction

SHORT FICTION: "Sac au dos" (English translation, 1907), in *Les Soirées de Médan*, 1880 (celebrated volume of Naturalist short stories by Émile Zola and his circle).

POETRY: *Le Drageoir aux épices*, 1874 (*A Dish of Spices*, 1927); *Croquis parisiens*, 1880 (*Parisian Sketches*, 1962).

NONFICTION: *L'Art moderne*, 1883; *Certains*, 1889; *La Bièvre*, 1890; *Sainte Lydwine de Schiedam*, 1901 (*St. Lydwine of Schiedam*, 1923); *De tout*, 1902; *Esquisse biographique sur Don Bosco*, 1902; *Trois Primitifs*, 1905; *Les Foules de Lourdes*, 1906 (*The Crowds of Lourdes*, 1925).

MISCELLANEOUS: *Oeuvres complètes*, 1928-1934 (23 volumes).

Bibliography

Baldick, Robert. *The Life of Joris-Karl Huysmans*, 1955.

Brandeth, Henry R. T. *Huysmans*, 1963.

Cogny, Pierre. *J.-K. Huysmans à la recherche de l'unité*, 1953.

Ellis, Havelock. *Affirmations*, 1922.

Issacharoff, Michael. *J.-K. Huysmans devant la critique en France*, 1970.

Laver, James. *The First Decadent: Being the Strange Life of J. K. Huysmans*, 1954.

Mathews, J. H. *Surrealism and the Novel*, 1966.

Ridge, George Ross. *Joris-Karl Huysmans*, 1968.

Murray Sachs

JEAN PAUL
Johann Paul Friedrich Richter

Born: Wunsiedel, Germany; March 21, 1763
Died: Bayreuth, Germany; November 14, 1825

Principal long fiction

Die unsichtbare Loge, 1793 (*The Invisible Lodge*, 1883); *Hesperus*, 1795 (*Hesperus: Or, Forty-five Dogpost Days*, 1865); *Blumen-, Frucht- und Dornenstücke: Oder, Ehestand, Tod und Hochzeit des Armenadvokaten F. St. Siebenkäs*, 1796-1797 (*Flower, Fruit, and Thorn Pieces: Or, The Married Life, Death, and Wedding of the Advocate of the Poor Firmian Stanislaus*, 1845); *Titan*, 1800-1803 (*Titan: A Romance*, 1862); *Flegeljahre*, 1804-1805 (*Walt and Vult: Or, The Twins*, 1846); *Der Komet*, 1820-1822.

Other literary forms

When, at the age of fifty-nine, Jean Paul took stock of his literary accomplishments, he arrived at the number of exactly fifty-nine books, one book for each year of his life—certainly a gratifying coincidence for a man who so clearly had lived in order to write. Jean Paul had started his career in literature with two collections of satires, *Grönländische Prozesse* (1783; Greenland lawsuits) and *Auswahl aus des Teufels Papieren* (1789; selections from the Devil's papers). After 1790, inspired by a new sympathy for the unavoidable follies of downtrodden men in their narrow circumstances, the youthful critic became less censorious in his view of world and society. Over the next twenty years, Jean Paul wrote several short narratives in which unique blends of satire and idyll create shades of the comical, reaching from the subtly subversive praise of steadfast endurance in *Leben des vergnügten Schulmeisterlein Maria Wutz in Auenthal* (1793; *Life of the Cheerful Little Schoolmaster Maria Wutz in Auenthal*, 1959) to the grotesque farce of capricious cowardice in *Des Feldpredigers Schmelzle Reise nach Flätz* (1809; *Army Chaplain Schmelzle's Journey to Flätz*, 1827).

During the turbulent years of the early nineteenth century, Jean Paul wrote a good number of important political essays. *Jean Pauls Freiheitsbüchlein* (1805; Jean Paul's booklet of freedom) attacks censorship; *Dämmerungen für Deutschland* (1810; twilights for Germany), published during Napoleon's occupation of Germany, counsels friendship with France and suggests that being governed by liberal foreigners might, after all, be preferable to being governed by illiberal compatriots. The same years saw the publication of comprehensive inquiries into what for Jean Paul were two closely related areas, inquiries into the theory and practice of art, his *Vorschule der Ästhetik* (1804; *Horn of Oberon: Jean Paul Richter's School for Aesthetics*, 1973) and into the theory and practice of education, his *Levana* (1807; *Levana: Or, The*

Doctrine of Education, 1848). Jean Paul's lifelong preoccupation with the experience of death and his research into man's sense of immortality found expression in two religious tracts, *Das Kampaner Tal* (1797; *The Champaner Thal,* 1848) and *Selina,* published posthumously in 1827.

Achievements

Jean Paul has often been called the greatest humorist in the German language. Yet despite this distinction, his fame continues to be transmitted by the lexicographer's assertion rather than by any impact that arises from a wide acquaintance with his work. Even among well-educated Germans, few have ever attempted to read one of Jean Paul's novels, and fewer still have persevered beyond the opening pages. Foreign readers have fared no better. Eric A. Blackall begins his analysis of Jean Paul's novels with the warning that Jean Paul "is of all German authors perhaps the most difficult to interpret to a foreign audience." What makes the appreciation of Jean Paul's art such a formidable task is that his style places enormous obstacles in the way of even the most expert reader. It is a style in which everything direct, precise, and unequivocal in the description of the world has been dismissed in search of the contradictoriness and contrariness of all human efforts to experience it. With maddening mastery, Jean Paul thus designed an anarchic, shapeless universe that tries to be as exhaustive of its multiple perplexities as it proves to be exhausting of the reader's sense of order and direction.

It is difficult to imagine how Jean Paul's reputation as one of Germany's foremost novelists could have survived had his works not attracted the attention of fellow writers. In the German language, the chain of his admirers stretches from the novelist Gottfried Keller, the poets Stefan George and Hugo von Hofmannsthal, and the essayist Karl Kraus to such modern writers as Robert Walser, Hermann Hesse, and Günter Grass. In England, Thomas Carlyle and Thomas De Quincey read and translated Jean Paul's works with enthusiasm; in France, Charles Baudelaire expressed his growing fascination with the curiously German charm of Jean Paul; while in the United States, Henry Wadsworth Longfellow even required his students to study the perplexing German author.

Critical assessments have varied greatly. During his own time, Jean Paul was hailed as the master of an idealistic, effusive emotionalism. Later generations saw in him, at times, a champion of the oppressed; at other times, a whimsical apologist of backward provincialism. Only in the twentieth century has it become widely acknowledged that Jean Paul's greatest achievement lies precisely in his attempt to combine all of these conflicting attitudes, as well as their conflicting literary styles, and thus capture man's disturbingly disharmonius way of life. A century which has learned to read Marcel Proust, James Joyce, and Thomas Pynchon with glossary in hand should no longer feel quite so overwhelmed by Jean Paul, this early virtuoso of the humorously conceived, pedantically prepared, and yet willfully written novel of infinite incongruities.

Biography

Johann Paul Friedrich Richter, who chose the pen name Jean Paul to honor the memory of Jean-Jacques Rousseau, was born in a remote town in what today is the northeastern part of Bavaria. He was the oldest child of a school-master who soon advanced to the modest position of a parson in one of the neighboring villages. Increasingly embittered by the stifling backwardness of his family and environment, the fifteen-year-old boy decided to embark on a course of indiscriminate reading with an obsession only the self-educating person would be able to sustain. There has probably never been a German writer who read more and read more widely than did Jean Paul. With the meticulous industry that was to become so typical of him, he collected in barely four years twenty volumes of excerpts culled from all fields of knowl-edge. This neatly indexed but largely undigested erudition was to provide Jean Paul in later years with the basis for his notoriously extravagant choice of metaphors.

After the death of Jean Paul's father in 1779, the family faced more than a decade of humiliating poverty. Jean Paul was, nevertheless, determined to break the stranglehold of his provincial upbringing and tried, in 1781, to eke out an existence as a student of theology at the University of Leipzig. Instead of pursuing this sanctioned career of the poor, he actually intended to make a name for himself as a writer of satires. Despite all efforts, however, his works went unnoticed, as did their ambitious and desperate author. His mounting debts finally forced him to return home, only to endure three demoralizing years during which he lived in one room with his mother and three brothers on a fare of bread and potatoes.

Undaunted by outward adversity, Jean Paul continued to write hundreds of pages of satires until an inward experience brought about an important change of mind. On November 15, 1790, Jean Paul had a vision of himself dead and was so shaken by it that he resolved from that moment to devote his art to the love of his fellow mortals. Filled with highly sentimental scenes of love and death, Jean Paul's first novel, *The Invisible Lodge*, promptly gained for him the long-elusive recognition.

Totally unknown until the publication of this novel, the thirty-year-old author became an almost instant celebrity. With childlike innocence, he let himself be swept up by the wave of adulation. There followed hectic years in the literary limelight of Leipzig, Weimar, and Berlin. Two engagements to ladies of the high nobility were quickly entered into and dissolved by him. In 1801, Jean Paul finally married Karoline Mayer, the daughter of a civil servant from Berlin, but—physically and mentally exhausted by the demands of his drawing-room existence—insisted that they return to the provincial life he had known before. Three years later, the growing family settled in Bayreuth, a town chosen by Jean Paul not for any cultural ambience, but for its excellent beer.

During the remaining twenty-one years of his life, Jean Paul retreated ever further into the eccentricities of a role which showed him to his contemporaries as half philistine and half prophet, half hypochondriac and half quack. Only once did he let his self-imposed idyll be disturbed when, in 1817, he proudly accepted an honorary doctorate which the University of Heidelberg—on the recommendation of the philosopher Georg Wilhelm Friedrich Hegel—had decided to confer upon him. The last years of Jean Paul's life were overshadowed by the tragic death of his only son in 1821. Plagued by intolerable nightmares and blind from cataracts, Jean Paul died of edema on November 14, 1825, almost thirty-five years to the day after the vision of his death had awakened his true artistic calling.

Analysis

Jean Paul turned toward the novel only after having slaved for more than ten years as a writer of satires. Much of what he had learned as a satirist continued to influence his novelistic art. In the eighteenth century, satire—the ridiculing of representative social vices—relied for its effect on the application of wit. Jean Paul naturally adopted the practice, and it is without doubt his peculiarly witty style that has proved to be the most prohibitive aspect of his novels.

Wit, for the eighteenth century, was defined as the intuitive power through which the mind links seemingly incomparable objects by revealing a similarity in their relation to a common, often more abstract concept or quality. To compare wise Greek philosophers with white clouds on a sunny day—an example Jean Paul used to explain his procedure—strikes the reader as witty only after he has made the connection that these two dissimilar sets of entities share their tendency to move with lofty serenity. Jean Paul, his volumes of excerpts organized under such abstract notions as rich and poor, big and small, could provide virtually every object, emotion, action, or thought with a whimsical commentary of remote analogues. He thus created a constantly shifting layer of references that could throw its foreshortening or elongating shadow on everything in this world. The problems for the reader are, of course, staggering. An encyclopedic knowledge and a sheer inexhaustible patience are only the most obvious prerequisites for following Jean Paul on his flights of combinatory imagination. Yet the rewards, faithful readers insist, are more than commensurate, as there arises a humorously bewildering universe in which all things are stripped of their pretensions to serious and weighty self-identity.

After 1790, no longer satisfied with a critique of representative vices, Jean Paul set out to study the shortcomings of human beings in all their uniqueness.

In the process, he became convinced that not only foolish men but all men are essentially absurd, because their lot is inherently incongruous. This incongruity stems from the fact that man must constantly try to square the infinitude of his desires with the finitude of his circumstances, marking everything he is, does, or achieves as ridiculously inappropriate. Jean Paul was, however, also convinced that the infinity—which usually surrounds humans as nothing but a mocking absence—can, on occasion, enter the life of "higher human beings" as an all-sustaining presence. He therefore incorporated into his humorous style lengthy passages in which starry-eyed young men and women experience moments of rapturous bliss in dreamlike landscapes of surrealistic beauty, leaving behind the oppressive "cottage smoke of human existence" for the recognition of an omnipresent harmony.

In spite of his belief that a mixture of styles is the truest representation of the human condition, Jean Paul did distinguish three types of novels according to the perspectives that dominate their style. Borrowing terms normally applied to schools of painting, he spoke of the "Italian novel" as one written in an elevated tone and narrating the actions and passions of noble heroes. The "Dutch novel," in contrast, focuses on the dull details in the life of humble people. Midway between these two stands the "German novel," which tries to mediate the opposing visions of the Italian and Dutch novels. Though Jean Paul was quick to admit that in his novels, as in a museum, Italian, Dutch, and German styles coexist, he stressed that he had written only Italian and German novels, the Dutch style in its pure form having been reserved for his shorter fiction.

Jean Paul listed three of his six novels as belonging to the Italian style: *The Invisible Lodge*, *Hesperus*, and *Titan*. It has often been observed that many parallels in form and content exist among these novels and that they are most appropriately considered as three versions of one theme. *The Invisible Lodge* tells of the emotional and political education of Gustav von Falkenberg. Brought up in total isolation from the world and its corruption, Gustav is sent to the court of the small principality of Scheerau to enter upon a military career. There he becomes friends with Amandus, the son of the physician, satirist, and political liberal Dr. Fenk. Their friendship, however, seems irreparably damaged when both young men fall in love with the same girl, the angelic Beata. In the end, the prolonged impasse is conveniently overcome as Amandus dies—not, of course, before he has reconciled himself with Gustav and has asked the friend to love Beata in his stead. Everything seems to have worked itself out when Gustav's and Beata's bliss is unexpectedly cut short. Gustav has apparently led a double life. Disenchantment with the court of Scheerau must have taken a drastic turn for him, because he has joined a secret society devoted to the overthrow of the government. The conspirators have been discovered, and Gustav is reported to be in prison. With these startling revelations, hastily communicated on the last three pages of the novel, *The Invisible Lodge* comes to an abrupt and premature end.

Considering that *The Invisible Lodge* was Jean Paul's first novel, it constitutes an amazingly complex achievement. A multiplicity of styles—Jean Paul's most distinguishing trademark—is orchestrated with a sure hand. Moments of high lyric intensity are followed by witty descriptions of court, town, and country, allowing Jean Paul to display his mastery over a wide range of comic moods. Still, something is seriously wrong with the novel: It does not advance convincingly the political education of its hero. Too much is withheld from the reader for too long, and by the time the political plot gets under way, the reader is no longer prepared to adjust to the required change of perspective. Because the novel was originally published in serial installments, radical revisions of the plot were impossible, the first parts of the novel having been published before the work was complete. Jean Paul did the only thing he could do at that point: He dropped the idea of finishing *The Invisible Lodge* and instead started all over again.

Hesperus, the most successful of his novels published during Jean Paul's lifetime, concerns a young man's education at the court of Flachsenfingen. This young man, Viktor, again has a close friend, Flamin, and again their friendship is jeopardized by their love for the same girl, Klotilde. This time, a happy ending is arranged not through the death of one of the rivals but through the discovery that Flamin is the illegitimate son of the Prince of Flachsenfingen and, besides, the natural brother of Klotilde. Viktor and Flamin promptly become reconciled, and Viktor is free to marry Klotilde.

Superimposed on this familiar plot is a political intrigue the outline of which Jean Paul took from a contemporary novel by Wilhelm Friedrich von Meyern with the fantastical title *Dya-Na-Sore* (1787). Adjusted to the demands of Jean Paul's own plot, the story runs like this: Discouraged by the philandering Prince of Flachsenfingen, Lord Horion—an English relative and adviser of the Prince—arranges for better things from the next generation. He kidnaps four illegitimate sons of the Prince and has them brought to England, where they are educated in the liberal ideals of that country. As the novel opens, these sons have grown up and, uninformed about their true identity, are encouraged to come to Flachsenfingen. There they form a revolutionary club and indulge in much rhetorical posturing and some haphazard violence. Viktor, recently appointed physician of the court, joins the club. When the hotheaded and jealous Flamin gets himself into trouble with the court and ends up in prison, his identity as one of the four illegitimate sons of the Prince is finally revealed, as are the identities of his three half brothers. The conservative court camarilla realizes that it has been outmaneuvered by Lord Horion and quickly abdicates.

To avoid the mistake of his first novel, Jean Paul reminded himself explicitly that he wanted to deal with three themes concomitantly: friendship, love, and republicanism. In contrast to *The Invisible Lodge*, *Hesperus* certainly contains much that relates to each of the three topics, and the success of the novel might well have resulted from the fashionable association of these very timely themes. Nevertheless, Jean Paul soon felt that he had not been able to fuse them into a coherent whole. Indeed, how much the ideals of friendship, love, and republicanism are at odds with one another becomes particularly clear from the conflicts resulting from the characterization of the novel's hero, the court physician Viktor.

As a character, Viktor represents an indisputable improvement upon the pale and schematic Gustav. Viktor combines in one complex personality the enthusiastic commitment of the idealist with the ironic distance of the satirist. Yet it is precisely this complexity which thwarts the intentions of the plot. In Jean Paul's novels, only commoners possess the ability to take a satiric attitude toward world, life, and society. Granting Viktor this talent, Jean Paul had to make him, in contrast to Gustav, a commoner. As a result, Viktor becomes unsuited for heroic action in a novel of the Italian style. Flamin, Viktor's friend, must therefore take up the slack. Unlike Amandus, he is not allowed to die; rather, he is made to advance the political plot and be the center of it. Still, Viktor is the more mature of the two friends, and it is poetically just that he should end up marrying Klotilde. Political and emotional education have, once again, gone their separate ways: Flamin's political success is not built on his emotional maturity, while Viktor's success in love has no implication for his sense of political responsibility. Jean Paul, unimpressed by the praise of his contemporaries, therefore felt compelled for a third time to write the book he had in mind.

Titan is Jean Paul's most elaborate novel. It occupied him for more than ten years, and when it was finished, he believed it to be his masterpiece. He had finally got his story straight. Albano, the younger son of the Prince of Hohenfliess, is removed from court as an infant by the scheming Gaspard. At twenty, Albano is allowed to reenter court society, believing himself to be the son of Gaspard. He falls in love with two beautiful young women, becomes disappointed by life at court, and travels to Italy, where the memories of republican Rome make him want to join the revolutionary armies of France. At that moment, Albano learns that he is the son of the Prince and, now being in love with a princess who shares his progressive views, accedes to the throne of Hohenfliess.

On his way to emotional and political happiness, Albano meets a number of fascinating characters who teach him by their examples the danger of everything excessive in life. The ethereal Liane shows him, through her unhappy fate, the debilitating influence of an unchecked sensibility. The misfortunes of the emancipated Linda disclose the destructiveness of unrestrained desire. Gaspard's political intriguing reveals that an unprincipled pursuit of ideals inevitably leads to a cynical disregard for human beings. Albano's friend Roquairol displays the suicidal desperation of an aestheticism that treats life as a charade in which everything is permissible on the condition that it will entertain. Finally, the fate of the librarian Schoppe demonstrates how the scorn of the satirist must—if not mitigated by human sympathy—end in self-disgust and self-negation.

Yet even with its rich assortment of characters, *Titan* remains a tour de force. Albano's aristocratic world is that of the *ancien régime*, Jean Paul's idea of a revolution from above, the typical illusion of that regime's vision of reform. Appearing eleven years after the French Revolution, Jean Paul's titanic plot had become obsolete at the moment that its author felt that he had perfected it. Disappointment with the long-awaited novel was general. Jean Paul's honeymoon with his reading public ended abruptly, as did his interest in the Italian novel.

Flower, Fruit, and Thorn Pieces: Or, The Married Life, Death, and Wedding of the Advocate of the Poor Firmian Stanislaus is the first of Jean Paul's German novels and was published only one year after the phenomenal success of *Hesperus*. When eager publishers clamored for more material from the new celebrity, Jean Paul promised a collection of shorter works with the title "Flower, Fruit, and Thorn Pieces." The faked death and burial of the lawyer and satirist Siebenkäs was planned as one of the "Thorn Pieces." Soon, however, the little story began to preoccupy Jean Paul, and in nine months of feverish writing he turned it into a "Goliath" of a book: the first important novel of German middle-class life, the first detailed account of a middle-class marriage.

The story is that of Firmian Stanislaus Siebenkäs, who marries the good-natured yet thoroughly conventional Lenette. His wife's inability to feel or think anything that goes beyond the narrow bounds of prescribed custom annoys and eventually tortures the sensitive Siebenkäs. After many attempts to achieve a *modus vivendi* between the spouses, Siebenkäs must admit to himself that he simply cannot tolerate the suffocating mediocrity of Lenette's aspirations. On the suggestion of a friend, the cynical idealist Leibgeber, Siebenkäs stages his own death and burial and leaves town. Lenette is now free to marry a man after her own heart. Siebenkäs takes on Leibgeber's name and station in life, while Leibgeber is glad to be rid of his last contact with society—his name—and disappears into the freedom of total anonymity. Siebenkäs, however, is guilt-ridden about his ruse. He returns home only to find that Lenette has recently died in childbirth. As he visits her grave, Siebenkäs meets Natalie, a girl with whom he had fallen in love at the height of his marital unhappiness but whom he had renounced after his flight from Lenette. The novel closes with hints of a new love and a happier marriage.

The world of Siebenkäs and his wife knows no political intrigue and contains few dramatic events. Instead, the reality of everyday life is depicted with a stifling accuracy which until then had been almost totally unknown in German literature. Indeed, Jean Paul accentuated the oppressiveness of middle-class existence by weighing down every detail with the crabbed erudition of his metaphorical associations. What arises before the reader is the struggle of a sensitive man against the deadening objectivity of his senselessly restrictive environment. The political and social message of Siebenkäs' quiet desperation could not go unnoticed. The same fashionable circles that had recently embraced the high-flying republicanism of *Hesperus* felt remarkably ill at ease with this novel on the curses of middle-class life in Germany. Austria's censorship, probably the most telling barometer in its day for anything smacking of political insubordination, quickly issued an order banishing the book from its territory.

Walt and Vult, Jean Paul's second German novel, had also not been intended as an independent work; it had originally been envisioned as a subplot of the already gigantic *Titan*, describing the education of a nontitanic, middle-class hero. Jean Paul finally separated the story from *Titan*, and, though unfinished, *Walt and Vult* is now generally considered his most mature novel and one of the best in the German language.

As the early sketches indicate, the novel was to tell how an innocent young man overcomes the machinations of a hostile world and builds for himself an idyllic enclave as a country parson. The story begins as the will of the rich van der Kabel is being opened for the greedy stares of seven anxiously waiting heirs. To their dismay, the lion's share of van der Kabel's wealth is bequeathed to an unknown twenty-four-year-old student of law and spare-time poet, Walt Harnisch. Walt, however, can claim his bequest only after he has fulfilled several rather outlandish stipulations, which van der Kabel designed apparently to teach the naïve dreamer how to advance his own best interest.

Into this situation comes Vult, Walt's twin brother, who ran away from home years before, traveling throughout the world as a flutist, and who, with his disillusioned realism, seems the right person to help his brother foil the schemes of van der Kabel's relatives. Yet as Vult's presence asserts itself, Walt's pursuit of the inheritance recedes into the background, and the novel focuses on the question of whether these dissimilar twins can learn from each other's outlook on life.

Vult provides a satiric commentary on Walt. He repeatedly tries to pierce the clouds on which Walt walks through life, but to no avail. Walt is too innocent even to understand his brother's critical perspective, and, oddly enough, he sidesteps all snares placed in his path with the assurance of a sleepwalker. What makes the conflict between the two well-meaning brothers so tragically comic is that their opposing temperaments lead to two equally valid, equally necessary, but fundamentally incompatible modes of perception. Vult leaves the incorrigible Walt with the parting words, "I leave you as you were, I go as I came." No resolution is in sight, no conclusion possible.

Of the ideals of friendship, love, and republicanism, which the young author had wanted to promote in his fiery *Hesperus*, republicanism already had given way to a dispirited faith in the revolution from above, political change by princely intrigue and incognito, while the ideal of love had suffered lasting harm in the petty squabbles of Siebenkäs' household. In *Walt and Vult*, Jean Paul's first and most cherished ideal, friendship, also proved unattainable. Begun as an affirmation of adolescent idealism in its power over reality, *Walt and Vult* becomes persuasive in the painful recognition that all such adolescent dreams have departed, never to return again.

After having written five lengthy novels in roughly twelve years, Jean Paul paused another twelve years before he started on his last, unfinished novel, the unjustly neglected comical coda to his oeuvre, *Der Komet*. Jean Paul initially had contemplated a veritable encyclopedia of the comic with the title "A Thousand and One Folly." The scope of this plan gradually intimidated him, however, and he settled on a more manageable plot, the story of the quixotic fool Nikolaus Marggraf. An apothecary by profession, Marggraf believes that he is a prince, surrounds himself with an entourage of fools, bon vivants, and swindlers, and sets out to find his true father and the princess he loves. Happy in his illusion, he comes across another madman, the Leather Man. While Marggraf uses his imagination to fashion for himself a universe of his own liking, the Leather Man uses the same power to create for himself a personal hell. It is quite possible that these two extremists of the imagination were destined to cure each other of their respective excesses. Marggraf, in any case, was to end up at the Rollwenzelei, an inn near Bayreuth where Jean Paul had for many years gone almost daily to eat his potatoes and to drink his beer, to write of the world and to imagine himself the idyllic hermit he would so much have liked to be.

Jean Paul's last novel, which he himself called an "anti-Titan," thus parodies not only the idealistic heroes of his earlier works but also their idealistic creator. Nevertheless, even this all-inclusive parody contains within itself a deep-seated sympathy for the illusions it ridicules. The reader is, of course, supposed to laugh at the pretentious antics of man's unbounded enthusiasm, yet he is also supposed to feel moved by those who wish for too much and wish for it too ardently. It is true that Jean Paul's satiric vein continued to flow long after his emotional idealism had dried up. Still, Jean Paul always resisted the most self-destructive urge of the censorious temperament, its seemingly inescapable turn toward misanthropy and cynicism. In Jean Paul's universe, no one is allowed to take himself too seriously, least of all he who claims to be a satirist.

Major publications other than long fiction

SHORT FICTION: *Grönländische Prozesse*, 1783; *Auswahl aus des Teufels Papieren*, 1789; *Leben des vergnügten Schulmeisterlein Maria Wutz in Auenthal*, 1793 (*Life of the Cheerful Little Schoolmaster Maria Wutz in Auenthal*, 1959); *Des Rektors Florian Fälbel und seiner Primaner Reise nach dem Fichtel-*

gebirge, 1796; *Leben des Quintus Fixlein*, 1796 (*Life of Quintus Fixlein*, 1827); *Der Jubelsenior*, 1797; *Des Feldpredigers Schmelzle Reise nach Flätz*, 1809 (*Army Chaplain Schmelzle's Journey to Flätz*, 1827); *Dr. Katzenbergers Badereise*, 1809 *Leben Fibels*, 1812.

NONFICTION: *Das Kampaner Tal*, 1797 (*The Champaner Thal*, 1848); *Vorschule der Ästhetik*, 1804 (*Horn of Oberon: Jean Paul Richter's School for Aesthetics*, 1973); *Jean Pauls Freiheitsbüchlein*, 1805; *Levana*, 1807 (*Levana: Or, The Doctrine of Education*, 1848); *Dämmerungen für Deutschland*, 1810; *Selina*, 1827.

Bibliography

Berger, Dorothea. *Jean Paul Friedrich Richter*, 1972.

Blackall, Eric A. *The Novels of the German Romantics*, 1983.

Brewer, Edward V. *The New England Interest in J. P. F. Richter*, 1943.

Bruyn, Günter de. *Das Leben des Jean Paul Friedrich Richter*, 1978.

Schneider, Helmut J. "Jean Paul," in *Deutsche Dichter der Romantik*, 1971. Edited by Benno von Wiese.

Schweikert, Uwe. *Jean Paul*, 1970.

Smeed, John William. *Jean Paul's "Dreams,"* 1966.

Joachim Scholz

JOHANNES V. JENSEN

Born: Farsø, Denmark; January 20, 1873
Died: Copenhagen, Denmark; November 25, 1950

Principal long fiction

Danskere, 1896; *Einar Elkær*, 1898; *Kongens fald*, 1900-1901 (*The Fall of the King*, 1933); *Madame d'Ora*, 1904; *Skovene*, 1904; *Hjulet*, 1905; *Den lange rejse*, 1908-1922 (includes *Bræen*, 1908; *Skibet*, 1912; *Norne-Gæst*, 1919; *Det tabte land*, 1919; *Christofer Columbus*, 1921; *Cimbrernes tog*, 1922; the series is translated as *The Long Journey*, 1922-1924, 1933, 1945, in 3 volumes [includes *Fire and Ice*, 1923; *The Cimbrians*, 1923; *Christopher Columbus*, 1924]); *Dr. Renaults Fristelser*, 1935; *Gudrun*, 1936.

Other literary forms

In addition to his novels, Johannes V. Jensen wrote an extensive number of essays dealing with evolutionary, anthropological, and historical topics. He was also a master of the shorter prose form, primarily seen in his series of Himmerland stories and myths. The stories are principally studies of characters from the Danish countryside, rendered with humor and irony but also permeated with a tragic view of life as meaningless, whereas the myths—embodying the core concept of Jensen's aesthetics—are lyric and symbolic sketches of mankind, nature, and animals. Three volumes of exotic stories contain for the most part travel descriptions from the Far East and the United States. In addition to his prose works, Jensen was the author of several poetry collections, the first volume of which, *Digte* (1906, 1917, 1921), established him as a pioneer in modern Danish poetry.

Achievements

Jensen is generally regarded as the most prolific and influential Danish author of the twentieth century. His reputation rests less on the ideological content of his work than on his unique power of observation and stylistic brilliancy when describing both tiny details and the vast macrocosmos with a conciseness which, in spite of its scientific precision, does not preclude artistic refinement and poetic expressiveness. With his roots in the self-centered, spiritual world of the 1890's, Jensen nevertheless began as a fanatic worshiper of progress and materialism, introducing motifs of modern technology into Scandinavian literature. After decades in which French and German philosophy and literature had been the major foreign sources of inspiration, Jensen advocated the entirely pragmatic and expansive view of life which he found in the Anglo-American world. His knowledge of American culture and society was unique. He was the first to introduce Jack London and Frank Norris in Scandinavia and Ernest Hemingway in Denmark; his translations of Walt

Whitman's poetry are as yet unsurpassed. The two trends of introversion and extroversion manifest themselves in a constant process of tension and inter- action, and they merge in the "mythic" aspect of Jensen's works into a sublime synthesis.

Biography

Johannes Vilhelm Jensen was significantly influenced by his parents. His mother had a prosaic and practical view of life, but she also possessed a vivid imagination—a double predisposition inherited by her son. His father's exten- sive botanical and zoological knowledge (he was a veterinarian) became an important source of information for Jensen's later studies of nature and encouraged his preoccupation with Charles Darwin's theories of evolution. A third formative element was the family's deep-rooted feeling for peasant culture.

After a few years in school in Farsø, followed by private tutoring, Jensen entered a cathedral school in Viborg in 1893. There he received his earliest contact with literature, in particular from reading Heinrich Heine, Knut Ham- sun, Rudyard Kipling, and the Danish neo-Romantic poet Johannes Jørgen- sen. Jensen studied medicine at the University of Copenhagen from 1893 to 1898, but then decided to become a professional writer. A short trip to the United States in 1896 was the first of Jensen's extensive travels. These journeys took him five more times to the United States; to Spain in 1898 as a reporter during the Spanish-American War; to Germany, France, and England in 1898 and 1899; and to the World's Fair in Paris in 1900. In 1902 and 1903, Jensen took a long journey around the world; in 1912 and 1913, to the Far East; and in 1925 and 1926, to Egypt and Palestine. Shortly before World War II, Jensen visited the United States for the last time, a trip described in the travelogue *Fra fristaterne* (1939). During the German occupation of Denmark from 1940 to 1945, Jensen burned his diaries and most correspondence from the previous thirty years, but he continued to write until his death. In 1944 he was awarded the Nobel Prize for Literature.

Analysis

"It is a force in itself, the love of my soil and my stock. . . . My entire life is a description of Himmerland." Thus does Johannes V. Jensen acknowledge the influence of his home region upon his life, and an understanding of that influence provides the key to Jensen's writing as well. The dream of the lost land of his childhood made him search both in the past and in distant places for milieus and conditions that would recall the life and traditions of his ancestors. This expansion, Jensen's mythic method, led him back to his home region and in his best works established a balance between an optimistic and a materialistic view of life, the latter influenced by Darwin's theories and the former by spiritual reflection.

This balance was not yet established when Jensen wrote his first novels. In his descriptions of students from the provinces and their confrontation with the modern metropolis, Copenhagen, both Buris in *Danskere* and the title character of *Einar Elkær* are afflicted with a paralyzing introspection. Their inability to accept life leads to cynicism and destruction. To be sure, it is suggested that Buris will escape the advancing process of disintegration, but Einar dies in a mental hospital. Preoccupation with the self remains a major problem in the fictitious travelogue *Skovene*, written in the capricious and ironic style of Heine; here, the contrast between the white man's civilization and the native's primitive life also shows the influence of Kipling. The work tells humorously of Jensen's stay among Malaysians during his world trip of 1902 and 1903, focusing on a tiger hunt which is supposed to affirm the author as a man of action. Scattered throughout the narration is a marvelous wealth of witticisms, brilliant animal and nature descriptions, and lyric passages full of beauty and color. The predominant mood is one of homesickness and longing, which, together with a penetrating introspection, haunts the narrator throughout the book. If *Skovene*—like Jensen's other youthful works—was an attempt to escape his preoccupation during the 1890's with soul and self, the attempt did not succeed.

A more successful attempt can be found in Jensen's Himmerland stories, the robust realism of which is continued in two of his novels, *Madame d'Ora* and *Hjulet* (the wheel), set in the splendidly depicted milieus of New York and Chicago, respectively. These works, however, are marred by lengthy monologues and dialogues attacking metaphysical speculation. Thus, in *Madame d'Ora*, a spiritualist seance to which the Faustian scientist and neurasthenic dreamer Hall falls prey, is revealed as pure swindle. In addition, Jensen employs stereotyped suspense effects in an unsuccessful attempt to parody the detective story, as well as grotesque character delineation in accordance with his wish to portray stages in man's evolution rather than individuals. The extremes of these stages are represented by the "ape-man" and religious charlatan Evanston, and by his opponent, the poet Lee, a man of Nordic descent who in *Hjulet* kills Evanston, now symbolically called Cancer. Lee is thereby changed from a passive spectator to a man of action who condemns any aestheticism as an illness preventing acceptance of reality and social commitment.

The Faust theme of *Madame d'Ora* was thus replaced with social motifs, clearly influenced by Norris, an author Jensen greatly respected and admired, although it was to resurface in the novel *Dr. Renaults Fristelser*. In contrast to the famous Faust story by Johann Wolfgang von Goethe, Jensen's "Faust" wins over Mefisto (here called Asbest) because he is willing to accept wholeheartedly the experience of the moment, life as it is. Structurally, the novel is one of Jensen's more uneven books. The explanation lies in his intention to write a philosophical treatise disguised as fiction, a goal he had set for himself in *Madame d'Ora* and *Hjulet*. Greater artistic strength is noticeable when Jensen gives rein to his mythic imagination. Masterful are his cinematic view of modern civilization, his description of modern technology and machinery, and his evocation of the magic power of nature over the human spirit.

Jensen's last novel, *Gudrun* is a contemporary portrayal of the Copenhagen woman and thus also a novel about the Danish capital. It is, however, completely different from *Danskere* and *Einar Elkær* The city is no longer seen through the eyes of an outsider. When he wrote *Gudrun*, Jensen had been a citizen of Copenhagen for many years—and a mature artist—and the novel delivers a splendid and profoundly personal eulogy of this city as a swarming, animated organism. As in Jensen's other realistic novels, the individualized portrait is only secondary; character delineation tends to be either caricatural or pale and blurred. Yet, typically, the portrayal of the woman is the exception: The picture of the full-blooded Gudrun is drawn with Jensen's usual gusto, which elevates it to a paean to woman as a sexual being.

A renewal of Jensen's writing had, however, already taken place in 1900 and 1901 with the novel *Kongens fald*. Here Jensen succeeded in merging into a mythic unity two factors: the introverted and spiritual elements of his writing and the extroverted and naturalistic aspects. The book can be read as a historical novel from the early sixteenth century—the most significant period in Danish literature—which attacks skepticism and the inability to act, traits regarded by Jensen as the major components of Danish mentality. This paralyzing skepticism is exemplified by the Renaissance king, Christian II, and by his companion, the mercenary Mikkel. Like the main characters of Jensen's first two novels, these men are lonely, self-divided, and therefore barren and destructive. Jensen does not, however, pay any attention to historical accuracy or detailed psychological characterization. The epic continuity is constantly disrupted either by lyric sequences of exquisite beauty or by scenes of violence and death rendered with harsh Naturalism. These sequences transform the work into a magnificent, deeply pessimistic vision of man's inability to find happiness. Mikkel, who is totally unable to devote himself to enjoying the present, can act only when hatred takes possession of him. He therefore must kill his antithesis, the sensuous Axel, who has happiness in abundance and who is not plagued by doubt or reflection. Thus, all human endeavor is in vain; only death brings the sought-for peace.

This disillusionment also concludes Jensen's multivolume novel *The Long Journey*, which was intended as an evolutionary history of mankind, a modern scientific substitute for the Bible. *Det tabte land* is a Darwinian Genesis myth about the transition from animal to man, resulting from the challenges of nature in the primeval Nordic rain forests. In *Bræen*, the Ice Age has forced man toward the south. Only Dreng returns in defiance to the north, founding a large family with Moa and becoming the inventor of various tools. After

Dreng's death, Hvidbjørn becomes the main character of the volume. He has inherited not only Dreng's ingenuity but also his longing for the south and the sea. This longing to travel leads to Hvidbjørn's invention of the ship and the family's voyage across the sea, bringing it to the Baltic region. There they meet the primitive people from the warm forests, modeled partly on Jonathan Swift's Yahoos and the Nietzschean *Untermensch*. In *Norne-Gæst*, Jensen follows the life of the Nordic people from the Stone Age to the era of the Great Migrations, focusing on the title character's insatiable longing to travel abroad and then to return home. This yearning drives Norne-Gæst around the world and through time, rendering him a mythic personification of "the long journey" itself. *Cimbrernes tog* takes place during the Great Migrations. Climatic deterioration sets in suddenly during the transition between the Bronze Age and the Iron Age; floods and famine threaten; and the Cimbrian tribe, living in Himmerland, sets off. We follow their everyday life on their raid down through Europe; intervening mythic scenes are observed and commented upon by the omnipresent Norne-Gæst. The Nordic longing to go abroad is represented in *Skibet* by the Vikings and their raids to the Mediterranean, and by the title character in the volume, *Christopher Columbus*, whom Jensen, in *Hjulet*, had described as a Nordic type, a Goth. Like Dreng, Hvidbjørn, and Norne-Gæst, Columbus is seen as the defiant individual, the source of cultural development. Yet he is driven by more than an urge for discovery: Like his Nordic ancestors, he is searching for "the lost land." Characteristic of the Northerners is the dream of warmth and sun. This dream, through which Jensen attempts to explain religious feeling, manifests itself in a longing to travel which, at the same time, is a longing for home. This search for paradise finds its concrete expression in the ship and the Gothic cathedral, but when Columbus sets out to find the India of his dreams, he discovers America, the land of reality, not an earthly paradise. The futility of his search is evident from his continued voyages of discovery; and Jensen lets him find happiness only in his memories, with life appearing in all of its splendor only in a vision illuminated by the light of eternity: the concluding prose poem "Ave Stella."

The Long Journey, therefore, does not submit to the common interpretation as a solely Darwinist epic about man's descent and the victorious march of the Nordic people through the ages. It is, rather, a collection of mythic texts, lyric fantasies with inserted essays, held together not by a pervasive plot but by a leitmotif: longing as a point of departure for the described expansion in time and space, and as an existential matter, a basic condition of life. The work stands out as a manifestation of the ages of history and of mankind, its struggle and defiance, its pain and precious dreams. It is grandiose in its concept, filled with provocative reflections and composed in a language of unique originality. By virtue of these elements, it occupies a special position in world literature.

During the 1930's, Jensen's fictitious works became increasingly sparse. The reason was a growing antipathy toward belles lettres, which resulted outwardly in a strong involvement in the current cultural debate and, in his own writing, in a preference for the newspaper article and the essay, for the sole purpose of popularizing the theories of evolution. Jensen's numerous essays are based primarily on questionable scientific theories and deductions, but they are often written in a fluent, vigorous, yet lyric style; his mythic technique frequently emerges with a single, concrete observation as the point of departure, opening up grandiose perspectives and unsuspected inner coherences. It is precisely as a lyricist and creator of myth that Jensen reaches perfection, particularly when he is able to combine these two elements, as in *Kongens fald*, *Skovene*, and *The Long Journey*—works which have shown him to be not only the greatest Danish writer of the twentieth century but also a sublime artist for all ages.

Major publications other than long fiction

SHORT FICTION: *Himmerlandsfolk*, 1898; *Intermezzo*, 1899; *Nye Himmerlands historier*, 1904; *Myter og jagter*, 1907; *Singaporenoveller*, 1907; *Nye myter*, 1908; *Himmerlandshistorier*, 1904, 1910; *Myter*, 1907-1944 (11 volumes); *Ved livets bred*, 1928; *Kornmarken*, 1932; *Møllen*, 1944.

POETRY: *Digte*, 1906, 1917, 1921; *Den jydske blæst*, 1931.

NONFICTION: *Den gotiske Renaissance*, 1901; *Den ny verden*, 1907; *Introduktion til vor tidsalder*, 1915; *Æstetik og udvikling*, 1923; *Fra fristaterne*, 1939.

Bibliography

Friis, Oluf. "Johannes V. Jensen," in *Scandinavica*. I (1962), pp. 114-123.

Ingwersen, Niels. "America as Setting and Symbol in Johannes V. Jensen's Early Works," in *American-Norvegica*. III (1971), pp. 272-293.

Marcus, Aage. "Johannes V. Jensen," in *American-Scandinavian Review*. XX (1932), pp. 339-347.

Rossel, Sven H. *Johannes V. Jensen*, 1984.

Wiehl, Inga W. *Johannes V. Jensen's Concept of America*, 1967 (dissertation).

Sven H. Rossel

UWE JOHNSON

Born: Cammin, Pomerania; July 20, 1934
Died: Sheerness, England; March 13, 1984

Principal long fiction

Mutmassungen über Jakob, 1959 (*Speculations About Jacob*, 1963); *Das dritte Buch über Achim*, 1961 (*The Third Book About Achim*, 1967); *Zwei Ansichten*, 1965 (*Two Views*, 1966); *Jahrestage: Aus dem Leben von Gesine Cresspahl*, 1970-1983 (4 volumes; *Anniversaries: From the Life of Gesine Cresspahl*, 1975, includes volume 1 and part of volume 2 of *Jahrestage*).

Other literary forms

Known almost exclusively for writing narrative fiction, Uwe Johnson published one book of short stories, *Karsch und andere Prosa* (1960; Karsch and other prose), and three volumes of essays and literary scholarship: *Eine Reise nach Klagenfurt* (1974; a journey to Klagenfurt); *Berliner Sachen* (1975; Berlin essays); *Begleitumstände: Frankfurter Vorlesungen* (1980; attendant circumstances: Frankfurt lectures). His most ambitious scholarly work, *Eine Reise nach Klagenfurt*, is a competent study concerning the Austrian writer Ingeborg Bachmann. *Berliner Sachen* contains the article "Berliner Stadtbahn" ("Berlin, Border of the Divided World") and other programmatic writings of his early career, while some of his most revealing theoretical utterances are found in *Begleitumstände: Frankfurter Vorlesungen*, the documents of his tenure as guest lecturer at the University of Frankfurt/Main in 1979.

Achievements

With his first published novel, *Speculations About Jacob*, Johnson became an instant success as a writer, and his subsequent novels brought him ever-widening acclaim as an important literary analyst of the tensions, pressures, adjustments, and contradictions that mold everyday life in the two postwar German states. Beginning in 1960, when he received the Fontane Prize of the City of Berlin for *Speculations About Jacob*, Johnson won many prestigious writing awards; among the most important were the International Publishers' Prize (1962), the Georg Büchner Prize (1971), the Raabe Prize (1975), and the Thomas Mann Prize (1978).

Despite predominantly positive response, there has been some controversy concerning Johnson's works. Most visible is the discomfort caused in both parts of Germany by the author's conscious attempts to remain objective in his portrayals. *Two Views*, for example, received favorable press in the East for its harsh picture of the Federal Republic but was panned for its "unrealistic" presentation of life in the workers' state. In West Germany, critics rejected its superficial treatment of postwar society under capitalism while praising the "objective" treatment of the Democratic Republic. In general, Johnson's novels are criticized sharply in East Germany because they are not accurate in their description of Socialist "reality."

Although all of his novels appeal more to an intellectual than to a general audience, this is especially true of Johnson's massive, four-volume novel, *Anniversaries*, the *magnum opus* on which he labored for some fifteen years, completing the last volume only a year before his death. Regarded by some critics as a masterpiece of postmodern literature, by others as a sterile exercise doomed to quick oblivion, *Anniversaries* demands comparison with such encyclopedic novels as Carlos Fuentes' *Terra nostra* (1975; English translation, 1976) and Thomas Pynchon's *Gravity's Rainbow* (1973).

Biography

After receiving his early schooling at a Nazi boarding school in Poland, Uwe Johnson fled to Mecklenburg with his family. There, he attended school in Güstrow until 1952. Before he entered the university, he joined the Free German Youth. He remained an uncompromising advocate of Marxism until postwar realities generated doubts about the advantages of Communism.

In 1952, Johnson entered the University of Rostock. He remained there for two years before moving to Leipzig to complete his studies in Germanic philology under Professor Hans Mayer. The lean university years, from 1952 until he received his diploma in 1956, were especially important for Johnson's development as an author. During the winter of 1953, he began writing, although he then viewed his fiction as secondary to his chosen profession as a literary scholar. Growing tensions with the political establishment almost made it impossible for him to complete his program of study. Eventually, these conflicts prevented him from obtaining secure employment in his field, even after Hans Mayer had made it possible for him to graduate. Johnson was then forced to look more seriously at writing as a primary occupation.

As a student in Leipzig, Johnson completed his first novel, "Ingrid Babendererde," which was never published. State-owned publishing houses rejected it for political reasons in 1956, and the author later abandoned it as an unsuccessful and immature product of his youth. Soon after graduation, he began composing *Speculations About Jacob*. Exposure to the works of William Faulkner, especially *The Sound and the Fury* (1929), and to James Joyce's *Ulysses* (1922) gave him significant stylistic insights that caused him to change his approach and rewrite the first chapter of the new book. Both Faulkner and Joyce had a profound impact on Johnson's literary development. While struggling with *Speculations About Jacob*, Johnson made a meager living through occasional work as an editor and translator. Requests that his second novel be revised to meet accepted political standards finally convinced him to break off negotiations with East German publishers. He decided to move to West Berlin, where he could work under more favorable circumstances.

Johnson was rapidly integrated into the West German literary mainstream. In 1959, he was introduced to other successful writers at a meeting of Gruppe 47 in Elmau. For a time, he maintained a warm friendship with Günter Grass, and he also became closely associated with Hans Magnus Enzensberger. Nevertheless, after his relocation, he systematically refused to take the side of the West or to renounce the East during public appearances, and until 1961, he maintained active ties with friends in the German Democratic Republic. In 1969, he became a member of the West Berlin Academy of Arts. The same year, he joined the West German branch of P.E.N., an international writers' organization.

Although he once felt that West Berlin might become a permanent home, it never did. Johnson had been something of a homeless wanderer since his first literary success in 1959. Two years after he settled in West Berlin, he visited the United States as the guest of Wayne State University and Harvard University. A year later, he received a grant to go to Rome. Following his marriage to Elizabeth Schmidt in 1962, he remained in Berlin for four years. He was finally given West German citizenship in 1965. A two-year stay in the United States from 1966 to 1968 proved especially significant for the genesis of *Anniversaries*, which is set in New York City. From 1975 until his death, at the age of forty-nine, on March 13, 1984, Johnson lived in England, excepting a period in 1979, when he visited West Germany as a guest lecturer in poetics at the University of Frankfurt/Main.

Analysis

Uwe Johnson described his writing as an attempt to discover the truth. The trail of clues that he followed in his quest leads from the environment of his youth in Mecklenburg, through the divided city Berlin and the two postwar German states, to the ultimate symbol for modern urban society, New York City. Each of his novels forms a step along his path and represents a fragment of the author's acquired understanding of a world rife with contradictions, confusion, and paradox.

In the essay "Berlin, Border of the Divided World," which first appeared in 1961, Johnson disclosed in detail the perceptions of literature that shaped his career, beginning with his unpublished novel "Ingrid Babendererde." Several important ideas compose the basis of his approach to fiction. Of special moment is the distinction he makes between discernible facts and reality as a whole. Johnson saw a potential danger in trying to make something "real" out of something that is only "factual." Reality is bound inseparably to the individual's internal nature and thus remains an elusive intangible that can never be circumscribed entirely by facts alone. The novelist's task, therefore, is to present his material with a precision that will allow the reader to examine the "facts" and draw personal conclusions about "reality." Accordingly, the author must not hide the truth that he has invented what he presents, nor should he suggest that his information is anything but fragmentary and incomplete. Inevitably, the material that he offers is subject to interpretation. Yet that in itself is the measure of true reality amid the ambiguities of life today.

The principal reason for Johnson's failure to place his early novels with East German publishers was his unwillingness to compromise in his literary search for truth. His desire to dig down to the heart of contemporary individual existence could not be reconciled with the Socialist Realist demand for a portrayal not of life as it is, but of life as it should be. The preconceived pattern prescribed by Socialist Realism precludes the objective illumination of society from a variety of viewpoints. Such a method, however, is the most characteristic trait of Johnson's literary technique. Moreover, the typical absence in his works of a definitive perspective, which makes total penetration impossible and allows the reader to arrive at an independent judgment, is quite unacceptable in the rigidly programmed literature of the German Democratic Republic.

Fundamental to Johnson's approach to postwar German reality is temporal context. The background of Germany's past is inescapable, and Johnson builds each story from a historical perspective. Each of his novels employs a major national event or situation as focus and external symbol for the central truth that is the narrative's target. In *The Third Book About Achim*, the pivotal experience is the workers' uprising of June 17, 1953; in *Two Views*, it is the erection of the Berlin Wall in August, 1961. The events themselves are nothing more than points of orientation, against which the lives of affected individuals are projected. It is the scrutiny of basic human reactions to the broad social and political happenings, the implications of international tensions and unrest for the everyday life of the common man, the concrete situation of people who perceive their world as natural and only in coming to grips with ideological positions discover that they are bound by politics that provide the raw material from which author and reader create a joint picture of the twentieth century world.

The literary impact of Johnson's prose fiction depends largely upon his stance vis-à-vis his audience. Like Bertolt Brecht, whose works he greatly admired, Johnson tells his story in a way that will force the reader to take it, think about it, and measure it against his own experience. Especially important is the continuing effort to resist producing illusion. That specific requirement had a fundamental formative influence on Johnson's style, the devices of which function as the narrative equivalent of Brecht's famous alienation technique in the drama.

Although *Speculations About Jacob* is especially marked in style by the influence of Joyce and Faulkner, even in that early work, Johnson made use of virtually all the literary techniques developed in the history of the novel. He experimented with syntax and punctuation, employing inverted, paratactic sentences, colloquial dialogue, narrative report, and internal monologue in unending variation. The transitions from one type of presentation to another are very often fuzzy and sometimes impossible to discern. Thus, the reader must constantly reflect on what has just been read in order to pin down the context. The books that followed *Speculations About Jacob* feature differences in language and approach which are specifically adapted to the needs of the particular novel. In almost all of them, however, the prevailing style is severe and soberly intense. The language, especially that of technology, is painfully precise. Metaphors are exact and symbols are few and simple. Rapid shifts in point of view and nonlinear plots force the troubled reader to search for the essence of the author's message. Only in *Two Views* did Johnson opt for a more conventional chronological development in order to portray the mundaneness of his characters' spiritual involvement with their surroundings.

Perhaps the most remarkable feature of Johnson's writing is his ability to give substance to his characters. Rarely are the characters themselves described in extensive physical detail, yet they are vibrantly real. The stiff, cumbersome language found in the Mecklenburg scenes of *Anniversaries*, for example, matches the nature of the central figure, Gesine Cresspahl's father, while the emphasis on superficial external detail in *Two Views* underscores the shallowness of the two central personalities in their interrelationships with each other and their respective social environments.

The creation of his first published novel, *Speculations About Jacob*, was for Johnson a process of refinement of personal experience through analytical challenge of external facts and appearances, in an effort to explain the ambivalence of his own feelings about the realities of life in postwar East Germany. As a result, *Speculations About Jacob* has something of the form of a judicial inquiry. Witnesses are called upon to testify, providing bits and pieces of informaton that illuminate the book's central problems from a variety of perspectives. The author serves as court recorder, meticulously noting the details of testimony in the varying forms in which they are given, but leaving it up to the reader as jury to organize the random elements into a coherent whole from which proper conclusions may be drawn.

The focus of the investigation is the peculiar death of Jacob Abs, an East German railroad dispatcher who is crushed between two trains while crossing the tracks in the morning mist. Following the classic pattern of the analytic fable, the plot is presented from the reference point of the story's end in an attempt to arrive at the genesis of Jacob's death and an answer to the question: Was it an accident or suicide? As is typical of Johnson's narratives, however, the puzzle that sets the story in motion remains unsolved. The point of departure serves merely as a pretext for an examination of Jacob's life, which is at best synthetically created from incomplete and undependable memories of others. A fragmentary picture of Jacob arises like an unfinished mosaic from the rapid shifts among narration, dialogue, memory, and stream of consciousness. These yield the impressions of him that are held by friends and acquaintances. The fact that individual motives are impenetrable magnifies the enigma of Jacob, leaving the result inconclusive.

From the clarification of a series of motivations, reasons, events, and relationships that probably play a role in Jacob's life, there emerges a sketchy outline of a man who arrived in a small town on the Baltic as a refugee in 1945, attempted to make a place for himself in East German society, found himself unable to cope with the demands of political reality, sought an acceptable alternative in West Germany but failed to find it, and returned to his job in the East, only to perish under mysterious circumstances. By themselves, the external details of his existence give no clear picture of the "reality" that is Johnson's ultimate goal in the novel. Only when superficial acts and relationships are viewed in the context of parallel international events do they assume the weight and meaning that allow the reader to understand what the author intends to communicate.

The focal political/historical occurrence of the novel is the Hungarian uprising of 1956. To Jacob and his friend Jonas Blach, the revolt signals hope, while the declared position of the East German regime serves as an immediate stimulus for Jacob's relocation in the West. Suppression of the rebellion gives an additional emphasis to the hopelessness of life under a governmental system in which realpolitik hides behind rhetorical socialism, yet the attractiveness of the Federal Republic is destroyed by the Western powers' concurrent involvement in the attack on the Suez. Jacob's return home and his subsequent "accidental" death take on a different light when viewed in that framework. The unfortunate railroad dispatcher becomes Johnson's first effective symbol for the absence of a clear-cut choice in the confrontation between East and West.

Like *Speculations About Jacob*, Johnson's second novel, *The Third Book About Achim*, takes the form of a search for the reality of the title figure's inner self. Whereas the elusive Jacob symbolizes the common individual who fulfills his function in society without initially understanding the true weight of the political forces that determine his fate, Achim typifies the few who perform their roles freely, in full awareness of the broader ramifications of what they do. Thus, although the investigation follows a pattern similar to that carried out in *Speculations About Jacob*, the revelation of the central figure's particular nature is complicated by a powerful added dimension: Achim's own subjective perception of his life and its meaning.

While difficult to penetrate because of Johnson's style, the basic framework of the narrative is relatively simple. A West German journalist, Karsch, attempts to write a biography of the East German bicycle racer, Achim T., about whom two books have been written already. As he explores the readily accessible details of the racing hero's life, Karsch finds that they yield no coherent picture. Each new fact is tied to a different point of view and suggests an alternate perspective for the descriptive analysis of Achim's past. As a result, the picture of Achim becomes progressively less comprehensible. Karsch's endeavor ultimately founders on the conflict between his sequential, causal approach to his task and Achim's insistence that everything be considered in retrospect from the point of reference of what he is now. Karsch, for example, sees the fact that he participated in the June 17, 1953, workers' revolt as a critical element in the substance of Achim's life. Achim, however, who has repented the sins of his youth, denies that those events are a part of the truth concerning him, because they have no bearing upon what he is now. In this light, the novel becomes a critical examination of the probleof falsely understood reality, an attempt to determine what is meant by "objective" history.

Despite the author's insistence at the end of the work that his figures are invented and that events are presented to illuminate the division between East and West in an abstract sense, *The Third Book About Achim* is a direct and concrete commentary on tangible personalities and situations. Achim T. is modeled after the East German bicycle champion Gustav Adolf Schur, about whom two books had actually appeared when the novel was written. Klaus Ullrich's biography of Schur served as a primary source for Johnson's narrative. The latter is in many respects a thinly veiled antibiography of Schur that employs the contradictions in Schur-Achim's nature and personality as a symbolic elucidation of the growth of the German Democratic Republic.

As a personal response to the building of the Berlin Wall, an event that at last deprived him of direct, active contacts with his East German friends and milieu, Johnson wrote the novel *Two Views*. It is at once his stylistically simplest, most conventional novel and his most devastatingly profound statement concerning individual response to the irrevocable division of Germany. Further, it is his only major narrative that is not tied to the others by the presence of one or more characters in common. To that extent, it is an anomaly in an otherwise continuous progression in the development of the author's basic raw material.

Unlike Johnson's earlier books, *Two Views* consists of the presentation of two clearly defined perspectives that illuminate the chronologically ordered events of the story. Although totally disparate, the characters' points of view complement each other to provide the reader with an overwhelmingly clear portrayal of what Johnson considers to be the great underlying tragedy of postwar German existence: the inability of the typical German citizen (East and West) to see beyond the meaningless superficiality of immediate surroundings, which in turn leads to passivity, indifference, and lack of awareness of true political reality. In his narration of the unlikely love story of a West German photographer and an East German nurse who have nothing whatsoever in common, the writer employs their peculiar relationship as a symbol for the way in which people are moved by the happenings of the times yet float on the surface of events without participating in them spiritually.

The kernel of Johnson's statement is contained in a vivid representation of the effect of the erection of the Berlin Wall upon the two characters' lives. They respond by going through the motions of coping with the stark reality of the Wall, yet they remain unaffected in any deep internal sense. The compelling account of the nurse's escape from East Germany, which stands for the many similar flights of the period, contrasts sharply with her pale, passionless life both before and after the events of the crossing. The manner in which she and her friend sink back into the complacency of their former states is Johnson's ultimate comment on the absurdity of modern man's failure to escape the façades and clichés that characterize present-day social interchange at the personal level. Perhaps nowhere else in his works does the idea erupt so strongly that even the most trivial differences between East and West are insurmountable.

Although still unresolved, some of the questions raised and left unanswered in *Speculations About Jacob* and *The Third Book About Achim* are given additional attention in Johnson's most extensive work of fiction, *Anniversaries*. Subtitled *Aus dem Leben von Gesine Cresspahl (From the Life of Gesine Cresspahl)*, this immense novel is in many respects a review, expansion, and summation of the themes and motifs that preoccupied Johnson throughout his career. Interwoven with new perspectives and information on the lives of characters from *Speculations About Jacob* and *The Third Book About Achim* are events and impressions from the author's encounter with New York City between 1966 and 1968, a personalized history of Germany from the 1920's to the postwar era, and much more.

In form, the novel is a diary, Gesine Cresspahl's private record of the daily events of her life as a bank employee and mother in the complex world of the big city; in substance, it is a panoramic analysis of the fate of the individual in the twentieth century. The story is conveyed on two levels. Gesine's experiences in her urban environment, including observations about her job, her relationship with her daughter Marie, her reunion with Karsch, who was depicted in *The Third Book About Achim*, and her association with a refugee German physicist are projected against current events of local, national, and international scope as reported in *The New York Times* to form the external framework of the narrative. Her memories of life in Germany, German history of the 1930's and the Nazi era, the persecution of the Jews, the personal needs of her ancestors and their experiences that ended in catastrophe, her former relationship with Jacob Abs, who was Marie's father, and with her own parents—all of these elements combine to provide a second, more important illumination of the central character as a representative of her origins. With Gesine serving as mediator, Johnson juxtaposes critical situations from her past, such as persecution of the Jews and the atrocities of the Nazis, with comparable events and circumstances in the present, such as racial discrimination and the horrors of Vietnam. The result is a mural of chaotic reality against which the individual can do nothing. Gesine's ultimate response is to retreat within herself, to avoid developing new interpersonal bonds that might renew the pains of past experience. In so doing, she makes of her love for her daughter a foil against the disorder and confusion around her and a symbol for the only hope that she has for the future.

Stylistically, *Anniversaries* is Johnson's most demanding work. The chronicle of Gesine's life is a never-completed mosaic of loose, colorful fragments: reports, newspaper clippings, memories, dialogues, monologues, authorial comment, thoughts, reflections, and endless minutiae. The author employs naked facts to suggest some sort of external order without revealing a meaning in the world's happenings. Devoid of meaning, however, time becomes empty form. The sequence of days cannot be altered, but the temporally organized events in the newspaper—political unrest, murders, and racial violence—are interchangeable. The reader is left unprotected against the deluge of events, facts, connections, and suffocating details, and he experiences the helplessness against the real power of history that is the backbone and substance of all of Johnson's novels.

Major publications other than long fiction
SHORT FICTION: *Karsch und andere Prosa*, 1960.
NONFICTION: *Eine Reise nach Klagenfurt*, 1974; *Berliner Sachen*, 1975; *Begleitumstände: Frankfurter Vorlesungen*, 1980.

Bibliography
Baumgart, Reinhard, ed. *Über Uwe Johnson*, 1970.
Boulby, Mark. *Uwe Johnson*, 1974.
Hye, Roberta T. *Uwe Johnsons "Jahrestage,"* 1978.
Lennox, S. J. K. *The Fiction of Faulkner and Uwe Johnson*, 1973.
Murphy, R. A. *The Dilemma of the Artist-Writer in the Novels of Uwe Johnson*, 1967.
Neumann, Bernd. *Utopie und Mimesis*, 1978.
Schwarz, Wilhelm J. *Der Erzähler Uwe Johnson*, 1970.
Wünderich, Erich. *Uwe Johnson*, 1973.

Lowell A. Bangerter

FRANZ KAFKA

Born: Prague, Czechoslovakia; July 3, 1883
Died: Kierling, Austria; June 3, 1924

Principal long fiction

Amerika, 1913, 1927 (*America*, 1938; better known as *Amerika*, 1946); *Die Verwandlung*, 1915 (novella; *Metamorphosis*, 1936); *Der Prozess*, 1925 (*The Trial*, 1937); *Das Schloss*, 1926 (*The Castle*, 1930).

Other literary forms

In addition to long fiction, Franz Kafka wrote numerous stories, the most famous of which are *Ein Hungerkünstler* (1924; *The Hunger Artist*, 1938) and *In der Strafkolonie* (1919; *The Penal Colony*, 1941). He also left behind extensive diaries and letters.

Achievements

What W.H. Auden wrote of Sigmund Freud—that to us he had become less a man than a climate of opinion—is equally true of Kafka. He is the twentieth century prophet of alienation, his name a household synonym for *Angst*. His stories—visionary, hallucinatory, yet very controlled artistically— have exerted their powerful influence over modern fiction. Few would dispute the assertion that he is one of the major literary figures of the twentieth century. None of this, however, could have been anticipated of a writer who was not widely known at the time of his death. Kafka's genius was difficult for him to harness: The fact is that he never completed any of his three novels. Before dying, he left instructions with Max Brod, his friend and executor, to destroy his manuscripts. Reasoning that Kafka was not committed to their destruction as much as he was ambivalent over their fate—could not he have destroyed them had he really wished to do so?—Brod preserved the manuscripts, arranged to have them printed, wrote a biography of his friend, and generously championed his cause. Thus, *The Trial* and *The Castle*, books which so remarkably capture Kafka's paradoxical vision of man's existence, came to light.

Biography

Despite the strange occurrences that animate Franz Kafka's fiction, the events of his life are colorless and mundane. Like Emily Dickinson or Henry Thoreau, however, Kafka could, by sheer imagination, transform the most ordinary life into fascinating reading. Tirelessly, he penned his impressions of his life, recording the nuances of his thoughts and actions in ethical and ontological terms.

Kafka was born into a bourgeois German-Jewish family in Prague. The

Czechs of Kafka's day felt oppressed by the Austrian-Germans and in turn oppressed the Jews, so from his earliest days Kafka was accustomed to the pain of a threefold prejudice—as non-Austrian, as non-Czech, and as Jew. Franz was the oldest child, the sole surviving son in a family that was later to include three girls. The father, Herrmann Kafka, struggled to achieve financial security for his family, and he succeeded, but the ordeal coarsened him; he became autocratic and irascible. Money and status were his chief passions, and he directed his considerable energy to their acquisition. Nevertheless, he had a zest for life which left its imprint on his son, who could admire though never attain it. Kafka's mother, on the other hand, came from a family of rabbis, scholars, and physicians, and from her Kafka probably inherited his sensitive nature and dreamy tendencies.

As Kafka was heir to divergent traditions in his family, so, too, the city of Prague offered him contrasting traditions. On the one hand, Prague, influenced by Austria, looked westward, toward rationalism and the Enlightenment; on the other hand, it gazed eastward, toward Russia with its semimystical fervor. In his Jewish studies, too, Kafka discovered similar tensions: the casuistic flavor of the Talmud straining against the impassioned piety of the mystics. These elements ultimately recombine themselves in Kafka's fiction.

Photographs of Kafka reveal him to be dark and slender, respectable in appearance, with a face that is intense and boyish, delicate and sensitive. Young Franz spent his school years in Prague—first at a German elementary school and later at a *gymnasium*; he ultimately was graduated from the German Karl-Ferdinand University. For two weeks, he specialized in chemistry but found it uncongenial; soon after, he succumbed to pressure from his friends and family, especially his father, and commenced the study of law. Unhappy, he described it as "living in an intellectual sense, on sawdust, which had, moreover, already been chewed for me in thousands of other people's mouths."

Kafka, however, needed some means to support himself, and the legal profession, then as now, was an eminently respectable career—especially appealing to Jews. Though he never cared for the practice of law, a major consideration was the hope of winning his father's long-withheld approval. In this, he never succeeded; here was a struggle that allowed neither victory nor retreat.

Reams have been written on the subject of Kafka and his father. Are not the fathers in his fiction oversize presences that visit judgment and wrath on their sons? Are not his protagonists accused persons, judged guilty of some undefined transgression against an all-powerful and implacable force that hounds the hero and destroys him? In story after story, in all of his novels, one finds Kafka returning, irresistibly, obsessively, to the theme of the judging father in an effort to exorcise this demon—in vain. Kafka's friend and biographer, Brod, first reported and later released an amazing document penned by the twenty-six-year-old Kafka, the *Brief an den Vater* (1952, written 1919; *Letter to His Father*, 1954). The manuscript was given to Franz's mother for delivery to her spouse. Hardly a letter—it is more than one hundred pages long—the document minutely scrutinizes the son's pained relations with his father. Its tone—mingling abjectness and defiance—can be heard in Kafka's fiction as well, where it expresses his protagonists' attitudes toward their parents. One can only speculate how Herrmann Kafka might have responded to the missive: His wife never delivered the letter.

Completing his studies, Kafka gained legal experience in a district, then in a criminal court, where he observed at first hand the workings of the law which he later fictionalized in *The Trial*. Soon after, he secured a position with the Workers' Accident Insurance Office, where he remained a respected and admired figure until illness forced his retirement in 1922. There he gained intimate knowledge of the operations of a bureaucracy, which he transferred to his novel, *The Castle*.

Though Kafka never married, he did seek romance and the consolation of women. In 1912, Kafka began courting a woman he had met at Brod's house, Felice Bauer. (Her initials are echoed both in *The Trial*, in the name of Fraulein Burstner, and in *The Castle*'s Frieda). Curiously, Kafka avoided contact with her, although he maintained a voluminous correspondence with her, sometimes writing as many as three letters a day. He feared that marriage would infringe both on his privacy and on his writing, and for three years the relationship waxed and waned; Kafka's ambivalence denied him the domestic peace he so desperately sought. In 1917, soon after their second engagement, Kafka discovered that he had tuberculosis, and once again he and his fiancée were disengaged. After several years of battling this disease, Kafka succumbed in June of 1924.

Though Kafka's life was marked by suffering, both intimates and casual acquaintances testify to the sweetness of his disposition, to his sympathy for others, to his unfailing humor and quiet courage. Brod's biography takes pains to overcome the impression that his friend's character was morbid; indeed, Kafka had a gift for finding wry humor both in his life and in the most dreadful predicaments of his characters. He had a gift for whimsy as well; Brod relates that once, when Kafka was about twenty years old, he came to visit Brod and inadvertently awakened Brod's father, who was napping on the sofa. "Please look upon me as a dream," murmured Franz as he glided by.

Analysis

The name Franz Kafka conjures up images of a world without a center, of man alienated both from his society and from himself. Kafka lived at the threshold of the modern technological world, and his stories are prophetic of the bewilderment and anxiety that typify modern man's frustrations and darkest moods: man increasingly out of touch with his essential nature or, when confronted by totalitarian oppression, man out of touch with his society. When Eugene O'Neill's hairy ape laments that "I ain't in heaven, and I ain't on oith, but takin' the woist from both woilds," he captured something of the spirit, if not the flavor, of Kafka's tragic vision. For Kafka, man is postlapsarian man—man with only glimmerings of his formerly blessed state, yet who desperately attempts to recover it.

With the story *Das Urteil* (1913, 1916; *The Sentence*, 1928; also as *The Judgment*, 1945), Kafka created the kind of fiction that characterizes his maturity, combining the unreality of dream states with images of startling vividness. In this early story, as in *The Trial* and *The Castle*, the protagonist faces a judgment on himself, a fate in which the horrible and the absurd intertwine. In Kafka's fiction, every interpretation begets an alternative— one that may contradict its predecessor. This is partly a result of narrative technique: In limiting the narrative to the protagonist's point of view, Kafka ensures that the reader will share his character's bewilderment without benefit of an omniscient author. In terms of literary form, Kafka's stories most closely resemble the parable: simple yet enigmatic. His work may be read for its historical and social import as the reflections of a German Jew living in Czech Prague, a city under Austrian influence. Neither Austrian nor Czech but Jewish, he was trebly an outsider. His work may be viewed psychologically, as an anxious son's efforts to deal with an accusing father. (Note that all the novels' protagonists bear the author's initial, "K.") Finally, his work may be read for its religious content, as Everyman's craving to reconcile the demands of the physical with the yearnings of the spiritual.

Characteristically, Kafka's protagonist is a man going about his normal domestic business when a violent and inexplicable eruption warns him that his life has gone astray. Often he awakens one morning to discover that some incomprehensible change has occurred. In *The Trial*, the protagonist discovers men in his room, mysterious functionaries who announce that he has been arrested on charges they will not explain. In the novella *Metamorphosis*, Gregor Samsa arises, or attempts to do so, only to discover that during the night he has been transformed into a giant dung beetle. No explanation is forthcoming. Is this a judgment on Gregor from above or from within, or is it caused by some force whose will is unknown and unknowable? Is the transformation a necessary but painful path to enlightenment or a punishment? One reads on, hoping for an explanation, a hint of rational purpose in such mysterious happenings; one watches fascinated as others respond to the protagonist's dilemma; one searches for clues in their responses; and one is disarmed at every turn by paradox piled upon paradox, an infinite regression of possibilities that welcome analysis but will never yield to it. Ultimately, the Kafka protagonist perishes or disappears, but whether he is enlightened remains obscure.

In 1911, Kafka began a novel that Brod later published under the title *Amerika*. The first chapter was released during Kafka's lifetime under the title *Der Heizer* (1913; the stoker), but his journals refer to it as "The Man Who Was Lost Sight Of." The most Naturalistic of Kafka's novels, *America* relates the story of an innocent youth, not yet sixteen, who is forced to leave home for an indiscretion: He was seduced by an older woman, who conceived a child. Like most of Kafka's fictional parents, Karl Rossmann's, too, harshly judge their loving son, who, despite their punishment of him, yearns to be reunited with them.

Rossmann's first intimation of what the new Eden of America will be like occurs when he sees the Statue of Liberty, holding aloft not a torch but a sword (justice? wrath? expulsion from Eden?). This is not the America of Emma Lazarus' poem "The New Colossus" (1883) but rather a capitalistic/ technological society replete with Mark Twain-like rogues—Robinson and Delemarche—and tycoons *à la* Frank Norris and Theodore Dreiser. At first, Rossmann seems blessed: His uncle Jacob, a politician and an industrialist, discovers him aboard a ship and takes the lad under his wing. Rossmann quickly perceives, however, that this highly industrialized state degrades all of those who come in contact with it—workers, rulers, and politicians. Through the familiar device of the picaresque novel, the hero undergoes a series of adventures loosely strung together—adventures among the rich and poor, insiders and outcasts. Rossmann himself is an innocent, hopelessly entangled in a fallen world, and this is the major problem of the work. Unlike the protagonists of the later novels, Rossmann is not part of the world he observes, merely its victim. The reader can pity Rossmann, impressed with Kafka's diagnosis of a world grown increasingly bureaucratic, but one is not astonished and mesmerized, as readers of the later two novels are. The nightmare in *Amerika* is someone else's nightmare, not the reader's. When Rossmann is vilified and loses his job at the Hotel Occidental for his momentary lapse from duty, the reader is too keenly aware of the injustice, too eager to protest on his behalf.

Compare this, for example, to Kafka's novella *Metamorphosis*, in which Gregor is transformed into a giant insect. At first, one shares the protagonist's shock—how could such a thing happen, and what does it mean?—but this is quickly succeeded by a more pressing question: How does Gregor know that he is an insect? Not through his senses, for he does not need to look at himself; rather he seems to have intuited the transformation, perhaps invited it. Whether the metamorphosis is a judgment, an injustice, or a signpost to salvation, Gregor's fate, unlike Rossmann's, is part of his character.

Still, in *Amerika* many of Kafka's familiar themes are developed, however embryonically. The theme of justice is manifest in the opening chapter, when Rossmann unsuccessfully attempts to aid the confused stoker in airing his grievances. As in many scenes that follow, Rossmann will be forced to leave those he cares about without succeeding in accomplishing his aims. His departure from the ship with his uncle Jacob marks the climax of his good fortune. (Indeed, most of Kafka's fiction climaxes in the opening chapter, with the rest of the story exploring the consequences of what proves to be an irreversible judgment.) For ingratitude, Rossmann is promptly disinherited by his uncle, a capitalist/exploiter with overtones of Yahweh (the sort of paradox in which Kafka delighted). The sword that the Statue of Liberty holds aloft adds to the impression that Rossmann is being expelled from his American Eden.

Like the stoker, Rossmann will have difficulties with authority. Soon after departing from his uncle, he is employed at the Hotel Occidental in Rameses—in other words, a symbol of civilization, whether Western or Eastern. Under the patronage of the Manageress, Rossmann does well at his menial job of elevator boy, but one evening he is caught in a minor infraction. As in the case of the stoker, his efforts to obtain justice—his attempt to justify himself, to minimize his error, to benefit from the help of the Manageress—come to naught, and he is dismissed. The author here creates the kind of nightmarish scene that has become known as Kafkaesque, one in which everything that can go wrong does. The accused cannot stand before authority and state with certainty that he is truly innocent, while the officials on whom his fate depends are blasé, bored, indifferent to petitions, sometimes mocking and malicious.

Leaving the hotel in disgrace (he is even suspected by the police, though no charges have been filed against him), Rossmann is forced once more into the company of the scoundrels Delemarche and Robinson, who have taken up with the former singer Brunelda, a gross embodiment of sensuality who enslaves all three in her love nest. Usually in Kafka's works, the artist points the way to transcendence, but this singer has given up her art to satisfy her lusts. In a memorable scene, she presses her huge body against Rossmann, literally pinning him to the balcony railing while they watch a political demonstration on the streets. The scene reveals man given over to the appetites: on the balcony, Brunelda pursues carnality; on the streets, the crowd pursues drunkenness. Though this scene is vividly delineated, it reminds the reader once again of the problem Kafka faces here: What has his protagonist to do with the gross bodily appetites which indeed appall him?

At the beginning of the uncompleted final chapter, Rossmann finds himself at the nature theater of Oklahoma. What the author intended here may be inferred from Brod's report that Kafka wished to end the book on a note of reconciliation. Had Kafka realized these intentions, this work would have been unique in his fiction for its promise of hope and transcendence. The extant fragment, however, suggests that Kafka was deviating from his announced plan. The paradoxes continue: The welcoming angels blowing their horns are not angels, or even good musicians, and they are elevated above common humanity with the aid of ladders which can be seen through their gowns. Rossmann does get a job, but again it is a lowly one, far from a profession. At the novel's end, he is on a train, presumably heading westward—to a promising future or, as the title suggests, simply to vanish?

"Someone must have denounced Joseph K., for without having done anything wrong he was arrested one morning." Thus begins Kafka's second novel, *The Trial*. What are the charges? K. never learns, though he encounters several functionaries of the court, attends preliminary hearings, and hires a lawyer to defend him. This might have been the opening of a novel of political repression, but one quickly discovers that the law here, unlike its operation in Arthur Koestler's *Darkness at Noon* (1941), for example, does not represent the state judiciary system but a shadow court, one that is paradoxically both loftier and seedier. When Kafka speaks of the law, he means what the Chinese philosopher Lao-tzu called The Way—that style of living which conduces to right conduct and enlightenment. Kafka's protagonists (and his readers) grope for truth along a path circumscribed by darkness.

Has K. really done nothing "wrong"? He is certainly innocent of civil or criminal wrongdoing. A respected bank official, his conduct has been apparently irreproachable. Yet he is under arrest—a curious form of arrest, in which he is not "prevented from leading [his] ordinary life." Curiously, the "criminal" must not only defend himself but also discover his crime. Critics diverge in their efforts to understand the nature of the charge against him. According to Brod, K. is unable to love; according to another commentator, his mediocrity condemns him. A third argues that his crime lies in his suppression of his guilt. For yet another, K. is one who refuses to act in accordance with his knowledge of good and evil because he lacks the strength for such action. No easy answer emerges. Whether man is indeed guilty or is falsely accused by a Divinity unable or unwilling to help him comprehend his own essence is never revealed. What is clear is that K. feels guilty even while defending his innocence.

What sort of man is K.? Like most Kafka protagonists, he is a bachelor, uncommitted to others. He dwells in a rooming house, ignoring both his cousin, who lives in town, and his mother, who lodges in the country. His friends are mainly business associates; his lover, a mistress visited once a week. No doubt, Kafka, in his diaries, often expressed contempt for such an existence ("My monotonous, empty, mad bachelor's life"), but is this K.'s crime? If so, he could easily have been informed of that by any number of the officials he encounters. Moreover, Joseph K. seems to be living a life similar to that of most of the officials of the court. Can the priest denounce him for bachelorhood? The Examining Magistrate or the painter Titorelli for womanizing? The Magistrates for vanity? Lawyer Huld for placing his profession before his personal life? Rather, Joseph K. is a flawed human being, flawed in some fundamental spiritual way, one who lacks self-confidence. The best clue to understanding his situation is the guilt he only halfway acknowledges. He is told: "Our officials never go hunting for guilt in the populace, but, as the Law decrees, are attracted by guilt, and must then send out us warders." The implication is that Joseph K. himself lured the warders to him in the interests of self-realization and self-extermination—the two are synonymous in Kafka's fiction.

Joseph K., respectable, even dignified in the world's eyes, experiences a number of humiliations, each of which will signify the hopelessness of his position. Arrested in his own bedroom by intruders who offer to sell his clothing (they confiscate his underwear), observed by a couple across the courtyard as well as by his landlady and three of his subordinates at the bank, K.'s privacy, self-respect, and professional competence are shredded. K. has indeed awakened to a nightmare.

Yet what authority has this court? It is independent of the civil judiciary system; K. is notified that his first hearing is to be held on a Sunday, in a shabby part of town. In fact, he discovers, he is being tried in an attic; most of the attics in the city, he learns, house divisions of this omnipresent bureaucracy. Very likely, Kafka is suggesting that most people are under indictment.

The hearing is alternately comic and maddening. At the outset, the judge mistakes the chief clerk of a bank for a house painter. Have they arrested the wrong man? Are they incompetent, or are they simply ignorant underlings blindly administering a form of justice they themselves do not comprehend?

K.'s efforts to denounce these outrageous proceedings, however, reveal that he does not grasp the nature or gravity of his situation. However clownish these officials may appear (the Examining Magistrate browses over obscene drawings throughout the hearing), their power should not be underestimated. K.'s speech mocking the court proceedings does not reveal confident self-sufficiency but swaggering ignorance. "I merely wanted to point out . . ." remarked the Examining Magistrate afterward, "that today . . . you have deprived yourself of the advantage an interrogation usually confers on an accused man." Unfortunately, this and all the other bits of information about the court that K. receives, whether valid or invalid (and how is he to distinguish between them?), are equally useless to him.

Of K.'s plight the philosopher Martin Buber remarked that, though man has been appointed to this world, he is forever caught in the thick vapors of a mist of absurdity. Is Divinity unwilling to reveal itself? Possibly. "The highest court . . . is quite inaccessible to you, to me, and to all of us," K. is told. It is equally possible, though, that it reveals itself every moment but that man either blinds himself or is simply ill-equipped to internalize the message. Near the novel's conclusion, the priest shrieks out to him, "Can't you even see two inches in front of your nose?" K. both can and cannot: Indeed, the tragedy of man's relations with Divinity is the near-impossibility of communication between them.

K. can never get beyond dealing with underlings; man lacks the spiritual strength and the understanding necessary for his quest. In the often-excerpted passage of the doorkeeper of the Law, the priest suggests that the petitioner might have merely stepped through the first door of justice had he the temerity and the wisdom. Presumably, the same applies to K., but all of his efforts to assert himself—to demonstrate that he is innocent or that the Law is in error—come to naught. Even the women from whom he has sought comfort have misled him. He has made many errors, and now, the priest informs him, his guilt is all but proved.

Earlier, K. had met another functionary of the court, the painter Titorelli. The name itself is a pseudonym, an amalgam of the names of famous Italian artists. In reality, he is a hack court painter, as degenerate as another artist, Brunelda, in Kafka's *Amerika*. Efforts that artists once dedicated to the glory of God, during an age of worship, Titorelli now dedicates to cynical aggrandizement of petty officials. From the painter, K. learns of the three possible directions for his case: definite acquittal, ostensible acquittal, and indefinite postponement. Even this, however, may be merely a joke: Definite acquittals do not occur. "I have never heard of one case," avers the artist. Ostensible acquittal grants provisional freedom, which may last for years or only for an hour, followed by rearrest. Postponement seems to be the tactic another accused man, Mr. Block, has resolved to follow, but such an approach would deny K. an opportunity to face his creator and accuser; it would reduce him to the status of a beggar, more a cringing beast than a man. Are the courts merely playing with man? Possibly: Titorelli's drawing of Justice makes her look "exactly like the Goddess of the Hunt in full cry."

Exactly one year after K.'s arrest, when K. is thirty-one years old (Kafka's age at the time the novel was written), two men come for him. Garbed in black, K. is prepared for his executioners. Somber as this scene is, however, it has comically grotesque elements. "Tenth rate old actors they send for me," he muses. ". . . Perhaps they are tenors." Joseph K. is led through the streets; at times he even does the leading, indicating acceptance of his fate. The final scene is richly textured and enigmatic. His executioners require that he lay down on the ground and intimate that he is to reach for the knife and execute himself. Wordlessly, K. refuses. Is this further evidence of his rebellious nature or his own judgment of the shameful justice rendered by the court. He is stabbed and dies "like a dog, it was as if the shame should survive him." As one critic has asked, whose shame, the man's or the courts'? On this ambiguous and troubling note, Kafka's unfinished novel ceases.

Sometime in 1922, less than two years before his death, Kafka began his final novel, the longest and most thematically complex of his narratives. In *The Castle*, Kafka's settings grow even sparer than those of his earlier works, reinforcing the parablelike nature of the tale. *The Castle* is the story of K., a land surveyor, who leaves his village to live and work near the castle. Unlike Joseph K., who is summoned to trial, K. seeks out the castle of his own volition: He wishes to be the castle's land surveyor. Unable to enter the castle, he attempts to secure an interview with the Court Official in charge of land surveyors, Klamm (the letter "K" again). Like the petitioner who has come to the Law in *The Trial*, K. finds his way barred. No matter what he attempts, he is no nearer the castle at the novel's end than he was on the first day. His quest wears him out, and though Kafka never concluded this novel, he did make it clear that K. was to die, exhausted by his efforts.

Again, Kafka's enigmatic art has kindled various interpretations. Brod interprets the castle theologically, as man's attempt to secure Divine Law and Divine Grace. Others assert that Kafka's novels describe man's efforts to overcome his limitations as a physical being in order to grapple with his spiritual self in a vain effort to unify the two sides. Another group perceives this novel as a denunciation of the bureaucracy that ruled Kafka's country. All sides can adduce strong arguments—more testimony to the paradoxical and allegorical nature of Kafka's art.

K. is an outsider, an Everyman attempting to find a meaningful life in a world that has lost its spiritual moorings. In doing so, he looks toward the castle, but whether the castle is even occupied, whether it has corporeal existence or is the inward world the narrator yearns to reach, must remain a mystery: At the novel's opening, K. stands "for a long time gazing into the apparent emptiness above him." This emptiness echoes and amplifies the spirit of T. S. Eliot's *The Waste Land* (1922) and Oswald Spengler's *Der Untergang des Abenlandes* (1918, 1923; *The Decline of the West*, 1926-1928). (The never-seen owner of the castle is named Count Westwest.)

Like many of Kafka's protagonists, K. is aroused from a deep sleep to face an identity crisis. He claims at the inn where he is staying that he has been summoned by the castle, but a telephone call to the castle brings a hasty denial; then, before K. can be ejected from the inn, another call reverses the first judgment. The issue of K.'s status is further complicated when he observes that the castle "was accepting battle with a smile."

The castle accepts the intruder's invasion but its smile is not easily decipherable. Much suggests that it is mocking. The assistants assigned to him are childish and troublesome, very likely dispatched as spies. The messages he receives are so ambiguous in language, so ill-informed regarding his activities, that he despairs after receiving them, despite the fact that he wants nothing more than to be acknowledged. One official, Bürgel, even informs him that the present moment holds the key to his hopes, implying that if he were to present his petition at once, it would be accepted. Alas, K. has fallen asleep.

As in *The Trial*, the protagonist's efforts to justify himself before officialdom prove fruitless. His superior, Klamm, is perceived by K. through a peephole, but all attempts to speak to him are rebuffed. To K.'s request for an interview comes the reply: "Never. Under no conditions!" Resolutely, K. determines to intercept Klamm at his carriage, but the official will not venture forth. Stalemated, K. feels he "had won a freedom such as hardly anybody else had ever succeeded in winning, as if nobody could . . . drive him away . . . [but] at the same time there was nothing more senseless, nothing more hopeless, than this freedom." K. cannot be driven away, but he will never be recognized.

By means of subplots, mainly involving the family of K.'s messenger, Kafka reinforces his theme that man is alienated from his society, his inner self, his God. The reader who is familiar with the Aristotelian formula of a protagonist who successfully completes an action will be disarmed by Kafka's novel, in which developments serve only to clarify the impossibility of a successful completion of his goal.

Like Joseph K. of *The Trial*, K. discovers some respite in women. Frieda (peace), the mistress of Klamm, represents domestic pleasure, the highest earth has to offer. Although she agrees to leave Klamm for K., his Faustian spirit is not satisfied. Forsaking the sensual and domestic comforts, K. continually leaves Frieda in pursuit of his goal, transcendence of the merely mundane, while maintaining that he does so in part for her. This paradoxical attitude probably mirrors Kafka's own relationship with Felice Bauer (note the two women's initials). Kafka was torn between committing himself to his fiancée and freeing himself for his art, an ambivalence reflected in K.'s inconsistent behavior with Frieda. After losing her, K. remarks that though he "would be happy if she were to come back to me . . . I should at once begin to neglect her all over again. This is how it is." Thus we see why K. can never know peace, why he is doomed to wear himself out.

In addition to Frieda, K. is intimate with Olga, Barnabas' sister. Like K., she is desperate to reach the castle to redress a wrong done to her family by one of its officials. Olga's sister, Amalia, has been grossly propositioned by one of the castle officials. Her family has worn itself out, as K. is doing, in a fruitless attempt to justify themselves before the authorities, to gain access to the Law; even the villagers find the authorities inaccessible. From K.'s perspective, the authorities seem impersonal, aloof. In ruling, they are attentive to trivial detail but bureaucratically indifferent to human considerations.

Though Kafka did not complete *The Castle*, his intended ending was communicated to Brod: "Round [K.'s] deathbed the community assembles and from the castle comes this decision: that K. has no claim to live in the castle by right—yet taking certain auxiliary circumstances into account, it is permitted him to live and work there." How ironic! With remarkable prescience, Kafka had sketched his own epitaph. Consider the treatment accorded his memory: Czech authorities have placed signs in five languages to mark his grave, yet they forbid sale of his works.

Major publications other than long fiction

SHORT FICTION: *Der Heizer*, 1913; *Das Urteil*, 1913, 1916 (*The Sentence*,

1928; also as *The Judgment*, 1945); *Ein Landarzt*, 1919 (*The Country Doctor*, 1940); *In der Strafkolonie*, 1919 (*The Penal Colony*, 1941); *Ein Hungerkünstler*, 1924 (*The Hunger Artist*, 1938); *Erzählungen*, 1946 (*The Complete Stories*, 1971).

NONFICTION: *The Diaries of Franz Kafka*, 1948-1949; *Tagebucher 1910-23*, 1951; *Brief an den Vater*, 1952 (written 1919; *Letter to His Father*); *Briefe an Milena*, 1952 (*Letters to Milena*, 1953); *Briefe an Felice*, 1967 (*Letters to Felice*, 1974).

MISCELLANEOUS: *Dearest Father: Stories and Other Writings*, 1954 (includes *Letter to His Father*).

Bibliography

Brod, Max. *Franz Kafka: A Biography*, 1937.
Emrich, Wilhelm. *Franz Kafka: A Critical Study of His Writings*, 1968.
Greenberg, Martin. *The Terror of Art: Kafka and Modern Literature*, 1965.
Pawel, Ernst. *The Nightmare of Reason: A Life of Franz Kafka*, 1984.
Politzer, Heinz. *Franz Kafka: Parable and Paradox*, 1962.

Stan Sulkes

YASUNARI KAWABATA

Born: Osaka, Japan; June 11, 1899
Died: Zushi, Japan; April 16, 1972

Principal long fiction

Izu no odoriko, 1925 (*The Izu Dancer*, 1964); *Asakusa kurenaidan*, 1930; *Matsugo no me*, 1930; *Kinju*, 1933 (*Of Birds and Beasts*, in *The House of the Sleeping Beauties and Other Stories*, 1969); *Hana no warutsu*, 1936; *Yukiguni*, 1937, 1947 (*Snow Country*, 1957); *Hokura no nikki*, 1940 (*The Mole*, 1955); *Meijin*, 1942-1954 (*The Master of Go*, 1972); *Utsukushii tabi*, 1947; *Otome no minato*, 1948; *Asakusa monogatari*, 1950; *Sembazuru*, 1952 (serialized 1949; *Thousand Cranes*, 1958); *Hi mo tsuki mo*, 1953; *Saikonsha*, 1953; *Suigetsu*, 1953 (*The Moon on the Water*, 1958); *Kawa no aru shitamachi no hanashi*, 1954; *Tokyo no hito*, 1955; *Yama no oto*, 1957 (*The Sound of the Mountain*, 1970); *Mizuumi*, 1961 (*The Lake*, 1974); *Nemureru bijo*, 1961 (*The House of the Sleeping Beauties*, in *The House of the Sleeping Beauties and Other Stories*, 1969); *Kyoto*, 1962; *Kataude*, 1965 (*One Arm*, 1967); *Utsukushisa to kanashimi to*, 1965 (*Beauty and Sadness*, 1975); *Shosetsu nyumon*, 1970; *Aru hito no sei no naka ni*, 1972; *Tampopo*, 1972.

Other literary forms

In world literature, Japan has the oldest tradition of the novel; there is, however, no significant qualitative distinction between the Japanese "novel" and the "short story." As a result, Yasunari Kawabata may be said to have been a writer of short stories, as well as novels, but the distinction is Western, arbitrary, and based merely on length. Some of the collections of works so designated are *Jojoka* (1938), *Shiroi mangetsu* (1948), *Maihime* (1951), *Bungei tokuhon Kawabata Yasunari* (1962), *Kogen* (1969), *Tenohira no shosetsu* (1969), *Shui yuch* (1971), *Tenju no ko* (1975), and *Honehiroi* (1975). His first non-fiction work was autobiographical, *Jurukosai no nikki* (1925; diary of a sixteen-year-old), and he is well-known as a literary critic. His essays have been published in *Bungakuteki jijoden* (1934), *Rakka ryusui* (1966), *Bi no sonzai to hakken / The Existence and Discovery of Beauty* (1969; bilingual), *Utsukushii nihon no watakushi / Japan, the Beautiful, and Myself* (1969; bilingual), *Isso ikka* (1973), and *Nihon no bi no kokoro* (1973). He also translated into modern Japanese a selection of ancient Japanese stories as *Ocho monogatari shu* (1956-1958), and *Aesop's Fables* as *Isoppu* (1968). His collected works have been published as *Kawabata Yasunari zenshu* (1948-1969).

Achievements

Yasunari Kawabata has been recognized as one of Japan's major novelists, short-story writers, and critics for more than fifty years. He is the only Japanese author to have received the Nobel Prize for Literature, after having received every major Japanese literary award, including the Bungei Konwa Kai Prize (1937) and the Geijutsuin-sho Prize (1952). He also received the Goethe Medal of Frankfurt, Germany (1959), and the Ordre des Arts et Lettres (1960) and Prix du Meilleur Livre Étranger (1961) of France. In 1954, he was elected to the Japanese Academy of Arts. Early in his career, Kawabata was instrumental in founding the avant-garde Neo-Sensualist movement of the 1920's and experimented with cubism, Dadaism, Surrealism, and Futurism. He was also influenced by the stream-of-consciousness techniques of James Joyce and the "automatic writing" of the Surrealists. Later, he abandoned these experiments and reverted to more traditional Japanese forms, developing a style that was unique and difficult to translate. His works are sensitive, delicate, and often difficult for readers without a full understanding of Japanese thought and culture; he is recognized internationally as one of Japan's, and the world's, greatest twentieth century authors.

Biography
Yasunari Kawabata's childhood was dogged by sadness and loneliness. Born the son of a doctor in Osaka, he was only two when his father died and three when his mother died. He went to live with his maternal grandparents but lost his only sibling, a sister, a few years later. When he was only seven, his grandmother died, and he was left virtually alone, at age sixteen, by the death of his grandfather. The latter's death became the subject of *Jurukosai no nikki*, a reminiscence of his sorrow-filled childhood and the affection he felt for his grandfather. In primary school, Kawabata was first interested in painting, but as he entered puberty, he became more interested in literature, especially the Buddhist writings of the Heian period of the 800's through the 1100's, valuing them more for their fantastic elements than religious teaching.

Kawabata became a secondary school student in Tokyo, where he enthusiastically read Scandinavian literature and became involved in a movement of writers interested in introducing Western artists such as Michelangelo, Leonardo da Vinci, Rembrandt, and Paul Cézanne to Japan. When Kawabata enrolled at Tokyo Imperial University in 1920, he first studied English literature but changed to Japanese literature a year later. He worked on the student literary magazine *Shinshicho* and impressed novelist and playwright Kikuchi Kan with the piece *Shokonsai ikkei* (1921; a scene of the memorial service for the war dead). He became Kikuchi's protégé and was later hired to work for his literary magazine *Bungei shunju*. In 1924, after graduating with a degree in Japanese literature, he, with Riichi Yokomitsu and others, founded *Bungei jidai*, a literary journal which became the primary organ of the Shinkankaku-ha movement.

Drawing on avant-garde Western literary movements of the 1920's such as Dadaism, cubism, Surrealism, and Futurism, the Japanese Shinkankakuha movement was also known as the Neo-Sensualist, Neo-Sensationist, Neo-Perceptionist, or Neo-Impressionist movement. Though the Japanese literary scene was dominated by realism and Marxism, members of the Shinkankaku-ha movement were primarily interested in the experience of the senses. Kawabata himself experimented with a long interior monologue—similar to that of James Joyce's Molly Bloom—in his short story *Suisho genso* (1934; the crystal fantasy). His main contribution to the movement, other than his writings, was to write the manifesto *Shin-shin sakka no shinkeiko kaisetsu* (1925; the new tendency of the avant-garde writers), calling for new perceptions, expression, and style. It also asserts the need for a new language to replace "lifeless, objective narrative" with a more sensual expression of thought and feeling. Much of the manifesto freely uses undefined terms from the literary movements in Europe and its arguments are largely borrowed from them. His literary reputation grew with the publication of his short novel *The Izu Dancer*, but by the middle of the 1930's, he had largely abandoned his experimental phase and was working in more traditional forms, beginning one of his major works, *Snow Country*, in 1934.

Never deeply interested in politics, Kawabata remained as aloof as possible during World War II. He traveled in Manchukuo and studied classics such as Murasaki Shikibu's *Genji monogatari* (c. 1004; *The Tale of Genji*, 1935), the great traditional novel of the eleventh century, thereby retreating from the chaos of the time. Kawabata explained his detachment from politics in his essay *Bungakuteki jijoden*: "I have become a person who can never hate or grow angry at anyone." After the war, he said he was going to immerse himself in tradition and "write elegies." His most celebrated works, with their elegiac tone, appeared in the years following the war. Although he had published one version of *Snow Country* in 1937, he had never been satisfied with it and finished a new version in 1947. In 1949, he published *Thousand Cranes* in serial form. Beginning in 1948, Kawabata became president of the P. E. N. Club of Japan; he also became the mentor of younger Japanese writers, notably Yukio Mishima.

By the mid-1950's, Kawabata's reputation had spread around the world, advanced in America by Edward G. Seidensticker's translations of *Snow Country* and *Thousand Cranes*; *The Izu Dancer* had appeared in abridged form in *The Atlantic Monthly* in 1955. Excerpts of *The Sound of the Mountain* were published in English in *Japan Quarterly* in 1962, the same year in which Kawabata published *Kyoto*, a novel about the Western corruption of Japan. As yet untranslated, it is considered by some critics to be his masterwork. He received the major Japanese literary awards, the Bungei Konwa Kai Prize in 1937 and the Geijutsuin-sho Prize in 1952, and was elected to the Japanese Academy of Arts in 1954. In 1957, he organized the twenty-ninth congress of the International P. E. N. Club in Tokyo, and he was elected vice president of that organization in 1959. In that capacity, he later made many trips abroad.

In 1960, he visited the United States and conducted seminars at several universities.

In 1968, on the centennial of the Meiji Restoration, Kawabata was awarded the Nobel Prize for Literature. With his usual modesty, he stated he was at a loss to know why he had been selected, crediting his translators and his background in Japanese tradition. He also expressed pleasure that Japanese literature had achieved recognition. Possibly foreshadowing his suicide, he added that for a writer "an honor becomes a burden." He spent his final years quietly with his wife, Hideko, except in 1971, when he emerged to support an unsuccessful conservative candidate for governor of Tokyo. In 1972, he took his own life by asphyxiating himself with gas in his workroom. He had been somewhat ill, though not seriously, and was sleeping poorly, but he left no explanation for the act, and there was much theorizing about the motive, including linking it to the ritual suicide of his student Yukio Mishima in 1970.

Analysis

When announcing the award of the Nobel Prize for Literature to Yasunari Kawabata, Dr. Anders Osterling praised him as a "worshipper of the beautiful and melancholy pictorial language of existence" who had "contributed to spiritual bridge-spanning between East and West." He also praised Kawabata's highly refined prose for "an eminent ability to illuminate erotic episodes, an exquisite sharpness in each observation and a whole net of small secretive values that often overshadow the European techniques of the narrative." In this statement, Osterling summed up the predominant characteristics of Kawabata's fiction, as viewed by Westerners. Kawabata's novels and short stories, despite their reference to subtleties of Japanese culture and other essential Japanese elements, seem to reach across the cultural gap between East and West. As Kawabata himself remarked, Japanese literature, which constitutes an unbroken tradition between the eleventh century and the nineteenth, opened to a torrent of Western influences in the twentieth. The influence of Edgar Allan Poe, Oscar Wilde, and other Decadent writers has often been noted in the works of Jun'ichirō Tanizaki, for example, and the influence of the artistic movements of the early 1920's upon Kawabata is crucial. Therefore, in the works of these and other authors so influenced, a Western reader recognizes familiar structures and motifs which also help make the foreign works seem less alien.

Nevertheless, things which are taken for granted in Japan acquire a gloss of mysteriousness in translation. A "whole net of small secretive values" manifests itself, so that what, at first glance, is very simple prose becomes complex because of the unfamiliar, implicit Japanese cultural assumptions. Kawabata, it must be noted, is mysterious even to Japanese critics—he deliberately maintains an enigmatic aura— but this effect is intensified when the works are transported to the West.

For example, Western criticism of Tanizaki, Kawabata, and Mishima often focuses on their "eroticism" (as in the Nobel Prize citation above), yet much of what is perceived as eroticism derives from the more sexually open traditions of Japan. Kawabata is, therefore, more relaxed in dealing with the erotic, achieving a naturalness in this regard which many Western writers have found elusive. Another example is Kawabata's characteristic air of melancholy. One may point to his lonely childhood, when virtually every member of his family died before Kawabata was sixteen. One might also point to his suicide as a sign of his basic unhappiness, although no convincing reason was ever presented for it. Yet, one must also consider the cultural context. As Gwenn Boardman notes, "sadness is characteristic of much Japanese literature, the *mono-no-aware* or *aware* that is a delicate perception of transience, of sadness, of the implication of the gesture, or of the intersection of silence and time." Others have asserted that melancholy is a pleasurable mood to the Japanese. Such subtle cultural differences obviously deeply affect one's reading of Kawabata. In translation, his eroticism, his *haiku*-like effects, the implications of a simple gesture may be easily misinterpreted. At the same time, this very strangeness is a source of considerable pleasure to the Western reader of Kawabata's fiction.

Snow Country, which Kawabata struggled with for some fourteen years, tells of the love of Shimamura, a jaded Tokyo writer, for Komako, a geisha at a mountain resort. Structurally, it is relatively simple. The novel begins as Shimamura is about to begin his second visit, then flashes back to their meeting the previous spring, then returns to the ground situation and progresses to his third visit, in which he takes the geisha's advice and leaves her. It is in Kawabata's suggestive imagery that *Snow Country* transcends the materials of the common love story. In particular, the theme of transience is highlighted in the novel's imagery. Despite Shimamura's desire to make the moment permanent, time passes. There is nothing he can do to slow it down. An image of a coach window early in the novel symbolizes this idea as he sees a girl reflected back to him, but the trees, mountains, and sky continue moving under her transparent face. Though the passage of time, aging, and death are inevitable, Shimamura feels his chest rise at the inexpressible beauty, especially when a light shines through the girl's face. Transience thus enhances the preciousness of beauty. Another striking image of impermanence is the scene in which Shimamura observes the death of a bee: "It was a quiet death that came with the change of the seasons." When he watches the bee struggle against the inevitable, he has an insight similar to that which he had at the coach window: "For such a tiny death, the empty . . . room seemed enormous." The imagery invites an existential interpretation: Even with the cerin knowledge of death and impermanence, it is mankind's fate to struggle against time.

The distinctly Japanese style of *Snow Country* has caused it to be compared to *renga*, or linked verse. Like all Japanese poetry, *renga* is characterized by its affective depth and its lack of didacticism and philosophical precision. This form derives in part from characteristics of the Japanese language, such as its imagistic, concrete nouns, and in part from the traditions of Shintoism and Buddhism, which led to a poetry concerned with different states of consciousness, marked by a complexity that is tonal rather than thematic. An appreciation of these traits contributes to a greater understanding of the elements of *Snow Country* and other Kawabata novels. Like *renga*, it is a progression of images, integrated more by association than by plot. As Masao Miyoshi describes it, "The 'shape' of the novel is thus not architectural or sculptural, with a totality subsuming the parts, but musical in the sense of a continual movement generated by surprise and juxtaposition, intensification and relaxation, and the use of various rhythms and tempos." This analysis helps explain Kawabata's publication of the novel over a long period of time, in sections in different periodicals, with later substantial emendations; it also accounts for the novel's lack of traditional Western structural unity. Like all of Kawabata's works, *Snow Country* is unified not by plot or action, but by imagery, suggestion, and, to an extent, characterization.

Even the main character, Shimamura, has been described as "insubstantial." The tale is told in the third person, but the narrator seems to imply no moral judgment of Shimamura's behavior toward the women in his life. Miyoshi points out references to the legend of Kengyu and Shokujo, who loved each other so much that God made them stars and placed them at opposite ends of the Milky Way, eternally separated. This imagery is indeed suggestive but does little to explain Kawabata's attitude toward the lovers Shimamura and Komako. Perhaps a clue to Kawabata's stance is to be found in his treatment of nature imagery: When he uses images of the natural world, he does so not to mirror the inner life of the characters but to show that the world is indifferent to their affairs. This stance is curiously reminiscent of the comments made by Alain Robbe-Grillet concerning the New Novel and its need to remove the Romantic imagery which implies that nature "cares" about human beings. This would further explain why a writer as traditional as Kawabata often seems so ultramodern.

Like Tanizaki's *Futen rojin nikki* (1962; *Diary of a Mad Old Man*, 1965), Kawabata's *The House of the Sleeping Beauties* is an exploration of an old man's sexuality. Eguchi, who is impotent, goes to a house where beautiful, drugged young girls sleep naked beside him. During these visits, he tries to understand the meaning of his existence and in drugged reveries remembers various incidents in his life. An atmosphere of doom is strongly evoked in the novel. There are locked doors and a red curtain that seem to conceal secrets. As he approaches the house, he wonders if the sleeping girl will resemble a drowned corpse. As the novel progresses, the weather turns colder, foreshadowing the approach of death, and the last section begins with Eguchi's sipping warm tea to fortify himself against the winter cold. On his last visit, the conversation in the house is all about an old man who died while sleeping next to one of the girls. Eguchi sleeps between two girls this time, one symbolically dark, the other fair, but awakens to find the dark girl, whom he had called "Life itself," dead. As the novel ends, he seems paralyzed, chilled by the knowledge of inevitable death. Mishima likened the book to "a submarine in which people are trapped and the air is gradually disappearing. While in the grip of this story, the reader sweats and grows dizzy, and knows with the greatest immediacy the terror of lust urged on by the approach of death." Particularly notable in this novel is Kawabata's use of color. As a painter, he employed it in all of his works, but the color red and the playing of light against dark stand out. The contrasting of fundamental opposites—ugliness and beauty, age and youth, life and death—is also done with extraordinary skill.

The major themes that reverberate through Kawabata's fiction are especially manifest in *The House of the Sleeping Beauties*. Loneliness, the hopelessness of love, impermanence, old age, death, and guilt all appear in evocative imagery. In keeping with Kawabata's Buddhist ethos, however, no conclusive statements on these themes emerge, except that the physical world consists of irreconcilable forces which mankind is ultimately unable to understand or transcend while in the human body. Kawabata reflects this worldview in a style that persistently hints at his meanings, particularly through visual imagery. He is a writer of suggestion. Arthur Kimball, for example, examines Kawabata's tension of opposing imagery in great detail and states that the persistent accumulation of this tension leads any reader who has identified with Eguchi to the same feeling of chilled numbness which Eguchi feels in the last scene.

Paradox follows paradox. Ugly old men sleep beside beautiful young women who are alive, yet drugged into a deathlike sleep. Though they are real, the girls are like inflatable dolls, toys for lonely men's amusement. One part of Eguchi's character is disgusted by all of this, and he thinks he will not return. Yet, these nights are as sexless—despite their obvious sexual overtones—as any night Eguchi has ever spent. On his second visit, Eguchi is given a girl described as being "more experienced," but what does her "experience" consist of? The old woman in charge makes mocking references to men she can trust. The girl's "prostitution" is apparently sexless. On his third visit, caught between his desire to stay awake to enjoy the beauty of the girl's body and his desire for a "sleep like death," he contemplates evil and thinks of the girl as a Buddha: She is a temptation to evil, yet her "young skin and scent might be forgiveness" for sad old men. In the face of death, however, Eguchi finds no answers. As Kimball remarks, "In his last extremity he stands, a chilly old man asking questions of himself."

The Sound of the Mountain also uses an aging man, Ogata Shingo, as its protagonist and focuses on his meditations on the meaning of his life. Written in very brief paragraphs, the novel consists of Shingo's thoughts and relates the form of the book to the traditional *haiku* and *renga*. It does not work in the way most novels do. The character of Shingo is subservient to the succession of themes and images, just as the settings (Kamakura, Tokyo, and Shinshu) serve, as Miyoshi observes, as spatial correlatives of Shingo's present and past. The novel is an accumulation of images, many of which center on Kikuko, Shingo's daughter-in-law, who becomes a distant as well as unattainable love, similar to women in several of Kawabata's works. Although Kawabata has been praised for his insights into feminine psychology, Kikuko, like Shingo, is not a fully developed character in the usual novelistic manner. She is part of a succession of images, expressing the transience of all natural phenomena. Without a clear plot line or climax, *The Sound of the Mountain* nevertheless is powerful in evoking Shingo's nostalgia and his inward voyage of regret.

Kawabata's legacy includes some of the finest, most sensitive fiction of the twentieth century. The exact meaning of his characters' gestures is never quite clear, yet they remain strangely evocative. Like the Japanese paintings which he so admired, Kawabata's fiction reveals the shadowy nature of reality and the subjectivity of all human observation. One of the most traditionally Japanese of novelists, he is also one whose works speak with great authority to contemporary concerns.

Major publications other than long fiction

SHORT FICTION: *Shokonsai ikkei*, 1921; *Suisho genso*, 1934; *Jojoka*, 1938; *Shiroi mangetsu*, 1948; *Maihime*, 1951; *Bungei tokuhon Kawabata Yasunari*, 1962; *The House of the Sleeping Beauties and Other Stories*, 1969; *Kogen*, 1969; *Tenohira no shosetsu*, 1969; *Shui yuch*, 1971; *Honehiroi*, 1975; *Tenju no ko*, 1975.

NONFICTION: *Jurukosai no nikki*, 1925; *Shin-shin sakka no shinkeiko kaisetsu*, 1925; *Bungakuteki jijoden*, 1934; *Rakka ryusui*, 1966; *Bi no sonzai to hakken / The Existence and Discovery of Beauty*, 1969 (bilingual); *Utsukushii nihon no watakushi / Japan, the Beautiful, and Myself*, 1969 (bilingual); *Isso ikka*, 1973; *Nihon no bi no kokoro*, 1973.

TRANSLATIONS: *Ocho monogatari shu*, 1956-1958 (of ancient Japanese stories); *Isoppu*, 1968 (of *Aesop's Fables*).

MISCELLANEOUS: *Kawabata Yasunari zenshu*, 1948-1969.

Bibliography

Boardman, Gwenn R. "Kawabata Yasunari: Snow in the Mirror," in *Critique: Studies in Modern Fiction*. XI, no. 2 (1969), pp. 5-15.

Kimball, Arthur G. "Last Extremity: Kawabata's *House of the Sleeping Beauties*," in *Critique: Studies in Modern Fiction*. XIII, no. 1 (1970), pp. 19-30.

Mishima, Yukio. "Introduction," in *The House of the Sleeping Beauties*, 1969.

Translated by Edward G. Seidensticker.
Miyoshi, Masao. *Accomplices of Silence: The Modern Japanese Novel*, 1974.
Obuchowski, Mary Dejong. "Theme and Image in Kawabata's *The Sound of the Mountain*," in *World Literature Today*. LI, no. 2 (1977), pp. 207-210.
Rimer, J. Thomas. "Kawabata Yasunari, Eastern Approaches: *Snow Country*," in *Modern Japanese Fiction and Its Traditions*, 1978.
Yamanouchi, Hisaaki. *The Search for Authenticity in Modern Japanese Literature*, 1978.

J. Madison Davis

NIKOS KAZANTZAKIS

Born: Heraklion, Crete; February 18, 1883
Died: Freiburg, Germany; October 26, 1957

Principal long fiction

Toda-Raba, 1933 (English translation, 1964); *De tuin der Rotsen*, 1939 (better known as *Le Jardin des rochers*, 1960; *The Rock Garden*, 1963); *Bios kai politela tou Alexe Zormpa*, 1946 (*Zorba the Greek*, 1953); *Ho Kapetan Michales*, 1953 (*Freedom or Death*, 1956); *Ho Christos xanastauronetai*, 1954 (*The Greek Passion*, 1953; also known as *Christ Recrucified*, 1954); *Ho teleutaios peirasmos*, 1955 (*The Last Temptation of Christ*, 1960); *Ho phtochoules tou Theou*, 1956 (*Saint Francis*, 1962); *Aderfofades*, 1963 (*The Fratricides*, 1964).

Other literary forms

Long before he began writing the novels for which he has won international acclaim, Nikos Kazantzakis had established a reputation in his own country and, to a lesser extent, throughout Europe as a playwright, essayist, translator, and poet. For years, he earned his living by writing about the many countries he visited and translating classics of Western civilization into his native tongue. His travelogues of Russia, Spain, and England combine vivid descriptions of these countries with observations on the political and cultural climate he found there. In addition to his original compositions, he translated a number of important works into modern Greek, among them philosophical writings of Henri Bergson and Friedrich Nietzsche, Jules Verne's novels, Dante's *La divina commedia* (c. 1320; *The Divine Comedy*), and Johann Wolfgang von Goethe's *Faust* (1808, 1833). For fourteen years, he wrote and revised *Odysseia* (1938; known in English as *The Odyssey: A Modern Sequel*, 1958), a 33,000-line continuation of Homer's *Odyssey* (c. 800 B.C.), showing Odysseus, still driven to wander in search of new experiences, traveling throughout the Mediterranean region and over the world in search of personal fulfillment.

Achievements

Kazantzakis' achievements as a novelist lie in two areas: his use of native demotic Greek as a medium of fiction and his transformation of philosophical materials into art.

The most revolutionary aspect of Kazantzakis' writing is often lost in translations of his work. Early in his career, he opted to write in demotic Greek, the colloquial language spoken by Greek workers, farmers, and fishermen. This devotion to the language of the common people often caused him to meet with sharp criticism from academics and other purists, who insisted that "acceptable" literature be written in a form of Greek highly stylized and often barely readable by the masses. Though some of his travel-writing and mid-career imaginative literature was written originally in French, Kazantzakis always sided with those in his country who wanted written Greek literature to mirror the living speech of the country. *The Odyssey* and his novels beginning with *Zorba the Greek* are written in the colloquial form of his native language; in fact, *The Odyssey* has been described by Peter Bien as a repository of demotic words and phrases, a kind of gloss on modern spoken Greek. The popularity of his works among the general public in Greece attests the success he has had in achieving his aim.

Another of Kazantzakis' major achievements is his capability to transform philosophy into art. The metaphysics of Nietzsche and Bergson find life in the characters that populate Kazantzakis' fiction, poetry, and drama. While no single work stands out as a masterpiece (though some have made such claims for *Zorba the Greek*), the body of Kazantzakis' work, taken as a whole, represents a remarkable accomplishment. In almost all of his works, he focuses on the plight of man struggling to make sense of a world that is essentially meaningless. Those who continue to struggle rather than accept their fate in life are set apart from the commoners, for whom Kazantzakis has only pity or contempt. These heroes often sweep the reader along with their enthusiasm. Additionally, as Bien has noted, Kazantzakis' novels resemble those of James Joyce, Marcel Proust, Thomas Mann, Joseph Conrad, D. H. Lawrence, and William Faulkner in their fusion of the language of poetry into the medium of prose. In his novels, Kazantzakis unites his own experiences with those of his countrymen and his adopted brothers of the Western world to create fiction that illuminates the mystery of human existence.

Biography

Nikos Kazantzakis once described himself as a follower of Odysseus, and his life bears out his claim. Always a Cretan at heart, he nevertheless spent the better part of his adult years wandering the European continent, traveling to Asia and the Far East, storing up experiences that made their way into the many works that seemed to pour from his pen.

He was born in 1883 in Heraklion, Crete, an island strife-torn for years by a bloody war of independence. His father was a freedom fighter against the Turkish forces that ruled by might over the Greek population; Nikos himself was introduced to the struggle as a young boy when Turkish marauders invaded his village in 1889, threatening the safety and the lives of his immediate family.

At nineteen, Kazantzakis went to Athens to study at the University. Four years later, armed with his degree, he went to Paris to pursue his interest in philosophy. There, he fell under the twin spells of Nietzsche and Bergson, a curious pairing but one which subsequently gave life to all of his writings. When he returned to Greece a year later, he had already become an Existentialist, convinced that, though life was meaningless, great men could distinguish themselves by pursuing a meaningful existence in this meaningless world. His dissertation on Nietzsche expresses his concept of "positive nihilism." Kazantzakis saw himself as a prophet who would use his art to educate others regarding the plight of mankind. His first literary attempts were in drama, though while he was writing, he was also working actively as a businessman and minor government official. In 1917, he ran a lignite mine with the real-life Alexis Zorba; for a brief period, he was a member of the Greek government under Prime Minister Venizelos, but when Venizelos fell from power, Kazantzakis, disillusioned, returned to Paris.

The remainder of Kazantzakis' life can be described as one of constant travel. Even during periods when he was settled on the island of Aegina, he was often away, either on the mainland of Greece or in other parts of Europe. He had wed Galatea Alexiou in 1907, but their marriage lasted only a short time. Always fond of women's company, he had for his "companion" a succession of women in the various places he visited during his sojourns. Some of these relationships were merely fleeting liaisons; others developed into life-long friendships, such as the one he formed in 1924 with Helen Samiou. They eventually were married in 1945.

After World War I, Kazantzakis began a series of journeys to countries throughout Europe and the Middle East, supporting himself by writing for magazines in his native country. At that time an active supporter of Communism, he traveled to Moscow to join other distinguished literary figures at the Soviet Union's tenth anniversary celebration in October, 1927. Though somewhat disappointed at the fate of the Russian Revolution, he nevertheless spent much time in the Soviet Union during the next three years and even considered emigrating there with Helen Samiou. From his experiences there, he produced a book in which he attempted to explain his own theory of "meta-communism."

Early in this same decade, Kazantzakis envisioned a scheme for expressing his personal philosophy in the form of a continuation of Homer's *Odyssey*. Begun in 1924, Kazantzakis' epic was to go through seven major revisions in fourteen years before he reluctantly allowed an edition of three hundred copies to be printed. While he labored over the work, he continued his wanderings and wrote other works as well. He spent a year in Gottesgab, Czechoslovakia, where he wrote his book on Russia and a novel, *Toda-Raba*, also based on the Russian experience. He worked on *The Odyssey* there, moved to Paris briefly to attempt to get some of his works published, returned to Crete, then went back to Gottesgab. In 1932, he completed a translation of Dante. The following year he visited Spain, where he gathered materials for his *Ispania* (1937; *Spain*, 1963). At the end of that year, he returned to Greece, to the island of Aegina, to revise once more *The Odyssey*, but was off again in 1935 to visit Japan and China, where his experiences found expression in the novel *The Rock Garden*. The fall of 1936 found him back in Spain, observing and writing about the Spanish Civil War.

Three years later, Kazantzakis was traveling abroad again, this time to England; the outbreak of war marooned him there for several months. In 1940, he returned to Aegina, where he spent the war years writing and translating and quietly supporting the Resistance movement against the German occupation force. Despite his expressed aversion to writing novels, he found himself in 1943 turning to that form to portray another side of the complex creature called man that so fascinated him. What proved to be the first of several prose fictions was also to be his best known: *Zorba the Greek*.

The post-World War II years were far from quiet ones for Kazantzakis. He was given a minor post in the Greek government and in 1947, he accepted a position as head of the newly created Department of Translation of the Classics for the United Nations. From that time until his death, he was a recurrent nominee for the Nobel Prize, and newfound friends Albert Schweitzer and Thomas Mann urged the trustees of the Nobel fund to select him. Bids for this honor were never successful, but Kazantzakis did not seem to mind. He worked diligently on a number of projects, including novels that raised his stature in international literary circles while bringing criticism and even condemnation in his native land.

The final years of his life were difficult ones for Kazantzakis. He refused to let physical impairment slow him down. Though diagnosed as having leukemia in 1952, he worked on undaunted, slowing down only briefly to take treatment in Freiburg, Germany, on occasion. Finally, while visiting the Far East, he became ill from a bad vaccination and was forced to return to the clinic in Freiburg, where he died on October 26, 1957.

Analysis

The reader interested in understanding any of the works of Nikos Kazantzakis would do well to begin by reading *Salvatores Dei: Asketike* (1927; *The Saviors of God*, 1960). In that short philosophical expostulation that Kazantzakis called his "Spiritual Exercises," he expressed succinctly his strange mixture of Nietzschean nihilism and Bergsonian optimism. For Kazantzakis, God is not dead, as Nietzsche proclaimed; rather, He is waiting to be created by men who think they need Him. The search for God becomes one of the ways that Existential man seeks to create meaning for his life. Hence, Kazantzakis' heroes are often dramatizations of Existential man trying to face up to the fact that God, as He has been traditionally conceived, does not exist. Rather than being overwhelmed by such knowledge, however, the hero simply posits the existence of God—one created more in his own image than in the traditional Judeo-Christian image. For example, in *The Odyssey*, Kazantzakis' Odysseus carves a harsh-looking mask that serves as the image of God, which the people who follow Odysseus revere. Odysseus, of course, knows who created the image, and he lives with the knowledge that this "god" is merely representative of his own imagination; yet he acts as if God is real, and this God is both friend and antagonist to the hero as he struggles to assert his identity and stake his claim to fame.

The actions of Odysseus in Kazantzakis' *The Odyssey* are repeated in a variety of ways by the heroes of his novels and plays. Indeed, the heavy emphasis on philosophy, and especially metaphysics, is often cause for artistic heavy-handedness in terms of plot and narration: The story is sometimes lost in the symbology, to the point where the reader not familiar with the whole of Kazantzakis' work, and especially with his nonfiction, may come away confused about the author's use of the techniques of realism to explore highly abstract philosophical issues. Indeed, his early works are often thinly disguised attempts to cloak philosophical discussion in the garb of imaginative literature.

What is surprising is that Kazantzakis' most famous novel, *Zorba the Greek*, represents an apparent reversal of the author's position that man must abandon pleasures of the flesh to achieve spiritual self-fulfillment. In that novel, the reader is forced to recognize the attractiveness of the hero Alexis Zorba, whose whole life is devoted to sensual gratification. Zorba is anti-intellectual and antireligious, having thrown off the shackles of paralyzing intellectualism that have bound the narrator, the Boss, within himself and caused him to be ineffectual in dealing with others except as "intelligences." The Boss is the consummate ascetic, a follower of Buddha who renounces the pleasures of the flesh because he believes that closeness to others only leads to pain. Zorba, on the other hand, is the epitome of Bergsonian élan vital. The Boss withdraws from commitment; Zorba seeks it.

The mining venture in which the two men engage is Kazantzakis' way of representing symbolically the vast differences between them and hence between the life-styles they represent. Mining, the act of taking from the earth the materials one needs to survive, is hard work, but Zorba relishes it, getting dirty along with his fellow workers, taking chances with them, even risking his life when necessary; the Boss's involvement is that of the dilettante, who occasionally pokes his nose in to see how things are going but who actually remains aloof from the work itself. Their different approaches to the mining operation characterize their approaches to other forms of involvement as well: Zorba is a great womanizer because he believes that only through such lovemaking can man be fulfilled (and besides, he tells the Boss, all women want a man to love them); the Boss is paralyzed by contact with women. The Boss's affection for books is paralleled by Zorba's penchant for dancing, playing the *santiri*, womanizing; where one learns of life secondhand through the writings of others, the other experiences it fully and directly.

Zorba's power to act, even in the face of overwhelming odds and with the knowledge that his actions will be of little real value, mark him as the kind of hero whom Kazantzakis admires. Failure does not deter him from action. When his elaborate scheme to bring down timber from the top of the mountain collapses (literally as well as figuratively), he shrugs off the experience and goes on to another venture. The death of the old whore Hortense, whom Zorba has promised to marry, disturbs him only momentarily: Death is the way of the world, and Zorba understands it. By the end of the novel, the Boss, too, has come to understand the inevitability of death and the need to live vigorously in the face of that knowledge. When he receives word that his good friend Stavridakis is dead, he accepts the information stoically; and when he learns that Zorba, too, has died, he chooses not to mourn but instead to turn his own talent for writing to good use by composing the story of his experiences with Zorba.

In the novels following *Zorba the Greek*, Kazantzakis moves from studying the contrast of opposing life-styles to concentrating on the figure of the hero himself. *Freedom or Death*, based on the Cretan revolt of the 1880's, focuses on Captain Mihalis, who is torn between self-satisfaction and service to country. Kazantzakis was always fascinated by the heroes of history and literature; often his novels and plays are attempts to retell the stories of heroes whom he has met in other works, to reinterpret their struggles in the light of his own theory of positive nihilism. It is not surprising, then, to find that he chooses for his subjects Odysseus, Faust, Columbus, Saint Francis, and even Jesus Christ.

The Christ story held a special fascination for Kazantzakis. In 1948, he recast the account of Christ's Passion in a contemporary setting in *Christ Recrucified*, a novel in which the hero, a Greek peasant named Manolios, is invested with Christlike characteristics. That particular rendition apparently did not satisfy him, however, for in 1950, he returned to the subject, and this time confronted the hero in his own milieu. The result is a novel that surely ranks as Kazantzakis' most controversial, *The Last Temptation of Christ*.

In *The Last Temptation of Christ*, Kazantzakis deals with the Gospel accounts directly, combining elements of mysticism with an extremely realistic treatment of the biblical characters to turn the Christ story upside down. The actors in the Gospel are humanized to a degree considered by some to be blasphemous; all are given human motives, not all of which are the highest, and the familiar characters of the Evangelists' accounts—Peter, Christ's mother Mary, Mary Magdalene, and especially Judas—are presented in a new light. The major episodes of the novel are based on biblical accounts, but these take on the particular philosophical cast that characterizes all of Kazantzakis' work: In the novel, each temptation that Jesus encounters is presented as a struggle in which the hero must choose between "flesh" and "spirit," between acquiescence to the tendencies to rest from the futile pursuit of human perfection and the drive toward self-fulfillment.

The plot of *The Last Temptation of Christ* loosely follows the Gospel stories. Structurally, the action is centered on a series of temptations, most of them drawn from the Gospels. The last temptation, which Jesus undergoes as he hangs on the Cross, is the ultimate test of his commitment to "spirit" over "flesh": For an instant, he imagines himself rescued from his fate, given the opportunity to live as other men, with a wife and children, and only through a heroic act of will does he overcome the temptation and accept his own death as part of his fate as Savior. The women in the novel, even Christ's mother, become temptations of the flesh. Mary wants her son first to disassociate himself from the Romans and later to give up the messianic folly that seems to be leading only to confrontation with the foreign powers; she constantly yearns for him to settle down to carpentry and fatherhood. When Jesus' special nature is reported to her, she says "I don't want my son to be a saint. . . . I want him to be a man like all the rest. I want him to marry and give me grandchildren. That is God's way."

Kazantzakis also expands the meaning of and challenges the accepted responses to the parables of the Gospels. For example, in recounting the story of the wise and foolish virgins, he remains close to his source until the end of the story. In Saint Matthew's account, the foolish virgins, who were out buying oil when the bridegroom arrived, returned saying, "Lord, Lord, open to us," to which the bridegroom replies, "Verily I say unto you, I know you not." Jesus then provides a moral for the tale: "Watch, therefore, for ye know neither the day nor the hour wherein the Son of Man cometh" (Matthew 25:11-13). In Kazantzakis' version, Jesus tells essentially the same story, up to the point at which the virgins return and beg entrance, dramatizing the plea of the maidens: "'Open the door! Open the door! Open the door!' and then . . . Jesus stopped. . . . He smiled. 'And then?' said Nathanael . . . 'And then, Rabbi? What was the outcome?'" Kazantzakis' Jesus provides no "moral." Instead, he asks his disciples to supply the answer. "'What would you have done, Nathanael?' Jesus asked, pinning his large, bewitching eyes on him, 'What would you have done if you had been the bridegroom?'" Jesus repeats the question, persisting in his stare, until Nathanael finally says, "I would have opened the door." Jesus replies, "Congratulations, friend Nathanael. . . . This moment, though you are alive you enter Paradise. The bridegroom did exactly as you said." Jesus is immediately challenged by the village chief, who screeches out, "You're going contrary to the Law, Son of Mary." Jesus answers him, "The Law goes contrary to my heart." For the reader who knows the source of the story in Matthew, this scene functions in a manner similar to the original Gospel accounts, but with an ironic twist: Now it is the traditional Gospels themselves that represent the "Old Law," which Kazantzakis' hero comes to challenge with a new gospel, founded even more firmly on human interaction and human sympathy than the message of Jesus as recorded by the Evangelists. In this approach, Kazantzakis is at his most daring theologically, and the captivating power of his art has prepared the reader to side with his hero and accept the new message of salvation: Men must help men if anyone is to attain paradise.

Nowhere is God's need of man made more apparent than in Kazantzakis' portrayal of Judas. Where the Evangelists have portrayed Iscariot as a weak, self-serving coward whose disillusionment with the Messiah led him to commit the crime of betrayal, Kazantzakis depicts Judas as a strong-willed zealot, filled first with the hope that Jesus will establish a political kingdom, then infused with faith that through the Crucifixion and Resurrection, God will accomplish His Messianic role. Kazantzakis' Judas is the strongest of the Apostles and the only one to whom Jesus directly reveals the way that salvation will be accomplished. Shortly before Christ's confrontation with the Sanhedrin and Pilate, he takes Judas aside and tells him, "I am the one who is going to die." When Judas appears confused and sees his dream of political rebellion slipping away, Jesus tells him "Take courage. . . . There is no other way; this is the road." To Judas, Jesus reveals the mystery of the Resurrection, because Judas is to play a key role in bringing it about. What Kazantzakis has seen in the Gospel story is a point that reinforces his own belief that God needs man: In order for Christ to be crucified and resurrected, he must first be betrayed. The betrayer, therefore, plays an all-important role in bringing about salvation, a role as important as that of the Messiah Himself. At first reading, such a reversal of character seems heretical, and in fact, Kazantzakis was seriously criticized by the Greek Orthodox bishops, who contemplated excommunicating him.

If one is able to approach this novel without prejudice, though, the author's achievements in characterization and exploration of theme will appear most remarkable. Kazantzakis' beliefs about the natures of man and of God are made most evident in the struggle of his hero, who *is* both God and man. His Christ is an unwilling savior. Presented first in a fantastical dream in which he sees himself pursued by a "tempter," Jesus is no heroic Messiah but rather a poor carpenter whose "mission" haunts him and prevents him from indulging in the pleasures of the flesh. One of his first acts is to build a cross upon which the Romans crucify a zealot, a member of the radical Jewish group working to overthrow Roman rule. At this crucifixion, Jesus is reviled by the crowd for assisting the occupation forces in their dirty work; even his mother is disturbed by his participation, and wants to rescue him from his association with the Romans. On the other hand, Kazantzakis' view of God as pure spirit is expressed by Jesus himself in his encounter with the woman at the well. "Where is God found? Enlighten me," she asks; Jesus replies, "God is spirit." Jesus' own ambivalence is highlighted in this scene, as the woman continues to question him: "'Can you be the One we're waiting for?' . . . Jesus leaned his head against his breast. He seemed to be listening to his heart, as though he expected it to give him the answer." The ambivalence of the Savior toward his own mission is made evident in other places as well.

For half the novel, Christ is a man pursued by a demon, a man whose every waking moment is a struggle between the flesh and the spirit. The drama of this pursuit is heightened for the reader by the constant confusion of the demon in Christ's mind with both God and the Devil; God and Christ seem to be at war with each other. He runs away from his home to escape the Tempter, only to find himself followed and harassed wherever he goes. He seeks refuge in a monastery, but is recognized by the dying abbot as the Savior and is thrust forward as the new abbot, a position he does not want. Always attracted by the prostitute Mary Magdalene, he seeks comfort at her home, but instead of losing himself in sensual gratification, he ends up leaving her, too, after engaging her in a discussion of his mission. Though others, notably the Apostles, flock to him because they recognize something in this young carpenter, Jesus himself only reluctantly accepts his role as Savior and even then is not free from the temptations of the world. Throughout his life, even when on the cross, the lures of "the flesh" are present to divert him from his redemptive mission.

The hero of *The Last Temptation of Christ* is both God and man, but throughout the novel, Kazantzakis emphasizes Jesus' humanity, often at the expense of the reader's preconceived concept of Christ's divine nature. Jesus feels the temptations of both the flesh and the intellect as fully as any character in a novel by Fyodor Dostoevski or D. H. Lawrence. He wrestles with a strong animal attraction for Mary Magdalene, desiring her body as much as he desires to save her soul. He runs from his mission as Savior because he recognizes the pain it will cause him; he wants to be like other men. In the end, however, he accepts his mission, gives in to God, and fulfills himself; spirit has won over flesh, and mankind is redeemed through the act of the hero. This is the ultimate message that Kazantzakis has for the reader in all of his novels.

Major publications other than long fiction

PLAYS: *Melissa*, 1939; *Kouros*, 1955; *Christophoros Kolomvos*, 1956; *Three Plays: Melissa, Kouros, Christopher Columbus*, 1969.

POETRY: *Odysseia*, 1938 (*The Odyssey: A Modern Sequel*, 1958); *Iliad*, 1955 (modern version, with Ioannis Kakridis); *Odysseia*, 1965 (modern version, with Ioannis Kakridis).

NONFICTION: *Salvatores Dei: Asketike*, 1927 (*The Saviors of God: Spiritual Exercises*, 1960); *Ispania*, 1937 (*Spain*, 1963); *Iaponia-Kina*, 1938 (*Japan/China*, 1963); *Anghlia*, 1941 (*England*, 1965); *Anaphora ston Greko*, 1961 (*Report to Greco*, 1965); *Ho Morias*, 1961 (serialized 1937; *Journey to the Morea*, 1965).

Bibliography

Bien, Peter. *Kazantzakis and the Linguistic Revolution in Greek Literature*, 1972.

_____ . *Nikos Kazantzakis*, 1972.

Durant, Will, and Ariel Durant. "Nikos Kazantzakis," in *Interpretations of Life*, 1976.

Journal of Modern Literature, II, no. 2 (Winter, 1971-1972). Special Kazantzakis issue.

Kazantzakis, Helen. *Nikos Kazantzakis: A Biography Based on His Letters*, 1968.

Laurence W. Mazzeno

GOTTFRIED KELLER

Born: Zurich, Switzerland; July 19, 1819
Died: Zurich, Switzerland; July 15, 1890

Principal long fiction

Der grüne Heinrich, 1854-1855, 1879-1880 (*Green Henry*, 1960); *Die Leute von Seldwyla*, 1856-1874 (2 volumes, novellas; *The People of Seldwyla and Seven Legends*, 1929, partial translation); *Züricher Novellen*, 1878 (novellas; *The Banner of the Upright Seven and Ursula*, 1974, partial translation); *Das Sinngedicht*, 1882 (novellas); *Martin Salander*, 1886 (English translation, 1964); *The Misused Love Letters*, 1974 (novellas).

Other literary forms

In addition to his novels and novellas, Gottfried Keller wrote some masterful lyric poems, published in the *Gedichte* (1846; poems) and *Neuere Gedichte* (1851; recent poems). He also wrote political, literary, and cultural essays, collected in volumes 21 and 22 of *Sämtliche Werke* (1926-1948; complete works). *Sieben Legenden* (1872; *Seven Legends*, 1911) is a delightful collection of stories based on Christian traditions but reflecting Keller's more worldly outlook. Keller also has produced autobiographical writings.

Achievements

Keller, a leading figure of poetic realism and considered by many the greatest Swiss writer of the nineteenth century, began his literary career in the 1840's with only modest outward success. Even at the publication of the second volume of *The People of Seldwyla* in 1874, only five hundred copies of the first volume had been sold. Not until after Friedrich Theodor Vischer, in that same year, published a favorable essay about Keller did the latter's work find a wider audience. After that his popularity grew rapidly, and today his novellas are regarded as one of the peaks in that art form. *Green Henry*, his *Bildungsroman* (novel of education), is generally thought to be the most important prose work of mid-century and is often compared to Johann Wolfgang von Goethe's *Wilhelm Meister's Lehrjahre* (1795-1796; *Wilhelm Meister's Apprenticeship*, 1824), by which Keller was influenced. Writing at a time when the effects of the Industrial Revolution were becoming evident, when the world was felt to be becoming more prosaic, positivistic, and ordinary, Keller nevertheless was able to suffuse his works with a sunny, worldly blessedness. Standing at that great moment in Western thought at which the Judeo-Christian tradition began to crumble, Keller represents the secular outlook of the coming age combined with a feeling of security and assurance that life is whole and chaos no serious threat. Much celebrated in his homeland, Keller's works have been translated into a number of languages.

Biography

Gottfried Keller spent most of his life in his native Zurich, where he was born into the family of a turner who died when Keller was five years old. The loss of his father had far-reaching and most unfortunate consequences for the imaginative boy's upbringing and education, even though his mother did the best she could for him, given her limited perspective and financial resources. What he lacked most was guidance and understanding. He attended an elementary school for poor children and then later the Cantonal Industrial School, from which he was expelled in 1834 for his part in a rather harmless student demonstration against an unpopular teacher. Thus, at a young age, he found himself with little chance for continued schooling and no particular prospects for the future.

He had been spending much of his spare time at home drawing and painting and announced that he wanted to become a painter. His mother arranged for him to take lessons in Zurich, and in 1840 he was able to leave for Munich to further his studies. In 1842, he returned home, apparently having accomplished little, unable to sell his paintings. In July of 1843, he recorded in his diary a strong desire to become a writer, a wish which he carried out by publishing political and other poetry, the first collection of which appeared in 1846. The Zurich government gave him in 1848 a stipend to enable him to attend lectures in Heidelberg, Germany. This proved to be a turning point in his life, for there he heard the atheist Ludwig Feuerbach, whose thoughts Keller welcomed as a release from the burden of the Christian past. Giving up his belief in personal immortality, Keller embraced a this-worldliness, a joy and celebration of life before death.

In 1850, he received a further stipend from the Zurich government that enabled him to go to Berlin to study theater. The Berlin years were fruitful ones, for there he finished the first version of *Green Henry*, the first volume of *The People of Seldwyla*, and planned other works. Upon returning to Zurich in 1855, he hoped to live from his writing, but this proved impossible, and he spent many days in depression and idleness. His financial worries were eased in 1861 when he allowed himself to be elected State Clerk for the Zurich Canton, an office he occupied with great conscientiousness until his retirement. The post provided not only the money but also the discipline he later needed to apply himself to his writing.

Although Keller felt attracted to several young women over the years, he was in matters of the heart quite shy, and given his rather odd appearance and small stature, around five feet tall, he had little success in love and remained a bachelor. His one engagement, in 1866, ended when Luise Scheidegger, his fiancée, committed suicide, ostensibly because of a negative article written about Keller. In friendship, Keller had similar, though somewhat better, luck. He was, however, not a close friend of any man or woman of his literary or cultural rank, although he did have some contact with the composer Richard Wagner and the architect Gottfried Semper. He avoided the other famous Swiss writer living in Zurich at the time, Conrad Ferdinand Meyer.

In his early years as State Clerk, Keller had neglected his fiction, but following his fiftieth birthday, which was celebrated by Zurich in a grand fashion, he once again took up his writing. In the next twelve years, he published four of his major works. After his retirement from office in 1876, he continued to live in Zurich but became more and more lonely, although his fame and popularity continued to grow. At his death in 1890, his funeral procession included the entire Zurich city government, the faculty of the University of Zurich, representatives from the Swiss national government and from all the large clubs in town, and large numbers of ordinary citizens from Switzerland and abroad.

Analysis

Gottfried Keller's prose sparkles with a robust, generous goodwill, a delightful irony, and a fertile imagination which were unexcelled in the second half of the nineteenth century in German. Although his literary settings are almost exclusively Swiss, he succeeded in giving them a significance and poignancy which saved him from being merely a regional writer. He did have a strongly didactic bent, but this rarely dominates a fiction which bubbles with rare warmth and luxuriates in concrete detail. The term "poetic realist" is particularly applicable to him since he was concerned with the boundary between the imaginary and the actual, appearance and reality.

In his fictive world, there is evil or, at least, human weakness and inconsistency, and these sometimes lead to tragedy, but taken as a whole, his writings exude faith in mankind and joy in life. This faith and joy manifest themselves most clearly in his humor, which Walter Benjamin says is as much at home in this world as Homer's was among the gods. It is a sovereign humor in which author and reader are able to see characters and situations bathed in a golden light of aesthetic enjoyment. Even when he exercises moral judgment over his characters, he still, as a poet, affirms them and refuses to give up on them entirely. Even though he believed in no life after death, he was not overwhelmed, as was his contemporary Theodor Storm, by the transitory and ephemeral quality of life. Drawing some of his optimism perhaps from faith in the democratic institutions of his homeland, he continued to insist on the worth of the human tragicomedy. Herein perhaps lies one of the reasons he has not won through to ultimate greatness. As Ernst Alker has suggested, he remains too much tied to the nineteenth century. In the twentieth century, the underlying tone has been one of threatened or real chaos. It was probably Storm, after all, with his brooding awareness of the vanity of existence, who presaged the coming age. Keller's humanism at its fullest, though based on the materialism espoused by Feuerbach, seeks, as Emil Ermatinger has noted, to be in touch with the ethics of Immanuel Kant and at the same time to take a joy in the senses as did Goethe. In the light of two world wars and under the threat of a third, even more horrible one, the twentieth century has had a difficult time sustaining that buoyancy.

In spite of this shortcoming, either in Keller or more likely in us, his works still have great appeal. This is true of the novel *Green Henry*, which exists in two versions and is clearly autobiographical. This *Bildungsroman* was first published in 1854-1855, written in first and third person. Keller rewrote it entirely in first person, changing the sequence to chronological, and reissued it in the authorized version of 1879-1880. The latter loses something in youthful freshness, but it gains in order and balance. Both versions are printed and read today, the later one being given preference and thus forming the basis for the following analysis.

Green Henry Lee gets his name from wearing almost exclusively green clothing, made from that of his father, who dies while Henry is still young. The father had been a successful stonemason, but, still, mother and son are left with the bare minimum of income. In a difficult childhood, which reflects Keller's own, Henry is sent first to a school for poor children, where he is one of the best dressed, and then to a middle school, where he cuts a much less imposing figure. In order to secure the pocket money that he feels he needs to keep up with his classmates and to prove his self-importance, he raids his savings bank. Upon discovering this, his mother is deeply troubled and wonders what is to become of him. She is unable to understand the rich imaginative gifts of a child who is regarded as taciturn and stubborn. His informal education, received in the home of a neighboring junk-and-antique dealer, speaks far more to his requirements. There he hears of human failure and exultation, of occult science, of gods and goddesses, and of a whole universe that somehow seems missing in his formal schooling. The conflict between Henry's fantasy and reality, a theme throughout the novel, causes the boy no end of troubles, finally resulting in his expulsion from school at age fourteen for taking part, mainly out of sheer exuberance, in a student demonstration.

Perplexed as to what to do with his life, he decides to become a landscape painter, a decision which he announces on a visit to his family's ancestral village. There he also feels the first stirrings of an ideal, ethereal love for Anna, daughter of a retired schoolmaster, and later the first, innocent rush of sexual desire for Judith, a young woman living in the village. The village is, in addition, the scene of his first acquaintance with the atheism of Ludwig Feuerbach, as propounded by a new, young village schoolmaster. Henry finds himself, as a result, opposed to Christianity and allows himself to be confirmed in the Church only to spare his mother's feelings.

His education as an artist is first undertaken by the hack Habersaat, from whom Henry learns little in two years, and next by the gifted Römer, who has studied painting in France and Italy and whose tutelage proves more fruitful. From reading the works of Goethe, Henry learns a love and appreciation for all that exists, an attitude he tries to incorporate into his painting. After Römer's departure for Paris, under circumstances that leave Henry feeling guilty, the latter sets out for Munich to further his studies, funded by a small inheritance from his father. Before he leaves, he witnesses the premature death of Anna and the departure of Judith for America.

In Munich, he becomes friends with the painters Lys and Erikson, both of whom eventually give up their art for a practical life, a course later followed by Henry. His art becomes more and more divorced from its Swiss roots, more abstract, until he is finally reduced to painting what looks like a giant spiderweb. He begins to attend lectures at the university, and he soon finds that he is more at home in discussion of history and philosophy, staying out late drinking, than he is among artists. He incurs debts, more than his self-sacrificing mother can send him money to pay, even though she mortgages her house.

A change of aspiration is indicated by his writing and having bound his autobiography, an act which exhausts his last money. He resorts, perhaps by divine inspiration, to selling his flute and finally his portfolio of drawings to a secondhand dealer. The death of his landlady reminds him of his old mother, from whom he has been away too long and who is pining to see him. Troubled by dreams, he sets out on foot for home but is soon sidetracked by a stay at the estate of Count Dietrich, who has bought his drawings from the junk dealer and who encourages Henry to do two more paintings, which are subsequently bought by his old friend, the now wealthy Erikson. In spite of the sale of the paintings and of his love for Dorothea, the adopted daughter of the Count, Henry once again sets out for home, determined to give up his career in art. He arrives home right before his mother's death. She is unable to speak, and he is filled with guilt at the thought of his neglect of her.

After her death, he sells the house, which, together with a inheritance he has received from the Munich junk dealer, leaves him enough money to live modestly but comfortably. Yet he is not satisfied, since he has done nothing to earn the money. His years have been spent in self-preoccupation, for which he feels the need to atone. A year later, he receives a governmental post and still later becomes Director of the Administrative District, tasks to which he applies himself with a quiet, selfless efficiency. Inwardly, he is, however, sad and at times longs for death, until Judith returns from America to become his loyal, though somewhat distant, friend.

Green Henry cannot truly be said to be a novel of the development of a young artist, for the result of his maturation is the abandoning of his art. It is more the story of the development of the social consciousness and responsibility of a whimsical, somewhat withdrawn and slightly selfish young man who is not without charm. The strength of the novel lies not only in Henry's education to responsibility, for this theme is submerged for long stretches, but also in the texture, atmosphere, and incident which Keller creates along the way. The plethora of richly imagined minor characters, the brilliance in choice of descriptive detail, both of landscape and of people, lend to the work an air of festiveness. It is, in the words of Roy Pascal, a novel "thronging with things, with material, psychological and social reality." In spite of its flaws of digression and a rather abstract ending, *Green Henry* remains the most important novel of mid-century in German.

Keller's next published work, in 1856, was the first volume of the cycle of novellas *The People of Seldwyla*, which is loosely held together by a frame. Seldwyla is an imaginary small town in which colorful, farcical characters live out their days in often self-deluded bliss. Although each novella can stand on its own, together they leave the impression of a human comedy of epic proportions, far exceeding the boundaries of small-town Switzerland. The novella from this cycle which has received the most critical attention is *Romeo und Julia auf dem Dorfe* (*A Village Romeo and Juliet*). Although it did not catch on when first published, in the years following 1874 it became hugely popular and has been a part of the standard German canon ever since. Based on a newspaper account of a drowned couple who had apparently spent the night floating downstream on a hay barge, Keller is able to relate the event to both William Shakespeare and the Swiss locale.

The novella opens in a scene of pastoral tranquillity. Two landed farmers, by a village close to Seldwyla, are plowing their fields, which lie on opposite sides of an abandoned one. Their meal is brought to them by their children, the seven-year-old son, Sali Manz, and the five-year-old daughter, Vrenchen Marti. The children play on the overgrown, rocky middle field, which is encroached on by the fathers as each continues plowing past his own boundary line and cultivates a section of the abandoned one. Every year the middle field becomes smaller, more filled with stones, and wilder. The fathers' greed causes the emerging love of their children to fall on stony ground, for when the field is finally auctioned off, a dispute arises between Manz, who buys the field, and Marti, who still claims an irregular section of it. They become bitter enemies, using every legal means to get back at each other, a quarrel that ultimately leads to the impoverishment of both. Their greed for land, of which Keller is more than a little critical, has been grist for the mill of Marxist critics in condemning the entire capitalist system, though Keller himself did not intend to go so far.

The farmers' children, Sali and Vrenchen, still feel an affection for each other which comes to the fore as the raging fathers confront each other, years later, across a wooden footbridge. In physically separating their fathers, Sali and Vrenchen touch hands in a flash of tenderness. The novella pivots on this incident, moving from focusing primarily on the farmers to focusing on their children. Sali, who is living with his family in Seldwyla after they have lost their farm, goes out to the village on the day after the bridge incident in order to find Vrenchen. He finds her at Marti's run-down house, and together they go to the field where they had played as children. Their happiness is disturbed, first by the Black Fiddler, to whom the field rightly belongs and who has been betrayed by their fathers, then by Vrenchen's father, who mistreats Vrenchen for being with Sali. Their tragic fate is conclusively sealed when Sali deals Marti a blow to the head with a rock. The old man becomes an imbecile and has to be institutionalized.

No permanent relationship is possible for Vrenchen and Sali now, but since Vrenchen must leave her father's farm because of a lost court case, the two decide to spend one day together and enjoy one small corner of happiness. In the face of a depressing reality, they give rein to their imaginations in order to claim a moment of innocence. Decked out in his best, Sali comes to her on a Sunday, bringing her a pair of shoes he has bought by selling his watch. Looking like a bridal couple, they set out for a neighboring village where they eat and buy each other gifts at a fair. Because they do not fit in with the villagers at the fair, who recognize them and their strange situation, they take refuge among the vagabonds and homeless who accompany the Black Fiddler to a remote forest inn, the Paradise Garden, where they are joined in mock matrimony as performed by this strange musician. Robbed of his rightful inheritance by the couple's fathers, the Black Fiddler is permitted to see the sad result of a love that has no place in the village and yet is too innocent and pure to remain a part of the wayward and loose life of the Fiddler's friends.

With their passions spurred on by the wild and reckless company, Sali and Vrenchen set out in the direction of the village. They pass by the river which runs by the cursed field and find there a hay barge which they loose from its moorings and make their bridal bed. Floating along with the stream, between dark forests, past villages and cottages, they slip, toward morning and while still embracing, down into the cold river.

A Village Romeo and Juliet shows some of the most negative sides of the Seldwylars and their neighbors: the desire for quick and easy gain, the grotesque comedy of two settled farmers making themselves ludicrous, the slightly good-for-nothing Seldwylars, who enjoy the spectacle a little too much. Set against this is the beauty and loyalty of the children's love and the life that might have been had not reality collided with imagination.

Die drei gerechten kammacher (*The Three Righteous Combmakers*), also from the first volume of *The People of Seldwyla*, represents a heightening of Keller's grotesque humor. Three combmakers—Jobst, Fridolin, and Dietrich—employed in a shop in Seldwyla, all have the ambition to buy the shop and become the master. This seems attainable to them, for all the previous masters—as typical Seldwylars—have wasted their time, have lived off their workmen, and after a few years, have sold out and moved on. The three combmakers are "righteous" in that they never bother anyone, save every penny they get their hands on, work like proverbial beavers, even nights and Sundays, sleep like three herrings in a double bed, and pursue their goal of ownership with a quiet, desperate intensity.

Dietrich, the youngest, is somewhat at a disadvantage, since he has no savings, but he attempts to remedy this by courting the twenty-eight-year-old maiden, Züs Bünzlin, who has inherited a bond worth seven hundred guilder. In addition, she is the proud owner of a painted chest filled with the oddest assortment of objects. Keller's ever-fertile imagination runs rampant here and leaves the reader with the impression that Züs must be a strange creature, as indeed she is, full of egotism and of a domineering spirit. Soon all three combmakers are her suitors and are much edified by her pseudowise admonitions. A choice in favor of one of the combmakers is forced by the intention of the master to dismiss two of them. It is decided that the three of them will leave and go a certain distance from town. The first one to return to the shop will be the one who stays and also, Züs decides, the lucky one who may have her hand in marriage.

Once they are outside the town, Züs reassures them one more time what a prize she will be, and then they are off and running. That is, Jobst and Fridolin are off and running, but Dietrich stays behind with Züs, who attempts to keep him from competing. As the other two approach their goal, they become entangled in a running fight with each other, much to the amusement of the Seldwylars, who are making a holiday of the desperation race. In a scene of high and grotesque tragicomedy, Jobst and Fridolin lose all sense of place and direction as they wrestle past the master's house and on out the opposite city gate. The next day, when they realize what fools they have made of themselves, Jobst hangs himself and Fridolin changes his whole life-style for the worse.

Dietrich is the winner, since he had stayed behind with Züs and, in a thicket into which she had lured him, had conquered the shallow and self-infatuated young lady in every way. Later he arrives at his master's house with his bride-to-be. They marry and buy out the master, but Dietrich lives to regret it, for Züs's tyrannical nature gives him no peace. As with the farmers in *A Village Romeo and Juliet*, too great concentration on material wealth and too little generosity of spirit lead to ludicrous caricatures of human life.

The second volume of *The People of Seldwyla* appeared in 1874 and contained the entertaining farce of the tailor who is mistaken for a Polish count, *Kleider machen Leute* (*Clothes Make the Man*). Wenzel Strapinski has lost his job in a tailor shop in Seldwyla, and although he is literally penniless, cold, hungry, and going by foot to Goldach, he is nevertheless very well clothed in a dark gray cycling cape and a Polish fur cap. On the way, he encounters an empty but new and comfortable coach, whose driver asks Strapinski if he would like a ride, which he accepts. Upon arrival in front of an inn in Goldach, Strapinski is mistaken by the innkeeper for a person of high rank and practically forced into the restaurant and served a fancy meal. All kinds of fanciful and humorous contortions by the innkeeper and his staff in their attempt to meet Strapinski's every surmised wish allow Keller to castigate all of those who grovel and toady before slick appearances.

Before the coachman leaves, he, being a mischievous fellow, tells the inn staff that Wenzel is Count Strapinski from Poland. They and the other Goldachers believe this, shower Strapinski with favors, and draw him into their midst. Strapinski, though essentially innocent, allows himself to participate in this charade and even falls in love with Nettchen, daughter of a local official. The only doubter in Goldach is Melcher Böhni, a bookkeeper and Strapinski's rival for Nettchen. Böhni notices Strapinski's pricked fingers and suspects something, but allows matters to take their course, in the hope of an even larger blowup later on. This he intends to achieve at the betrothal celebration of Wenzel and Nettchen, which is to take place at the beginning of Lent in late-winter snowy weather, at an inn two hours away, halfway between Goldach and Seldwyla. Very calculating in the way he proceeds, Böhni recruits the Seldwylars for his plan, has them act out, using masks, a play in which a tailor-count appears, then stands before the engaged couple and reveals Strapinski's secret by calling on the Seldwylars to come and greet their former acquaintance. Even Strapinski's master from Seldwyla is there and shakes his hand heartily.

Events at this point almost turn from sad to tragic. Strapinski walks out through the crowd and into the snowy night and, taking the road toward Seldwyla, he soon disappears in the forest. Tormented by his thoughts, he lies down in the snow and falls asleep. Nettchen, desiring to speak one more word with him, sets out by sleigh to find him and does so. She saves his life by taking him to a nearby farmhouse, where he tells her his story, from which she recognizes his honorable intentions and good heart, even if he is not a nobleman. She is herself a person of strength and loyalty, and his story awakens again her love for him. They go together that night to Seldwyla, where on the next day Nettchen declares her desire to marry Strapinski, which she does. Using the sizable inheritance she has from her mother, she and Strapinski open a fabric shop in Seldwyla and are so successful that after ten or twelve years they are able to double her inheritance and move to Goldach with their ten or twelve children. Strapinski becomes a respected citizen of Goldach, but he does not leave one penny behind in Seldwyla.

The ending, so different from *A Village Romeo and Juliet*, puts the petty and fawning Seldwylars and Goldachers in their place, yet Keller does it with such magnanimity that even thoroughgoing villains such as Melcher Böhni are somehow forgivable and even pitiable in their malevolence. There is room in Keller's universe for a whole host of characters. Determining who is respectable and who is not, however, takes close observation. The theme of appearance and reality, of imagination and fact, is woven into this story in such a way that the Goldachers, though wrong in mistaking Strapinski for a nobleman, are right insofar as he has a basically noble soul.

Keller's novel *Martin Salander*, published in 1886, continues the theme of appearance and reality, but with less success. Generally regarded as dry, overly didactic, and lacking tension, the novel does not share the redemptive humor that pervades Keller's work at its best. In its disillusionment and pessimism, *Martin Salander* represents the aged Keller's resignation and his anxiety for the future of his country. Beginning it in 1881, Keller put the work aside for a while for fear that if published then, it would be seen as a political pamphlet. Keller himself had reservations about the novel and would have given up on it had it not already been announced. Since Keller's time, it has, in fact, been seen as a political statement but with differing interpretations. The National Socialists claimed that Keller had thereby renounced his faith in democracy, whereas the Marxist critic Georg Lukács takes the view that the novel indicates that, after the respite given by the successful revision of the Swiss constitution in 1848, capitalist greed was once again beginning to choke Swiss freedom.

The work opens as Martin Salander, returning to his native Münsterburg from Brazil after a seven-year absence, meets Möni Wighart, an old friend, and learns from him that the Swiss bank to which Salander had sent his funds from Brazil is insolvent and owned by the devious Louis Wohlwend,who seven years before had caused Salander to lose his sizable fortune. Now three-quarters of the money he had made in the seven years in Brazil is lost to him through the Swiss bank's insolvency and the concurrent failure of the corresponding bank in Rio de Janeiro. The sacrifices made in his absence by Salander's wife and three children have largely been in vain. Nevertheless, Salander returns once more to the New World to try to recover his money or make more. A former teacher and for some years now a businessman, Salander is able in three years to recoup his losses, and he returns to Switzerland and becomes active in local politics as an ardent democrat.

The Salander family settles into a comfortable, middle-class existence, freed from the unscrupulous Wohlwend, who has now gone to Hungary, where he has married the daughter of a rich swine dealer. Salander's two daughters, Setti and Netti, who are now in their twenties, are courted in secret by the superficial, silly Weidelich twins, Julian and Isidor, who are also interested in politics and make their choice of party by the roll of the dice. After the courtship is discovered, the girls are forbidden to see the twins. The boys' father is a simple, quiet gardener, but their mother, Amalie, has all sorts of pretentious ambitions for them, even though the boys are not particularly bright and lack all character and soul. Given the climate of the day, however, the twins succeed in becoming notaries, with their own offices and homes, and are soon, through sheer cunning, elected to the Cantonal Parliament. At this point, Mr. and Mrs. Salander reluctantly give their consent to the marriage of Netti and Setti to the twins. The double ceremony is celebrated largely out-of-doors in the manner of a folk festival, in keeping with Martin's democratic sentiments. The event is so popular that Martin himself is elected to the Cantonal Parliament, where he proves to be a conscientious and hard-working public servant, while his sons-in-law, who are so alike they can only be told apart by their earlobes, continue to play fast and loose with their public trusts.

In private life, the twins turn out, as Salander and his wife have feared, to be egotistical, narrow, and insensitive to their wives' needs and wishes. Their homes give the appearance of success and tranquillity, but Netti and Setti are miserable, and, in their shame, avoid each other and their parents. Even after the Salanders find out about their daughters' unhappiness, there seems to be no legitimate reason for asking for a divorce, until the twins are accused of misappropriation of funds, convicted, and sentenced to twelve years in prison. Their mother, who wanted so much to see them climb socially, suffers a fatal collapse at hearing the news, and their father is saved from near-bankruptcy only when Salander pays the large bond for which Mr. Weidelich was responsible as a result of his sons' crimes. The twins' conviction is only one of the rash embezzlements at the time. All of this makes Salander wonder about the future of his country.

In the meantime, Louis Wohlwend is back in town with his Hungarian family, which includes a beautiful, unmarried, and unintelligent sister-in-law, through whom he hopes to reattach himself to Martin Salander. Wohlwend begins by appearing at Salander's office and offering to pay off, in five-thousand-franc yearly installments, the original amount Salander lost through him. Martin is almost taken in again when he accepts the money, becomes acquainted with Wohlwend's family, and begins to feel an infatuation for the sister-in-law. He is saved by the return of his son, Arnold, who has been away for years, first studying law, then living in London, Paris, and Brazil. Arnold has come home to participate in the family business. He quickly recognizes the beauty for the simpleton she is and foils Wohlwend's plans. Wohlwend and family are last seen boarding a train leaving his homeland.

What kind of future faces the Salanders and Switzerland? Netti and Setti are back home and comfortably settled, and Arnold is back, so prospects for the family look good. Martin also has reason to hope for his country as well, for in spite of so many recent betrayals of trust and evidences of greed, there appears to be in Arnold and his circle of friends a moderation, sophistication, and integrity that bode well for the future. Thus, the novel ends on what some critics have called a forced note of confidence. Keller's plan to write a sequel focusing on Arnold Salander was never realized.

Major publications other than long fiction

SHORT FICTION: *Sieben Legenden*, 1872 (*Seven Legends*, 1911); *Nachgelassene Erzählungen*, 1946.

POETRY: *Gedichte*, 1846; *Neuere Gedichte*, 1851.

NONFICTION: *Autobiographien*, 1947; *Gesammelte Briefe*, 1950-1954.

MISCELLANEOUS: *Sämtliche Werke*, 1926-1948 (22 volumes).

Bibliography

Bernd, Clifford A. *German Poetic Realism*, 1981.

Boeschenstein, Hermann. *German Literature of the Nineteenth Century*, 1969.

Breitenbruch, Bernd. *Gottfried Keller in Selbstzeugnissen und Bilddokumenten*, 1968.

Hauch, Edward. *Gottfried Keller as a Democratic Idealist*, 1916.

Lindsay, James M. *Gottfried Keller: Life and Works*, 1968.

Pascal, Roy. *The German Novel*, 1956.

Reichert, Herbert. *Basic Concepts in the Philosophy of Gottfried Keller*, 1949.

Thomas P. Baldwin

YASHAR KEMAL
Yaşar Kemal Gökçeli

Born: Adana, Turkey; 1922

Principal long fiction

İnce Memed, 1955 (Memed, My Hawk, 1961); Teneke, 1955 (novella; English translation in Anatolian Tales, 1968); Ortadirek, 1960 (The Wind from the Plain, 1963); Yer demir, gök bakir, 1963 (Iron Earth, Copper Sky, 1974); Ölmez otu, 1968 (The Undying Grass, 1977); İnce Memed II, 1969 (They Burn the Thistles, 1973); Ağrıdağsı efsanesi, 1970 (The Legend of Ararat, 1975); Binboğalar efsanesi, 1971 (The Legend of the Thousand Bulls, 1976); Çakircali efe, 1972; Akçasazın Ağaları, 1973-1975 (The Lords of Akchasaz; includes Demirciler çarşısı cinayeti, 1973 [Murder in the Ironsmiths Market, 1979]; Yusufouk Yusuf, 1975); Al gözüm seyreyle Salih, 1976 (Seagull, 1981); Yilani öldürseler, 1976; Kuşlar da gitti, 1978; Deniz küstü, 1979.

Other literary forms

A prolific author, Yashar Kemal has also published collections of journalism, essays, and short stories. His reportage appeared in Yanan ormanlarda 50 gun (1955; fifty days in burning forests), Çukurova yana yana (1955; the Chukurova up in flames), and Peri bacaları (1957; fairy chimneys); these works were consolidated in Bu dijar baştan başa (1972). Further collections of journalism are Bir bulut kayniyor (1974) and Allahin askerleri (1978). Kemal's essays appeared in Taş çatlasa (1961) and Baldaki tuz (1974). His short stories have been collected in Sarı sıcak (1952), Üç anadolu efsanesi (1967; three Anatolian legends), and Bütün hikâyeler (1967; Anatolian Tales, 1968). An enlarged edition of Bütün hikâyeler was published in 1975.

Other writings include poetry and folklore material contributed to Turkish periodicals. Kemal's first work was a collection of folk elegies, Ağıtlar (1943), and he has also turned some of the folk material into screenplays. In addition, Kemal created stage versions of his novella Teneke (in 1965) and the novel Iron Earth, Copper Sky (in 1966).

Achievements

Yashar Kemal has often been called Turkey's foremost novelist, but such praise has problematical value in a country with no tradition in the novel. For models, Kemal has sometimes had to look abroad; in particular, he is an admirer of William Faulkner, but in his best work Kemal's imagistic description, narration of action, and tough-minded attitude are more reminiscent of Ernest Hemingway. Like Hemingway, Kemal began as a newspaper reporter, and his novels show the influence of his reportage, especially in their documentation of local color. Perhaps the most important influence on Kemal, however, has been the native tradition of songs, legends, and other folklore. In Turkey, plagued by illiteracy, the oral tradition has remained strong, especially in rural areas, and as a child Kemal imbibed this tradition from village minstrels and storytellers.

Kemal's work reveals the strengths and weaknesses suggested by his background. His original forte was the genre called the "Village Novel," exemplified by the early novels *Memed, My Hawk* and *The Wind from the Plain*, which provide fascinating glimpses into the lives and minds of Anatolian peasants. As Kemal repeated himself and grew further away from village life and legend, he was faced with the need to develop. In the 1970's, he branched out into new forms and transferred his political attitudes to new settings, but his recent efforts have not equaled his original success. The later novel *Seagull*, for example, is a monument of sentimentality, confusion, and dullness. Whether Kemal will work out his problems remains to be seen, inasmuch as he is still a practicing novelist.

Biography

Yashar Kemal is the Anglicized form of Yaşar Kemal; the author's full name is Yaşar Kemal Gökçeli. His parents were Sadik and Nigar Gökçeli, descendants of landlords and brigands, respectively. Kemal grew up in the region of Turkey featured in his early novels, the Taurus Mountains and the coastal plain (the Chukurova) around Adana, and he personally experienced the conditions about which he writes. At the age of five, he witnessed his praying father's murder in a mosque. In the same attack, one of young Kemal's eyes was put out, and he had a severe stutter for years afterward. His stutter temporarily disappeared only when he sang, an activity at which he excelled, sometimes improvising his own songs.

There was no school in young Kemal's small village, Hemite, so at the age of nine, he began walking to the neighboring village to attend a three-class school. Later, he stayed with relatives in Kadirli, where he completed primary school and two years of secondary school (equivalent to the eighth grade) before he had to start working. He held numerous jobs—farm laborer, construction worker, factory worker, clerk, substitute teacher—but was driven out of them by the powerful landowners, the Aghas, who labeled him a Communist because he openly criticized the rural tenant-landlord system. When he became a public letter writer (a respectable type of employment in countries where most people cannot read or write and so need help with correspondence), the harassment intensified: In 1950, he was charged with disseminating Communist propaganda and was thrown in jail, where an attempt was made on his life. Although acquitted in a trial, Kemal continued to be persecuted by landowners and police. Finally, in 1951, he fled to Istanbul.

In Instanbul, he shortened his name to Yaşar Kemal, to avoid detection, and began writing for *Cumhuriyet*, a leading daily newspaper. His journalism—reports, feature stories, travel pieces—soon caught on, and so did his short fiction. His first novel, *Memed, My Hawk*, won the 1956 Varlik Prize. His growing public esteem, which eventually became international, insulated him somewhat from persecution but also infuriated his right-wing enemies. As a continuing critic of the landowning system and a leader of the Turkish Labor Party, Kemal has been imprisoned several times for his political views, most notably in 1966 and 1971.

On the domestic side, Kemal married Thilda Serrero in 1952; they have one son, Rasit. Thilda has translated a number of Kemal's books into English. Kemal stopped writing for *Cumhuriyet* in 1963 in order to spend his time on politics and writing fiction.

Analysis

Whatever political and literary sophistication Yashar Kemal has achieved since becoming a writer, his fiction grows essentially out of his village background. Until the 1970's, he specialized in Village Novels showing the brutal conditions of peasants in the Adana region where he grew up—the Taurus Mountains and the Chukurova. In the 1970's, Kemal moved on from the Village Novel to legendary tales and to novels set in the Istanbul area. Yet the legends were ones Kemal had heard as a child, and the Istanbul novels reflect political attitudes Kemal began forming based on what he saw of village life, particularly from the archetypal relationship of tenant and landlord.

Kemal's special achievement is his depiction of what could be called the peasant mentality, which prevails even in his later works. His picture of a small-minded, vindictive peasantry might distress some Marxist intellectuals, but Kemal clearly connects the peasant mentality and the peasants' condition. In Kemal, the Turkish peasants are victimized by an appalling range of scourges which include the weather, hunger, hard labor, ignorance, superstition, disease, green flies, landlords, and one another.

Among the few things which the peasant has to fall back on is the close-knit structure of family and village life. This structure, however, is based not so much on love as on dependency and familiarity, often manifested in some vicious form—gossip, grudges, backbiting, spite, quarreling. Feuding keeps the family going, and cursing develops verbal skills (an admonition to children is "Eat poison!"). Emotional displays, including tantrums and fainting spells, are the order of the day.

Another outlet for the peasant is his imagination. Within his imagination, the peasant can daydream and fantasize, can satisfy his wishes and right wrongs. One happy result of such imagination is vigorous folk art—songs, designs on knitted socks, stories, and legends. One of the unhappy results is superstition—belief in jinn, peris, folk cures, holy trees. Perhaps religious belief also fits in here, considering that among Kemal's peasants it so often leads to passive acceptance or fatalism—the attitude that whatever happens must have been decreed by Allah. Yet the work of the imagination does not necessarily inspire inaction, for the songs and legends sometimes speak out against oppression and glorify rebels. A favorite fantasy is the revenge fantasy, which calls for revenge on a personal basis and is frequently directed at the landlord or *muhtar* (village leader).

The revenge motif looms large in Kemal's first and most popular novel, *Med, My Hawk*. The story of *Memed, My Hawk* begins in the isolated little world of Dikenli, the Plateau of Thistles, where cluster the five villages owned by Abdi Agha. In the largest village, Deyirmenoluk, live both the Agha and the boy Memed, a tenant whose father is dead and who must work like a man to support his mother, Deuneh. All day long Memed plows the fields of thistles, which leave his legs bloody, and endures the unmerciful beatings of the Agha. When he is eleven, Memed runs away across the mountain but is eventually discovered and driven back home by the Agha on horseback. Thereafter, the Agha bears down harder: He takes three-fourths instead of the customary two-thirds from Memed and Deuneh's yearly harvest. Thus, Memed and his mother have even less to live on than the other tenants, who regularly starve in the winter. So it goes, Memed laboring mostly for the Agha and growing up stunted but bitter and tough as a mountain oak. Still, Memed finds some happiness in the arms of Hatche, his sweetheart since childhood.

The turning point comes when Abdi Agha tries to force Hatche to marry his nephew Veli. Memed and Hatche elope and are pursued by the Agha's gang. In a shootout, Memed kills Veli, wounds Abdi Agha, and then escapes, but Hatche is captured. Thereafter, unfairly charged with Veli's death, Hatche languishes in a terrible Turkish jail, while Memed pursues a life of brigandage. Memed also pursues Abdi Agha, who, after stomping Deuneh into the mud (she eventually dies from the beatings), fears increasingly for his own life. Memed pursues him into the Chukurova and burns a whole village around him, but the Agha miraculously escapes—only to deteriorate further psychologically. Meanwhile, Memed recues Hatche, distributes the Agha's land to the villagers, and earns a fabulous reputation for his daring exploits and generosity toward poor people. As Memed's reputation grows, so does the Agha's paranoia. Finally, when Abdi Agha's hirelings kill Hatche, Memed rides straight into town, marches upstairs in the Agha's house, and shoots the quivering Agha. Then Memed rides off into legend.

Despite Memed's disappearance into legend, the novel has a suspiciously autobiographical cast. The reader here may be sharing one of the author's youthful fantasies—Kemal identifying with his hero and seeing himself as a sort of Robin Hood figure. With one eye missing, Kemal certainly looks enough like a brigand. In any event, *Memed, My Hawk* is full of realistic details of village life and landscape, such as the fields of thistles which, in a symbolic act of liberation, are burned at the end. Like his hero, Kemal grew up fatherless, and he no doubt heard inspiring tales from his own mother, who was descended from a family of brigands.

The political implications of brigandage in *Memed, My Hawk* are fairly clear. In a society where the law merely legitimates organized violence against the peasantry, large numbers of peasants are driven by desperation outside the law. Most of them join the brigands, who constitute a social underground. Morally, the brigands are no better than the Aghas, with whom they sometimes hire out and form political alliances, but at least they are free and empowered, as symbolized by their colorful dress bristling with daggers, cartridge belts, and grenades. They attain moral legitimacy only by following the path of Memed, turning their violence against the Aghas and becoming, in effect, guerrillas. ("Slim Memed," by the way, does not actually disappear into legend forever; he returns in a sequel, *They Burn the Thistles*, to help oppressed peasants quell another mean, greedy Agha.)

The main fault of *Memed, My Hawk* is the slightly rough mixing of legendary and realistic levels, resulting in some uneven narration and characterization. Kemal's next novel, *The Wind from the Plain*, does not have such unevenness; it is unrelentingly realistic throughout. It details the annual migration of Anatolian villagers across the Taurus Mountains to the Chukurova, where they hope to pick cotton and thereby earn enough to keep going for another year. The story would be utterly depressing if the villagers' disasters did not sometimes lead to black, bitter humor.

When the villagers migrate, the whole village goes along—animals, pots and pans, the sick and old. The migration is a ritual demonstration of village solidarity, perhaps, or a return to an ancestral nomadic existence, but it is also a motley scene with its basis more in custom than in common sense. Any solidarity is only on the surface, because the migration exacerbates old frictions into inflamed sores. The villagers are trying to rebel against the *muhtar*, who is plotting as usual to sell their labor cheap in return for a fat bribe. Dredging up grudges from many years before, an old couple (who are not related but know each other well) squabble over who will ride a decrepit horse—until the horse falls dead. The old woman, Meryemdji, then spitefully blames her son, Long Ali, to whom she refuses to speak (instead, she addresses rocks or trees) and who has to travel the road three times (once in carrying his goods forward, and twice in returning to pick up the old woman and then carrying her forward, too). Scattered along the road and fearing they will be late for the harvest, Long Ali and his family fall several days behind the other villagers. When they finally come upon the others in the Chukurova, they discover that the whole village is late, that the rebellion has failed, and that the *muhtar* has sold them out to a cotton field full of weeds. Thus the novel ends, in total frustration for the villagers. (*The Wind from the Plain* is the first novel of a trilogy, followed by *Iron Earth, Copper Sky* and *The Undying*

Grass; the full trilogy shows, among other things, a much better cotton harvest the next year and scores being settled with the *muhtar*.)

A similar theme of frustration marks *Seagull*, an example of Kemal's later work. In arriving at the theme, readers of *Seagull* will likely experience frustrations of their own, since Kemal experiments unsucessfully with fictional techniques such as flashback, interior monologue, and limited point of view. In the best Faulknerian manner, *Seagull* is narrated from the point of view of an eleven-year-old boy, Salih, but Kemal violates that point of view by including sexual, political, and social satire beyond the boy's understanding. Worse, it is sometimes difficult to distinguish the present from flashbacks or the boy's juvenile fantasies from what is really happening. Such confusion could be rationalized on the theory that technique recapitulates theme; unfortunately, here technique recapitulates tedium. Either Kemal does not know eleven-year-old boys or this particular eleven-year-old boy is not all that interesting. Either way, Kemal's efforts to create a Turkish "New Wave" drown the reader in sentimentality and dullness.

Yet, on a symbolic level, Salih's story is highly revealing. He lives in an unnamed Black Sea coastal town, relatively prosperous, which caters to tourists and supplies fish and smuggled goods to Istanbul. Salih's family, however, does not share in the prosperity: His father is an alchoholic, a gambler, and a beater of wife and children, and the family exists on the earnings of Salih's mother, sister, and grandmother, who weave all day on shuttles in the home. Salih clashes constantly with his grandmother, who is embittered because her husband, Halil, left forty years before (she still meets every ship in the hope that he will return). To escape this family situation, Salih wanders about the town (he cannot afford school), watching the blacksmith and the fishing boats, helping Skipper Temel, playing with other boys, and fantasizing about his neighbor Metin (a dashing smuggler) or the snake boy. The snake boy—a boy in a huge snake's body—is an unhappy prince who kills his playmates and, later, loves his wives to death, until he meets a compatible mermaid.

Identifying with animals, especially birds, which are slaughtered for fun by the town's hunters, Salih finds his soulmate in a baby seagull with a broken wing. Told by everyone that wounded seagulls invariably die, Salih nevertheless cares for the chick and, with Skipper Temel's help, cures the broken wing. His grandmother, who had smugly predicted the bird's death, is infuriated by its recovery, especially when it actually flies. In turn, Salih's happiness is brief. For innocently wearing a Che Guevara T-shirt that a tourist gave him, Salih is beaten within an inch of his life by three teenagers, self-styled "Turkish commandos." In addition, his hero Metin is killed, which causes his grandmother to gloat. Salih taunts her back when his father joins the smugglers and leaves home: Salih announces his intentions to leave and never return, like his father, like his grandfather Halil. Enraged, the grandmother first tries to choke Salih, then twists off the head of his seagull and, still squeezing the bloody bird, dances frenziedly about the garden—like a whirling dervish—until she crumples to the ground. Salih ends up not leaving home: He misses Skipper Temel's boat to Istanbul and instead becomes the blacksmith's apprentice.

As unsuccessful as *Seagull* is on the literal level, the novel's images sum up Kemal's message about Turkey. In the same way that James Joyce thought Ireland was an old sow which devoured its own litter, so Kemal depicts Turkey as a wounded bird (birds frequently have symbolic or metaphorical meaning in Kemal's works, as in the translated title *Memed, My Hawk*, from an epithet in the novel). Despite valiant efforts to achieve a modern democracy, Turkey still struggles against the cruel legacy of the Ottoman Empire, "the Sick Man of Europe." As Kemal's novels show, the old social structures, the old ways, the old frustrations hang on tenaciously, forming a self-perpetuating cycle. As soon as some young fellow cures the bird, enabling it to fly, along comes an old grandmother to wring its neck.

Major publications other than long fiction

SHORT FICTION: *Sarı sıcak*, 1952; *Bütün hikâyeler*, 1967, enlarged, 1975 (*Anatolian Tales*, 1968; includes *Teneke*); *Üç anadolu efsanesi*, 1967.

PLAYS: *Teneke*, 1965; *Yer demir, gök bakir*, 1966.

POETRY: *Ağitlar*, 1943.

NONFICTION: *Çukurova yana yana*, 1955; *Yanan ormanlarda 50 gun*, 1955; *Peri bacaları*, 1957; *Taş çatlasa*, 1961; *Bu dijar baştan başa*, 1972; *Baldaki tuz*, 1974; *Bir bulut kayniyor*, 1974; *Allahin askerleri*, 1978.

CHILDREN'S LITERATURE: *Filler sultani ile kirmizki sakalli topal karinca*, 1977.

Bibliography

Halman, Talat Sait. "Tamberlaine Country," in *The Times Literary Supplement*. No. 3765 (May 3, 1974), p. 465.

_____ . "World Literature in Review: *Kuşlar da gitti*," in *World Literature Today*. LII, no. 4 (Autumn, 1978), p. 689.

_____ . "World Literature in Review: *The Undying Grass*," in *World Literature Today*. LI, no. 4 (Autumn, 1977), pp. 676-677.

_____ . "World Literature in Review: *The Wind from the Plain*," in *Books Abroad*. XLIV, no. 1 (Winter, 1970), pp. 181-182.

Pollitt, Katha. "Turkish Trouble," in *The New York Times Book Review*. LXXIX (June 18, 1978), pp. 14, 37.

Theroux, Paul. "Turkish Delight," in *The New York Times Book Review*. LXXVII (July 10, 1977), pp. 11, 40.

Thwaite, Anthony. "Turkish Delights," in *The New York Times Book Review*. LXXXI (August 19, 1979), pp. 13, 21.

Harold Branam

TADEUSZ KONWICKI

Born: Nowa Wilejka, Poland; June 22, 1926

Principal long fiction

Władza, 1954; *Z oblężonego miasta*, 1956; *Rojsty*, 1956; *Dziura w niebie*, 1959; *Sennik współczesny*, 1963 (*A Dreambook for Our Time*, 1969); *Wniebowstąpienie*, 1967; *Zwierzoczłekoupiór*, 1969 (*The Anthropos-Specter-Beast*, 1977); *Nic albo nic*, 1971; *Kronika wypadków miłosnych*, 1974; *Kompleks polski*, 1977 (*The Polish Complex*, 1981); *Mała apokalipsa*, 1979 (*A Minor Apocalypse*, 1983).

Other literary forms

Tadeusz Konwicki launched his literary career with *Przy budowie* (1950), an example of the "fact literature" wedged between fiction and journalism that was characteristic of Socialist Realism of the late 1940's and the early 1950's. At this early stage of his career, he also published two more books, each of which can be defined as a long short story. Since the publication of *Władza*, however, he has devoted himself to longer genres, among which the novel occupies the central place. It should be noted, though, that his later novels lean more and more toward a peculiar kind of fiction bordering on nonfiction, in which narrative sections are interspersed with essayistic ones. (This blend of fiction and essay has been increasingly popular among Polish prose writers.) Two of his books published in the 1970's and the 1980's, *Kalendarz i klepsydra* (1976; the calendar and the hourglass) and *Wschody i zachody księżyca* (1982; *Moonrise, Moonset*, 1985), should be classified as nonfiction, since their core consists of the writer's diary; the diaristic notation of events serves, however, merely as a starting point for essayistic reflection and narrative anecdote.

Konwicki is also a prolific screenwriter and a director in his own right. Besides screenplays written for other directors, he has written and directed four films—*Ostatni dzień lata* (1958; the last day of summer), *Zaduszki* (1961; Halloween), *Salto* (1965), *Jak daleko stąd, jak blisko* (1971; how far it is and yet how near)—each of which was a much-discussed event in modern Polish cinema; scripts for these movies have been published in book form. Konwicki returned to the cinema after a ten-year absence to direct *Dolina Issy* (the Issa Valley), which he adapted from Czesław Miłosz's novel of the same title.

Achievements

The publication of *A Dreambook for Our Time* in 1963 marked the moment since which Konwicki has been universally considered one of the most prominent novelists of postwar Poland. This novel, having met with rave reviews in Poland, was soon translated into several foreign languages and established Konwicki's international renown. A period of relative relaxation in the cultural policies of the Polish regime, initiated in 1956 and continued throughout the early 1960's, made it possible for the writer to enjoy, at least for a while, both a wide readership and tolerance on the part of the authorities; he was even awarded a few state prizes for his novels and films. Since the mid-1960's, however, Konwicki, increasingly disappointed with the theory and practice of Communism, has experienced a growing number of censorship troubles and has gradually assumed a dissident stance. After a state publisher's attempt to censor extensive parts of his novel *The Polish Complex* in 1977, the writer decided to publish his book beyond the reach of censorship, as a special issue of the underground journal *Zapis*. His next novel, *A Minor Apocalypse*, was written from the start with the same method of publishing in mind. Despite their underground beginnings, both novels are undoubtedly the most widely known to date among Konwicki's books, both in Poland and abroad; critical opinion views them as controversial but highly original and revealing reflections of Polish reality in the 1970's. Among Konwicki's earlier novels, *Wniebowstąpienie* (ascension) and *The Anthropos-Specter-Beast* in particular, although less known in the West, enjoy a high reputation among Polish critics and readers.

Biography

Tadeusz Konwicki was born into a worker's family in 1926 near the city of Vilnius in Polish Lithuania. He attended a high school in Vilnius and, under the Nazi occupation, continued his study in a clandestine study group. In July, 1944, he joined a guerrilla unit which fought both the retreating Nazis and the approaching Soviet troops. In 1945, his native region having been annexed by the Soviet Union, he went to Krakow, where he managed to conceal his anti-Communist past and began to study Polish literature at the Jagiellonian University.

Konwicki made his debut as a journalist in 1946 and in the same year joined the editorial board of a literary weekly, *Odrodzenie*. In 1948, he moved to Warsaw, where he has lived ever since. Between 1950 and 1958, he was on the editorial board of another leading weekly, *Nowa Kultura*; like several of his colleagues, he resigned to express his protest against what he considered the return to Stalinist tactics in the cultural policy of the regime. Since that time, Konwicki has often taken part in the protest actions staged by Polish intellectuals. After a writers' protest against censorship in 1968, Konwicki's newly published novel *Wniebowstąpienie* received no critical response—all reviews were "silenced" by the censorship office, which had blacklisted Konwicki. Although he managed to have his next few books appear in the official circuit and be reviewed, Konwicki eventually found it unacceptable to try continuously to reconcile his writing and filmmaking with censorship's ubiquitous control. Since 1977, the first editions of all of his books have been issued in the underground press and have subsequently been reprinted in the West.

Analysis

Like the majority of Polish writers of his generation, Tadeusz Konwicki went through a period of "mistakes and misjudgments" in his Stalinist youth before he was able to find a more authentic voice of his own. When he entered the literary arena in 1946, however, he brought with him the burden of his past—his experience of fighting Soviet troops in a Home Army guerrilla unit— which he had to repudiate in a painfully self-denying way in order to reconcile himself with the new political reality. This inner moral conflict caused Konwicki to lead a double life as a writer during the immediate postwar years: While publishing propagandistic literature and reportage, he was secretly writing a novel about his guerrilla experience, *Rojsty*, which he was able to publish only eight years after its completion. The year 1956—the year of the famous "thaw" in Polish political and cultural life—marked Konwicki's authentic debut; since that time, he has remained true to his underlying obsessions and recurring themes.

The constant subject of his novels is the reality of contemporary Poland, but reality seen in a highly subjective way, through the eyes of an individual who obsessively confronts it with his personal memories and with what he knows about his country's historical past. Moreover, a characteristic device of Konwicki is his frequent use of a first-person narrator who does not fully belong to the reality he describes; thus, his primary task is to find a key to a world that seems alien and absurd to him. This strategy is carried out in a variety of ways. The narrator, for example, may be a child whose perversely naïve way of seeing things as they are exposes the hypocrisy of the adult world (*The Anthropos-Specter-Beast*); he may be a man who mysteriously wakes up in a remote town where he has never been before (*A Dreambook for Our Time*) or who regains consciousness after having been beaten up by hooligans in the center of Warsaw, only to discover that he has lost his memory (*Wniebowstąpienie*). The common effect of these various points of departure is the cognitive and narrative situation of an *outsider*, who perceives the surrounding realm of everyday life as something absurd and incomprehensible. This perception makes him view the existing world (and particularly the reality of contemporary Poland) in a way which is as grotesque as it is apocalyptic; the absurdity he encounters provokes his nervous laughter as well as his eschatological fear. A world so absurd cannot possibly exist for long, and thus there is only one conclusion: Doomsday must be nigh.

A Dreambook for Our Time became an instant sensation in 1963 because Polish readers, used to reading between the lines, quickly grasped the intrinsic paradox of Konwicki's art: It was precisely his intensely subjective way of telling the story that enabled him to give the fullest account to date of the objective reality of postwar Poland. What had happened to Poland since World War II was a nightmare—and this nightmare could be related only by a novelistic "dreambook" with all of its nightmarish rules of narration and plot construction. At the outset of the novel, the main character wakes up from a poison-induced coma (he has attempted suicide) in a sleepy provincial town somewhere in Poland. Trying unsuccessfully to find some common ground with the twisted characters that inhabit the place, the hero feels increasingly overwhelmed by the absurdity of their lives. At the same time, he is chased by his own memories, which time and again rouse deeply hidden feelings of guilt apparently connected with his guerrilla past. The narrator's continuous flight from himself coincides agonizingly with his attempts at understanding himself and the surrounding world. Justly described by Miłosz as "one of the most terrifying novels in postwar Polish literature," *A Dreambook for Our Time* is, however, by no means a nihilistic revelation of the void: It is, rather, a tortuous search for the meaning of life and for salvation.

The same can be said about Konwicki's subsequent novels, which consistently employ the same structural patterns while continuously filling them with more and more concrete and overtly expressed observation of contemporary reality. *Wniebowstąpienie*, for example, describes a Dantesque pilgrimage of the narrator through Warsaw of the mid-1960's. Tormented by his amnesia and accompanied, instead of by a Vergil, by some shady characters that apparently wish to take advantage of him, the hero ascends symbolically from Hell through Purgatory to Paradise (the latter grotesquely identified with the observatory deck at the top of the kitschy Palace of Culture, built by the Soviets in the center of Warsaw). All of its symbolism notwithstanding, *Wniebowstąpienie* was perhaps the most realistic novel to emerge in Poland during the 1960's. The device of amnesia made it possible for the narrator to perceive reality without any presuppositions or prior knowledge and thus describe it without any evaluation or justification; within such utterly objective description, any discrepancy, abnormality, or absurdity of the external world is automatically more conspicuous and striking.

Only in the late 1970's, however, did Konwicki begin to speak without inhibition and without spending his artistic energy on finding intricate ways to confuse the censor. As far as their political import is concerned, both *The Polish Complex* and *A Minor Apocalypse* are as overt and direct as a novel possibly can be. In both, the narrator is closely identified with Konwicki himself, the narration is often interrupted by ideological digressions expressing the author's point of view, and the reality presented is clearly that of contemporary Poland, despite occasional elements of caricatural exaggeration (and also despite the fact that the action of *A Minor Apocalypse* takes place in an unspecified future). Nevertheless, both novels are far from serving chiefly political purposes; their aim is rather to offer a condensed artistic image of a certain society in a certain country at a certain time. In both novels, this aim is achieved in the first place by highly eccentric yet highly convincing opening situations which provide a point of departure for the plot as well as the key metaphor for each novel.

In *The Polish Complex*, such a key metaphor appears on the very first page. The narrator stands twenty-third in a long line in front of a state jewelry shop. In spite of appearances, this scene is more realistic than grotesque: In Poland of the 1970's, suffering rapid inflation, gold was a highly valued and sought-after commodity. The waiting for merchandise (cheap Soviet rings) drags on, and in the line, which contains a cross section of society, social acquaintances as well as sympathies and antipathies form. The line appears to be a reflection of the state of affairs in the country, with a worker, a student, an undercover policeman, and a wealthy proprietress of a private farm all united by a common desire to obtain unattainable goods. The class differences and opposing viewpoints play a decidedly smaller role here than the problem of how to win a better place in the line. Next to the author-narrator stands his erstwhile would-be assassin, a man who immediately after the war was ordered by the anti-Communist underground to shoot the "traitor"; behind him stands a former agent of the Stalinist secret police, a man who once imprisoned and tortured the would-be assassin. These old tragedies, however, have been forgotten, replaced by an overwhelming feeling of sense-lessness and impotence. The only thing which still counts is the acquisition of scarce material goods.

The contemporary plot of the novel, however, constitutes only one of its layers. Another layer consists of lengthy digressions and even separate short stories inserted in the course of the narration. In particular, two such stories, both referring to a defeat in one of the many spurts of liberation in Polish history, the 1863 Uprising, apparently bear no relation to the main line of the plot, yet they are functional in showing yet another version of the motif of "amnesia"—in demonstrating, by way of contrast, the degree to which the contemporary citizen of a Socialist state has become alienated from ethical imperatives.

While the action of *The Polish Complex* occasionally shifts back to the historical past, the action of *A Minor Apocalypse* is moved forward, to some unspecified (though ominously near) future. The reality presented here is again that of Poland in the 1970's, yet it is subject to dreamlike distortion and grotesque, often blackly comic exaggeration. Communism appears here as a still powerful system, but it is powerful by the force of inertia—its actual condition can only be defined as one of prolonged collapse.

Like *The Polish Complex*, *A Minor Apocalypse* opens with a startlingly absurd, yet in a sense plausible, situation: The narrator-author is visited by two literary acquaintances who propose that, as a respected and well-known Polish writer, he should set himself on fire in front of the Party Central

Committee building as an act of protest against the incorporation of Poland into the Soviet Union, which is to take place that very day. Initially shocked, the narrator grudgingly acknowledges their point and sluggishly sets off to meet the dissidents who will provide him with gasoline and matches (Swedish matches—not the shoddy variety foisted upon the general public). The narrator's weary progress through Warsaw streets, apartments, and restaurants parodies the Stations of the Cross, and the end of the novel is deliberately inconclusive, so that the author's attitude toward the proposed martyrdom remains highly ambiguous; one can only guess that the act of self-immolation finally does take place.

In its diagnosis of the state of Polish society, *A Minor Apocalypse*—written toward the end of the 1970's—is more bitter than any of Konwicki's previous works, yet even here he appears as a moralist rather than as a nihilist, as someone who writes to improve the world rather than to condemn it.

Major publications other than long fiction

SHORT FICTION: *Przy budowie*, 1950; *Godzina smutku*, 1954; *Klucz*, 1954.

SCREENPLAYS: *Ostatni dzień lata*, 1958; *Zaduszki*, 1961; *Salto*, 1965; *Jak daleko stąd, jak blisko*, 1971.

NONFICTION: *Kalendarz i klepsydra*, 1976; *Wschody i zachody księżyca*, 1982 (*Moonrise, Moonset*, 1985).

Bibliography

Fuksiewicz, J. *Tadeusz Konwicki*, 1967.
Krzyżanowski, J. R. "The Haunted World of Tadeusz Konwicki," in *Books Abroad*. XLVIII (1974), p. 3.
Pawłowski, J. "Świat Tadeusza Konwickiego," in *Lektury i problemy*, 1976. Edited by J. Maciejewski.
Rostropowicz Clark, J. "Introduction," in *The Polish Complex*, 1984.
Wegner, J. *Konwicki*, 1973.

Stanisław Barańczak

MILAN KUNDERA

Born: Brno, Czechoslovakia; April 1, 1929

Principal long fiction

Žert, 1967 (*The Joke,* 1969, revised 1982); *La Vie est ailleurs,* 1973 (*Life Is Elsewhere,* 1974; in Czech as *Zivot de jinde,* 1979); *La Valse aux adieux,* 1976 (*The Farewell Party,* 1976; in Czech as *Valčik no roz oučenou,* 1979); *Kniha smíchu a zapomnění,* 1978 (*The Book of Laughter and Forgetting,* 1980); *Nesnesitelná lehkost byti,* 1984 (*The Unbearable Lightness of Being,* 1984).

Other literary forms

Apart from Milan Kundera's novels, of particular interest are his three linked volumes of short stories, *Směšné lásky* (1963; laughable loves), *Druyh sešit směšných lásek* (1965; the second book of laughable loves), and *Třetí sešit směšných lásek* (1968; the third book of laughable loves), which were published together in a definitive edition, *Směšné lásky* (1969); seven of these stories appear in English translation in *Laughable Loves* (1974). Kundera started his literary career with poetry, publishing three collections of that genre. His most important contribution to literary criticism is *Umění románu: Cesta Vladislava Vančury za velkou epikou* (1960; the art of the novel: Vladislav Vančura's search for the great epic), a study of the Czech novelist Vladislav Vančura. Kundera contributed to the revival of Czech drama with *Majitelé klíčů* (1962; the keys), *Ptákovina* (1969), and *Jacques et son maître: Hommage à Denis Diderot* (1970; Jacques and his master: an homage to Denis Diderot). Kundera's speech to the Union of Czechoslovak Writers' Congress of 1967 was one of the high points of the cultural-political movement known as the Prague Spring; the essayistic talent revealed there has since been put to use in a series of striking essays, among the best known of which are "The Tragedy of Central Europe" (*The New York Review of Books,* April 26, 1984) and "The Novel and Europe" (*The New York Review of Books,* July 19, 1984). Finally, Kundera has also collaborated on a number of screenplays, the most notable of which was written for the film *Žert* (1969), based on his novel of the same title.

Achievements

Kundera became rather well-known quite early in his career on account of his poetry. He became famous for the wrong reason, so to speak, and this he tried to undo by switching to prose, experimenting in drama, and finally, by taking a lively interest in the literary-political scene in Prague at the time of great excitement caused by the liberalization of the Communist regime.

As far as Kundera was concerned, the time of his great breakthrough in literature and on the cultural scene that involved him also in politics came in 1967, following the publication of *The Joke*, a novel exemplifying the cultural and political sophistication of its author as well as of his country. This confluence of art and life, private and public, philosophical and political domains is the principal characteristic of Kundera's fiction, refined and finely honed in his subsequent novels.

Each of his five novels—as well as his cycle of short stories, *Laughable Loves*—is a fresh approach to his abiding concern: his search for authenticity defined as an unmasked, demythologized, yet philosophical parable of the existence of a Czech intellectual in a given historical time. Against the background of modern Czech fiction, Kundera appears as a worthy follower of the three main directions of Czech prose, associated with the names of Jaroslav Hašek, Karel Čapek, and Vladislav Vančura. It is the mark of Kundera's genius that he has been able to alchemize the best that these authors had to offer him into his own original prose, surpassing them all.

Biography

Milan Kundera was born into a highly cultured and sophisticated family of a Brno pianist, Milada Janosikova, and a distinguished professor of Janáček's Academy of Music, Ludvík Kundera. Thus, among those early interests that he took seriously was music as well as literature. In 1948, the year of a Communist coup in Czechoslovakia, Kundera began his study at the Charles University in Prague. He was forced to interrupt his studies, and for some time he hesitated between music and literature, having studied music composition with Václav Kaprál. Finally, he was allowed to switch to the famous film school of the Prague Academy of Music and Dramatic Arts, from which he was graduated in 1958. The Prague film school was also his employer: There, he taught world literature. In 1963, he married Vera Hrabankova.

Having associated himself strongly with the movement known variously as the Prague Spring or "socialism with a human face," Kundera fell into disfavor following the invasion of Czechoslovakia by the Soviet Union. His works were put on the censor's index and withdrawn from the libraries, and he was left without any means of support when forced out of his professorship in 1970. He was allowed to go to France, in 1975, as a visiting professor at the university in Rennes, and it was in France that he learned, in 1979, of the Czechoslovak government's decision to take his citizenship from him. Hence, Kundera continues to teach and write in Paris.

Kundera has been the recipient of many prestigious literary prizes, including the Czechoslovak State Prize (1964), the Union of Czechoslovak Writers' Prize (1968), the Czechoslovak Writers' Publishing House Prize (1969), the Prix Médicis (1973), the Premio Mondello (1978), and the Common Wealth Award for Distinguished Service in Literature (1982).

Analysis

None of Milan Kundera's novels fits into the traditional concept of the novel. Each is an experimental foray into the unknown, even though well prepared and supported by the literary legacy of Hašek, Čapek, and Vančura. This is particularly visible in the structure of Kundera's novels, which strikes one as that of a loosely organized group of short stories which have in common not so much recurring characters as a central theme of which each story illustrates a single facet.

Thus, Kundera's first novel, *The Joke*, seems to grow out of the short-story collection *Laughable Loves*. They have in common the central device of a "joke"—that is, an intended and performed hoax, a prank—which misfires and, like a boomerang, hurts the perpetrator rather than the intended victim. Consequently, in one of the stories of *Laughable Loves*, "I, the Mournful God," the narrator wants to punish a pretty girl who has resisted his advances by punishing her vanity. He approaches his Greek friend, who acts the role of a foreign impresario attracted by the talent of the girl, who happens to be a music student. The girl is easily seduced, and the affair is consummated the same day on the narrator's couch, to the narrator's wrenching and never-ending dismay. Hoist with his own petard, the narrator waxes philosophical about the important lesson he has learned about life.

This device becomes central in the novel *The Joke*, wherein it is enriched and used to probe deeply into the realms of character motivation past and present, the political order (with the attendant zigzags of the Party line), and the sensitive area of emotional and erotic relationships, the highs and lows of which Kundera captures with singular detachment bordering on misanthropy and misogyny.

The Joke consists of four narratives of the same event, or rather a set of events centering on the "joke": Ludvík Jahn, the central character, sends his naïve activist girlfriend a postcard that is politically compromising; his intention is to make fun of her seriousness and steer her toward erotic rather than political interests. The girlfriend reports him to the Party organization, and Ludvík is thrown out of the university as a politically unreliable element, his life derailed for years during which he has to work as a mine laborer, first as a draftee in a punishment battalion, then as a volunteer without much choice. In revenge, the "rehabilitated" Ludvík, now a scientist in Prague, decides to seduce the wife of his archenemy who engineered his dismissal from the university. Like the first joke, the second misfires: The enemy's wife falls in love with Ludvík at a time when her husband is estranged from her; to add insult to injury, the enemy, Zemánek, is a thoroughly reformed man, now as fond of ideas as is Ludvík and embarrassed for his past—all in all, a different man, one who is involved with a young woman and glad that Ludvík is interested in his unwanted wife. Philosophically, the novel explores the fluidity, the inconstancy of people's characters and ideas; Kundera also suggests that the nature of justice is undermined by the element of time. Perhaps in some timeless corner of the universe, an exact justice prevails, but how can one implement it in a world crucified by time?

Ludvík Jahn is also an ideal personification of the reformist ideas sweeping Czechoslovakia in 1967 and 1968. Historically, the novel is a literary summing-up of the Czechoslovak experience with socialism from its very outset, in 1948. The sensational quality of *The Joke*, from the political point of view— and it is clear that this point of view is relevant to the understanding of the novel—stems from the near-documentary quality with which Kundera depicts successive stages of modern Czech history, taking into account the many different moves and countermoves of cultural, social, and existential aspects of the Czech reality. What each of the four character-narrators documents, Kundera the author transcends, so powerfully does one feel the controlling intelligence behind the scene, pulling the strings that direct the literary "god game."

While the novel was immediately praised for its literary qualities, it also served to polarize Czech critics along political lines, dividing them into dog-matists and reformists: The former decried Kundera's wholly irreverent atti-tude toward Communist taboos, while the latter praised his candor.

Kundera himself has noted the danger of ideological interpretations of the novel that obscure the more subtle love story between Ludvík and the tender girl, Lucie, whom he met while he was a laborer—a love story at the center of the complex novel but for that very reason easily overlooked when weightier and more topical concerns clamored for attention. In the novel's first recep-tion, few critics noted Ludvík's failure to lead an authentic existence. Impris-oned by his grudge and his ambiguous attitude toward women as a result of the decisive, treacherous act by the female Party activist, Ludvík blinds himself even to such timeless aids as Moravian folk music—which, in a key passage omitted from the original English translation, opens his eyes to the authen-ticity he missed.

This powerful concern with authentic life is developed masterfully in *Life Is Elsewhere*. Where, then, is life? Rather, what is life? Kundera's second novel answers this question by way of a negative example of a young poet living the life of precocious maturity conventionally found admirable in Arthur Rimbaud, Vladímir Mayakovsky, Sergei Esenin, or the Czechs Jiří Wolker and Jiří Orten, embodying Romantic conventions of the genius and of the indivisibility of art and life. Is it then possible for the Poet, this higher being, to become a wretched masturbator and police informer, as well as a clumsy bungler of everything but his verses?

Kundera magisterially answers these and other questions by giving an inde-cent history of the young poet Jaromil: his life, beginning with his conception, all the way up to his pathetic and bathetic death. On the way, Kundera demolishes the Romantic myth of the poet as the truth-seeker, or truth-sayer.

Instead of a prophet, he shows us a pervert. That, however, is only the consequence of Jaromil's inability to lead an authentic life, precisely because he is and remains all the time a poet. The lyric quality so necessary for a poet is seen as the greatest obstacle to authenticity, to life as it should be lived.

The unlikely counterpart of Jaromil is a man with whom Jaromil shares a girlfriend. The authentic man, however, is selfless, whereas Jaromil is possessive; he is attached to timeless traditional art, whereas Jaromil seeks absolute modernity. Needless to say, in the political sphere, Jaromil repeats Communist inanities, though he is sufficiently intelligent to see how flawed they are. Lyricism *contra* logic: This is the conflict at the heart of the painful demolition of the poet. He, the poet Jaromil, even dies without understanding the harm he has done to others and himself through his fateful lyricism.

So much for the poet; but what if Jaromil's condition is generally present among people at large? Kundera turns to this question in the wry, tragicomic novel *The Farewell Party*. Instead of following one causal chain, he traces several, crisscrossing them in order to show how, like billiard balls, individual fates meet and are bounced in a yet more unexpected direction. Though the plot is too complex to recount in detail, in simplified form, *The Farewell Party* deals with the issue of self-deception on a group scale, up from the previous novel's individual scale.

A musician is arranging his mistress's abortion with a doctor who heads a fertilization clinic in an unorthodox manner: He impregnates his patients artificially, using his own semen. The man whose mission it is to fertilize then kills, and the man who wants to free himself supplies poison to a woman, the same musician's mistress, who, not knowing about the poison, kills herself. Further complications follow. This novel is far more dramatic than anything else written by Kundera, but it does have the operatic quality of some of his early tales. The obvious tragic aspect of the happenings is countered step by step with genuinely comic happenings, accidents, and a jovial set of characters, almost all of whom preclude the kind of tragic tension that the mere plot implies.

Without any doubt, *The Farewell Party* is Kundera's most cynical and misanthropic literary performance. At the same time, it announces the arrival of supernatural elements in his fiction, in the guise of an American, Bartleff. Without the somewhat absurd supernaturalism of Bartleff, which injects into the novel a modicum of warmth, the novel would be hard to bear. Thematically, it is possible to place the work into the tense, Kafkaesque atmosphere of postinvasion Bohemia with its ever-growing demoralization.

Kundera's next novel was like a breath of fresh air. A daring experiment, *The Book of Laughter and Forgetting* features the return of a more aggressive narrative with documentary elements, more authorial intrusion and manipulation of the narrative with autobiographical elements, quotations from an eccentric array of thinkers, attempts at the theory of laughter, and incursions into the domains of musicology and philosophy of history.

First, Kundera manages to introduce and establish very successfully the plight of a dissident and an émigré, though in ways that run contrary to political clichés. There is then a considerable dose of "reality": Historical events are recounted; politicians—dead and alive—are quoted and described; and snippets of what purports to be Kundera's life are offered in a very appetizing smorgasbord, where the wound of history is treated with the balm of a new mythology, created by Kundera in a feat of magic to vanquish the old—people dance the hypnotic circle and rise into thin air. Finally, there is a "theory of laughter" that distinguishes between the laughter of the Devil and the laughter of angels. At the same time, structurally, the novel solidifies around seven key tales with a limited number of characters, some of whom are present in more than one tale; the tales themselves are introduced as variations (in musical fashion) on the common themes of laughter and forgetting. The dangers of forgetting and the necessity of laughter are often illustrated roughly, subtlety being reserved for a sustained criticism of the modern malaise of indifference, lack of compassion, and the frittering away of a precious cultural heritage.

Above all, Kundera's concern with authenticity is present here in force, as is his attempt to do away with the sentimental glorification of youth, of childhood even—as if he believed that he had not finished the job properly in *Life Is Elsewhere*. To get his message across in a definitive fashion, he places his favorite heroine, Tamina, on an island inhabited by children who ogle her, pounce on her, take away her privacy, rape her, and finally kill her—naïvely, sincerely, purely, without malice, but full of curiosity. The island of children, the children's paradise, is a beautiful parable of the horrors of totalitarianism.

Kundera wanted to impress the Western reader with the issue of totalitarianism, and the avenue he chose was a parable. The totalitarian system, however imperfect, tries to turn adults into children in yet another parody of a perfectly legitimate and profound traditional idea found in many sacred traditions—above all, in Christianity. The primitivism of the totalitarian ideology, the simplicity of its propaganda, has thus acquired a profound meaning: It harks back to the children imprisoned within adults, and therein lies its success, no matter how banal, how simple, how trivial.

To resist the totalitarian temptation, to become a "dissident," is desirable, but in Kundera's world, the dissident is a man who exemplifies in miniature the larger political processes existing on a large scale in his society, for one is but a part of the whole. Thus, even a dissident feels the need to tamper with his past in order to bring it more in line with his present: The past embarrasses him. Kundera justifiably resents labels such as "dissident" or "émigré" as applied to him, for he has spent his entire adult life peering at what is hidden behind the label, behind the mask, knowing that a label—any label—does not absolve one from anything. At the depths in which Kundera operates, such labels are meaningless.

It is curious to see, then, in Kundera's *The Unbearable Lightness of Being*, an attempt to present a character who, according to all indications, does lead an authentic life. Yet when Kundera portrays someone who is living an authentic life, as his main character Tomas and Tomas' love Zdena do, it is only to suggest that ultimately life itself has been emptied of meaning, of authenticity. Kundera introduces this theme in the surprising opening of the novel, which spells out the consequences of Friedrich Nietzsche's frightful idea of eternal recurrence: If everything is to be repeated, then any individual event, no matter how tragic, loses its uniqueness, its unrepeatable quality, and consequently does not matter; it is no longer heavy, but "light." The problem is, can human beings bear this lightness—or is it, as the title suggests, unbearable?

Tomas and Zdena, as authentic and as unobjectionable as Kundera could make them, are frustrated by the accidents of history. They understand the personal and the social tragedy which they witness. They feel compassion. When the great traumatic event of their life happens, the Soviet invasion of Czechoslovakia in 1968, they decide to emigrate to Switzerland. Because Tomas is a natural Don Juan, Zdena, who loves him deeply, decides to return to Czechoslovakia, unable to share Tomas with other women. Zdena's absence weighs heavily on Tomas, and he returns to Czechoslovakia to join her, though the price is high: A skillful surgeon, he is fired from his hospital and forced to work as a window washer. Yet he does not mind, feeling even more free, and the new occupation seems especially useful from the point of view of his easier access to potential erotic adventures. Finally, Tomas and Zdena move into a benighted village, where Tomas works as a truck driver. During a weekend outing, Tomas and Zdena are accidentally killed in the truck.

Far away from Tomas, in America, lives his former love, Sabina, who also suffers from the burden of "lightness." She influences one of her lovers, Franz, a Swiss professor, into adopting a more authentic life and then drops him. Franz looks for a cause, is attracted to a humanitarian mission in Southeast Asia, and while there is killed in a mugging. Tomas, Sabina, and Franz all have something in common, irrespective of their accomplishments as authentic beings, inasmuch as the meaning has been decanted from life itself. This common feature is the Nietzschean *amor fati*, love of life as it is in all of its merciless fatefulness. Kundera never announces this theme, but after his Nietzschean opening, it is only logical to translate the surrender of all of these characters to life as it is, without preconditions, as a literary adaptation of this Nietzschean conceit.

Mention should be made of Kundera's superlative satire of leftism and its kitsch. In this connection, the conclusion serves as a magnificent counterpoint to Kundera's discussion of many varieties of kitsch, including the political. What could promise more in the way of kitsch than the death of a dog improbably named Karenin? After all, pets, whatever kind, are the beneficiaries of the most absurd type of maudlin sentimentality and kitsch. It takes courage to lecture about kitsch and then, in a truly inspired and unforgettable passage, after showing why the death of millions of human beings no longer has power to move people, describe the death of Tomas and Zdena's dog Karenin as a genuinely moving event that restores, through acceptance of tragedy, meaningfulness to life. This is the most unbearable event of the novel. As such, it pokes a hole through the all-embracing curtain of Tomas' *amor fati* and reestablishes the primary importance of authenticity.

Major publications other than long fiction

SHORT FICTION: *Směšné lásky*, 1963; *Druyh sešit směšných lásek*, 1965; *Třetí sešit směšných lásek*, 1968; *Směšné lásky*, 1969 (combined edition of preceding volumes; *Laughable Loves*, 1974, partial translation).

PLAYS: *Majitelé klíčů*, 1962; *Ptákovina*, 1969; *Žert*, 1969 (screenplay); *Jacques et son maître: Hommage à Denis Diderot*, 1970.

POETRY: *Clovĕk zahrada šira*, 1953; *Poslední máj*, 1955; *Monology*, 1957.

NONFICTION: *Umění románu: Cesta Vladislava Vančury za velkou epikou*, 1960.

Bibliography

Goetz-Stankiewicz, M. *The Silenced Theatre: Czech Playwrights Without a Stage*, 1979.

Harkins, W. E., and P. I. Trensky, ed. *Czech Literature Since 1956: A Symposium*, 1980.

Porter, R. C. *Milan Kundera: A Voice from Central Europe*, 1981.

Peter Petro

MADAME DE LA FAYETTE
Marie-Madeleine Pioche de la Vergne

Born: Paris, France; March(?), 1634
Died: Paris, France; May 25, 1693

Principal long fiction

Madame de La Fayette is the author of two novels: *Zayde* (also as *Zaïde*), in two volumes, published under the name of Segrais in 1670-1671, and *La Princesse de Clèves*, published anonymously in 1678 (*The Princess of Clèves*, 1679). She is also the author of two shorter works of fiction, often called historical novellas: *La Princesse de Montpensier*, published under the name of Segrais in 1662 (*The Princess of Montpensier*, 1666) and *La Comtesse de Tende*, published posthumously in 1724. Two other shorter works of fiction, published in 1909, have been attributed to her but are not generally recognized as authentic: *Histoire de Don Carlos D'Astorgas* and *Histoire espagnole*. The three works of fiction published during her lifetime appeared without her name apparently because of questions of decorum involved in women's literary activities. Although La Fayette explicitly denied having written *The Princess of Clèves*, the attribution is not seriously contested.

Other literary forms

Madame de La Fayette also wrote the following historical works: *Histoire de Madame Henriette d'Angleterre* (1720; *Fatal Gallantry*, 1722) and *Mémoires de la cour de France pour les années 1688 et 1689* (1731).

Achievements

Madame de La Fayette is frequently described as the first person to write a modern novel (as opposed to a romance) in French. *The Princess of Clèves* is considerably briefer than the pastoral and chivalric prose romances, often filling thousands of pages, that were fashionable earlier in the seventeenth century. La Fayette's plot construction clearly distinguishes between the main characters and those involved in the many subplots. The resultant concentration on the heroine allows readers to follow the development of her character and her motivations. Because the reader's attention is not dispersed over many plots, as in the romances, suspense and empathy are more intense. In fact, the public's identification with the novel's heroine reached such proportions that a torrent of letters and pamphlets appeared, taking passionately held positions on the rightness or error of the heroine's conduct. It is said that engagements were broken off because couples could not agree about the conduct of the Princess of Clèves.

In purely literary terms, *The Princess of Clèves* constitutes a major change in the way fiction relates to history in French literature. Instead of placing her story in the distant past or in an exotic Oriental or African country, La Fayette blended real historical persons, well-known to her readers, with purely imaginary characters. This proximity of the story to the life of the reader awakened an expectation of verisimilitude or realism that made the reader compare himself or herself with the characters. Reading thus became a critical activity of a new sort, for the reader could claim that a character behaved in an unlikely way or, on the contrary, could decide to identify with the character and try to model real-life action on the fictitious pattern. The so-called "quarrel of *The Princess of Clèves*" marks the historical beginning of the attempt to use the novel as a serious tool of social examination, an attempt that culminated two centuries later in Émile Zola's "experimental novel."

Biography

Born in Paris and baptized on March 18, 1634, Marie-Madeleine Pioche de la Vergne was well connected with the royal court. Her mother, Isabelle Pena, was the daughter of the physician of Louis XIII. La Fayette's father had an honorable career in the royal army until his death in 1649. Her mother's second husband, Renaud-René de Sévigné, was involved in the aristocratic rebellion known as the Fronde and was exiled from the court in 1652. Three years later, Marie-Madeleine married François, Comte de La Fayette. Madame de La Fayette spent less than four years at her husband's estate in the Auvergne. By 1659, the couple was back in Paris, where their second son was born. In 1661, the Count returned to the Auvergne, leaving Madame de La Fayette to live in the house built by her father and to participate in the life of the court. She was close to Madame de Sévigné and to Princess Henrietta of England, wife of Philippe d'Orléans, brother of the King. She frequented the salon of the literary Du Plessis-Guénégauds, held at the Hôtel de Nevers. In 1665, she began a long friendship with the Duc de La Rochefoucauld, a former leader of the Fronde and author of the well-known *Maximes* (1665-1678; *The Maxims*, 1670, 1706). After his death in 1680 and her husband's death in 1683, she renewed her friendship with the active literary figure Gilles Ménage. In the later 1670's, she was active in secret diplomatic negotiations with the Duchy of Savoy. After 1689, she turned toward religion under the direction of the Abbé de Rancé.

Analysis

Although it is frequently neglected by readers because of its exaggerated reputation as a difficult and complex novel, Madame de La Fayette's *Zayde* (often spelled *Zaïde*) is a highly polished, thoughtful work, containing many of the elements of La Fayette's undoubted masterpiece, *The Princess of Clèves*. Like the latter, *Zayde* contains a principal plot interrupted with less important plots appearing in inserted tales—that is, stories told by the characters. The inserted tales in *Zayde* are longer than those in *The Princess of Clèves* and differ also in that the characters in *Zayde* tell their own stories and not stories about other people. This constant changing of narrative voice and of character does make *Zayde* somewhat harder to follow than the later novel, but *Zayde* is simple and clear by comparison to such earlier works as Honoré d'Urfé's *L'Astrée* (1607-1628; *Astraea*, 1657-1658).

Thematically, *Zayde* is closely linked to *The Princess of Clèves* by the characters' probing of the nature of reality in contrast to their presuppositions and fears about it. The heroes are their own worst enemies. They are paralyzed by assumptions about life and other people that simply do not match experience. In *Zayde*, La Fayette's hero Consalve is literally afraid of himself, for the novelist has used a banal motif of Baroque literature—the lost portrait—and has treated it as a metaphor for man's division from himself, his alienation, in his fears and desires.

At the beginning of the novel, Consalve, a younger courtier from one of the two most powerful families of the court of León, leaves the court to seek utter solitude on the Spanish coast. There he meets another gentleman, Alphonse, who offers him a place to stay. The two exchange their stories of disenchantment. Consalve's story concerns his betrayal by his two best friends, the Prince Don Garcie and Ramir. The three of them had discussed whether love arises most strongly in a man for a woman he knows well or for someone he does not know until the moment of surprise, when he finds himself totally and irrationally attracted. Consalve claimed that he could not love a woman he did not know well, adding that he would prefer that she not have any prior sentiment for another. His two friends argued that acquaintance defeats love, and Ramir added that the desirability of the loved object increases if she already is attached to another. When Consalve tells Alphonse this story, he demonstrates the illusory character of the knowledge of his beloved, because he did not know that she had the capacity to leave him for Ramir, and of the knowledge of other people in general, since he was betrayed by his two best friends as well.

Alphonse's story follows the pattern of Consalve's, for Alphonse, too, had developed a general concept of human conduct that subsequently failed him. He had decided that he would not marry a beautiful woman, because women in general are faithless and because a beautiful woman, having more temptation to infidelity, would make him unhappy by making him jealous of his rivals. In spite of this resolve, Alphonse had fallen in love and become jealous—to such an extent that he killed his best friend and drove his beloved into a convent. Yet no one was at fault except Alphonse, whose ideas about women were so rooted in his mind that he did not need any real reason to be jealous. In many ways, Consalve's and Alphonse's stories are symmetrical. Consalve was betrayed by others in whom he placed excessive trust; Alphonse killed his best friend and ruined the life of his beloved because of an excessive lack of trust. Consalve believed that he knew Nugna Bella well enough to love her; Alphonse did not believe that he knew Bélasire well enough and, indeed, could never be satisfied, no matter how great a quantity of information was supplied to him.

If the vanity of trying to guide one's life by preconceived notions is not already clear, it becomes abundantly evident in the course of the novel, which is largely devoted to Consalve's love for Zayde. She is a young woman whom Consalve finds washed up on the beach after a violent storm. Only Zayde and her woman companion have survived a shipwreck. Although they are dressed in Moorish costumes, the hero, accustomed to Arabic because of his frequent military encounters with the foe, does not recognize their tongue. For months, he tries to converse with Zayde and fails, except by using gestures and paintings. He intuits that Zayde finds in his face the likeness of someone else she has loved. Because Consalve is in love, by now, with this person of whom he knows only the name and the "fact" that she has loved someone else, he is jealous when Zayde looks at him with tenderness. He thinks that she sees him only as the image of her absent lover. The hero has, of course, proved that his initial assumptions about the relationship of love and knowledge are entirely wrong. His "maxim" of conduct does not correspond to his experience. Knowledge and love are, however, related in *Zayde*, but it takes many adventures and many more inserted tales before Consalve discovers what the relationship is. At the end of the novel, when he and Zayde meet after a long separation, they are able to speak to each other. She has learned Spanish, and he has discovered that her language is Greek and has learned it. He finds that she recognized in him the face from a portrait that had been identified for her as that of the Prince of Fez, to whom she had been promised in marriage. This resemblance explains her emotion on seeing Consalve. The portrait, however, is actually a lost portrait of Consalve. La Fayette concludes her novel with this trite mechanism for undoing complicated plots, but she uses the lost portrait for a specific reason that is quite original. One aspect of love, one that has afflicted both Consalve and Alphonse, is the attempt to impose on the outside world a conception of the way things are or ought to be. In a sense, both Consalve and Alphonse are seeking in love someone who will mirror themselves. Alphonse is punished by his inability to see that Bélasire is not the mirror of his jealousy. Her actions and his jealousy are unrelated. Consalve's purgatory is the long quest to discover that it is his own image that stands in the way of his love for Zayde.

Although *The Princess of Clèves* is briefer than *Zayde* and has a less difficult plot, this acknowledged masterpiece addresses problems that are fully as complex as those in *Zayde*. In her second novel, La Fayette also treats the relationship between general assumptions and individual experience, but she does so by tracing the life of a woman, Mademoiselle de Chartres (the heroine has no first name), who comes to the court as an adolescent with her mother, who wants to arrange a good and prestigious marriage for her daughter.

Although the setting of this story gives La Fayette the opportunity to analyze the political intrigues of the French court, a milieu she knew intimately, the principal focus in *The Princess of Clèves*, as in *Zayde*, is on the relationship between knowledge and experience. Since Mademoiselle de Chartres arrives at the court with neither opinions about nor acquaintance with its ways, she relies entirely on her mother to form her. In her educational endeavor, the mother uses two approaches: plain assertion and illustrative narration. The problem, however, is that the mother's assertions about the way a woman can be happy (the sole means of obtaining feminine happiness, she says, is to love one's husband and to be loved by him) and the story she tells about Madame de Valentinois (Diane de Poitiers), the mistress of King Henri II, do not coincide. The King's mistress is the most powerful woman at the court. She is faithful neither to her husband nor to her lovers, yet there is no indication of unhappiness on her part. There is a further contradiction between the mother's claim about happiness and her struggle, largely out of personal vanity it seems, to arrange a marriage that will show the whole court that she and her family are important.

This contradictory maternal pedagogy is the starting point for one of the structural problems of the novel, a problem that was noted shortly after publication. Valincour, one of the earliest critics of *The Princess of Clèves*, felt that the internal narratives told by various characters to the heroine simply did not hold together. Surely, if the novelist wanted simply to create local color, she would not have needed to interrupt her narrative repeatedly to have characters fill in the gaps in the heroine's knowledge of court intrigue. The heroine could learn about these things without the reader of the novel having to listen verbatim to all the accounts given of the life of Mary Stuart or of Madame de Tournon, among others. It is more probable that the act of listening to such stories and trying to apply them to one's own life as models of conduct is a matter of interest in its own right. The heroine is trying to fit her general ideas about life—including such notions as that men are never faithful—to these stories in search of confirmation of her expectations. Even when she does not find her assumptions borne out, she clings to the instructions given to her by her mother.

The heroine's marriage to the Prince of Clèves does not give her happiness, but it does give her someone to talk to after her mother dies. This is not a small matter in this novel, nor indeed in the court milieu that La Fayette knew. Her friend La Rochefoucauld wrote, "Nothing flatters us so much as the confidences of the great, since we see them as the consequence of our merit, without considering that they usually come only from vanity or from the inability to keep a secret." The "inability to keep a secret" is a frequent problem in *The Princess of Clèves*, as several of the internal stories show. The Princess, however, has a special reason for not being able, or not wanting, to keep a secret. She has learned to seek guidance by using stories as examples of conduct and is accustomed to telling her own life, as a story, to her mother. When the Princess falls in love with the Duke of Nemours, she fails to tell her mother, who nevertheless notices her daughter's infatuation and is mortally grieved by the silence that covers this one event in her daughter's life. The Princess' husband becomes the only person in whom she can confide. After trying to keep her love for Nemours secret, even from Nemours, the Princess believes that she must either yield to her passion or tell it to someone. The confession scene at Coulommiers, where she tells her husband that she is in love with someone else, is therefore a logical consequence of the mother's (and the novel's) insistence on telling stories.

One of La Fayette's contemporaries, the Count of Bussy-Rabutin, wrote, "The wife's confession to her husband is extravagant and can only be told in a true story." His opinion was widespread, for the readers of the novel generally thought that no woman would ever make such a confession. On one hand, their opinion was based on the social mores of the time. Women were generally married very young (often to older men) by their parents. Love and marriage were therefore strictly separate, despite the teachings of the Church and the somewhat utopian doctrine presented by the Princess' mother that women should love their husbands. Husband and wife frequently had little to do with each other, living separate lives, as did Madame de La Fayette and her husband, the Count. Under these circumstances, it would be either superfluous or imprudent for a wife to tell her husband about a love affair. Beyond the sociological aspect, the confession raises the specifically literary problem to which Bussy-Rabutin alluded when he claimed that it could be told only in a true story. Here a distinction is being made between "true" and "verisimilar." Seventeenth century French classical theory distinguished these two categories (in an application of Aristotle's *Poetics*). Many things could happen in real life, it was thought, that were so improbable as to render a story suspect. Therefore, unlikely events could be recounted only in authentic historical narratives, whereas fiction should limit itself to the probable.

To make matters worse, from both the sociological and the literary standpoints, La Fayette multiplied the improbabilities of her novel. If the confession is in itself unlikely, how likely is it that Nemours, the object of the wife's adulterous passion, should be hidden in the trees, listening to everything she says? If his presence there is already stretching one's capacity to suspend disbelief, Nemours' secret return to the Clèves estate to spy on the Princess another time is certainly hard to credit. Finally, in the list of improbabilities detected by the early readers, the Princess' refusal to marry or to have an affair with Nemours after her husband's death (caused by a broken heart) raised numerous objections.

La Fayette seems to be playing with the reader's assumptions about what is normal. She can do so only by locating her novel in a time and space sufficiently close to the reader's own for the reader to apply the same standards to both book and world. If the Princess had been a figure in a romance such as Ludovico Ariosto's *Orlando furioso* (widely read in France at the time), readers would probably have accepted anything she did as no less credible than the flying steed and the magic palace of Ariosto's work. In *The Princess of Clèves*, however, there is a real tension between what Bussy-Rabutin, Valincour, and other readers found unbelievable and the historical accuracy of most of the setting. La Fayette herself, in a celebrated letter, denied her authorship of *The Princess of Clèves*, adding that "what I find in it is a perfect imitation of the world of the court and of the way in which one lives there. There is nothing novelistic [Romanesque] and high-flown about it; thus it is not a novel [*roman*]: it is rather a book of memoirs." Whatever one thinks of the author's sincerity in this letter, the tension between the novelistic and the realistic, or "perfect imitation," is evidently maintained.

The key to this puzzle may very well lie in the last sentence of *The Princess of Clèves*, when, after having left the court for a remote country house, the widowed Princess dies and leaves the world "inimitable examples of virtue." The notion of example belongs both to literary or rhetorical theory and to everyday assumptions about life. The many inserted stories of this novel are used by the heroine as examples of conduct at the court. As such, they must be supposed in some way representative of general truths, and they must be useful as guides to conduct. La Fayette has clearly used the inserted stories as a counterpoint to the heroine's own behavior. Despite the apparent educational value for the young woman in these stories, they serve a strictly negative function, showing her, if anything, what kind of conduct does not conform to her mother's precepts about feminine happiness. Furthermore, throughout the novel—the confession is only the most notable instance—the Princess is described by her husband, by her mother, and even by herself as being unlike others. La Fayette squarely poses the problem of the usefulness of examples by confronting exemplary stories of the court with a heroine who is unique and who leaves behind examples that cannot be imitated.

The Princess of Clèves has been described as the first novel of psychological analysis. Although this description is in some ways a projection into the seventeenth century of late nineteenth century approaches, it does have the merit of emphasizing the heroine's role in seeking to understand her own desires and the conduct of those around her. She does this by talking about it, and this verbal approach does have similarities to the "talking cure" of modern psychotherapies. Yet there are considerable areas of the mind and emotions of the principal characters that remain ambiguous. Even the heroine's decision to leave the court and not to marry Nemours remains a subject of great controversy. Some critics claim that she follows a basically religious impulse that leads her to flee from the man who led her to the brink of sin and, in doing so, apparently precipitates the death of her husband. Others see this ultimate refusal of love as a utilitarian flight from unhappiness in view of her conviction (based on her mother's teaching) that men are never faithful when they are satisfied both emotionally and sexually.

Perhaps in trying to find a single reason for her actions, readers are being too simplistically psychological, forgetting that the heroine does not really have a psyche because she is entirely a fictive creation. Perhaps, too, readers forget the seventeenth century discovery of the dispersion of the self as it unfolds in La Rochefoucauld's work, particularly in reflections such as the one that was first in the original edition of *The Maxims*, where self-love is described as multiform and so contradictory that it can even effect self-hatred. One of the intercalated stories in *The Princess of Clèves*, the one about Madame de Tournon and her lover Sancerre, portrays a character whose conduct is composed of layers of actions and motivations so dissimilar that no one seems to be able to seize the totality of her personality.

The persistence of mystery in the self is a link between *The Princess of Clèves* and *Zayde*. For all of their attempts to compress human conduct into clear definitions and rules, Consalve, Alphonse, and the Princess are never really certain what will happen or even precisely what passes through their own minds.

Major publications other than long fiction
NONFICTION: *Histoire de Madame Henriette d'Angleterre*, 1720 (*Fatal Gallantry*, 1722); *Mémoires de la cour de France pour les années 1688 et 1689*, 1731.

Bibliography
Durry, M. J. *Madame de La Fayette*, 1962.

Genette, Gérard. *Figures of Discours*, 1982.

Haig, Sterling. *Madame de Lafayette*, 1970.

Horowitz, Louise K. *Love and Language*, 1977.

Langaa, M. *Lectures de Madame de La Fayette*, 1971.

John D. Lyons

PÄR LAGERKVIST

Born: Växjö, Sweden; May 23, 1891
Died: Lidingö, Sweden; July 11, 1974

Principal long fiction

Människor, 1912 (novella); *Det eviga leendet*, 1920 (novella; *The Eternal Smile*, 1934); *Gäst hos verkligheten*, 1925 (novella; *Guest of Reality*, 1936); *Bödeln*, 1933 (novella; *The Hangman*, 1936); *Dvärgen*, 1944 (*The Dwarf*, 1945); *Barabbas*, 1950 (English translation, 1951); *Sibyllan*, 1956 (*The Sibyl*, 1958); *Pilgrimen*, 1960-1964, 1966 (includes *Ahasverus död*, 1960 [*The Death of Ahasuerus*, 1960]; *Pilgrim på havet*, 1962 [*Pilgrim at Sea*, 1964]; *Det heliga landet*, 1964 [*The Holy Land*, 1966]); *Mariamne*, 1967 (*Herod and Mariamne*, 1968).

Other literary forms

Though he is known primarily for the full-length novels which began appearing near the end of World War II, Pär Lagerkvist has also achieved great recognition in Scandinavia for his numerous short stories, novellas, poems, and plays. Little of this early work is available in translation. Lagerkvist's short fiction and miscellaneous prose have been collected in *Prosa I-V* (1956). Some of the pieces in this work have appeared in translation in *The Eternal Smile and Other Stories* (1954), *The Eternal Smile: Three Stories* (1971), and *The Marriage Feast and Other Stories* (1955). Lagerkvist's nine volumes of poetry have been collected in *Dikter* (1965). This portion of his work is the least known outside Scandinavia; only one volume, *Aftonland* (1953; *Evening Land*, 1975), has been translated in its entirety. Lagerkvist also wrote plays, as well as dramatic adaptations of two of his fictional pieces: *Bödeln* (1934; *The Hangman*, 1966) and *Barabbas* (1953). These plays are collected in *Dramatik I-III* (1956). A selection of his plays has been translated in *Modern Theatre: Seven Plays and an Essay* (1966). His diaries and unpublished notes were edited by his daughter, Elin Lagerkvist, under the title *Antecknat* (1977).

Achievements

Lagerkvist is perhaps the most important figure of Swedish modernism, a tradition which is little known outside Scandinavia itself. Though Lagerkvist's influence on literature outside this region has been slight, his work has exerted a great influence on the Nordic tradition of which he is a part.

Despite Lagerkvist's relative unfamiliarity to readers of modern European literature, he is the most widely translated Swedish author since August Strindberg. Though various portions of his work have been translated into at least thirty-four other languages, large portions remain inaccessible. Only one other Swedish writer, Ingmar Bergman, rivals the degree of international recognition Lagerkvist has achieved, and Bergman is not so much a literary artist as a filmmaker.

Lagerkvist's importance to literary history lies in his influence on the development of the unique characteristics of Swedish modernism which distinguish it from the modern literature of other countries. Lagerkvist's influence in this regard has not been limited to his role as a leading novelist but applies to his poetry and drama as well.

In 1941, Lagerkvist received an honorary doctorate from the University of Gothenburg. In addition to being elected to the Swedish Academy of Literature in 1940, Lagerkvist received the Nobel Prize for Literature in 1951, the year following the publication of his novel *Barabbas*.

Biography

Pär Fabian Lagerkvist was born on May 23, 1891, in Växjö, Sweden, a small town in the southern region of Småland. His father, Anders Johan Lagerkvist, was the railway agent at the station in Växjö, and the family lived in a small apartment above the station's restaurant. His mother, Johanna Blad, was, like her husband, from a simple peasant family. Lagerkvist was the youngest of seven children, and like the others, he attended the local primary and secondary schools, spending summer vacations with his maternal grandparents in the country. Though normally reticent about biographical disclosure, Lagerkvist has described his early environment as a mixture of the fundamentalist conservatism of his parents with the radical nonconforming Calvinism of his maternal grandparents. Between these two competing religious attitudes, the young Lagerkvist was torn, and his inability to reconcile their contradictions eventually resulted in his abandonment of both.

During his secondary education at the Växjö *gymnasium*, Lagerkvist's rebellious attitude toward his family's conservative influence began to surface. Together with four of his friends, he formed a study group named the Red Circle. Wearing the broad-brimmed hat and flowing bow tie that indicated their affiliation with the growing Socialist movement, they met each Sunday morning at eleven o'clock—the precise hour that services were held at the nearby cathedral. With the Red Circle, Lagerkvist studied the works of Charles Darwin, Camille Flammarion, Thomas Huxley, Peter Kropotkin, Strindberg, and Henrik Ibsen—purveyors of a new view of the world which, Lagerkvist later said, "was sweeping God and all hope aside . . . laying life open and raw in all its nakedness, all its systematic absurdity."

Following his graduation from the *gymnasium* in 1910, Lagerkvist left home, going to live with his older brother, Gunnar, who was a schoolteacher in western Sweden. In the fall of 1911, Lagerkvist entered the University of Uppsala, where he studied art history and literature briefly, leaving in dissatisfaction after only one semester.

In this prewar period, from 1908 to 1914, Lagerkvist's lifelong attitude of rebellion against conformity in thought and traditional values in literature became increasingly apparent. Among his earliest published works are the idealistic "revolutionary songs of struggle," in which he identified with the developing Swedish workers' movements. Many of these early poems, essays, and prose sketches—which were first published in *Fram* and *Stormklockan*, two Socialist journals—were later collected in *Motiv* (1914). In 1912, Lagerkvist's first novella, *Människor*, appeared, and the following year, in the spring of 1913, he forsook the artistic isolation of Sweden for the avant-garde fashions of Paris, where he was much impressed by cubism. After a few months, he returned home and began to write the reviews of modern European novelists in which the earliest expression of his own personal aesthetic is to be found. Later in 1913, he published "Ordkonst och bildkonst"—his first important polemical work—in which he presented his critique of "the decadence of modern literature" against "the vitality of modern art."

With the outbreak of World War I, Lagerkvist fled to Denmark, settling in Copenhagen in 1915, where he remained until the Armistice was declared in 1918. During this period, he became intensely involved in the theater, and began reviewing drama for the local newspapers. In 1915, *Järn och människor*, his first volume of short stories, appeared, and in 1917, *Sista mänskan*, his first published play, appeared.

In 1918, Lagerkvist published the essay "Modern teater" ("Modern Theatre," 1966), which attacked the dominant mode of Naturalism in drama at that time, emulating August Strindberg's powerful experiments with Symbolism and ritual in his later plays. In the same year, he married a Danish woman, Karen Sörensen, with whom he returned to Sweden after the Armistice, where he served as drama critic for *Svenska dagbladet*, a Stockholm newspaper, during 1919. The following year, he traveled to Italy, France, and North Africa and published *The Eternal Smile*, a novella. Three years later, *Onda sagor* (1924; evil tales), his most famous collection of stories, appeared.

In 1925, Lagerkvist divorced his first wife and married Elaine Hallberg, a Swedish widow. The same year, his autobiographical novella *Guest of Reality* appeared. Lagerkvist was also active in the Swedish theater following the war, and in 1930, he and his wife settled permanently in Lidingö, an island community near Stockholm. In 1933, Lagerkvist published *The Hangman* and in the same year traveled to Palestine and Greece. This journey resulted in the publication of *Den knutna näven* (1934), a volume of travel essays which reflect Lagerkvist's intense interest in the early history of the religions of the Mediterranean region. In 1934, his dramatic adaptation of *The Hangman* was produced with great success—first in Norway and then in Sweden. In 1940, he was chosen to succeed Verner von Heidenstam as one of the "Eighteen Immortals" of the Swedish Academy of Literature, and in 1941, he received an honorary doctorate from the University of Gothenburg.

In 1944, *The Dwarf* appeared. This work was the first of a series of full-length novels that, through their translation into many other languages, brought Lagerkvist increasing recognition outside his own country. His growing international reputation was secured by the appearance in 1950 of *Barabbas*, which was immediately published in several translations. The following year, he was awarded the Nobel Prize for Literature. *Barabbas* has been the most popular of Lagerkvist's novels and has reached the widest audience by far. A dramatic version, which appeared in 1953, and a film version, released in 1960, were both very successful. Another novel, *The Sibyl*, which appeared in 1956, drew on Lagerkvist's interest in ancient Greek religion. In 1960, Lagerkvist began publishing a series of novels which critics later called "the Tobias trilogy." Comprising *The Death of Ahasuerus*, *Pilgrim at Sea*, and *The Holy Land*, the trilogy was later published in a single volume entitled *Pilgrimen*. Lagerkvist's last novel, *Herod and Mariamne*, appeared in 1967, the year of Elaine's death. On July 11, 1974, Lagerkvist died in Lidingö at the age of eighty-four.

Analysis

In his first critical work, "Ordkonst och bildkonst" (1913; word art and picture art), Pär Lagerkvist argues, as Thomas Buckman says, "that the naturalistic portrayal of reality in literature is completely inadequate for the representation of modern experience." The argument of this programmatic essay is divided into two parts—"On the Decadence of Modern Fiction" and "On the Vitality of Modern Art"—which indicate Lagerkvist's approach to his subject. Emulating the treatment of "simple thoughts" in literature—the themes of timeless, universal application which he found in the Bible, the Koran, the Egyptian Book of the Dead, the *Kalevala*, and the *Eddas*—he attacked what he called "the planless improvisations" of the psychological realism that dominated Swedish fiction at the beginning of the century. To escape the state of lifeless decadence into which literature had fallen, Lagerkvist suggested modern fiction should appropriate the nonrepresentational methods of modern art. He was particularly interested in the strongly stylized picture of reality in the works of the cubist painters—whose compositions he had just seen in Paris. In these works, he found a clear example of what he believed to be the most important aspect of art: the element of "constructivity"—which he placed in opposition to the mechanical imitation of reality practiced by the Naturalists and realists.

The aesthetic reform proposed in "Ordkonst och bildkonst" was elaborated in "Modern Theatre," an essay which appeared together with a series of three one-act plays entitled *Den svåra stunden* (*The Difficult Hour*, 1966) in the volume *Teater* (1918). In "Modern Theatre," Lagerkvist presented more fully his analysis of the situation of art in the modern world:

> Our time, in its lack of balance, its heterogeneity . . . is baroque and fantastic. . . . What a sea of brutality has broken over us, sweeping away and recreating! Is not every inner problem of mankind . . . now suddenly transformed into objective, threatening realities?

In such a world, with its "violent and abrupt contrasts," Naturalistic and realistic means of expression seemed increasingly inadequate. Lagerkvist attempts to convey this new experience of the world as both fantastic and threatening in *The Difficult Hour*, the three brief plays which make up the remainder of the volume. It is in these plays that the portrayal of man's experience of bewilderment before the "violent and abrupt contrasts" of modern life is successfully accomplished in mature and complex symbolic terms.

Equally important to Lagerkvist's work is the effect of this symbolic aesthetic upon the content and form of his fiction. In looking for symbolic analogues of modern man's experience and forms in which to express these experiences, Lagerkvist plunders many different mythological systems. Predominant among these, of course, is the Judeo-Christian heritage, though he also draws on the symbolic heritage of such diverse traditions as the dualistic and polytheistic religions of the ancient Near East, the Osirian religion of the ancient Egyptians, the mystery religions of the Hellenistic world, and the Norse mythology of his native Scandinavia.

Lagerkvist, in drawing on myths and legends from man's past, employs the material he finds there not to reconstruct that past so much as to reinterpret it from the perspective of life in the twentieth century. For Lagerkvist, the remote past in which nearly all of his novels are set is a symbolic world, as opposed to a historical one. It is through the activity of shaping the historical material to this purpose that Lagerkvist reveals the worldview that underlies his work.

Lagerkvist seems to prefer to treat legendary subjects about which the reader knows little, thus allowing himself greater freedom in shaping the material. Many times during his career, he has demonstrated the ability to take one of the marginal characters of a well-known story—about whom the original source provides only a bare minimum of facts—and then fabricate around it a plausible psychological and social context into which those few details are carefully woven. By an act of imagination, Lagerkvist provides marginal figures from the Bible and from the Apocrypha—figures such as Barabbas, Lazarus, Ahasuerus, Tobias, and Mariamne—with a past, with complex motivation arising out of that past, and, above all, with an individual consciousness which is both appropriate to the character in question and distinctively modern in its sensibility. It is this latter quality of Lagerkvist's characters that has led critics to call them "mouthpieces" for their author; this twentieth century sensibility in historical characters has also encouraged critics to read the stories themselves as allegories or fables of man's experience in the modern world.

Of all the important elements of Lagerkvist's work, however, it is not the aesthetic values, the subject matter, or the form of his work that has attracted the most attention, but rather the philosophical ideas and patterns of thought that they express. The questing protagonists whom he portrays in his novels are alienated outsiders who wander through life as strangers trapped in a world to which they do not belong. As many critics have pointed out, Lagerkvist's response to the spiritual questions is a curiously ambivalent one. While seeming to accept the objective truth of nineteenth century determinism—which swept God aside as an unnecessary appendage to a purely material universe—he continues to probe man's relentless quest for God in a world stripped of spiritual values.

Within this philosophical framework—which many critics have described as a form of religious existentialism—two particular tendencies of thought are prominent. The first of them is Lagerkvist's dualistic perspective on the world, which leads him to characterize himself, in *Den knutna näven*, the account of his travels to Greece and Palestine, as "a believer without a faith, a religious atheist."

For Lagerkvist, the god that most men worship is a false, inferior, and evil deity—which his character Ahasuerus in *The Death of Ahasuerus* describes as a twisted abortion of the human imagination. Beyond this god is the true God, an absolutely transcendent deity Who is wholly alien to man and, in His separation from the world, equally dissatisfying. This characteristic of Lagerkvist's thought has created much confusion among many of his critics, who, being unfamiliar with this type of theology, attempt to force the dualistic ideas and paradoxes expressed in his work into a more conventional Christian theological framework.

The second pattern of thought which is prominent in Lagerkvist's work is that of dialectical reasoning, which affects not only the arrangement of characters in the plot but also the structure of the novels themselves. This dialectical tendency is apparent in Lagerkvist's practice of presenting contrasting pairs of characters; examples of such contrasting pairs are the Sibyl and the Wandering Jew in *The Sibyl*, Barabbas and Sahak in *Barabbas*, and Tobias and Ahasuerus in *The Death of Ahasuerus*. Though there are frequently minor characters that are also contrasted in this way, Lagerkvist's novels almost always focus on a central pair of contrasting characters.

Typically, these contrasting characters become involved in debates as they tell their life stories to one another. As many critics and readers have observed, Lagerkvist is a novelist of ideas, and the argument and counterargument of these contrasting characters is typical of the way in which he engages his readers' indecision about such questions as the goodness of God, the origin of evil, the justification of earthly suffering, and the forgiveness of sins. In his trilogy comprising *The Death of Ahasuerus*, *Pilgrim at Sea*, and *The Holy Land*, this dialectic is carried on not only within the individual novels themselves but also from one novel to the next, much like what critics have seen in *The Sibyl*, an antithesis to *Barabbas*. Of this continuation of the dialectic from one volume to the next, Lagerkvist said: "I constantly conduct a dialogue with myself; one book answers the other."

For many readers, Lagerkvist's portrayal of human existence in his novels is the supreme expression of the mood of Nordic despair which pervades the last plays of Strindberg, Lagerkvist's direct literary ancestor, and the mature films of Ingmar Bergman, his best-known descendant. Prominent in this somber view of life is a Manichaean strain, a metaphysical dualism in which good and evil are eternally warring principles. In some of Lagerkvist's novels, these forces exist simultaneously within the same character, while in other novels, the forces are represented by contending groups or individuals. Regardless of how they are distributed, however, their opposition is not resolved, for the world that Lagerkvist portrays in his fiction is not, despite its historical trappings, a dynamic one capable of change; it is a profoundly static world composed of symbolic forms that move in an unchanging pattern of eternal conflict.

Lagerkvist's novel *The Dwarf* is in many ways the most atypical of his novels. Of the many novels he has published, it is the only one that does not draw upon biblical sources. *The Dwarf*, moreover, marks an important turning point in Lagerkvist's career, for in it one can see both where he has been and where he is going. The subject matter of *The Dwarf* is drawn from the Middle Ages, as was his most successful novella, *The Hangman*, a decade before. In form, however, *The Dwarf* approaches the dialectical method of his mature novels. Unlike most of his earlier fables and satires, which employ an omniscient perspective, *The Dwarf* uses the first-person point of view, allowing the dwarf Piccoline to tell his own story in the form of a memoir. Piccoline's account of his experiences is told after the fact; he tells his story from the confines of a dungeon where he has been imprisoned by his master, Prince Leone.

The debates about the nature of power, the relativity of good and evil, and the effects of conscience upon human behavior in which the dwarf engages are, by necessity, arguments with himself—since he is alone in the dungeon. Through the device of retrospection, however—a technical strategy which Lagerkvist uses in all of his subsequent novels—Piccoline is able to re-create his scenes of conflict with Prince Leone, Princess Angelica, his rival, the dwarf Jehoshaphat, and many others. The outcome of all of these conflicts is always the same: The dwarf is triumphant—though it is important for the reader to remember that he is an unreliable narrator and that his account of the events is clearly distorted by egotism. He strangles the rival Jehoshaphat during a wrestling match; he repays Angelica's innocent curiosity about his condition by killing her favorite cat; and he "helps" the Prince to overcome his vacillating conscience by poisoning his enemies for him.

In all of these actions, the dwarf comes to embody the force of evil loose in the world; yet, as Piccoline comes to realize, the malevolent, destructive impulses embodied in himself are present in all humans as part of our earthly heritage: "They think I scare them, but it is the dwarf within them, the ape-faced manlike being who sticks up its head from the depths of their souls." The deformity of the dwarf externalizes this intrinsic evil. As the dwarf concludes his story, he reminds the reader of the eternal nature of the conflicts that he has described: "I shall have an opportunity of continuing my chronicle by the light of day as before, and my services will be required again. If I know anything of my lord, he cannot spare his dwarf for long."

In this novel, then, one sees not only the dualistic character of Lagerkvist's thought but also the beginnings of his search for an adequate form in which to convey these ideas. For some readers, the cyclical movement displayed here—the suggestion that nothing has really changed—is very dissatisfying, since it violates the expectations they have about the dynamic character of the world derived from their experience with novels of psychological realism. This is perhaps the greatest ideological challenge Lagerkvist's work presents to its reader.

Lagerkvist's second novel, *Barabbas*, introduces important changes in subject matter and technique that influenced the remainder of his career. In this novel, he uses for the first time the body of legends surrounding the life of Christ, upon which all of his subsequent novels draw. He also begins to develop the complex narrative strategy of alternating first-person accounts spoken by the characters themselves with detached omniscient commentary. Such shifts in point of view are employed with increasing sophistication in his later novels.

Considered from the perspective of subject and form, then, *Barabbas* is the first of Lagerkvist's novels to combine successfully all the essential features of his mature style within a single work. Certainly, it is by far his most popular novel—though that is only in part the result of its aesthetic qualities. Of all of his novels, it has captured the largest and most diverse reading audience—who, attracted for the most part by its biblical subject matter, treat it as a conventional work of religious devotion.

Regardless of the reasons for its success, *Barabbas* was the first of Lagerkvist's novels to reach a large international audience, to whom his work was previously unknown. Within a year after its appearance in Sweden, *Barabbas* had been translated into nine other languages, and on the strength of its appeal to this huge new audience, Lagerkvist was awarded the Nobel Prize for Literature in 1951.

Perhaps the two most interesting features of the novel are the method of extrapolation Lagerkvist has employed in telling the story of Barabbas and the persistent ambiguity with which the facts of that story are presented to the reader. Taken together, these elements reveal the intense irony which pervades the book, a quality often missed by readers who, unfamiliar with the attitudes and patterns of thought reflected in Lagerkvist's other works, read the book as a pious, factual narrative.

The plot of *Barabbas* is almost entirely fabricated. The central character, Barabbas, is little more than a name in the biblical sources upon which Lagerkvist draws: The reader of the Gospel accounts is told only that Barabbas was the name of a notorious criminal of the time, who was pardoned at the Passover feast instead of Jesus. Building around this minimal core of information, Lagerkvist carefully arranges a grouping of characters designed to reveal the personality of the protagonist, whom he provides—by the method of extrapolation from the legendary material—with a personal history and a symbolic destiny.

In developing the character of Barabbas, Lagerkvist divides his novel into three discontinuous episodes, each of which presents an important stage of Barabbas' symbolic journey through life. The first section of the novel focuses on the consequences of his unexpected release from prison. Though he immediately returns to his old way of life when he is freed, his friends notice that he has lost the brash self-assurance which characterized his former life as a criminal. During this episode, he witnesses at first hand the Crucifixion and the mysterious darkness which falls upon the city at the last hour of Christ's Passion. As he is considering the rumors he has heard that this man who died in his place is the Son of God, he encounters a harelipped woman who is a faithful follower of this self-proclaimed Messiah. Her unquestioning faith in the authenticity of this Savior—who allowed Himself to be crucified in order that mankind might be redeemed—has an ironically literal application for Barabbas, the man who was pardoned at Christ's expense. The ironic interplay between the details of Barabbas' seemingly random experiences in the world and the symbols of the Christian doctrine of Salvation is a pervasive element in the novel, which abounds with such surprising coincidences.

This dramatic irony arising from the plot is intensified by the verbal ambiguity with which Lagerkvist calls the very facts of Barabbas' story into question. In the majority of instances, this is done by inserting hypothetical qualifications into the statements of the omniscient narrator. This stylistic strategy forces the reader to participate consciously in the imaginative construction of the text by constantly requiring judgments concerning the validity of the narrator's inferences about the perceptions, actions, and motivations of the characters described in this manner. The most hotly debated of these ambiguous statements is the concluding sentence of the novel, which describes the last thoughts of the dying protagonist, Barabbas: "When he felt death approaching, that which he had always been so afraid of, he said out into the darkness, as though he were speaking to it: 'To thee I deliver up my soul.'" Though many critics, in their zeal to discover the religious or existential meaning of the story of Barabbas, have tried to resolve the ambiguity of this statement, upon which the validity of their particular interpretation usually depends, the "as though" bracketing of the facts of the story resists all attempts at final reduction to such a meaning. In *Barabbas*, the potential of these complex strategies of verbal and dramatic irony is fully explored for the first time.

In *The Sibyl*, his third novel, Lagerkvist develops the technique of the narrative debate which reaches its perfected form in the Tobias trilogy. Of all Lagerkvist's novels, *The Sibyl* has the most self-conscious formal structure, alternating a detached omniscient narration with the first-person accounts of the two principal characters.

The novel begins with an omniscient expository prologue reminiscent of the opening formula of traditional fairy tales—a generic similarity which is apparent throughout the entire course of the novel. The prologue is followed by a brief expository introduction in which Ahasuerus, the Wandering Jew of biblical legend, arrives at the Sibyl's hut; in the section that follows, he recounts his experiences to her. Having completed his story, Ahasuerus engages the Sibyl in a debate about its significance, and then the Sibyl tells him the story of her experiences as the Delphic Pythia. In the epilogue, they again engage in a debate about the meaning of their experiences, and the novel is brought to a close by the comments of the moralizing narrator, who sorts out the objective "truth" of the characters' situation by means of his privileged position of omniscience, completing the circular pattern of the novel's formal movement.

In form, then, *The Sibyl* is a balanced compromise between the total objective detachment of the omniscient narrators employed in Lagerkvist's early fables and satires and the total subjectivity of the viewpoint employed in *The Dwarf*, with its unreliable narrator. By mingling the two modes of narration to tell a single story, Lagerkvist found a satisfying novelistic form that enabled him to present human experience in all of its complex ambiguity. In this way, he managed to avoid the abstraction into which his desire to treat man's experience in symbolic terms constantly threatened to fall. On the other hand, he was not limited by the technical restrictions of psychological realism—a "realism" incapable of expressing the baroque and fantastic quality of experience in the modern world.

The questing protagonist of the novel, Ahasuerus, who later reappears in *The Death of Ahasuerus*, the first of the Tobias novels, is never identified by name in *The Sibyl*, where he is simply referred to as "the stranger." It is clear from the story he tells, however, that he is the legendary Wandering Jew, supposedly condemned to this fate by Jesus, the Christian "savior" who cursed Ahasuerus for refusing to let him rest against his house on his way to Calvary. Reflecting on the misfortunes this curse has brought upon him, Ahasuerus comes to see the contradiction between the compassionate image of God as Christ and the vengeful malice that this curse of eternal retribution reveals in his nature. As he considers this contradiction in his discussion with the Sibyl—which follows the tale of his misfortunes—he relates it to the paradox of the Crucifixion, about which he had heard many puzzling rumors: "I can't make out either what good it was supposed to do. But I've heard it said that his father wanted him to suffer."

In his questioning of the justice and benevolence of a deity who could treat man in such a vengeful fashion as he has treated the Wandering Jew, and who is apparently so jealous of the forces of evil loose in the world that he would send down a son to recapture those who had rejected him, Ahasuerus is posing questions which are at the heart of Lagerkvist's dualistic view of the world, questions which are echoed by the dwarf, by Barabbas, and by the protagonists of all of his subsequent novels.

Whatever the challenges and difficulties presented to the reader by the aesthetic values which inform his work, Lagerkvist has, for many readers, successfully challenged the dominant mode of psychological realism in modern literature. In restoring the symbolic, mythic function to modern literature through the example of his own work, he has no doubt provided inspiration for many others.

Major publications other than long fiction

SHORT FICTION: *Järn och människor*, 1915; *Onda sagor*, 1924; *The Eternal Smile and Other Stories*, 1954; *The Marriage Feast and Other Stories*, 1955; *Prosa I-V*, 1956; *The Eternal Smile: Three Stories*, 1971.

PLAYS: *Sista mänskan*, 1917; *Teater*, 1918 (includes the essay "Modern Teater" ["Modern Theatre," 1966] and *Den svåra stunden* [*The Difficult Hour*, 1966]); *Himlens hemlighet*, 1919 (*The Secret of Heaven*, 1966); *Han som fick leva om sitt liv*, 1928 (*The Man Who Lived His Life Over*, 1971); *Bödeln*, 1934 (*The Hangman*, 1966); *Mannen utan själ*, 1936 (*The Man Without a Soul*, 1944); *Låt människan leva*, 1949 (*Let Man Live*, 1951); *Barabbas*, 1953; *Dramatik I-III*, 1956; *Modern Theatre; Seven Plays and an Essay*, 1966 (includes the essay "Modern Theatre" and *The Difficult Hour*).

POETRY: *Motiv*, 1914 (includes essays and prose sketches); *Ångest*, 1916; *Kaos*, 1919 (includes the play *The Secret of Heaven*); *Den lyckliges väg*, 1921; *Hjärtats sånger*, 1926; *Vid lägereld*, 1932; *Genius*, 1937; *Sång och strid*, 1940; *Hemmet och stjärnan*, 1942; *Aftonland*, 1953 (*Evening Land*, 1975); *Dikter*, 1965.

NONFICTION: *Teater*, 1918 (includes the essay "Modern teater" ["Modern Theatre," 1966] and plays); *Den knutna näven*, 1934; *Antecknat*, 1977.

Bibliography

Buckman, Thomas. "Introduction," in *Modern Theatre: Seven Plays and an Essay*, 1966.

Budd, John. *Eight Scandinavian Novelists*, 1981.

Henmark, Kai. *Främlingen Lagerkvist*, 1966.

Jonas, Hans. *The Gnostic Religion*, 1963.

Ryberg, Anders. *Pär Lagerkvist in Translation: A Bibliography*, 1964.

Scobbie, Irene. *Pär Lagerkvist: An Introduction*, 1963.
Sjöberg, Leif. *Pär Lagerkvist*, 1976.
Spector, Robert Donald. *Pär Lagerkvist*, 1973.
Weathers, Winston. *Pär Lagerkvist: A Critical Essay*, 1968.
White, Ray Lewis. *Pär Lagerkvist in America*, 1980.

Steven E. Colburn

SELMA LAGERLÖF

Born: Mårbacka, Sweden; November 20, 1858
Died: Mårbacka, Sweden; March 16, 1940

Principal long fiction

Gösta Berlings saga, 1891 (*The Story of Gösta Berling*, 1898; also as *Gösta Berling's Saga*, 1918); *Antikrists mirakler*, 1897 (*The Miracles of Antichrist*, 1899); *Jerusalem I: I Dalarne*, 1901 (*Jerusalem*, 1915); *Jerusalem II: I det heliga landet*, 1902 (*The Holy City: Jerusalem II*, 1918); *Herr Arnes penningar*, 1904 (*The Treasure*, 1925); *En saga om en saga*, 1908 (*The Girl from the Marshcroft*, 1910); *Liljecronas hem*, 1911 (*Liliecrona's Home*, 1914); *Körkarlen*, 1912; *Kejsaren av Portugallien*, 1914 (*The Emperor of Portugallia*, 1916); *Bannlyst*, 1918 (*The Outcast*, 1922); *Löwensköldska ringen*, 1925-1928 (*The Ring of the Löwenskölds: A Trilogy*, 1928; includes *Löwenskölda ringen*, 1925 [*The General's Ring*, 1928]; *Charlotte Löwensköld*, 1925 [English translation, 1928]; *Anna Svärd*, 1928 [English translation, 1928]); *Höst*, 1933 (*Harvest*, 1935).

Other literary forms

Selma Lagerlöf's first novel, *Gösta Berling's Saga*, is a cycle of stories with a common setting and a shared cast of characters; short stories, particularly tales drawn from oral traditions of her native Värmland, are Lagerlöf's most characteristic form. Lagerlöf published several volumes of stories, and two of her works, *The Treasure* and the trilogy *The Ring of the Löwenskölds*, could be classified as tales. Two of Lagerlöf's major story collections, *Osynliga länkar* (1894; *Invisible Links*, 1899) and *Drottningar i Kungahälla* (1899; *From a Swedish Homestead*, 1901; also in *The Queens of Kungahälla and Other Sketches*, 1917) followed the publication of her first novel. In *Invisible Links*, Lagerlöf relies on plots from Swedish folk legends. *The Queens of Kungahälla* is based on the Norwegian royal sagas—the *Heimskringla* (twelfth century) and others—which record the careers and legends of medieval Scandinavian kings. Lagerlöf has presented these well-known stories from the point of view of the women in them.

Lagerlöf is also the author of the classic of Swedish children's literature, *Nils Holgerssons underbara resa genom Sverige* (1906-1907; *The Wonderful Adventures of Nils*, 1907; *The Further Adventures of Nils*, 1911). Commissioned by the National Teachers' Association of Sweden, this work was "to present in story form the geography, folklore, flora and fauna of the various Swedish provinces." Lagerlöf chose to do that through a story of a lazy and mischievous boy who is brought down to size by elves he has troubled. Nils becomes acquainted with a barnyard goose, much larger than he, and the two join a migrating flock of wild geese, Nils traveling on the gander's back.

Lagerlöf's *Kristuslegender* (1904; *Christ Legends*, 1908) although not explicitly a children's book, has had a worldwide response from children. Clemence Dane once called this work "the truest Christmas book of all." The simple, compassionate stories of Christ's life are described as if they might be ordinary neighborhood occurrences. The Christmas season is central to many of Lagerlöf's stories and novels. Of the eleven stories in *Christ Legends*, seven of them deal with Christ's birth and childhood.

In 1915, Lagerlöf wrote a volume of short stories entitled *Troll och människor* and completed a second volume of the same title in 1921. The subjects of most of these tales are drawn from Värmland lore. In 1920, Lagerlöf wrote a book-length biography of Zacharias Topelius, the Finnish poet who had been a major influence on the author's literary development.

Several of Lagerlöf's later works are autobiographical, among them her memoirs, which are collected in the three so-called Mårbacka volumes: *Mårbacka* (1922; English translation, 1924), *Ett barns memoarner* (1930; *Memories of My Childhood*, 1934), and *Dagbok, Mårbacka III* (1932; *The Diary of Selma Lagerlöf*, 1936). *Liliecrona's Home*, Lagerlöf's novel published in 1911, also has an autobiographical basis.

Achievements

Lagerlöf spent years searching for the right poetic form in which to present the stories that became *Gösta Berling's Saga*. In an age dominated by Henrik Ibsen, August Strindberg, and other realists whose plays and novels were strongly Naturalistic and often addressed current social issues, Lagerlöf found her own artistic energies frustrated. She did try writing for a time in a realistic style and, for many years, conceived of all of her works as poems. Her talent, however, was not to be realized as a debater of contemporary problems, nor was she to become an explorer of psychological consciousness. Rather, Lagerlöf yearned to express what she believed were the heroic, elemental, and spiritual strains running through daily life. Thomas Carlyle's *Heroes and Hero-Worship, and the Heroic in History* (1841) gave her a sense of what was to become the epic fairy-tale atmosphere so characteristic of her mature work. In contrast to her contemporaries, many of whom examined their characters' psychological sensibilities in elaborate and often painful detail, Lagerlöf created characters marked by tragedy, sorrow, and joy, but who move through their lives with a stately dignity given them by an author who, as a matter of decorum and aesthetic choice, does not violate a character's privacy.

With the appearance of her first book, Lagerlöf's distinctly unmodern aesthetic, perhaps more at home in the ninth century than the nineteenth, was warmly received by her countrymen, who, time and time again, communicated to her their gratitude that she expressed her subject matter in a mode entirely absent from contemporary literature.

In 1909, the Swedish Academy awarded to her the Nobel Prize for Literature, commending her noble idealism, the richness of her imagination, and the generosity and beauty of forms that characterize her work. She was the first woman to win the prize. In characteristic fashion, her speech to the Nobel Commission took the form of a story: of a journey she made to Heaven to tell her father about winning the prize. In the course of this address, Lagerlöf reviewed the several influences that had kindled her imagination, particularly honoring the "old country folk" who had taught her "to cast the glamour of poetry over grim rocks and grey waters." Five years later, Selma Lagerlöf became the first woman to be elected to the Swedish Academy. Her works are widely translated.

Biography

Selma Ottiliana Lovisa Lagerlöf was born on November 20, 1858, at Mårbacka in Värmland, Sweden. Her parents, both members of aristocratic families, had moved to the estate of Mårbacka after Selma's father, Lieutenant Erik Gustav Lagerlöf, had failed to inherit the important post of Regimental Paymaster from his father. Lieutenant Lagerlöf became a gentleman farmer with many progressive ideas, few of which proved practical. Lack of success at farming seemed relatively unimportant to the Lieutenant, who, according to various memoirs, was a true son of the gay-hearted Värmland gentry. Among other celebrations held at Mårbacka, Lieutenant Lagerlöf's annual birthday party, enlivened by pageants, theatricals, poetry recitations, dancing, and singing, became a social affair famous throughout the province. Adolph Noreen, later a noted philologist, attended some of these holiday affairs at Mårbacka and remembers how Lieutenant Lagerlöf, in his office as host, made everyone feel "what an unspeakable happiness [it was] just to live!" Selma herself, as her fiction widely attests, shared this exuberant perspective. Her father's character plays a part in her creation of the cavaliers in *Gösta Berling's Saga*.

As a child, the future writer was more aware of such doings than other children because she was more observer than participant. At the age of four, the little girl had been stricken by a paralysis that left her lame, although she regained the ability to walk. The special care dictated by her condition allowed her to ripen her natural inclination for intellectual and imaginative pursuits. Lagerlöf later noted that the greatest sorrow of her childhood came with the death of her grandmother, who, as she remembered, had told her stories "from morning until evening." Other family members, particularly a sister of Lagerlöf's father, were also gifted storytellers.

Tales told from memory and read aloud at night—from local legend, from Hans Christian Andersen, and from Scandinavian sagas—were the essence of Selma Lagerlöf's early education; neither she nor her sister attended school. By early adolescence, Lagerlöf had determined that she would be a writer. During the next several years, she wrote novels, plays, and poems. In 1880, she attracted the notice of Eva Fryxell, a young author of the day, when she read an occasional poem at a friend's wedding. Despite Fryxell's sponsorship, Lagerlöf failed to place any of her work in literary journals. Fryxell encouraged the girl to broaden her education, a plan to which Lagerlöf eagerly subscribed. After a year's preparation at Sjöberg's Lyceum in Stockholm, Lagerlöf entered a teachers' college. During her years of training there, the idea of cavaliers living at a manor house, the germ of what was to become *Gösta Berling's Saga*, first came to her. It was to be ten years before it attained final form.

In 1885, Selma Lagerlöf began a career as a teacher at a high school for girls at Landskrona. According to students' reports, Lagerlöf was an unusually gifted teacher. She taught school for ten years, during which time she wrote several stories which became part of *Gösta Berling's Saga*. In 1888, three years after her father's death, Mårbacka was sold. It was while she was at the homestead, watching her childhood home and family heirlooms sold, that she finally realized that her story of the cavaliers should be told in a series of tales. With the five chapters she had completed by July of 1890, Lagerlöf won a competition sponsored by the women's paper *Idun*. She finished *Gösta Berling's Saga* by December of 1891, and it was published. While sales in Sweden were at first sluggish, the Danish version attracted the attention of the Danish critic and literary historian Georg Brandes, who immediately recognized it as a work of genius. His critical acclaim won widespread recognition for the book. By the time the second Swedish edition appeared, in 1895, recognition had come to Lagerlöf from all quarters.

In 1895 and 1896, Lagerlöf visited Italy, Switzerland, Germany, and Belgium, supported by a Royal Traveling Scholarship. Her visit to Sicily provided inspiration for *The Miracles of Antichrist*. Other travels followed. Of particular importance was Lagerlöf's journey to the Orient, partly in response to her desire to learn about a group of peasants from Dalecarlia, who had emigrated to the Holy Land in pursuit of a fundamentalist Christian vision. While in Palestine, Lagerlöf gathered material for the second volume of *Jerusalem*, the plot of which is based on the Dalecarlian colony.

Lagerlöf's growing reputation as a writer never discouraged her from offering her talents in support of causes in which she believed. In June, 1911, she delivered a speech before the World Congress on Women's Suffrage; during World War I, she gave her full support to relief work; and after the war, she wrote on behalf of the Red Cross.

After Lagerlöf was awarded the Nobel Prize in 1909, nearly all other literary honors offered in Sweden were awarded to her. The income associated with her success allowed her to repurchase the estate of Mårbacka, to which she moved with her mother. Until Lagerlöf's death in 1940, she oversaw the estate, entertained admirers and visitors from all over Europe and America, and sustained a large correspondence. She died at Mårbacka on March 16, 1940.

Analysis

Although Selma Lagerlöf wrote many distinguished novels, her countrymen have always considered the first to be her masterpiece. Whatever other merits later novels have—and they are more sophisticated in plot construction and theme—none compares to *Gösta Berling's Saga* for sheer concentration of vitality and idealism. The paeans of praise to Värmland's landscape and the detailed knowledge of Sweden's natural history, hallmarks of Lagerlöf's prose style, first appear here. As in later novels, the narrative voice in *Gösta Berling's Saga* is more prominent than those of the characters. The narrator is a storyteller; the raconteur never fades unobtrusively into the background. A reader knows that he is but a listener: The teller will make the story and say what it signifies. Characters do not, as in more realistic fiction, resemble living persons with lives of their own; rather, they are like marionettes, pulled up to their feet to dance only when the storyteller commands. One would never speculate about what a Lagerlöf character might be thinking when that character is not in the immediate scene. Characters, because they are so fully bound to the scenes in which they appear, simply do not exist when they are not "onstage." In Lagerlöf's novels, an air of reality surrounds the story but not the individual characters in it. In turn, the reader must listen, accept as final what information the narrator provides, and, above all, agree to be entertained.

The opening scene of *Gösta Berling's Saga* is characteristic of Lagerlöf's epic sweep, her comic tone, and, particularly, her eccentric character portraits. Gösta Berling, a young pastor, mounts the pulpit, pauses momentarily for inspiration, giving his congregation time to notice his exquisite features. His voice grows rich and strong as his images of God's glories ring through the chancel. At sermon's end, he has convinced the visiting bishop of his extraordinary merit; Gösta's triumph is particularly notable because on the previous Sunday he was not in church, nor was he there for many Sundays before that—each time he had been too drunk to preach. This day appears to be his redemption. One of Gösta's overzealous drinking companions, however—fearing that the bishop might still dismiss Gösta—takes the bishop on a carriage ride over ditches and half-plowed fields, counting on physical coercion to accomplish what the brilliant sermon may have fallen short of accomplishing. Hearing of his friend's misplaced loyalty, Gösta despairs of his future as a preacher and runs away. When next seen, he is stealing a sled loaded with grain from a child in another village.

In Lagerlöf's novels, human destiny is prey to violent turns of the sort Gösta's takes; the sheer speed with which a woman loses her beauty or a pastor becomes a derelict gives the work the flavor of fairy tale or allegory. This is particularly true in this first novel, in which Lagerlöf was finding a style suitable to her Carlylean vision. Later novels possess a greater aura of realism but operate essentially upon the same premises.

Gösta is rescued by the Mistress of Ekeby, the pipe-smoking, gracious, and powerful owner of seven mines and hostess to a group of pensioners. She makes Gösta one of her cavaliers. (This situation is based on an actual custom prevalent in Sweden after the Napoleonic Wars, when families on the great estates often did take in war veterans who had little to do. They were given room and board in exchange for their appearance at social functions in the district. A cavalier was expected to sing, dance, or be socially charming in some other way.)

Although the novel does have a plot of sorts, the power of the story is primarily its ability to render the life at the manor houses of a Sweden which was vanishing during Lagerlöf's childhood. The beautifully embellished descriptions of great balls and sleigh rides suggest a nostalgic longing for a life more elegant in manner and more mythic in perception than that of later eras.

The main body of *Gösta Berling's Saga* loosely centers on Gösta's reformation as he endures his humbled station as a pensioner. Gösta, "the strongest and weakest of men," is the center of provincial society, winning the affection of four of the district's loveliest women. The gentle influence of these good women and the subtler chastening of the Almighty lead Gösta from his impetuous youth to the verge of maturity.

The *Bildungsroman* begins on Christmas Eve, when the cavaliers—Gösta signing for them—make a pact with Sintram, a jealous blacksmith who comes to the cavaliers disguised as the Devil. Sintram's predictions of doom are realized when the cavaliers take over the estate, bringing it to the brink of ruin through their wild dissipations and neglect of the industries. In turn, the district is blighted; unemployment, drunkenness, and general stagnation reign. In the novel's terms, God's Storm Year breaks over the countryside.

Nearly every main character—most are treated in separate vignettes—suffers a life-changing tragedy or loss, and these events represent a kind of spiritual cleansing. In the end, Sintram is arrested, and the Mistress of Ekeby returns home to die.

The thirty-six chapters of the book divide roughly into three sections. The first is dominated by Gösta's love affairs and the prosperous days the cavaliers enjoy before Ekeby slides toward destruction. The second section, centered on the sorrowful fate of the Countess Elizabeth, records the ongoing brilliant exploits of the cavaliers against scenes of impending doom. The cavaliers are in the background in the third section, which features great crowd scenes, emphasizing the desperate plight of the people during the year of devastation. This desolate course is altered at last by the noble Lennaert, who gives his life to defend a group of children and women. In the end, the chastened Mistress of Ekeby dies peacefully, and Gösta sets forth with his new wife to rebuild the district's fortunes.

In *Gösta Berling's Saga*, as in all of Selma Lagerlöf's novels, dramatic scenes of daily life give way to mythical, epic moments or insights. Neither mode prevails for long, and it is the tension between them that is the hallmark of Lagerlöf's style in this early novel. No event, however small, is conceived apart from the metaphysical claim that God's Storm Year has broken over the land. The morality implicit in such an idea emanates with epic force from natural causes—wind, storms, ice, and blizzard—and from the lake, invoked by the narrator as the district's guardian muse. Handsome Gösta is little more than a human embodiment of the same idea.

In the two-part novel *Jerusalem*, Lagerlöf employs another native Swedish setting but peoples it with sober, pious Dalecarlian peasants, profoundly unlike their lighthearted countrymen from Värmland. In their ability to see visions and interpret dreams, and in their earnest regard for life, the Dalecarlians resemble Old Testament Hebrews. While it is the narrator in *Gösta Berling's Saga* who gives voice to mythical and epic components at work, in *Jerusalem* it is the characters themselves. Many have the power to see from one world into the other, and they pass easily between the two. The point of view in this novel is more specifically religious but as undoctrinaire and humane as the one in *Gösta Berling's Saga*.

The first book opens as Ingmar Ingarsson is plowing his fields, engaged in contemplation. His farm is prosperous and the activity salutary, but Ingmar has much on his mind. Several years before, Ingmar's fiancée, Brita, troubled because the wedding she never wanted had been postponed until "after the christening," ran away, gave birth to a child, and strangled it. After years in prison, she is due to be released, and Ingmar must decide if he will meet her. After "deliberating" with his dead father and making a conscious decision not to meet her, Ingmar nevertheless brings Brita home, and the two share a long, happy life. Ingmar and Brita's children become the central subjects of the second half of the first volume.

Even while Ingmar is still living, various fundamentalist religious sects spring up within the district. Efforts are made to counteract the movement, but to little avail. Hellgum, the husband of one of the Ingmarsson daughters, forms one communal society. Another daughter is convinced to join when a paralysis she has suffered is miraculously cured as her little daughter is about to wander into a fire. In a scene reminiscent of the God's Storm Year motif from *Gösta Berling's Saga*, a cataclysmic storm, known as the Wild Hunt, breaks over the district one night, convincing many doubters to join the sect.

The group of believers, to the great sorrow of their families, decides to go to Jerusalem to live in closer concord with their beliefs. The departure of the group breaks up the community, splits homes, and parts lovers. One of the most powerful scenes is the final one in the first volume, in which the train of pilgrims sets forth, leaving their ancestral homes. Lagerlöf said she modeled this portion of the story on the Scandinavian sagas; the profound attachment to the soil and the determination visible in the lives of the simple farmers are depicted in heroic terms.

Volume 2, *The Holy City*, is set primarily in Jerusalem. It opens with an imaginary dialogue between the Dome of the Rock and the Holy Sepulchre, which summarizes the long history of the country that was once fertile and flowering and now is barren, that once was a religious center for many religions and now is cruelly divided between competing religious factions. Much of this book is devoted to a history of the colonists, who eventually reach a deeper understanding of their purpose in Jerusalem when young Ingmar arrives and encourages them to take up their old livelihoods. In a scene not unlike the one in which the smithy is fired up and the mill wheels set in motion at Ekeby, the colonists in Jerusalem begin making cloth, shoes, and bread, the wares of their old livelihoods. Ingmar's purpose in traveling to Jerusalem is to rescue his former love, Gertrude, from madness. Like many colonists, Gertrude suffers from fevers, and her desire for rapturous experiences are bound up with delirium. In the end, she and her new fiancé return to Sweden with Ingmar, where Ingmar is reunited with his estranged wife.

In the Jerusalem books, Lagerlöf's fictional treatment of the fundamentalist ideas which divide the Dalecarlian community is a balanced one. While the most compelling scenes are set in Sweden, not Jerusalem, the sympathy Lagerlöf creates for the fervent pilgrims is considerable. In the trilogy of her maturity, *The Ring of the Löwenskölds*, she attempts with less success to achieve the same tone of compelling objectivity.

The Ring of the Löwenskölds, the first novel of the trilogy, which bears its name, is a ghost story, generically similar to Lagerlöf's novella *The Treasure* but less violent. This tale traces the fate of a ring given to the district hero by Charles XII and stolen from his grave by a simple country farm couple. Disaster follows immediately: The couple's house burns and they lose all their possessions. Nevertheless, they are afraid to return the ring, and it passes to the next generation. Three men who find a former owner dead in the woods are accused of his murder. Although they are innocent and pass an ordeal to prove it, they are all put to death. Unknown to them, the ring was sewn into a cap that one of the men picked up in the woods near the dead man's body. A young servant girl eventually frees the Löwenskölds from the curse.

This first part, the shortest segment of the trilogy, is a story replete with fairy-tale motifs and repetitions. It ends with a romantic and comic moment. After the servant girl saves the young master of the house from the general's ghost by returning the ring to the general's grave, the two seem destined for one another. Yet when the girl appears in the baron's room to receive his thanks, she learns that he is engaged to another. She herself is relatively untroubled by this turn of events and continues to serve the household for years. In a rather unbelievable twist of plot, her daughter, Thea Sundler, emerges in the sequel books to take revenge on later generations of Löwenskölds. This tenuous connection is all that links *The Ring of the Löwenskölds* to the later books of the trilogy, which are among Lagerlöf's finer realistic novels.

The whole of *Charlotte Löwensköld* and the first two-thirds of *Anna Svärd* form a compelling story of a young minister and the two women he courts. The final third of *Anna Svärd* reverts from realism to the fairy-tale tone that opens the trilogy. When the storyteller attributes Thea Sundler's jealousy of Charlotte Löwensköld and Anna Svärd to the ring's curse, the realistic development of the novel is broken. To achieve this unity with the first book, Lagerlöf systematically dismantles characters, sending them into the final pages as two-dimensional versions of themselves. Anna disappears from view to reappear in a single scene in which we are to believe she has forgotten what she learned during hard years of experience; Charlotte lingers, but her character is of little consequence.

Such narrative oddities serve to point up the fact that, although Lagerlöf wrote "novels," she was preeminently a teller of tales. Her plot structures are simple ones, based on reversals of fate and characters' growing awareness of the larger cosmic design against which all human events play. Lagerlöf's strengths as a novelist are most obvious in the openings and development of her works. She is unmatched at setting a scene; there, the storyteller finds her natural medium. She creates in the reader the sense that he is present at an oral rendition of the story. Each chapter begins afresh, as if the storyteller has been out for air and has returned to address a band of eager listeners. Her confidence allows her to risk a long, pregnant suspension. The introductory material might be a scrap of folk philosophy pertinent to the tale, a description of a landscape, or a bantering dialogue between narrator and an imaginary audience.

After such a lead, the action typically springs forward, the author weaving into an unforgettable spectacle precise descriptions of houseware, blossoming hedges, or the contents of a peddler's pack. Information about a character and his motives is invariably sketchier. In *Charlotte Löwensköld*, for example, one chapter is devoted to the preparations the manorial staff make for the arrival of Schagerström and Charlotte on their wedding day. Floors are scrubbed, great arches of flowers are braided and hung along the road, and the manor folk, dressed in costumes matching their trades, line the pathway to cheer the new bride. Yet for all the attention devoted to the advent of Charlotte's tenure as mistress of Schagerström's manor, the theme is never mentioned again. Characters may be at the heart of the action in one scene but may then disappear with little ado; likewise, a scene may be drawn with an exactitude that commands the reader's attention but may have little to do with the direction of the plot. To a modern novelist, this shuttling of characters in and out, combined with the care taken to create lavish background scenes for their own sakes, is an eccentric narrative habit. As noted, this aesthetic is defined by the persona of the omniscient storyteller. She and she alone determines what belongs to the story. Motives are revealed as the narrator sees fit; otherwise, the reader has no access to them.

Something of Lagerlöf's development as a novelist can be understood by comparing Gösta Berling and Karl Arthur Ekenstedt. Despite the titles *Charlotte Löwensköld* and *Anna Svärd*, the two novels are primarily the story of Karl Arthur Ekenstedt. Charlotte is his fiancée for five years and Anna Svärd is his wife; Thea Sundler is his confidante and later his illicit companion. Karl Arthur's mother, the Baroness, is the fourth woman whose life is interwoven with Karl Arthur's.

In many ways, Karl Arthur is a more realistic Gösta Berling. The four women in his life are interwoven throughout the story and are not simply a string of romantic attachments, as Gösta's women are. While Karl Arthur has a more believable biography, he is neither as lovable nor as intrinsically capable of reform as is Gösta. Ekenstedt's characterization embodies a mature and realistic version of a theme touched only lightly in *Gösta Berling's Saga*. In the early novel, it is primarily a comic invention to have Gösta appear as a drunken preacher. Once he runs from his parish, Gösta's spiritual life is left behind, simply a passing stage of his youth. On the other hand, in Lagerlöf's more realistically conceived later work, Karl Arthur's concept of religion and his identity as a pietist are given a much larger part, and Lagerlöf, the most devout and optimistic of novelists, treats this theme both seriously and severely.

Karl Arthur Ekenstedt is a Löwensköld, a distant cousin to Charlotte. He is the youngest of three children, the apple of his mother's eye. Because she is the Baroness, the most popular woman in the district, outshining her daughters in all ways, her adoration of Karl Arthur becomes a district affair. Everyone knows that Arthur is off at the university taking Latin examinations or preparing for this or that degree. In fact, he is an ordinary boy, utterly spoiled by his mother's attentions. His extreme handsomeness, like Gösta's, attracts others to him, particularly women. While carrying out a mediocre study program at the university, Karl Arthur becomes acquainted with a young pietist who initiates him into the religion of austerity. Because Karl Arthur is unable to succeed in other ways, he determines to become a man of God. In subsequent years, his destructive jealousies, fired by a religious fanaticism, become the cover for his own weakness and also threaten to destroy others. Like Gösta, Karl Arthur is a gifted preacher under certain inspirations. More often, however, he is confused and quick to believe that he must reform those near him in order to become more devout and thus more popular.

Despite his family's position and the possibility of acquiring a prestigious parish, Karl Arthur is content to remain at the deanery as curate. While there, he meets Charlotte, who is companion to the dean and his wife. Although Charlotte is amused by Karl Arthur's pietism, they become friends and Karl Arthur proposes. Five years pass, and Karl Arthur has made no attempt to take his career in hand. Not knowing that Charlotte is engaged, a wealthy gentleman from the countryside asks for Charlotte's hand. Charlotte, a spirited and loyal woman, refuses him. When Karl Arthur hears about the proposal, he remembers a single occasion when Charlotte suggested that he might try to find a post of his own, and he is furious at the thought. He uses what he terms Charlotte's "ambition" as an excuse for breaking with her, and she attempts to bring about a reconciliation. After Charlotte offers to accompany him to the poorest parish and to live in a humble hut, Karl Arthur is calmed, but a jealous thought sends him swiftly out the door, vowing that he will marry the first woman he sees.

Karl Arthur tells himself that he is submitting completely to God's Will, but once out on the road, he begins to regret his rash vow. The moment is one of Lagerlöf's most comic. The woman Karl Arthur meets is (to his great relief) a pretty Dalecarlian peasant girl, Anna Svärd, unschooled in the ways of the gentry but a skillful peddler woman, both bright and good-hearted—an acceptable alternative to Charlotte. Meanwhile, Karl Arthur's fierce jealousy of Charlotte and his overweening pride are both encouraged by Thea Sundler, wife of the church organist. Thea, who is herself in love with Karl Arthur, manages to convince him that Charlotte is unfaithful to him.

In the opening pages of *Anna Svärd*, Lagerlöf delineates life in the northern village where Anna lives, and the segment is as sympathetic and beautifully drawn as that describing Charlotte's life among the gentry. Lagerlöf lavishes scene after scene on Anna's wedding preparations, her acquisition of manners fitting to a minister's wife, and her innocent adoration of her handsome fiancé in the south. Great plans are made for the wedding, which Anna's uncle, a man of some means, will provide. Anna is believed to be favored above all peasant women; she will have "horse and cow, manservant and maidservant."

Karl Arthur has something quite different in mind. He arrives in the village one day, insisting that the marriage take place immediately, without ceremony. As the bailiff's wife quickly perceives, Karl Arthur is looking for a wife who is both manservant and maidservant. Anna, too stunned and too enamored of Karl Arthur to protest, sets off with him. Anna arrives at her new home to find that it is no more than a hut refurbished for the couple by Thea Sundler. To help keep Karl Arthur true to his pietist ways, Thea has prepared a comfortable couch for Karl Arthur in his study and a narrow cot for Anna in the kitchen. As she will do many times over the next several years, Anna outwits Thea and has her wedding bed. Years later, however, after Karl Arthur has callously ignored her feelings again and again, Anna finally leaves him. Karl Arthur himself, his preaching not going well, determines that God wants him to be out on the road preaching to the traveling folk, so he decides to take God's Word to the markets and fairs.

At this point, the novel loses its realistic foundation. Thea runs away to follow Karl Arthur, and the two become derelicts of the road; Anna, pregnant with Karl Arthur's child, finds a group of ten orphans, adopts them, and buys a farm with money from Karl Arthur's parents. Charlotte has long since married the country gentleman whose proposal she rejected when she was engaged to Karl Arthur.

Karl Arthur's pietism is equivalent to weakness of character. His absorption in himself, disguised as an ongoing search for God's way, is brilliantly portrayed and satirized. His is a more complex portrait than Gösta Berling's. At the depth of his misfortune, Karl Arthur says, "I hate mankind"—given his behavior, an apt and honest summation. Lagerlöf's description is sure and revealing. In the end, however, the narrator does not take her theme to a fittingly dismal conclusion. She attempts in the last chapters to thread Karl Arthur's tragedy and the deaths of other Löwensköld barons back to the ring's curse. The portrayal of a flawed man surrounded by good women is finally more memorable than the cursed ring motif; nevertheless, it is typical of the storyteller's mode not to wish any of her characters ill. In the final scene, Karl Arthur is planning to go to Africa to preach. Anna goes to church to hear him make his appeal and, recalling her youthful love, drops her wedding ring into the collection plate. The novel closes as Karl Arthur arrives at Anna's door, the storyteller asking, "How shall she answer him?"

In characteristic Lagerlöf style, then, the story resolves itself with a suggestion of enlightenment and joy. In this case, the ending and much of the narrative are also comic. Lagerlöf's use of comedy bypasses her more serious themes rather than bringing them to a resolution. Even so, *Charlotte Löwensköld* and *Anna Svärd* are Lagerlöf's masterworks of character portrayal; they have been favorably compared to those of Jane Austen.

Major publications other than long fiction

SHORT FICTION: *Osynliga länkar*, 1894 (*Invisible Links*, 1899); *Drottningar i Kungahälla*, 1899 (*From a Swedish Homestead*, 1901; also in *The Queens of Kungahälla and Other Sketches*, 1917); *Kristuslegender*, 1904 (*Christ Legends*, 1908); *Troll och människor*, 1915, 1921 (2 volumes).

NONFICTION: *Zachris Topelius*, 1920; *Mårbacka*, 1922 (English translation, 1924); *Ett barns memoarner*, 1930 (*Memories of My Childhood*, 1934); *Dagbok, Mårbacka III*, 1932 (*The Diary of Selma Lagerlöf*, 1936).

CHILDREN'S LITERATURE: *Nils Holgerssons underbara resa genom Sverige*, 1906-1907 (2 volumes; *The Wonderful Adventures of Nils*, 1907, and *The Further Adventures of Nils*, 1911).

Bibliography

Berendsohn, Walter A. *Selma Lagerlöf: Her Life and Work*, 1931.

Gustafson, Alrik. *Six Scandinavian Novelists: Lie, Jacobsen, Heidenstam, Selma Lagerlöf, Hamsun, Sigrid Undset*, 1950.

Larsen, Hanna Astrup. *Selma Lagerlöf*, 1936.

Vrieze, Folkereina Steintje de. *Fact and Fiction in the Autobiographical Works of Selma Lagerlöf*, 1958.

Helen Mundy Hudson